ROUTLEDGE HANDBOOK ON ARAB MEDIA

This handbook provides the first comprehensive reference book in English about the development of mass and social media in all Arab countries. Capturing the historical as well as current developments in the media scene, this collection maps the role of media in social and political movements.

Contributors include specialists in the field from North America, Europe, and the Middle East. Each chapter provides an overview of the history, regulatory frameworks and laws governing the press, and socio-political functions of the media. While the geopolitical complexities of the region have been reflected in the expert analyses collectively, the focus is always the local context of each member state. All 38 chapters consider the specific historical, political, and media trajectories in each country, to provide a contextual background and foundation for further study about single states or comparative analysis in two or more Arab states.

Capturing significant technological developments and the widespread use of social media, this all-inclusive volume on Arab media is a key resource for students and scholars interested in journalism, media, and Middle East studies.

Noureddine Miladi is Professor of Media and Communication at Qatar University, Qatar. He is former head of department of mass communication and president of the Arab Media & Communication Network (AMCN). He is editor of *JAMMR*, the first Arab-refereed journal in Arab media and society.

Noha Mellor is Professor of Media at the University of Bedfordshire, UK, and Adjunct Professor of Middle Eastern Studies at Stockholm University, Sweden. She is the author of several books about Arab media and journalism.

ROUTLEDGE HANDBOOK ON ARAB MEDIA

Edited by
Noureddine Miladi and Noha Mellor

LONDON AND NEW YORK

First published 2021
by Routledge
2 Park Square, Milton Park, Abingdon, Oxon OX14 4RN

and by Routledge
52 Vanderbilt Avenue, New York, NY 10017

Routledge is an imprint of the Taylor & Francis Group, an informa business

British Library Cataloguing-in-Publication Data
A catalogue record for this book is available from the British Library

Library of Congress Cataloging-in-Publication Data
Names: Miladi, Noureddine, editor. | Mellor, Noha, 1969– editor.
Title: Routledge handbook on Arab media / edited by Noureddine Miladi and Noha Mellor.
Description: London ; New York : Routledge, 2020. | Includes bibliographical references and index.
Identifiers: LCCN 2020027207 (print) | LCCN 2020027208 (ebook) | ISBN 9781138385481 (hardback) | ISBN 9780429427084 (ebook) | ISBN 9780429762925 (adobe pdf) | ISBN 9780429762918 (epub) | ISBN 9780429762901 (mobi)
Subjects: LCSH: Mass media—Arab countries. | Social media—Arab countries.
Classification: LCC P92.A65 R68 2020 (print) | LCC P92.A65 (ebook) | DDC 302.230917/4927—dc23
LC record available at https://lccn.loc.gov/2020027207
LC ebook record available at https://lccn.loc.gov/2020027208

ISBN: 978-1-138-38548-1 (hbk)
ISBN: 978-0-429-42708-4 (ebk)

Typeset in Bembo
by Apex CoVantage, LLC

CONTENTS

Contents

Contents

United Arab Emirates   **473**

Yemen   **489**

CONTRIBUTORS

Joel W. Abdelmoez is a researcher working on Arab media, gender politics, and feminist activism in the Middle East, with focus on Egypt and Saudi Arabia. He is a former adjunct lecturer and director of studies for Middle Eastern languages and cultures at Stockholm University, as well as chairman of the Swedish MENA association and co-founder of MENAtidningen.se. He holds a BA and MA in Middle Eastern studies from Stockholm University and an MPhil in multidisciplinary gender studies from the University of Cambridge.

Bahjat Abuzanouna is an independent media researcher. He earned his PhD from University of Westminster. Prior to obtaining his PhD, he worked in many places, including Palestinian News Agency (WAFA), Reuters, and others. He worked as Assistant Professor in Faculty of Media at Al-Aqsa University. His research focuses on Palestinian media, media and conflict, media and democracy, and media ethics. He has participated in a number of academic conferences and researches related to media and politics. His doctoral research was subsequently transformed into *Enhancing Democratic Communication? Television and Partisan Politics in Palestine* (2012).

Akshatha Achar is a 2019 graduate of Emory University, where she pursued a double major in international studies, with a focus on the Middle East and Africa. During the course of her studies at the Emory College of Liberal Arts and Sciences, she was initiated into Pi Sigma Alpha, the National Political Science Honor Society. She was appointed as a Junto Fellow in the Franklin Fellows Program for Democracy and Citizenship.

Ismail Sheikh Yusuf Ahmed obtained his MA and PhD in mass communication from International Islamic University Malaysia (IIUM). At IIUM, he won the "Best Doctoral Student" award. He is currently affiliated with the Mass Communication Department, Qatar University (QU). He has published scores of refereed articles and authored book chapters and encyclopedia entries. His research interest areas include new media, media history, political communication, news consumption, and media effects.

Najat AlSaied holds a PhD from the University of Westminster, UK, and two master's degrees in health promotion disease prevention and computer information systems from the American

University, Washington, DC. She is an independent researcher at the Emirates Centre for Strategic Studies and Research (ECSSR) in Abu Dhabi, UAE. She is a columnist in *Al Ittihad* (UAE) and in *Al Hurra* (USA), and she was previously Assistant Professor at Zayed University in Dubai. AlSaied has over 20 years of experience in media industries, development organizations, and the diplomatic service. She is the author of *Screens of Influence: Arab Satellite Television and Social Development* (2015).

Awad Ibrahim Awad is Professor of Communication at King Khalid University, Kingdom of Saudi Arabia. He obtained a PhD in mass media and English language from the University of Malaya, Malaysia, and was a professor of communication and linguistics in Malaysia, USA, Sudan, and Saudi Arabia. He is member of the board of trustees at three universities, and served as director of Al-Amal TV Satellite Channel, Al-Ala Satellite Miya TV Satellite Channel, and Radio Africa. He authored 40 books in various media and social topics, and his research interests center mainly on broadcasting in Sudan and Africa.

Saida Kheira Benammar is a lecturer in media studies at the University Center of Relizane in Algeria and a research member at the Laboratory of Communication, Media Studies and Discourse Analysis. She got her PhD (2016) from the University of Mostaganem in Algeria on journalists and social network sites. She has also been in a fellowship program at the University of Naples in Italy (2014–2015). Her main research interests include social media studies, digital platforms, media and communication's science problematic, and the sociology of the Web 2.0.

Belkacem Amin Benamra is a researcher at the Laboratory of Communication, Media Studies and Discourse Analysis (LCMSDA) at the University of Mostaganem, Algeria. He took part in several research projects of multidisciplinary research in several fields, including media studies, cultural studies of technology, and cyber ethnography. His research revolves mainly around problematics related to the political significance of social media, democratization challenges, and the digital public sphere in the Algerian context.

Moez Ben Messaoud is Associate Professor in the Department of Mass Communication, College of Arts and Sciences, Qatar University. He got his PhD from the Sorbonne in France and served previously as Head of Department of Communication at the Institute of Journalism, University of Manouba, Tunis. Ben Messaoud was editor-in-chief of the *Journal of Communication Sciences*, and he has coordinated various research projects both in Manouba University, Tunisia, and Qatar University. His research interests include social media networks and social change, public service broadcasting, and media and democratic transition.

Mohamed Ben Moussa is Associate Professor at the College of Communication, University of Sharjah. Before joining UOS, he was an associate professor at the Canadian University Dubai and a post-doctoral fellow at McGill University, Canada. His research interests revolve around new media and social movements, media convergence and journalism, multimodal discourse analysis, and gender and communication, among others.

Sam Cherribi holds his PhD from the University of Amsterdam. He is currently a senior lecturer in Middle Eastern studies, sociology, and economics at Emory University, as well as a former member of the Dutch House of Representatives. His most recent book in English is *Fridays of Rage: AlJazeera and the Arab Spring*, published by Oxford University Press. For his chapter in this volume, he was assisted by Drew Siegal (Boston), a current undergraduate student at Emory, and Akshatha Achar (Dubai) and Patrick Harris (New York), both undergraduates.

Ali A. Dashti is Associate Professor in the Department of Mass Communication and Media at Gulf University for Science and Technology in Kuwait. He has published numerous papers related to journalism, women studies, public relations, and social media studies. He earned his PhD from the University of Stirling in Scotland and an MS from Kansas State University. In 1990, he served in the US Army during Operation Desert Shield and Desert Storm as a translator for the 66th Military Intelligence (MI) 3rd Armored Cavalry Regiment. He is the author of "Sergeant over One Week" and "How 0.10 Can Change Your Life" and co-author of *Media Law in Kuwait*.

Aziz Douai is Associate Professor at the Faculty of Social Science and Humanities, Ontario Tech University. He has published more than 40 peer-reviewed journal articles and book chapters in international periodicals and book volumes. He is the author of *Arab Media and the Politics of Terrorism: Unbecoming News* (in press), co-editor of *New Media Influence on Social and Political Change in Africa* (2013), *Mediated Identities and New Journalism in the Arab World: Mapping the "Arab Spring"* (2016).

Mokhtar Elareshi is Assistant Professor in the College of Communication and Media, Al Ain University, UAE. He is the author of *News Consumption in Libya* (Cambridge Scholar, 2013), the co-author of *The Future of News Media in the Arab World* (2014), and the co-editor of *Social Media in the Arab World* (2016). His research interests include news consumption, young adults' media habits, new media, mobile phone use, and satellite TV news.

Abdelmalek El Kadoussi, PhD, is Assistant Professor of Media and Communication at Ibn Toufail University, Kenitra, Morocco. Over the last 15 years, he has conducted research on different layers of media scholarship, including but not confined to media and democratization, media political economy, and media production and reception. He has presented papers in national and international congresses and published on national and international journals.

Elsayed Abdelwahed Elkilany received his PhD in electronic publishing from Helwan University, Egypt. He is currently Lecturer at the Mass Communication Department, Qatar University. He is the author of "eLearning Quality," and his articles appeared in *Global Media Communication* and *Journal of Arab and Muslim Media Research*. His research interests include interactive multimedia, print and online journalism, advertising, graphic design, and education quality. He is the recipient of the award of distinguished faculty member in teaching from Sharjah University (2009) and from Qatar University (2015).

Nahed Eltantawy is Associate Professor of Journalism and Associate Dean in the Nido R. Qubein School of Communication at High Point University. Eltantawy graduated from Georgia State University with a PhD in public communication in December 2007. Her research interests include media representation, gender issues, social media activism, Middle East media, and critical and cultural studies. Her work has been published in *Communication and Critical/Cultural Studies*, *Feminist Media Studies*, and the *International Journal of Communication*.

Nour Halabi is Lecturer of Media and Communication at the University of Leeds and the Vice-Chair of the MeCCSA Race Network. Her research focuses on social movements, migration, and global media. Recent publications include "The Spatial Politics of the Syrian Revolution" in *Middle East Critique* (2019) and "The Contingency of Meaning to the Party of God: Carnivalesque Humor in Revolutionary Times" in *The International Journal of Communication* (2017). She holds a PhD from the Annenberg School at the University of Pennsylvania and a master's from The London School of Economics.

Andrew Hammond teaches late Ottoman and Turkish history at the University of Oxford, where he obtained his doctorate in modern Islamic thought. His publications include *The Islamic Utopia: The Illusion of Reform in Saudi Arabia* (2012), *Popular Culture in North Africa and the Middle East* (2017), "Producing Salafism: From Invented Tradition to State Agitprop," in *Salman's Legacy: The Dilemmas of a New Era in Saudi Arabia*, ed. M. Al-Rasheed (2018), and "Salafi Thought in Turkish Public Discourse since 1980," *International Journal of Middle East Studies* 49 (2017). Previously he worked for the European Council on Foreign Relations, BBC Arabic, and Reuters news agency in Saudi Arabia and Egypt.

Patrick Harris is a research assistant for Dr. Sam Cherribi. Harris graduated from the College of Arts and Sciences at Emory in 2019 and previously interned at the Carter Center Peace Program. While at the Carter Center, Harris worked on projects that provided technical assistance and advice to the Liberian government and Liberian civil society on the implementation and use of Liberia's Freedom of Information Law. Harris currently works at PIMCO in their Financial Institutions Group.

Christina Zacharia Hawatmeh is Assistant Professor and Chair of the Department of Languages and Literature and the Department of Translation in the Faculty of Languages and Communication at the American University of Madaba since 2016. Previously, she served as Senior Writer and Issue Analyst in the Office of His Majesty King Abdullah II. With an MA and PhD in sociology from the American University of Washington, DC, and a BA in sociology from the University of California at Berkeley, Hawatmeh has authored and co-authored numerous journal articles and two books in the fields of Palestine and Arab studies.

Mohammed Ibahrine, PhD, is Associate Professor for Integrated Marketing Communication at the American University of Sharjah, UAE. His research interests cover technology and marketing, entrepreneurship, innovation, and the technologies of the fourth industrial revolution.

Khalid Al-Jaber earned his MA and PhD from the USA and UK respectively. He also holds a postgraduate diploma from Fordham University, Stanford University, and Georgetown University. Al-Jaber is director of the MENA Center in Washington, DC. Previously, he served as editor-in-chief of *The Peninsula*, Qatar's leading English-language daily newspaper. Al-Jaber is also Assistant Professor of Political Communication in the Gulf Studies Program (GSP) at Qatar University. His research focuses on Arab and Gulf Studies, as well as public diplomacy, international communications, and international relations. He has published scholarly works in several academic books and journals.

Ildiko Kaposi is a social scientist whose work focuses on issues of democracy from the perspective of media and communication. She has studied the roles of the press and Internet in fostering participation in emerging or transitioning democracies in post-communist Europe and the Middle East. Employing mainly qualitative methods, she specializes in in-depth explorations of the intersections of democratic principles and their interpretations in specific social, legal, political, and cultural contexts. She is Assistant Professor at the Mass Communication and Media department of the Gulf University of Science and Technology, Kuwait, where she teaches media law.

Magdalena Karolak is Associate Professor of Humanities and Social Sciences at Zayed University, UAE. She received her PhD in linguistics, MA in political science, and MA in Latin American studies. Prior to working at ZU, Karolak held positions in Bahrain and Saudi Arabia. In 2014–15, she was an American Political Science Association MENA Fellow. Her research interests include transformations of societies in the Arabian Gulf and comparative linguistics. Karolak has published more than 40 articles and chapters on the gender relations, social media, culture and identity, and political transformations in the GCC. She is the author of two scholarly monographs.

Nermeen Kassem is an Assistant Professor in the Mass Communication and Media Department at Gulf University for Science and Technology (GUST), Kuwait, and Faculty of Women for Arts, Science and Education-Ain Shams University. Kassem specializes in new media, mediated mobilization, and political participation. She was a visiting professor at the University of Texas at Austin in 2019. Kassem was also a Research Associate in the Five College Women's Studies Research Centre at Mount Holyoke University (USA). She joined the Annenberg-Oxford Media Policy Summer Institute in 2017 at the University of Oxford, and she was also member of the team on a large policy-making project with the Open Society Foundations and Issam Fares Institute for Public Policy and International Affairs at the American University of Beirut.

Natalie Khazaal is Assistant Professor at Georgia Institute of Technology. Khazaal studies the links among disenfranchisement, media, and language. Her latest book, *Pretty Liar: Television, Language, and Gender in Wartime Lebanon* (2018), is a cultural study of the role of audiences in redefining trust in the media during violent crises and deep social divisions. Her contribution to *Global Media and Strategic Narratives of Contested Democracy* (2019, Routledge) explores how international audiences in the Arab world engaged with the 2016 US presidential elections. Khazaal is an American Council of Learned Societies (ACLS) fellow for her work on the engagement of Arab atheists with the media.

Abdullah K. Al-Kindi is Professor of Journalism and Electronic Publishing at Sultan Qaboos University, Oman. He obtained his MA in journalism from Cardiff University, Wales, in 1995, and his PhD from Reading University in 2000. In the period 2011–2017, he served as a dean of the College of Arts and Social Sciences at Sultan Qaboos University. In his research, he focuses on media policies, media coverage of wars and crisis, and Omani media. He authored or co-authored several books, of which the most recent is *Omani Pioneer Journalists* (2020).

Mongi Mabrouki is Lecturer in Communication and Cultural Studies at Carthage University, Tunisia. Since March 2020, he has been serving as advisor on research and strategies to the minister of Youth and Sport. Mabrouki also taught at the High Institute of Arts and the University of Sousse and served as director of the National Youth Radio and the National Tunisian Radio (2012–2014). He published numerous articles and research papers on media and communication in Tunisia. Among his research interests are Al Jazeera and public opinion, media and democratic transition in Tunisia, and the youth and new media.

Ebtihal Mahadeen is Lecturer in Gender and Media Studies with a focus on the Middle East, based at the University of Edinburgh. Her research focuses on the intersection of gender, sexuality, and media within an Arab context, and she has a professional background in reporting and online media.

Ibrahim Al-Marashi is Associate Professor of Middle East History at California State University San Marcos. His research focuses on 20th-century Iraqi history and the post-Baathist Iraqi state. He has worked on various media initiatives in Iraq with the United Nations and Iraq's Communication Media Commission. He is co-author of Iraq's *Armed Forces: An Analytical History* (Routledge, 2008), and *The Modern History of Iraq*, with Phebe Marr (Routledge 2017), and *A Concise History of the Middle East* (Routledge, 2018).

Noha Mellor holds a PhD from Copenhagen University, Denmark. She is currently Professor of Media at the University of Bedfordshire (UK) and Adjunct Professor of Middle Eastern Studies at Stockholm University (Sweden). She is the author of several books about Arab media and journalism including *Making of Arab News* (2005), *Modern Arab Journalism* (2007), *Arab Media* (2011), and *Voice of the Muslim Brotherhood* (Routledge, 2017).

Noureddine Miladi is Professor of Media and Communication and former Head of Department of Mass Communication, College of Arts and Sciences, Qatar University. He previously taught at the University of Westminster in London and Northampton University, UK. He is editor of *Journal of Arab and Muslim Media Research*, an international peer-reviewed journal specialized in Arab and Middle Eastern media and society. He is co-author of *Media and the Democratic Transition in the Arab World* (2019) and *Mapping the Al Jazeera Phenomenon 20 Years On* (2017). He currently serves as president of the Arab Media and Communication Network (AMCN).

Mohamed Elamin Musa is Associate Professor of Online Journalism at the Department of Mass Communication in Qatar University. Previously, he taught at Ajman University of Science and Technology, Sharjah University, and Al Dar University College (UAE). He has authored eight books and has written several refereed articles on online journalism, graphic design, visual media, new and social media, and media ethics. His research covers new media, online journalism, print journalism, graphic and web design, nonverbal communication, and the psychology of communication.

Ibrahim Natil is a lecturer at Dublin City University, teaching politics and business at Centre for Talented Youth, CTY Ireland at Dublin City University (DCU). Natil is also a research fellow at Institute of International Conflict Resolution and Reconstruction (Dublin City University) and an international development consultant for many civil society organizations. He has managed more than 56 human rights, women's and youth empowerment, and peace-building programs since 1997. He is co-editor of *Power of Civil Society: Peacebuilding, Change and Development in MENA* (Routledge 2019) and the author of more than 20 academic papers/chapters about peacebuilding, human security, conflict resolution, civil society, international relations, and political violence.

Ahmed Al-Rawi is Assistant Professor of News, Social Media, and Public Communication at the School of Communication at Simon Fraser University, Canada. He is the director of the Disinformation Project that empirically examines fake news discourses in Canada on social media and news media. His research expertise is related to social media, global communication, news, and the Middle East with emphasis on critical theory. He authored three books and over 70 peer-reviewed book chapters and articles published in a variety of journals like *Information, Communication & Society, Online Information Review, Social Science Computer Review, Telematics & Informatics, Social Media+Society, Journalism, Journalism Practice, Digital Journalism, International Journal of Communication, International Communication Gazette,* and *Public Relations Review.*

Sarah El-Richani is Assistant Professor of Mass Communications in the School of Global Affairs and Public Policy, The American University in Cairo. She was visiting fellow and academic visitor at the Centre for Lebanese Studies and St. Antony's College, University of Oxford, during the academic year 2016–2017. El-Richani obtained her BA from the American University of Beirut, where she received the Penrose Award, and her MA from the University of Westminster courtesy of the Quintin Hogg Scholarship, and she completed her doctoral studies in 2015 at the University of Erfurt, courtesy of a DAAD Scholarship. Her monograph, *Lebanon: Anatomy of a Media System in Perpetual Crisis,* was published by Palgrave Macmillan in 2016.

Haider al-Safi, PhD, is an author, journalist, and media consultant specializing in the political, religious, and security affairs in the Middle East. He contributed to the Independent, ITV, Channel 4, APTN, and the BBC. He joined the BBC Arabic in 2009, and in 2018 he moved to the Turkish TRT Arabic Service. Al-Safi holds a PhD from City University, London, and he is the author of *Iraqi Media: From Saddam's Propaganda to American State-Building* (2013).

Mohammed Al-Sheikh is a Mauritanian researcher and a PhD candidate in media and communication at Al Jazeera University in Sudan, and he is also senior editor in the public relations department at Qatar University. He worked for over 20 years as a journalist in various Arab newspapers. His research interests include Mauritanian media, broadcasting and public opinion, and African journalism.

Drew Siegal is an undergraduate student at Emory University. Outside of academia, Siegal competes on the national university Model United Nations debate circuit, receiving awards from several of the nation's top universities, including Harvard University. He also is a leader of Emory's International Relations Association (EIRA), one of the largest student organizations on campus, with over 500 registered members.

Fahed Al-Sumait is the Vice President for Academic Affairs at the Gulf University for Science and Technology in Kuwait. He has served as a visiting fellow at the Middle East Centre in the London School of Economics and a post-doctoral research fellow at the Middle East Institute in the National University of Singapore, and he was previously a Fulbright-Hays fellow for his research into contested discourses on Arab democratization. He is the current president of the Association for Gulf and Arabian Peninsula Studies. He teaches various courses on strategic communication, as well as several offerings in mass communication and media studies.

Deborah L. Wheeler teaches political science and Middle East studies at the United States Naval Academy in Annapolis. She is the author of *Digital Resistance in the Middle East* (2018) and *Internet in the Middle East* (2006). She has conducted fieldwork on gender, resistance, food security, and digital politics in Kuwait, Oman, Qatar, United Arab Emirates, Saudi Arabia, Jordan, Lebanon, Israel/Palestine, Egypt, Tunisia, and Morocco. She has held visiting positions at Oxford University, Sciences Po, Bergen University, American University in Cairo, The King

Faisal Center for Research and Islamic Studies, Kuwait University, and American University in Kuwait.

Bouziane Zaid, PhD, is Associate Professor of Global Communication at the University of Sharjah, UAE. His research interests are in the areas of media technologies, media law and policy, media advocacy, and corporate communication. He presented his research in more than 20 countries in North and South America, Asia, Europe, the Middle East, and Africa. Zaid authored and co-authored two books and numerous journal articles, country reports, and book chapters, and he served as a consultant for UNESCO, Open Society Foundation, Freedom House, and other international organizations.

INTRODUCTION

Noha Mellor and Noureddine Miladi

Despite the burgeoning interest in Arab media, there is still a paucity of historical studies that trace the development of media industries in the region to demonstrate the continuities, disruptions, and significance of key historical events, from colonial and anti-colonial discourses to the recent ruptures that ravished the region since 2011. The volume provides an overview of the historical development of news media in all Arab states. There are several reasons behind this narrow focus on news media: firstly, the majority of higher education courses about Arab media tend to focus on the journalistic field and news discourse, and this volume aims to serve as an accessible one-stop source about the media in each Arab state. Secondly, Western commentators and journalists still draw on Arab media and journalistic sources in their writings about the region, and they can use this volume as a source of knowledge about the historical development of news media in each state. Thirdly, despite the tight control on press freedoms in most of the Arab states, news media is ironically one of the thriving media sectors in the region, as seen in the increasing number of journalism courses across the region, compared to, for instance, courses in performing arts (Nashmi et al., 2018). Fourthly, Western think tanks have dedicated a great share of interest and budgets to Arab media programs, as demonstrated in the steady funding provided by media donors to support journalism projects in the region including investigative journalism (Kalathil, 2017). This interest is also underpinned by the belief in media and democracy and seeing journalism as a site of a power struggle among various political actors. Finally, the field of journalism has attracted even more interest since the 2011 uprisings with the emergence of "citizen journalism" and hence the porousness of the professional boundaries in this field in the Arab region.

In this volume, we refrain from using the term "Middle East" as a label for the region, not least because it refers to a large area including the Arab states, Turkey, Iran, and Israel; besides, such terms like the "Middle East" and "Near East" were coined by the former imperial powers in the 19th and early 20th centuries (Keddie, 1973: 257) and did not originate from the region. Instead, we use the term "Arab region" to refer to members of the League of Arab States and those who share Arabic as the official language. Despite sharing common linguistic code, however, the Arab states do not represent a homogenous group, as their cultural boundaries have partly changed throughout the past 50 years (Hopkins and Ibrahim, 2003: 4). This is seen, for instance, in the joining of Mauritania, Somalia, and Djibouti to the League of Arab States in the 1970s, followed by the Comoros Islands in the 1990s. In this book, we cover the media trajectories in the following states: Algeria, Bahrain, Egypt, Iraq, Jordan, Kuwait, Lebanon, Libya, Mauritania, Morocco, Oman, Palestine, Qatar, Saudi Arabia, Somalia, Sudan, Syria, Tunisia, the UAE, and Yemen.

One aim of this volume is to integrate descriptive case studies prevalent in area studies with the findings of media studies research about single Arab states, including research into the use of media to bolster national identity or the use of digital media as a tool for raising awareness about acute social problems. The focus of this volume then is the local context of each member state, considering the specificity of the historical, political, and media trajectory in each country, to provide contextual background and a foundation for future studies about single states or comparative studies that juxtapose media trajectories in two or more Arab states. Such a "trans-local" perspective may "establish local-to-local connections," which is sorely missed in today's global media studies (Kraidy, 2011: 50). While zooming in on the local context in each state, this volume also links these local contexts to the overall regional, and indeed transnational, media scene. In so doing, we follow Korany's (2016: 83) call for the analysis of the Arab region based on the conceptual lens of "intermestics" or the "overlapping between INTERnational and doMESTIC dimensions of socio-political process and interactions." Most chapters in this volume draw on Arabic-language, in addition to English-language, sources, to engage with "indigenous" research and deliberately move away from the pervasive Eurocentric perspectives.

This volume also attempts to go beyond works done before on media systems in the Arab states such as Boyd (1999), Hafez (2001), and Rugh (2004). Although Boyd's comprehensive work on broadcasting in the Arab world was unique when it appeared in 1995, it is limited in terms of the media sector it covered (broadcasting). Moreover, Rugh's typology was significant in attempting to analyze the media systems in various Arab countries by organizing them according to specific categories, but it does not discuss the relationship of these media systems with the social and political changes in the region, not to mention that his proposed typography has now become obsolete due to the transformations in journalism due to satellite technologies and the Internet revolution. Most importantly, the aforementioned works fall short of capturing the significant technological developments in the region, especially with the widespread use of social media networks as alternative platforms of news production and dissemination and their impact on journalism and public opinion.

Debunking the myth of exceptionalism

We agree with Fawcett (2016b: 16) that to understand the region, scholars must understand the historical context, the domestic actors, and the inadequacy of Western political models to explain the developments within the region. In this volume, we move away from the notion of "exceptionalism" which continuously highlights the divergence of the region from ethnocentric normative standards, and we look beyond the East/West and developed/underdeveloped dichotomies. Instead, we argue for the need to analyze Arab media within the specific historical trajectory in each country. For instance, Western scholarship tends to focus on the role of the state as a coercive power imposing their rules of media censorship, but such an analytical lens is based on analyzing media and politics as two independent categories, which is not always the case in the Arab region. The chapter on Kuwaiti media, for example, argues that the government and market are not a dichotomous pair as the two spheres are intertwined through multiple personal and familial linkages. Yet, the concentration of media owners in the Gulf Cooperation Council (GCC) states has meant the dominance of Gulf capital, not only on the structural media development in the region but also on articulating mass media messages.

Moreover, the traditional liberal theory advocates the role of media as a watchdog that holds the state to account, but this model does not take account of other shareholders; in the case of Arab media, private media ventures have contributed to increasing competitiveness among local and regional media outlets (Mellor, 2020). This means that the Arab media scene is indeed complex, given the intertwinement of local, regional, and global media, in addition to the fact that national security interests play a pivotal role in shaping the media power (Mellor, 2020). This interconnectedness of the regional economy and its integration into the global economy, coupled with national security interests, makes it rather difficult to analyze the Arab media as an independent or autonomous field.

This, however, does not mean that the analysis of media power should be based solely on the external power of wealth while ignoring the power of the media to generate meaning (Hardy, 2014: 197). National media discourses are based not only on the historical trajectory of each state but also on the ideologies, or sets of assumptions, prevailing in that state. Such ideologies form the intellectual foundations behind media discourses, disseminated in media policies, and media professionals' engagement with these policies. Seen through this prism of ideology and discourse, media provides different roles within Arab societies: it relays state hegemonic discourse, establishes media professionals' symbolic power as mediators, and serves as a site of contested ideas shared by diverse media users. The contributions in this volume share a focus on four main acute themes, namely the role of Arab media in shaping national identity, the intensifying rivalry among Arab states, the role of media as a national security tool, and the role of media as a medium for digital transformations. The remainder of this introductory chapter reviews each of these themes.

Identity politics

Identity politics is pivotal in understanding the region and its media landscape, as it informs each state's conception of its interests, especially with calls of irredentism and revisionism (Hinne-busch, 2016: 174). For instance, most Arab states were colonized or were treated as protectorates of former European colonial powers which drew arbitrary borders and formed new states. The porous borders resulted in irredentism and several inter-regional territorial disputes, such as the disputes between Egypt and Sudan, Lebanon and Syria, Oman and Yemen, Saudi Arabia and Yemen (settled in 2000), Qatar and Bahrain over the Hawar islands (settled in 2001), and Saudi Arabia and Egypt over Tiran and Sanafir islands (settled in 2017). This also means that the whole region is factionalized, "as are most of its countries, and many of the deepest ethnic, religious, linguistic, and tribal divisions overlap borders, further accentuating the region-wide problem of national interpenetration" (Springborg, 2020: 23).

In this volume, we adopt a definition of identity, and particularly national identity, as leaning on coherent discursive practices, including collective memory and the construction of in-group solidarity about a shared past or even a shared trauma. Indeed, national identities are relational constructs, meaning that they depend on the presence of an *Other* for their significance. Such constructs then are based on the "dialectic of identification: how we identify ourselves, how others identify us, and the ongoing interplay of these in the process of social identification" (Jenkins, 2000: 7). This process of identification relies on an ideology defined as the shared values used for mobilizing the majority of populations in one society and as interpreted by the custodians of collective memory, whether they be heads of state or media professionals. Media discourse functions as a tool through which we understand our national and community's histories and present practices, and mediat(iz)ed accounts of conflicts as well as heritage, for instance, constitute an important component of identities and histories (Garde-Hansen, 2011).

The following chapters provide several examples of the identity discourse disseminated via national media. For instance, the chapter about the UAE media argues that the unique federal nature of the state has sustained a traditional role for national media as a guardian of national identity and as a catalyst for economic development. Similarly, Yemeni media have been utilized as a tool to produce a sensitized narrative in a polarized country that was historically divided into different regions. The Yemeni media then were used to amplify differences in times of war and to claim unity in times of peace.

Moreover, the Arab mediascape presents a case of the intertwining media-politics nexus where politicians communicate with citizens through mass media using the latter instead of the waning party-political system. Examples abound of the use of media in the region as a tool in accentuating discord among Arab states, which further divided the region into sectarian, economic, and political loyalties, as demonstrated in the blockade against Qatar. There are several recent examples of Arab outlets, particularly Saudi Arabia, UAE, Egypt, and Bahrain, which stand in opposition to Qatar and Turkey, and the former states have called for a revisit of the historical accounts of Ottoman rule and its perceived negative role in the region. Some states like Syria have called for a stop to the flow of Turkish TV series, which used to be dubbed in Syrian dialect before being broadcast on many Arab television networks, following Turkey's intervention in the war in Syria and its hosting of anti-Assad media ventures (Mellor, 2018).

Thus, key regional events tend to fuel not only revisionism but also sectarianism. For instance, the 1979 revolution in Iran was arguably one key event that fuels anti-Shi'a discourse in the region, facilitated by generous funding from the GCC states (Hashemi and Postel, 2017: 10–11). Both Iran and the Kingdom of Saudi Arabia (KSA) have since battled for the leadership of the Islamic world leading the GCC to fund Saddam's war against Iran (1980–1988). However, when Saddam Hussein invaded Kuwait in 1990, Arab media coverage of the 1991 war tended to depict Iraqis as disloyal to their Arab brethren in neighboring Kuwait. The war was not supported by all Arab populations, however, which prompted the GCC to call for banning Arab intellectuals and artists who opposed the war from appearing in any media outlets owned by businessmen from the Gulf states (Mattar, 1992: 230–231). The subsequent war on Iraq in 2003, the rise of Hezbollah in Lebanon, and the 2011 Arab uprisings have marked several other turning points in further fueling rivalries in the region (Hashemi and Postel, 2017: 12).

Regional rivalry

Post-independence, several Arab countries sought to enforce a unified Arab identity, and some formed federations such as the short-lived union between Egypt and Syria (1958–1961). Arab nationalism was then a political reaction to European colonialism during the late 19th and early 20th century (Haddad, 1994: 217). However, the Arab region, argues Springborg (2020: 16) "has regionalization without regionalism," where the former refers to a bottom-up process and formal and informal networks, and the latter is a top-down process with formal institutions leading the process of integration. The region has always lacked a framework that can secure its security, political, and economic integration; such a framework for regional integration should guarantee many gains for the individual member states such as "increasing the region's collective political bargaining power in extra-regional issues," not to mention "meeting security concerns and preventing future conflicts" (El-Erian and Fischer, 1996: 1).

Thus, despite geographical and cultural unifiers, the Arab region is not economically integrated. Labor mobility is conditioned by national regulations, with intraregional trade and investments being rather limited. The only exception is the pan-media sector, where Arab journalists and writers have been able to move across the diverse pan-Arab outlets that have proliferated in the region since the mid-1990s.

Moreover, the Arab region is characterized by being the stage for rivalries not only among global powers but also among regional actors, such as Egypt and Saudi Arabia, competing "to shape the MENA environment" (Korany, 2016: 98). For instance, following the Arab defeat in the 1948 war, (Trans)Jordan was suspected of harboring expansionist ambitions, heightened by the annexation of the West Bank in 1950, while the Saudis were concerned that the Hashemite ruler might want to revive his family's old hegemony on parts of the Arabian Peninsula. Syria feared that (Trans)Jordan might wish to recapture Damascus to resuscitate the old Greater Syria plan (Haddad, 2018: 53–61). Most recently, the Gulf states' meddling in the Syrian conflict, regarded as a proxy war between Iran and Syria supported by Russia, on the one hand, versus the Gulf states and the US, on the other, further fractured the relations among the Gulf states, igniting the ongoing blockade against Qatar. The ongoing conflict has demonstrated the deployment of media discourse as one pivotal tool in imbuing patriotic sentiments on states' policies, and this discourse was also evident on social media platforms which were also used as a site of a virtual proxy war with Iran (Mellor, 2018).

The following chapters provide several examples of this rivalry, and the Arab states' active use of media to extend their regional influence. For instance, Saudi Arabia paying in subscription fees in publications in other GCC states and Yemen or using Hajj/pilgrimage visas as two tools to promote its policies; Qatar's promotion of its policies via its own growing media empire such as Al Jazeera network and later al-Araby network in London; or the pro-Syria outlets in Lebanon, particularly al-Manar and al-Mayadeen television channels, promoting Hezbollah, with its links to both Syria and Iran, as a resistance movement. Thus, the Arab states have not only failed to integrate politically and economically, but they also failed to coordinate their efforts in the media sphere largely due to the increasing insecurity in each state.

National security and media policies

In the Arab region, national security and state interests tend to overlap, and the interests of single states may be entangled with those of other states (Korany et al., 1993: 26–27). In the media sector, Arab governments tend to cite national security as one main reason for curtailing media, as well as political freedoms. Such a crackdown has sustained for decades partly due to the incessant conflicts and wars that have impacted the region since 1948, and this has been exacerbated by the pervasiveness of the war-on-terror discourse. True, muddled within these national security interests are the long-held conspiracy theories about the threat of several foreign actors, but such theories are often linked with the region's colonial history (Gray, 2010).

Seen against this background, Arab military powers have managed in several countries to sustain their grip on power thanks to their role as guardians of individual states' security. As many states weakened, citizens longed for protection, and they ended up seeking it "from the very institution responsible for state decay – the military," and this explains the findings of recent public opinion surveys which indicate higher public trust in the national militaries (Springborg, 2020: 22). For instance, the Arab Barometer survey (2016–2017) showed that the public trust in Arab armies increased to 88% in 2016/17, compared to 71% in 2011; the percentage is higher in countries like Egypt and much lower in countries suffering from civil wars such as Libya and Syria (ibid.). In Egypt, for one, the army is often depicted as the vanguard and savior of the nation and even the whole region, and this depiction is reinforced in Egyptian popular culture such as songs and drama (Mostafa, 2017). The heroic depiction of the army has urged media professionals to declare their support to the military lest they are accused of betraying the nation

(Mellor, 2020). This form of military backing demonstrates that media capture is not only the result of coercive action by individual governments but can also take a non-coercive form where media institutions back up the ruling elites (Mellor, 2020). Similarly, in Saudi Arabia, the rulers held several Saudi media tycoons against their will before they were allegedly released on the condition of releasing control of their media empires (Mellor, 2020).

The security interests are also visible in transitional media ventures which seek to promote different factions, as will be discussed in the chapters about Libya and Yemen. Likewise, the chapter about Syrian media demonstrates how the Syrian media scene has not only witnessed rival discourses between pro- and anti-government discourses but has also been a chaotic scene for international, mostly European, media donors who set up hundreds of outlets in the wake of the civil war in 2011, only to shut down the majority of them later due to abrupt withdrawal of funding. The result was an unnecessary competition among those outlets and a failed attempt to bolster solidarity.

Digital transformation

With the increasing digital literacy of the Arab youth under 24, who constitute 50% of the region's populations, digital media consumption and production across the region are notably high, particularly in well-connected societies such as the GCC states (Dubai Press Club, 2016). The rate of connectivity is particularly highest in Saudi Arabia, which is YouTube's largest market worldwide in terms of per capita consumption. Digital media and amateur digital content distributed via platforms such as YouTube, produced by the new generation of social media influencers and budding artists, is arguably the fastest-growing segments in the region (Dubai Press Club, 2016: vi). It is estimated that the digital market could add USD 95 billion per year to the region's annual GDP already by 2020 (Digital McKinsey, 2016).

The following chapters shed light on the development of digital media in each Arab state, demonstrating the discrepancy in connectivity across the region (e.g., Yemen versus Saudi Arabia) and the emerging role of digital media in shaping the media landscape and in consolidating the region's integration within the global digital economy. The chapter on Saudi new media, for instance, demonstrates the impact of the high connectivity of Saudi youth and the use of social media beyond activism such as to spread public health awareness. Moreover, the chapter on new media in Morocco argues that new and social media have facilitated a new form of engagement among Moroccans concerning issues such as Amazigh/Berber rights and gender-based violence. In Syria, the number of Syrians connected to the Internet has increased significantly since the mid-2000s and the civil war, which began in 2011, contributed to raising that number following the escape of millions of Syrians to neighboring and Western countries and the subsequent rise of independent media ventures by Syrians in diaspora communities. However, tens of online news services were launched only to end soon thereafter due to unsustainable funding. Another obvious consequence of increasing digitization is the shrinking press market in the region, coupled with the high price of paper; for instance, in Egypt, several newspaper editors claim that the total circulated copies of all Egyptian newspapers are around 300,000 daily (Meghawer, 2018). Nonetheless, media reports such as Arab Media Outlook (issued by Dubai Press Club) tend to provide inflated circulation figures despite the absence of independent audit of newspaper circulation, which makes such figures hard to verify. Additionally, the COVID-19 crisis exacerbated the decline of the print press with the temporary suspension of printing facilities and distribution operations and the shutdown of restaurants and cafés, where people used to congregate and pass on their copies of newspapers. Finally, digitization seems to be the future for the print industry, but this too comes with the challenge of cyber hacking as was demonstrated in the 2015 hacking of the *Tahya Masr* newspaper in Egypt by a terrorist group (Egypt Independent, 2015).

Limitations

There are limitations to the ambitious aim of this volume to cover the historical development of news media in each Arab state and their role in social and political changes. One main limitation is that several other key themes were not covered here, mainly due to the restricted length of the volume, and which need to be covered in separate issues. These include, for instance, the development of other cultural industries such as cinema and performing arts and the significance of these industries post-2011. Also worthy of a separate research inquiry is the definition and role of the so-called Islamic journalism, as well as the role of media ventures affiliated with Islamist movements. Moreover, the recent discussion about a possible "deal of the century" as a solution to the long-standing Israel-Palestine conflict will undoubtedly have a long-lasting impact on the region and the media discourse about the conflict for years to come.

The ongoing political turmoil affecting the region has certainly reshaped the current media market organization in those countries. The civil wars in Libya, Yemen, and Syria have loosened the grip of the state on media ownership and brought up new voices, albeit each representing a faction in the conflict. Yet as those conflicts come to a settlement, so will the shape of the media market. Mainly radio and TV will witness a reorganization that follows the challenges of newly born democracies such as Tunisia. The significant transformations in the media scene during the democratic transition since the revolution of 14 January 2011 have highlighted Tunisia as a model for the region with the changes in ownership and regulations and consolidation of the public service media governed by an independent council away from the influence of the government meeting international standards in well-established democracies.

As the media scene keeps evolving, we believe many other themes can shape a future research agenda about Arab media, covering many other genres, professional communities, and ongoing conflicts. Such an agenda will depart from the hitherto narrow focus on Arab media as an example of "under-developed" media striving to emulate Eurocentric standards. Instead, as this volume seeks to demonstrate, the media trajectory of each state is very much tied to the historiography, the development of national identity, and the integration of each state into a global media economy.

References

Boyd, Douglas (1999), *Broadcasting in the Arab World*. Ames: Iowa State University Press.

Digital McKinsey (2016), *Digital Middle East: Transforming the Region into a Leading Digital Economy*, October. Washington, DC: McKinsey & Company.

Dubai Press Club (2016), *Arab Media Outlook 2016–2018 Youth, Content, Digital Media*. 5th edition. Dubai: Dubai Press Club.

Egypt Independent (2015), *Newspaper Restores the Facebook Page Hacked by IS*, 16 April. Retrieved from www.egyptindependent.com/newspaper-restores-facebook-page-hacked/

El-Erian, Mohamed, and Fischer, Stanley (1996), *Is MENA a Region?* IMF Working paper, WP/96/30. International Monetary Fund.

Fawcett, Louise (2016a), Alliances and Regionalism in the Middle East. In Louise Fawcett (ed.), *International Relations of the Middle East*. 4th edition. Oxford: Oxford University Press, pp. 196–217.

Fawcett, Louise (2016b), Introduction: The Middle East and International Relations. In Louise Fawcett (ed.), *International Relations of the Middle East*. 4th edition. Oxford: Oxford University Press, pp. 1–17.

Garde-Hansen, Joanne (2011), *Media and Memory*. Edinburgh: Edinburgh University Press.

Gray, Matthew (2010), *Conspiracy Theories in the Arab World. Sources and Politics*. London: Routledge.

Haddad, Mahmoud (1994), The Rise of Arab Nationalism Reconsidered. *International Journal of Middle East Studies*, 26(2), pp. 201–222.

Haddad, William W. (2018), *The Arab-Israeli Conflict in the Arab Press: The First Three Decades*. Bristol: Intellect.

Hafez, Kai (2001), *Mass Media, Politics, and Society in the Middle East*. Cresskill, NJ: Hampton Press.

Hardy, Jonathan (2014), *Critical Political Economy of the Media. An Introduction*. London and New York: Routledge.

Hashemi, Nader, and Postel, Danny (eds.) (2017), *Sectarianization. Mapping the New Politics of the Middle East*. Oxford: Oxford University Press.

Hinnebusch, Raymond (2016), The Politics of Identity in the Middle East International Relations. In Louise Fawcett (ed.), *International Relations of the Middle East*. 4th edition. Oxford: Oxford University Press, pp. 155–175.

Hopkins, Nicholas S., and Ibrahim, Saad Eddin (2003), *Arab Society. Class, Gender, Power & Development*. 3rd edition. Cairo: The American University in Cairo Press.

Jenkins, Richard (2000), Categorization: Identity, Social Process, and Epistemology. *Current Sociology*, 48, pp. 7–25.

Kalathil, Shanthi (2017), *A Slowly Shifting Field: Understanding Donor Priorities in Media Development*. CIMA Digital Report, 25 April. Retrieved from www.cima.ned.org/publication/slowly-shifting-field/

Keddie, Nikki (1973), Is There a Middle East? *International Journal of Middle East Studies*, 4(3), pp. 255–271.

Korany, Bahgat (2016), The Middle East since the Cold War: The Multi-Layered (in)security Dilemma. In Louise Fawcett (ed.), *International Relations of the Middle East*. 4th edition. Oxford: Oxford University Press, pp. 79–98.

Korany, Bahgat, Noble, Paul, and Brynen, Rex (eds.) (1993), *The Many Faces of National Security in the Arab World*. New York: Palgrave Macmillan.

Kraidy, Marwan (2011), Globalizing Media and Communication Studies: Thoughts on the Translocal and the Modern. In Georgette Wang (ed.), *De-Westernizing Communication Research. Altering Questions and Changing Frameworks*. London and New York: Routledge, pp. 50–57.

Mattar, Khawla Mohammed (1992), *Silent Citizens: State, Citizenship, and Media in the Gulf*. Unpublished PhD thesis, Durham University. Retrieved from http://etheses.dur.ac.uk/5768/

Meghawer, Mohamed (2018), Raising the Price of Newspapers (in Arabic). *Arabi21*, 9 August. Retrieved from https://bit.ly/2rKfxvG

Mellor, Noha (2018), *The State of Arab Media since 2011. Mediterranean Yearbook 2018*. Barcelona: IeMED.

Mellor, Noha (2020), Analyzing Media Power in the Arab World. In Naila Hamdy and Phil Auter (eds.), *Communication as an Agent of Change in the Modern Arab World*. Lanham, MD: Rowman & Littlefield.

Mostafa, Dalia (2017), *The Egyptian Military in Popular Culture. Context and Critique*. London: Palgrave Macmillan.

Nashmi, E. A., Alkazemi, M. F., and Wanta, W. (2018), Journalism and Mass Communication Education in the Arab World: Towards a Typology. *International Communication Gazette*, 80(5), pp. 403–425.

Rugh, William (2004), *Arab Mass Media: Newspapers, Radio, and Television in Arab Politics*. Westport, CT: Praeger Publishers.

Springborg, Robert (2020), *Political Economies of the Middle East and North Africa*. Cambridge: Polity.

Algeria

1

MASS MEDIA IN ALGERIA

Saida Kheira Benammar

Introduction

Despite the early appearance of radio and TV broadcasting in Algeria, the pace of media advancement was slow, particularly on the organizational and legal levels. Radio and TV broadcasting appeared in Algeria during the French occupation (1830–1962) to spread colonialist principles and especially impose a news blackout on the Algerian cause. Radio broadcasting had begun under the French colonialist rule before members of the Algerian revolution started a clandestine radio to serve the aims of their cause.

The press as a traditional media tool was also made part of the political events in Algeria since its emergence with the outset of French colonization in 1830, in which the first newspaper for political purposes was issued. In the same period, the press had been transformed into a tool that served the colonization objectives in misleading Algerian public opinion with bilingual issues directed to Algerians for their inclusion. As a reaction to these practices, the indigenous press has emerged in its various states to maintain Algerian rights and to reject repression without demanding independence explicitly, as it was an unthinkable risk. We may also notice the presence of integrative press that demanded integration and naturalization and ultimately turned to manifest resistance and revolutionary ideas that culminated in proclaiming independence. Television was likewise established by the French to advance their propaganda against the Algerian revolution. After independence, the Algerian Radio and Television institution were restored as an Algerian state establishment under Algerian administration.

The post-independence era took two decades or, until 1982 for the first media legislation to appear. However, its codes supported the state's monopoly on the media sector putting it under the service of the ruling party. The media became a reflection of the socialist ideology of the Algerian regime at that time.

Following the 1988 October riots, a new constitution was adopted in 1989 allowing a multiparty system that led to the establishment of different political organizations, which led accordingly to issuing the second media law in Algeria in 1990. This legislation provided space for more media pluralism and freedom of newspapers and publications but excluded the privatization of TV and radio, which remained under the monopoly of the state until 2012.

The 2012 media law came under specific political conditions similar to that of the 1988 period context, as in 2011, Algeria witnessed a series of protests in the context of the Arab

11

Spring revolutions, in addition to the protests in neighboring Arab countries (Tunisia, Egypt, and Libya), which prompted the government to settle on pressing choices in April 2011 discourse and allude to some political and media changes. The Media Code of 2012 was viewed as the beginning of broadcasting pluralism in Algeria, yet the legal positions of these media establishments were problematic, especially as they were institutions with foreign links that are broadcast from outside Algeria. A few of them have been closed for financial and political reasons, to be followed by another code in 2014 to control audiovisual activities and to clarify the functions of the audiovisual regulatory authority.

In terms of financial regulation, the Algerian public media (press, radio, and television) rely heavily on government support and also on advertising revenues, while private press and TV outlets face a plethora of financial difficulties, but they continue to operate as long as they do not oppose the regime.

Emergence and development of print media in Algeria

The appearance of print media in Algeria is linked to the French occupation, where the first newspaper was published in 1830, a year that coincided with the French invasion of the country. *L'Estafette de Sidi Ferruch* appeared as the first newspaper and a platform for the support of the French colonization. The first newspapers to appear in Algeria were under the control of the colonial power that invaded Algeria in 1830 (Ihaddaden, 2014: 91). In 1847, the colonial authority also issued *El-Mobasher* as an official bilingual newspaper for colonial political purposes oriented to indigenous readers to inform them about the instructions and orders of the colonial power (Nacer, 2006: 11).

While the colonial press was fully supportive of the French occupation, indigenous initiative appeared by launching *El-Montakheb* in 1882, which was the first Islamic newspaper to extensively treat Muslim affairs (Ihaddaden, 2014: 91). In 1881 the French government promulgated a new law on press freedom in France; this law stipulated that the text applies to Algeria also. Once the first Arabic newspaper appeared by a nongovernmental body, however, the authorities refused it in with an act of aggression against the *El-Montakheb* newspaper (Nacer, 2006: 12).

The third type of press was newspapers led totally by Algerians. After the various individual contributions of Algerians in French newspapers dating back to 1874, the first attempt of what can be called as "indigenous press" was in 1893 in Annaba department when *"El-Haq"* newspaper launched. It was the first platform to defend the rights of Algerians (Delliou, 2014: 46).

Other newspapers worth mentioning here were those issued by non-French settlers, especially the well-known press of Spanish immigrants to Algeria, which is usually ignored in the history of Algerian press. Delliou (2014: 65) recorded about 30 newspapers between 1880 and 1931, in addition to a few limited Italian and Maltese attempts, such as French-Italian Brothers (*La Fraternité-Fratellanza*) in 1906 and the French–Italian Association (*La Lega Franco-Italiana*).

The following phase witnessed the emergence of the reformist and political press that appeared between 1919 and 1954, as these issues were divided into the production of individual activities such as newspapers of Abd el Hamid Bin Badis, Mohamed Al Said Al Zahri, and Abu Al-Yaqdhan, among others. In the political resistance press period between 1937 and 1954, a group of reformist newspapers appeared as the *El-Maghreb El-Arabi* newspaper (1937) and *Al-Wifaq* weekly newspaper (1938) (Delliou, 2014: 103).

The last phase of print media before independence was characterized by the appearance of the revolution press (1954–1962) that accompanied military activity in the context of the liberation revolution. This stage was marked by the suspension of most Algerian newspapers two years after the eruption of the revolution in 1954 when the National Liberation Front leadership was called upon to do so. The most prominent newspaper during this period was *The Algerian Resistance* (1955–57). *El Moujahid* replaced *The Algerian Resistance* with its two versions scheduled to be stopped at the Soummam conference of 1955 and merged into one newspaper (Delliou, 2014: 116).

The aforementioned typology is certainly not the only one classification of the development of the Algerian press during French colonial rule. Other classifications that can be taken into consideration are a language-based classification, or a classification based on editorial choices, such as colonial press, indigenous press, reformist press, and the integrative press, in addition to the foreign press that was published in Algeria (such as Spanish, Italian, and Maltese) and Algerian press activity outside the country.

Algerian press after independence

The Algerian authorities kept the French Press Law of 1881, which recognized the freedom of the press; however, this did not prevent it from turning to the termination of all French and foreign newspapers that were issued in Algeria. Between 1962 and 1963 there were about 11 newspapers in Algeria, with a total of 300,000 copies, all in the French language (Ihaddaden, 2014: 96). In September 1963, the Political Bureau of the National Liberation Front (FLN) met and decided to nationalize these newspapers and for others made up new names such as *AlNasr* and *AlJoumhouria*, except for *Alger Républicain*'s newspaper, which was run by Algerians (Ihaddaden, 2014: 96).

From 1962 to 1965 numerous daily and weekly newspapers were issued, such as *Elchaab* in 1962; *El-Moudjahid*, the army magazine in 1963; and the *African Revolution* magazine in 1963. This also coincided with the decision of the Political Bureau of the National Liberation Front to nationalize the French dailies on 18 September 1963 (Delliou, 2013: 284). This period also witnessed the publication of the first evening daily newspaper, *Al-Massae*, as well as two daily regional newspapers, *AlNasr* in 1963 and *Aljoumhouria* in 1963.

The socialist political system embraced by the Algerian regime at the time was not compatible with the freedom of the press, as the authorities attempted in various ways to control the press sector. On 19 August 1966, the government decided to establish the National Publishing and Distribution Company to give it monopoly power in the field of newspaper distribution (Ihaddaden, 2014: 97). After this decision, the government became able to impose its dominance on distributing newspapers. Thus, the post-1966 period did not witness the existence of any private newspaper (Ihaddaden, 2014: 98). The third phase, which lasted from 1979 to early 1989, was marked by some openness and clarity regarding the legal status of the media by the promulgation of Media Law of 6 February 1982 (Delliou, 2013: 285).

The events of October 1988 and the emergence of the constitution of February 1989 led to the appearance of the Media Law of 3 April 1990, which allowed the establishment of private and party newspapers. Under this law, the private press was created. It was supported by the government in various ways, including giving journalists in the public sector who wanted to create private newspapers three years' salary in advance, among other financial incentives (Layadi, 2016: 175). This led a large number of journalists to launch daily journals which increased the number of press releases, some of which became influential like *Echorouk Elyawmi*, with an estimated 500,000 copies, *Elkhabar*, 400,000 copies, *Ennahar eljadid*, 300,000 copies, and *El Watan*, 150,000 copies (Taiebi Moussaoui, 2016: 63). Because of the political crisis that appeared in the summer of 1991, the Algerian press entered a new stage marked by total suspension, threat, and assassination. This phase witnessed the withdrawal of private newspapers compared to the public newspapers issued in French at the expense of Arabic. (Delliou, 2013: 287). Although Algeria has moved to media pluralism, which was approved by the Media Law 90–7, it has not put in place the regulatory instruments that preserve it. The public authorities have been monopolizing the public advertising sector, a practice that impede the citizen's right to information (Layadi, 2016: 176).

The last stage was accompanied by the move of Algerian newspapers towards online platforms. Algeria has been engaged in the electronic press experience since the mid-1990s to free itself from political pressures. This was initiated by online newspapers since November 1997 by publishing the *El Watan* daily online (www.el-watan.com), followed by other newspapers in 1998 including *Elyawm*, *La Tribune*, *ElKhabar*, *Horizons*, and *Le Matin*. These electronic editions were gradually developed using the PDF and HTML formats to be shown on the Internet in creative, hetero style (Delliou, 2014: 203).

During 2000, which is considered the period of the Internet boom in Algeria, digitization significantly transformed print and electronic journalism, which began to emerge as one of the main sources of news, and offers sphere for political discussion, with dozens of independent electronic newspapers appeared such as *TSA Algérie*, *Algérie Patriotique*, *Algérie 1*, *Impact24*, *Sabq-Presse*, and *Maghreb Emergent*. These platforms have become important production centers for public news (Dris, 2017: 262). In 2005 the newspaper *Echorouk-Alyawmi* established its website – *Echorouk Online* – which is considered as the most advanced website, as it ranks 13th in the Algerian websites list (Layadi, 2016: 179). It was followed by many public and private newspapers that became focused on electronic visibility and digital content, especially after the integration of the Internet and social network sites in newsrooms.

Radio and television in Algeria (establishment and development)

Before independence, radio broadcasting in Algeria went through three major phases. The first phase was the colonial radio, which was founded by the French occupation and started to resonate in Algeria. The second phase was the Algerian independent radio programs, but this time from outside Algeria through a few Arab radio stations, most notably in Egypt and Tunisia. In the third phase, and to promote the Algerian independence movement, clandestine radio was established with humble technical potential on the Algerian-Moroccan border to support the Algerian revolution between 1954 and 1962.

In 1924, a private French company set up a 100-watt transmitter in the capital Algiers and began broadcasting in French on the medium wave, as recorded by Henry Gaillod (Rezagui and Rashad, 2012: 22). It rose to 600 watts in 1928 as a personal initiative. On the occasion of the centenary of French occupation in 1929, the first real transmission station with a power of 12 kilowatts on the medium wave was set up (Sabri and Abdou, 2008: 24), to expand in 1940 to four provinces: the capital (Algiers), Oran and Tlemcen (western Algeria) and Constantine (eastern Algeria). Broadcasting was initially limited to the French minority in Algeria, and could not spread because the language used was not the language of the Algerian population and Arabic was prohibited until 1947 (Rezagui and Rashad, 2012: 22). Since 1948, studios have been established to produce radio programs in Constantine, Oran, and Bejaia, with several stations connected to several other Algerian cities (Tetouani, 2019: 163). The radio stations generally aimed to promote colonial power.

According to Zahir Ihaddaden (2012), the year 1948 witnessed the launch of genuine Algerian radio. In addition to the establishment of new channels, the French authorities stepped up programming studios in various Algerian cities such as Constantine, Oran, and Bejaia. Technical reforms were also introduced to transmission and multiplication stations with a total transmission capacity of 322 kW in 1954, while it was only 25 kW in 1946, on medium and short wave (Rezagui and Rashad, 2012: 24).

Pan-Arab radio broadcasting played a great role in supporting the Algerian revolution with the establishment of several radio programs that were broadcast on Arab radio waves such as Voice of the Arabs in Cairo, Radio Tunis, and Radio Damascus, among others. Those outlets attempted to publicize and support the Algerian revolution, especially Voice of the Arabs with dedicated radio programs in support of the Algerian revolution. Because it again became impossible to establish Algerian radio within Algeria at the time, radio programs concerning the Algerian cause were presented by Algerians abroad.

The only available alternative at the hand of the FLN (National Liberation Front), the party fighting the war of independence against France, was to establish a clandestine radio station in Algeria, because Algeria's voice from pan-Arab radio stations did not reach the Algerian people inside. That was decided at the Soummam Conference in August 1956, but it had not begun its actual activity until early 1957. It started with a mobile radio station, which traveled into the mountains and borders (Abd el-Rahman, 1985: 59).

The clandestine radio was the first Algerian radio service that started its broadcasting with an Algerian administration. It aimed to promote the Algerian revolution and to communicate with the Algerian people. As for TV broadcasting, it can be argued that Algeria had its first TV service in the mid-1950s, or on 24 December 1956, with the establishment of a television station in Algiers by the French colonial authority. The service included news about France and various political, economic, cultural, and sports events (Tetouani, 2019: 166).

The Algerian Radio and Television Corporation (RTF) and French Television were only a regional station of the French Radio and Television service, which was later established under the name ORTF and operated according to the regulations of French media (Chettah, 2010: 424). The broadcast was available 31 hours a week in Arabic and French, with the possibility of choosing between them by a device placed within each receiver (Zaatar, 2008: 85). The French authorities worked to expand the transmission networks to cover the country's qualified areas (Zaatar, 2008: 86). Because of the importance of television as a means of communication and in light of the development of media activity of the liberation movement through clandestine radio, France sought to focus on the media pressure locally and internationally. They did this through establishing a television channel which aimed to spread misinformation among the public and to present the French occupation as a civilized one.

Algeria gained its independence on 5 July 1962, but 28 October 1962 was considered the real date of the liberalization of Algerian (audiovisual) media, albeit still under French authority according to the Evian Agreement. Article 1 of the Convention, in section 10, states, "Radio and television shall devote part of their broadcasts in French commensurate with the importance of this language in Algeria" (Chettah, 2010: 425). Also on 28 October 1962, the Algerian army stormed and regained the headquarters of Radio and Television since it believed that the Algerian media's dependence on France ran counter to the principles of national sovereignty. All French workers withdrew from the television building as part of a media blockade to thwart the start of Algerian Radio and Television.

Radio and Television of Algeria (RTA) witnessed a significant development in 1968 by establishing two radio services (Radio Constantine in 1968; Radio Oran in 1973). Thus, since 1976, it has been possible to listen to radio throughout the Algerian homeland (Ihaddaden, 2012: 40). At the programming level, however, Algerian television was experiencing weak production due to several technical and administrative issues. By 1986, and to revitalize the Algerian media, a major separation took place in the RTA following the restructuring decision of the audiovisual sector through the decree of 1 July 1986, which resulted in four media institutions: National

Television Corporation (ENTV), National radio Corporation (ENRS), National Broadcasting Corporation (TDA), and National Audiovisual Production Corporation (ENPA).

Under the decision of restructuring and separation between Algerian radio and television institutions, the National Radio Broadcasting Corporation was granted financial, technical, and organizational independence, which enabled it to develop its capabilities and improve its performance in the field of public service. By transforming it into a public institution, as stipulated in the decree of 20 April 1991, Algerian radio has become an industrial and commercial presence that exercises a public service function in the field of radio broadcasting (Chelouch, 2014: 9).

Since 1991, Algerian Radio has started to diversify its program offerings by establishing a regional and thematic radio network, gradually forming the Algerian radio system and completing the way it is now: 48 regional radio stations and four thematic radio stations (youth radio, Holy Quran radio, cultural radio, and international radio). In addition to these, three national Arabic-speaking channels have been added: Amazigh, French, and digital radio or Algerian multimedia radio, which is now the homepage of Algerian Radio on the Internet (Chelouch, 2014: 10). Although a new media code was passed, promoting the establishment and ownership of private newspapers and publications, the radio sector remained uninterested in this development.

Despite the promulgation of Organic Law 12–05 on private sector owning audiovisual media, there was no interest in the radio broadcasting field except for the emergence of some private radio channels belonging to private TV channels such as Echorouk Radio or various digital radio channels. The most prominent private digital radio channels in Algeria are Voice of Women Radio, which is the first electronic radio station in the Arab world to deal with women's issues and broadcasts five hours a day in Arabic and French, and Radio M, which is the first private web radio in Algeria, launched in 2013.

Following the restructuring of the RTA, the National Television Corporation (ENTV) was established by Decree 01–86–146 on 1 July 1986, with an economic and socio-cultural tone (Zaatar, 2008: 89). The same decree included the establishment and organization of national television as a publicly owned and financially independent institution, thus helping to combat the public services monopoly (Zaatar, 2008: 90).

As of the executive order No. 91–101 of 20 April 1991, the basic legal reference for Algerian television, ENTV became a public institution with an industrial and commercial nature but was dominated by an element of public service. The executive order was authorized by the Algerian Public Television Corporation (EPTV) to broadcast advertising and finalize agreements and production contracts (Bouzegaou, 2011: 60). Since 1991, the National Television Corporation of Algeria has not issued any decrees to its rules of procedure, despite the establishment of Canal Algérie and the third Algerian TV (A3) channels. Despite this, the preliminary draft of the Media Code of 2002, which did not see the light of day, hinted at the possibility of opening the industry to the private sector (Chettah, 2010: 426).

The third Algerian channel broadcasts 24 hours on Hotbird and Nilesat 102 satellites and is directed to Arab countries (Chettah, 2010: 438). In comparison, Canal Algérie broadcasts its programs in French, with some programs in Arabic and Tamazight, especially news bulletins, miscellaneous programs, and some religious ones, which are largely dedicated to Algerian immigrants in France (Chettah, 2010: 436). In addition, two thematic channels were established on 18 March 2009, namely Channel 4, an Amazigh-speaking channel, and Channel 5, designated for Quran.

It is noteworthy that the Organic Code of Information issued in 2012 came after a wave of political protests in Algeria, prompting former President Abdelaziz Bouteflika's speech on 16 April 2011, which promised reform. The reforms were introduced after 2012 and involved opening the audiovisual field to the private sector after decades of closure. Many channels appeared equivalent to 50 channels; only five channels were approved. These channels have developed in a gray legal field where they enjoy the freedom of foreign institutions, allowing them to broadcast to Algeria.

Allegedly, it was the absence of any legal regulation of these channels that made authorities close down El Watan TV. However, it was more likely due to a guest, Madani Merzag, the former leader of the Islamic Salvation Front, making statements against the Algerian regime (Reporters sans frontières: 8). The authorities proclaimed that El Watan Tv did not owned a license as the Article of 20 of the Audiovisual Code stipulates.

In 2015, businessman Mahieddine Tahkout, manager of the ETHRB Group, bought Numedia-News channel, while the Algerian Channel El djazairia belonged to the management of Oueld Zemerli family. Isaad Rebrab, ranked among the 10 richest personalities in Africa, bought *Liberté* newspaper, while Ali Haddad, the president of the FCE business forum and president of the BTP building complex, has two television channels, Dzair TV and Dzair News, and two daily newspapers, Le Temps d'Algérie and Wakt eldjazair (Reporters sans frontiers: 24). These channels were indeed formed with Algerian capital, but they are not considered institutions with Algerian rights, although they are managed from the homeland (Dris, 2014: 10).

Since the emergence of public television, the Algerian state has sought to embody a network program that reflects the national identity, but it has not been able to do so, especially when they began television broadcasting due to the weakness of financial and human resources. In 1987, for instance, the national production of documentaries, children's programs, and entertainment shows totaled only 23% of the programming (Boucherit, 1988: 17). However, with the availability of human and material resources, the Algerian public television institution managed to integrate 100% of national production into Channel 4 (Amazigh channel) and the Holy Quran channel, according to the general manager of the public television institution, Tewfik Khelladi (Ministry of Communication, 2018). As for private media, the principle of preserving the values and principles of Algerian society and promoting national dialects has been defined in each channel's "cahiers de charge" which the audiovisual regulatory authority works to achieve. As for radio broadcasting, the program network for the distribution of radio stations is working to refine the Algerian identity, with 48 local radio stations supporting local dialects as well as Arabic (Rezagui and Rashad, 2012: 61).

Media laws and regulations in Algeria

Numerous laws and decrees (1963–1981) do regularize media in Algeria, but we can limit the most important to the following.

The general structure of the Media Code of 1982 consists of five sections containing 128 articles. These articles conclude that the 1982 code did not deviate from serving the one party, especially its ideology, principles, and symbols of the Algerian revolution. This law, although delayed, came to monopolize the media, not liberate it. While the second article states, "The right to media is a fundamental right for all citizens," Article 3 sets limits: "The right of information shall be exercised freely within the scope of the ideological choices of the country, the moral values of the nation, and the directives of the political leadership emanating from the National Charter" (Chettah, 2006: 293).

The 1988 October riots provided a strong impetus to political and economic reforms in the country. Among them was the popular vote on a new constitution ratified on 23 February 1989.

The media code came in line with the country's new constitution and opened the field for political pluralism. Article 2 of the Constitution states:

> The right to information is embodied in the right of the citizen to be informed completely and objectively, on the facts and opinions of interest to society at national and international levels, and the right to participate in the media by exercising fundamental freedoms of thought, opinion, and expression following Articles 35–39–40 of the Constitution.

In Article 3, the document speaks about the freedom to exercise the right to information: "The right to information shall be exercised freely while respecting the dignity of human personality and the requirements of foreign policy and national defense" (Chettah, 2006: 195).

What is new in this code is its emphasis on the freedom to own newspapers and publications, but it excludes the audiovisual sector in Article 56 which states, "The distribution of sound or television broadcasting quotas and the use of electric radio frequencies shall be subject to licenses and a general record prepared by the Department after consultation with the Higher Media Council."

Between 2010 and 2012, a set of internal and neighboring conditions caused the bulk of protests. Algeria's protests of January 2011, along with the Arab Spring, helped force the Algerian state to make quick decisions to open the field of audiovisual media for Algerian citizens. The Media Code of 2012 is the true opening of audiovisual media in Algeria, despite the preliminary draft being submitted in 2002. For the first time, the state explicitly endorsed the opening of the audiovisual industry and not simply a state monopoly. The Audiovisual Regulatory Authority was then established as an independent body with the task of ensuring the free exercise of audiovisual activities – within the constraints laid down in code No. 14–04 of 24 February 2014 (Rebouh, 2017: 270).

Financial regulation of media in Algeria

The public audiovisual media institutions in Algeria rely mainly on state subsidies. Funding sources of Algerian Radio and Television come from the following sources:

- Government subsidy – provided by the State Treasury, so that the state media can complete their annual production plans and achieve their objectives.
- State subsidies are specifically directed towards the costs of management, wages, and other running costs (Bouzegao, 2011: 98). The state started to provide subsidies to the broadcasting sector immediately after independence especially between 1962 and 1967, where the smallest budget amounted to 2,000,000 DZD in 1965, while the highest in 1966 was 14,000,000 DZD (Ihaddaden, 2012: 37).
- Fees/licenses on radio and television transferred directly to radio and television institutions.
- Corporate revenues.

The subsidy allocated to television is the highest compared to other media. The lowest rate recorded at the end of the 1960s was 68% in 1966 decreasing to 46% in 1968, peaking to 88% in 1979, and falling to 62% in 1985. A large part of the budget for television went to pay for the operating costs and technical installations for national television coverage (Mostefaoui, 1988: 57).

The magnitude of the television budget may be because television is the most far-reaching medium, not to mention its costly technical equipment. As the significance of the medium increased, a higher television budget was needed. Business objectives were also behind the establishment of other public channels, and transition to satellite broadcasting along with digitization all meant an even higher budget was needed. From 2001 to 2003, the state's support for Algerian television was stable and increased slightly, but it did not exceed 80 million dinars. However, this support doubled and increased significantly in 2008, reaching 270 million dinars, peaking in 2009 and 2010, where the state subsidy exceeded 296 million dinars (Akroud, 2012: 72). These specific increases can largely be attributed to coverage of election campaigns and sporting events (African Cup and the World Cup). In 2009, the Algerian television budget amounted to five billion DZD (Saidani and Lafqiri, 2016: 11). Fees and licenses are often used to cover the lack of funding for management costs that should be covered by state subsidies: The National Broadcasting Corporation receives 30%, radio stations receive 30%, and the Algerian Public Television Corporation receive 40% (Bouzegao, 2011: 99).

Algerian public media rely financially on state subsidies, while the private print press is subjected to the terms of private advertising stipulated by the Agency for Publication and Advertising (ANEP). Many Algerian opposition newspapers have stopped printing because of the withdrawal of advertising subsidies by the state; because private television channels are financially linked to some newspapers, they are equally affected by lack of funding. Private television channels, established under the Media Code of 2012, are linked to the advertising revenues of their newspapers because they form one institution, for example, *Ennahar* newspaper is connected to Ennahar TV. Thus, there are two categories of private TV channels in Algeria: The first is owned by Algerian executives, such as Numedia News owned by Mahieddine Tahkout, or Dzair News and Dzair TV owned by Ali Haddad. The second category of private channels is linked to newspapers, such as Echorouk, Ennahar, and Elbilad.

There is no declared financial support for these two kinds of channels except the advertising revenues received by newspapers. Despite the ambiguity of funding, private media in Algeria have managed to capture a large share of the Algerian audience, thus becoming the most popular channels in Algeria. Sigma Conseil's study (2014) shows that the Algerian public channel *A3* ranked first among Algerian viewers at 15.5% market share, followed by Ennahar TV channel with 13.3% and Echorouk TV channel at 13%, with a total absence of French channels (Almanach, 2015). By 2016, private TV channels had dominated the media scene with Ennahar TV leading at 34%, Echorouk TV with 32%, followed by the pan-Arab channel MBC and Algerian public television with 11.5% (Zitouni, 2016). By 2019, three Algerian channels were leading the scene: Echorouk TV at 41%, Ennahar TV at 40%, and the public channel A3 at 33.5% (Almanach, 2019). Echorouk TV especially dominated in May 2019, during Ramadan, with a market share of nearly 43% (Bourse-dz, 2019). As for radio audience, there were more than 284 million listeners in 2017, up from 140 million in 2016, and the most popular radio stations were Radio Al Bahja, Jil FM, and La Chaine Une (Radio Algérie, 2018).

Conclusion

The Algerian official decision to delay the privatization of media institutions has had a significant impact on the development of Algerian media, adding to that a variety of legal, economic, and professional obstacles. Among the legal obstacles is the narrowing field of work due to the earlier mentioned legal decrees as well as the media restrictions imposed by the government. As a result of these major obstacles a group of Algerian channels failed immediately after their emergence: for example, the Audiovisual Regulatory Authority's pressures caused the shutdown of the Atlas channel in 2014 and El-Watan channel in 2015, as the Authority objected to their political content. In the absence of a culture of investment in the media sector, some media institutions were led to bankruptcy as a result of insufficient funding, since obtaining governmental or private financial support is rather difficult. Moreover, the slow pace of the Algerian technological advances pressured the Algerian media to use dated practices. With the recent protests in Algeria since February 2019, in response to former president Abdelaziz Bouteflika's candidacy for a fifth term, private media channels have been pushing for obtaining more freedoms while asking the government to guarantee them adequate sources of funding.

References

Abd el-Rahman, A. (1985), *Arab Journalism in Algeria (Analytical Study of the Algerian Revolutionary Newspapers (1954–1962) (AR)*. Algeria: National Book Foundation.

Akroud, S. (2012), *Organization of Advertising Sponsorship and its Relationship to TV Programs in Algerian Television* (AR). Magister thesis, University of Algiers 03, Algeria.

Almanach (2015), Communication – Television- Audimat – classement sigma 2014. *Almanach-dz*, 15 February. Retrieved from www.almanach-dz.com/index.php?op=fiche&fiche=4179. Accessed 26 September 2019.

Boucherit, A. (1988), Complexité linguistiques des programmes à la télévision algériennes: Essai d'analyse d'une production locale. *Revue de l'occident musulman et de méditerranée*, 47, pp. 35–46.

Bourse-dz (2019), Audience des chaînes TV: Echourouk indétrônable. *Bourse-dz,* 22 May. Retrieved from https://bourse-dz.com/audience-des-chaines-tv-echourouk-indetronable/. Accessed 26 September 2019.

Bouzegaou, N. (2011), *Financial Management of Public Audiovisual Institutions, Case Study: Algerian Public Television 2000–2010 (AR)*. Magister thesis, University of Algiers 03, Algeria.

Chelouch, M. (2014), Algerian Radio: Origin and Track (AR). *Algerian Radio*, 15 December. Retrieved from www.radioalgerie.dz/culture/sites/default/files/pdf/Koteyb%20Radio%2016%20dec%202014pdf. Accessed 14 October 2019.

Chettah, M. (2006), Legislation of Audiovisual Media in Algeria, Reading in Laws and Legislation (AR). *Al-Mieyar Journal*, 6(12), pp. 288–312.

Chettah, M. (2010), Identity and Dialogue with other's Issue in Arab Satellite Channels (AR). *Journal of Research and Studies in Humanities*, 5, pp. 423–444.

Delliou, F. (2013), *History of Media and Communication Tools (AR)*. Algeria: Dar Elkhaldounia.

Delliou, F. (2014), *History of Algerian Press 1830–2013 (AR)*. Algeria: Dar Houma.

Dris, C. H. (2014), Les médias en Algérie: un espace en mutation. *Maghreb – Machrek*, 3(221), pp. 65–75.

Dris, C. H. (2017), La presse algérienne: une dérégulation sous contraintes (les nouvelles formes de contrôle ou la "main invisible" de l'état. *Questions de communication*, 32, pp. 261–286.

Ihaddaden, Z. (2012), *L'information en Algérie: de 1965 à 1982*. Algérie: OPU.

Ihaddaden, Z. (2014), *Introduction to Media and Communication Sciences* (AR). Algérie: OPU.

Layadi, N. (2016), Algerian Press in the Web: Change Indicators (AR). *Algerian Journal of Social and Human Sciences*, 3(6), pp. 171–193.

Ministère de la communication (2018), Télévision publique: priorité à la production nationale dans la grille des programmes du mois de Ramadhan. *Ministère de la communication*, 13 May. Retrieved from www.ministerecommunication.gov.dz/fr/node/5048. Accessed 28 September 2019.

Mostefaoui, B. (1988), Tendance actuelles de l'audiovisuelle en Algérie: A propos de brèches dans le monopole de l'état. *Revue de l'occident musulman et de la méditerranée*, 47, pp. 53–72.

Nacer, B. (2006), *The Algerian Arabic Press 1847–1954 (AR)*. Algeria: Alpha.

Radio Algérie (2018), Plus de 284 millions de nombre d'écoutes des programmes de la Radio Algérienne sur le web en 2017: Une progression de 52% en une année. *Radio Algérie*, 26 January. Retrieved from www.radioalgerie.dz/news/fr/article/20180126/132015.html. Accessed 26 September 2019.

Rebouh, Y. (2017), Media Activities in Algeria, from Unilateralism to the Liberation of Audiovisual Sector (AR). *Journal of Human and Social Sciences*, 29, pp. 265–272.

Reporters sans frontières (2016), Algérie: la main invisible du pouvoir sur les médias. *Reporters sans frontières*, 21 December. Retrieved from https://rsf.org/fr/rapports/rsf-publie-son-rapport-algerie-la-main-invisible-du-pouvoir-sur-les-medias. Accessed 19 October 2019.

Rezagui, A., and Rashad, A. (2012), The Role of Local and Regional Radio Broadcasting in Raising Awareness of Community Issues and Problems: Algeria, Sudan, and Egypt (AR). *Research Series and Radio Studies*, 72, pp. 1–192.

Sabri, A., and Abdou, K. J. (2008), The Status and Role of Government Radio Broadcasting in Light of the Competition of Private Radio (AR). *Radio Research Series and Studies*, 62, pp. 1–149.

Saidani, S., and Lafqiri, L. (2016), *The Algerian Experience in Ownership of Audiovisual Media: Algerian Television ENTV as a Model* (AR). Proceedings of paper presented to the First National Forum on: Media profession between Public Service, Professional Pressure and Economic Investment Requirements, 26–27 October, University Center of Ahmed Zabana, Relizane.

Taiebi Moussaoui, F. (2016), Le développent de la presse électronique en Algérie: dispositifs aux pratiques journalistiques (étude d'un échantillon de journaux en ligne). *L'Année Maghreb*, 15, pp. 61–76.

Tetouani, H. (2019), Media in Algeria under French Occupation: Beginnings of Newspapers, Radio and Television (AR). *Journal of Communication and Press*, 10, pp. 158–174.

Zaatar, M. (2008), *Advertising in the Algerian TV: Content Analysis of the ads of the National TV Channel* (AR). Magister thesis, Constantine University, Algeria.

Zitouni, A. (2016), Le duo Ennahar-Echourouk domine les audiences TV au 3ème jour de Ramadhan (IMMAR). *Huffpostmaghreb*, 13 June. Retrieved from www.huffpostmaghreb.com/entry/le-duo-ennahar-echourouk-domine-les-audiences-tv-au-3eme-jour-de-ramadhan-immar_mg_10434962?utm_hp_ref=mg-audiences. Accessed 2 October 2019.

2

NEW AND SOCIAL MEDIA IN ALGERIA

Belkacem Amin Benamra

Introduction

Social media is at once an artifact, a milieu, and a complex system of participatory interaction that is incessantly affecting all areas of human activity and impacting the ensemble of social and cultural dynamics both online and offline. In the Middle East and North Africa (MENA), social media, amid its exponential growth, is opening up vast fields of possibilities, where the disruptive user-driven technologies are being reinvented and used innovatively under the persistence of long-standing authoritarian regimes. As such, Arab users do not engage with social media for the mere sake of connectivity, rather, they crucially employ its affordances for varying trajectories, including self-expression, collective identity building, and the construction of alternative spaces of political protest.

Set in this context, the present chapter seeks to analyze the emergence and development of Internet and social media in Algeria, focusing on its patterned usage routines, regulatory ecology where it exists, and most importantly socio-political outputs afforded to social actors.

Respectively, this chapter consists of three sections. The first section tracks the development of the Internet from its emergence to present-day status, centering attention on landmark changes and adoption tendencies, in addition to the sectoral landscape of telecommunications management. The second section provides an analytical framework where social media patterns of usage in Algeria are addressed based on contextual and statistical data, as well as the regulatory ecology and regime de facto policies towards social media platforms. The last section discusses the socio-political significance of social media with more nuances, through exploring modes of Algerians engagement with social media platforms, and socio-technical modalities of employing its affordances as discursive mechanisms to frame their protests and to challenge the status quo. As the context requires, this section also looks at the intersections between social media usage and the ongoing *Hirak* movement, whether regarding its triggering, continuity, or consolidation.

Internet development in Algeria

The Internet made its debut in Algeria in 1991, through concerted efforts of the Algerian Association of UNIX Users in collaboration with the Association of Algerian Scientists, and via a wired network connection coming from Italy (Doudi et al., 2004: 3). By 1993, the Center of Research and Scientific Information (CRSI), an Algerian public research institute, was the first and exclusive Internet service provider (ISP), operating in reliance on poorly developed infrastructures that were well below international standards at that time. The monopoly of CRSI on Internet service ended by 1998, after issuing the ministerial decree No. 98–257 of 5 August 1998, which implemented some new measures, ending full state exclusive management of the telecommunications sector and allowing private companies to provide Internet and fixed telephony services.

Following that, law No. 2000–03 was issued on 5 August 2000, with the main aim of separating regulatory functions of traditional postal services from those of telecommunications and Internet services. This is why, by 2000, the investment in the Internet sector was partially open to private competitors who reached 18 ISPs by the first trimester of the same year and to 28 by the third trimester. At the time, Internet service was processed via analog telephone lines, of which there were only six lines per 100 inhabitants, while the average ratio in the developed countries was approximately 80 lines per 100 inhabitants (Doudi et al., 2004: 6). The asymmetric digital subscriber line (ADSL) service was launched in November 2003, following an agreement signed by the state-owned enterprise Algérie Télécom and the Algerian private Internet service provider Eepad (ibid.: 134). In 2005, Algérie Télécom launched an ambitious initiative of the project 1533 with the target of providing access to 300 000 new subscribers via a prepaid card system. By the end of 2005, the number of Internet users reached 1.9 million, which represented about 6% of the population at that time (ibid.: 136).

In the framework of a medium-term development programme for the period 2005–2010 adopted by Algérie Télécom in early 2005, modems with integrated routers that guaranteed wireless access in domestic spaces had been commercialized, adding a new dimension of mobility to the connectivity experience and leading to a significant increase in laptop ownership (Akli, 2006).

On the regulatory side, the governmental body responsible for the management of the telecommunications sector is the Ministry of Post and Telecommunications, which was created on 27 September 1962 and renamed the Ministry of Post and Information and Communication Technologies in June 2002. Once again, the name was changed in May 2017 to the Ministry of Post, Telecommunications, Technology, and Digitalization. However, the concrete management of the sector is dominated by the Regulatory Authority of Posts and Telecommunications (RAPT) and Algérie Télécom, with both bodies operate under the Ministry. The RAPT, which was created also by Law 2000–03, must, in theory, ensure the regulatory flexibility and healthy competition within the information and communications technology (ICT) sector; yet, it is usually viewed as the blameworthy of bureaucratization and overregulation of the sector. On the other hand, Algérie Télécom is the state-owned enterprise that monopolizes fields of fixed telephony, mobile telephony, Internet, and satellite telecommunications until the present day. It was created jointly by Law 2000–03 of 5 August 2000, and it presents itself as a public joint-stock company SpA with a capital of 61,275,180,000 Algerian dinars and a workforce of 21,408 employees in 2019 (Rédaction AE, 2019).

At the level of the Algerian society, the initial stage of Internet implementation was marked by a tangible explosion in the number of Internet users in less than three years (150,000 in 1999, 400,000 in 2001, one million at the end of 2002), which truly reflects the dimension and magnitude of the societal demand for Internet services and the enthusiastic reception of ICT in general (Djelti, 2008: 132).

Another aspect worth considering within the Algerian Internet landscape is cybercafés. Internet cafés or cybercafés are cost-effective techno-spaces that provide access to computers and the Internet and permit people to get familiar with computing equipment and Internet navigating experience (López-Bonilla et al., 2016). The first Internet café was launched in the center of Algiers in September 1997 by a private sector initiative, and then the number increased significantly to reach 5,000 cybercafés within the national territory by 2007 (Djelti, 2008: 135).

Cybercafés were the only cheap and accessible alternative to access Internet and computers because of the limited Internet penetration rate and the unaffordable price of desktop computers, which were the only way to connect during the 2000s. As a consequence, such cafés became very popular spaces in record time, far beyond any sort of leisure spaces, as they offered the very first interaction with Internet accessing experience and the initial informal technical learning to large segments of the Algerian population, especially to the youth. Nowadays, cybercafés are slowly disappearing as technological infrastructures have become more accessible and due to official authorities' systematic plan to restrict their activities right after the outbreak of Arab Spring incidents. In the process, a decree was promulgated by the Ministry of the Interior in the summer of 2011 placing them under the category of sensitive establishment, setting serious prohibitive conditions on continuing exercising the activity or opening new cybercafés (Nasri, 2018). As a result, by 2012 more than 50% of these cybercafés all across the country, open for years, had shut down this business activity permanently (Rahmouni, 2012).

Over the past decade, the development of the Internet in Algeria has followed a bumpy course as there was endless back and forth, with slow-paced progress at the level of installing new fiber optic cables or upgrading Internet services and regularly maintaining the infrastructure. Nevertheless, the number of Internet users kept increasing steadily until 2014, when it took an explosively upward turn, due to the adoption of mobile broadband technology. This new element marked the whole cluster of Internet adoption and usage practices in Algeria; hence, with the implementation of mobile broadband, whether the third (3G) or the fourth generation (4G), large segments of society became able to access to relatively high-speed Internet through low-cost mobile network subscription.

The 3G was released belatedly in December 2013. The three mobile operators, namely Mobilis, Nedjma, and Djezzy, were officially accredited by the RAPT to start the service. Best offers at that time were forwarded by the two public mobile operators Mobilis and Nedjma; the first one offered a monthly bitrate ranging between 500 MB and 4 GB for a sum between 750 DZD and 3,000 DZD and the second operator offered a monthly bitrate of 750 MB for 1,000 DZD and 3 GB for 3,000 DZD (Ananna, 2018). The 4G was officially launched by the public mobile operator Mobilis in October 2016, with an established deployment schedule of five years, were Mobilis to ensure a minimum coverage of 10% of the Algerian territory in the first year (Wakli, 2016a).

It is worth noting that the pace of adopting mobile broadband technology has ranged between stalling and a complete standstill. This could be interpreted as a clear sign of authorities' traumatic apprehension from the rapidly growing democratizing significance of ICTs, especially in the aftermath of the Arab Spring outbursts, where the prevailing assumption was that social media platforms had provided the decisive impetus for the Arab protestors. Add to that the security concerns related to cyber terrorism proliferation and the potential resort of Algerian Jihadist groups to the Internet as vital logistic support.

According to figures provided by the RAPT, the penetration rate rose insignificantly to 10.18% in 2008 following the lowering of tariffs to the half; however, after the adoption of 3G technology, the rate has climbed to 28% in 2014 and then to 71.17% in 2016, which reflects a remarkable trend towards the mobile broadband service. Similarly, the last updated statistical figures provided by *Internet World Stats* in December 2019 indicated that Algeria has a penetration rate of 58%, which is the equivalent of 25,428,159 Internet users (Internet World Stats, 2019).

This is slightly above the average penetration rate in the region of North Africa, which amounts to 50%, although more than 80% of the Algerian territory is already covered with fiber optic infrastructure. The minimum fixed broadband Internet, since 1 January 2019, is 2 megabits, from 2,600 DZD to 1,600 DZD monthly for the service (Belgacem, 2018).

Tracing the trajectory of Internet development in Algeria indicates clearly that the experience of Internet connection for the average user was and remains a *casse-tête quotidien*, since it is still marked by connectivity issues, frequent Internet interruptions and state sector's failure to meet increased maintenance requirements, not to mention exaggerated tariffs compared to the poor service. On the other hand, although serious constraints, including underdeveloped ICT infrastructures and weak processing of fiber optic technology, have been significantly overcome, the monopolistic state-management of the ICT sector is still plagued by a critical lack of clear strategy for development, unmet challenges imposed by previous failed policies, and to a lesser extent, the inability to invest competently in the sector.

Social media usage in Algeria, emerging trends and regulatory ecology

Social media constitutes the ensemble of Internet-based applications which are built on the techno-epistemic foundations of Web 2.0, which allow the participative creation and exchange of user-generated content (Kaplan and Haenlein, 2010: 61). Since its appearance, social media usage has exponentially increased over the past years to the point of becoming a vital part of the whole Internet usage experience on a global scale.

Although in the Algerian context no previous evidence-based research can be found on patterns and adoption extent of social networking technologies, we may assume that first attitudes were characterized by excitement and readiness for adoption. However, the extensive proliferation of Internet access technologies paired with accelerated access to mobile phones had led to an intensified adoption and use of social networking sites, creating new socio-technical habitus and practices in the daily routine of millions of users.

Back in the initial stage of social media growth, the *Arab Social Media Report* released in July 2012 estimated that the number of Facebook users in Algeria between June 2010 and June 2012 was around 1,413,280, with a penetration rate of only 3.99%, while the number of active Twitter users barely reached 8,415 registered users in June 2012 with a penetration rate of 0.2%. In the same vein, the sixth edition of the *Arab Social Media Report* (2014) indicated that the total number of Algerians on Facebook exceeded 6.8 million users by June 2014, with a whole one million new registered users between the period of January and May 2014, in addition to Facebook's penetration growth from 12.27% in May 2013 to 18.1% in May 2014, positioning Algeria as the sixth in rank among Arab countries. Also, Twitter has witnessed a rise towards 37,500 users in the first half of 2014.

However, by 2017, conforming to the seventh edition of the *Arab Social Media Report* (2017), Algeria witnessed the second-largest growth in the Arab region in terms of the number of new users joining Facebook, with approximately 9.4 million users. Moreover, Algeria witnessed the largest growth in terms of the number of new active users on Twitter since 2014, with around 774,000 new users. This data attests to visible transformations in adoption rates and the increasingly dynamic engagement with social media offerings.

According to the most recent data provided by *StatCounter Global Stats* in October 2019 concerning social media usage trends in Algeria, Facebook is the most popular social media platform with a penetration rate of 51.03%, followed by YouTube with an estimated penetration rate at 36.56%, while Twitter is still conditioned by a slow-paced evolution with a penetration rate of 4.05%, which is similar to Instagram that falls behind the curve with a penetration rate of 3.23%.

Within this context, the spiraling growth in the usage of social networking sites can be correlated with the arrival and expansion of mobile broadband service in Algeria after December 2013, since we assume that there is a direct link between the increasing percentage of subscribers to the 3G and 4G service and the increasing number of social networking users, as the mobility component has rendered those sites progressively more present and intrusive in the everyday socio-technical routines of individuals.

On another level, when approaching the legal aspect of social media, we have first to acknowledge that social media platforms in their essence are tools of communication which provide the average citizen with the possibility of exchanging and disseminating information in a public or semi-public fashion; thus, making full use of its affordances is related to the flexibility of the regulatory setting that regularizes the freedom of expression.

In every respect, the Algerian formal legal system dedicates significant space to freedom of speech and expression, granting them full constitutional guarantee (the Constitution of 1963, Article 4; the Constitution of 1976, Articles 53, 54, and 55; the Constitution of 1989, Articles 35, 36, 39, and 40; the Constitution of 1996, Articles 36, 38, 41, and 42; the constitutional revision of January 2016, Articles 49 and 50). However, regulatory frameworks, do not mirror reality, since the Algerian regime erects laboriously formal regulations while adopting a modality of action that could be qualified, least of all, as political banditry, according to the expression of Luis Martinez (1998).

Against this background, the de facto power avoids being fully subject to the constraints of the constitutional law in the case of freedom of expression and related liberties, inevitably weakened, by using the defamation pretext to restrict freedom of expression and harass people with dissenting opinions. This is especially the case of social media where the government uses the defamatory allegations as an oppressive mechanism to stifle independent voices and to impose strict control over targeted cyber activists, journalists, and ordinary citizens (Mostefaoui, 2016).

In this regard, the defamation in Algeria is codified by two main legal texts: the Penal Code (*le Code pénal*), promulgated on 10 June 1966, in which Article 296 touched upon forms of defamation, and Article 298, which determines penalties related to defamation. In parallel, the Law of Information (*Code de l'Information*) No. 90–07 of 3 April 1990, in which the Article 40 addressed several issues related to defamation committed by journalists, and after the amendment, the Organic Law of Information No. 12–05 of 12 January 2012 on information, in which defamation is covered by Article 93. Both texts do not provide a clear terminological definition of the defamation, in addition to imposing repressive and stiff penalties.

In this regard, it would be useful to cite a few examples, which are not exhaustive, but only indicative. We start with the case of *Djamel Marih* in December 2018, who was given a custodial sentence of six months and a fine of 50,000 DZD for having criticized local authorities' mismanagement of the province where he lives (Tiart, west of Algeria), through comments and sharing of press articles on his Facebook wall (Djouadi, 2018).

Another case in point is that of *Salah Dabouz*, the Algerian human rights lawyer who is facing systematic judicial harassment, and who has been subjected to judicial scrutiny since September 2018, for having criticized the functioning of Algerian courts on his Facebook page (Djamel, 2019). Also, *Zoulikha Belarbi*, member of the Algerian League for the Defense of Human Rights, who has been convicted of criminal defamation and undermining the state symbols and given three months suspended prison sentence with a fine to pay, for having published on her Facebook wall a satirical photo montage that depicts the ex-president Bouteflika in a king's *accoutrement*, surrounded by his ministers in October 2015 (Abane,

2015). A further case was that of the independent journalist *Mohamed Tamalt*, who was sentenced in July 2016 to two years of custodial imprisonment for having insulted the president and public institutions in his Facebook publications. He had started a hunger strike in June 2016, falling into a coma in August and dying in hospital in December 2016 (Bozonnet, 2016).

Another distressing issue is the promulgation of Law N°09–04 on 5 August 2009, which authorizes the public authorities to carry out preventive surveillance operations of electronic communications under imperatives of protecting the public order, national defense, or the strategic interests of the national economy. Other than that, Article 10 of the law puts the private Internet service providers and mobile operators under the obligation of assisting the judicial authorities, in the context of investigations, with the collection, retrieval, and sharing of electronic data of their customers (Law N° 09–04 2009).

Furthermore, Article 13 of the same law announced the creation of a national body for confronting ICT-related offenses and combatting cyber criminality under the authority of the Ministry of Justice. In June 2019, however, this body has been placed under the authority of the Ministry of National Defence, while reinforcing it with advanced technological equipment that facilitates the traceability, collection, and safeguarding of digital data. In this context, Rachid Zouaimia, Professor of Law at the University of Bejaia, cautioned in an interview delivered to the francophone daily newspaper *El Watan* that this specialized body, under the pretext of carrying out preventive surveillance, may be converted into a branch of digital political police whose primary mission is to restrict civil and political rights and asphyxiate any opposition to the regime (Ait Ouarabi, 2019).

On the substance of what has previously been discussed, restrictions on freedom of speech online or violations of the right to privacy or unwarranted access to personal data through online surveillance are probable scenarios in Algeria, due to the repressive approach the regime has developed regarding Internet-based technologies, and the existing absence of counterbalancing and effective legal protection measures that sustain users' rights.

Socio-political significance of social media: potential and challenges

It has become clear that ICT's adoption and implementation trajectories in societies governed by authoritarian political structures, as is the case of Algeria, are bound to a large extent by the definitions and representations that authoritarian regimes bestow on these technologies and the concrete approaches they choose to deal with. To build a more nuanced understanding of ecologies where the Internet and social media exist and function, we should break down the key elements of the political regime modus operandi.

After the independence of Algeria in 1962, the top priority for the new regime was, and still is, to restore the operational structure of the state, materializing its coercive dominance over all spheres of Algerian society (Rouadjia, 1995: 352). In other words, the notion of "the restored state" has been always considered in purely material terms. So for the state to regain its power and dominance, it has to possess well-equipped forces of order, stringent legal frameworks that organize and regularize every single aspect of the society (ibid.: 361). The second element that shaped the operating mode of the regime has to do with the Jacobin sense of a state that the Algerian power structures retained and translated into brutal legal and politico-administrative machinery. The concept designates a variety of attributes coming together, such as the absolute governmental and administrative centralization and the indivisibility of national sovereignty, side by side with the sacred vocation of state to transform society into a uniform entity (François and Ozouf, 1992: 243).

After attaining a working understanding of the Algerian regime, we should point out that examining the socio-political role of social media from the perspective of conventional mediators like civil society associations will prove fruitless, due to the significant weight of the rentier economy on public life and its actors, since the regime succeeds continuously in co-opting them and winning them to its side. In this respect, Roth (2004) pointed out that associative organizations are very potential supporters of autocratic regimes, which is the same conclusion drawn by Liverani (2008), who noted that a significant portion of Algerian associations are unambiguous supporters of the authoritarian regime. Similarly, when examining state-association complex relationships, Dris-Aït Hamadouche (2017) claimed that the Algerian political regime has created its civil society. A pertinent statement that is reaffirmed by Cavatorta (2015), who sees civil society associations as annexed entities to the current Algerian political system.

It would be therefore more fruitful to focus on ordinary users of social media, in their concrete way of appropriating technological artifacts and charting social media's course of adoption and putting to use in daily life contexts. Seen from this perspective, a good point of departure would be the mobilization of February 2019 or the *Hirak* movement,[1] as fertile ground to situate possible scenarios of social media effects on the incidents, whether regarding its triggering, continuity, or consolidation. However, as we reject technologically deterministic views in interpreting social movements, we should identify the existing socio-economic and political variables to be able to understand the real significance of social media on the course of events. This is a social setting characterized essentially by the intensification of sectoral and socio-economic demands, especially after the collapse in crude oil prices since mid-2014, and the imposition of acute austerity measures that affected the Algerian society at large, adding to that high levels of unemployment among the youth and other marginalized groups. In this instance, the Algerian League for the Defense of Human Rights stated in its annual report of 2016 that the number of social protests exceeded 16,000 per year, which emphatically reflects the fragility and conflagration of the social front (LADDH Report, 2016).

Politically speaking, it is increasingly recognized that many of the dilemmas that Algeria is facing are in significant part the fruit of the authoritarian nature of the political regime, which still preserves its ineradicable attributes (Tlemçani, 2012). And since the arrival of Bouteflika into power in 1999, the situation reached such a level of severity and gravity that irreversible consequences were to follow suit (Hachemaoui, 2015).

At the technological level, the Algerian techno-social landscape is rich and complex in its dimensions and manifestations, since it consists of a confluence of appropriating practices, a reservoir of techno-symbolic representations, and technological artifacts. In more concrete terms, intensive connectivity to social networking sites is an essential part of the everyday routine, associated essentially with the massive growth in mobile phone ownership, with a penetration rate of 111% by the end of 2016 (Semmar, 2017) and the implementation of 3G and 4G mobile broadband technology since 2013, two factors that have revolutionized the Algerian social media scene, stepping up the ritualized ubiquitous connectivity.

By reflecting upon social media affordances and its technological essence, we figure out that its tools as instantaneous, horizontal, and interconnected means of communication (Derieux and Granchet, 2013) and as being less subjected to authoritarian control measures than traditional media are easily accessible alternative spaces of collective expression and discussion of subjects of public topicality. In this context, the production, exchange, and dissemination of independent information or counter-information in a two-step flow represent an essential component of protesting dynamics (Sedda 2015).

Viewed in this way, social media platforms are regarded as a privileged locus for collective and individual freedom of expression, especially when this freedom is lacking in real-world settings, and as such, these platforms guaranteed primary material for confronting authoritarian regimes. (Fleury, 2015). Aside from that, social media has generated new counter-legitimacies and new counter-discourses that disrupted conventional power relations, at the discursive level at least.

In the Algerian context, social media gave rise to two major dissenting dynamics that have permitted approaching and discussing public issues from a critical and indignant perspective, granting them public visibility and attention. In the first place, the digital spaces incubate intensive discussions concerning micro societal problems, like the dilapidated state of public infrastructures, housing problems, power outages, lack of good quality drinking water, and the deterioration of healthcare services. At a macro level, the public online discussions focus usually on the Algerian political system and its modus operandi, like infringements of constitutional laws, electoral fraud, and other forms of political abuse.

Two dynamics are contextually significant – the restricted access to public information and the controlled media, which serve as the regime mouthpiece instead of operating according to the normative principles as independent bodies that should concentrate on problems and deficiencies encountered in day-to-day public life. It is equally true that the Algerian traditional media system is marked by the failure in responding to citizens' real concerns and expectations in matters of the right to information and public debate (Merah and Boudhane, 2012).

Moreover, the Algerian public sphere is adversarial and hostile to any socio-political action or citizen participation that is discordant with the official discourse (Merah and Meyer, 2015). In such contexts, social media tools created an emancipated sphere of collective action that builds on vigilance towards political abuse and functions as an efficient whistleblowing mechanism (Flichy, 2010). One of the fruits of such a nascent sphere was the *Hirak* movement which erupted across the country on 10 February 2019 and which has continued ever since, even after Bouteflika's resignation, rejecting political abuse of power and aspiring to genuine change.

What distinguishes the *Hirak* movement resides in the dynamic combination of both traditional forms of mobilization, like mass demonstrations, street rallies, and planned vigils, and the targeted use of social media platforms. This combination facilitated coordination at the ground level and provided visibility to the protests by permitting participants to transmit events via live streaming and video uploading to compensate for the limited media coverage. At the digital level, it opened up horizontal spaces where users can generate dissenting content to solidify the legitimacy of their cause.

Faced with challenges imposed by the intensified use of social media platforms by protestors, the regime responded with an adaptive set of measures designed to deal with long-term mobilizations, revealing technological sophistication in filtering online content and consolidating its control over digital spaces. In this respect, since the very beginning of the *Hirak* movement, social networking sites were in the crosshairs of the regime. That is exactly why Facebook was flooded with trolls,[2] fake accounts, and newly created Facebook profiles, camouflaged under pseudonyms or random nicknames to remain anonymous, in addition to hundreds of Facebook pages that present itself as pro-*Hirak* and in reality work to foster social fissures and confrontations among Algerians.

The automated trolls are programmed to generate repeatedly identical content under certain publications in specific pages and groups. This content tends generally to contain an excessive degree of verbal violence, virulence, and racial statements. Many Algerian activists suspect that private communication and marketing companies owned by businessmen close to the Algerian regime are the origin of these trolls (Aichoun, 2019).

It can also be noted that few fake profiles and pages are managed by human agents, focusing on specific frames of action, like attacking political opposition figures on Facebook, lampooning and commenting negatively on publications of pro-*Hirak* activists, or posting and sharing intimidating messages that tend to discourage the Algerians from manifesting by evoking the catastrophic scenarios of Syria and Libya. They proliferate more frequently in the event of controversial issues and they stand on the side of the regime, disseminating its arguments and defending its claims.

As the Algerian regime struggles with digital activism, it employs a dual strategy, targeting digital spaces with well-orchestrated disinformation campaigns, while suppressing every possible source of validation of information, through minimizing meaningful official communication and exercising censorship on traditional media channels, rendering it *caisse de résonance* of its official theses.

On another front, the regime has resorted to shutting the Internet down, from partially decreasing connectivity to completely switching it off. As a general rule, every Thursday and Friday, accessing Facebook and other digital platforms is severely disrupted or blocked entirely, especially in case of accessing through ADSL service. With the 3G or 4G connection, access is possible but still considerably perturbed. The strategy was intended to prevent protestors from streaming live videos or sharing content from the demonstrations field. In specific cases, and during the rest of weekdays, Internet disruption may occur as a reaction to specific contexts, for instance, YouTube and Google services have been blocked on the evening of Thursday, 8 August 2019, immediately after the publication of a video by the Algerian ex-defense minister Khaled Nezzar in which he addresses the army officers, requesting them to remove the Chief of the Army Staff Ahmed Gaid Salah (Boko, 2019).

In the recent period, the Algerian regime has undergone a structural metamorphosis in the direction of consolidating its grip on digital spaces. Now it is capable of employing the new technologies to launch counter mobilizations, process cyberattacks, and flood social media platforms with disinformation campaigns. We may argue then that we are exploring a new variant of authoritarianism, *technologically savvy authoritarianism*, that can develop the resilience that was lacking in former traditional authoritarian regimes in the MENA region.

Conclusion

The implementation of the Internet and ICT was within the scheme of enhancing the organizational efficiency of governmental bodies and maximizing its viability and performance, not to reaffirm the legitimate societal right of benefiting from ICT outputs. However, with its inevitable diffusion and divergence of its applications, the Internet and social media developments largely exceeded the Algerian regime's capacity of containing its implications, at least long enough for its users to chart its socio-technological trajectories.

In this sense, social media usage occupies a privileged part in the entire experience of connecting to the Internet, due to its varying functionalities and services and owing to the prevalence of mobile access technology and the affordability of handheld digital devices. Nevertheless, making optimum use of social media offerings is still hampered by the regime's systematic efforts to impose censorship and surveillance on digital spaces and to track down political opponents and cyber activists in a formalized banditry-like atmosphere.

Social media platforms constitute emancipatory communicative territories that enacted new possibilities of interaction and debate for average citizens (Sedda, 2015), permitting them to engage with each other in new horizontal forms of open exchange. In a certain way that the previously excluded individuals now enjoy new political agency in a bottom-up model of citizen action, particularly if we consider that traditional political and associative actors are an integral part of the regime's logic of clientelism, and play themselves the role of its *agents consolidateurs*.

In a context properly Algerian, the main idea we can retain is that routine use of social media has led to its appropriation as a new mechanism of collective protesting, resulting from accelerated awareness of existing injustices and political corruption. That is precisely why social media has been converted into structured channels for authentic counter-democracy (Mathieu, 2007), notably in the sense of disrupting authoritarian fabricated legitimacies and accessing to alternative information sources, a sine qua non for enlightened collective action.

The ultimate conclusion extracted from analyzing the ongoing *Hirak* movement is that social media offers a compendium of empowering tools, that once collectively employed by *citizen-agents* in a context of mobilizations, in the presence of triggering contextual elements, with the parallel resort to classical forms of protestation at street level, will lead to the formation of a citizen counter-force that can alter rules of the political game. However, as argued earlier, unlike authoritarian regimes' conventional approaches towards new technologies, which range between rejection, control, and repression (Heeks and Seo-Zindy, 2013), the Algerian régime is manifesting coping mechanisms to devitalize the emancipatory dynamism of social media platforms, using its technological affordances to amplify disinformation and polarization and to control the flow of online content.

Once again, it should be stressed that social media cannot overcome the *democratic deficit* at the institutional level or renew the social contract between those governing and the governed, nor can it guarantee the emergence of a public sphere à la Habermas. In this scheme, the effects of social media, both positive and negative, must be evaluated on a case-by-case basis, considering the intersection between individual technology appropriation, the socio-cultural environment of its users and above all the nature of political structures found in their societies.

Notes

1 *Hirak* in English stands for social mobilizations/protests.
2 The Algerians label the anti-*Hirak* trolls as "*doubab ilktrouni*" (electronic bots).

References

Abane, M. (2015), Le président de la Laadh, Salah Dabouz, accuse l'Etat de répression contre les défenseurs des droits de l'homme. *El Watan*, 23 October. Retrieved from https://www.elwatan.com/edition/actualite/le-president-de-la-laadh-salah-dabouz-accuse-letat-de-repression-contre-les-defenseurs-des-droits-de-lhomme-23-10-2015. Accessed 8 July 2019.

Ait Ouarabi, M. (2019), Il était sous l'autorité du ministère de la Justice: L'Organe de surveillance des TIC passe sous la tutelle du MDN. *El Watan*, 27 June. Retrieved from https://www.elwatan.com/edition/actualite/il-etait-sous-lautorite-du-ministere-de-la-justice-lorgane-de-surveillance-des-tic-passe-sous-la-tutelle-du-mdn-27-06-2019. Accessed 24 July 2019.

Akli, M. (2006), Reseaux d'acces haut debit d'algerie télécom. *Séminaire régional sur l'accès hertzien mobile et fixe pour les applications large bande dans la région des Etats arabes*. Co-organisé par UIT/BDT et Algérie Télécom, Alger19 au 22 juin. Retrieved from www.itu.int/ITUD/tech/events/2006/Algiers2006/Presentations/Day%201/Algiers_Presentation_5_MAkli.PDF. Accessed 25 August 2019.

Ananna, C. (2018), Voici les meilleures offres 3G/4G à 1000 DA et comment les activer. *Android-DZ*, 6 December. Retrieved from www.android-dz.com/voici-les-meilleures-offre-3g-4g-a-1000-da-et-comment-les-activer-39108. Accessed 21 July 2019.

Belgacem, F. (2018), Internet: 2 mégas à 1 600 DA dès janvier 2019. *Liberté*, 17 November. Retrieved from www.liberte-algerie.com/actualite/Internet-2-megas-a-1-600-da-des-janvier-2019-303816. Accessed 22 July 2019.

Boko, H. (2019), En Afrique, les coupures très politiques des réseaux sociaux et Internet. *France 24*, 11 August. Retrieved from https://bit.ly/2qCvkMn. Accessed 16 August 2019.

Bozonnet, C. (2016), Le journaliste algérien Mohamed Tamalt meurt en prison. *Le Monde Afrique*, 11 December. Retrieved from https://bit.ly/2pHoTHg. Accessed 26 July 2019.

Cavatorta, F. (2015), *Civil Society after the Uprisings: The Case of Algeria.* Singapore Middle East Papers 15. The National University of Singapore. Retrieved from https://mei.nus.edu.sg/themes/site_themes/ agile_records/images/uploads/SMEP_15_-_Cavatorta.pdf. Accessed 27 July 2019.

Derieux, E., and Granchet, A. (2013), *Réseaux sociaux en ligne: Aspect juridiques et déontologiques.* Paris: Editions Lamy.

Djamel, K. (2019), L'avocat Salah Dabbouz placé sous contrôle judiciaire. *El Watan,* 08 April. Retrieved from https://www.elwatan.com/edition/actualite/lavocat-salah-dabouz-libere-08-04-2019. Accessed 03 August 2019.

Djelti, M. (2008), *L'implantation de l'Internet en Algérie, enjeux et perspectives.* Master thesis, Oran University, Algeria.

Djouadi, F. (2018), Le facebookeur Djamel Marih condamné à 6 mois de prison ferme suite à une plainte du wali de Tiaret. *El Watan,*16 September. Retrieved from www.elwatan.com/edition/actualite/le-facebookeur-djamel-marih-condamne-a-6-mois-de-prison-ferme-suite-a-une-plainte-du-wali-de-tiaret-16-09-2018. Accessed 17 July 2019.

Doudi, L, Khentout, C., and Djoudi, M. (2004), Place de l'Algérie dans le monde des TIC. *International Conference on Electronic Commerce 15 and 17 March 2004.* University of Ouargla, Algeria. Retrieved from https://bit.ly/2T6G3su. Accessed 9 July 2019.

Dris-Aït Hamadouche, L. (2017), La société civile vue à l'aune de la résilience du système politique algérien. *L'Année du Maghreb,* 16, pp. 289–306.

Fleury, C. (2015), Formes anciennes et nouvelles de la désobéissance civile. *Pouvoirs,* (4), pp. 5–16.

Flichy, P. (2010), La démocratie 2.0. *Etudes,* 412(5), pp. 617–626.

Furet, F., and Ozouf, M. (1992), *Dictionnaire critique de la Révolution française.* Paris: Flammarion.

Hachemaoui, M. (2015), *Clientélisme et patronage dans l'Algérie contemporaine.* Paris: Karthala Editions.

Heeks, R., and Seo-Zindy, R. (2013), *ICTs and Social Movements under Authoritarian Regimes: An Actor-Network Perspective.* Manchester: University of Manchester. Retrieved from https://www.escholar. manchester.ac.uk/jrul/item/?pid=uk-ac-man-scw:192723. Accessed 09 August 2020.

Internet World Stats (2019), *Internet Usage and Population Statistics in Algeria,* December 2019. Retrieved from https://www.internetworldstats.com/africa.htm#dz. Accessed 26 May 2019.

Kaplan, A. M., and Haenlein, M. (2010), Users of the World, Unite! The Challenges and Opportunities of Social Media. *Business Horizons,* 53(1), pp. 59–68.

Law 09–04 of 5 August 2009 (2009), *Special Rules on Prevention and Fight Against TIC Related Crimes.* Retrieved from https://bit.ly/33QEnrn. Accessed 18 July 2019.

Law 2000–03 of 08.05.2000 (2003), *General Rules on Post and Telecommunications.* Retrieved from https:// bit.ly/2qwqPTD. Accessed 10 July 2019.

Ligue Algérienne pour la Défense des Droits de l'homme (2016), *le rapport sur les droits de l'homme en Algérie.* Retrieved from https://laddh-algerie.org/?lang=fr. Accessed 9 July 2019.

Liverani, A. (2008), *Civil Society in Algeria: The Political Functions of Associational Life.* London: Routledge.

López-Bonilla, G., Yáñez-Kernke, M. D. C., and Vidauri-González, G. (2016), Cybercafés as Constellations of Social Practices: Exploring "Place" and "Technospace" in Cybercafés in México. *Cogent Social Sciences,* 2(1).

Martinez, L. (1998), *La guerre civile en Algérie.* Paris: Editions Karthala.

Mathieu, L. (2007), L'espace des mouvements sociaux. *Politix,* (1), pp. 131–151.

Merah, A., and Boudhane, Y. (2012), Espace public médiatique en Algérie: À la recherche d'un modèle. *Revue arabe de la communication et du développement,* 1(6), pp. 367–383. Lebanon.

Merah, A., and Meyer, V. (2015), *La communication publique et territoriale au Maghreb. Enjeux d'une valorisation et défis pour les acteurs.* Paris: L'Harmattan.

Mostefaoui, B. (2016), Note sur la régulation des médias en Algérie. *L'année du Maghreb,*15, pp. 25–28.

Nasri, R. (2018), Les cybercafés, un commerce en voie de disparition. *Le Soir d'Algérie,* 4 July. Retrieved from www.lesoirdalgerie.com/actualites/les-cybercafes-un-commerce-en-voie-de-disparition-6117. Accessed 15 July 2019.

Rahmouni, K. (2012), Les cybercafés en Algérie: des espaces en voie de disparition? *n'tic web,* 5 March. Retrieved from www.nticweb.com/it/6514-les-cybercafes-en-algerie-des-espaces-en-voie-de-dispari tion-.html. Accessed 18 July 2019.

Rédaction, AE. (2019), *Algérie Télécom prévoit de doubler son chiffre d'affaires en quatre ans.* Retrieved from telecom-prevoit-de-doubler-son-chiffre-daffaires-en-quatre-ans/. Accessed 31 December 2019.

Roth, R. (2004), Die dunklen Seiten einer Zivilgesellschaft. Grenzen einer zivilgesellschaftlichen Fundierung der Demokratie. In A. Klein, K. Kern, B. Geißel, and M. Berger (eds.), *Zivilgesellschaft und Sozialkapital. Herausforderungen politischer und sozialer Integration.* Wiesbaden: VS Verlag, pp. 41–64.

Rouadjia, A. (1995), L'Etat algérien et le problème du droit. *Politique étrangère*, pp. 351–363.

Sedda, P. (2015), L'Internet contestataire. Comme pratique d'émancipation: Des médias alternatifs à la mobilisation numérique. *Les Cahiers du numérique*, 11(4), pp. 25–52.

Semmar, A. (2017), Les prix baissent et les ventes explosent/La révolution des Smartphones en Algérie. *Algérie Part*, 19 April. Retrieved from https://algeriepart.com/2017/04/19/prix-baissent-ventes-explosent-revolution-smartphones-algerie/. Accessed 31 July 2019.

StatCounter Global Stats (2019), *Social Media Stats in Algeria – October 2019*, November. Retrieved from https://gs.statcounter.com/social-media-stats/all/algeria. Accessed 3 November 2019.

Tlemçani, R. (2012), Algérie: un autoritarisme électoral. *Tumultes*, 1(38), pp. 149–171.

Wakli, E. (2016a), Lancement de la 3G en Algérie: l'offre de Mobilis est jugée la meilleure. *Algérie focus*, 17 October. Retrieved from www.algerie-focus.com/2013/10/lancement-de-la-3-g-en-algerie-loffre-de-mobilis-est-jugee-la-meilleure/?cn-reloaded=1. Accessed 18 July 2019.

Wakli, E. (2016b), Internet. La 4G officiellement lancée/Et après? *Algérie focus*, 1 October. Retrieved from www.algerie-focus.com/2016/10/Internet-4g-officiellement-lancee-apres/. Accessed 19 July 2019.

Bahrain

3

MEDIA IN BAHRAIN – A CONTESTED SPHERE

Magdalena Karolak

Introduction

With a territory of roughly 770 km² and a population of 1.2 million inhabitants, Bahrain is the smallest country in the Middle East and North Africa. It is an island nation scattered over roughly 30 islands, most of them now artificially interconnected. Its population is diverse and subject to global migratory patterns. As of 2019, it comprises more than 50% of expatriates, with the majority coming from the Indian subcontinent. Native Bahrainis are heterogeneous. The community is divided among several superimposed cleavages: tribal or community-based organization, Arab or Persian background, Sunni or Shi'a denomination, as well as patterns of settlement, namely, city or village. Khuri (1980) enumerated the following social groups: tribal Sunnis, rural Arab Shi'as (*Baharna*), urban Sunnis of Persian origin (*Hawala*), urban Sunnis of nontribal Arab origin (*Najdi*), and urban Shi'as of Arab origin. There are also more recent Persian Shi'a migrants (*Ajam*). The local civil society has experienced remarkable levels of activism since Bahrainis enjoy a high level of educational attainment. Bahrain was the seat of ancient civilizations; in modern times, it became independent from Britain only recently, in 1971. In 2002, Bahrain was proclaimed a constitutional monarchy. Despite its limited land and population size, the recent history of the country and the complex social fabric make it an interesting case to study, among others, the development of mass communication in the region.

This chapter aims at analyzing the evolution of the media sector, looking at the print press, radio, television, and social media. While the main focus of the study is the last 60 years, a historical background is necessary to understand the development of each type of media.

The growth of media in Bahrain can be divided into three periods. The first one encompasses the emergence of media during the period of colonial rule until proclaiming independence in 1971. Subsequently, Bahrain experienced maturing of the media sector but within the constraints of the authoritarian regime until 1999. At the turn of the 21st century, Bahrain witnessed important political reforms that brought about liberalization, among others, of the media sector and market, and consequently, the expansive growth of the social media and satellite channels. Following this chronological order, the study will highlight the major developments in mass communication based on data gathered through the literature review.

Historical background

To begin with, the role of the social context in the development of media should be explained. Literacy is, for instance, primordial for the growth of printed press, and access to technology is necessary for the emergence of radio, television, and the Internet. Here, it is important to highlight that Bahrain has the oldest public education system in the Arabian Gulf, and the literacy rates are among the highest in the Arab world (Nydell, 2002: 2). Established for the first time in 1919, Bahraini schools have provided free public education on the elementary level for male students and since 1928; they included female students too. Secondary education was initiated in 1936 for boys and in 1951 for girls. In the late 1960s, Bahrain experienced the establishment of its first institutions of tertiary education. Despite the country having the earliest education system in the Arabian Gulf region, which entails increased literacy rates, the establishment of print media in Bahrain was relatively belated. Neighboring Saudi Arabia witnessed the emergence of its first newspapers in the 1920s, while Bahrainis had to wait till 1939 to see the first print edition of a local newspaper, *Jaridat Al Bahrain*, published in Arabic. Thus, the progress of media in Bahrain should be understood within the historical period and the political context that influenced technological development, regulatory frameworks, and audience needs over time.

The initial development of media was impacted by the British colonial presence and the discovery of oil. Firstly, the development of the press was hindered by the colonial British rule that lasted till 1971. *Jaridat Al Bahrain* had a short-lived success being a private venture of Abdallah Al Zaid. His printing press faced many economic challenges during the WWII period, such as shortages of paper, and the newspaper ceased with his death in 1944 (Al Khatir, 2014: 383). Also, the technology used for printing was very primitive. Subsequently, the colonial rulers thwarted the efforts to establish other, as many as 10, national Arabic newspapers in the decades of the 1930s–1960s (Jawad, 2001: 169). The reasons were due to the anti-colonial and nationalist stance of these publications, which prompted the colonial power to curtail the spread of ideas challenging its vital interests in the region (Al Shaikh and Campbell, 2013: 156). Even if some Arabic newspapers managed to emerge over the years, the anti-colonial riots of 1956 led to their closure. With the colonial rule nearing its end, three Arabic weeklies were established, namely *Al Adwa* in 1965, *Sada al-Usbu'a* in 1969, and *Al Mujtama al-Jadid* in 1970 (Rugh, 2004: 60). They presented topics of general interest and continued their print into the years of Bahrain's independence.

Nonetheless, the colonial presence gave a boost to the development of the English language press. The English language was introduced in the country, and the growing presence of expatriates encouraged the establishment of English language media. The trend was exacerbated since the 1930s, as the Bahraini society was gradually transformed by the discovery of oil and the shift to an oil-dependent economy. Oil revenues furthered the rapid development of the country, with the creation of modern industries and a vast range of services, exacerbating the demand for labor. In the 1930s, Bahraini society hardly had enough of a workforce to warrant the need for growth. Foreigners filled various occupations, from manual labor to highly qualified professional jobs, and their numbers have continued growing. According to Bahrain Open Data Portal, the number of native Bahrainis constituted more than 82% of the population back in 1971, but the figure was reduced to 68% in 1981, 62% in 2011, and only 46% in 2016.

The increase in foreign workers made English the lingua franca of Bahrain. Since the time of colonial rule, English-language publications were in demand, providing information to the ever-growing population of foreigners who did not master Arabic and relied primarily on English-language media for information. The impact of the connection between the presence of the colonial power and the discovery of oil on media development is visible in the establishment of the first English-language newspaper, *The Islander*, in 1954. It was published by Bahrain Petroleum Company (BAPCO). While Bahrain was a British protectorate, BAPCO was created by the American company Standard Oil (Commins, 2012: 142). BAPCO employed American and British professionals in the managerial and higher technical cadre, and since the 1930s it began to import large numbers of Indian skilled and semi-skilled workers to complement its workforce (Kumar, 2016: 76). *The Islander* was a weekly till 1956 when it was converted into a daily. Until its last edition in 1969, *The Islander* reported local news and other BAPCO-related information (Abdulla, 2004). In the year it ceased operations, three new English-language newspapers were launched. Subsequently, the first successful commercial English-language newspaper, *The Gulf Mirror*, saw the light of the day on 3 January 1971. It was published as a weekly, initially on Sundays, and later Thursdays. It included local news, business, and sports coverage. The editorial team was led by a Briton, Andrew Trimbee (Trimbee, 2009).

Along with the development of the print press, radio broadcasting was initiated in the Middle East by the British at the onset of WWII. As the war front expanded, both sides of the conflict strived to reach audiences in the Middle East to gather support for their cause. To begin with, the British started broadcasting in the Arabic language from London; but to better compete with the German wavelengths, in November 1940, they established the Bahrain Broadcasting Station. Ulaby (2010: 117) notes that its program included Koranic recitations, poetry recitations, music performances, and news favorable to the British. The station was closed after the end of the war in 1945. A governmental radio station opened in Bahrain only 10 years later broadcasting in Arabic. Nonetheless, broadcasts in Arabic from Cairo would reach Bahrain, and after the Egyptian Revolution in 1952, Egyptian wavelengths would spread the Arab nationalist message, which became popular among Bahrainis, fueling anti-British sentiment (Fuccaro, 2009: 182). The beginnings of radio had an important impact on the society as listening to the broadcasts became a major pastime for Bahrainis. Radio devices were available on the market before 1940, but the majority of Bahrainis would not have a personal set. Consequently, large audiences would gather in coffee shops to listen or in the homes of prominent local personalities who had a radio set and guests would visit according to the radio transmission timings (Fuccaro, 2009: 182). Radio brought people together and the topics influenced these gatherings, leading to debates on social and political topics. Ultimately, radio broadcasts fueled with nationalism and the growing social and economic grievances among Bahrainis led to the emergence of anti-British and anti-government movements that culminated in the riots of 1956 (Fuccaro, 2009: 184).

All in all, the beginnings of media in Bahrain were heavily influenced by the British presence. The colonial rulers could limit the circulation of unfavorable ideologies to a certain extent, which explains the slow progress of the local Arabic press. They allowed, however, English-language publications necessary to fulfill the needs of the growing class of expatriates; and the importance of the English language press only continued to grow after 1971 linked to the influx of foreigners to Bahrain. The constraints to the media imposed under the British rule resurfaced, however, in another form after independence in 1971.

Media post-independence

Bahrain declared independence from Britain on 15 August 1971, following a survey conducted by the United Nations. The subsequent political developments in Bahrain had, ultimately, an important impact on the media. The formative years of independence marked a failed experiment with a parliamentary system of government. With the withdrawal of the colonial power, Emir Isa bin Salman Al Khalifa (1961–1999) proclaimed a law concerning the formation of the Constitutional Assembly. The Assembly, composed of elected and appointed members, drafted the constitution. The very first constitution of Bahrain, adopted in 1973, stipulated that the legislative power would be vested in a unicameral parliament elected in general elections, while the executive would be controlled by the emir through appointments of the prime minister and the cabinet. The first election to the parliament took place in 1973. However, two years after its inception, the parliament was permanently dissolved for almost 30 years. Lack of consent related to the issues of foreign policy, US naval base presence in Bahrain, and especially the State Security Law promulgated in 1974, led to a split between the parliamentarians and the emir. As a result, Bahrain was ultimately ruled singlehandedly by the emir under the emergency law. Opposition to his rule grew throughout the years and left Bahrain in a state of permanent upheaval known as the Intifada (1994–1999). Open clashes with security forces were predominant in Shi'a villages, while urban Sunnis and Shi'as petitioned the emir for change (Herb, 1999: 175). The regime responded with more coercion, incarcerations, and deportation of opposition leaders. Under such circumstances, the development of media faced new constraints from the ruling establishment. The emerging mediascape became either government-owned or, if private, strictly controlled concerning the political ideas disseminated.

A regulatory body, Bahrain Radio and Television Corporation (BRTC) was formed in 1971. In 1973 the government established Bahrain Television that began a daily broadcast of an initially five-hour-long program. Radio broadcasting, functioning since 1955, continued its operations under a national agenda. In 1976, the governments of the Arabian Gulf countries established an official media agency, Gulf News Agency (GNA). It was made up of ministers of information from the countries in the region and provided an official account of the news. The agency was combined with the Ministry of Information in 1985 and the name was changed to Bahrain News Agency (BNA) in 2003. The reforms in the sphere of media saw the promulgation of the Press Law in 1979 restricting, among others, the licensing of publishers, permissions for content publications and even for events promoting literary readings, as well as imposing penalties for offenders to the long list of sensitive subjects (Jawad, 2001: 169).

Independence of Bahrain encouraged the growth of media, but the political events put a hold on their full development. The State Security Law mentioned earlier had an even more important impact on media than did the Press Law. It made dissent risky, and publicizing opposing voices carried severe penalties. Press censorship was set in place. In these circumstances, two new daily newspapers emerged, and the situation remained the same until 1989. One of them is the longest still functioning Arabic newspaper in Bahrain, *Akhbar Al Khaleej*. It was established in 1976, while its sister English language publication, *Gulf Daily News* (GDN), began in 1978, the year when *The Gulf Mirror* ceased its operations. Both operate as private ventures and were set up by Al Hilal Corporation. The latter was established initially to import and distribute international magazines and newspapers before widening its portfolio to other publishing activities. The corporation was launched, among others, by Mahmood Al Mardi, who became the first editor-in-chief of *Akhbar Al Khaleej* and was succeeded upon his death by Anwar Abdulrahman, another businessman and founder of the corporation. The team also stood behind the publication of *GDN*. The newspaper was the brainchild of Ronnie Middleton, Al Hilal Publishing and Marketing Group managing director. Its first editor-in-chief was Mahmood Al Mardi, while Anwar Abdulrahman is the *GDN* chairman. Printing and publication of both newspapers are done by Dar Akhbar Al Khaleej Printing and Publishing House. In their news coverage, both newspapers adopt a nationalist stance. They cover a wide range of topics from international and national news to sections devoted to business, sports, classifieds, and entertainment. Both

newspapers remain close to the government, which explains their commercial success and continuity on the market, as for a long time they faced no viable competition. While in the decade
of the 1990s Bahrain was engulfed in anti-government protests, the opportunities for the operations of local media were still constrained. *Akhbar Al Khaleej*, despite its pro-government stance,
ran occasionally into trouble. In 1993 the newspaper was suspended after showing a map of the
disputed island of Hawar as belonging to the State of Qatar rather than Bahrain. In the same
year, one of its editors was fired for attempting to interview with one of the main Shi'a opposition figures (Sakr, 2003: 109). The lines of what was allowed were rather vague.

Despite media constraints, the 1990s saw a new global phenomenon, namely the emergence
of satellite TV. Passing across borders, satellite channels faced fewer limitations concerning local
censorship, although jamming of the signal occasionally occurred. While in theory possessing
a satellite receiver in Bahrain was not allowed without approval from the government (Jawad,
2001: 171), in practice many Bahrainis were connected. The Arabic channels, such as the Egyptian Satellite Channel broadcasting from Egypt and the Saudi-owned Middle East Broadcasting
Center (MBC) from London, aired their transmissions in the Arabian Gulf. Sakr (2003: 109)
noted, however, that such channels were not interested in breaking the political status quo in the
region even if they reported events unfolding on the ground in Arab countries. Besides, some
channels were largely devoted to entertaining the audiences rather than spreading political ideas.
Hence, other pan-Arab channels that joined the scene in the mid-1990s had a bigger impact
in this domain. Such was the case of the Qatari Al Jazeera network that began broadcasting in
1996 (Rugh, 2004: 235).

The death of the former emir on 6 March 1989 marked a turn in the history of Bahrain.
The day following his death, on 7 March 1989, another daily appeared on the market, the
Arabic *Al Ayam*. It adopted, unsurprisingly, a pro-government stance, as political reforms were
announced. Yet it differed from *Akhbar Al Khaleej* in its approach to modern journalistic editing
and inclusion of a greater variety of topics, with supplements dedicated to specialized areas, such
as business and cultural affairs. All in all, *Al Ayam* was a commercial success, and it soon became
the most-widely circulated Arabic daily in Bahrain. Al Ayam Publishing and Printing also established the English language daily, *Bahrain Tribune*, in 1997 (Rugh, 2004: 62), relaunched later
as *The Daily Tribune*.

By the end of the 1990s, Bahrain had three dailies and seven weeklies. The latter were of
general interest or catered to more specific topics such as engineering, *Al Muhandis*, or commerce, *Hayat Al Tejariya* (Jawad, 2001: 169). The volume of daily newspaper publication was
estimated at 70,000 (Youssry and Fikri, 2002: 1041). Radio and television were state-owned.
The reforms of the successor to the late emir, namely, his son Shaikh Hamad bin Isa Al Khalifa,
help explain the fast development of the Bahraini media in the 21st century.

Regulating the media

The end of the 20th century marked a new beginning in Bahraini politics with the introduction of sweeping liberalization reforms. In 2000, the new emir, Hamad bin Isa Al Khalifa,
initiated a plan to establish the National Action Charter. The document upheld, among others,
the rights to freedom of expression, publication, and belief as well principles of democracy.
It was submitted afterward for approval in a national referendum and was overwhelmingly
accepted by the society with 98.4% of Bahrainis voting in favor. The Constitution promulgated
subsequently in 2002 saw Bahrain becoming a constitutional monarchy. With further political reforms such as Decree of Amnesty and abolishment of the State Security Law in 2001,
civil rights were restored, and political dissidents were allowed to return to the country. The

Press Law promulgated in 2002 eased the regulations for operating the private press. Bahraini authorities did not recognize political parties; however, they allowed the creation of political associations that mushroomed along with various nongovernmental organizations (NGOs). The opposition was pleased with the announcement of reforms. Shi'a clerics called on their followers to stop skirmishes with security forces and remain calm.

Nonetheless, the initial euphoria of the civil society soon turned into disappointment. A parliament was re-established but as a bicameral body with only the Council of Representatives, the lower house, elected in universal suffrage. The upper house of the parliament, selected directly by the king, would approve bills proposed by the lower house before they are implemented. Moreover, ultimately the king would have the right to veto all bills. In comparison to the Constitution of 1973, the role of the parliament was reduced. In a show of discontent, Shi'a political associations boycotted the parliamentary elections in 2002. This step allowed Sunni candidates to dominate the parliament. Ultimately, the most significant change brought about by the controlled political liberalization of the country is that it contributed to a growing split within the society with Sunnis almost overwhelmingly backing the new reforms, while the majority of the Shi'as called for further progressive amendments. The growing political ferment and the deepening of the sectarian split culminated in the 2011 Arab Spring uprising that was contained by the government with the help of neighboring countries. Yet, its aftermath has led to an era of increased censorship and incarcerations of dissidents.

New regulations that came into place at the beginning of the 21st century set the foundations for the operations of modern Bahraini media. While promising extensive freedom of expression, provisions limiting the latter were also introduced. Their weight increased at the end of the 2000s when the political climate witnessed a sharp increase of political confrontations between the pro-government and various opposition groups. Within Bahrain's legal framework, freedom of speech is guaranteed. The Constitution of 2002 has three articles that specifically relate to media and freedom of speech, but limitations were also set in place. Article 23, for instance, guarantees "freedom of opinion" and "scientific research." The article stipulates further,

> [e]veryone has the right to express his opinion and publish it by word of mouth, in writing or otherwise under the rules and conditions laid down by law, provided that the fundamental beliefs of Islamic doctrine are not infringed, the unity of the people is not prejudiced, and discord or sectarianism is not aroused.

The Press Law (Decree-Law No. 47 of 2002) provides additional limitations to the contents allowed for public circulation. Article 19 specifies,

> it is possible to prohibit the circulation of publications instigating hatred of the political regime, encroaching on the state's official religion, breaching ethics, encroaching on religions and jeopardizing public peace or raising issues whose publication is prohibited by the provisions of this law.

In the initial climate of political liberalization, the Press Law opened the opportunity for licensing of further newspapers. Licensing, controlled by the Ministry of Information and Broadcasting, required its consent and minimum capital investments to begin operations. Daily newspapers require BD 1 million (US $2.65 million) paid-up capital, BD 250,000 (US $662,000) for non-dailies, and BD 50,000 (US $132,000) for "specialized" newspapers (Internet Filtering in Bahrain, 2005: 4). Publishers took this opportunity, and new daily newspapers emerged. These are *Al Wasat* (initiated in 2002 and closed down in 2017), *Al Watan* (2005), *Al Waqt* (2006), and

Al Bilad (2008). Among these newspapers, *Al Wasat*, founded by a leading dissident Mansoor Al Jamri and Karim Fakhrawi, stood out as the only opposition newspaper in circulation. In addition, due to a large presence of Malayalam speakers from Southern India, dailies in this language were also established. Finally, the 2000s saw the emergence of new press catering to special interests as well as glossy print devoted to entertainment, leisure, and celebrity lifestyle, which include English-language titles such as *Woman, Gulf Insider, Fact Bahrain, Bahrain This Month, Time Out Bahrain*, and *Ohlala Magazine* and Arabic *Layalina*. Some of these publications followed global trends of reporting photographs of participants of various events, restaurants, and bars, and ceremonies held in the country.

With regard to the development of television, the situation has not changed. Bahrain Radio and Television Corporation controls all the TV channels, and private licenses are not issued. Bahrain saw, however, the establishment of headquarters of satellite TV channels on its soil. Orbit Communications Company, a Saudi-owned satellite TV network, opened its doors in Manama in 2004 and operated till 2009 when it merged with Showtime Arabia to form OSN. It offered subscriptions to various satellite channels and presented its own broadcasts. Channels progressive in terms of political ideas found it more difficult to prosper. In 2015, Al Arab television operated by Saudis under the direction of the late Jamal Khashoggi was suspended on its first day after inviting a Bahraini opposition figure to the studio. Al Jazeera network operated a bureau from Manama, but it was also closed down after a dispute over the coverage of developments in Bahrain back in 2002. To counter such restrictions, Bahraini opposition launched a satellite TV channel LuaLua TV in London in 2011. It should be noted that 99% of Bahraini households have a satellite connection and access international media channels (Reporters Without Borders, 2013).

The development of new technologies prompted legislation in other areas. Telecommunications Law was promulgated in 2002. It stipulates severe penalties for an individual who

> uses telecommunications equipment or the telecommunications network intending to send any message in the knowledge that the contents of the message are false, misleading, offensive to public policy or morals, endanger the safety of third parties or prejudice the efficiency of any service.
>
> *(Legislative Decree No. 48 Promulgating the*
> *Telecommunications Law 2002)*

Political reforms were accompanied by liberalization and privatization of the telecom industry in 2004. Bahrain experienced a strong growth in the ICT sector, placing the country at the top of the Gulf Cooperation Council (GCC) region in terms of phone and Internet connectivity (Bahrain Economic Development Board, 2009). Consequently, various forms of communication became available to the majority of the inhabitants of Bahrain. Already in 2010, up to 88% of Bahrain's inhabitants were connected to the Internet (Internet World Stats, 2010) and mobile phone penetration rates reached 158% (Gulf Daily News, 2012). While the telecommunications market was liberalized and private operators allowed to enter the market, they must "provide all technical resources, including telecommunications equipment, systems, and programs relating to the telecommunications network . . . to allow security organs to have access to the network for fulfilling the requirements of national security" (Internet Filtering in Bahrain, 2005). In practice, the network operators are thus required to submit personal information about the users of their telephone and Internet services. The Internet is filtered to assure that the legal provisions are not breached. Local Internet providers ban particular websites at the request of the governmental regulators. The list of prohibited websites is often updated. On the one hand, sites displaying pornographic or erotic content and proselytizing religions other than Islam to

Arabs have been blocked. But Islamic morality is only one of the factors in determining access, as many websites with political content were closed down or banned for their criticism of the government or alleged sectarian content. As a result, the websites of some opposition political organizations, NGOs, and blogs of various individuals remain blocked. In the past, the list of blocked pages included also proxy websites and some Google applications.

Widespread access to the Internet among Bahrainis had an important impact through the digitalization of the already existing newspaper publications and especially the emergence of alternative media, as will be analyzed in the next section.

Further reforms saw the transformation of governmental bodies that regulate the circulation of the news. In 2010, the Ministry of Culture and Information was split and the Information Affairs Authority (IAA) began regulating the kingdom's press and controlling the state TV and radio services through BRTC. Bahrain News Agency became an extension of IAA broadcasting official accounts of national and international news in Arabic and English. In 2014, IAA was merged as part of the Ministry of Information.

All in all, the effects of the political liberalization reforms were limited. On the one hand, the promises and provisions guaranteeing freedom of expression were set in place. The amendments to the Press Law in 2008 announced even more room for media freedom, but major obstacles to journalism remained (Reporters Without Borders, 2008). On the other hand, the growing conflict surrounding the political developments antagonized the pro- and anti-government groups, leading to an outbreak of popular unrest in February 2011. Bahrain Independent Commission of Inquiry (BICI) that assessed the disputed events of 2011, concluded,

> It is clear that the media in Bahrain is biased towards the GoB [Government of Bahrain]. Six of the seven daily newspapers are pro-government and the broadcasting service is State-controlled. The continuing failure to provide opposition groups with an adequate voice in the national media risks further polarising the political and ethnic divide in Bahrain.

Consequently, the lack of viable opportunities for self-expression in the official channels contributed to the creation of alternative media online. The latter are controlled with much more difficulty by national governments due to the possibility of using nicknames, external servers, VPN software, and encrypted messaging. Indeed, the introduction of the Internet to Bahrain in the mid-1990s slowly tilted the power to disseminate information in the kingdom from the state to the citizen. The Internet provided Bahraini activists with a new information tool and produced a generation of online activists who began to express their opinions in public forums. Soon, the Internet became a platform to exchange critical views, organize popular mobilization, and spread the news of events that would have been otherwise omitted from the local media channels (Desmukh, 2010). Subsequently, since the 2000s, the rift between the official and unofficial media has been growing.

Challenges post-2011

Media play an important role in any society, providing credible information but also contributing to the socialization of its members. The Internet has revolutionized the opportunities for individual broadcasting and access to information. What is observed in Bahrain is a dual model of media: one that is official and supports the government, and the other that is grassroots and opposes or at least discusses the official news accounts. It relies most often on the Internet to spread to avoid gatekeepers. Bahraini activists tested the boundaries of free speech in Bahrain in the early 2000s. Open criticism of government officials and calls for political reforms resulted in a wave of trials of bloggers and journalists well before the Arab Spring began. Trials of activists are based on the provisions of the Bahraini Penal Code. It specifies that punishment of

> imprisonment for no more than 2 years and a fine not exceeding BD [Bahraini dinar] 200, or either penalty, shall be imposed upon any person who willfully broadcasts any false or malicious news reports, statements or rumors or spreads adverse publicity, if such conduct results in disturbing public security, terrorizing people or causing damage to the public interest [Article 168],

and the same penalty is dictated for

> any person who publishes by any method of publication untrue reports, falsified or forged documents or falsely attributed to other people should they undermine the public peace or cause damage to the country's supreme interest or the State's creditworthiness [Article 169].

The latter also applies to defaming the country's image abroad, for instance during international conferences. The legal provisions related to media safeguard the integrity of the political system, prevent the spread of voices critical to the government. This function of the official media to support the government is paramount and has only increased since 2011. Nonetheless, *Bahraini Monitor*, an online independent newspaper, was established in 2011 and produces English and Arabic news complementing the opposition-led LuaLua TV.

The Arab Spring exacerbated the crackdown of online and offline activists. Reporters Without Borders, an independent NGO, reported that several Bahraini activists were arrested and prosecuted in the aftermath of the uprising (Reporters Without Borders, 2011). The detained activists included bloggers, citizen journalists, and professional journalists of the opposition newspaper *Al Wasat*. In addition, it was reported that some activists died in custody or in other circumstances that were unaccounted for. Such is the case of Karim Fakhrawi, mentioned previously, who died while being interrogated by the security. Bahraini activists were tried for the alleged attempt to overthrow the regime. Their trials resulted in lengthy sentences, ranging from 15 years to life imprisonment, that in some cases were subsequently changed to house arrest; at times Bahraini citizenship was withdrawn. Moreover, the crackdown led to the detention and deportation of foreign journalists reporting the Arab Spring events and of foreign human rights activists.

After the violent clampdown on the opposition, foreign correspondents were gradually expelled from the country and Bahrain disappeared from the headlines of international newspapers. The authorities tried to preserve the image of the "island of golden smiles," as Bahrain was once known, by cutting out the flow of unfavorable and disapproving information abroad. Foreign journalists were accused of exaggerating the unrest and inciting violence. Foreign journalists have been allowed to return only after BICI was set up by the king as an independent body to assess the events of the Arab Spring in Bahrain. Secondly, the Arab Spring exacerbated the censorship of media. As mentioned, BICI found that media coverage was biased in favor of the regime (2011: 411). Yet new legislative changes limiting free expression were approved in 2013. A new law stated that anyone who in any way defames the king, Bahrain's flag or coat of arms, could be jailed for up to five years and handed a fine of 10,000 Bahraini dinars (26,500 USD). Recent developments affected Bahrain's position in the Press Freedom Index, causing a sharp drop in the freedom of expression rankings.

Despite BICI's recommendations that censorship be relaxed and the opposition allowed greater access to television and radio broadcasts and to print media, the situation has not improved since the Arab Spring. On the contrary, the year 2017 marked a return to the crackdown on activists. The challenge posed to the monarchy was still present, as activism did not stop with the containment of the protests on the Pearl Roundabout (Karolak, 2017). Subsequently, in 2017 *Al Wasat* was ordered to close down, marking the end of the only opposition newspaper on the market. Various political associations, NGOs, and websites faced a similar fate and many activists, among them journalists, were convicted by military courts on terrorism charges (Reporters Without Borders, 2017). In 2019, it was announced that following opposition media and accounts is a criminal offense. The pro-government media remain thus the only channel of information originating officially within the country. While presenting the image of the country as "business as usual," they help preserve the status quo on the political level.

Conclusion

The case of Bahrain is illustrative of the constraints in which media operate in the MENA region. The colonial past and the subsequent installation of authoritarian regimes had a profound impact on the mediascape. Bahraini media lie at the center of the dispute about the scope of the political liberalization reforms and their role in maintaining the status quo. Bahrain is also illustrative of the Gulf Cooperation Countries where the access to the Internet is widespread. The latter contributes to the proliferation of alternative media that bypass the official gatekeepers. Yet, it is also clear that any real challengers to the regime will be prosecuted. All in all, Bahraini media remain a contested sphere.

References

Abdulla, H. (2004), *Bahrain's English Newspapers an Illustrated History*. Manama: BAPCO.

Al Khatir, M. (2014), The Art of Printing in Bahrain 1913–1948. In Shaikh A. bin Khalid Al Khalifa and M. Rice (eds.), *Bahrain Through the Ages: The History*. London: Routledge.

Al Shaikh, E. A., and Campbell, V. (2013), News Media and Political Socialization of Young People: The Case of Bahrain. In B. Gunter and R. Dickinson (eds.), *News Media in the Arab World: A Study of 10 Arab and Muslim Countries*. New York: Bloomsbury Publishing USA, pp. 153–172.

Bahrain Economic Development Board (BEDB) (2009), *Arab Advisors Group Reveals Bahrain's Communications Connectivity Leading the Region*. Retrieved from www.bahrainedb.com. Accessed 6 January 2010.

Bahrain Independent Commission of Inquiry (BICI) (2011), *Report of the Bahrain Independent Commission of Inquiry*. Retrieved from www.bici.org.bh/BICIreportEN.pdf. Accessed 8 April 2011.

Bahrain Open Data Portal (2016), *Bahrain in Figures Booklet*. Retrieved from www.data.gov.bh./ Accessed 8 January 2019.

Commins, D. (2012), *The Gulf States: A Modern History*. London: I.B. Tauris.

Desmukh, F. (September 21, 2010), *The Internet in Bahrain: Breaking the Monopoly of Information*. The Middle East Channel. Retrieved from http://mideast.foreignpolicy.com/posts/2010/09/21/. Accessed 1 May 2013.

Fuccaro, N. (2009), *Histories of City and State in the Persian Gulf: Manama since 1800*. Cambridge: Cambridge University Press.

Gulf Daily News (2012), *Bahrain Mobile Phone Users Top 1.9 Million*, 30 December. Retrieved from www.gulf-daily-news.com/NewsDetails.aspx?storyid=344673. Accessed 3 May 2013.

Herb, M. (1999), *All in the Family: Absolutism, Revolution, and Democratic Prospects in the Middle Eastern Monarchies*. New York: State University of New York.

Internet Filtering in Bahrain 2004–2005 (2005), Retrieved from www.opennetinitiative.net/studies/bahrain/. Accessed 5 February 2010.

Internet World Stats (2010), Retrieved from www.Internetworldstats.com/middle.htm. Accessed 10 January 2010.

Jawad, F. (2001), Bahrain. In D. Jones (ed.), *Censorship: A World Encyclopedia*. London: Routledge, pp. 169–173.

Karolak, M. (2017), Social Media and the Arab Spring in Bahrain: From Mobilization to Confrontation. In C. Cakmak (ed.), *Making of Arab Spring: Assessing Role of Civil Society through Cases of Innovative Activism*. New York: Palgrave Macmillan, pp. 81–119.

Khuri, F. (1980), *Tribe and State in Bahrain*. Chicago: The University of Chicago Press.

Kumar, K. (2016), Indian South Asian Migration to Gulf Countries: History, Policies, Development. In P. C. Jain and G. Z. Oommen (eds.), *South Asian Migration to Gulf Countries*. New York: Routledge, pp. 71–92.

Nydell, M. (2002), *Understanding the Arabs: A Guide for Modern Times*. Boston: Intercultural Press.

Reporters Without Borders (2008), *Press Law Amendments Hailed but Journalists Still Face Jail and Websites Risk Closure*. Retrieved from https://rsf.org/en/news/press-law-amendments-hailed-journalists-still-face-jail-and-websites-risk-closure/. Accessed 3 January 2019.

Reporters Without Borders (2011), *No Concessions to Media as Indiscriminate Repression Continues in Countries with Pro-democracy Protests*. Retrieved from http://en.rsf.org/bahrain-no-concessions-tomedia-as-12-04-2011,40009.html. Accessed 30 March 2013.

Reporters Without Borders (2013), *Bahrain*. Retrieved from http://en.rsf.org/report-bahrain,148.html. Accessed 30 June 2013.

Reporters Without Borders (2017), *Bahrain Sentences Journalist to Life . . . with no Evidence*. Retrieved from www.ifex.org/bahrain/2017/11/12/journalists-convicted/. Accessed 3 January 2019.

Rugh, W. A. (2004), *Arab Mass Media: Newspapers, Radio, and Television in Arab Politics*. Westport, CT: Praeger Publishers.

Sakr, N. (2003), Dynamics of GCC Press – Government Relations in the 1990s. In T. P. Najem and M. Hetherington (eds.), *Good Governance in the Middle East Oil Monarchies*. London: Routledge.

Trimbee, A. (2009), *The Inshallah Paper*. London: Quartet Books.

Ulaby, L. (2010), Mass Media and Music in the Arab Persian Gulf. In M. Frishkopf (ed.), *Music and Media in the Arab World*. Cairo: The American University in Cairo Press, pp. 111–128.

Youssry, H., and Fikri, H. (2002), The Middle East. In J. McDonough and K. Egolf (eds.), *The Advertising Age Encyclopedia of Advertising*. Chicago: Fitzroy Dearborn Publishers, pp. 1038–1043.

Egypt

4

PRESS IN EGYPT

Impact on social and political transformations

Elsayed Abdelwahed Elkilany

Historical background

The Egyptian press dates back to the end of the 18th century, when Napoleon Bonaparte, during the French occupation (1798–1801), introduced *Al-Hawadith Al-Youmiyya* newspaper. After the occupation ousting, the Ottoman governor Muhammad Ali founded the Egyptian newspaper *Al-Waqa'e al-Masria* in 1828, which was distributed to specific groups including army officers, mission students, and state employees (Sternfeld, 2014: 26). In 1882, Egypt entered into 40 years of British occupation. Despite the censorship of newspapers, especially articles criticizing the occupation, newspapers and magazines increased, and Cairo saw more than 90 such publications in 1890 (Goldschmidt and Johnson, 2012). With the increase in literacy, regional newspapers began to emerge in 1886 and were typically controlled through individual ownership and some bilateral ownership.

Some chronicle the regional press in five stages: nascence (1866–1900), youth (1901–1920), maturity (1921–1938), deflation (1939–1960), and contraction (1961–1987) (see Fadel, 2016: 16). In the last two decades, statistics show that the number of newspapers issued in Egypt has increased from 44 (2004) to 142 (2010) but decreased to 102 in 2011 and then to 76 in 2016 (Egyptian Central Agency for Public Mobilization and Statistics 'CAPMAS', 2017: 9).

With the technological advancement at the end of the 20th century, online journalism entered the field, where it contributed 45% of news content in the Arab world. In 2010–2011, Forbes ranked *Al-Youm Al-Sabe'a* as the most visited online news site in the Middle East. Dubai Press Club (2012: 140, 144, 2015: 139) reported that 24.7% of readers use the Internet to browse journalistic content. Egyptian citizen journalists began to use forums as a space for expression in 2003, and switched to social media platforms in 2006 (Rizk, 2016: 5). Social media users increased from 60% (2009) to 83% (2012); Facebook came at the forefront of social media applications, as YouTube did for video sites (Allam, 2018: 9).

Egyptian press business models

Egyptian press business models aligned with the established social and political structure and the political ideology of successive regimes that defined the press regulatory framework. First, in terms of ownership models, there were mixed models with some newspapers owned by the state and others by individuals and private corporations, in addition to partisan press.

Newspapers owned by individuals

This first model remained prevalent throughout the 19th century and continued until President Gamal Abdel Nasser issued the "Regulation of the Press" Law 156/1960, which transferred the ownership of *Al-Ahram*, *Akhbar Al-Youm*, *Rosal Youssef*, and *Al-Hilal* newspapers to the state. *Al-Ma'aref* followed in1963 and *Al-Tahrir* in 1967.

Most studies regard the press during that era as marking the golden age of the press industry, where the concept of modern management was rooted; the "professional manager" concept replaced the "owner-manager" and the concepts of "specialty," "division of labor," and "separation of ownership and management" emerged (Ghali, 2008: 157–158).

State-owned newspapers (national newspapers)

Such newspapers are also referred to as "governmental" and "semi-official" newspapers, and these designations reflect the government's control over them. Egypt is second to China with regard to state-owned media institutions (Rizk, 2016: 103). The legal ownership of these newspapers was entrusted to several entities, including the Shura Council (SC) (1980–2013), the Supreme Press Council (SPC) (2013–2016), and then to the National Press Authority (NPA) (2016–present). See also the following chapter on Egyptian broadcasting.

According to the executive regulation adopted by the SPC in November 1985, the national press corporation was administratively, editorially, and financially represented in three bodies: the board of directors, the editorial board, and the general assembly (Ghali, 2008: 163). This type of organization defined the way national press worked for decades. Both the National Union (NU) and then the Socialist Union (SU), "the legal owner," limited their role to appoint, but not to monitor, heads of boards of directors and editors. They were almost "the actual owner," which paved the road for corruption, creating administrative and economic imbalances and failures (Ghali, 2008: 159). This period also witnessed increased nepotism in recruitment and a predominance of the centralized management style because of long-term presidents, members of boards of directors, and editors (26 years in some cases) (Ghali, 2008: 186–187).

Moreover, economically this pattern indicated an imbalance of economic structures, reliance on the state to cover budget deficits, the rigidity of administration in dealing with distribution policies or press marketing, and a lack of clear rules governing national press subsidies by the state. This led to increasing losses reaching 7 billion and 184 million pounds in 2006 (Ghali, 2008: 188–196). On the other hand, national newspapers faced financial difficulties in 2017 due to a 40% reduction in government subsidies, 60% in advertising spending, and the unsustainable business model prevailing in these institutions (Allam, 2018: 3).

Newspapers owned by political parties (partisan newspapers)

Political parties issue these newspapers under the Political Parties Law 40/1977. The law entrusted the "Committee of Political Parties Affairs" to receive requests for the party establishment, decide on them, and follow up on the performance of existing parties. The committee, which was governmental par excellence, acted as a guardian and censor capable of stopping partisan newspapers and investigating what they published (Ghali, 2008: 222). In 30 years, it refused to form more than 60 parties, which is why people called it the "Committee for Parties Prevention" (Shaqir, n.d.).

A pattern continued of the central administration dominating administrative and editorial decisions, as well as creating a lack of separation between the management of the party and the newspaper. The party leaders considered themselves responsible for the performance and the agenda, which turned some newspapers into special "bulletins" for party leaders (Ghali, 2008: 219).

Due to financial weakness, partisan newspapers could not own printing presses and distribution outlets, which caused them to stop their operations on various occasions because of the government's dissatisfaction. Most parties merely published major publications reflecting their political and intellectual orientation, which was reflected in the lack of professionalism in hiring journalists, not to mention that transparent promotion criteria were generally missed (Ghali, 2008: 186–218).

Most partisan newspapers published weeklies, while Al-Wafd and Al-Ahrar parties published dailies. Al-Sha'ab party's newspaper appeared twice a week before recently moving online (Allam, 2018: 4).

Newspapers owned by companies (private newspapers)

This type of newspaper is referred to as the "independent" press. Public or private owners can own these outlets, under Law 148/1980, where the owner can be cooperatives, joint-stock companies, or trust funds. However, a serious restriction contained in Law 3/1998 required the Council of Ministers' approval to establish companies whose purposes include issuing newspapers. On 5 May 2000, the Supreme Constitutional Court considered the restriction aggression on the press and ruled to abolish it (Orabi, 2015: 83–86).

Ownership of private newspapers was subjected to licensing laws, high establishment costs, and restrictions on published content. This led many to establish their companies outside Egypt (Cyprus in particular). To censor these newspapers, the Authority established an office dedicated to the censorship of foreign publications. In line with the economic openness program, the privately owned *Al-Masry Al-Youm* newspaper was published in 2004, and the private sector used this opportunity to obtain licenses for other new newspapers (Rizk, 2016: 7–10).

Competition: audience and market share

Egyptian newspapers allege that they distribute over one million copies daily, which represents 70%–80% of their income sources (Dubai Press Club, 2015: 137). However, even if this figure was true, this constitutes about 1% of the Egyptian population. Most recently, one prominent Egypt editor, Madgi al-Gallad, claimed that the total circulation for all newspapers in Egypt does not exceed 300,000 copies (Meghawer, 2018). The decreasing readership could be due to the illiteracy rate (which constituted at least 20% in 2018) combined with the level of poverty, where more than 18% of Egyptians live with an average of $2 a day, while the average newspaper price is $0.15–$0.35. This means that one in five Egyptians will not be able to purchase the paper due to limited income (Sternfeld, 2014: 84–85).

According to the Egyptian statistics bureau (CAPMAS), there were around 96 national or state-owned newspapers in 2016, compared to only four partisan newspapers. Private newspapers usually compete with national newspapers. For example, in mid-2011, *Al-Masry Al-Youm* newspaper ranked first in terms of readership, ahead of the state-owned *Al-Akhbar* and *Al-Ahram* (Dubai Press Club, 2012: 29, 139). This is could be due to their focus on citizens' problems, corruption cases, and new interactive features on their website. However, *Al-Masry Al-Youm* ranking allegedly declined in 2015 to third place after *Al-Ahram* and *Al-Akhbar* (Dubai Press Club, 2015: 136), which can be explained by the different political environment during those two years and its impact on the private newspaper's performance, and thus the readership figures.

On the other hand, both partisan and private newspapers lose 35%–40% of distribution revenue because they do not own their printing presses and distribution outlets, so they depend on the national press institutions for printing and distribution operations. In addition, the SPC restricts the number of copies for each private newspaper, which further curtails the distribution of the latter in the main governorates such as Cairo and Alexandria, not to mention in other governorates (Sternfeld, 2014: 86–87). This loss of income intensified after *Al-Ahram* increased its printing costs by 80% in 2017, following the decision to float the Egyptian pound, which depreciated against the dollar (Allam, 2018: 4).

When the trend towards digital space increased before and after the 2011 uprising, most Egyptian newspapers maintained both print and online versions. Private newspapers were more active online and outperformed national newspapers in their level of online activity; for example, the number of *Al-Masry Al-Youm*'s online visitors increased from 900,000 in 2013 to 1.2 million in 2017, while *Al-Ahram* online readership dropped from 850,000 in 2005 to 71,000 in 2017. However, online presence, contributing 10%–15% of the income, still did not compensate for the decline in the printed market (Allam, 2018: 8).

With regard to advertising, or the most important financial source for press institutions, the government has continuously used it to curtail the partisan and private newspapers' capabilities. Most state advertising contracts were awarded to national newspapers, while few went to those who refrained from criticizing the state (Ghali, 2008: 171–172). Although several private newspapers have moved online and hence bypassed the monopoly over offline distribution, neither private nor national newspapers succeeded in developing a purely online journalism business model, and their advertising revenues remained rather limited (Rizk, 2016: 73).

Meanwhile, university journalism programs increased in number: from two programs in the 1930s and 1940s at the American University in Cairo, and later Cairo University, to about 15 programs in public and private universities by 2019. There are also training centers affiliated with major institutions such as Dar Al-Ahram, Journalists Syndicate, Middle East News Agency, and National Council for Broadcast Media (NCBM). However, there are mounting criticisms of the quality and capability of these programs to qualify trainees for the modern media market (Allam, 2018: 15–16).

Laws and legislation

The Egyptian press regulations began with the first Publications Law in 1881; it was enacted for two years and then suspended by Lord Cromer,[1] but Sir Eldon Gorst reinstated it in 1909 (Al-Masry Al-Youm, 2009). Two publication laws followed: Law 98/1931 and Law 20/1936. During this period, individuals had the right to issue newspapers, which was the dominant business model.

The legal organization of the Egyptian press entered a new era when President Nasser issued Law No. 156 in 1960. Although the law did not contain an explicit provision prohibiting individuals from issuing and owning newspapers,[2] it cited an important restriction on this right, which was that the owner should obtain a license from the Nationalist Union, thus making licenses dependent on political loyalty to the regime, and thereby excluding opponents.

Moreover, the Political Parties Law, which affirmed the right of each party to issue one or more newspapers, was followed by Law 36/1979, which stipulated that the party should have at least 10 seats in the People's Assembly to enjoy the right to issue its publications. This restriction persisted until abolished by the Supreme Council of Armed Forces (SCAF), which seized power after Mubarak stepped down on 11 February 2011.

Regulatory bodies

The Egyptian press has been subject to several regulatory bodies created by laws, each of which has had its impact. These bodies can be defined in terms of their establishment, legal organization, and relationship to the government, as follows:

A Journalists Syndicate (1940–present)

The idea of establishing a syndicate for journalists began in 1900 when Sheikh Ali Yusuf, through his newspaper *Al-Mu'ayyad*, called for the establishment of a trade union for press workers, but his efforts did not materialize. Egyptian journalists later established several associations under different names such as "Press Syndicate," "Journalists Syndicate," "Editors' Association," and "Newspaper Owners Association" (Orabi, 2015: 144–145).

The organization of journalism syndicates has been through several laws, the most important and comprehensive of them are Laws 10/1941, 185/1955, and 76/1970. The revision of these laws shows the regime's influence and dominance of trade union work. According to the "Association for Freedom of Thought and Expression (AFTE)" (Shawqi, 2017: 5), the laws required a journalist to be nominated by a recognized newspaper to be enrolled in a syndicate, a requirement that is discriminatory and unconstitutional since membership is individual/personal and should not be controlled by the labor market. According to Allam (2018: 10), the latest statistics show that the syndicate has 8,951 journalists registered in its lists, 6,127 males and 2,824 females in 2018. Importantly, the state outlets such as *Al-Ahram* are the largest voting bloc with 1,700 members (19.76%) followed by *Akhbar Al-Youm* and Dar Al-Tahrir.

The syndicate's struggle for freedom of expression and press was manifested in several situations, most notably the threat of strike action and the suspension of newspapers in opposition to the so-called Suspicious Press Law No. 93/1995, which included provisions allowing for pre-trial detention of journalists in publishing cases. This led the government to issue Law No. 96/1996, which, according to some, made a qualitative leap in the Egyptian press system (Ghali, 2008: 177–178).

Supreme Press Council (1978–2018)

After the enforcing of Law 156/1960, the call to establish a Supreme Journalism Council emerged, but its formation began in 1975 and continued until replaced by the Supreme Council for Media Regulation (SCMR) in 2018. The council formations clearly show the Authority's control, which some interpret as circumventing the democracy slogans raised by the successive regimes (Orabi, 2015: 118).

The Council's competencies as defined by laws show that it is an effective authority in the press industry as it is eligible to express opinions on all draft laws, coordinating between press institutions, following up their economic performance, and determining their shares of papers. It also monitors and evaluates what newspapers publish, reviews complaints against them, and authorizes journalists who wish to work in a non-Egyptian press institution, either inside or outside Egypt.

National Press Authority (2016–present)

The NPA was established under Law 92/2016 to manage the state-owned press institutions, as an alternative to both SC and SPC. It was first formed by Presidential Decree 159/2017 and then was issued a separate law No. 179/2018. The revision of those laws shows that the state continues to dominate the press. The NPA is formed of nine members; the state selects at least five of them. The NPA has been authorized to have full control over press institutions, including appointing and dismissing the head of the board of directors of national press institutions and the editors of newspapers.

Press freedoms

When the British occupation came to Egypt, it began to restrict press freedom by applying the 1881 Publications Law. It confronted newspapers that were fanatical to Orabians[3] and abolished and disrupted some newspapers. Afterward, Lord Cromer, who opposed press restrictions, disrupted the implementation of the 1881 Law, giving the Egyptian press freedom unknown in North Africa or West Asia at the time. Newspapers numbered to 200 periodicals. When Sir Eldon came to power, he reinstated the 1881 Law, which sparked public outrage in the Boutros Pasha Ministry, and demonstrators chanted for the fall of the Publications Law. However, police forces suppressed it (Al-Masry Al-Youm, 2009).

The Egyptian press worked erratically under the various publications laws. Khalil (1995: 3–38) observed that Egyptian newspapers' interest in various issues and problems fluctuated over the years between 1945 and 1952, and she attributed this to the change in power behavior towards press freedom.

After overthrowing the monarchy in July 1952, the Free Officers (coup leaders) received considerable popular support due to strong discontent against the monarchy. To impart its voice to people, the new authority established *Al-Gomhouria* (or Republic) newspaper in December 1953, which was then replaced by *Al-Ahram* after President Nasser nationalized newspapers in 1960. The nationalization homogenized newspapers, resulting in similar content supporting the regime. Opposition newspapers were threatened with closure, as indicated by the distribution of the *Ros Al-Yousif* newspaper dropping from 80,000 to 22,000 copies during that period (Sternfeld, 2014: 30–31).

When Al-Sadat came to power in 1970, he gave the press more freedom. He abolished newspaper censorship in 1974, and the great writers who emigrated during Nasser's rule returned and practiced their work relatively freely. This period did not last long, however. In 1976, Sadat could not bear the national newspapers' criticism of his policies; so he replaced their leaders with others who were more loyal to him and also replaced the editors of some private newspapers. As the criticism continued, Sadat passed laws to restrict press freedom, such as 33/1978 on Protection of the National Security, 95/1980 on Protection of Values from Defect, and 148/1980 on Press Authority. In September 1981, he dismissed some opposition journalists, transferred others to non-journalistic posts, and closed down some newspapers and magazines. This phase ended with the assassination of Sadat on 6 October 1981 (Orabi, 2015: 62–65, 76).

When Mubarak came to power on 14 October 1981, he tried to mitigate the negative effects of Sadat's recent press decisions. He released the detained party leaders and journalists, returned 30 journalists to their institutions, and reinstated some banned newspapers. When partisan newspapers increased their criticism of the government policies, particularly in corruption cases, Mubarak aimed to restrict press freedom by resorting to some provisions of the Penal Code to use against newspapers and journalists. The SPC, for its part, filed complaints in limited cases against some newspapers and journalists to the Supreme State Security Prosecution (Orabi, 2015: 65–66, 78). Freedom House's indicators showed that the press was "not free" in the years between 2002 and 2007, and improved to only "partially free" in the last three years of Mubarak's rule, while the Internet was "partially free" in 2009.

This improvement in press freedom was attributed to the emergence of a new player, namely the private press owned by new businesspersons who benefited from the state's privatization drive under the "economic openness policy" and the "structural adjustment program," initiated by Mubarak in the late 1990s (Sternfeld, 2014: 75–89). Nine new private newspapers entered the Egyptian market in 2004/5, all of which sought to gain the public's trust, increase distribution, and ensure marketing for their services and goods. They did this by increasing the space dedicated to entertainment, by publishing gossip news about celebrities, and by relatively focusing on the economic and political corruption in the state agencies. On the other hand, the government reduced restrictions on national newspapers' content to give them more credibility. Nevertheless, Rizk (2016: 75) ruled out associating political freedom with economic freedom on Mubarak's regime agenda. With the 2011 uprising, the state tried to control the demonstrations, shutting down the country's Internet and mobile networks on 27 January and returning them on 2 February 2011 (Freedom House, 2013b: 16).

Mubarak stepped down from power on 11 February 2011 and entrusted the SCAF with running the country during a transitional period. According to Freedom House reports (2011a), (2012a), (2011b), (2012b), the SCAF continued to follow Mubarak's approach to restricting press freedom and widening the scope of legal cases under the pretext of protecting the country from "false information that would harm national security" while activating the emergency law. In March 2011, the SCAF warned journalists against publishing materials criticizing the armed forces, and in October 2011, it appointed a military censor to the press, which forced several prominent columnists to abandon their columns in the daily press. In November 2011, the SCAF suspended the English edition of *Al-Masri al-Youm* newspaper for containing sensitive articles about the council.

According to Freedom House's reports, the year 2011 was the most dangerous for Egyptian journalists with some of them killed and many activists and bloggers brought to military trials on charges of "insulting the military establishment" and "threatening social peace." In addition, journalists working for foreign media were attacked too, their devices confiscated or broken, and some were temporarily detained. Internet freedom was described as "partially free" in 2011 and 2012, but the Freedom House reported that the SCAF, rather than completely shutting down the Internet and mobile networks, deliberately limited access to the Internet and weakened online communication. This happened especially during the clashes with the military forces such as the "Maspero massacre" in October 2011, "Mohamed Mahmoud" incident in November 2011, and during the elections for the People's Assembly in 2011/12.

On 30 June 2012, Mohamed Morsi came to power after winning the first democratic elections, following the 2011 uprising. During this period, increased press freedom can be seen through several indicators such as Morsi's ordering of the release of journalist Shaimaa Adel, who was detained in Sudan. Morsi was keen to return with Adel on the presidential plane from Addis Ababa as a symbol of his interest in journalists (Reuters, 16 July 2012). Moreover, when an Egyptian court ordered one newspaper editor-in-chief to be jailed for "insulting Morsi" and "promoting rumors undermining security," Morsi issued a law that same evening abolishing pre-trial detention for journalists and released the journalist (Al-Nahar Online, 23 August 2012). Also, to enhance national newspapers' independence, members of the boards as well as editors were selected in a competitive manner (Rizk, 2016: 9). Subsequently, and within five months of his rule, new licenses were issued for 59 newspapers and 22 channels (YouTube, 21 April 2013: 9: 05–10: 02). The Freedom House report in 2013 (2013a) stated that during Morsi's government, no Internet content was filtered, and many bloggers and activists freely criticized the government and debated contentious issues.

On the other hand, Freedom House also recorded the gradual decline of press freedom during the same period/year, with many journalists being killed or injured during coverage of protests that increased during Morsi's rule, Islamic groups' besieging the media production city,[4] and many lawsuits being launched against journalists and media institutions with charges such as "insulting the president."

After the 2013 coup and the appointment of Adly Mansour as interim president, there was a strong polarization of two groups: the first was the 30 June movement backed by the army to overthrow Morsi, and the second was the group of defenders of Morsi's legitimacy. The interim president Mansour ratified a bill that abolished prison sentences for "insulting the president," and the amended constitution adopted in January 2014 abolished imprisonment for publishers – but with a broad exception for censorship in "war" and "emergency" periods. However, in reality, there was a marked decline of press freedom, including the arbitrary arrests of journalists without a warrant, closing satellite channels, and preventing some media from attending press conferences and official events "due to their expressed sympathy with the Brotherhood." In addition, Egyptian and foreign journalists were injured, killed, or imprisoned while covering demonstrations in support of Morsi (Freedom House, 2013a).

Egyptian press freedom declined the most after Abdelfattah al-Sisi came to power on 8 June 2014. It declined from "partially free" in 2014 to "not free" in the period between 2015 and 2019. In 2018, the Reporters Without Borders organization listed Egypt as part of the dark circle referred to as "media phobia" ('Egyptian Observatory for Press and Media, 2019: 1). The entire media landscape regressed, whether in legislation, laws, or practices, negatively impacting local and foreign press operating in Egypt.

> In terms of legislation and laws, despite the 2014 Constitution encouraging arti-
> cles relating to free expression and free press, restrictions prevailed. Some examples
> include Article 7 of the Anti-Terrorism Law (issued August 2015) which gave inves-
> tigators the power to block websites if they deemed the published content to consti-
> tute a crime or threat to national security or economy. In February 2018, the public
> prosecutor issued a decree instructing public defenders and prosecutors to continue
> monitoring media and social networking sites. The statement demanded all citizens
> to report abuses of media workers, turning all citizens into "informers" who report
> against media workers according to their whims and personal interpretations (EOJM,
> 2019: 12). The Cybercrime Act (enacted August 2018) expanded the criminaliza-
> tion of numerous online offenses, threatening human rights activists and govern-
> ment critics (Freedom House, 2019: 25). Article 19 of Law 180/2018 mandates the
> SCMR to monitor citizens' social media and blogs when the account exceeds five
> thousand followers, and SCMR can block accounts (Abdelsalam, 2019). Article 70
> of Law 180/2018 regulates the intervention of the State Information Service (SIS)
> as a censor on foreign media. It imbues SIS with the power to control foreign cor-
> respondents and foreign media offices operating in Egypt. For some, this regulation is

unconstitutional, and it contradicts the essence of law and the provisions of the Egyptian Constitution, which stipulates in its Article 211 that SCMR is an independent body. However, due to the subordination of SIS to the presidency, this runs counter to SCMR's independence.

(Abdelsalam, 2019: 25)

As for practices against the local press, various violations were recorded, such as banning coverage, breaking into a press facility, seizing and breaking press equipment, stopping the printing of an issue, confiscating and chopping issues, trespassing or threatening, assault, beatings, unlawful detention, and housebreaking. Violations also included imprisonment, the prohibition of entry into the country, arbitrary dismissal, the prohibition of writing and articles, and modification of articles without the knowledge of its author (Ata, 2016: 3). However, two cases were prominent during that period: the first was the storming of the Journalists Syndicate by security forces in 2016 and arresting several journalists on charges of "incitement to demonstrate," and the incident had symbolic significance as it resulted in the loss of the dignity attributed to the Egyptian journalistic profession (Moussa, 20 December 2017: 4). The second case was the closure of *Al-Masryoun* newspaper in September 2018 and the assignment of a committee from *Al-Akhbar* to manage it. This was part of the decision of a special committee entrusted with seizing the Brotherhood funding and closing outlets affiliated with the Brotherhood (EOJM, 26 January 2019: 2). The repression and harassment of the local press influenced its performance, leading to the further decline of objectivity and balance, and the shift of journalism from a community of watchdogs to "pets" controlled by the Authority (Harb, 2019: 110–111). In addition, this led to replacing the censorship roles that dominated the early stages of the post-Mubarak era in favor of a radical role, where private newspapers' journalists have demonized their political opponents, especially the Islamists, and portrayed them as the ultimate enemy. At the same time, the new military regime was respected and celebrated, which led to further destabilizing democracy's fragile transition (El Issawi and Cammaerts, 2016: 549).

The foreign press operating inside Egypt also suffered harassment under Al-Sisi's rule. It was systematically attacked in 2018–2019, specifically when Diaa Rashwan[5] was appointed as the SIS Chair. The SIS exerted pressure on the foreign press on two levels: firstly by issuing official statements on specific events to criticize foreign media, and secondly by using local media to lead defamation campaigns against foreign media (Abdelsalam, 2019: 19–20). There were at least scores of statements issued by the SIS, and those statements tended to criticize the foreign media's professionalism and made specific demands, such as deleting or modifying content or formally apologizing to the Egyptian government. Further, the directors of Reuters and BBC were summoned to the office of the SIS chair, where the meeting seemed more like an investigation into the foreign media's use of certain terms, as well as the sources of their information. Moreover, the SIS chair called state officials and the business elite to boycott the BBC, after the latter published news about the enforced disappearance of a young woman named "Zubaida Ibrahim," which was categorically denied by the government.

The most prominent results of the restriction on the foreign press led journalists to fear prosecution, which in turn forced many of them to leave Egypt. Moreover, the increased harassment of correspondents in the streets, with aggressors accusing them of betrayal, and the delayed access granted to the foreign journalists to sites as well as sources, all contributed to the declining role of the foreign press in Egypt.

The role of the press in social and political change

Throughout its history, the Egyptian press has worked in a context that made it a subordinate to the regime, either by offering incentives or with threats of intimidation.

Between the years 1906–1914, Egyptian newspapers presented the ideas of the new nationalists and their perceptions about Egypt's future. With the outbreak of WWI, Egyptian newspapers led debates about the culturally distinct and politically viable Egypt (Goldschmidt and Johnson, 2012). After the end of the World War, newspapers and magazines focused more on efforts for independence from British rule, which then occurred in 1922 (Sternfeld, 2014: 27).

Between 1945 and 1952, the press tackled acute problems such as class inequality, social justice, labor problems, education, supply and price increases, housing problems, and other social ills. This period showed that the 1952 coup was not merely an idea that grew in the minds of the Free Officers, but was a direct result of the socio-political development in Egypt during that period (Khalil, 1995: 3–38).

According to a study about the role of the Egyptian press in the prelude to the 2011 uprising, Egyptian newspapers attempted to tackle acute problems such as corruption and lack of civic freedoms (Zaki, 2015). However, there were differences among newspapers in how they handled issues, and here ownership might have played a role in this difference. For instance, *Al-Dustour* (private) had a daring and sometimes ferocious style, while *Al-Wafd* (partisan) and *Al-Masri Al-Youm* (private) were less daring in their coverage (ibid.). Meanwhile, national newspapers such as *Al-Ahram* aimed to enhance the regime's image and refute the messages of partisan and private newspapers (Zaki, 2015: 216–229).

By 2019, polarization has prevailed in the Egyptian press market with national newspapers still being deployed as the propaganda tool of power for decades, save for the last months of Morsi's rule (2013) when it turned against the regime. During 2013, most Egyptian national, partisan, and private newspapers focused on distorting Morsi's image and the Muslim Brotherhood in general, honing in on the failure to secure the needs of citizens for fuel and other goods and services. Meanwhile, the Brotherhood's newspaper *Al-Hurreya wa Al-Adala*, owned by the Brotherhood's Freedom and Justice Party, kept on supporting Morsi while largely ignoring other societal problems, which weakened readers' confidence in the outlet (Zaki, 2015: 242).

Conclusion

This chapter provided an overview of the Egyptian press market with regard to its origins and development and business models as well as regulation. It reviewed the status of press freedom and the role it played in accelerating the socio-political changes in modern Egypt. Indeed, the Egyptian press presents a model of the press in non-democratic developing countries. According to Freedom House indicators, the Egyptian press was described as "non-free" between 1972 and 2018, save for the period between 1974 and 1992 and briefly in 2012 where it was "partially free." Overall, the Egyptian press has been subjugated to the state's control and subsequently to decades of marginalization.

Notes

1 The de facto English ruler of Egypt in 1883–1907.
2 Depriving individuals from the right to own newspapers effectively started from Law 148/1980.
3 Named after Ahmed Orabi, who led a revolution in 1879–1882 against Khedive Tawfiq and foreign intervention in Egypt.
4 A facility that includes all private satellite TV studios in Egypt.

5 A politician, journalist, and researcher who held several positions, most notably the director of Al-Ahram Center for Political and Strategic Studies and the Journalists Representative.

References

Abdelsalam, M. (2019), The Egyptian Authorities' Attack on Foreign Media, Two Years of Threats, and Smear Campaigns. *AFTE Egypt*, 31 July. Retrieved from https://afteegypt.org/publications_org/2019/07/31/17965-afteegypt.html. Accessed 16 October 2019.

Allam, R. (2018), Egypt – Media Landscape. *European Journalism Centre (EJC)*. Retrieved from https://medialandscapes.org/country/egypt. Accessed 23 November 2019.

Al-Masry Al-Youm (2009), Publications Law: 128 Years of Shackling the Egyptian Press. *Almasryalyoum,* 14 August. Retrieved from www.almasryalyoum.com/news/details/62120. Accessed 10 November 2019.

Ata, W. (2016), Second Semi-Annual Bulletin, Media Freedom July – December 2016. *AFTE Egypt.* Retrieved from https://afteegypt.org/media_freedom/2016/02/01/11562-afteegypt.html. Accessed 20 October 2019.

Central Agency for Public Mobilization and Statistics (2017), *Annual Bulletin of Cultural Statistics 2016*, November. Retrieved from www.capmas.gov.eg/Pages/Publications.aspx?page_id=5104&Year=23213. Accessed 5 October 2019.

Dubai Press Club (2012), *Arab Media Outlook 2011–2015*. Retrieved from www.dpc.org.ae/Portal/en/amo/editions/request.aspx?v=5. Accessed 9 November 2019.

Dubai Press Club (2015), *Arab Media Outlook 2016–2018*. Retrieved from www.dpc.org.ae/Portal/en/amo/editions/request.aspx?v=5. Accessed 9 November 2019.

Egyptian Observatory for Journalism and Media (2019), *Annual Report 2018, Violations of Press and Media Freedoms in Egypt*, 26 January. Retrieved from https://tinyurl.com/ugz9dam. Accessed 6 November 2019.

El Issawi, F., and Cammaerts, B. (2016), Shifting Journalistic Roles in Democratic Transitions: Lessons from Egypt. *Journalism*, 17(5), pp. 549–566.

Fadel, A. (2016), Regional Press in Egypt: Reality and Future. *Journal of Media Research*, 43(43), pp. 9–26.

Freedom House (2011a), *Egypt, Freedom of the Press 2011*. Retrieved from https://freedomhouse.org/report/freedom-press/2011/egypt. Accessed 8 October 2019.

Freedom House (2011b), *Egypt, Freedom on the Net 2011*. Retrieved from https://freedomhouse.org/report/freedom-net/2011/egypt. Accessed 8 October 2019.

Freedom House (2012a), *Egypt, Freedom of the Press 2012*.Retrieved from https://freedomhouse.org/report/freedom-press/2012/egypt. Accessed 8 October 2019.

Freedom House (2012b), *Egypt, Freedom on the Net 2012*. Retrieved from https://freedomhouse.org/report/freedom-net/2012/egypt. Accessed 8 October 2019.

Freedom House (2013a), *Egypt, Freedom of the Press 2013*. Retrieved from https://freedomhouse.org/print/43758. Accessed 8 October 2019.

Freedom House (2013b), *Egypt, Freedom on the Net 2013*. Retrieved from https://freedomhouse.org/report/freedom-net/2013/egypt. Accessed 10 October 2019.

Freedom House (2019), *Freedom and the Media: A Downward Spiral*. Retrieved from https://freedomhouse.org/report/freedom-media/freedom-media-2019. Accessed 22 October 2019.

Ghali, M. H. (2008), *The World's Press Industry, the Challenges of the Current Situation and Future Scenarios*. Cairo: Egyptian Lebanese House.

Goldschmidt, A., and Johnson, A. J. (2012), *Re-Envisioning Egypt 1919–1952*. Cairo: University Press Scholarship Online. Retrieved from https://tinyurl.com/rakhzga. Accessed 5 August 2019.

Harb, Z. (2019), Challenges Facing Arab Journalism, Freedom, Safety and Economic Security. *Journalism*, 20(1), pp. 110–113.

Khalil, N. H. (1995), *Egyptian Society before the Revolution, in the Egyptian Press 1945–1952*. Cairo: General Egyptian Book Organization (in Arabic).

Meghawer, Mohamed (2018), Raising the Price of Newspapers (in Arabic). *Arabi21*, 9 August. Retrieved from https://bit.ly/2rKfxvG

Orabi, A. R. (2015), *Press Freedom between Legalization and Criminalization in Constitution, Law and Judiciary*. Cairo: Egyptian National Library and Archives.

Reuters (2012), Morsi Takes on his Way Home an Egyptian Journalist Detained in Sudan. *ara.reuters,* 16 July. Retrieved from https://ara.reuters.com/article/newsOne/idARACAE86F0BC20120716. Accessed 16 November 2019.

Rizk, N. (2016), Media Ownership and Concentration in Egypt. In M. N. Eli (ed.), *Who Owns the World's Media? Media Concentration and Ownership around the World*. Oxford: Oxford University Press.

Shaqir, S. (n.d.), Committee on Party Affairs and Freedom to Form Political Organizations. *aljazeera. net*. Retrieved from www.aljazeera.net/specialfiles/pages/87cb801a-530f-4ebd-83ad-caea5722dd00. Accessed 14 October 2019.

Shawqi, M. (2017), A Prejudiced Feeling of Defeat – Elections for Journalists: A Different Vision. *AFTE Egypt,* 15 May. Retrieved from https://afteegypt.org/media_freedom/2017/05/15/13011-afteegypt. html. Accessed 9 September 2019.

Sternfeld, R. A. (2014), *Political Coalitions and Media Policy: A Study of Egyptian Newspapers*. Unpublished PhD thesis. University of Texas, Austin.

Zaki, K. (2015), *al-Sahafa wal Tamheed lil-thawarat* (*Press and the Prelude for Revolutions*). Cairo: Alarabi for Publishing and Distribution.

5

THE EGYPTIAN BROADCASTING SECTOR BETWEEN 1920 AND 2020

Joel W. Abdelmoez

Introduction

This chapter covers the history and development of broadcasting technologies in Egypt and the regulations imposed by the Egyptian state, as well as the political and social functions of these technologies. The chapter aims to demonstrate those functions in the cultural, political, and social spheres in Egypt. To illustrate the diversity of this sector in Egypt, this chapter will provide examples of various genres such as educational and entertainment programs, popular music, and streaming services. This is because the broadcasting sector includes terrestrial, cable, and satellite channels as well as digital streaming of radio and TV services. I begin with a short overview of the history of radio and television before moving on to discussing the broadcasting sector post-2011.

History of Egyptian radio

Egyptian radio broadcasting dates back to the 1920s when the first local radio services began transmitting, mainly in Cairo, Alexandria, and Port Said. These were small private radio stations, run by amateurs who received radio licenses from the Ministry of Transportation. The first such licenses were issued in 1926, after a royal decree on 10 May, which allowed for the establishment of local radio stations. There were over 100 licenses issued to these amateur stations and, although it began haphazardly, permission to operate such stations was controlled by the colonial authorities and the government (Ayish, 2011a). The first national service, Egyptian Radio – also referred to as Radio Cairo and well-known for its jingle "this is Cairo" ("*huna al-Qahira*") – began broadcasting on 31 May 1934 (Frishkopf, 2010). This radio service is sometimes called *el-bernameg el-'am*, or the General Program. It was initially run by the British Marconi Company and later came under the full control of the Egyptian government. A large portion, or 40% of its revenues from collected fees, went to the government, while 60% went to Marconi (Tayie, 1989). In 1943, the contract to run the station was renewed, but it was later canceled on 4 March 1947, when the government became its sole operator, placing it under the Ministry of Social Affairs and later the Ministry of Internal Affairs. In 1952, the Egyptian government established the first Ministry of Information, following the Free Officers' ascension to power, and all radio services were placed under the army's auspices (Tayie, 1989).

During the early 1930s, there was limited news radio service, and it was not until the British Broadcasting Corporation (BBC) began its Arabic service in 1938 that news became a large part of radio broadcasts in Egypt (Armbrust, 2012). Generally, radio programming had a cultural and educational focus, which included Qur'an recitations and music programs. This was because the contract with the Marconi Company stipulated that the radio service was limited to entertainment and education. According to that contract, the government retained the right to broadcast news bulletins and public directives, as well as other announcements, deemed to be of public interest. The station was not allowed to broadcast commercial advertising until that restriction was removed by a presidential decree that came in effect in 1959 (Abdel Rahman, 2010; Tayie, 1989). Post-1952 radio services continued to mix entertainment and education (or edutainment) and political talk shows disseminating anti-colonialist messages, such as the speeches by Muhammad Naguib, Gamal Abdel Nasser, and other leaders of the 1952 revolution (Ayish, 2011a).

One of the most well-known radio stations in Egypt, Voice of the Arabs (*sawt al-Arab*), was launched on 4 July 1953, as the first regional radio service. It started as a half-hour daily service, but it quickly grew and became the most popular service across the Arab world, drawing much of its popularity from its broadcast of Arab nationalist songs, combined with popular music from Egyptian singers like Umm Kulthum (James, 2006; Boyd, 1975). In addition to Voice of the Arabs, which was the first pan-Arab radio service, targeting audiences across the Arab region, Radio Cairo also aimed at audiences outside Egypt. This was perhaps why European powers at the time, mainly France and Britain, saw Egyptian radio services as a serious threat to its hegemony (Boyd, 1975). However, when French and British airstrikes halted Egyptian radio broadcasts during the Suez Crisis in November 1956, Radio Damascus showed its solidarity by opening its programs with this jingle, "From Damascus, this is Cairo" (Ahram Weekly, April 19, 2018).

Voice of the Arabs demonstrated President Nasser's pan-Arab ambitions, which became the defining feature of his rule. It is not clear who was behind the decision to launch this service, but Boyd (1975) argues that it was Mohammed Abdel-Kader Hatem, who later became the minister of information. Radio broadcasting has been highly centralized and controlled since 1934, but its scope and ambitions were significantly expanded under Nasser's rule, reflecting the government's desire to use radio for political and ideological gains. One oft-cited reason for this is that radio played a pivotal role and had a broad impact on the illiterate population compared to the print media, which usually targeted educated elites. While the print press was not nationalized until 1960, the radio service had been under the government's control since 1952 (Boyd, 1975; Armbrust, 2012; Ayish, 2011a). Radio services increased their broadcasting hours, and Egyptian popular music and culture were shared across the region, which contributed to consolidating a shared media experience and effectively uniting Arab listeners outside Egypt (Frishkopf, 2010).

The 1960s saw a rapid expansion of radio services. Following the invention and affordability of transistor radios, Egyptian audiences gained access to international broadcasts from Europe and America, in addition to their local services. For one, the BBC Arabic Service was launched on 3 January 1938, in response to the anti-British broadcasts from the Italian Radio Bari in 1934 from its headquarters in Bari in Southern Italy. During World War II, the Germans also began broadcasting in Arabic, from their radio facilities in Zeesen (Ayish, 1991; Seul and Ribeiro, 2015). Several international radio stations followed suit, and the most popular of them was Voice of America Arabic service, and Radio Monte Carlo (RMC) in Arabic. With the national radio sector under the Egyptian government's control, audiences tuned in to the international radio stations to access a more varied information diet. International broadcasting services were particularly important as the main sources of accurate information about the Six-Day War in 1967 when Voice of the Arabs resorted to reporting false information about an alleged Egyptian victory against Israel (James, 2006; Lahlali, 2011). Nevertheless, Egyptian radio services continued to grow during the Cold War era, both in terms of airtime and number of stations, with the main aim of promoting a sense of cultural and political unity that transcends national borders. Indeed, one can refer to the Arab world as "a self-conscious community, sometimes interpretable as a nation" (Frishkopf, 2010: 23), or as it is known in the Ba'athist slogan: "*Umma Arabiyya Wahida Dhat Risala Khalida*," or "the one Arab nation with an immortal mission" (Ajami, 1978: 355).

During the 1970s and 1980s, radio services still relied on terrestrial broadcasting, but the new satellite and digital broadcasting technologies provided new ways of transmission (Ayish, 2011a). Consequently, new stations were launched during the 1990s when the government loosened its monopoly on national radio broadcasting (Frishkopf, 2010).

The most popular private radio station in Egypt now is Nogoum FM, which was established in 2003 and is based in the Media Production City. According to its website (www.nogoumfm.net), the station has 30 million listeners tuning into the variety of content ranging from music to political shows. The station launched Nogoum FM TV channel in 2015, live streaming to reach as many audiences as possible and providing interactive service via social media platforms.

History of Egyptian television

The first Egyptian TV network was launched on 21 July 1960, with three channels. The third channel, however, was terminated in 1967 in the wake of the Six-Day War, and some of its programs were moved to the other two channels. The first channel aired Egyptian productions, while the second channel aired foreign shows in English (Tayie, 1989). Egyptian television also aired live and pre-recorded concerts, and during its first year, 1960, the first television orchestra was launched, under the leadership of conductor Rif'at Garana (Nassar, 2010). During the 1960s, pan-Arab nationalistic songs such as *el-watan el-akbar* (The Great Homeland) were broadcast repeatedly and sung by an ensemble of famous Egyptian and other Arab singers. The state television in Egypt broadcast entertainment and family content to promote pan-Arabism while dedicating limited airtime for news. This shows the significant power of popular music during the post-independence era (Abdelmoez, 2016; Frishkopf, 2010).

Private broadcasting was not allowed in Egypt during Nasser's era, and the government maintained its grip over the media industries. However, due to scarce public resources, the actual operation of television broadcasting was delegated to the Radio Corporation of America, which was a point of contention throughout the 1960s and 1970s. The financial problems were compounded by limited advertising, which made the television channels almost entirely dependent on public funding. During the early years of Egyptian television, radio was still more popular, and it dominated the media landscape (Ayish, 2011b). As such, the television industry was initially slow to grow, and it was not until 6 October 1985 that the government managed to relaunch the third television channel, broadcasting for the region of Greater Cairo (Tayie, 1989).

In addition to its long history of cinema production, Egypt also became the regional center for television drama, which was widely viewed alongside American and European productions across the region (Ayish, 2011b). By 1989, five of the 12 national television studios in Egypt were dedicated to drama productions, while only one studio was used for news production (Tayie, 1989). That does not mean that television drama was apolitical or unaffected by the state's political agenda. On the contrary, television drama was highly political, "disseminating moral messages inflected by local political ideologies" (Abu-Lughod, 2008: 113).

In October 1990, the first Egyptian cable channel, Cable News Egypt (CNE), was launched. This was an agreement with CNN, with the main purpose of retransmitting CNN content to an Egyptian audience. However, the chairman of the Egyptian Radio and Television Union (ERTU) was also the chairman of CNE (Amin, 2009), which reflected the government's unwillingness to loosen its grip over the broadcasting sector. As such, CNE was not run as a private television channel but was an early example of the government's new policy, which allowed private media outlets as long as the latter was placed under the state's regulation and oversight.

On 12 December 1990, the Egyptian Space Channel (also called the Egyptian Satellite Channel, or ESC) was founded, partly motivated by the Iraqi invasion of Kuwait. As Egypt sent troops to support Kuwait, the ESC aimed to boost the morale of the Egyptian troops and counter the media propaganda broadcasted by Iraq (Brynen et al., 2012). The ESC was the result of broadcasting cooperation among the Arab states initiated during the 1960s and the launch of the Arab Satellite Communications Organization (Arabsat), in April 1976, and the subsequent launching of the other Arab satellites: Arabsat 1-A and 1-B in 1985 (Kraidy, 2002). Another Egyptian satellite channel, Nilesat 101, was launched on 28 April 1998 and aired content aimed at the entire Arab world. Sana Mansour, the former head of the ESC, argued that terrestrial channels could attend to local issues, while satellite channels, such as ESC1, ESC2, and NileTV, needed to function as ambassadors for Egypt. The ESC was later renamed *Al Masriya* and is still operated by the Egyptian government (Sakr, 2001; Allam, 2018).

With the proliferation of satellite channels, Egyptian audiences have had access to a plethora of outlets beaming from outside Egypt, provided by the major satellite operators, Nilesat and Arabsat. It is argued that the most viewed satellite in Egypt is the Nilesat with more than 40 million viewers, and the large market share is due to the broad range of services and content available via Nilesat (OECD, 2013: 85). Nilesat is owned by the ERTU (40%), state enterprises (40%), and private owners (20%), and its board of directors have representatives from the ERTU (ibid.).

The satellite channels offered slightly different content than did the terrestrial ones. For example, in political talk shows, the state-terrestrial channels would often invite a guest to answer questions by the show's host, whereas the satellite channels adopted an open forum-approach with live audience involved in debating various social and political issues (Lahlali, 2011). The introduction of satellite television also meant to liberalize the media landscape, and the Egyptian government issued a decree in 2001 allowing private ownership of television channels, with the condition that such new outlets would be based in the Media Production City in the outskirts of Cairo, that the private outlets would be partially owned by the ERTU, and that they would not be allowed to produce news. Thus, the government retained its control of television broadcasting, whether state or privately owned. The first private stations in Egypt were Dream TV and El Mehwar, and both outlets attempted to circumvent the journalism ban by providing political talk shows for analysis and commentary, without any "news-gathering" activities (Sakr, 2013; Allam, 2018).

As the number of satellite channels increased, many print journalists moved to work in those channels, hosting entertainment shows without prior experience in the field (Nassar, 2010). Former president Hosni Mubarak, like Nasser, acknowledged the power of music and entertainment, and he had commissioned jingoistic musical performances to be aired on state television, such as the song *ikhtarnah* (or "we chose him") in 1999, which was meant to proclaim and garner support for Mubarak. Such songs were referred to as *obrette*, or operettas – probably because of their use of grandiose style (Abdelmoez, 2016). After the 2011 uprisings, Egyptian artists produced songs and music videos showing their support or conversely opposition to either Mubarak or the military. Examples abound, but they include the superstar Tamer Hosny's song in support of the military promoting the term *"id wahda,"* or "one hand" referring to the

2011 slogan "the army and the people are but one hand" (Abdelmoez, 2016). Indeed, as Gilman (2014) argues, there is an interconnectedness of the popular music industry and the television sector in Egypt, especially with the dependency of the music industry on the state, which makes many musicians wary of any regime change that may threaten their economic livelihood.

The increasing popularity of satellite television channels prompted producers to launch new daring shows questioning state policies that antagonized the Egyptian government. In 2008, Arab governments joined forces to adopt a common charter for satellite television, in an attempt to bring these channels in closer alignment with those states' politics. Specifically, the charter aimed to curb content that promoted sexual activity and consumption of alcohol, but it mainly targeted programs deemed offensive to religious or political leaders or subversive to traditional values and culture, the interpretation of which was too broad and was left to each state to determine. The charter deliberately used ambiguous language in banning content that could "damage social harmony, national unity, public order, or traditional values,"[1] to justify governments' interference in the televised content (Kraidy, 2008; Ayish, 2011b).

Post-2011, it was argued that the Egyptian uprising in 2011 was driven by the proliferation of social media; while it is true that social media provided a new tool for mass mobilization, it is important to remember that Internet penetration was still low in Egypt in 2011, with only 26.7 Internet users per 100 inhabitants (Brynen et al., 2012), and in 2013, the number of Internet users reached up to 37 per 100 (Abdelmoez, 2017). As such, most Egyptians relied on traditional media, particularly television, for news and updates about the country's political situation during the uprising. Alterman (2011) argues that television was more important than social media, with its live broadcasting of images of the large masses of demonstrators and thus attracting more people to join the protests. Increasingly, however, Egyptian newsrooms intensified their use of social media content and reporters cited "citizen journalists," which further blurred the line between journalism and activism (Sakr, 2013).

While the 2008 charter had laid the grounds for the government's interference in private channels' content, the Egyptian government also resorted to imposing additional legal measures to control the broadcasting sector (Brynen et al., 2012). This was illustrated in the 2011 protests, when the majority of journalists injured while reporting were affiliated with private outlets, while journalists affiliated with state outlets were mostly unharmed (Sakr, 2013). After the 2013 coup, media suppression intensified, as demonstrated in the termination of the successful Bassem Youssef show *el-Bernameg* (The Programme), which began on YouTube in March 2011 and was quickly picked up by ONTV channel and later MBC Egypt, owned by a Saudi businessman. President Morsi, a recurring target of the show, had Youssef arrested and interrogated, but Youssef continued with his show until Morsi was ousted by the army and was later replaced by the interim President Adly Mansour. Youssef then began targeting the military in his satirical program, which led to the termination of his show by ONTV in October 2013. In February 2014, the show was broadcast on MBC Egypt, but shortly after al-Sisi had officially begun his first term as president the program was canceled altogether, and Youssef moved abroad, citing harassment and security concerns as the main reasons motivating his move (Kraidy, 2016). Post-2013, there were also reports of imprisonment and intimidation of journalists and private television outlets being shut down, which prompted many media producers and journalists to resort to self-censorship (Abdulla, 2016: 4223).

Ownership in the broadcasting sector

The major owner of the broadcasting sector was the Egyptian Radio and Television Union headquartered at the famous Maspero building in central Cairo, and it received its mandate by Law No. 13 of 1979, or what is coined "ERTU Law."[2] A decade later, the government amended that law to grant RTU monopoly over TV and radio stations in Egypt (OECD, 2013: 83); the law stipulated that ERTU would be in charge of all audiovisual media and broadcasting services in Egypt, and it granted ERTU the power to lay out policies for the planning, delivery, and execution of television content (Rozgonyi, 2014).

In February 2000, the Egyptian government issued a decree to create a media free zone (Article 29 of the Investment Law 84), and private broadcasting outlets began operations shortly after that. By 2001, several Egyptian businessmen, known for their close ties to Mubarak's regime, established their private media ventures. Radio was open to private operators in 2003, with Nile Radio Productions (NRP) becoming the first private radio company in Egypt, running two stations: one in English (Nile FM) and one in Arabic (Nogoum FM). They later began distributing via the Internet and, therefore, could reach a larger audience base. The two outlets only air entertainment content, as they were barred by the government from broadcasting news. In 2010, the NRP had only 10.4% of the market share of audiences, compared to ERTU's share of 85.4%. Nevertheless, ERTU considered NRP a serious threat and therefore set up a media agency, Voice of Cairo (*sawt al-qahira*), in 2009 to transform its services and produce commercially attractive content (Rizk, 2016). It is worth mentioning that Voice of Cairo, also known as SonoCairo, had existed before that point, as a record company, producing cassettes and CDs of Egyptian music (Al Wassimi, 2010).

After the 2011 uprising, the minister of information in Mubarak's government, Anas el-Fiqqi, was forced to resign and was placed under house arrest, while the head of ERTU, Osama el-Sheikh, was also arrested on 24 February. The military then took control of ERTU and appointed General Tarik el-Mahdi as its transitional head before the position was given to Samy el-Sharif, who at the time was a professor at the Faculty of Mass Communication at Cairo University. Together with the new prime minister, Essam Sharaf, the two men restructured the union and appointed new heads of its various divisions. The changes triggered the protests by approximately 43,000 employees of ERTU, who went on strikes in 2011 demanding an end to nepotism and corruption in ERTU (Guaaybess, 2013).

In 2014, the National Media Authority (NMA) was created to replace ERTU, although it was not until 2018 that NMA received its new mandate, by the enactment of Law No. 178 of 2018. In 2016, the government decreed the establishment of three media regulators, namely the Supreme Council for Media Regulation (SCMR), the National Press Authority (NPA), and NMA. The SCMR is responsible for regulating private media and is subject to Law 180/2018. Thus, the SCMR can censor media content and has the power to grant licenses to individuals or entities for setting up websites. Moreover, both the NPA and NMA are answerable to the SCMR.

The series of laws introduced by the government in 2018 has been heavily criticized by NGOs such as Article 19 (2019) because such laws were feared to provide sweeping powers for the SCMR, NMA, and NPA to block journalists' work and hinder the freedom of expression in Egypt. For instance, The SCMR has the power to block websites and social media accounts but does not make public a list of blocking orders issued. This lack of transparency, warns Article 19 (2019), makes it difficult for individuals and media outlets to challenge the SCMR's decisions. Moreover, the NMA is tasked with appointing the heads of public media outlets, overseeing the quality of content provided by state media, taking decisions concerning new investments such as purchasing companies, or entering joint ventures in accordance with the objectives and strategy of the NMA.

As per Law 180/2018, referred to as the SCMR law, the SCMR is granted massive powers to prevent media outlets or websites from publishing content deemed to violate public morals or incite violence and hatred. The decree covers publications distributed from abroad if their content is deemed to threaten the country's national security or spread false news, in addition to content issued by individuals online which is a threat to individuals' freedom of expression (TIMEP, 2019).

In terms of ownership, NMA has the largest share of power among other stakeholders in the broadcasting sector, although Saudi owners control the largest shares of the sector in Egypt. Saudi outlets include the Middle East Broadcasting Center (MBC), and Rotana Group, which own and run several channels, aired via satellite and broadcasting entertainment content aiming at Egyptian audiences inside and outside Egypt; their portfolio in Egypt includes MBC Masr and Rotana Masriya. Another important stakeholder in the Egyptian media is Naguib Sawiris, a billionaire and businessman who is a majority shareholder of the Melody Entertainment Holding and the chairman of Orascom Investment Holding, which until 2018 was known as Orascom Telecom Media & Technology (Rizk, 2016; Guaybess, 2015). In 2007, Sawiris launched OTV channel, and in 2009, he launched ONTV, which would later host Bassem Youssef's successful satirical show post-2011. By the end of 2012, Sawiris sold ONTV to the Tunisian Tarek Ben Ammar, in an attempt to move his assets abroad, and selling off other companies of the Orascom group (Sakr, 2015).

Beyond the channels and networks that are directly owned by the state, there are also those under the control of the General Intelligence Service, a branch of the secret service, disguised as part of the Egyptian Media Group (EMG). Since its foundation in 2016, EMG has successfully acquired several TV channels such as Al Hayah, ON E (previously ONTV), and Extra News.[3]

Other media businessmen in Egypt include Ahmed Bahgat, who founded the private satellite television channel Dream TV, and Mohamed Gohar who together with Hassan Rateb founded El Mehwar. Gohar had also been part of several other media ventures, such as Al Jazeera Egypt and Orbit TV, and after leaving El Mehwar, he went on to launch a new channel in 2011, called 25TV. The latter was affiliated with the Muslim Brotherhood and claimed to be rooted in the mission of the 2011 uprising calling for social justice, but it was shut down in 2012 by the Supreme Council of Armed Forces (SCAF) after the channel's license was revoked (Ibrahim, 2017; Guaybess, 2015).

During Mubarak's rule, the media liberalization discourse was limited in scope favoring mainly a few businessmen close to Mubarak and his family and with the Ministry of Information and ERTU as the main power holders in the sector. However, in pursuit of their business interests, several Egyptian businessmen shifted their allegiance from Mubarak to Morsi and later to al-Sisi. One example is Mohamed Aboul Enein – he is a famous investor, is owner of Cleopatra Group, whose portfolio includes several companies in the ceramics, tourism, and aviation sectors, and served as MP for 15 years (1995–2011). Post-2011, Abul Enein attempted to curry favor with the Muslim Brotherhood by, for example, publishing advertisements in several newspapers congratulating president Morsi for winning the presidential elections in June 2012 and ordering his media outlets (*Sada al-Balad* television network and website) not to criticize the MB (El Tarouty, 2015: 79). When Aboul Enein realized that the MB government would not accept his investment proposals, he used his media outlets to wage criticism against the MB and supported the 2013 coup to topple Morsi. In 2014, Aboul Enein funded an outdoor advertising campaign supporting al-Sisi, and he later announced his investment in new industrial schools to support al-Sisi's aim of educating a new cadre of professionals to aid the Egyptian manufacturing sector (El Tarouty, 2015: 80). Another businessman is Ahmed Bahgat, owner of Dream TV; he set up his channel mainly to advertise his products and to save himself the 40 million EGP that he used to spend annually on marketing his products. The channel got involved in several controversies such as broadcasting a lecture by the Egyptian veteran Mohamed Hassanien Heikal (d. 2016) in 2002 criticizing Mubarak's succession plan and airing a show by the famous journalist Ibrahim Eissa, who criticized the performance of the government and was eventually dismissed from Dream TV (El Tarouty, 2015: 88). Following the overthrow of Mubarak, Bahgat faced severe financial difficulties with the banks confiscating his assets to pay for his debts, worth more than 3 billion EGP; this shows that Bahgat's debts were used as a card in the hands of Mubarak's regime to threaten Bahgat and ensure his support (El Tarouty, 2015: 89). These examples show that private ownership worked in tandem with the successive regimes rather than challenging them.

As mentioned, the 2014 constitution (Articles 212, 211, and 210) approved the abolition of the Ministry of Information, the Supreme Press Council, and the Radio and Television Union, replacing them with the SCMR, NPA, and NMA. However, in April 2020, a new ministerial reshuffle included the (re)creation of a Ministry of Information to be headed by former Minister of Information Osama Heikal, head of Parliament's Culture, Information, and Archaeology Committee. The decision was attributed to the inability of the SCMR to regulate the Egyptian media (Shawky, 2020).

Finally, a notable recent development in the television sector is the proliferation of streaming services, such as Netflix and HBO Go. While these services are mainly American, streaming foreign content to Egyptian subscribers (although Netflix's Arab catalog grows larger every day), Netflix announced on 23 May 2019 that they would be producing their first-ever Egyptian drama. This is a TV series called *The Paranormal* (or *Ma Waraa Al Tabiaa*), based on the 81-volume series of horror-thriller novels written by the late Egyptian novelist Ahmed Khaled Tawfiq. While Netflix has previously acquired streaming rights to many Arab and Egyptian productions, this was the first time they produced their own Egyptian TV drama, which was seen as a sign of the revival of Egyptian drama production (Fouad, 2019; Egyptian Streets, 2019). There is now also a streaming app called WatchIt, owned by the Omani UMS Group, and it competes with Netflix for a share of the Egyptian market.

Conclusion

The broadcasting sector has played a pivotal role in promoting the ideologies and policies of Egypt's successive regimes, beginning with Nasser (1954–1970) through al-Sisi's government. It was no coincidence that one of the primary sites of protest in 2011 was the Maspero building, which is the headquarters of Egypt's state television and the epicenter of Egyptian state propaganda. Even under Mubarak's liberalization policies, which was limited in scope, state television still enjoyed a unique position as a link between the regime and the general public. This does not mean that state television served the public (Abdulla, 2016), but that state broadcasting media controlled the dissemination of public information and news. When private licenses were granted, the new private stations were barred from engaging in newsgathering, and those who overstepped this line quickly lost their licenses. The hope for political changes after the overthrow of Mubarak has largely dissipated, as media censorship has continued under the Supreme Council of the Armed Forces and the Brotherhood's Mohamed Morsi, and it has intensified under al-Sisi's presidency. Egypt is second only to China in the percentage of state ownership of media (Rizk, 2016).

In December 2018, the Committee to Protect Journalists reported the increasing number of Egyptian journalists arrested and subjected to mass trials (Beiser, 2018). Moreover, Reporters Without Borders coins Egypt as "one of the world's biggest prisons for journalists."[4] Kraidy (2016) argues that Egypt under al-Sisi closed down television channels and withdrew broadcasting licenses, thus limiting the diversity of media outlets in the country while consolidating the government's control of the media sector.

In terms of technological development, Egypt is following the global trend of audiovisual media going from satellite, cable, and terrestrial transmission to digital transmission and reception (Kelly, 2017). While YouTube podcasts now rival traditional broadcasts, television content is becoming more and more associated with streaming services rather than with mainstream channels, and this content can be viewed on demand, which makes it accessible anytime to audiences inside and outside Egypt. While it is part of the mission of ERTU and its successor NMA to keep up with broadcasting technologies and modernize state media institutions, it is still to be seen whether the Egyptian government will attempt to jump on the bandwagon of live TV streaming services.

Notes

1 See Reporters Without Borders. Retrieved from https://rsf.org/en/egypt (last accessed November 19, 2019).
2 See BBC News report on the charter. Retrieved from http://news.bbc.co.uk/2/hi/middle_east/7241723.stm (last accessed November 30, 2019).
3 The full text of the law can be read in English here: www.law-democracy.org/wp-content/uploads/2010/07/Law.ERTU_.No-13-of-1979.pdf (last accessed November 30, 2019).
4 See the Media Ownership Monitor, Egypt, from Reporters Without Borders. Retrieved from https://egypt.mom-rsf.org/en/owners/ (last accessed December 1, 2019).

References

Abdel Rahman, Haidi M. K. (2010), *Women, Regional Radio and Development: The Role of North Upper Egypt Radio in the Struggle of Females Towards Development in North Upper Egypt*. Unpublished M.A. thesis, American University in Cairo, Egypt.

Abdelmoez, Joel W. (2016), *"Bless These Hands" – Egyptian Military, Masculinities, and Music*. Unpublished working paper, Nordic Africa Institute, Uppsala, Sweden.

Abdelmoez, Joel W. (2017), Is it a Revolution or a Coup? Scandinavian Media Representations of the Ousting of Egyptian President Mohamed Morsy. *Journal of Applied Journalism and Media Studies*, 6(2), pp. 109–131.

Abdulla, Rasha (2016), Navigating the Boundaries Between State Television and Public Broadcasting in Pre- and Post-Revolution Egypt. *International Journal of Communication*, 10, pp. 4219–4238.

Abu-Lughod, Lila (2008), *Dramas of Nationhood: The Politics of Television in Egypt*. Chicago: University of Chicago Press.

Ahram Weekly (2018), Arab Citizens More Confused than their Governments over Syria. *Ahram Online*, 19 April. Retrieved from http://english.ahram.org.eg/News/297999.aspx. Accessed 29 November 2019.

Ajami, Fouad (1978), The End of Pan-Arabism. *Foreign Affairs*, 57(2), pp. 355–373.

Al Wassimi, Mounir (2010), Arab Music and Changes in the Arab Media. In Michael Frishkopf (ed.), *Music and Media in the Arab World*. Cairo: The American University in Cairo Press.

Allam, Rasha (2018), Egypt – Media Landscape. *European Journalism Centre*.

Alterman, Jon B. (2011), The Revolution Will Not Be Tweeted. *The Washington Quarterly*, 34(4), pp. 103–116.

Amin, Hussein (2009), *Report on the State of the Media in Egypt*. Cairo: The Arab Center for the Development of the Rule of Law and Integrity. Retrieved from https://www.arabruleoflaw.org/Files/PDF/Media/English/P2/Egypt_MediaReportP2_En.pdf. Accessed 30 November 2019.

Armbrust, Walter (2012), History in Arab Media Studies: A Speculative Cultural History. In Tarik Saby (ed.), *Arab Cultural Studies: Mapping the Field*. London: I.B. Tauris.

Article 19 (2019), *Egypt: 2018 Law on the Organisation of Press, Media, and the Supreme Council of Media*. London: Article 19.

Ayish, Muhammad (1991), Foreign Voices as People's Choices: BBC Popularity in the Arab World. *Middle Eastern Studies*, 27(3), pp. 374–388.

Ayish, Muhammad (2011a), Radio Broadcasting in the Arab World. In Noha Mellor, Muhammad Ayish, Nabil Dajani, and Khalil Rinnawi (eds.), *Arab Media: Globalization and Emerging Media Industries*. Cambridge: Polity.

Ayish, Muhammad (2011b), Television Broadcasting in the Arab World. In Noha Mellor, Muhammad Ayish, Nabil Dajani, and Khalil Rinnawi (eds.), *Arab Media: Globalization and Emerging Media Industries*. Cambridge: Polity.

Beiser, Elana (2018), Hundreds of Journalists Jailed Globally Becomes the New Normal. *Committee to Protect Journalists*, 13 December. Retrieved from https://cpj.org/x/7504. Accessed 29 November 2019.

Boyd, Douglas A. (1975), Development of Egypt's Radio: 'Voice of the Arabs' under Nasser. *Journalism Quarterly*, 52(4), pp. 645–653.

Brynen, Rex, Moore, Pete W., Salloukh, Bassel F., and Zahar, Marie-Joëlle (2012), *Beyond the Arab Spring: Authoritarianism & Democratization in the Arab World*. Boulder, CO: Lynne Rienner Publishers.

Egyptian Streets (2019), *Netflix Announces Production of First Egyptian Drama 'Paranormal'*. Retrieved from https://egyptianstreets.com/2019/05/28/netflix-announces-production-of-first-egyptian-tv-drama-paranormal/. Accessed 3 November 2019.

El Tarouty, Safinaz (2015), *Businessmen, Clientelism, and Authoritarianism in Egypt*. New York: Palgrave Macmillan.

Fouad, Ahmed (2019), Will NETFLIX Boost Stagnant Local TV Industry? *New African*, 597, pp. 58–59.

Frishkopf, Michael (2010), Introduction. In Michael Frishkopf (ed.), *Music and Media in the Arab World*. Cairo: The American University in Cairo Press.

Gilman, Daniel J. (2014), *Cairo Pop: Youth Music in Contemporary Egypt*. Minneapolis: University of Minnesota Press.

Guaaybess, Tourya (2013), Reforming Egypt's Broadcasting in the Post-25 January Era: The Challenges of Path Dependence. In Tourya Guaaybess (ed.), *National Broadcasting and State Policy in Arab Countries*. London: Palgrave Macmillan.

Guaaybess, Tourya (2015), Broadcasting and Businessmen in Egypt: Revolution is Business. In Donatella Della Ratta, Naomi Sakr, and Jakob Skovgaard-Petersen (eds.), *Arab Media Moguls*. London: I.B. Tauris.

Ibrahim, Dina (2017), The Birth and Death of 25TV: Innovation in Post-Revolution Egyptian TV News Formats. *Arab Media & Society*. Retrieved from https://www.arabmediasociety.com/wp-content/uploads/2017/12/20170130123517_25TV.pdf. Accessed 30 November 2019.

James, Laura (2006), Whose Voice? Nasser, the Arabs and 'Sawt Al-Arab' Radio. *Arab Media & Society*. Retrieved from www.arabmediasociety.com/whose-voice-nasser-the-arabs-and-sawt-al-arab-radio/. Accessed 30 November 2019.

Kelly, J. P. (2017), The Temporal Regimes of TVIII: From Broadcasting to Streaming. In *Time, Technology and Narrative Form in Contemporary US Television Drama*. London: Palgrave Macmillan.

Kraidy, Marwan M. (2002), Arab Satellite Television Between Regionalization and Globalization. *Global Media Journal*, 1(1).

Kraidy, Marwan M. (2008), Emerging Consensus to Muzzle Arab Media. In *Carnegie Middle East Center*. Retrieved from https://carnegie-mec.org/sada/20619. Accessed 29 November 2019.

Kraidy, Marwan M. (2016), *The Naked Blogger of Cairo*. Cambridge, MA: Harvard University Press.

Lahlali, El Mustapha (2011), *Contemporary Arab Broadcast Media*. Edinburgh: Edinburgh University Press.

Nassar, Zein (2010), A History of Music and Singing on Egyptian Radio and Television. In Michael Frishkopf (ed.), *Music and Media in the Arab World*. Cairo: The American University in Cairo Press.

OECD (2013), Competition Issues in Television and Broadcasting, 28 Oct 2013.

Rizk, Nagla (2016), Media Ownership and Concentration in Egypt. In Eli M. Noam and The International Media Concentration Collaboration (eds.), *Who Owns the World's Media? Media Concentration and Ownership around the World*. Oxford: Oxford University Press.

Rozgonyi, Krisztina (2014), *Assessment of Media Legislation in Egypt*. MedMedia Report. Retrieved from https://www.menamedialaw.org/sites/default/files/library/material/medmedia_egypt.pdf. Accessed 30 November 2019.

Sakr, Naomi (2001), *Satellite Realms: Transnational Television, Globalization, and the Middle East*. London: I.B. Tauris.

Sakr, Naomi (2013), *Transformations in Egyptian Journalism*. London: I.B. Tauris.

Sakr, Naomi (2015), Naguib Sawiris: Global Capitalist, Egyptian Media Investor. In Donatella Della Ratta, Naomi Sakr, and Jakob Skovgaard-Petersen (eds.), *Arab Media Moguls*. London: I.B. Tauris.

Seul, Stephanie and Nelson Ribeiro (2015), Revisiting Transnational Broadcasting. *Media History*, 21(4), pp. 365–377.

Shawky, Mostafa (2020), *Position Paper: On the Creation of the State Ministry of Information, Association of Freedom of Thought and Expression (AFTE), Egypt*, 21 April. Retrieved from https://afteegypt.org/en/media_freedom-2/2020/04/21/18632-afteegypt.html#

Tayie, Samy Abdel Raouf Mohamed (1989), *The Role of Egyptian Mass Media in the Formation of Young Egyptians' Images of Foreign People and Foreign Countries: A Content Analysis and Audience Studies.* Unpublished PhD thesis, University of Leicester, UK.

TIMEP/Tahrir Institute for Middle East Policy (2019), *TIMEP Brief: The Law Regulating the Press, Media, and the Supreme Council for Media Regulation*, 15 May. Retrieved from https://timep.org/reports-briefings/timep-brief-the-law-regulating-the-press-media-and-the-supreme-council-for-media-regulation/

6

SOCIAL MEDIA IN EGYPT

The debate continues

Nermeen Kassem

Introduction

For the past few years leading to the revolt in Egypt in 2011 and shortly afterwards, social media has become a powerful tool used by citizens to unveil corruption, mobilize for protests, and act as a real watchdog over the mainstream media and the government. Egypt's netizens arguably succeeded in mobilizing for the 25 January uprising using social media. The revolution, which started as an event on the social networking site Facebook, took the world by storm when Egyptians succeeded in overthrowing former President Mubarak, who ruled the country for almost three decades. Yet, although social media have mostly been used by citizens as a platform for public opinion expression and mobilization, they have also become important propaganda tools used by governments. In the case of Egypt, the successive post-revolt governing entities starting by the Supreme Council of the Armed Forces (SCAF), which ruled Egypt for a transitional period of 16 months, then former presidents Adly Mansour and Mohamed Morsy, up to current President al-Sisi, realized the need to speak the same language of the Egyptian youth, to communicate with them electronically, as well as to issue counter-revolutionary discourse. This has resulted in significant investments in the telecom market, leading Egypt to acquire a unique position as one of the largest telecom markets in Africa and the Arab world. Nonetheless, the same political and social potential of social media has led to (de)veloping a set of laws and regulations that mainly aim at not only regulating social media platforms, but also halting future endeavors of dissent.

This chapter provides an overview of social media since they have appeared in Egypt at the beginning of the century. It also focuses on different regulatory bodies and policies and how they might relate to and influence the functionality of social media within the Egyptian context at the socio-political level prior to and after the Arab Spring revolts. It provides an overview of social media in Egypt with a special focus on recent development in infrastructure, legislation, and social and political aspects of the environment within which these media are expected to operate. The chapter argues that while the current government tries to catch the train of technological innovation by investing in the Internet and social media infrastructure, this investment is being undermined by the many laws. It seems that what is being given by one hand is taken, or at least undermined, by the other. Several laws have been recently imposed with the intention of suffocating and monitoring cyberspace and crippling netizens. Several consequences and technology-enabled circumvention precautions taken by civil society are also discussed.

Historical background

The Internet service appeared in Egypt in 1993 with a cable connection to France of a 9.6 kilobits per second (kbps) bandwidth to the Egyptian Universities Network (EUN) and the Cabinet Information & Decision Support Center (IDSC) with the National telephone organization (predecessor of Telecom Egypt) providing the infrastructure. The number of users at that time was estimated to be between 2,000 and 3,000 (Freedom on the Net, 2011).

In 1994 the Egyptian domain (.eg) was divided into three subdomains, (.eun.eg) for the Egyptian Universities Network, (.sci.eg) serving the scientific research institutes, and (.gov. eg) for governmental bodies. The IDSC acted as Internet service provider. Digital data access was provided to the end user using digital multiplexors. Interconnectivity has been drastically improved by the setup of a number of digital multiplexors as the first digital backbone for data communication in the country. Fiber international connectivity was made available on SE-ME-WE-2 or satellite via Intelsat (Kamel, 1997).

In 1996, the gateway speeds have been increased by nearly 20 times. The user numbers have increased to 20,000 users. IDSC/RITSEC (Regional Information Technology and Software Center) started to provide connectivity to private service providers under the (.com.eg) domain, while some providers had their own international gateways. Internet service providers (ISPs) had reached 40 by the end of 1996 providing Internet services to end users in Cairo, Alexandria, Sinai, and the Red Sea area.

In 2000 the integrated services digital network (ISDN) service was introduced in Egypt. ISDN is an added feature to the existing normal telephone line. It converts the normal, analog, and slow telephone line to digital, fast, and reliable telephone line. Available speeds were 64 kbps and 128 kbps (Reda, 2018a).

With the implementation of the digital subscriber line (DSL) technology in Egypt, many businesses and end users changed their subscriptions to utilize the high speed and affordable new service. Today, speeds of up to 24 megabits per second are available to customers in their homes by many ISPs. The largest of these ISPs are TEdata and LinkdotNet, which are two shareholdings, companies providing Internet services to subscribers in all regions in Egypt (Rashad, n.d.). Over the next three years, copper cables will be replaced with fiber optic cables, which can transfer digital data at a rate of 100–200 Mbps (Reda, 2018a).

It is worth noting that Egypt was the first country to request the registration of domain names in the Arabic language (International TLD [International Top Level Domain] ".Masr") immediately after the Internet Corporation for Assigned Names and Numbers (ICANN) had approved a new multilingual address system (and the registration of domain names and websites in several languages other than the English language. It is expected that this great property will enhance the usage of Arabic websites and open up new areas of investment in this concern (NTRA, 2010).

Main providers

Egypt is one of the largest telecom markets in Africa and the Arab world. The national telecom market is highly dynamic and is characterized by a sustainable and steady growth in the demand for various telecom services in general and broadband services specifically (MCIT, 2019a).

Broadband Internet access was introduced commercially to Egypt in 2000 as ADSL. The service was offered in select central offices in big cities such as Cairo and Alexandria and gradually spread to cover more governorates of Egypt. There are numerous (220 according to regulatory authority numbers) Internet service providers in Egypt offering an ADSL service. Seven companies used to own the infrastructure and are called Class A ISPs: Egynet, LINKdotNET, TE Data, NOL, Vodafone data, Noor communication, and Yalla. Etisalat Egypt has bought both NileOnline and Egynet to expand their Internet presence. They sell to Class B ISPs which, in turn, sell to the rest of the 208 ISPs (NTRA, 2016).

The Ministry of Communications and Information Technology (MCIT), through its regulatory arm, the National Telecommunication Regulatory Authority (NTRA), launched the "eMisr National Broadband Plan" in 2011. The eMisr National Broadband Plan is committed to increasing broadband Internet penetration in Egypt and endorsing the development of a digital society. It proposes different strategic directives to meet Egypt's broadband service needs. NTRA announced a tender for the Broadband pilot project in 2014 (MCIT, 2019b). The project aims to provide high speed broadband service for around 1,600 institutions affiliated to eight ministries and government bodies in addition to the Public Prosecution, the central administration for the Central Agency for Public Mobilization and Statistics and the Information Technology Institute (ITI) (MCIT, 2019b). eMisr is the second initiative after the government's broadband initiative in 2004, through which the number of broadband connections increased tenfold within four years and brought 24 Mbps ADSL2+ access to residential households (MCIT, 2019b).

In 2014, GPX Global Systems Inc., a provider of state-of-the-art, neutral Internet eXchange (IX) facilities in emerging Internet markets, partnered with Egyptian Class A ISPs which joined the GPX Middle East Internet Exchange (MEIX). By joining the GPX MEIX, these ISPs have access to a broad range of customers wishing to expand their marketplace – content providers, DNS service providers, online brokerage companies, and others (GPX Global Systems Inc. 2014).

On May 10, 2018, Telecom Egypt announced that its board of directors approved the acquisition of MENA Cable that is licensed in Egypt and Italy to operate a submarine telecommunications system connecting Europe to the Middle East and Southeast Asia (Telecom Review, 2018).

Audience share in a competitive market

Except for Nigeria, Egypt's Internet penetration is higher than that of the rest of Africa (Internet Live Stats, 2016). In December 2017, Egypt's Internet penetration reached 49.5% according to Internet World Stats, compared to an overall penetration rate of 35.2% in the continent (Reda, 2018a).

According to *ICT Indicators in Brief* by MCIT (March 2019), the number of mobile subscriptions slipped from 100.24 million subscriptions during February 2018 to 93.13 million subscriptions with a penetration rate of 100.62% to the total population during February 2019. In contrast, the number of mobile Internet users increased from 5.43 million subscriptions in 2018 to 6.74 million subscriptions in 2019, with 1.88% monthly growth rate and 24.20% annual growth rate (MCIT, 2019a). These results reflect a significant development in the Egyptian ICT market when compared to results from 2011. For example, during October 2011, the number of mobile subscriptions in Egypt was 80.98 million subscriptions with a penetration rate of 100.06% to the total population, while mobile Internet users recorded 35.06 million, with 2.01% monthly growth rate and 6.93% annual growth rate. The number of Internet users totaled 27.75 million, with 34.29% penetration rate (MCIT, 2011).

According to the latest Similar Web ranking of top websites accessed by Egyptians, the first 10 websites suggest, when aggregated, that the Internet is mostly used for searching information, followed by social media usage, checking news and media, and online shopping (Similar Web, 2019). Digital in 2018 puts active social media users at 39 million distributed between 37% female and 63% male users. Facebook is by far the preferred platform among Egyptian users (81.25%), followed by YouTube (13.11%), Twitter (3.4%), Pinterest (1.71%), Google+ (0.2%), and Instagram (0.16%) (Stat Counter, 2019). It is also worth noting that the total number of Egyptian users that publish content on Facebook in Arabic is 34 million, while only nine million are publishing their content in English (Digital Marketing Community, 2018).

Based on research done by consultancy and analysis platform Global Web Index, the digital landscape in Egypt is characterized by key indicators that marketers need to know (Buckle, 2017):

1   The smartphone is the most important device: 86% of Egypt's Internet population own a mobile phone.
2   Social media is dominating the online space: across the 40 tracked markets, Egyptian Internet users are devoting more time to social networking than many of the studied world's digital consumers.
3   Local is key for online TV entertainment: linear TV is still king in Egypt, but this market is among the top five for online TV consumption. Sound Cloud is also becoming more popular in Egypt with a preference for local content.
4   Offline transactions are driving online commerce: Egyptian Internet users are less likely than the global average to engage with all the commerce activities listed in the study. Context is key here: Egypt is a primarily cash-driven economy with a relatively undeveloped financial infrastructure, something which has dramatic implications on how people are able to purchase online. For example, Egyptian consumers may under-index significantly for visiting Amazon each month, but they are over three and a half times as likely to be visiting OLX monthly (requires offline transactions for its listed items).
5   Egyptian consumers are open to online ads: Internet users display a remarkably – if somewhat rare – susceptibility to online ads despite the proliferation of ad-blocking software. Looking at how Egyptian consumers typically discover new brands or products, their highest over-indexes are for personalized purchase recommendations on a website or for ads seen online.

It is worth noting, however, that the significant Internet growth in numbers and underlying infrastructure that Egypt has witnessed between 2011 and 2019 does not seem to reflect an opportunity for a better Internet and social media experience for Egyptian users due to recent, escalating legal procedures and regulations that render users prey to serious consequences if they breach the *red lines*. This also influences the degree to which users trust the Internet and social media as a source of information, especially about the government. For example, while 26.77% use the Internet to communicate with others via social networks, only 6.57% of Egyptian Internet users use the Internet to obtain government-related information.

Regulatory environment after 25 January uprising

The aforementioned numbers show that the Egyptian government has successfully sought to expand access to the Internet as an apparatus of economic growth. However, Egypt's security forces have increasingly attempted to restrain the use of new technologies for sharing sensitive political information. The video-sharing site YouTube, social networking sites such as Facebook and Twitter, and numerous international blog-hosting services are freely available. No laws specifically granted the government the power to censor the Internet, and Egypt's constitution and the 2003 Law on Telecommunications uphold freedom of speech and citizens' right to privacy and require a judicial warrant for surveillance. Articles of the penal code and the Emergency Law – which has been in effect without interruption since 1981 and was extended for another two years in 2010 – give security agencies broad authority to monitor and censor all communications, and to arrest and detain individuals indefinitely without charge. Since 2010, however, the central goal for Egyptian Internet activists and bloggers has been political change. Concurrently, rather than tightening laws or relying on technical content filtering or monitoring, Egyptian government typically employed "low-tech" methods such as intimidation, legal harassment, detentions, and real-world surveillance of online dissidents (Freedom on the Net, 2011).

This tendency has extended to the period following the January 2011 uprising, during which the regime of ousted president Hosni Mubarak blocked access to a number of websites before it shut down the Internet on 27 January 2011 (Internet Monitor, 2017). However, authorities who feel threatened by domestic reform efforts or criticism after the overthrow of authoritarian regimes in Tunisia, Egypt, Libya, and Yemen in 2011 have fiercely cracked down on online journalism and freedom of expression more broadly. As the euphoria of the Arab Spring has given way to the sobering challenge of creating rights-respecting democracies, the willingness of new governments to respect rights are key indicators to whether those uprisings would give birth to genuine democracy or simply spawn authoritarianism in new forms (Human Rights Watch, 2013).

The last several decades have seen increasing skepticism toward the state, ultimately leading to the uprising and very polarized and unstable debates and policies in the post-Mubarak phase until the presidency of al-Sisi (Transformation Index BTI, 2018). The Internet is no longer as welcoming to independent journalism as non-democratic governments erase the legal distinctions between speech online and off. The digital space for independent journalism and free speech is likely to be constricted further by the impact of restrictive laws, surveillance, and ensuing self-censorship. In this environment, laws against disrupting public order and spreading false news have been passed or updated to apply to online expression – all in the name of preserving stability, preventing terrorism, and avoiding anarchy. Journalists who violate these regulations face criminal penalties, sometimes including lengthy prison sentences and fines (Radsch, 2015).

Since President Abdel Fattah al-Sisi secured a second term in the presidential election in March 2018, the government continued to silence critics through arrests and prosecutions of journalists and bloggers, and the parliament issued severely restrictive laws that further curtail freedom of speech and access to information (Human Rights Watch, 2019).

The Egyptian constitution guarantees freedom of thought, opinion, and expression (Art. 65), prohibits concretely any kind of censorship, suspension, or closure of media (Art. 71), and is expressly committed to international human rights agreements ratified by Egypt (Art. 93). De facto civil rights have been under severe pressure since the beginning of the transition process until the present and severely deteriorated since the crackdown of the Muslim Brotherhood and its affiliates in 2013. The social climate has been increasingly shaped by a general security threat, identifying any critic and any opposition as an enemy of the state or harming state security (Transformation Index BTI, 2018). According to Freedom on the Net Report (2018), Egypt's score of Internet freedom has fallen from "partially free" in 2014 to "not free" in 2015. Internet freedom further declined in 2018 as online censorship increased dramatically, with little to no transparency. Numerous individuals were arrested or imprisoned for critical online posts and commentary. For example, the disappearance of former Member of Parliament and journalist Mostafa al-Naggar highlighted the dangers faced by individuals who speak out against the regime. Naggar had been sentenced to three years in prison for "insulting the judiciary" before his disappearance in September (Freedom House Report, 2019).

A recently approved set of laws (Anti-Cyber and Information Technology Crimes Law and Media Regulation Law) grant the government broader powers to restrict freedom of expression, violate citizens' privacy, jail online activists for peaceful speech, allow censorship without judicial orders, and levy severe monetary fines for violating the law's articles, in addition to prison sentences for cases related to "inciting violence" (Human Rights Watch, 2019).

Regulatory bodies

Mobile service providers and ISPs are regulated by the National Telecom Regulatory Authority and governed by the 2003 Telecommunication Regulation Law (Law 10/2003). The law also regulates the licensing procedures, permits for importation, and manufacture or assembly of telecommunications equipment, as well as the frequency spectrum management sector. The law also describes cooperation between NTRA and other authorities for national security purposes (MCIT, 2018).

The NTRA's board is chaired by the ICT minister and includes representatives from the defense, finance, and interior ministries; the state security council; the presidency; workers' unions; and public figures, experts, and military representatives (NTRA, 2017a). Officially, the NTRA is responsible for regulating the telecommunications industry, ensuring a competitive environment in the market, and managing the frequency spectrum, standardization, and interconnection agreements (NTRA, 2017b). In addition, it aims to enhance and integrate advanced telecommunications and broadband technologies (Bannerman, 2017). The NTRA has led reforms to upgrade the telecommunications infrastructure by installing fiber optic cables to increase Internet speeds and, in October 2016, auctioned 4G frequencies to all mobile providers (Noureldin, 2016).

NTRA also has the power to monitor the performance of operators and penalize deviations from licenses, as well as to manage frequency utilization for commercial and governmental use (MCIT, 2018).

In June 2018, Egypt's parliament approved three draft laws regulating the media, including social media. The laws regulate the three government bodies – the Higher Council for Media Regulation (HCMR), the National Press Authority (NPA), and the National Media Authority (NMA) – tasked with regulating the media (Essam El-Din, 2018). The laws contain a number of new restrictions on online media. For example, stipulating that no websites may be set up or managed in Egypt without a license from the HCMR. Moreover, the law considers blogs and personal social media accounts to be websites, which would be subject to account removal, fines, and imprisonment if found to be spreading false news. The country has already blocked hundreds of websites, including local media like the independent Mada Masr and rights groups like Human Rights Watch (The Telegraph, 2018).

According to Reporters Without Borders (RSF), the new "cybercrime law" legalizes and reinforces the existing censorship and blocking of websites and criminalizes both those who operate sites and those who use them (IFEX, 2019). Ranked 161st out of 180 countries in RSF's 2018 World Press Freedom Index, this law presents Egypt as one of the world's biggest jailers of journalists, with at least 36 professional and non-professional journalists detained in connection with the provision of news and information (RSF, 2018).

The new "cybercrime law" – passed to "protect citizens and safeguard their freedom," according to head of Parliament's Communications and Information Technology Committee Nidal al-Saeed – defines a broad scope of penalties that apply to a wide range of persons or an everyday act like publishing a photo of a celebrity or public figure in a public place (Mada Masr, 2018). For example, posting without consent original content – videos, photos, or texts – on websites or social media platforms, that violates the privacy of others would result in no less than a six-month prison term and/or a LE 50,000 to LE 100,000 fine.

Additionally, the cybercrime law renders service providers legally liable to no less than a year in prison and/or a fine of up to LE20 million for overlooking censorship orders, storing and sharing client data, sharing users' data, and failing to report crimes against companies that use their services. The law also stipulates a number of additional punishable acts for a subset of service providers that includes security service providers and hackers. For instance, a cybersecurity infrastructure specialist who discovers security vulnerability in the civil registration database is an offender in the eyes of the law. Lighter penalties are provided for hacking into personal accounts and emails, but the motive is also disregarded. The law holds liable web, account, email, or information system administrators for a special set of offenses, i.e., if the space s/he administers publishes content that is prohibited by the law and/or if it is used to commit any crime that is punishable by the cybercrime law. The law also regulates conciliation for a select set of punishable offenses.

The regulations aiming at combating the Internet and social media were incited by the role those platforms played in steering the events leading up to, during, and after the Egyptian and other Arab Spring uprisings. Epithets such as "Facebook revolutions" (Talbot, 2011) and "Twitter revolutions" (Brunner, 2014) refer to the central role that social media seemed to have played in bringing them about. The argument was twofold. On one hand, researchers chimed in, arguing that social media platforms had transformed the dynamics of movements organizing in the Arab world, making these "revolutions" possible (Howard and Hussain, 2013). Others were more skeptical. They pointed out that revolutions had been organized many times in the past without the help of these digital tools, and that though social media was clearly used during the Arab Spring, it was hard to show that it had any real effects (Lynch, 2011).

Social and political functions of social media

At times during 2011, the term Arab Spring became interchangeable with "Twitter uprising" or "Facebook revolution," as global media tried to make sense of what was going on (Shearlaw, 2016). Nearly a decade later, researchers revisit the question: did Facebook and Twitter play any meaningful role in bringing down the Mubarak regime? In a recent study, Clarke and Kocak (2018) found that social media importance was more limited than some of the breathless early coverage suggested. Looking specifically at how social media was used to organize the key event of 25 January 2011, "Police Day" protests in Egypt, Clarke and Kocak argue that Facebook and Twitter helped bring about three aspects of this protest's success: its considerable turnout, its national scope, and its grassroots appeal. These two platforms contributed to what has been termed "first-mover mobilization" through three mechanisms: (1) protester recruitment, (2) protest planning and coordination, and (3) live updating about protest logistics. Given the specification of the cultural milieu and political context in Egypt, it has been argued that "social media have [enabled] the young activists to urge citizens to take their first steps on the participatory ladder" (Sayed Kassem, 2013: 229).

Although the role of the Internet and social media in steering the events towards Tahrir Square could not go unnoticed, "it is an oversimplification to frame the Egyptian uprising exclusively as either a 'Facebook revolution' or a 'people's revolution'" (Lim, 2012: 232). In fact, it has been argued that social media played a fairly unimportant role in comparison to other factors, such as the Muslim Brotherhood's participation, the enthusiasm generated by the preceding revolution in Tunisia, the military's disillusionment with Mubarak, and the impact of other mobilization tools such as SMS and satellite media (Rugh, 2004, in, Tkacheva, 2013).

Mediated mobilization and participatory journalism during the uprising

The entrance of social media on the scene from 2007 onwards has brought to the fore a new generation of Internet activists. These activists were less interested in the long treatises on political developments that the blogger community had tirelessly created and were instead quick to act, exploiting the capability of social media for mediated mobilization (Eaton, 2013: 7). The new forms of media have generated what Henry Jenkins (2006) referred to as a "participatory culture" that fundamentally "contrasts with older notions of passive media spectatorship" (p. 3). The participatory culture is an outcome of the advancement of technology that has produced an inevitable convergence in the media (Hamdy and Gameel, 2018). Through social media, citizen journalists are telling their own stories and utilizing the networked design of social media as tools for threatening authoritarian regimes (Howard, 2011: 182).

Leading up to and during the 18-day uprising, the Internet and social media have constituted a repertoire of mobilization that afforded opposition online presence and dissemination of information about events to their online circles, shared awareness and counterculture, an opportunity to cultivate movement entrepreneurs and build leaders' reputation in the virtual world, and equally important, create publicity and news coverage and alternate the state-controlled media's point of view (Tkacheva, 2013). Upon the eruption of the 2011 protests and during the events in Tahrir Square, the volume of information in circulation was unprecedented. The ability to bridge the gap between new media and traditional media was crucial. As concluded by Sayed Kassem (2013: 295), "social media are apparatuses for mobilization that are instrumentally used with respect to given factors (or opportunities) at each stage of the life span of the youth social movement and the context within which it emerged." For example, activists relied on social media as a medium of visibility; for those who were not active in the political sphere, social media have been instrumental in educating them about the political process (Sharbatly, 2014).

However, it is worth noting that different types of social media contributed to different types of mobilization. Twitter (#jan25) and the Facebook page We Are All Khalid Said (WAAKS) variously mediated mobilizations and provided for participatory journalism. First, Facebook had a mass impact compared to Twitter, given the significant difference of the numbers of users for each platform. Second, Twitter facilitated perpetual connectivity while Facebook was able to effect mass mobilization on its own. Third, Facebook is more suited for advocacy of a cause and was most important in the build-up to the protests, while Twitter was a far more effective tool for activists once on the ground, as they were often able to use the Twitter interface through their mobile phones. Fourth, in terms of providing activists with information in almost real time, Twitter is more efficient with its 140-character limit micro-blogs compared to WAAKS's Facebook interface, which required administrator approval of postings. Furthermore, on Twitter, contact with the entire community is nearly instantaneous while delays could occur when sending SMS messages of similar length, as the time that it takes the phone to send will increase as the number of recipients multiplies (Eaton, 2013). This explains why the Egyptian uprising was declared the Twitter "news moment" of the year (Friedman, 2011). In the words of one protester, Fawaz Rashed, "We use Facebook to schedule the protests, Twitter to coordinate, and YouTube to tell the world" (Shearlaw, 2016).

During the transition period in Egypt (February 2011–June 2012), different social media networks have been used differently by adherents of different political orientations. They partially reinforced organized structures of mobilization (El Gendi, n.d.). Indeed, in the months following Mubarak's resignation in 2011, there were hopeful signs that Egypt might achieve enduring reform. The Supreme Council of the Armed Forces, which assumed control of the government until elections could be held, presided over an Egypt in which civil society was at its zenith and the independent media were rapidly expanding. Dozens of news outlets and hundreds of nongovernmental organizations (NGOs), trade unions, political parties, and coalition groups were established. Revolutionary activists, NGO leaders, and artists were dominating the public sphere (Mansour, n.d.).

Civil society and social media after Tahrir

Following a brief opening after the 2011 uprising, media independence and freedom of speech show the discrepancy between the promise of the 2011 revolt and the reality of repression. More clearly, repression against journalists and autonomous outlets helped return Egypt to a system of authoritarian stagnation. Human rights groups and activists were represented in the government media as "foreign agents" working to incite chaos in Egypt. Conspiracy theories about activists having military training, ties to the US Central Intelligence Agency, and weapons in their offices were repeated constantly on state television and on privately owned channels known to be close to the military regime. In late December, security forces raided the offices of 17 Egyptian and international NGOs whose work included advocacy on media and freedom of expression issues (Mansour, n.d.).

In 2014, the Egyptian Ministry of Interior announced a tender offer for equipment and technology capable of conducting surveillance on various social media and networks. These networks included specific smartphone applications such as Viber and WhatsApp, as well as content analysis tools that can identify political opinions on social media websites (Al-Gallad, 2014).

The offer would also set up social media accounts for the Ministry of Interior that would provide a platform for it to contradict opinions it sees as dangerous. The announcement of such an offer roused criticism from not only human rights activists in Egypt, but also from some pro-government media outlets, which viewed the announcement as a confirmation of the security apparatus's desire to control the digital space. Despite this criticism, the fate of the project remains unknown (Ezzat, 2014). However, the recent ratification of the Anti-Cyber and Information Technology Crimes Law seems to pave the path for such surveillance to be "legally" practiced in the name of national security as it ultimately boosts the government's ability to conduct surveillance on its citizens and facilitates the banning of websites (Miller, 2018).

Starting in May 2017, the censors have begun to block websites of regional human rights groups such as the Cairo-based Arabic Network for Human Rights Information (ANHRI) and the international advocacy organization Reporters Without Borders (Internet Monitor, 2017).

The Egyptian government blocked access to the website of Human Rights Watch (HRW) on 7 September 2017 one day after the organization released a report critical of Egypt's policing practices, torture by security forces, and forced disappearance (Human Rights Watch, 2017a, 2017b). Filtering of such prominent international human rights and advocacy websites is rare, even in some countries known for pervasive filtering of political content; only China and Iran are known to have blocked both RSF and HRW (Tilton et al., 2017).

In the course of the filtering campaign, the censors also blocked access to the entire publishing platform Medium.com, which has been used by authors to bypass Internet blocking of smaller independent websites (Tilton et al., 2017). As filtering of political content continues to expand, the censors have also blocked websites of hundreds of circumvention tools, which netizens can use to bypass the filtering regime and to surf the Internet anonymously (AFTE, 2018). By September 2017, the number of websites known to be blocked reached 432 (AFTE, 2018).

Moreover, the Egyptian government has also been scrutinizing social media firms such as Facebook and Twitter, which resulted in the removal of multiple accounts involved in what Facebook terms "coordinated inauthentic behaviour." Facebook defined this behavior as "when groups of pages or people work together to mislead others about who they are or what they are doing" (Huang, 2019).

In response to this dramatic increase of Internet filtering in Egypt, Internet users have taken to social media and Google Drive to "protest filtering." Their efforts center on disseminating banned content through platforms protected by encrypted HTTPS connections such as Facebook and Google Drive, which makes individual objectionable URLs challenging for the censors to block.

Internet Monitor (2017) examined how users react to Internet filtering and their attempts to bypass the technical filtering regime. Specifically, they examined the conversation about the blocking of websites in Egypt on Twitter, identified spikes in conversation volumes, and examined if users resorted to alternative means to disseminate banned content between May 2008 and September 2017. For example, users tweeted excessively at times of blocking a number of websites before shutting down the Internet during the January 25 revolt, after the Court ordered a 30-day ban of YouTube in February 2013 and in May 2017 in the shadow of blocking a large number of local and regional sites including Al Jazeera and Mada Masr. The conversation also reveals interesting observations about URLs shared by users between April and September 2017. For example, the most frequently shared URL is a website that reposted the HRW report as an alternative to the blocked website (Human Rights Watch, 2017a). This website has been accessible since it was first widely advertised on Twitter.

Using Google Trends, Internet Monitor (2017) also examined if there has been any notable increase in searching for Internet circumvention tools in Egypt since the recent filtering wave began. It was found that since the start of the selective political blocking in late 2015, there has been an increase in search queries for circumvention tools such as Psiphon and VPN services. The study infers from the Google Trends data that there has been an aggregate increase in demand for circumvention and privacy tools to bypass the technical filtering regime and to surf the Internet anonymously. The proportion of this demand that is due to the blocking of websites in Egypt was not determined, but the correlation is noteworthy.

It might be true that much of Egypt's most independent news coverage and analysis is found on the Internet given the difficult operating environment for traditional media. However, online activity brings both positive and negative attention. It is possible to build an audience online, but doing so risks attracting the unwanted gaze of the security services (Freedom on the Net, 2014). As Egyptian public opinion has become polarized between pro- and anti-government voices, political discourse online has also become highly contentious. Verbal harassment is common, and many activists have been chased offline by aggressive pro-government social-media campaigns (Mansour, n.d.).

However, social media seem to still have the power to mobilize people behind political causes, even if in smaller numbers. Recently, (September 2019) Egypt has seen some of its first political demonstrations in years after political videos shared by a businessman and actor Mohamed Ali alleging state corruption went viral on social media (NetBlocks, 2019). Facebook

Messenger, Facebook image CDN servers, as well as BBC News and other news sites in Egypt accordingly became unavailable on two leading providers (Telecom Egypt and Raya) amid the heightened political tensions that followed the publication of the videos.

Social media have also opened more doors for influencer marketing (IM) to become the most effective form of advertising given the constant release of new features on its platforms, additional to the rise of ad blockers, decline in radio and TV viewership, and significant increase in billboard prices. Facebook and Instagram are the two big players in the field, but it all depends on the content, audience type, the content's lifespan, and the experience intended (Reda, 2018b). However, the bigger Instagram and other social platforms became, the more features they added for users to manage accounts, the more users crave the popularity and money that come from having a huge following. As a result, fake followers accounts are being created and sold to celebrities and politicians, as well as average "want-to-be" influencers, which in turn mars the online reputation for the social media influencer (Hausman, 2019).

Conclusion

The latest Anti-Cyber and Information Technology Crimes Law demonstrates the Egyptian government's effort to institutionalize online repression and restrict Internet freedoms through legislation that infringes on citizens' rights in the name of national security. The broad definition of national security is in keeping with other measures put in place in recent years, including a draconian NGO Law (Aboulenein, 2017), and anti-terror provision (Carnegie Endowment for International Peace, 2017) that contribute to the weakening of freedom of expression and civil society, the facilitation of human rights abuses, and increasing immunity for state authorities stifling dissent (Miller, 2018).

Civil society actors come together in these social networks from across several divides and special and temporal divisions in the spirit of Habermas's positive and vibrant public sphere where none who are able and wish to join are excluded (Habermas, 1989: 27). This helps social media serve as public place (Juris, 2012) while also making social media a place in and of itself (Narayan, 2013). The use of such media in political deliberations, however, associates with a number of problems. One such problem is the lack of sustainability in online campaigns, which should ideally convert into offline collective action. This is essential for a sustainable civil society and a truly diverse public sphere, which can indeed bring about significant changes in the Egyptian political sphere (Sharbatly, 2014).

There are five critical challenges facing today's social media (Ghonim, 2015) and impeding their contribution to creating an enabling environment for constructive dialogues that contribute to democratic transformation. First, social media is a fertile environment for spreading rumors and fake news that confirm people's biases, yet we don't know how to deal with rumors. Second, via social media, people create their own *echo chambers*. They tend to only communicate with people that they agree with, and mute, unfollow, and block everybody else. Third, online discussions quickly descend into angry mobs causing polarization and shaky networks. Fourth, social media is an environment where opinions are formed hastily, and it becomes really hard to change our opinions. Because of the speed and brevity of social media, users are forced to jump to conclusions and write sharp opinions in 140 characters about complex world affairs. And once they do that, it lives forever on the Internet, and we are less motivated to change these views, even when new evidence arises. Fifth, and most critically, today, social media experiences are designed in a way that favors broadcasting over engagement, posts over discussions, shallow comments over deep conversations. It is a space where people tend to talk at each other instead of talking with each other.

References

Aboulenein, A. (2017), *Egypt Issues NGO Law, Cracking Down on Dissent*. Retrieved from www.reuters.com/article/us-egypt-rights/egypt-issues-ngo-law-cracking-down-on-dissent-idUSKBN18P1OL. Accessed March 2019.

AFTE (2018), Decision from Unknown Body: On Blocking Websites in Egypt. *afte Egypt*. Retrieved from https://afteegypt.org/en/right_to_know-2/publicationsright_to_know-right_to_know-2/2017/06/04/13069-afteegypt.html. Accessed February 2019.

Al-Gallad, M. (2014), The Ministry of the Interior Imposes 'an Electronic Fist' on Social Networking Crimes (in Arabic). *El-Watan News*. Retrieved from www.elwatannews.com/news/details/495659. Accessed March 2019.

Bannerman, N. (2017), 4G Frequencies Given to Egypt's Telcos. *Capacity Media*. Retrieved from www.capacitymedia.com/articles/3727608/4G-frequencies-given-to-Egypts-telcos. Accessed February 2019.

Brunner, E. (2014), Asking (new) Media Questions: Thinking beyond the Twitter Revolution. *Explorations in Media Ecology*, 13(3–4), pp. 269–283.

Buckle, C. (2017), 5 Things Every Marketer Should Know About Online Consumers in Egypt. *Global Web Index*. Retrieved from https://blog.globalwebindex.com/trends/5-things-every-marketer-should-know-about-online-consumers-in-egypt/. Accessed March 2019.

Carnegie Endowment for International Peace (2017), *Institutionalized Repression in Egypt*. Retrieved from https://carnegieendowment.org/2017/05/18/institutionalized-repression-in-egypt-pub-69959. Accessed March 2019.

Clarke, K., and Kocak, K. (2018), Launching Revolution: Social Media and the Egyptian Uprising's First Movers. *British Journal of Political Science*, 1–21.

Digital Marketing Community (2018), *Social Media Users in Egypt: Facebook Insights and Usage in Egypt, 2018*. Retrieved from www.digitalmarketingcommunity.com/indicators/facebook-insights-usage-in-egypt-2018/. Accessed March 2019.

Eaton, T. (2013), Internet Activism and the Egyptian Uprisings: Transforming Online Dissent into the Offline World. *Westminster Papers in Communication and Culture*, 9(2).

El Gendi (n.d.), Social Media in Egypt's Transition Period. *Y.A.S.* Retrieved from http://schools.aucegypt.edu/huss/pols/Khamasin/Documents/Social%20Media%20in%20Egypt%27s%20Transition%20Period%20-%20Yosra%20El-Gendi.pdf. Accessed March 2019.

Essam El-Din, G. (2018), Egypt Parliament Approves Three New Draft Laws Regulating Media, Press Authorities. *Ahram Online*. Retrieved from http://english.ahram.org.eg/NewsContent/1/64/302160/Egypt/Politics-/Egypt-parliament-approves-three-new-draft-laws-reg.aspx. Accessed March 2019.

Ezzat, A. (2014), *Social Media and Online Surveillance: Egypt and Abroad*. The Tahrir Institute for Middle East Policy. Retrieved from https://timep.org/commentary/analysis/online-surveillance-egypt-abroad/. Accessed January 2019.

Freedom on the Net (2011), *Egypt*. Freedom House. Retrieved from https://freedomhouse.org/report/freedom-net/2011/egypt. Accessed November 2019.

Freedom on the Net (2018), *Egypt*. Freedom House. Retrieved from https://freedomhouse.org/report/freedom-net/2018/egypt. Accessed January 2019.

Freedom on the Net (2014), *Egypt*. Freedom House. Retrieved from https://freedomhouse.org/sites/default/files/resources/Egypt.pdf. Accessed January 2019.

Freedom on the Net (2019), *Egypt*. Freedom House. Retrieved from https://freedomhouse.org/country/egypt/freedom-net/2019. Accessed April 2019.

Friedman, U. (2011), The Egyptian Revolution Dominated Twitter this Year. *Foreign Policy Magazine*. Retrieved from https://foreignpolicy.com/2011/12/05/the-egyptian-revolution-dominated-twitter-this-year/. Accessed February 2019.

Ghonim, W. (2015), *Let's Design Social Media that Drives Change*. Geneva: TED Global. Retrieved from www.ted.com/talks/wael_ghonim_let_s_design_social_media_that_drives_real_change/transcript?language=en#t-503904. Accessed March 2019.

GPX Global Systems Inc (2014), GPX Global Systems Inc. Partner with Egyptian Class A Internet Service Providers (ISPs) to Expand Marketplace. *GPX Global*. Retrieved from www.gpxglobal.net/gpx-global-systems-inc-partner-with-egyptian-class-a-Internet-service-providers-isps-to-expand-marketplace/. Accessed March 2019.

Habermas, J. (1989), *The Structural Transformation of the Public Sphere: An Inquiry into a Category of Bourgeois Society*. Cambridge, MA: MIT Press.

Hamdy, N., and Gameel, M. (2018), Egyptian Youth: Networked Citizens but Not Fully Engaged Politically. *Arab Media & Society*, (26).

Hausman, A. (2019), *The Rise and Fall of the Social Media Influencer: Hidden Dangers of Influencer Marketing*. Retrieved from https://marketinginsidergroup.com/influencer-marketing/the-rise-and-fall-of-the-social-media-influencer/. Accessed December 2019.

Howard, P. N. (2011), *The Digital Origins of Dictatorship and Democracy: Information Technology and Political Islam*. Oxford: Oxford University Press.

Howard, P. N., & Hussain, M. M. (2013), *Democracy's Fourth Wave?: Digital Media and the Arab Spring*. New York: Oxford University Press.

Huang, Esurance (2019), *Facebook Removes 'Coordinated' Fake Accounts in UAE, Egypt, Nigeria and Indonesia*. Retrieved from www.cnbc.com/2019/10/04/facebook-removes-coordinated-fake-accounts-in-uae-egypt-nigeria-and-indonesia.html. Accessed December 2019.

Human Rights Watch (2013), *World Report 2013*. Retrieved from https://www.hrw.org/world-report/2013. Accessed 9 August 2020.

Human Rights Watch (2017a), *Egypt Blocks Human Rights Watch Website*. Retrieved from www.hrw.org/news/2017/09/07/egypt-blocks-human-rights-watch-website. Accessed January 2019.

Human Rights Watch (2017b), *"Here, We Do Unbelievable Things": Torture and National Security in Egypt under Sisi (in Arabic)*. Retrieved from https://fqadi.files.wordpress.com/2017/09/egypt0917ar_web_1.pdf. Accessed March 2019.

Human Rights Watch (2019), *World Report 2019*. Retrieved from https://www.hrw.org/sites/default/files/world_report_download/hrw_world_report_2019.pdf. Accessed 10 August 2020.

IFEX (2019), *Twitter*. Retrieved from https://twitter.com/ifex/status/1032643831156695042. Accessed January 2019.

Internet Live Stats (2016), *Internet Users by Country 2016*. Retrieved from www.Internetlivestats.com/Internet-users-by-country/. Accessed November 2019.

Internet Monitor (2017), *The Slippery Slope of Internet Censorship in Egypt*. Retrieved from https://thenetmonitor.org/pages/the-slippery-slope-of-Internet-censorship-in-egypt. Accessed January 2019.

Jenkins, H., and American Council of Learned Societies (2006), *Convergence Culture: Where Old and New Media Collide*. New York: New York University Press.

Juris, J. S. (2012), Reflections on #Occupy Everywhere: Social Media, Public Space, and Emerging logics of Aggregation. *American Ethnologist*, 39, pp. 259–279.

Kamel, T. (1997), *Internet Commercialization in Egypt: A Country Model*. Retrieved from https://web.archive.org/web/20160103124917/www.isoc.org/inet97/proceedings/E6/E6_2.HTM. Accessed November 2019.

Lim, M. (2012), Clicks, Cabs, and Coffee Houses: Social Media and Oppositional Movements in Egypt, 2004–2011. *Journal of Communication*, 62(2), pp. 231–248.

Lynch, M. (2011), After Egypt: The Limits and Promises of Online Challenges to the Authoritarian Arab State. *Reflections*, 9(2), pp. 301–310.

Mada Masr (2018), *How You Will Be Affected by the New Cybercrime Law: A Guide*. Retrieved from https://www.madamasr.com/en/2018/08/21/feature/politics/how-you-will-be-affected-by-the-new-cyber-crime-law-a-guide/. Accessed 10 August 2020.

Mansour, S. (n.d.), Stifling the Public Sphere: Media and Civil Society in Egypt. *National Endowment for Democracy*. Retrieved from www.ned.org/wp-content/uploads/2015/10/Stifling-the-Public-Sphere-Media-Civil-Society-Egypt-Forum-NED.pdf. Accessed February 2019.

MCIT (2011), *ICT Indicators in Brief: December 2011 Monthly Issue*. Arab Republic of Egypt Ministry of Communication and Information Technology. Retrieved from www.mcit.gov.eg/Upcont/Documents/Publications_3012012000_Eng%20Flyer-December-3.pdf. Accessed February 2019.

MCIT (2018), *Telecom Act – Law 10/2003*. Arab Republic of Egypt Ministry of Communication and Information Technology. Retrieved from www.mcit.gov.eg/TeleCommunications/Telecom_Act_Law/Telecom_Act. Accessed February 2019.

MCIT (2019a), *ICT Indicators in Brief: March 2019 Monthly Issue*. Arab Republic of Egypt Ministry of Communication and Information Technology. Retrieved from www.mcit.gov.eg/Upcont/Documents/Publications_3042019000_EN-ICT-Indicators-in-Brief-March2019.pdf. Accessed November 2019.

MCIT (2019b), *National Broadband Plan*. Arab Republic of Egypt Ministry of Communication and Information Technology. Retrieved from www.mcit.gov.eg/telecommunications/national_broadband_plan_emisr. Accessed February 2019.

Miller, E. (2018), *Egypt Leads the Pack in Internet Censorship across the Middle East*. Atlantic Council. Retrieved from www.atlanticcouncil.org/blogs/menasource/egypt-leads-the-pack-in-Internet-censorship-across-the-middle-east. Accessed January 2019.

Narayan, B. (2013), Social Media Use and Civil Society: From Everyday Information Behaviours to Clickable Solidarity, *Cosmopolitan Civil Societies: An Interdisciplinary Journal,* 5(3), pp. 32–53.

National Telecom Regulatory Authority (NTRA) (2010), *Egypt is the First Country to Use Arabic Internet Domain Name 'Masr'*. Retrieved from www.tra.gov.eg/en/media-center/news/Pages/Egypt-is-the-First-Country-to-Use-Arabic-Internet-Domain-Name-'-Masr'.aspx. Accessed November 2019.

National Telecom Regulatory Authority (NTRA) (2016), *Licenses Chart*. Retrieved from https://web.archive.org/web/20160307205342/http://tra.gov.eg/presentations/licensedtelecomtree27032014_en.pdf. Accessed January 2019.

National Telecom Regulatory Authority (NTRA) (2017a), *Board Members*. Retrieved from http://bit.ly/2y4tGoh. Accessed January 2019.

National Telecom Regulatory Authority (NTRA) (2017b), *Scope of Work*. Retrieved from http://bit.ly/2yudQEo. Accessed January 2019.

NetBlocks (2019), *Facebook Messenger, Social Media and News Sites Disrupted in Egypt Amid Protests*. NetBlocks: Mapping Net Freedom. Retrieved from https://netblocks.org/reports/facebook-messenger-social-media-and-news-sites-disrupted-in-egypt-amid-protests-eA1Jd7Bp. Accessed October 2019.

Noureldin, O. (2016), Egypt Completes Long-delayed 4G Mobile License Deals. *Reuters*. Retrieved from www.reuters.com/article/us-egypt-etisalat-4g-idUSKBN12G0AB. Accessed February 2019.

Radsch, Courtney (2015), Treating the Internet as the Enemy in the Middle East. *Committee to Protect Journalists (CPJ)*. Retrieved from https://cpj.org/2015/04/attacks-on-the-press-treating-internet-as-enemy-in-middle-east/. Accessed March 2019.

Rashad, M. (n.d.), *History of the Internet in Egypt*. Mohamed Rashad Low Cost Web Design. Retrieved from www.mohamedrashad.com/Internet_history_egypt.html. Accessed January 2019.

Reda, L. (2018a), Fiber Optic Technology to be Introduced in 2,350 Schools. *Egypt Today*. Retrieved from www.egypttoday.com/Article/2/61940/Fiber-optic-technology-to-be-introduced-in-2-530-schools. Accessed January 2019.

Reda, L. (2018b), The Rise of Social Media Influencers: A New Age of Marketing. *Egypt Today*. Retrieved from www.egypttoday.com/Article/3/44582/The-Rise-of-Social-Media-Influencers-A-New-Age-of. Accessed December 2019.

RSF (2018), *One of the World's Biggest Prisons for Journalists. Reporters without Boarders for Freedom of Information*. Retrieved from https://rsf.org/en/egypt. Accessed February 2019.

Sayed Kassem, N. (2013), *Young Egyptian Activists' Perceptions of the Potential of Social Media for Mobilization*. Doctoral dissertation, University of York.

Sharbatly, A. (2014), *Social Media: A New Virtual Civil Society in Egypt?* Doctoral dissertation, University of Bedfordshire.

Shearlaw, M. (2016), Egypt Five Years on: Was it Ever a 'social media revolution'? *The Guardian*. Retrieved from www.theguardian.com/world/2016/jan/25/egypt-5-years-on-was-it-ever-a-social-media-revolution. Accessed March 2019.

Similar Web (2019), *Top Sites Ranking for All Categories in Egypt*. Retrieved from www.similarweb.com/top-websites/egypt. Accessed March 2019.

Talbot, David (2011), Inside Egypt's "Facebook Revolution." *MIT Technology Review*. Retrieved from https://www.technologyreview.com/2011/04/29/194993/inside-egypts-facebook-revolution/. Accessed January 2019.

Telecom Review (2018), *Egyptian Operator Expands its Submarine Cables Network*. Retrieved from www.telecomreview.com/index.php/articles/telecom-operators/2321-egyptian-operator-expands-its-submarine-cables-network. Accessed February 2019.

Tilton, C., Zittrain, J., Clark, J., Faris, R., Morrison-Wesphal, R., and Noman, H. (2017), The Shifting Landscape of Global Internet Censorship. *Harvard Public Law Working Paper*, No. 17–38. Berkman Klein Center Research. Retrieved from https://cyber.harvard.edu/publications/2017/06/GlobalInternetCensorship. Accessed February 2019.

The Telegraph (2018), *Twitter Users in Egypt with More than 5,000 Followers will be Classed as Media Entities Amid Crackdown on Dissent*. Retrieved from www.telegraph.co.uk/news/2018/07/17/twitter-users-egypt-5000-followers-will-classed-media-entities/. Accessed March 2019.

Tkacheva, O. (2013), *Internet Freedom and Political Space*. RAND Corporation. Retrieved from www.rand.org/pubs/research_reports/RR295.html. Accessed February 2019.

Iraq

7

IRAQI PRESS – BETWEEN PROPAGANDA AND SECTARIANISM

Haider al-Safi

Introduction

Much has been written on the formation of Iraq and on the turbulent history and politics of the country, from the 19th-century Ottoman ruling through to the formation of Iraq as a modern state (Tripp, 2002). During the 19th century, specifically in 1869, Iraq saw its first newspaper. The newspaper was entitled *Al Zawra*, which is one of the names for Baghdad. The restrictions imposed on the press were declining at the beginning of the 20th century, as there were many changes in the Ottoman Empire, such as the constitutional revolution in 1908. In a matter of few years, approximately 61 newspapers were launched in Baghdad, Basra, Mosul, Najaf, and 12 other Iraqi cities. These newspapers "were variously published in Arabic, in both Arabic and Turkish, and in both Arabic and French. Among such publications were dozens of dailies, weeklies, and literary magazines, including a satirical newspaper, *Habez Bouz*, that was very popular" (Noor Al Deen, 2005: 3).

After World War I, Iraq fell under British occupation. The occupiers supported the establishment of many daily newspapers in Arabic (Ayalon, 1995). Some newspapers were financed by the mandatory power and voiced a pro-British position, supporting the various versions of treaties proposed by Britain to the antagonistic nationalists (Ayalon, 1995). But the expansion of the press also reflected the growth of nationalism during the 1920s and 1930s;

> The founding of *As-Sahifah* (The Journal) by Husayn Rahhal, Mohammed Ahmed Al Sayyid and a group of leftist thinkers in 1924, *Al Ahali* (The Public) in 1932, *Sawt Al Ahali* (Voice of the Public) in 1934, and the Iraqi Communist Party's *Kifah Al Sha'ab* (The People's Struggle) in 1935, created a core of nationalist newspapers.
>
> *(Davis, 2005: 75)*

Newspapers like these attacked the British role in Iraq, and some of them called for the immediate evacuation of British troops (Davis, 2005) while also serving as the means to introduce new ideologies, and they played an essential role in forming revolutionary movements. This chapter sheds light on the development of the Iraqi press, particularly post-1958 or the end of the monarchical rule in Iraq.

The press after the fall of the monarchy in July 1958

On 14 July 1958, General Abdul-Karim Kasim led a military coup against the monarchs. Despite many promises of freedom of expression, the Iraqi media continued to suffer from state censorship, under the control of military regimes. Their professional prejudice led the military governments to view journalists as "irresponsible and almost traitorous since they are continually criticizing" (Janowits, 1977: 164). Journalists and military regimes hold different attitudes about freedom. The military, in general, tends to have "specific and firm" thinking about the right order of society. It offers no room for discussions, criticism, or debate, and everything is dealt with by a "firm hand" (Shils, 1962). The period of Kasim's rule ended with another bloody coup staged by other officers in the army on the 8th of February 1963.

In 1967, the government decided to nationalize the press, through Law 155. This law gave the ministry of culture a guiding role and the sole privilege to launch political publications while depriving the private sector of the right to launch political publications. The law was introduced on 3 December 1967, and there were then 10 daily newspapers, two weekly newspapers, and 25 monthly magazines and newspapers (Al Bakri, 1994). The cabinet justified the nationalization of the press because Iraq was not the only Arab country that nationalized the press; several Arab countries like Egypt, Tunisia, Syria, Libya, and Saudi Arabia pursued similar policies (Al Fahdawi, 2001). Law 155 of 1967 allowed individuals to launch their publications, but the General Foundation for Journalism and Press refused 89 requests from different journalists to launch their publications. The authorities then refused to explain the reasons behind the denial of issuing those licenses (Batti, 1970).

On 5 January 1969, the official *Al Waqaaeaa* newspaper published the text of Press Law 206 of 1968, which remained active until the fall of Saddam's regime on 9 April 2003. That decree contained 35 articles on organizing the press and publications. For political publications, the minister had to forward proposals for political publications to the Revolutionary Command Council, as it was the only authority that could grant such a license (Al Bakri, 1994). In the 10 years between 1958 and 1968, the number of publications reached 267; most of them were in Arabic, save for 15 which were in other languages including Kurdish, Turkish, and English (Al Bakri, 1994).

The Iraqi press under the Ba'ath Party 1968–1979

Due to nationalization, there were no independent newspapers, and the Ba'athist government effectively had the entire print media working for the benefit of the regime, as part of their propaganda machine (Kadham, 1997). The Ba'ath regime kept the same newspapers that were published earlier, with the addition of the following Ba'ath party's outlets:

Al Jumhuriya newspaper

This was the official newspaper, launched in 1958. It continued to be published under the authority of the Ba'ath, but under new management and presenting ideas consistent with the new regime's ideology (Saleh, 2008).

Al-Thawra newspaper

On 18 August 1968, the Arab Ba'ath Socialist Party published its first newspaper edition under the name *Al-Thawra*. It was headed by Tariq Aziz (Minister of Foreign Affairs in Saddam's government) and was published in a tabloid size, although the rest of the country's newspapers were broadsheets (Batti, 2010). A big budget was allocated to it, in addition to huge buildings and a big printing house, bringing on board Iraqi and Arab writers who endorsed the regime's ideas and the ideology of the Ba'ath Party. However, many of those writers were communists.

Al Thawra became one of the most popular newspapers, printed in photo-offset, and almost 100 journalists were working in it (Saleh, 2008).

Baghdad Observer

This was an English-language daily newspaper published by Al Jamahir House. The editor was Jalal Abdel Kader, and it was published by Naji Sabri Al Hadeethi (Batti, 2010).

The partisan press

The political parties in Iraq reached to a deal with the Ba'ath party to form the National Advanced Front in Iraq in 1973. The parties participating in the Front launched their press in the the same year. However, the Ba'ath authority had control over the press sector, and the other parties' publications were not allowed to criticize government policies or to form any real opposition. Under this understanding, the Ba'ath Party allowed the following partisan publications:

Tareeq Al Shaab, representing the Iraqi Communist Party, but was shut down in 1979 when the government banned the party.

Al Taakhi, representing the KDP, which later became *Al Iraq* newspaper, one of the official political daily newspapers in Iraq.

Al Iraq newspaper: When the coalition between the Ba'ath Party and the KDP ended in 1974, *Al Taakhi* newspaper closed down, but the government replaced it with *Al Iraq* newspaper under new management. *Al Iraq* used the same facilities as *Al Taakhi* but embraced the ruling party's views especially concerning the Kurdish issue. *Al Iraq* newspaper was part of the official press and continued until the 2003 invasion (Saleh, 2008).

Iraqi media under Saddam 1979–2003

In July 1979 Saddam Hussein was appointed as the president and the leader of the Ba'ath Party, after serving as the head of the National Information Bureau since 1973 and continuing in this role until the fall of his regime after the US invasion in 2003. When he was vice president, he actively contributed to decisions of the activities and direction of the bureau and to the discussions that took place in its weekly meetings (Al Alwai, 2010). The official press continued to glorify Saddam and his leadership of the country.

In the mid-1980s, *Al Ba'ath Al Riyadi* newspaper (Ba'ath Sport) was launched. Uday, the son of the president, supervised this newspaper. It grew over the years and became a huge institution in itself, and it included Al Rashid Sports Club. *Al Ba'ath Al Riyadi* was first published on 2 June 1984 and campaigned against corruption in the Iraqi sports. Not long after this paper was launched, Uday personally headed the Olympic Committee, but, surprisingly, the newspaper continued to be critical of administrative corruption within the Ministry of Youth and the Olympic Committee despite Uday's position in it.

Abbass Al Janabi, who was the press secretary for Uday Hussein for a long period, stressed at the time that Uday was aware of the campaign that was taking place in the newspaper; "There was a pre-arrangement with Uday that 70% of the reports would attack officials in the Ministry of Youth and the Olympic Committee, whereas 30% of them would be personally initiated," said Dr. Abbass Al Janabi (Al Janabi, 2010).

Babil newspaper – a special experiment in the history of Iraqi press

During the first Gulf War 1991, all newspapers cover the political and military issues. After the end of the war on 28 February 1991, *Al-Ba'ath Al-Riyadi* newspaper returned to its normal sports coverage, but the idea of having a political newspaper was rooted in the mind of Uday Saddam Hussein. A few weeks after the end of hostilities, he launched a political newspaper, which was initially called *Al Ba'ath Al Siyasi*, as a twin newspaper to *Al Ba'ath Ariyadi*. The first edition was published on 24 March 1991. The head of the administrative council was Uday Saddam Hussein, while the editor-in-chief was Mudehir Aref. The publication was called Babil and launched under the slogan, "A Newspaper for Everyone."

The influence that Uday enjoyed gave the journalists freedom to criticize the ministers and corruption in the public services; "Uday was very close to the decisionmaker, so he was a powerful man who could protect us, but at the same time he was the main source of information," said Abbass Al Janabi (Al Janabi, 2010). Uday built up a media empire, which included his newspaper, radio, and TV stations, and "he was the only one who could publish anything without fearing any reaction" (Al Janabi, 2010).

The sanctions and the Iraqi press

The sanctions imposed on Iraq by the UN before and after the first Gulf War had a great effect on Iraq, with many Iraqis suffering as a consequence – except for Saddam and his regime. The sanctions harmed the daily life of all individuals – both socially and financially.

For the first time in more than 20 years, Iraqis saw tabloid newspapers again (*Al Qadissiya*, 1996; *Al Jumhuriya*, 1996). The official newspapers were printed in the small tabloid size because printing paper started to run out. The circulation number was reduced for all newspapers from 250,000 and 150,000 to 25,000 for each newspaper. The editor-in-chief of *Al Thawra* newspaper, Sabah Yassin, confirms the destructive effect of the embargo:

> Because of the sanctions, many cultural and art publications were closed, the periodicals of all institutions were reduced to 10% or changed from weekly to monthly. The number of pages was reduced by half. Everything came under the control of the government, even the ink and printing blades.
>
> *(Yassin, 2010)*

In the middle of the 1990s, a wave of weekly newspapers appeared. These newspapers were connected to the Journalists' Union, and they were named as "publications of the weekly newspaper committee," which was headed by Uday Saddam Hussein. All the weekly newspapers put Uday's name on their headings as a mark of influence and protection from criticism by local authorities. From the early days of their launch, these weeklies highlighted the fact that they were different from other newspapers, claiming to have a margin of freedom much greater than the official newspapers. Their reports discussed issues that were never before explored – especially issues of corruption (Al Ruba'e 2007). Hashim Hassan, the chief editor of *Nabdh Al Shabab*, said,

> Many journalists joined the weekly press. They took this chance to revive the principles of journalism and they managed to publish many reports. Those newspapers were popular, and they exceeded the circulation of the official press. Many journalists were fooling the officials by criticizing their ministries or directorates, who would then think it was under Uday's instructions.
>
> *(Hassan, 2010)*

The new publications gained a large audience by publishing leaked information on topics important for the Iraqis, such as land distribution, or news which might affect the economy. Many of the leaks turned out to be accurate. Uday's former press secretary, Al Janabi, confirms this fact that "Uday used to buy news resources, we could not say it was a bribe, but we called it gifts, according to Uday's preference, so we had sources everywhere" (Al Janabi, 2010). After a while, these newspapers started to cover Uday's activities on their front pages, and "They were covering Uday in the same way as the daily official newspapers were covering his father's activities" (Abdul Majid, 2010).

Iraqi newspapers after the American invasion 2003

Following the US and UK led invasion of Iraq in 2003, the appointed American Administrator of Iraq, Paul Bremer, signed a decree to abolish the Iraqi Ministry of Information and dismiss all its employees, within a few weeks of capturing Iraq. Based on previous experience in Germany and Japan, the Americans planned to fill the gap left by the collapse of the official press through creating their means of communication with the public. Khalil (2006) observes that, at the end of any conflict, there will be an opportunity to lay the foundations for a free, democratic, and diverse media landscape; but in the case of Iraq, the US planners were thinking of monopolizing the information spectrum with the help of a "friendly" Baghdad government, as Joyce Battle has documented (Battle, 2007). However, their plans lacked any consideration of independent media, or the role of new media and the Internet (Battle, 2007). Information policy became a "weapon" of war that was considered as "full-spectrum dominance" in the official US strategy (Miller, 2004).

The media landscape broadened dramatically, and newspapers, magazines, and periodicals were launched by several different bodies. Political parties and religious groups, who were seeking to expand their base of supporters, launched many publications. A considerable number of those newspapers were issued in Kurdistan after 1991, but they moved to Baghdad after the collapse of the regime. Meanwhile, many individuals aspired to establish influence in the new regime after years of deprivation from political activities. Other groups of rich merchants and tribal leaders, who were capable financially, launched newspapers hoping that their voices would be heard. For example, *Al Rabetah* (The Connection) newspaper represented the national gathering for the sheikhs and tribal leaders in Iraq (*Al Rabetah*, 2004). The occupation forces joined those groups by issuing their publications or funding other newspapers (Al Azawi, 2008). Baghdad set the biggest example of media expansion, but other provinces witnessed the same phenomenon on a smaller scale. This flourishing media environment provided work opportunities for many writers, reporters, editors, photographers, administrators, technicians, and others who worked in the media sector (Thamir, 2008).

The American forces began distributing *Azzaman* newspaper to Iraqis after controlling massive territories; the troops were also distributing flyers containing messages from the coalition leaders Bush and Blair. The first issue of *Azzaman* entered Iraq on 8 April 2003, and it was labeled the "Basra edition." The newspaper was distributed in Baghdad and Basra, Nassiriya, and other southern provinces of Iraq (Al-Mljawi, 2009). *Azzaman* was then followed by other newspapers of the Saddam oppositions who moved back to Iraq, especially those who had publications printed in the Kurdistan region of Iraq. The mouthpiece of the Iraqi Communist Party, Tareeq Al Shaab (the People's Road), was one of the early newspapers that hit the streets of Baghdad (Al Jazaeeri, 2011). Other newspapers decided to leave Kurdistan permanently and move into Baghdad, like *Nedaa Al Mostaqbal* newspaper (The Future Call) (Eijam, 2011).

The Patriotic Union of Kurdistan reclaimed control of the printing house of *Al Iraq* newspaper to launch their publication, *Al Etehad* (The Union); it was named *Al Iraq* until 8 April, but on 10 April 2003, the newspaper was published as *Al Etehad*. Thus, the newspaper changed its political direction within only 24 hours, according to Dr. Abdul Amir Al Shemari, a former editor of *Al Iraq* and later *Al Etehad* newspaper (Al Shemari, 2010); the staff remained the same in the new publication, except two managers, namely the editor-in-chief and the directing editor (Al Shemari, 2010).

Publications carried promising names, such as *Al Shahed* (the Witness), *Al Akhbar* (the News), *Al Haqiqa* (the Truth), among others. Some of these newspapers were published with the same names as well-known newspapers of the monarchy era, as well as of the time of the first republic, such as *Al-Manar* (the Beacon), *Al Belad* (the Country), *Habsboz* (a satirical publication), and *Azzaman* (the Time) (Al Ruba'e, 2007).

Due to the return of religious political parties from exile joining the newly formed opposition inside Iraq, the printing market witnessed a relatively high stream of religious books, circulars and leaflets, and newspapers, such as *Al Bassaaer* (the Foresight), *Anssar Al Hawza* (supporters of Al Hawza), *Al Daawah* (Advocacy), *Al Bayan* (the Declaration), *Al Majles* (the Council), *Qamar Bani Hashem* (nickname for Imam Hussein), *Al Kufa* (the name for a city), *Sawt Al Jumaah* (the Sound of Friday), *Al wefak Al Islami* (the Islamic Harmony), among many others, which represented different religious Islamic factions (Al Ruba'e, 2007). These publications urged turning Iraq into an Islamic state, which was the same demand for many publications previously published in exile (Batti, 2006). Competing ideas among political factions surfaced on the pages of these publications, which reflected a conflict of ethno-sectarian agendas (Al Marashi, 2007). For example, *Al-Saah*, headed by Sheikh Ahmed Al Kubaisi, is regarded as a platform for Sunni Iraqis. A newspaper like *Al-Da'wa* represented the *Al-Da'wa* Party, which is an Islamic Shi'a political party; *Al-Adalah* is the organ of the Supreme Council of the Islamic Revolution in Iraq, which is another Shi'a party. Rohan Jayasekera of the London-based "Index on Censorship" gives this reason for the boom of such publications: "Iraqi media became very sectarian very quickly, not only because of the political situation but simply because of the income to sustain the media there; they became reliant on political factions, who have the money" (Jayasekera, 2011).

The Iraqi media experts attribute the increase in the number of publications to the low cost of launching a newspaper or other publications. An amount of USD 1,000 was enough to publish a daily tabloid-size newspaper of 16 pages. The publisher could put his name on the front page as the chairman of the board or the general director, publisher, or editor. Many had done this, but these publications existed for only a few editions (Al Azawi, 2008). Nearly 100 news publications and a handful of news broadcast outlets were available in Baghdad by the end of May 2003 (Isakhan, 2009). These figures increased substantially throughout the year, all over

Iraq. For example, in a small city like Najaf, more than 30 newspapers were serving the population of only 300,000 people (Whitaker, 2003).

The coverage of the new press

The new newspapers were obsessed with Saddam and the Ba'ath Party's ruling days. Articles about his atrocities and the discovery of mass graves filled the pages. Newspapers were breaking the old taboos about Saddam and his family; for example, one newspaper headline read: "Qussay Grabbed $1 Billion and 70 Billion Euros Before the War" (Daragahi, 2003). On the other hand, newspapers criticized the Americans too, and their plans in Iraq, but not in an overly bold or challenging way. *Al Ahrar* (the Liberal) newspaper published a picture of the American president George W. Bush with this caption, "Will you be the finest dream come true for all Iraqis as you promised, or will you be occupier No 1?" *Al Adalah* newspaper published an article once, under the headline, "Security Has Become a Dream That Will Never Come True," arguing that Iraq would not gain security if the Americans stayed in Iraq (Daragahi, 2003).

One of the factors contributing to the failure of these newspapers was the flood of state-backed and partisan newspapers, which began to offer more and better content and were cheaper to buy. Many newspapers that could not provide good content quickly disappeared from the market. One strange factor was the correlation between circulation rates and the number of pages in a newspaper; thus, the newspaper that had the largest number of pages coupled with the lowest price would usually attract more readers. Readers, generally, were being drawn towards the government press as a "reliable" news source, unlike the private newspapers, which lost their credibility (Jasim, 2009). Most of the newspapers were using a fairy-tale style of storytelling in their coverage, which was usually highly opinioned – emulating a style normally used by columnists (Emara, 2009).

There have been some incredible paradoxes and ironic moments experienced by the Iraqi press after 9 April 2003. As mentioned before, many of the historical media names that had a memorable presence before the Ba'ath Party era began to reappear, but under new management that had no tie with the founders of those newspapers. Iraqi law reserved the names for the concession owners, but when the Ba'ath Party closed those publications, these concessions were terminated. *Azzaman* (the Time), *Al Hawadith* (the Events), and *Al Manar* were old titles, which reappeared, but the owners of the original concessions were either dead or their heirs were not interested in relaunching the publications. Some of these publications wanted to keep the connection with the founder of the newspaper, like *Al Manar*, which kept publishing the name of the founder, Abdulaziz Barakat, who set it up in the middle of 1945. Such repetition of the old well-known titles was a clear attempt to attract readers by reprinting familiar names in the history of Iraq (Khudur, 2008). But for some families, these titles became a historical privilege and maybe a legal heritage. In one event, Dr. Adnan Pachachi, a senior Iraqi politician, wanted to revive *Al Nahdhah* newspaper (the Renaissance) (Al Nahdhah, 2004), which was founded by his deceased father Muzahim Pachachi together with Ibrahim Helmy in Baghdad in 1913, following the first Arab conference in Paris before WW1. Dr. Adnan Pachachi decided to republish *Al Nahdha* in Baghdad in June 2003 as the mouthpiece for his political movement, the Liberal Democrats. However, another newspaper was issued under the same name, Al Nahdha, in Basra claiming to be "the voice of the South" (Khudur, 2008).

Distributors, who are affiliated with different political factions, could also control the number of papers in circulation or stop the distribution of any publication. Using different methods of intimidation, the powerful distributors would stop other distributors who might represent a differing political view from buying into a newspaper. Sometimes these marketing companies delayed distributing certain publications to make them lose their value. In some cases, thousands of copies of some publications would be bought and then burned to prevent a piece of news from being read (Sinjari, 2006).

Azzaman and *Al Sabah* newspapers

Despite the huge number of publications that flooded the Iraqi streets, only a few publications hit a recognizable circulation figure. The only two newspapers to circulate over 40,000 copies per day were *Azzaman* and *Al Sabah*. *Azzaman* can be argued to be a profit-motivated newspaper representing the private sector while *Al Sabah* is a politically motivated newspaper representing the government. Both newspapers have maintained the same political line they followed since 2003 and have a strong presence in the Iraqi market.

Azzaman is an Iraqi international Arab-facing independent daily newspaper, published by the Azzaman Foundation for Press, Publishing, and Information. It is one of the leading Arab newspapers in Europe and was founded by the Iraqi journalist, Saad Al-Bazaz, a former press secretary of Saddam, and former editor of *Al Jumhuriya* daily newspaper before he formally opposed Saddam's regime and fled to London in 1995. The first pilot issue was published on 10 April 1997, and many stories were leaked to *Azzaman* newspaper from within Saddam's tight circle. Some of these stories were not true, but the publication would publish an apology on the front page if the editorial team found out, as *Azzaman*'s editor Dr. Fateh Abdul Salam (Al-Bazaz's brother) said: "It was difficult to get the news from Iraq, but we had some reporters who were working for us secretly" (Abdul Salam, 2011).

After 2003, the first edition distributed inside Iraq was on 8 April 2003 in Basra by the British troops (Falhi, 2006). *Azzaman* was distributed in Iraq earlier than April 2003, but it was limited to the provinces of Kurdistan in northern Iraq (Khudur, 2008).

Moreover, *Al-Sabah* (the Morning) newspaper was launched as part of the American media project in Iraq and then became part of the Iraqi Media Network (IMN), which was formed in the early days of the US occupation of Iraq in April 2003. The first issue of *Al Sabah* newspaper was published on 17 May 2003. The newspaper, at the time, was accused of speaking on behalf of the coalition forces in Iraq (Al-Dahan, 2006). Theoretically, *Al Sabah* was formed to be independent, as many articles confirmed in the new codes of the IMN, but the publication was effectively a mouthpiece for any party representing the authority (Mukhlif, 2008). The first chief editor was the Iraqi journalist, Ismael Zayeer, a former journalist at Radio Free Europe (Kareem, 2007). For Zayeer, *Al Sabah* was the idea of one of the American advisors, Mike Furlong, who suggested this name to Paul Bremer and Jay Garner.

The newspaper was published in tabloid size twice a week, Monday and Wednesday from 17 May 2003 until 2 July 2003. Next, it was published three times a week: Sunday, Tuesday, and Thursday from 3 July 2003 until 1 August 2003. Finally, from 3 August 2003, the newspaper became a daily publication, printed every day of the week except Friday, because it is a public holiday in Iraq (Falhi, 2006).

Conclusion

The Iraqi press was widely controlled by the successive regimes which ruled the country. It was in many cases the tool of the state to control and communicate with the public. It was one of the most effective tools until very few years after the US-led invasion in 2003. After the fall of Saddam's regime, the Iraqi press witnessed an era of expansion. The Americans supported many publications, official periodicals, and private titles, and they hoped that with such support, they would polish the image of their forces. In addition, the US forces tried to use these publications to publicize their propaganda. But the impact of these newspapers and the paid articles by the US intelligence unit might have been limited due to the growth in the number of satellite television channels. Many of the Iraqi newspapers closed down because of the loss of revenues compounded by the fierce competition with the partisan press, driven by ideology, not financial gain. In general, the newspapers in Iraq are now declining while new and social media platforms are attracting many segments of the Iraqi audiences.

References

Al Azawi, K. J. (2008), *Iraqi Press under the American Occupation*. Baghdad: publisher house not known.

Al Bakri, W. E. (1994), *The Development of the Press System in Iraq 1958–1980*. Baghdad: Cultural Events Publishing House.

Al Marashi, I. (2007), The Dynamics of Iraq's Media: Ethno-Sectarian Violence, Political Islam, Public Advocacy and Globalization. *Cardozo Arts & Entertainment*, 25(95), pp. 95–140. Retrieved from www. cardozoaelj.net/issues/07/Al-Marashi.pdf. Accessed 2 August 2009.

Al Nahdhah (2004), Adnan Al Pachachi Auspices the Graduation of Officers and Soldiers. *Al Nahdhah* (7 January), p. 1.

Al Ruba'e, D. H. (2007) *Political Trends of the Headings in the Iraqi Press*. Unpublished MA thesis, College of Media, Baghdad University, Iraq.

Ayalon, A. (1995), *The Press in the Arab Middle East*. New York and Oxford: Oxford University Press.

Batti, F. (1970), *14th of July Press and Iraq's Political Progress*. Baghdad: Al Adeeb Baghdadi Press.

Batti, F. (2006), *The Iraqi Press in Exile*. Damascus: Al Mada Publishing House.

Batti, F. (2010), *The Iraqi Press Encyclopaedia*. Damascus: Al Mada Publishing House.

Battle, J. (2007), Iraq: The Media War Plan. *George Washington University*, 8 May. Retrieved from www. gwu.edu/~nsarchiv/NSAEBB/NSAEBB219/index.htm. Accessed 23 June 2009.

Daragahi, B. (2003), *Rebuilding Iraq's Media*, Columbia Journalism Review. *All Business*, 1 July. Retrieved from www.allbusiness.com/buying_exiting_businesses/3483775-1.html. Accessed 23 June 2009.

Davis, E. (2005), *Memories of State: Politics, History, and Collective Identity in Modern Iraq*. Berkeley and London: University of California Press.

Isakhan, B. (2009), Manufacturing Consent in Iraq: Interference in the Post-Saddam Media Sector. *International Journal of Contemporary Iraqi Studies*, 3(1). Retrieved from http://deakin.academia. edu/BenjaminIsakhan/Papers/99701/Manufacturing_Consent_in_Iraq_Interference_in_the_post-Sad dam_media_sector. Accessed 12 January 2010.

Janowits, M. (1977), *Military Institutions and Coercion in the Developing Countries*. Expanded edition. Chicago and London: The University of Chicago Press.

Jasim, N. (2009), *Extracts of Iraqi Press History after 2003*. Baghdad: publisher house not known.

Khalil, J. (2006), *Diversity and Islam in Post Conflict Broadcast Policy: The Case of Afghanistan and Iraq*. The American University in Cairo in 2006. Retrieved from http://www1.aucegypt.edu/conferences/ iamcr/uploaded/5Finished%20.PDF/CD_Joe_ F._Khalil.pdf. Accessed 5 October 2010.

Khudur, S. (2008), *Iraq's Newspapers after the 10th of April 2003*. 2nd edition. Mosul: Al Jaeel Al Arabi.

Miller, D. (2004), Information Dominance: The Philosophy of Total Propaganda Control. *Global Policy Forum*, 23 December. Retrieved from www.globalpolicy.org/component/content/article/154/26581. html. Accessed 8 August 2011.

Noor Al Deen, H. (2005), Changes, Changes, and Challenges of the Iraqi Media. *Global Media Journal* (Spring). Retrieved from http://lass.calumet.purdue.edu/cca/gmj/oldsitebackup/submitteddocu ments/spring200 5/non_referreed/al-deensp05.htm. Accessed 10 September 2006.

Saleh, A. (2008), *Iraq's Press in the Second Ba'ath Era*. Retrieved from http://urfreeandme.blogspot. com/2008/07/1968-2003.html. Accessed 10 August 2011.

Shils, E. (1962), The Military in the Political Development. In J. Johnson (ed.), *The Role of the Military in Underdeveloped Countries*. Princeton, NJ: Princeton University Press.

Sinjari, H. (2006), *Arab Media in the Information Age*. Abu Dhabi, UAE: The Emirates Centre for Strategic Studies and Research.

Tripp, C. (2002), *A History of Iraq*. Cambridge: Cambridge University Press.

Whitaker, Brian. (2003), Getting a Bad Press. *The Guardian*, Mon 23 June 2003. Retrieved from https://www.theguardian.com/world/2003/jun/23/worlddispatch.iraq.
Yassin, S. (2010), *Iraqi Press*, e-mail to H. Kadhum, 6 April.

Unpublished studies

Al Fahdawi, A. (2001), *The Iraqi Press from 18th of November 1963–17th of July 1968*. Unpublished Master's thesis, College of Media, Baghdad University, Baghdad.
Al Ruba'e, D. H. (2007), *Political Trends of the Headings in the Iraqi Press*. Unpublished Master's thesis, College of Media, Baghdad University, Baghdad.
Emara, F. (2009), *The Attitudes of the Iraqi Press Towards the Migration of the Intellectual National Elite*. Unpublished Master's thesis, College of Media, Baghdad University, Baghdad.
Falhi, E. J. (2006), *Trends of the Iraqi Press over Woman Issues*. Unpublished Master's thesis, College of Media, Baghdad University, Baghdad.
Kadham, A. (1997), *Mass Media and the Process of Decision Making in Iraq*. Unpublished Master's thesis, College of Media, Baghdad University, Baghdad.
Kareem, Q. (2007), *The Development of The News Lead in Iraqi Dailies*. Unpublished Master's thesis, College of Media, Baghdad University, Baghdad.
Mukhlif, M. A. (2008), *Editorial of Al Sabah Newspaper (Analytical Study of Al Sabah Editorial)*. Unpublished Master's thesis, College of Media, Baghdad University, Baghdad.
Thamir, A. Q. (2008), *The Role of the Iraqi Press in the Formation of the Political Attitudes of Baghdad University Students*. Unpublished Master's thesis, College of Media, Baghdad University, Baghdad.

Interviews

Abdul Majid, A. (2010), *Interview with Dr. Ahmed Abdul Majid on 5 May 2010*. Baghdad. [Audio recording in possession of researcher]
Abdul Salam, F. (2011), *Interview with Dr. Fateh Abdul Salam on 22 February 2011*. Baghdad. [Audio recording in possession of researcher]
Al Alwai, H. (2010), *Interview with Hassan Al Alwai on 28 April 2010*. Baghdad. [Audio recording in possession of researcher]
Al Janabi, A. (2010), *Interview with Abbass Al Janabi on 25 February 2010*. London. [Audio recording in possession of researcher]
Al Jazaeeri, M. (2011), *Interview with Mofeed Al Jazaeeri on 20 January 2011*. Baghdad. [Audio recording in possession of researcher]
Al Shemari, A. (2010), *Interview with Dr. Abdul Amir Al Shamari on 27 April 2010*. Baghdad. [Audio recording in possession of researcher]
Eijam, A. (2011), *Interview with Ali Eijam on 20 June 2011*. London. [Audio recording in possession of researcher]
Hassan, H. (2010), *Interview with Dr. Hashim Hassan on 5 May 2010*. Baghdad. [Audio recording in possession of researcher]
Jayasekera, R. (2011), *Interview with Rohan Jayasekera on 14 July 2011*. London. [Audio recording in possession of researcher]
Zayeer, I. (2011), *Interview with Ismael Zayeer on 1 July 2011*. London. [Audio recording in possession of researcher]

8

BROADCASTING IN IRAQ – FROM PLURALISM TO ETHNO-SECTARIANISM

Ibrahim Al-Marashi

Introduction

During periods of Iraq's monarchy, from 1920 to 1958, the nation enjoyed a pluralistic media environment, able to report with relative independence. Once the Iraqi republic was established in 1958, various military governments cracked down on media freedoms, particularly after the 1968 coup that brought the Iraqi Ba'ath Party into power. Until 2003, the media in Iraq was subject to draconian state control, as the government and the state Ba'ath Party tightly controlled and owned all news agencies and broadcast media.

After the invasion of Iraq in 2003, the diverse Iraqi media that emerged in post-Ba'athist Iraq collectively presented a range of views, but most outlets were established by political parties and ethnic factions, often leading to sharply partisan coverage. Although the new Iraqi constitution of 2005 protects freedoms of speech and expression, related media legislation is vague and often contradictory, and the unstable security situation during Iraq's violence undermined legal and physical protections for journalists. Political tensions have been detrimental to independent reporting, and media outlets face pressure from the authorities. Journalists have been regularly denied access to government officials, and fear of reprisals, from fatal violence to criminal defamation suits, has resulted in pervasive self-censorship.

When the Islamic State of Iraq and Syria (ISIS) declared an Islamic State that encompassed vast swathes of territory in northwestern Iraq from 2014 to 2018, the ensuing violence and repression made Iraq one of the world's most deadly countries for media practitioners, both Iraqi and foreign, a problem that persists even after the militant group's loss of territory. Throughout these years, particularly in territory under de facto ISIS rule, reporters were detained and either forced to work with them or, if not, executed. While ISIS militants lost control over the major Iraqi cities and towns towards the end of 2018, it remains to be seen how the Iraqi media will play a role in the reconstructions of the nation.

The chapter charts the evolution of the Iraqi media from the Ottoman Empire to the Islamic State, examining the continuity and change in terms of the relationship between the state and the fourth estate, the legal environment regulating communications, business, and economic systems, and finally, the social roles these outlets provide, particularly in the light of the violence that has plagued Iraq since 2003.

Historical background

In August 1921 Faysal was installed by the British as Iraq's first king, ushering in a monarchy that lasted until 1958 and the most liberal period in the nation's press history. The newly emerging parties established affiliated newspapers during the 1920s, while the British mandatory authorities sought to financially co-opt journalists. Kurdish newspapers also began to be published during this decade. In 1930, Iraq became formally independent, coinciding with the establishment of the first government-controlled radio station (Al-Rawi, 2012).

Once the Iraqi republic was established in 1958, its military governments cracked down on media freedoms. General Abd al-Karim Qasim imported sophisticated radio equipment to communicate with the Iraqis, and also with the greater Arab world, to counter the challenge from Jamal Abd al-Nasir's "Voice of the Arabs" program from Egypt (Boyd, 1982: 401). After the 1968 coup that brought the Iraqi Ba'ath Party into power, a press act was passed prohibiting the writing of articles that criticized the president, then General Hassan al-Bakr, Saddam Hussein's cousin, the Party, and the highest executive arm of the state – the Revolutionary Command Council (RCC). The sole mission of the Iraqi News Agency and the Iraqi press was to relay state propaganda. Laws enacted during that era broadly restricted expression and punished violations harshly. In 1986, the RCC stipulated the death penalty for any journalist insulting the president, Saddam Hussein. Iraqi press and broadcasters were controlled through the Ministry of Information, essentially allowing the Ba'ath party to dominate the media landscape. There were five daily newspapers, four radio stations, and two television channels, with no views opposed to Saddam Hussein, who ruled Iraq from 1979 to 2003 (Amos, 2010: 4–5). The systematic suppression of any alternative voices was the norm, and all indigenous media was the preserve of the state. Satellite dishes were illegal, yet a few Iraqis sought to defy the ban with black market dishes hidden on rooftops.

In the aftermath of the 2003 Iraq War, the collapse of the Ba'athist state represented the end of authoritarian control and information hegemony. The restrictions placed by the Ba'ath on public discourse disappeared overnight and a plethora of newspapers, radio stations, and television networks emerged, free to debate and criticize public affairs, yet the regulatory framework had to be built anew. Iraq witnessed a burgeoning of both broadcast and print media in the post-war period, with a proliferation of hundreds of privately owned television, radio, and print media outlets in languages including Arabic, Kurdish, Syriac, and Turkmen. Since then Iraq's post-2003 media falls into four broad categories: (1) media owned by the Iraqi state, (2) media owned by political Islamist groups, (3) media owned by ethnic political parties, and (4) media owned by independent entities.

The first category emerged as the US Coalition Provisional Authority (CPA) abolished Iraq's Ministry of Information in the aftermath of the Iraq War to signal a break from the Ba'athist past. Under its auspices, the CPA established the Iraqi Media Network, an umbrella organization that includes Al-Iraqiya satellite TV channel, terrestrial TV channels, Republic of Iraq Radio station, and *Al-Sabah*, the national newspaper. While initially the Network served as media akin to an emergency broadcaster for CPA communications to the Iraqis, it eventually emerged as a public service broadcaster that sought to reflect the interests of the Iraqi state without being under the direct control of the state, at least in theory. Rather than mimicking the centralized broadcast system of the Ba'athist order, where most of its staff formed part of the public-sector bureaucracy, the post-2003 state is primarily responsible for financing this public service broadcaster and choosing its directors.

The second and third categories are a product of Iraq's post-2003 security vacuum within a fragile political system dominated by exiled and opposition organizations, for the most part, formed along ethno-sectarian lines. As Iraq pursued democratization after 2003, the post-war chaos led to political parties seeking to mobilize fractured identities based on ethnic, sectarian, and tribal divisions. These political parties and ethnic factions funded most media outlets, deeming it necessary to have a TV channel to convey political propaganda and to inspire their constituents. Thus, while most of the stations in Iraq are now independently owned, many operate as extensions of ethno-sectarian political institutions.

The second category, media owned by political Islamist groups, includes media holdings of the Shi'a and Sunni Islamist parties, which broadcast in Arabic. These holdings are numerous, but prominent examples include Al-Furat satellite channel, based in Baghdad, which began broadcasting in November 2004. This channel was established then by the Supreme Council for the Islamic Revolution in Iraq (SCIRI), a Shi'a-Islamist opposition group to Saddam Hussein, which was based in Iran before 2003. While this party has all but collapsed in Iraq's political electoral cycles, the station continues to broadcast.

The Iraqi cleric Muqtada Al-Sadr leads the Sadrists, a movement among the poorer tribes and marsh dwellers of Amara and Nasiriyya and in semi-urbanized areas like Saddam City and the poorer quarters of Basra. His media holdings include several newspapers, such as the *Ishraqat al-Sadr* (*The Dawn of Sadr*) paper, *Al-Hawza al-Natiqa* (*The Active Hawza*) weekly paper, Al-Salam radio station, and Al-Salam TV station. When US military forces tried to close down *Al-Hawza* for allegedly inciting violence, pitched battles broke out between them and his militia. While the content of these media in early 2003 was opposed to the American occupation, by 2016 they focused on government corruption and the cleric's embrace of the protest movement in Baghdad that emerged in 2015.

Iraq Shi'a militias such as Asaib Ahl al-Haq operate Al-Ahd TV, while other militias prefer to communicate to audiences via social media and creating their own YouTube clips to demonstrate their progress in combatting ISIS or their aid in reconstruction projects. Other Iraqi Shi'a militias, such as the Iraqi Hizballah, publish the *Al-Bayyina* newspaper. Both of the aforementioned militias are also supported by the Islamic Republic of Iran, and thus would have a pro-Iranian tilt in the news coverage.

The third category includes media owned by ethnic political parties. Within the Kurdistan Regional Government in northern Iraq, the Kurdistan Democratic Party (KDP) operates the Kurdistan Satellite Channel, and the Patriotic Union of Kurdistan (PUK) operates the satellite channel KurdSat. Both the KDP and PUK also publish newspapers in Kurdish, *Khabat*, and *Kurdistan Nuwe* respectively, as well as two Arabic newspapers, the KDP's *al-Taakhi*, and the PUK's *al-Ittihad*. All these media are non-profit and financed by their parties. While the directors of these media stress that their media holdings have editorial independence from the PUK and KDP respectively, the content suggests that both channels serve as mouthpieces for the parties. The Kurdish channels NRT TV, established by a Kurdish entrepreneur, and KNN TV, affiliated with the Goran Party, form the media affiliated with Kurdish political opposition to the KDP and PUK.

In the fourth category, the four most widely watched independent stations are Al-Sharqiya, Al-Sumaria, Al-Baghdadia, and Al-Fayha. While these channels are Iraqi-owned, with content directed towards an Iraqi audience, Al-Sharqiya and al-Fayha are headquartered in Dubai, Al-Baghdadia is in Cairo, and Al-Sumaria has facilities in Lebanon and Jordan. All stations have a Baghdad bureau. These channels primarily broadcast entertainment as well as political news. All these channels claim that they have no connections with any political, ethnic, or religious faction and refuse to air any programming that encourages sectarianism. In terms of reception among Arabic-speaking audiences that have been surveyed in Iraq, Al-Sharqiya, Al-Sumaria, and Al-Baghdadia are widely watched and trusted, with Al-Sharqiya ranking first, followed second by the state-owned Al-Iraqiya.

Market competition

As many as 97% of homes in Iraq have a satellite dish, and according to a 2012 BBC survey, more than 90% of Iraqis receive most of their information, whether it is news or entertainment, from satellite TV stations (Awad and Eaton, 2013: 22). Two-thirds of Iraqis stated they do not read newspapers (Freedom House, 2017).

Al-Iraqiya is the only national public service channel and its financing comes from the coffers of the Iraqi state, and the Ministry of Finance approves the channel's budget. As a state-run national news network, it does not accept paid campaign advertisements. The political parties representing sectarian and ethnic groups provide financing for their media outlets. Militias provide funding for their channels and allegedly receive financing from Iran.

The independent channels do not receive funding from the state, or any political or religious groups, but depend on advertising revenues and financing by wealthy Iraqi or Arab investors. Al-Sumaria is owned by the Iraqi company CET (Communication Entertainment and Television) and depends on advertising revenues from both Iraqi and Arab companies. Al-Fayha is an independent Iraqi channel owned by an Iraqi Shi'a businessman. Al-Sharqiya is owned by the media entrepreneur Sa'ad al-Bazzaz, the former editor of the newspaper *Al-Jumhuriyya* in Ba'athist Iraq, and his holdings also include the *Al-Zaman* newspaper, which competes with the state-owned *Al-Sabah* for the most widely read Iraqi daily in Arabic. It has been alleged that Saudi Arabia has provided financing for al-Bazzaz's media group. Al-Baghdadia's founders were former Ba'athists, and their financing comes from Iraqi entrepreneurs. These channels are independent, yet their funding sources are not transparent, and critics argue that due to sectarian ownership, Al-Baghdadiyya and Al-Sharqiyya have an Arab Sunni bias, while Al-Fayha has an Arab Shi'a bias.

Laws and regulations

Iraq's constitution protects freedoms of speech and expression, but vague and redundant laws govern the media. The 1968 Publications Law, still in effect, prescribes up to seven years in prison for insulting the government, and the 1969 penal code criminalizes defamation and insult. In 2010, the Supreme Judicial Council created a special court to prosecute journalists despite a ban on the creation of special courts in Article 95 of Iraq's post-2003 constitution. This Federal Publishing and Media Court allows government entities to pursue cases against journalists and media outlets for alleged defamation and insults. Journalists investigating corruption are often summoned before this court to divulge their sources, and as a result, journalists can face heavy fines and be placed on a national security blacklist (Freedom House, 2017).

In areas under the control of the Kurdistan Regional Government (KRG) in northern Iraq, the 2008 Kurdistan Press Law protects journalists' right to obtain "information of importance to citizens and with relevance to the public interest," and while it abolished imprisonment as a penalty for defamation, KRG public officials have often used the region's penal code to sue journalists for libel, usually for stories about corruption. The KRG passed legislation guaranteeing access to information in 2013, but critics note that the law contains vague language and vast exceptions and rarely helps journalists (Freedom House, 2017).

Iraq has no national law guaranteeing access to government information, and this information is difficult for journalists to obtain. Reporters are regularly prevented from covering sensitive stories or denied access to officials and news events. For example, when ISIS made advances into Iraq in Anbar and Ninawa provinces in 2014, the Iraqi government imposed a media blackout there, denying access to independent journalists to cover the fighting. Later, journalists seeking access to cover the front lines against ISIS forces were denied access unless they belonged to media outlets deemed loyal to the government.

The Coalition Provisional Authority disbanded the Saddam Hussein-era Ministry of Information and its Order 65 created of an Iraqi Communications and Media Commission (CMC), modeled on the American Federal Communication Commission (Isakhan, 2009: 15). The CMC is responsible for regulating broadcast media, with the power to close or revoke the licenses of critical media outlets, such as stations within Iraq that covered the government in a negative fashion. It even silenced Iraqi-owned media stations outside of Iraq that gave a platform to critical Iraqi politicians, particularly those who denounced former Prime Minister Nuri al-Maliki, who led the country from 2006 to 2014. During his tenure, 10 stations had their license revoked. For example, charges were brought against the Egypt-based, Iraqi-owned Al-Baghdadia TV station, which was closed by the CMC in 2010 as it allowed airtime to speakers critical of the Al-Maliki government. The station was allowed to reopen its Baghdad office in 2014, after appealing its case in the Iraqi court system. Even though the channel's headquarters are in Cairo, the Iraqi government approached Egyptian officials, who pressured Nilesat, Egypt's main satellite system, to drop the channel from its broadcasting lineup. In 2016 the Iraqi police, accompanied by a CMC employee, closed this station's Baghdad bureau and withdrew its license again. The Ministry of Interior did not provide details as to why it was reclosed, only stating that the channel had been operating in Iraq "illegally." The closure occurred two days before demonstrations in Baghdad were to take place against government corruption and failure to deliver public services. The channel had been sympathetic to the protestors, and its Facebook page broadcasted videos of these demonstrations (Freedom House, 2017).

An example of the CMC's relationship to the media sector was illustrated after the government declared a state of emergency amid the ISIS offensive in 2014. The CMC issued "mandatory" guidelines for media "during the war on terror" with a series of vague stipulations that placed arbitrary restrictions on coverage. One provision required the media to "hold on to the patriotic sense" and to "be careful when broadcasting material that may express insulting sentiments" or does "not accord with the moral and patriotic order required for the war on terror." Another forbade the broadcasting or publishing of material critical of the security forces and instead obliged journalists to focus on their accomplishments. Media in Iraqi Kurdistan issued similar guidelines.

The 2014 CMC guidelines had sparked fears about increasing self-censorship. After these guidelines were released, the CMC and other government officials had threatened to close or revoke the licenses of critical media outlets, particularly those with foreign ties that gave a platform to Sunni politicians, carried denunciations of the government, or provided live coverage of the fight against ISIS. The CMC revoked the license of Qatar-based Al Jazeera for one year, as a result of violating the 2014 guidelines for allegedly inciting violence and sectarianism (Freedom House, 2017).

Throughout Iraq, the KRG, and the former ISIS-occupied territories, Iraqi journalists faced harassment, intimidation, and violence from a variety of actors in the course of their reporting. Journalists in Iraq and the KRG faced phone threats, were beaten by security forces, or worse, assassinated if they had been critical of politicians, generals, or the various security and militia forces. TV and radio stations and newspapers that opposed the government have been raided by security forces.

Under Iraqi law, officials are required to investigate incidents in which journalists are injured or killed as a result of their work, although few journalists' deaths have been investigated since 2003. Not only have Iraqi and the KRG governmental authorities failed to follow up on investigations of murdered journalists, but they failed to provide adequate protection measures for journalists covering the military campaign against ISIS from 2014 to 2018 or protests within the nation, such as those that occurred in Baghdad as of 2015 or Basra in 2018.

In the ISIS-occupied territories, journalists were attacked or murdered for allegedly serving as spies or otherwise undermining the group's mission. The group arrested and executed journalists working for privately owned television stations in Mosul or Tikrit, like Al-Mosuliya TV, Sama Mosul TV, and Sama Salaheddin TV, or the Mosul newspaper, Rai' al Nas (Freedom House, 2017). Other journalists embedded with Iraq's security forces covering the conflict with ISIS were also killed in the course of their reporting.

Government control versus market rules

Commercial advertising revenues alone are too small to sustain Iraq's private media, and the government shapes the editorial content of some outlets by manipulating public advertising or pressuring private advertisers. Journalists have also allegedly slanted the news in return for bribes from officials, who offer money and other rewards. In KRG areas, independent media suffer from lack of advertising and are unable to compete with outlets that are subsidized by the major Kurdish parties.

An example of how the state media attempted to co-opt independent media occurred during the military campaign against ISIS. In 2016 the state-owned Iraqi Media Network established a national media coalition with a group of media outlets as part of a "national media strategy" to foster public support of the military campaign against ISIS. This strategy was designed to "counter rumors" that could sap the morale of the national military campaign. The media partners of this coalition included the state-owned Al-Iraqiya and independent channels such as Al-Sumaria, Hona Baghdad, Al-Rasheed, Al-Furat, Al-Hadath, and ANB TV, and in exchange, these media were provided technical and material support by the state. These channels produced joint evening TV news programs and output for social media networks, such as Facebook (Freedom House, 2017). Such an arrangement precluded channels in the coalition from providing news that may critique the state and excluded channels that had been critical of the government from entering this arrangement.

Iraqis have turned to digital and social media to spread information and consume news. However, poor infrastructure and sporadic access to electricity continue to make Iraq's penetration rate for terrestrial Internet access one of the lowest in the region, with overall Internet penetration at around 20%, leading the majority of Iraqi users to use wireless technology (Freedom House, 2017).

Until the crisis created by the ISIS offensive in the summer of 2014, the Internet had largely operated without government restriction. Shortly after the militant group gained control of Mosul in June 2014, the prime minister's office ordered the Ministry of Communications to shut down Internet service in ISIS-occupied provinces, ostensibly to prevent the group from using social media to plan attacks and release propaganda. However, access to websites such as Facebook, YouTube, and Twitter was also blocked intermittently throughout the whole of Iraq in 2014 and during other crises, in both Iraq and the KRG (Freedom House, 2017).

Social and political functions of broadcasting: politics and media economics

After 2003, the Iraqi media developed in a complex state and nation-building processes that continue in the present, where there are fundamental disagreements among political elites about the nature of the Iraqi state, both in terms of its identity and the distribution of power. Power-sharing and dialogue are keys to resolving Iraq's conflicts, and from a normative perspective media could make dialogue more effective; however, Iraq's media are far from fulfilling this role. Rather, the media has evolved where it is deeply polarized, especially in the aftermath of the rise of ISIS. Ethno-sectarian media were established to represent political positions and mobilize constituents, not necessarily as instruments of dialogue. However, the pluralistic media environment that emerged in the chaos of the post-war period has allowed more dialogue to occur than would otherwise. While no party seeks to break up the Iraqi nation, each party argues that it is best suited to be at the helm of power and knows what is best for Iraq. Paradoxically, while each party stresses its commitment to Iraqi unity, the ethno-sectarian media have exhibited the potential to widen the gap between Iraq's communities and weaken national belonging.

The curious life of the Al-Zawra satellite is emblematic of how Iraq's media developed and its relationship to violence. The Al-Zawra channel was owned by the family of Mish'an al-Juburi, which first emerged as an entertainment channel and a money-making enterprise, and later served as a mouthpiece for Mish'an's December 2005 parliamentary bid (Al-Marashi 2007: 113–117). With Mish'an's expulsion from the Iraqi National Assembly on charges of embezzlement, the channel's focus also changed.

When former Iraqi president Saddam Hussein's death sentence was announced in November 2006, Al-Zawra featured videos and songs supportive of the outlawed Ba'ath Party, as well as exhortations for Iraqis to join groups fighting the US "occupation forces," and the Iraqi government and its "sectarian gangs." The Iraqi government ordered the station closed down on charges of "inciting violence." The closure order came from the Iraqi Interior Ministry invoking the Anti-Terrorism Law, not from the CMC.

However, the station was able to circumvent the closure through its broadcasting from an unknown facility, either in Iraq or abroad. After the government closed its office, the channel's content focused on footage of insurgent attacks against US and Iraqi forces. The channel produced its announcements that directly incited violence by calling on Iraqis to join the "jihad" against "The U.S. and Iranian occupation." Its attacks on Iran reflected a pro-Iraqi Arab Sunni sentiment that alleged Iran was aiding its co-religionists in Iraq. Announcements on the channel denounced the "crimes of Muqtada and the gangs of Aziz al-Hakim," a reference to Muqtada al-Sadr and Abd al-Aziz al-Hakim, leader of the SCIRI group. The station called upon the "free youth of Iraq" to join the groups that are "defending" the nation to keep "Baghdad free from the Safawis," referring to the 16th- to 18th-century Safavid Empire of Iran but meant as a derogatory characterization of Iraq's Shi'a. The channel also featured footage of what it alleged were "Sunni civilians" being attacked by Shi'a militias.

Al-Zawra's news anchors, a man and a veiled woman, dressed in military uniforms and regularly read statements delivered by Iraq's insurgent groups. Most of their news footage was provided directly by groups such as the Islamic Army in Iraq, an Islamist insurgency primarily comprised of Iraqis. It also carried relatively sophisticated documentaries produced by the insurgent groups, which featured English subtitles and were directed to Western viewers. The station also carried video footage of attacks carried out by Nizar al-Juburi, who achieved notoriety in Iraq as the "Baghdad Sniper." However, though the channel often featured grisly footage of insurgent activity, it had never aired videos produced by the Al-Qaeda Organization in Iraq, the precursor to ISIS.

Mish'an al-Juburi claimed that the Al-Zawra channel broadcast in an area between Mosul and Al-Ramadi, using mobile transmission equipment. With their satellite truck, they could beam their programming to the Egyptian satellite distributor Nilesat, which then retransmitted the channel across the Middle East. The Iraqi and US governments tried to have Nilesat shut down the channel's satellite transmission over its transponders. Nilesat, bowing to pressure, had stopped transmitting new Al-Zawra broadcasts sent from the undisclosed locations in Iraq.

The case of Al-Zawra, an entertainment channel that evolved to an insurgency channel, represented a worst-case scenario for the Iraqi media, demonstrating the ineffectiveness of punitive measures, such as the closure of its Baghdad office, in the face of new transnational transmission technologies. It also foreshadowed ISIS's media strategies, which often broadcast the same message as Al-Zawra, particularly anti-Shi'a content and calling for Iraqis to rise against their government, content which it further spread due to social media technologies like YouTube, Facebook, and Twitter. The case of Al-Zawra and ISIS, or Iraqi Shi'a militias establishing their own media channels, demonstrated that while Iraq had become a literal battlefield since 2003, so too did communications become weaponized. It also demonstrated the transnational dimension of Iraq's media where both Al-Zawra and then ISIS media could inspire followers both inside and outside Iraq, and how media that emerged to counter these messages also sought to inspire Iraqis in the nation, as well as the Iraqi diaspora.

From 2003 to the present, the notion of an Iraqi nation is contested and still in flux, and its media sought to inculcate contested national identities immediately following the collapse of Saddam Hussein's government, amongst Iraqis living within the state and its large diaspora. The state-owned Al-Iraqiya channel stands for a unified country, but according to its critics, the station, reflecting its relationship with the incumbent Shi'a prime ministers, has an inherent bias. However, the station has tried to encourage dialogue by allowing more of its content to be devoted to Arab Sunni guests, who use the channel to express their grievances, if not criticize the government directly. Furthermore, the station has attempted to minimize the differences between Iraq's Sunni and Shi'a by broadcasting live coverage of Friday sermons in which religious leaders from both communities preach against the nation's sectarian divide and stress "Iraqi unity." It also holds televised meetings between Shi'a and Sunni leaders as a means of intersectarian dialogue, particularly during the conflict with ISIS.

As a public service broadcaster, Al-Iraqiya is inclined to portray the vision that there a viable state capable of governing. As a result, the channel's programming features mostly progovernment programs that stressed optimism in the fight against ISIS and progress being made in reconstruction and security. In its depictions of violence, the station's pro-government line is represented with features on the operations of the Iraqi security forces that gave viewers the impression that they were protecting the nation from ISIS. The channel featured continuous updates on battles against ISIS, showing maps of the front line, continuous interviews with military commanders, and an image of then Prime Minister Hayder Al-Abbadi superimposed on a screen while the news anchor delivered status updates on the military situation.

The channel also sought to frame state violence as legitimate by featuring public service announcements, advertisement-length pieces, in between the news programs, to rally the viewers behind the government's fight against ISIS. For example, one public service announcement on Al-Iraqiya opens with a voice that declares, "Instead of resolving their problems, they infiltrated our country filled with rancor and criminality. They sought to delude our children into believing they came to defend them." This is read along with an image of what is assumed to be a Wahhabi, depicted with a long beard, a flowing red-and-white kaffiyya over his head, and a short *thowb*. In the announcement, he is shown delivering money to Iraqi youth for what is assumed to take part in insurgent activity, an indirect way of accusing Saudi Arabia's Wahhabis of Iraq's domestic woes. Another features an image of an elderly Iraqi man lifting a heavy stone to drop it on a slithering snake, a recurring symbol of ISIS in these ads. Another announcement is animated, with a roaring lion taking on a swarm of rats, another animal-like avatar of ISIS.

Even entertainment on this channel was consumed by the fight against ISIS. Al-Dawla Al-Khirifa was a satirical program first broadcast in September 2014. Translated as the "Superstitious State," it is a play on the word "*khilafa*" or "caliphate," and depicted Abu Bakr al-Baghdadi as the love child of the devil and a Jewish woman, arranged by an inebriated CIA agent, dressed as a cowboy. The program featured former Republican Guard officers of Saddam Hussein alongside the "Caliph," suggesting that ISIS emerged as a result of a conspiracy between the US, Israel, and the Ba'athists (Al-Marashi, 2016: 95). The show has relatively high-quality production values, a legacy of the team of American advisors to the Al-Iraqiyya channel in the early years after the 2003 invasion – ironic, given that they have left Iraq with a legacy to produce programming that now critiques the US.

The state and media have used the rise of ISIS to rally the nation. However, recent protests in Iraq have demonstrated that despite a dedicated and consistent media campaign to mobilize the nation, such messages can only go so far to alleviate dissatisfaction with the Iraqi government. The channel had provided a space for Iraq's citizens to interact and communicate with politicians and the government, providing an alternative for the acts of violence that are in themselves protests against the Iraqi state. The channel featured coverage of protests that began in August 2015, criticizing corruption in the government that has led to daily difficulties, such as no electricity or AC during the brutal summer, but then sought to minimize them after then Prime Minister al-Abbadi made some cosmetic reforms after a cabinet reshuffle.

Ethno-sectarian factions, from 2003 to the crisis with ISIS, rallied support among its audiences on a platform of promising to protect each community's identity-based interests, which can be characterized as "mediated patronage." After 2003, most Iraqi Islamist parties used their media to stress unity among Iraq's communities (Price et al., 2010: 237). However, from 2004 to 2007, and particularly following the February 2006 bombing of the revered Shi'a Al-'Askariyya shrine in the city of Samarra, and then the 2014 to 2018 conflict with ISIS, when intercommunal violence between Shi'a and Sunni was at its highest, the various sectarian and ethnic factions used their media outlets to legitimize the violence and portray their respective groups as victims, encouraging both Shi'a and Sunni to defend themselves in the ensuing sectarian conflict.

Shi'a TV channels had sought to blame Sunni Muslims for targeting their communities, not Iraq's Sunni population per se, but rather foreign Arab fighters who came to Iraq who subscribe to the Wahhabi or Salafist ideologies, and those Iraqis who cooperated with them. Thus, even though the Shi'a are in power, ISIS's targeting of the Shi'a in suicide bombings and mass executions created a visual discourse that provides continuity with a past marred by "victimization" and a community "oppressed" since the Ottoman Empire and the creation of the Iraqi state in 1920. Shi'a channels have called on their co-religionists to have faith in the security forces and the militias that rose to prominence after the 2014 ISIS offensive into Mosul. On the other side, the Arab Sunni discourse focuses on a notion of "disempowerment," which also expresses a sense of victimization at the hands of first the US "occupying forces," and then the "militias" and security forces of former prime ministers Nuri al-Maliki and then al-Abbadi.

Iraq's televised state media was almost entirely devoted to news about the front line during the war with ISIS, with hourly updates on battles (Al-Marashi, 2016: 95). During the war with ISIS, parties demonstrated that they could provide security through their media, highlighting the successes of their security forces, whether it is the Shi'a militias or Kurdish Peshmerga, against ISIS. Thus, rather than seeking to promote or foster dialogue, the party and militia that owned each channel promised protection from the inimical other, whether it is ISIS or the Iraqi government itself.

Media and development

The Iraqi media since the end of the 2003 Iraq War have emerged as a space for public affairs. These channels also provide a space for covering local and national electoral campaigns and encourage voting. Issues such as government corruption, poverty, and unemployment may be taboo subjects in Middle Eastern countries with only a handful of state-owned channels; in Iraq, various media have addressed these challenges directly. The Iraqi media have taken on a public advocacy role, pressing policymakers to address deficiencies and shortcomings in providing security and infrastructure needs by highlighting these problems and giving Iraqi citizens a platform to express their views. Ethno-sectarian channels conduct public advocacy as well, but primarily on behalf of their communities. Iraq's media have also allowed citizens through various outlets, such as talk shows, call-in programs, and man-on-the-street interviews, to express their desires, complaints, and frustrations. Additionally, newsmakers and prominent members of civil society have used televised panel discussions to give their opinions about salient issues in the nation's development. Various media outlets have challenged the incumbent government for its shortcomings. Specific programs often carried out this role by highlighting the daily difficulties faced by the average Iraqi, with channels calling on the government to address their needs.

In contrast with many Arab states, with an official state channel owned by a Ministry of Information, Al-Iraqiya seemed to be moving toward a role as public service broadcaster. For example, the channel fostered a space for Iraq's citizens to interact and communicate with politicians and the government, providing an alternative for the acts of violence that are in themselves protests against the Iraqi state. Since its founding, al-Iraqiya broadcasted shows such as "The Iraqi Podium," which had a live call-in segment where viewers can direct questions about political affairs to the guests, ranging from various civil society leaders to journalists, academics, and intellectuals. The program "Open Encounter" hosted government officials and political leaders to discuss elections, military operations, and the agendas of various Iraqi political parties, with studio audience participation. Corruption, a topic rarely discussed on state channels in the Arab world, is addressed on programs such as "You and the Official." Other programs deal with local socio-economic issues: in "The People's Concerns," the viewer can phone in to express opinions on unemployment, as well as government corruption. "Al-Iraqiya with You" served as a forum for public advocacy where the hosts of the program seek to capture on film the poverty and unemployment among the Iraqis and then call upon the Iraqi government to address these social problems (Al-Marashi, 2007: 108).

While corruption can be discussed on the state-owned channel, the state has cracked down on private channels that do so. One of the alleged reasons for the CMC revocation of al-Baghdadia's license, according to its staff, is the "9 O'Clock" program which focused on government corruption (Freedom House, 2017). Additionally, some Iraqi channels feature entertainment (either locally produced or imported), particularly humor, music, and drama, to relieve the stresses of Iraq's post-war society. The satirical *Albasheer Show* on Sumaria, modeled on the US *Daily Show*, used humor and satire to mock Iraq's politicians, militias, and ISIS, which approximately 60% of Iraqis viewed regularly. Often the shaming of politicians nudged them to follow up and implement policies as a result of the show's segments. The show was broadcast from Sumaria's Amman, Jordan, facilities, but in August 2017 the CMS approached its production company informing them of broadcast "violations," including making fun of one of Iraq's clerics, and was eventually shut down (Freedom House, 2017).

Conclusion

More than a decade after the Iraq War, the nation's new newspapers, radio, and satellite TV stations have proliferated, but news and even entertainment were consumed by coverage of Iraq's conflicts: the insurgency that began in 2003, the sectarian civil war that began in 2006, and then the conflict with ISIS up to 2018. For most of Iraq's post-2003 era, the media were on a war footing, fostering a sense of a garrison society, besieged by threats posed by ISIS and other regional states, where militarism and violence pervaded the Iraqi public sphere.

While the initial plurality of Iraq's media after 2003 raised hopes for freedom of speech in Iraq, this same plurality allowed space for ethno-sectarian entrepreneurs to take the air. The rise of media controlled by Iraq's Shi'a, Sunni, and Kurdish parties has been one of the results of the collapse of the Ba'athist monopoly on the media. Pluralism also allowed Iraqi media with no political affiliation and agenda to emerge; these media are trying to provide an alternative to the ethno-sectarian media. The media independent of Iraq's political mosaic sought to provide a public space for education, entertainment, and cathartic release for the daily violence that dominates Iraqi public life. Furthermore, politicized control of Iraq's media does not neatly correspond to Iraq's society and how everyday Iraqis consume media, who often turn to non-Iraq media, both regional and international, to escape the realities of everyday life.

Media practitioners in Iraq will most likely face various forms of pressure from the authorities. Fear of reprisals, from fatal violence to criminal libel suits, will make self-censorship among journalists common. The Iraqi state faces daunting challenges in preventing assault and the harassment that media workers face in the course of their work and protecting them from retaliatory attacks for their reporting.

Despite the challenges, Iraq's media still has the capability of evolving, fostering a sense of national unity and encouraging dialogue and constructive debate among its citizens and the state, as well as among its fractured political landscape.

References and further reading

Al-Marashi, Ibrahim (2007), The Dynamics of Iraq's Media: Ethno-Sectarian Violence, Political Islam, Public Advocacy, and Globalization. *Cardozo Arts and Entertainment Law Journal*, 25(95) (Summer), pp. 96–140.

Al-Marashi, Ibrahim (2016), Les médias irakiens dans l'ombre de Daech. *Les Cahiers de l'Orient*, 121(1), pp. 91–98.

Al-Rawi, Ahmed K. (2012), *Media Practice in Iraq*. New York: Palgrave Macmillan.

Amos, Deborah (2010), *Confusion, Contradiction, and Irony: The Iraqi Media in 2010*. Discussion Paper Series D-58, Joan Shorenstein Center on the Press, Politics and Public Policy, June.

Awad, Abir, and Eaton, Tim (2013), *The Media of Iraq Ten Years On: The Problems, The Progress, The Prospects*. BBC Policy Briefing 8, March.

Boyd, Douglas A. (1982), Radio and Television in Iraq: The Electronic Media in a Transitionary Arab World Country. *Middle Eastern Studies*, 18(4) (October), pp. 400–410.

Freedom House (2017), *Iraq. Freedom of the Press*. Retrieved from https://freedomhouse.org/report/freedom-press/2017/iraq

Isakhan, Benjamin (2009), Manufacturing Consent in Iraq: Interference in the Post-Saddam Media Sector. *International Journal of Contemporary Iraqi Studies*, 3, pp. 7–25.

Price, Monroe, Al-Marashi, Ibrahim, and Stremlau, Nicole (2010), Media in Peace-building processes: Ethiopia and Iraq. In Pippa Norris (ed.), *Public Sentinel: News Media and Governance Reform*. Washington, DC: World Bank.

9

SOCIAL MEDIA AND SOCIAL CHANGE IN IRAQ

Ahmed Al-Rawi

Introduction

The Internet was only lately introduced in Iraq, since Saddam Hussein's regime did not offer it to the public until the early 2000s due to security and surveillance concerns. Even when introduced, the Internet was very limited in terms of speed and access; for instance, Yahoo and Hotmail emails were blocked, and the only open email account that could be created was via uruklink.net, the official Iraqi provider linked to the Ministry of Information (Al-Rawi, 2012: 24). There were, of course, other means to obtain emails by bypassing government censorship; the author of this chapter, for instance, created his email through a news website called myway. com, which was regarded as illegal at that time. The same applied to acquiring and using satellite TV dishes, which were also regarded as illegal. After the 2003 US-led invasion of Iraq, dial-up Internet connection remained in use, and the US administration introduced a free-of-charge service that was hard to connect to through landlines, but it still offered some limited Internet access to Iraqis. Yet the service was discontinued shortly afterward as some Iraqis complained about it being uncensored, for anyone could access pornographic sites. Later, hundreds of Internet cafés in Iraq offered Internet access for both genders and at relatively low fees (Alexander, 2005), although the cafés were dominated by men, while new rules were enacted that included blocking websites promoting sectarianism, pornography, and terrorism (Salaheddin, 2009). It is important to mention here that the situation in Iraqi Kurdistan's semi-autonomous region was different, as Internet cafés existed long before 2003. In general, the current Internet penetration in Iraq is low in comparison to other countries in the Middle East region as well as in those around the world. As of 2018, the Iraqi population's percentage of Internet users is around 47%, making the country the third lowest in the region after only Yemen (23.8%) and Syria (32.6%) (Internet World Stat, 2018a), which both witnessed some deterioration in Internet use after the civil wars that ravaged them in the previous few years (Internet World Stat, 2018b). Iraq's poor Internet service is due to several factors, including "the continuous disruption of electricity supply, the lack of stable governmental Internet services, the relatively high costs, and poor maintenance" (Al-Rawi, 2012: 70). In other frequent cases, the Iraqi Ministry of Telecommunications orders Internet shutdown from time to time, which often happens during protests, during general elections, and generally when there are high school exams, allegedly to prevent cheating, though there is no evidence on its effectiveness (Hameed, 2017).

Today, some of the top websites in Iraq include Google.com followed by YouTube, Google. iq, Facebook, Shabakaty.com (TV show provider), Yahoo, and Wikipedia, while porn websites like Xhamster.com and porn.hub (Alexa, 2019) are also among the top sites visited by Iraqis, despite all the Internet censorship and firewalls imposed by Iraqi authorities. Iraq is regarded as among the top Arab countries in Google Arabic searches for "sex," preceded only by Yemen, Sudan, Syria, Libya, Egypt, and Jordan respectively (Google Trends, 2019). This is also evident in YouTube trending searches, as will be discussed later. As a conservative country in which public relationships between the sexes are regarded as a social taboo, many Iraqis resort to watching porn whether online or through DVDs (El-Tablawy, 2010) as a means of education, entertainment, and compensation for the lack of such relationships. This is, in fact, a phenomenon that existed during Saddam Hussein's rule, as pornography was widely disseminated through VHS videos including a few that featured Iraqi women. Today, policymakers, including the Iraqi Communications and Media Commission, have clear rules on blocking porn sites (CMC, 2012: 16; Williams, 2009), while many Iraqi religious groups like Shiite militias and Sunni extremists imposed strict rules on Internet porn surfing as many incidents of abduction and even murder were documented in the country (Al Jazeera, 2007).

Social media use

In Iraq, YouTube is the top social media site not solely because of its interactive features but mostly due to its video providing service; next are listed some interesting and successful examples of channels that became popular in the country. For instance, a TV program called *Melon City Show* is the second most popular YouTube channel in Iraq with over 2 billion views and 6.6 million subscribers (Social Bakers, 2019). The show, which originally aired on Dijlah TV, uses dark comedy to criticize the political and social conditions in the country. Other popular channels include that of the Shiite singer, Bassem Al-Karbalai, that has over 1.4 billion views and 4.7 million subscribers, making it the third most viewed channel in Iraq, and that of Ameer Alabadi, a comedian whose YouTube channel has the fourth highest number of subscribers at over 3.4 million and almost 1 billion views. To qualitatively investigate what Iraqis mostly watch on YouTube, I examined the top 10 trending videos every day for one month from 11 November to 10 December 2015. I found three main patterns: (1) Shiite songs, especially by Bassem Al-Karbalai, as well as flagellation scenes, (2) sex videos, and (3) songs. For the sexy videos, they are similar to semi-porn clips which are viewed due to censoring porn sites in Iraq, mostly featuring Indian and Arab actors.

As for Facebook, it is the second top social media site in Iraq. By using Facebook ads manager and specifying Iraq, we can see that there are currently 17 million Facebook users whose ages range between 13 and 65+ years old. In this regard, 12 million are male users in comparison to 4.5 million females, while the remaining ones are not identified. Amongst the overall users, 4.4 million are interested in newspapers. 1.2 million in dating, 6.8 million in religion, and 4.6 million in politics. By examining the most popular Facebook pages and without taking into account the religious-political channels like Karbala TV Facebook page, we can find that religious social media sites are very popular in Iraq, especially Shiite ones. For example, Ammar Al-Hakim's Facebook page is ranked number two with over 4.5 million likes. Al-Hakim was previously the head of the Iraqi Supreme Council of Iraq and remains politically active as a Shiite religious leader. Another Shiite celebrity is the singer Bassem Al-Karbalai, whose Facebook page is ranked 19 in the country with over 2.9 million likes. Other pages include Sheikh Ahmad Kaka Mahmood (2.5 million likes), Hanan Al-Fatlawi (2.2 million likes) – an outspoken and often divisive Shiite female politician, Al-Shiaa (1.4 million likes), and Abdul Hameed Almuhajir (1.2 million likes) (Social Bakers, 2019). Some promising examples of social media use in Iraq include the popular Facebook page "Iraqi Anchorwomen," which has over 1.1 million likes and is ranked 76 in the country, according to Social Bakers (2019). The page is allegedly run by Iraqi female journalists, although it is difficult to determine the identity of those who manage the page despite the author's personal efforts to get more information from them. This page is unique in several aspects, including the overall critical remarks towards certain cultural and political practices in Iraq and more importantly the frequent publications of leaked government documents that reveal state corruption and malpractices. I argue here that this Facebook page functions as an alternative media space for Iraqi women journalists to speak, cover important events, provide exclusive reports and breaking news items, and potentially bridge sectarian divisions. Another Facebook page belongs to a female Iraqi journalist called Sahar Abbas Jameel (ranked 80 with over one million likes) whose popular TV show *It's Your Decree* on Dijlah channel attempts to disclose issues of public interest through one-to-one interviews with Iraqi politicians. Also, *Albasheer Show* is another successful example of a social media project that started on YouTube as a satirical program, imitating the Egyptian comedian Bassem Youssef. Despite its limitation in criticizing some Shiite figures like the Ayatollahs in Najaf and Karbala as well as Muqtada Sadr, it garnered the Iraqi public's attention as well as the Arab one, for the state-run German channel, DW Arabic, lately began producing the weekly show in Amman, Jordan (ranked 23 with 2.6 million likes). The show attempts to provide criticism on diverse issues in Iraq like terrorism, corruption, and sectarian policies by making fun of the political process, corruption, and politicians. On YouTube, it has the sixth-highest number of views in Iraq at 344 million and the fifth-highest number of subscribers at over 2.6 million users.

Regarding Twitter, it is not as popular in Iraq as it is Saudi Arabia and a few other Arab countries. The top Iraqi Twitter accounts mostly include celebrities like Kadhim Al-Sahir, a famous singer with 6.9 million followers and ranked number one, and Younis Mahmoud, a footballer, with 2.6 million followers and ranked number three, while Iraqi politicians and TV channels come later. Some of the Iraqi Twitterati politicians include Hanan Al-Fatlawi with over 1.1 million followers and ranked 8 and the former prime minister, Haider Al-Abadi, with over one million followers and ranked 9 (Social Bakers, 2019).

Finally, and in terms of the top mobile apps in Iraq, Facebook messenger and WhatsApp come first followed by a video game app, Instagram, Viber, and other mobile games. Indeed, mobile social media apps, especially those that offer free phone calls, are highly popular in Iraq. They include TikTok (no. 9), Telegram (no. 13), Facebook (no. 14), Facebook Lite (no. 28), and IMO (no. 30) (SimilarWeb, 2019), for they do not only save money for local calls, but they are also used to connect with the Iraqi diaspora that is estimated to be in the several millions, due to the ongoing conflicts in the country since the 1980s.

Iraqi Media Laws

In terms of media freedom, Iraq is ranked as one of the least free countries in the world. According to the 2019 World Press Freedom Index, it is ranked as 156 out of 180 countries (Reporters Without Borders, 2019). Freedom House, for instance, ranks Iraq at number 32 out of 100 (most free is 100) based on three criteria: freedom ratings 5.5/7, political rights 5/7, and civil liberties 6/7 (1 being most free) (Freedom House, 2019a). One of the problems Iraq faces is that many laws that are still applied in the country are archaic and often rely on the 1969 Iraqi Penal Code (Najjar, 2009), which makes it challenging to apply it to issues related to social media use. At the moment, Iraqi media is governed by Communications and Media Commission (CMC) rules. According to Article 103 of the 2005 Iraqi constitution, CMC is regarded as a "financially and administratively independent" body that was established by the Coalition Provisional Authority (CPA) after the US invasion of the country in 2003. Yet CMC unfortunately remains a tool used by the different Iraqi governments and prime ministers to further their agenda and support their rule (Al-Rawi, 2018). During the US occupation of Iraq, the CPA published many media laws that would theoretically and on paper safeguard media activities and ensure its independence (Coalition Provisional Authority, 2004), though this was far away from reality since the US administration, including the Pentagon, pressured, bribed, and often punished Iraqi media outlets that criticized the Coalition (The Bureau of Investigative Journalism, 2016). For instance, Order No. 14 issued on 10 June 2003 by the CPA, entitled "Prohibited Media Activity," stated that media organizations are prohibited from publishing or broadcasting content which:

a   incites violence against any individual or group, including racial, ethnic or religious groups and women;
b   incites civil disorder, rioting or damage to property;
c   incites violence against Coalition Forces or CPA personnel;
d   advocates alterations to Iraq's borders by violent means;
e   advocates the return to power of the Iraqi Ba'ath Party or makes statements that purport to be on behalf of the Iraqi Ba'ath Party (Coalition Provisional Authority, 2003).

Since the language remained vague, especially regarding what is interpreted as incitement, it gave US and later Iraqi authorities wide jurisdiction and flexibility in arresting journalists, filing libel suits, and closing media outlets (Kim and Hama-Saeed, 2008). After Iraq gained its independence from the US and inked the 2005 constitution, most of the older regulations remained effective. Once again, the laws ensured several types of freedom like assembly, the press, and movement, but this was mostly on paper. For instance, the following articles are relevant here:

> Article 38: The State shall guarantee in a way that does not violate public order and morality: A. Freedom of expression using all means. B. Freedom of press, printing, advertisement, media, and publication. C. Freedom of assembly and peaceful demonstration, and this shall be regulated by law.
> Article 39: First: The freedom to form and join associations and political parties shall be guaranteed, and this shall be regulated by law. Second: It is not permissible to force any person to join any party, society, or political entity, or force him to continue his membership in it.
> Article 40: The freedom of communication and correspondence, postal, telegraphic, electronic, and telephonic, shall be guaranteed and may not be monitored, wiretapped, or disclosed except for legal and security necessity and by a judicial decision.
>
> *(Iraqi Constitution, 2005)*

Due to the periodic absence of the rule of law in Iraq and the widespread corruption, tribal laws often apply as well, which further limits freedom of expression. Ali Yasser, a young Iraqi man, for example, once liked a Facebook post written by his friend in which he criticized a local politician and accused him of corruption. After a day, he encountered a group of men who were related to the local politician's tribe, demanding a financial settlement to solve the issue. Yasser ended up paying around $4,200 to the politician's tribe to avoid further trouble (Woodruff and

Stein, 2017). Numerous other cases are meant to silence people and prevent them from talking about corruption or state malpractices.

Politics, culture, and social media

Though it is still under-researched, the Arab Spring events influenced Iraqis in different ways, for many citizens began actively voicing their dissatisfaction with the Iraqi government's performance and corruption, leading up to the popular protests that started in February 2011. The former Shiite prime minister of Iraq, Nouri Al Maliki, used violence, intimidation, and libel suits to silence dissent, often accusing his opponents of being terrorists or sympathetic towards terrorism (O'Driscoll, 2017). It is the same technique used to counter legitimate political activism in other parts of the Arab world, as in the case of Bahrain, whose Sunni monarchy often accuses Shiite protesters of being extremists supported by Iran (Friedman, 2012), or Syria's Assad's regime that regards oppositional Sunni groups as terrorists to justify the deadly attacks against civilians and insurgents which ultimately create fear among civilians (Pearlman, 2016). Aided by his own media channels and supported by CMC, Al Maliki continued his general control over media coverage to attack his enemies and any criticism against his regime, which was also manifested in the way he violently reacted against the peaceful protests in Sunni provinces in 2014 which aided in the rise of ISIS (Al-Marashi, 2018). Often, Al Maliki would block Internet access during the crackdown on protesters, which made the latter resort to mobile apps like Firechat that do not require an Internet connection to connect (BBC News, 2014). Currently, many social media outlets are also employed by political and state actors to serve their agenda. Political trolls, for instance, are secretly hired by Iraqi officials, foreign embassies, and religious parties to silence opposition and dissent with the use of systematic and organized efforts, often involving mean-spirited comments, insults, and curses on social media by hired agents (Al-Rawi, 2019; Alaraby, 2017).

During election times, these online activities are greatly enhanced, sometimes evoking polarized (inter-)sectarian discourses to attract attention and win more votes. Hanan Al-Fatlawi, cited earlier, is known to employ such populist and divisive language, while Nouri Al Maliki often used polarizing discourses during the different Iraqi general elections to secure more support. He used slogans like "No man but [Imam] Ali, and no ruler but Al Maliki" as well as "Vote for the age's chosen one (Mukhtar)," about the historical figure of Al Mukhtar Al Thaqafi who fought those who killed Imam Hussein over a thousand years ago. The intended message behind these slogans is to invoke extremely old Shiite–Sunni divisions, presenting Al Maliki as a populist savior whose election can guide Shiites towards peace, protection, and prosperity, which also reveals Al Maliki's "Shiite supremacist" ideology (Arango, 2016).

Al Maliki's Internet policies continued even after Adel Abdul Mahdi, the following prime minister, came to power, for social media venues often are blocked by the government if there are popular protests. For example, when peaceful protests erupted in Basra, a Shiite-majority city in southern Iraq, in mid-July 2018, the Internet was blocked. The protests, which led to the death of several people, were meant to raise awareness about the high rates of unemployment in the country and state corruption (Goran, 2018; Netblocks, 2018; Freedom House, 2019b).

The other compelling issue is the Iraqi state's online surveillance efforts. On 15 September 2014, WikiLeaks released a series of Spyfiles, which is a trove of hacked documents and emails from the German FinFisher (formerly known as Gamma Group International) and the Italian Hacking Team (https://wikileaks.org/spyfiles/). The examination of these files shows that almost all Arab states, except for a few like Yemen, have purchased services from these hacking companies. For instance, the Iraqi counter-terrorism unit (www.ctsiraq.com) as well as the ministries of Defense and Interior and the Iraqi Intelligence Agency were seeking the information as well as the service from the Hacking Team, especially in relation to the Remote Control System (RCS) Galileo tool, which provides a backdoor to monitor the computer desktop, phone, and work computer. The Hacking Team video tutorial for RCS Galileo is freely available on YouTube and is used for promotional purposes.

On its website (www.hackingteam.com), the company states the following in relation to this tool: "Our historical solution, Remote Control System, is used by 50+ major governmental institutions for critical investigations, in more than 35 countries." In Iraq, an intermediary called Al-Qiffaf scientific company contacted the Hacking Team on behalf of the Iraqi government and asked for methods to hack Iraqi citizens. In the email sent to the Hacking Team by the Iraqi Al-Qiffaf company on 24 December 2014, the following is mentioned:

> our VIP customer in government sector asking [for] training for [sic] 10 people for how to be government hacker and the training most be including 1) Wifi hackers, 2) Network hackers, 3) Mobile hackers, 4) Mobile apps. Like (Viber, whatsup [sic], tango and other apps.) hackers, 5) Email hackers, 6) Website hackers, 7) Facebook, Twitter, Instagram [sic] hackers.
>
> *(WikiLeaks, 2015a)*

Another Iraqi intermediary company called Al Seraj and Al Safa Co. Ltd. mentioned the following in an email dated back in 2014 regarding their connection to the Iraqi government:

> We have good relationships with the IRAQ Government Institutes and Ministries. This relation concern to provide [sic] them the last version of security solutions (Hardware & Software) addition to that given training in mother companies [sic]. In this days [sic] we have project with them about Remote Monitoring and Deployment Solutions. that the help governmental [sic] customers to Track suspects monitor their online and offline activities realize other specific requirements [sic].
>
> *(WikiLeaks, 2014)*

A third company called Sedam IT, which partnered with INGRA – a Croatian construction company, contacted the Hacking Team on behalf of the Iraqi National Intelligence Service (INIS) as the latter requested the following:

> Specialized equipment and systems in the field of penetration of computers and networks, wired and wireless is a physicist and through the deployment of spy programs to monitor targets and remote computers and mobile and collect and extract sensitive information and analysis. Specialized devices breaking the password without change and hacking e-mail and monitor social networking sites of target.
>
> *(WikiLeaks, 2015b)*

As can be seen, Iraqi security agencies have been trying to secure spying devices to monitor people in Iraq, and there is little to no oversight or transparency regarding such activities. Online privacy is not a pressing or concerning issue in Iraq because the main preoccupation is fighting terrorism and maintaining security.

The second major and ongoing issue that Iraq faces is (cyber) terrorism and sectarianism. After the 2003 US invasion of the country, Al-Qaeda as well as other terrorist Sunni groups infiltrated the country and created havoc in it, often attacking Shiite mosques and considering anyone who opposes them as an infidel. As a result, Iraq had to control access to online violent content and its dissemination, which was extremely difficult to manage. Sectarian tension was enhanced with the Sunni terrorist groups' frequent attacks on Shiite targets, including innocent civilians, yet many Shiite militias involved in numerous killings were overlooked, especially in state-sponsored TV programs like *Terrorism in the Grip of Justice* (Al-Rawi, 2012: 75–76). With the emergence of ISIS, sectarianism worsened, especially due to the slaughter of thousands of Shiites in the different cities that the terrorist group controlled, and this sectarian tension was also manifested on social media and online forums; during that time, many Shiite figures fighting ISIS were regarded as heroes even if they were involved in the murder of innocent Sunni civilians (Fisk, 2016). Videos of atrocities from both sides are often shared on social media, serving as a warning that more violence might come and a reminder of the fragile sectarian relationships. Here, social media transformed the conflict into a mediated one (Al-Rawi and Jiwani, 2017) because some viewers who are not involved in the actual fight were actively engaged in inflaming and spreading hate against the opposite sect.

To further understand state favoritism and biased policies regarding social media use, it is important to refer to the recent case of Aloosh Jirmanah, an Iraqi Shiite man who owns a café in Najaf city. During the annual commemoration of Imam Musa Al Kadhim in 2019, Jirmanah posted a live video on Facebook saying that he does not participate in this celebration and prefers instead to listen to secular songs. He sarcastically added that Al Khadim died a long time ago, and he is not related to him, so he is not interested in the Shiite popular event. Yet, this was regarded by many politicians and religious clerics as a major insult against the Shiite doctrine and Imam Al Kadhim, and Jirmanah was momentarily detained by Iraqi security forces and charged with being a member of ISIS (NRTTV, 2019; BBC Trending, 2019). This was done although Jirmanah himself was a member of the Shiite Popular Mobilization Forces that were sent to different parts of Iraq and Syria to fight ISIS (Masr Alarabia, 2019), and he did not curse or insult the Shiite figure. In contrast, another Shiite man called Thaer Al Daraji, who has some connections to Iraqi militias and politicians, has been active on different social media outlets like YouTube, Instagram, Facebook, and Twitter in publicly cursing and insulting Sunni figures, and considering all Sunnis terrorists who should be collectively and continuously punished. Al Daraji would often go to Sunni neighborhoods in Baghdad and film himself cursing and insulting famous religious Sunni figures and posting the videos online. Al Daraji has never been detained though there has been an arrest warrant against him, and he remains active on social media (Al Sumeria, 2013). He has even been featured and interviewed in a BBC documentary about hate speech and the spread of sectarianism in the Arab world (BBC, 2014).

Finally, the issue of gender is important to be highlighted here. Similar to the majority of Arab countries, Iraq is a highly patriarchal society, and women are expected to take marginal leading roles in society. This gap can be observed in the online sphere as women remain less visible than men, which is partly observed in the large difference in the number of Facebook male and female users in Iraq, as stated earlier. This does not mean, however, that Iraqi women are not taking active roles in social media, for the few examples provided earlier show another promising insight on women's roles in Iraqi society. In my study on women and social media use in the Arab world (Al-Rawi, 2020), I provide many accounts on the way some human rights NGOs are employing social media to raise awareness about social injustice and equality between men and women. For instance, Thuraya Rufaat, the manager of Iraqi Women's Rights NGO, mentions the following regarding her organization's social media use:

> It has served the NGO a great deal especially that it is based outside Iraq. Social networking sites helped in conveying the views and ideas of IWR. They also assist many

women to connect with us and communicate their suffering as many of them are subjected to great amounts of violence; some of whom cannot leave their homes and use traditional telecommunication means [e.g., phone calls] to report their sufferings.

Rufaat also refers to the kind of social media interactions, stating that some men attack the NGO's mission and ideas, accusing it of "corrupting the girls' minds and agitating them to rebel," though some women also attack the NGO for the same reasons. Rufaat considers these women "victims of the patriarchal nature of the society because they are resisting those who want to free them from masculine chains" (Email Communication, 2017). Another popular feminist Facebook page is called "Iraqi Liberal Women," which is an online community carrying the motto of "Yes for freedom to women." The Facebook page organizer, who often cites well known liberal Arab thinkers like Nawal El Saadawy, Ali Al-Wardi, and Nazar Qabani, frequently attacks sexual harassment, underage marriage, religious hypocrisy, domestic violence, and women wearing the niqab. There are also many screenshots from fiery messages sent by Iraqi men who oppose the idea of the "Iraqi Liberal Women" community that are often posted on the Facebook page to shame them as well as discredit their claims. These messages provide insight into the way some Iraqis, mostly men, misunderstand the concepts of "liberal thought" and "freedom of ideas" in connection to women, since they often clash with traditional cultural views on the role of women in conservative societies (Al-Rawi, 2020). Unfortunately, this confusion, lack of education, ignorance, and patriarchy can often lead to violence. For example, Tara Fares, a famous female Instagram influencer who had over 2.7 million followers, was shot dead on 27 September 2018 in Iraq after receiving death threats to leave the country. Her lifestyle was regarded as obscene in conservative Iraqi standards but very normal in the Western world (Specia, 2018). Fares used social media to freely express herself and benefit from its affordances, yet it was used against her by conservative male extremists whose authority and power are threatened by mere Instagram posts. The other social media challenge is surveillance, which can endanger the lives of Iraqi women as well as homosexuals (Daly, 2019) whose online activities are often monitored and tracked. Finally, it is important to note here that the lives of Iraqi women who reside in Kurdistan, which is relatively safer and more stable than the rest of the country, have different concerns than Sunni women living in internally displaced camps in Western Iraq or Shiite women living amid the lack of public services in the south of the country. In other words, Iraqi women's experiences are extremely varied, and I cannot claim to present an overall assessment of their lived experiences.

In a more recent positive development, the largest anti-sectarian and most intense popular protests occurred in Iraq in late September 2019 and are still ongoing at the time of writing this chapter in December of the same year. Also called the TukTuk Revolution because of the use of rickshaws to carry the wounded, the pro-democracy rallies, demonstrations, and sit-ins led to the death of over 480 people and hundreds more injured. These protests spread all over the center and south, mostly led by students who asked for an end to state corruption, foreign intervention especially by Iran, and lack of public services and employment opportunities. Though the Iraqi government blocked Internet access once more for a long period to prevent any dissenting voices, the protesters found alternative methods of conveying their messages to each other and the outside world. For example, they use virtual private networks (VPNs) which also helps in avoiding state surveillance, private Internet cafés, and international mobile SIM cards to make use of their Internet roaming service. Also, other social media outlets became important, such as Telegram, WhatsApp groups, and Instagram, allowing more dissemination of information and more engaged people, especially women. In general, the protesters demanded the resignation of the whole government, and after several causalities and national as well as international pressure, the Iraqi prime minister, Adil Abdul Mahdi, resigned. Despite state-sponsored violence, intimidation, numerous arrests, and targeted assassinations against human rights activists conducted by Shiite militias allied to the Iraqi state, the protesters continued their demonstrations and sit-ins, often calling for canceling classes at all Iraqi universities and schools. I argue here that the widespread violence that happened in Iraq is one form of state terrorism. In this regard and according to the conceptual state terror models discussed by Gus Martin (2017), the assistance model fully applies to the events surrounding the Iraqi protests, for this model involves implicit state participation in terrorist behavior such as ordering security forces to directly fire live ammunition and tear gas at protesters, asking for foreign and domestic participation and indirect support, and arming and training of extremist proxies like the armed militias as well as providing them with sanctuary and protection (Martin, 2017: 75–77).

Conclusion

To sum up, Internet penetration in Iraq remains low in comparison to other countries in the Middle East and around the world, while social media has been playing important roles in raising awareness about political and social injustices, especially during and after the Arab Spring events, and several issues like women's empowerment and freedom. Despite government surveillance and social media restrictions imposed by powerful political and religious leaders, Iraqis can still use social media as alternative media outlets for political expressions, though political polarization and self-censorship are often widely practiced. The popular YouTube channels and Facebook pages in Iraq provide insight into the types of shows that are appealing for Iraqi audiences, most of which are comedies. However, a few Iraqi politicians have a large numbers of followers on Facebook and Twitter, and they sometimes disseminate controversial messages that have the potential of igniting (inter-)sectarian sentiments. In other words, the Internet has been weaponized by political figures and religious parties to promote their policies and agenda, which can ultimately enhance societal divisions. Due to the constant lack of security and the threats of terrorism, Iraqi security agencies have been trying to monitor dissent and any Iraqi citizens they deem suspicious, without any transparency or regard to online privacy. The online ecosystem in Iraq is constantly and swiftly evolving, which offers cautious optimism because it can provide more opportunities for expression and online community building, yet it can also be exploited by malicious actors to spy on, undermine, attack, or discredit their opponents.

References

Al Jazeera (2007), *Vigilantes Target Iraq Porn Surfers*, 29 June. Retrieved from www.aljazeera.com/news/middleeast/2007/06/2008525183917746213.html. Accessed 17 April 2019.

Al-Marashi, I. (2018), Iraq and the Arab Spring: From Protests to the Rise of ISIS. In Mark Haas (ed.), *The Arab Spring: The Hope and Reality of the Uprisings*. London: Routledge, pp. 147–164.

Al-Rawi, Ahmed (2012), *Media Practice in Iraq*. London: Palgrave Macmillan.

Al-Rawi, Ahmed (2018), Social Media & the 2014 Hostilities in Iraq. In Juliet Dee (ed.), *From Tahrir Square to Ferguson: Social Networks as Facilitators of Social Movements*. New York: Peter Lang, pp. 39–58.

Al-Rawi, Ahmed (2019), The Gulf Information War | Cyberconflict, Online Political Jamming, and Hacking in the Gulf Cooperation Council. *International Journal of Communication*, 13, pp. 1301–1322.

Al-Rawi, Ahmed (2020), *Women's Activism and New Media in the Arab World*. New York: State University of New York Press.

Al-Rawi, Ahmed, and Jiwani, Yasmin (2017), Mediated Conflict: Shiite Heroes Combating ISIS in Iraq and Syria. *Communication, Culture & Critique*, 10(4), pp. 675–695.

Al Sumeria (2013), *Abu Risha Reveals that Al Daraji Fled to Turkey with "State Facilitation,"* 22 October. Retrieved from www.alsumaria.tv/news/84746. Accessed 18 April 2019.

Alaraby (2017), *Iraqi Cyber Army: A Tool for Embassies and Religious Clerics,* 12 July. Retrieved from https://bit.ly/3giOagY. Accessed 19 April 2019.

Alexa The Web Information Company (2019), *Top Sites in Iraq.* Retrieved from www.alexa.com/topsites/countries/IQ. Accessed 18 April 2019.

Alexander, A. (2005), Website Review: Iraqi Websites. *Global Media and Communication,* 1(2), pp. 226–230.

Arango, Tim (2016), Days of Chaos in Baghdad: Protest or Meltdown? *The New York Times,* 2 May. Retrieved from www.nytimes.com/2016/05/03/world/middleeast/baghdad-iraq-green-zone-pro tests.html?_r=0. Accessed 19 April 2019.

BBC (2014), *The Hate Airwaves: Channels of Sectarian Incitement,* 19 March. Retrieved from www.bbc.com/arabic/tvandradio/2014/03/140319_close_up_broadcasting_hate. Accessed 19 April 2019.

BBC News (2014), *Iraqis Use Firechat Messaging App to Overcome Net Block,* 24 June. Retrieved from www.bbc.com/news/technology-27994309. Accessed 17 April 2019.

BBC Trending (2019), *Solidarity in Iraq with Aloosh Jirmanah after being Arrested for Insulting Imam Musa Al Kadhim,* 9 April. Retrieved from www.youtube.com/watch?v=TThoCflVO3k. Accessed 18 April 2019.

CMC (2012), *ISP Internet Licenses Regulations in the Republic of Iraq.* Retrieved from www.cmc.iq/ar-iq/wp-content/uploads/2017/12/ISP.pdf. Accessed 29 September 2019.

Coalition Provisional Authority (2003), *Prohibited Media Activity.* CPA/ORD/10 June 2003/14.

Coalition Provisional Authority (2004), *Transition of Laws, Regulations, Orders, and Directives Issued by the Coalition Provisional Authority.* CPA/ORD/28 June 2004/100.

Daly, Michael (2019), Murdered for "Looking Gay": How LGBT Iraqis are Fighting for their Lives. *The Daily Beast,* 7 June. Retrieved from www.thedailybeast.com/murdered-for-looking-gay-how-lgbt-iraqis-are-fighting-for-their-lives?ref=scroll. Accessed 19 April 2019.

El-Tablawy, Tarek (2010), In Porn, a Story of Iraq's Politics. *The Seattle Times,* 23 August. Retrieved from www.seattletimes.com/nation-world/in-porn-a-story-of-raqs-politics/. Accessed 18 April 2019.

Email communication (2017), Personal Correspondence with Thuraya Rufaat on 27 May and 10 June.

Fisk, Robert (2016), Iraq's Hangmen are Back and this Time they're Becoming More Efficient. *The Independent,* 25 August. Retrieved from www.independent.co.uk/voices/iraq-sunni-shia-nasiriyah-prison-hangman-excutions-back-and-they-re-becoming-more-efficient-a7208816.html. Accessed 18 April 2019.

Freedom House (2019a), *Freedom in the World 2019- Iraq.* Retrieved from https://freedomhouse.org/report/freedom-world/2019/iraq. Accessed 18 April 2019.

Freedom House (2019b), *Iraq.* Retrieved from https://freedomhouse.org/report/freedom-world/2019/iraq. Accessed 17 April 2019.

Friedman, B. (2012), Battle for Bahrain: What one Uprising Meant for the Gulf States and Iran. *World Affairs,* pp. 74–84.

Google Trends (2019), Retrieved from https://trends.google.com/trends/yis/2019/. Accessed 15 April 2019.

Goran, Baxtiyar (2018), Official: Iraq Ends Weeks-long Social Media Ban. *Kurdistan24,* 25 July. Retrieved from www.kurdistan24.net/en/news/a4ad1e05-d53a-426d-b6a2-78564bf45abf. Accessed 17 April 2019.

Hameed, Muhannad (2017), *Despite Everything, Iraq is still Shutting Down the Internet for School Exams in 2017,* 25 September. Retrieved from www.accessnow.org/despite-everything-iraq-still-shutting-Inter net-school-exams-2017/. Accessed 17 April 2019.

Internet World Stat (2018a), *Middle East.* Retrieved from www.Internetworldstats.com/stats5.htm#me. Accessed 16 April 2019.

Internet World Stat (2018b), *Iraq.* Retrieved from www.Internetworldstats.com/me/iq.htm. Accessed 16 April 2019.

Iraqi Constitution (2005), Retrieved from https://www.refworld.org/pdfid/454f50804.pdf. Accessed 8 August 2020.

Kim, H. S., and Hama-Saeed, M. (2008), Emerging Media in Peril: Iraqi Journalism in the Post-Saddam Hussein Era. *Journalism Studies,* 9(4), pp. 578–594.

Martin, G. (2017), *Understanding Terrorism: Challenges, Perspectives, and Issues.* Thousand Oaks, CA: Sage.

Masr Alarabia (2019), *Aloosh Jirmanah: The Café Owner who Erupted Iraq,* 9 April. Retrieved from www.masralarabia.com/العرب-1502254/والعالم-علوش-أشعل-العراق-الذي-المقهى-صاحب-جرمانة. Accessed 18 April 2019.

Najjar, O. A. (2009), The Pathology of Media Intervention in Iraq 20032008: The US Attempt to Restructure Iraqi Media Law and Content. *International Journal of Contemporary Iraqi Studies*, 3(1), pp. 27–52.

Netblocks (2018), *Study Shows the Extent of Iraq Internet Shutdown and Social Media Restrictions during Protests*, 15 July. Retrieved from https://netblocks.org/reports/study-shows-extent-of-iraq-Internet-shutdown-and-social-media-restrictions-during-protests-zPyXjzAE

NRTTV (2019), *NRT Publishes Exclusive New Details about Aloosh Jirmanahs Case and his Companion*, 10 April. Retrieved from www.nrttv.com/AR/News.aspx?id=11422&MapID=2. Accessed 18 April 2019.

O'Driscoll, D. (2017), Autonomy Impaired: Centralization, Authoritarianism, and the Failing Iraqi State. *Ethnopolitics*, 16(4), pp. 315–332.

Pearlman, W. (2016), Narratives of Fear in Syria. *Perspectives on Politics*, 14(1), pp. 21–37.

Reporters Without Borders (2019), *World Press Freedom Index*. Retrieved from https://rsf.org/en/ranking_table. Accessed 19 April 2019.

Salaheddin, Sinan (2009), Iraq to Impose Controls on Internet Content, Sparking Freedom of Speech Debate. *AP*, 4 August.

SimilarWeb (2019), *Iraq*. Retrieved from https://www.similarweb.com/.

Specia, Megan (2018), A Social Media Star is Shot Dead in Baghdad: Iraqis Fear a Trend. *The New York Times*, 29 September. Retrieved from www.nytimes.com/2018/09/29/world/middleeast/tara-fares-iraq-model-death.html. Accessed 14 April 2019.

The Bureau of Investigative Journalism (2016), *Fake News and False Flags*, 2 October. Retrieved from www.thebureauinvestigates.com/stories/2016-10-02/fake-news-and-false-flags-how-the-pentagon-paid-a-british-pr-firm-500m-for-top-secret-iraq-propaganda. Accessed 19 April 2019.

WikiLeaks (2014), *RE: RE: Remote Monitoring and Deployment Solutions*. Retrieved from https://wikileaks.org/hackingteam/emails/emailid/12832. Accessed 17 April 2019.

WikiLeaks (2015a), *R: Hackers Training*, 8 July. Retrieved from https://wikileaks.org/hackingteam/emails/emailid/12534. Accessed 17 April 2019.

WikiLeaks (2015b), *Hacking Team*. Retrieved from https://wikileaks.org/hackingteam/emails/. Accessed 17 April 2019.

Williams, T. (2009), Iraq Censorship Laws Move Ahead. *The New York Times,* 3 August. Retrieved from www.nytimes.com/2009/08/04/world/middleeast/04censor.html. Accessed 29 September 2019.

Woodruff, Betsy, and Stein, Sam (2017), Iraqi Tribes Go to War With Facebook Trolls. *The Daily Beast*, 27 July. Retrieved from www.thedailybeast.com/iraqi-tribes-go-to-war-with-facebook-trolls. Accessed 18 April 2019.

Jordan

10

THE PRINT AND ONLINE MEDIA IN JORDAN – BETWEEN LIBERALIZATION AND CONTROL

Ebtihal Mahadeen

Introduction

The Jordanian mediascape is characterized by cycles of liberalization and control in response to local and regional political dynamics. Over the last two decades, technological advances such as the advent of the Internet, improvements in communication infrastructures, high Internet connectivity rates, and the rise of new media have altered this landscape in Jordan as they have elsewhere. Furthermore, events such as the Arab Spring protests as well as International Monetary Fund conditions and austerity measures have created opportunities for expansion in media freedoms and, in turn, strong responses from the regime and regulatory bodies to control and moderate such freedoms.

The regulatory and legal framework that governs the media in Jordan is characterized by a clear tension between the Jordanian constitution and the various sets of laws that affect the media in the country. On the one hand, the Jordanian constitution of 1952 (amended in 2011) recognizes freedom of expression and the press within the limits of the law and maintains that laws must abide by the essence of the rights protected within it. For instance, the Jordanian constitution states, "the State shall guarantee freedom of opinion, and every Jordanian shall freely express his opinion by speech, writing, photography and the other means of expression, provided that he does not go beyond the limits of the law" (1952) and "the State shall guarantee the freedom of the press, printing, publication and information media within the limits of the law" (1952). The constitution also maintains in Article 128.1, "the laws issued in accordance with this Constitution for the regulation of rights and freedoms may not influence the essence of such rights or affect their fundamentals" (1952). On the other hand, as will be evident in this chapter, a host of laws not only chip away at freedom of expression and freedom of the press but also blatantly contradict constitutional provisions and the essence of the rights protected by the constitution.

This chapter provides an overview of the current state of play in the Jordanian print and online mediascape, focusing on four main areas: the history and political economy of print and online media, the regulatory environment and legal frameworks that govern these outlets, the political economy of these media, censorship, and soft containment, and finally, the potential of these media for social and political change.

A brief history of Jordanian print and online media

The bulk of the available scholarship on Jordanian media has focused on media freedoms (Jones, 2002; Tweisi, Suleiman et al., 2015) and the political economy of the Jordanian mediascape (Najjar, 1998; Sakr, 2002; Rugh, 2004; Najjar, 2008). In both sets of work, scholars agree that local and regional politics play a pivotal role in creating moments of openness (read increased freedoms, media diversification, and liberalization, freezing of restrictive regulatory and legal provisions) and constriction (crackdowns on freedom of expression and freedom of the press, activation of restrictive regulatory and legal provisions and the introduction of new ones, and punitive approaches to the media more generally). Yet this dynamic must not be taken to mean that the liberalization/control cycle is merely responsive to political events. As Robinson argues, the Jordanian regime regularly engages in what he terms "defensive democratization," that is, "a series of pre-emptive measures designed to maintain elite privilege in Jordan while limiting the appeal of more fundamental political change" (Robinson, 1998: 387). A key arena for defensive democratization has been and continues to be the media. The press and publications law has traditionally been a key tool with which the Jordanian regime has responded to ongoing or anticipated political crises, yet in recent years other laws have also been modified or introduced that affect the media with the direct remit of the press and publications law.

The recent history of Jordanian media can be charted along four main stages: (1) pre-1989, an era of total state control over the media, (2) 1989–1995, when Jordanian media witnessed relative openness due to broader political liberalization, (3) 1995–2010, a time of great technological advancement and the introduction of the Internet in Jordan, and finally (4) 2011–2017, characterized by the Arab Spring protests and their aftermath for the media landscape in the county.

In the pre-1989 era, the Jordanian state maintained a state of martial law for 22 years (1967–1989) and parliamentary life was frozen, large public gatherings were banned, and freedom of speech was heavily restricted. The state also maintained total control over the media: authorities could close newspapers at any time and had financial hegemony over the media, controlling major media outlets in the country. The press and publications law empowered the government to close newspapers without providing a reason for doing so and did not offer a right of appeal. Furthermore, the role of the General Intelligence Department (*Mukhabarat*) was entrenched in Jordanian media through its involvement in vetting potential members of the Jordan Press Association, which acted as a gatekeeper to the profession by licensing journalists and media professionals. The grip of the state was clenched tight on Jordanian media, as Jones notes, "the high degree of government ownership was matched by an authoritarian tradition of punitive legislation and direct regime oversight" (Jones, 2002: 176).

From 1989 to 1995, the country witnessed a wave of political liberalization accompanied by media diversification and openness. Beginning with the restoration of parliamentary life and the lifting of restrictions on the formation of political parties, this moment of democratization and liberalization reflected positively on the Jordanian mediascape. Sakr traces the flourishing of Jordanian media under the 1993 press and publications law: the government reduced its stake in newspapers and numerous new papers emerged, including many tabloid and opposition papers, and the government's power to close any media institution at will was withdrawn. However, it is recognized that this law was still "illiberal" (Sakr, 2002: 110) and "schizoid" (Jones, 2002: 180) primarily for its (further) entrenching of the role of the Jordan Press Association as a gatekeeper, but also for Article 40 of the press and publications law, which repeated earlier prohibitions on publishing materials revolving around the king and the royal family, the armed forces, heads of Arab, Islamic, or friendly states, as well as religious and social matters deemed to "violate ethics" or infringe on "public decency"(Jones, 2002: 181). Jones notes the particular animosity directed by the Jordanian government, as well as the Jordan Press Association, against tabloid newspapers during the 1990s as a type of "class queasiness" (Jones, 2002: 182) anchored in the government's distrust of these publications and their target audiences more broadly.

The third stage in the development of the Jordanian mediascape (1995–2010) was characterized by the advent of the Internet in Jordan in 1995, which ushered an era of investment in information technologies and a rapid growth in Internet access rates, culminating in the emergence of news websites in the early 2000s. The privately owned *Al Ghad* newspaper was a pioneer in this regard and launched its online version in 2004 alongside its paper version. Independent and privately owned news sites soon followed: the first of which was *Jordan Zad* (2005), *Ammon News* (2006), and *Khaberni* (2008). Internet access in Jordan improved in this period, also leading to the country's first blogs appearing in 2004. Simultaneously, in 1998 a new press and publication law was passed and was later amended in 1999 and 2010. The key features of this law and its amendments included the nullification of content restrictions from previous laws (Najjar, 2008) but maintaining a specialist "press and publications" chamber in the relevant courts. Simultaneously, however, the government amended the penal code in 2001, introducing articles restricting media freedoms in an attempt to tackle terrorism and keep the media in check. Some of these new provisions in the penal code mirrored earlier prohibitions in the press and publications law of 1993, including punitive measures for publishing insulting or false statements about the king or the royal family, as well as publishing "false or libelous information" and undermining national unity or harming the "honor" of individuals (Najjar, 2008: 225). A critical change here was the provision for the trial of journalists and media professionals in State Security Courts, as well as including, for the first time, materials published on the Internet within the remit of the penal code (Najjar, 2008).

In the fourth stage (2011–2017), a series of local and regional political events drove significant changes in the Jordanian mediascape as well as its regulatory framework. News websites were numerous and well-established by this point, and social media became important channels for communication and information exchange. In particular, these two types of media were instrumental in covering and amplifying the Arab Spring reform protests in Jordan (2011–2013). Due to the wider political upheaval in the region, Jordanians felt emboldened to make radical demands of the regime by criticizing the king and the royal family openly and calling for a serious move to democratization and more robust anti-corruption measures. The intensification of political mobilization and the absence of an extreme censorious response by the regime resulted in a marked uptick in press coverage of previously taboo subjects and a newly found boldness in Jordanian media to push the boundaries of freedom of expression. This was aided, however, by the rather loose regulation of news websites and social media through the press and publications law – a state that the Jordanian regime quickly reversed in 2012 through amendments to this law.

Legal frameworks and the current regulatory environment

The legal frameworks governing the media and the Internet in Jordan are multiple and complex. As indicated earlier, tensions exist between constitutional provisions and the various laws regulating the media in the country. Furthermore, the trajectory of the media and media laws in Jordan indicates a tendency to rein in any media law reforms in one piece of legislation through the introduction of restrictive and vaguely worded provisions in another. In brief, the various laws that impact on press and online freedoms in Jordan are the press and publications law, penal code, press association law, counter-terrorism law, cybercrimes law, audiovisual media law, state security court law, contempt of court law, telecommunications law, law on access to information, protection of state secrets and documents law, and law on the prevention of crimes. In this section, a brief exploration of the key laws is presented as an overview of the legal and regulatory environment in Jordan.

The most significant and widely cited piece of legislation in this complex matrix is the press and publications law. As evident in the discussion of media history in Jordan, the law has undergone many amendments in response to or to pre-empt political tensions. Currently, the press and publications law No. 8 (1998) with its latest amendment in 2012 guarantees the freedom of press and publication and individuals' freedom of expression yet at the same time greatly limits such freedoms. In the aftermath of the Arab Spring protests in Jordan and the instrumental role played by online news and social media in informing and mobilizing Jordanians, the 2012 amendments to the press and publications law directly attacked online media freedoms. They extended the jurisdiction of the law to online websites by making it applicable to websites as well as print publications, regardless of their type and purpose. It also required, for the first time, that websites obtain registration licenses from the government and that they are registered as companies in Jordan. Furthermore, the amendments introduced several new hurdles to online publishing, including considering online comments "press material" and requiring moderation of such content, as well as holding the owner(s) and chief editor responsible for comments published on their websites. The amendments also empowered the director of the press and publications department to close down and ban the publication of any website, as well as impose a fine of between US $1,400 and $7,000 on the owner.

The penal code is another key piece of legislation that is routinely used to curb freedom of the press and freedom of expression in Jordan. It includes several articles which directly impact on such freedoms. For instance, Article 118 dictates a prison sentence of no less than five years for anyone who

> commits acts, or produces writings or speeches unauthorized by the government and which may place the kingdom under the threat of hostile actions, damage its relationship with a foreign country, or subject Jordanian citizens to acts of revenge directed against them of their property.
>
> *(1960)*

Likewise, Article 150 criminalizes "any writing, speech, or action that is intended to instigate or instigates sectarian or racist strife or that encourages conflict between the different sects or elements of the nation" (1960). The penal code also criminalizes libelous and defamatory speech, as well as mandating a prison sentence of one to three years for anyone convicted of lèse-majesté, including "sending a written, oral, or electronic message, or a picture or a caricature, to the king, or placing such messages or pictures or drawings where they tarnish the king's dignity" or if they publish such content (1960). Furthermore, provisions aiming at protecting religious expression criminalize the publication of content that might offend "the religious sentiment" or "religious belief" of others, mandating a prison sentence of no more than three months and a small fine of no more than US $28 (1960). A further restriction on freedom of speech in the penal code is the criminalization of printing, selling, or displaying symbols or images or drawings that "give an incorrect impression about Jordanians or offends their dignity or standing" (1960).

Complicating this picture even further, the press association law, which regulates the affairs of the Jordan Press Association (JPA) and its members, sets very specific conditions for the practice of journalism in Jordan and reinforces the role of the JPA as a gatekeeper to the profession.

The law applies to practicing and non-practicing journalists as well as those in training or wanting to practice journalism. The impact of these conditions becomes apparent as soon as we consider the extent and applicability of the law: for instance, Article 16 prohibits media organizations from employing any individual who has not been registered in JPA records (i.e., satisfied the conditions stated) and paid the necessary dues, and Article 18 prohibits Jordanians from "corresponding with foreign media or presenting themselves as journalists" (1998). The law also mandates that to be considered a journalist and registered with the JPA, individuals must not have any other profession or business and must "be effectively dedicated to practicing journalism" (1998). The implications of these restrictions are severe, as they mean that ordinary citizens sharing content with foreign media are subject to one to three months' imprisonment and/or a fine of between US $280 and $700, and they also impose strict penalties on journalists in training who are treated in the same way as more established professionals. Most importantly, the law imposes a narrow definition of a journalist, virtually prohibiting part-time work in journalism and simultaneously establishing a monopoly for the compliant JPA over the profession.

Jordan's counter-terrorism law, issued in 2006, also includes provisions that can limit freedom of the press and freedom of expression. According to the law, a terrorist act is a deliberate act or the abstention from such an act or the threatening to commit such an act, either individually or collectively that (a) jeopardizes the security of Jordanian society, (b) creates strife by disrupting the public order, (c) intimidates people or puts their lives in danger, (d) damages the environment and public infrastructures or private property or the facilities of international or diplomatic missions or entails occupying or taking over such resources, (e) endangers national or economic resources, (f) forces a legitimate authority or an international or regional organization to do any work or abstain from it or, finally, (g) disables the application of the constitution or valid laws and regulations (2006). Furthermore, similarly to the press and publications law, amendments to the counter-terrorism law in 2014 criminalized any action that puts the kingdom at risk of hostile acts, jeopardizes its relationship with foreign states, or puts Jordanians at risk (2006). The very broad provisions of the law, therefore, can lead to the prosecution of journalists and writers, or publishers, who produce critiques of Jordanian strategies or foreign policy or even the regimes of other "friendly" states. Indeed, the provisions are so vague and expansive that they can be applied very liberally. The State Security Court, which is a military court, is given full jurisdiction over all such cases. It is noteworthy that the Human Rights Committee had recommended that Jordan abolish this court as far back as 1994, then again in 2010, as it was not seen as independent from the executive and had close ties to the Jordanian General Intelligence Department (OHCHR, 2017).

The state of the legal framework governing the media in Jordan is complex and designed to ensure that dissident and critical voices remain muted. Indeed, as noted earlier, the many possible avenues for suppressing freedom of the press and freedom of expression, in print and online, not only give the Jordanian regime plenty of leeway to practice its control of the press but also enable and empower it to actively prosecute journalists, writers, publishers, and ordinary citizens who adopt a line that goes against its agenda. There have been numerous cases of various laws, not just the press and publications law, being mobilized to achieve exactly this purpose. For example, in 2017 the editor-in-chief and editor of news website *Jfranews* allegedly violated Articles 5, 7, and 38 of the press and publications law and Article 11 of the cybercrimes law, having published a piece accusing the finance minister of tax evasion (CPJ, 2018). Likewise, the publisher and editor of another news website, *Al Wakeel News*, were arrested in 2018 and charged with inciting sectarian strife as per the provisions of the penal code for publishing a doctored image of *The Last Supper* painting deemed offensive to Christians (IFJ, 2018). Similarly, the counter-terrorism law was deployed repeatedly to curtail media freedoms. In 2015, a journalist for *Al Rai* newspaper was arrested for allegedly violating a gag order by publishing a piece on a foiled terrorist plot. The journalist was held for investigation for several days and then released on bail (HRW, 2015). In the same year, Jamal Ayoub, a freelance journalist, was detained for four months after publishing an article criticizing the Saudi-led war on Yemen. Ayoub was charged with damaging Jordan's relationship with Saudi Arabia under the counter-terrorism law (HRW, 2015). Numerous other cases of arrests and detention evidence the efficacy of Jordan's approach to media legal frameworks: the multiplicity of laws that allow the regime to crack down on media freedoms empowers it to do so under legal cover, and enables several different authorities to enact these various laws, including the prosecutor general, the press and publications department, the Jordan Press Association, the State Security Court, and the Audio-visual Commission, amongst others.

But control over the press (be that print or online publications) extends beyond restrictions on content and indeed pre-empts that. The press and publications law places significant hurdles in the way of establishing a print or online publication. While Article 11 maintains that every Jordanian and every Jordanian-owned company or licensed political party has the right to issue a publication, Article 13 limits this right by mandating that such a publication be "licensed as a company." Article 16 further limits this right by requiring that a director is appointed who "has attained qualifications or expertise that match the needs of the organization they will manage," and this is amplified in Article 23 which mandates that a chief editor must be appointed who satisfies the following conditions: they must be a journalist and have been a member of the JPA for at least four years, they must be Jordanian and resident in the country, and they must be working full-time for a single publication. Effectively, these conditions restrict the ability of ordinary Jordanians to launch publications and result in the concentration of media ownership in the hands of a few. Registering a publication as a company is a complex and costly process, and requiring full-time dedication to the publication means that freelancers, part-timers, and others are unable to fulfill the role of chief editor. Furthermore, the requirement of JPA membership, given its very specific conditions, introduces additional limitations.

The political economy of Jordanian print and online media

Despite the liberalization of the media landscape in Jordan, the government still retains considerable power through ownership or part-ownership of key media outlets. The government owns the country's only news agency, Petra, and is the main shareholder in three of the country's seven daily newspapers: it owns a 55% stake in the most widely read daily newspaper *Al Rai* (as well as the English-language daily *The Jordan Times*) and owns a 35% stake in *Addustour* daily, the third most widely read newspaper in the country (Mendel, Shukkeir et al., 2015). It also plays a major role in subsidizing print and online publications through ad revenue. On the other hand, three daily newspapers (*Al Ghad, Al Anbat,* and *Al Diyar*) are privately owned, and ownership of weekly newspapers (which stood at 30 in 2015) is also concentrated in the private sector. Likewise, the 300 or so news websites based in Jordan are owned privately by journalists and writers, even though some are also owned by government institutions. Very importantly, Jordan does not have any laws or rules on the concentration of media ownership, and this applies both to print/online as well as broadcast media (Mendel, Shukkeir et al., 2015). Aside from the obvious power retained by the government over the print publication landscape, this has led to the creation of clusters of ownership and power in privately owned print and online media; for instance, Zaid Jum'a and Mohannad Khalifah jointly own Al Faridah For Specialised Publications as well as Al Kawn for Radio and TV Broadcasting which together produces 10 monthly magazines, six weekly magazines, a news website, and several radio stations (Zaideh, 2015).

Such concentration of ownership produces power asymmetries and, like government dominance, has ramifications for media agendas as well. As Zaideh rightly notes, "media ownership by businesspeople has allowed them to play a political role through being elected to parliament, . . . or through promoting products owned by their other businesses" (Zaideh, 2015). In the absence of legal provisions that tackle this and bearing in mind that the Jordanian government itself remains one of, if not the most influential players in the print media landscape, the imbalance in media ownership is unlikely to be addressed any time soon.

Besides outright and part ownership, the Jordanian government exercises significant control over print and online media through channeling or withholding advertising revenue. As the biggest advertiser in the country, this places a tremendous amount of power in the hands of the government. Not surprisingly, the daily newspapers *Al Rai* and *Addustour* have traditionally held a monopoly over government advertising, thereby also increasing their financial health and ensuring a return on the government's investment in their shares. However, in early 2019 *Al Ghad* was also designated as an acceptable outlet for the publication of governmental ads and notices, as it was deemed to be one of the three most widely circulated newspapers. Other daily newspapers, such as the Muslim Brotherhood's *Assabeel*, are excluded from this arrangement despite their constant protestations against this exclusion. Indeed, although *Assabeel* is the mouthpiece of the major opposition party in Jordan, it regularly pleads with the government to increase its share of governmental advertising revenue and to review its criteria for determining the most popular newspapers. At this juncture, it is worth noting that there are specific stipulations for the publication of government advertisements and judicial notices, the latter of which is set out in the amended Judicial Execution Law published in 2017. According to a statement by JPA president in 2018, each of the three dailies (*Al Rai, Addustour,* and *Al Ghad*) stands to make around US $141,000 monthly from advertising judicial notices (*Jordan Times*). Notwithstanding the government's awareness of a broader financial crisis facing daily newspapers in Jordan and the challenges posed by online news websites to their circulation and readership, it selectively chooses to directly support only three of these papers, leaving the others to tackle the crisis on their own.

Furthermore, the government has routinely used the pricing of advertisements as a tool to mitigate financial crises in *Al Rai* and *Addustour*. For example, the two newspapers suffered a major financial crisis starting in 2011 when *Addustour* stopped producing its English weekly *The Star* and laid off tens of employees. Simultaneously, *Al Rai* stopped paying annual bonuses to its employees. The crisis intensified in the two newspapers over the following years, with *Addustour* whittling down its staff to 274 in 2015 and being unable to pay salaries for several consecutive months, and with *Al Rai* reducing the number of its columnists from 53 to eight in 2013 and later closing down some of its bureaus outside Amman in 2015 (Mendel, Shukkeir et al., 2015). In response to this crisis, the government raised the rate for advertising, as well as resuming the subscription mechanism by which each governmental department or ministry subscribes to the two main dailies and buys several copies of each (Mendel, Shukkeir et al., 2015). In 2017, the government raised the advertising rate again by a significant 120% after lobbying by the JPA and the management of daily newspapers *Al Rai* and *Addustour*. The decision was hailed as a major win for the two newspapers, especially since it introduced the largest increase ever in the rates of government advertising.

Weekly newspapers and online news websites do not receive government subsidies through government advertising revenue. They have to rely on private advertisers and, in the case of weekly newspapers, subscriptions, or direct sales revenue. As such, these media outlets are significantly more financially vulnerable, and this has translated into the closure of some weeklies and news websites over the years. In addition to this, given the large number of news websites, competition for advertising is fierce and the personal connections of their owners play as important a role as their reach in securing advertising deals. Understandably, most private advertisers choose more popular websites such as *Ammon News*, *Saraya News*, and *Khaberni* to maximize the reach of their ads. However, there is anecdotal evidence of some underhanded tactics used by some news websites to secure private advertising revenue through pressuring business owners to place advertisements with them in return for removing any particularly damaging content that may harm their businesses. Aside from the government, the major private advertisers in Jordan are telecommunications companies, banks, and property developers.

Censorship and soft containment

The complex regulatory and legal restrictions placed on the media in Jordan, and particularly the growing limitations placed on online media, have resulted in not only a stifling of media freedoms but have also fostered a culture of censorship and "soft containment." Indeed, these conditions have encouraged ever-increasing levels of self-censorship. In its 2017 report on media freedoms in the country, the Centre for Defending the Freedom of Journalists found an increase in the percentage of journalists who practice self-censorship, reaching an incredible 94.1%. Perhaps not surprisingly, the topics that journalists were most inclined to censor themselves about or avoid altogether were the Royal Court (therefore, the monarchy and the royal family), security services (the Intelligence Department), the armed forces, and religious issues (Ghunaim, Zahra et al., 2017). Indicating that media professionals know the red lines, these topics align to a large extent with the texts of the various laws, and therefore it can be argued that the laws are quite effective at reinforcing self-censorship amongst Jordanian journalists and writers.

Censorship and self-censorship are also widely practiced in Jordanian online news media, particularly since the introduction of the amendments to the press and publications law in 2012. Considering readers' comments "press material" and holding website owners and editors responsible for them has greatly restricted the freedom of ordinary Jordanians to express themselves online but has also changed the role of the owners and editors into gatekeepers eager to remain on the right side of the law. Further, hundreds of websites were blocked in Jordan since 2013 mostly because they have not been licensed following amendments to the law. And, to paint an even grimmer picture, under the 2015 cybercrime law, media professionals and citizen journalists can be punished by jail sentences or pre-trial detention on account of articles published in online newspapers or posts on social media networks (Reporters Without Borders, 2019).

"Soft containment," or the use of multiple non-coercive tactics to influence media professionals, has also emerged as a major detriment to media freedoms and independence in Jordan. In a survey of 504 journalists and opinion leaders (editors-in-chief, directors, columnists, and others in senior and influential media positions), Al Quds Centre for Political Studies found that 82% of the journalists and 84% of the opinion leaders surveyed believed that the government was deploying soft containment tactics to get media professionals on its side. Indeed, of the journalists surveyed, 35% had had such tactics used on them, with the percentage increasing to 45% of so-called opinion leaders (Fouad and Ammara, 2012). Forms of soft containment include gifts and bribes, the facilitation of government paperwork and other procedures, appointment in governmental or semi-governmental positions, invitations to accompany government officials on travels, regular invitations to important government-organized meetings or events, the facilitation of information flows, and finally customs exemptions or the provision of free education or healthcare services to journalists or their dependents (Fouad and Ammara, 2012). However, the study also found that the government is not the only user of soft-containment. Businesspeople, the security services, political parties, civil society organizations, and members of the lower and upper houses of parliament have also been identified as using soft-containment to influence media coverage (Fouad and Ammara, 2012).

The potential for social and political change

In a testament to the concentration of media power in the capital, the vast majority of Jordanian newspapers, print publications, and online news websites are published in Amman. Such geographical clustering not only excludes residents of other cities and towns from working in Jordanian media but also negatively reflects on the media's ability to effectively cover the issues that are relevant to people in these locales. In addition to this, mainstream Jordanian media shy away from addressing controversial topics that touch on sexuality, religious matters, and social conventions. These limitations are compounded by the precarity experienced by many journalists, especially freelancers, part-timers, and those working for news websites and smaller media outlets on insecure contracts, which render their working conditions unstable at best and, at worst, non-conducive to any critical engagement with pressing issues.

However, the Arab Spring wave of protests and demands for reform in the country did usher a moment, albeit brief, of increased media freedoms. The potential for Jordanian media to play a crucial role in political change (not social, however) was evident: news websites published reports on corruption, bold columns critiquing the monarchy, and coverage of the *Hirak* movement. Newspapers followed suit, especially *Al Ghad*. Independent websites such as 7iber.com were also instrumental in instigating critical dialogue and in organizing discussion groups and other activities that took full advantage of the opening in media freedoms in the country. This was, nonetheless, short-lived, as the government soon cracked down on websites through amendments to several laws, as noted earlier.

Challenging social norms is extremely difficult and fraught with risk in Jordan. Specifically, matters relating to sex, sexuality, religion, or social customs are routinely avoided by journalists and writers. Given the legal frameworks, this is not surprising; however, the practice of censorship extends beyond anxiety about the legality or illegality of discussing certain topics to what possible social reactions and ramifications such coverage might have not just for the writers of these materials but also for the publishers and editors. Very often, moral panics resulting from such coverage are exploited by the government to tighten control over the media and restrict freedoms further under the pretext of protecting public morals. For example, a media-focused grassroots social campaign was organized to lobby the government to block pornographic content in the country in 2012 and resulted in the government using the same moralistic discourse to tighten its grip on Internet access.

Conclusion

Jordan's media landscape is fraught with complexities. Print and online media face an evolving matrix of legal and regulatory frameworks that are designed to curb media freedoms, and, as a result, damaging practices such as soft containment and self-censorship, as well as more direct restrictions such as blocks, arrests, fines, and myriad other punitive measures, have become part of the general experience of doing media work in the country. And, while the brief opening in media freedoms in 2011–2012 energized the scene and allowed Jordanian media to play an unprecedented role in supporting calls for political reform, this was merely a blip in the trajectory of Jordanian media that soon passed with the attacks on media freedoms, particularly the focus on reining in online media. Given its history and the current political landscape, both domestically and regionally, it is unlikely that Jordanian media will move past being held hostage by these dynamics.

References

CPJ (2018), *Jordan Arrests Two Journalists over Report on Finance Minister*. Retrieved from https://cpj. org/2018/01/jordan-arrests-two-journalists-over-report-on-fina.php. Accessed 11 June 2019.

Fouad, H., and Ammara, S. (2012), *A Study on the Impact of Soft containment on the Freedom and Independence of the Press*. Amman, Jordan: Al Quds Centre for Political Studies.

Ghunaim, M., W. H. Zahra, R. Al-Huwaydi, H. Habayeb, B. Wala;, K. Al-Mallah and J. Al-Mallah (2017), *Media Freedom Status in Jordan 2017*. Amman, Jordan: Center for Defending Freedom of Journalists.

HRW (2015), *Jordan: Journalists, Writers Facing Terrorism Charges*. Retrieved from www.hrw.org/ news/2015/07/15/jordan-journalists-writers-facing-terrorism-charges. Accessed 11 June 2019.

IFJ (2018), *Jordan: Publisher and Editor Detained over Retouched Publication of Last Supper Painting*. Retrieved from www.ifj.org/media-centre/news/detail/category/press-releases/article/jordan-publisher-and-editor-detained-over-retouched-publication-of-last-supper-painting.html. Accessed 11 June 2019.

Jones, A. (2002), From Vanguard to Vanquished? The Tabloid Press in Jordan. *Political Communication*, 19(2), pp. 171–187.

Mendel, T., Y. Shukkeir, D. Baslan, M. Shalabieh, and S. Zaide (2015), *Assessment of Media Development in Jordan Based on UNESCO's Media Development Indicators*. Paris and Amman, Jordan: UNESCO.

Najjar, O. A. (1998), The Ebb and Flow of the Liberalization of the Jordanian Press: 1985–1997. *Journalism & Mass Communication Quarterly*, 75(1), pp. 127–142.

Najjar, O. A. (2008), *Media Policy and Law in Egypt and Jordan: Continuities and Change. Arab Media: Power and Weakness*. K. Hafez (ed.). New York: Continuum, pp. 217–236.

OHCHR (2017), *Human Rights Committee Examines the Report of Jordan*. Retrieved from www.ohchr. org/EN/NewsEvents/Pages/DisplayNews.aspx?NewsID=22269&LangID=E. Accessed 10 May 2019.

Reporters Without Borders (2019), *2019 World Press Freedom Index: Jordan*. Retrieved from https://rsf. org/en/jordan. Accessed 22 April 2019.

Robinson, G. E. (1998), Defensive Democratization in Jordan. *International Journal of Middle East Studies*, 30(3), pp. 387–410.

Rugh, W. (2004), *Arab Mass Media: Newspapers, Radio, and Television in Arab Politics*. Westport, CT: Praeger Publishers.

Sakr, N. (2002), Media Reform in Jordan: The Stop-Go Transition. In M. E. Price, B. Rozumilowicz, and S. G. Verhulst (eds.), *Media Reform: Democratizing the Media, Democratizing the State*. London: Routledge.

The Jordanian Anti-Terrorism Law (2006), Amman.

The Jordanian Constitution (1952), Amman.

The Jordanian Penal Code (1960), Amman.

The Jordanian Press Association Law (1998), Amman.

Tweisi, B. M., R. J. Suleiman, and A. S. Al-Garallah (2015), Jordanian Journalists' Awareness of the Concepts and Standards of Journalistic Quality within Jordanian Media Institutions. *Journal of Arab & Muslim Media Research*, 8(1), pp. 55–78.

Zaideh, Sawsan (2015), *Who Owns the Media in Jordan?* Retrieved from www.7iber.com/politics-economics/who-owns-media-in-jordan/?%3E. Accessed 1 July 2019.

11

BROADCAST MEDIA IN JORDAN AND THE (RENTIER) STATE

Christina Zacharia Hawatmeh

Introduction

The Hashemite Kingdom of Jordan is often portrayed by both international observers and domestic actors as an island of stability – resilient, safe, and moderate – surrounded by a sea of regional conflict and turmoil. Given the fact that Jordan has been one of the region's main destinations for wave after wave of refugees from neighboring countries, this metaphor is rather apt (Ghazal, 2017). Moreover, it showcases Jordan as a key geopolitical and strategic linchpin in the security of the entire region.

The "island" metaphor also serves to contextualize and explain the kingdom's own internal setbacks and struggles, especially in justifying what seems to be perpetually stalled, economic, social, and political progress on a national level. After all, so the narrative goes, to itself and its regional and international allies, slow or no developments on a politically democratic, economically liberal, and socially progressive vision are minor – even understandable – in comparison with the chronic chaos, regression, and oppression plaguing the Arab region. At the same time, Jordan's achievements and advancements in any area, however modest, are often celebrated and highlighted against the backdrop of this same narrative.

The media in Jordan is one such institution that shapes and is shaped by this dual narrative and quite arguably objective situation of the Jordanian state. Since the emergence of the Hashemite Kingdom, in particular its nationally owned broadcast media, which has been tightly controlled and regulated by various levels of the state, tells the larger story of Jordan's historical development and current circumstances, which not only reflects domestic political, social, and economic developments but regional and international events and pressures as well.

Since its inception, with a few notable exceptions, Jordan has increasingly taken a highly adaptive, middle-of-the-road approach in a factional, fragmented, and often conflicted region. A relatively small-sized country, with few natural resources apart from a barely tapped solar energy field, Jordan has relied heavily on regional and international alliances and partnerships for its economic viability, in periods of both growth and stagnation. Many have argued that Jordan's survival strategy has turned it into a "semi-rentier" state, one that heavily depends on external sources of revenue – mainly expatriate remittances, foreign investments, aid, loans, grants, and in-kind assistance – rather than homegrown productive industries that require large-scale, vertically and horizontally integrated, employment of its population (Al Razzaz, 2013; Muasher, 2011; Saif, 2007; Brand, 1992; Brynen, 1992).

A hallmark of the patriarchal rentier state model is that the bulk of its government's budget and spending is not based on domestic taxation and, therefore, not particularly accountable to the citizens they serve. In this bargain, the relationship between the citizen and the government gets distorted into one of the servants and the patron. Lack of accountability and impetus for productivity spreads and becomes embedded throughout the society's institutions, values, and norms, fostering a culture mired in unmeritocratic hierarchies, latent cynicism, and routine corruption. Another inherent feature of the patriarchal rentier state is that it tends to keep tight control of public spaces – including the media, education, and political associations – since it can become particularly susceptible to criticism, crisis, and/or collapse if it becomes unable to continue to subsidize and appease what inevitably becomes a bloated, redundant, and unproductive public sector that is out of sync with a privileged, frustrated, and uncompetitive private sector.

Jordan, as a semi-rentier state – one that depends on using its strategic geopolitical position to serve an array of international interests, without possessing enough of its own natural resources – has seemed determined to resist completely falling into the region's authoritarian tilt. In other words, while it used many tactics of the classic rentier state, it also has taken various steps to democratize its political systems, and the key to that has been the media and press freedoms. As a 2011 report published by the Jordan Media Strengthening Program notes,

> On the one hand, there has been a broad commitment to democratization and press freedoms; on the other hand, there has been an impetus toward controls, prompted by concerns that increasing democratization and openness could unleash expressive activity (particularly within privately owned media) detrimental to Jordan's international relations, internal stability and other interests.
>
> *(Center for Global Communication Studies, 2011: 17)*

So, at least on paper, Jordan subscribes to key international charters, conventions, and norms on best media practices and press freedoms, even as the implementation and actualization of them have been inconsistent or nonexistent on the ground.

What is essential to understanding how Jordan's media system operates is to first recognize that media institutions and regulatory bodies have been instrumental in mitigating tension between the state and the public, by limiting debate and controlling the national narrative. This chapter traces out the development of this historically close and symbiotic relationship between the semi-rentier state and broadcast media in Jordan. It further examines the inherent contradiction in tying the state's authority and the media's credibility to each other, since if one is weak the other is likely to be too, opening real gaps for alternative and oppositional narratives to emerge.

Broadcast media and becoming a nation

Since its independence from the British mandate in 1946, the Hashemite Kingdom of Jordan has sought to create for itself its own identity as a nation and people. From the beginning of Jordan's nation-state building, the impetus to establish a national broadcasting system was essential to allowing the voice of the regime to be heard, not only in the kingdom but also in the region. Especially during the reign of Egyptian President Jamal Abdul Nasser, who effectively used *Sawt*

Al Arab (Voice of the Arabs) radio station to broadcast his views of pan-Arabism to neighboring countries, Jordan's broadcast media allowed the Jordanian regime to tout its achievements and rally its people behind them. Following World War II, against the backdrop of the Cold War, the young kingdom also wanted to assert its strategic position, which was on the side of the Western allies, contrary to the pan-Arab nationalist movements that tended to ally with the Soviet bloc. Moreover, radio was an effective way to counter Israel's aggressive media tactics that used radio to broadcast programs in Arabic to its neighbors.

During the 1950s, television became a powerful form of mass media in Western countries, particularly in the United States. Throughout the Arab world, however, radio broadcasts were a much more common and popular source of news mixed with political views and activism. According to Betty S. Anderson, in Jordan, the spread of this technology throughout the population was rapid and pervasive, as

> the number of people owning radio sets increased throughout the 1950s, with two sets per 1,000 inhabitants in 1950 and 12 per 1,000 in 1953. In poor villages, radios were often set up in coffee shops, while in some refugee camps loudspeaker broadcast the news during the day.
>
> *(2005: 128)*

At that time, broadcast media were entirely Arab governments' official outlets, with the notable exception of BBC Radio, which represented a credible alternative in the polarized region as it tried to present news and views of all sides of the political spectrum in what was becoming a complex equation. The Jordanian government began its national broadcasts out of Ramallah Radio in 1950 (see Sahhab, 2004: 52), which had been established in Palestine under the British Mandate and had come under Jordan's rule in April 1949 until June 1967.

The newly crowned monarch of Jordan, King Hussein bin Talal, started in 1953 to introduce a series of reforms to bolster free speech and the liberalization of the press, which reverberated throughout the entire information ecosystem. In 1956, the government went further in the liberalization process, as it legalized the formation of political parties. In that same year, Jordan Radio, the state-owned corporation that was to oversee the entire distribution of the country's radio network, was established. In 1959, Jordan Radio's first official station went on air from a small building in its Amman headquarters.

A section of the official website of King Hussein gives an interesting window into the state's perspective on the competing interests facing Jordan during the 1950s, as well as its regressive impact on the development of the country's media system. It says:

> Three days after his coronation in May 1953, King Hussein called upon newly-appointed Prime Minister Fawzi al-Mulqi to introduce a series of liberal reforms, including freedom of speech and freedom of the press. However, a sense of civic responsibility had not yet permeated the Jordanian populace as a whole. Radical groups exploited the reforms and relentlessly attacked the regime, thus undermining the stability and integrity of Jordan. Sometimes they even cynically initiated riots to provoke reprisals. Nasser's propaganda broadcasts, in particular, incited massive riots that undermined domestic order.
>
> Throughout his long and fruitful reign, King Hussein tried to govern according to the precepts and ideals of democratic liberalism, while at the same time maintaining the necessary prerequisite of public order. This balancing act was not always easy.
>
> *(HM King Hussein's Official Website, n.d.)*

These political openings, which had begun to spark a lively and outspoken print and broadcast media environment, closed abruptly in 1957, when a failed assassination attempt by external actors prompted King Hussein to draw back liberal reforms, taking Jordan effectively into a state of martial law lasting until 1993. This early historical period proved to be formative in shaping the performance of a more passive, yet not completely subdued, media, bound by direct state control and a tangled web of legal restrictions, for decades to come.

State-led broadcasting: laws and regulations

The Jordanian government was a relative latecomer to television broadcasting, even compared to other countries in the region, particularly Syria and Egypt, which both established national TV services in 1960. According to the Fanack Chronicle (n.d.), "by the time the Jordanian government established the first national channel in 1968, the country already had an estimated 10,000 TV sets receiving broadcasts from neighboring countries." In the beginning, Jordan Television Corporation (JTV), aired in black and white for three hours a day, mainly news bulletins, with its editorial policies dictated by the government. By 1972, JTV introduced a second channel, the first in the region to carry international programing, including a news bulletin in English (Drbseh, 2013), targeting Israelis, foreign missions, and the Jordanian political and economic elite. It wasn't until 1975 that JTV's coverage reached the entire kingdom. In 1978, several hours of French-language programming was added.

The government's monopoly over Jordan's broadcast media institutions was enshrined in a 1985 law passed by Parliament, effectively preventing the establishment of privately owned terrestrial stations in the kingdom. Moreover, the law merged Jordan Radio and Jordan Television into the Jordanian Radio and Television Corporation (JRTVC), as a department within the Ministry of Information, under the direct administrative control of the minister of information. Under this law, still basically in effect until today, JRTVC's entire budget is under government control, which is mainly derived from a one Jordanian dinar fee collected by the national electric company, another state-controlled entity, on each household's monthly electricity bill as well as from advertising, sales, and other revenues. By law, as like any other government department, these funds go directly to the Treasury Department within the Ministry of Finance. The management of JRTVC would put together an annual budget, go to the government, and discuss it to receive its allocation. In its heyday, JRTVC could keep 30% of its commercial revenue to spend at its discretion, but that practice stopped in 1993. At a later stage, JRTV's budget spending came under the purview of the Audit Bureau.

By the late 1980s, Jordan had a tightly controlled media system, consisting of a total of three radio stations and two television channels, all state-owned, four daily newspapers, three with government-majority ownership as well as direct control of the country's only news agency, PETRA, which was established in 1969, also under the auspices of the Ministry of Information (founded in 1964).

The government's ability to keep a hold on the local media started to weaken during the financial crash and near economic collapse Jordan experienced in the late 1980s, culminating in the 1989 April Bread Riots that started in the southern city of Ma'an and quickly spread throughout much of the country. Accompanying a series of economic "structural adjustments" induced by the International Monetary Fund, the early 1990s witnessed a burst of liberalization and political reforms throughout the state. Observers characterized this political response as "defensive democratization," a pre-emptive survival strategy employed by semi-rentier states in times of economic crisis, whereby the regime initiates "sufficient reform to assure its political longevity, but without altering the core structures of power" (Robinson, 1998: 387; Lucas, 2003).

Liberal reform to the media was codified in the 1993 Press and Publications Law (PPL) No. 10, which shifted regulations limiting media ownership, speech, and licensing towards greater competition and editorial freedom. In particular, significantly reduced licensing barriers for ownership of print news outlets led to a proliferation of 35 weekly newspapers with a wide range of editorial perspectives across the political spectrum. Many of the newborn weeklies could be considered tabloids, attracting audiences and advertisers, while "pushing the boundaries of what the government was prepared to tolerate and testing previously established red lines" (Mendel, 2016: 4). On the other hand, a number of these new publications were credible and offered a real alternative source for news and views from the long-dominant daily newspapers.

Within this period, for the first time in the country's history, the government's grip on its national broadcasting media loosened and partly followed public opinion. Jawad Zada, then director of Radio Jordan's English service, reflected on these changes as they were happening in an important book, called *The Role of Media in a Democracy: The Case of Jordan*, published in 1995. He says:

> The democratic process in Jordan has no doubt had a positive impact on the official media, i.e. the Jordan Radio and Television Corporation. The unique coverage of the 1991 Gulf war and the focus on domestic affairs in the past few years are manifestations of the way in which the democratization process has impacted the media.
>
> *(Zada, 1995: 46)*

Indeed, especially after the dinar had lost two-thirds of its value against the US dollar in 1989, the 1991 Gulf War rejuvenated JRTVC, as Jordan became a hub for international broadcasters reporting from the region that rented its studios and equipment, bringing in an estimated US $10 million in revenue (UNESCO, 2015: 138, footnote 492).

According to Ghadeer Taher, also in *The Role of Media in a Democracy*, JTV submitted a modest proposal to the government in a bid to gain some financial and administrative independence from the Ministry of Information (Taher, 1995: 42). These recommendations ranged from introducing a new system for salary scales to allowing travel of personnel for events outside of the country without the minister's prior approval. At the time, there were even discussions on ways and means to turn JRTVC into a public broadcaster, overseen by an independent commission, along the lines of the BBC (Sakr, 2013). As it stood, no one was optimistic that JRTVC would ever be able to function effectively as a state institution that genuinely serves the public interests, if it stayed so closely bound to governments and the individuals within it. In other words, "If we remain tied to the government bureaucracy, we will always lag behind," as JTV's general director at the time put it (Taher, 1995: 42).

Accompanying domestic pressure on the government to open the country's media system, regional and international satellite stations began to break into Jordan's broadcast media market. CNN, launched in 1980, and found its teeth during the 1991 Gulf War, using Jordan as it reporting base, followed by the Middle East Broadcasting Center (MBC), the first private free-to-air satellite company founded in London in 1991, the Saudi privately owned Arab Radio and Television (ART) Network established in 1993, to the Qatari Al Jazeera, launched in 1996, not to mention the Internet, which made its first appearance in Jordan in 1995 − all proved to be formidable competitors to the heavily restrained JRTVC, which did try to keep pace by launching its satellite channel in 1993 as well as opening new facilities in 1997.

Against the backdrop of the post-Iraq War, which gave way to the 1991 Madrid peace process and eventually the 1994 peace agreement between Jordan and Israel, the early 1990s became a kind of free-for-all evolution of the media in Jordan, but the regime was not ready for it. The printed press was especially critical of Jordan's peace treaty with Israel, prompting King Hussein to openly complain about the "deteriorating morals" of journalists who tarnish the image of Jordan (Bookmiller, 2001: 1286). State-media outlets, particularly JRTVC, came under scrutiny for its heavy dependence on state-protocol news and staying too close to the government's line in its coverage of the unfolding events around the peace agreement. Especially opposition parties and figures criticized JTV for failing to include their point of view in news and talk show programs and for appearing to prematurely celebrate the peace process as a success (Fariz, 1995: 63).

The debate took a sharp turn in May 1997, when, after the Parliament had just been dissolved, the government issued a provisional PPL No. 27, strengthening content controls and penalties for violations of the law. Particularly targeting the vocal weekly newspapers, the government prescribed a steep increase of minimum paid capital requirement for licensing newspapers, from JD 15,000 to JD 300,000, immediately putting 13 weeklies out of business. A year later, the Higher (Administrative) Court of Justice issued what was considered a landmark decision that the amendments to the PPL were unconstitutional, not in principle, but on procedural grounds, invalidating both the new provisions in the law and the closures. The ruling was short-lived, however, as a newly elected Parliament enacted the regressive PPL No. 18 of 1998, which was nearly identical to the 1997 provisional law (Human Rights Watch, 1997; Campagna, 1998).

Change brings the same: the social and political functions of broadcasting

Suddenly, within less than one year, a new era emerged, not just for the media in Jordan, but for the entire kingdom, when King Abdullah II ibn Al Hussein was crowned on 7 February 1999, the same day that his father, King Hussein, passed away.

Early in King Abdullah's reign, there were clear signs that many of the country's economic pillars would be transformed under a process of privatization, liberalization, and globalization. Alongside these economic reforms were promises of enhancing democratic processes and public freedoms. In a November 1999 interview (Sharbel, 1999), King Abdullah laid out a comprehensive, progressive, and optimistic vision for Jordan, where economic development and political freedoms went hand in hand. Addressing the controversial 1998 PPL, the king said:

> We have finished laying a modern and contemporary publication law, consistent with Jordan's democratic direction, the protection of the freedom of the press, freedom of expression, and the openness of media without restriction or hindrance. The Jordanian press representatives have contributed to the drafting of this law. The domestic press writes what it desires without any barriers or restrictions, and we do not exercise any censorship on foreign press coming into Jordan.

The amendments that were introduced did ease some restrictions on the press but did not go all the way in eliminating "barriers or restrictions" on national press and "censorship" on foreign media in Jordan. Perhaps these early pronouncements and attempts to change the laws were never going to be enough to immediately uproot a media system that was deeply entrenched within the semi-rentier state and patriarchal social hierarchies. After all, legal mechanisms are just one means of control, and not necessarily the most effective ones either.

It is widely recognized that the enabling environment for the growth of privately owned media did emerge early during King Abdullah's reign. It can be argued, however, that those moves towards liberal reform were merely a cosmetic rebranding of the image of the regime's role in the media system. Lack of substantive change in the executive structures and legal autonomy of bodies regulating the media has kept them essentially under direct government control. Until today, crucial components of institutional independence – such as appointments, dismissals, budgets, licensing policies, etc. – all come under the purview of the Council of Ministers, headed by the prime minister, who are themselves appointed by Royal Decree, and other less visible entities of the state. It is also common to see key positions in both government and independent media organizations rotated around a small network of public personalities and officials, who could hold a post or board membership in more than one outlet at the same time.

In 2001, the government dissolved the Ministry of Information and replaced it with three new entities: the Audio-Visual Commission (AVC), responsible for the exercise of regulatory authority over the broadcast media sector; the Press and Publications Department (PPD); and the Higher Media Council (HMC), which was tasked by Royal Decree "to act as a regulatory, non-executive commission" to support the independence, freedom, plurality, and responsibilities of Jordan's media organizations (Al Hussein II, 2002). The HMC, however, was abolished in 2008; and the AVC and PPD were merged in April 2014 under one administrative umbrella called the Jordan Media Commission (JMC). According to UNESCO, the AVC, now JMC, is clearly "accountable to the government rather than the public." By law, the director of the JMC is appointed by the Council of Ministers, the body's budget is entirely allocated by the government, it is not required to report to either the public or Parliament, and the Council of Ministers retains the final word on its recommendations for granting broadcasting licenses (UNESCO, 2015: 65).

As for JRTVC, the 1985 law was also replaced. Now, it currently operates under Law No. 35 (2000), which in Article 3 states that the corporation shall be financially and administratively independent. In practice, however, the management is appointed by and accountable only to the government: the chair of the board of JRTVC holds the rank of a minister, reporting directly to the prime minister, and whose appointment is approved by Royal Decree; JRTVC board members and director general are approved by the Council of Ministers. It is important to note that frequent changes of government in Jordan have also meant frequent turnovers of JRTVC's top management. As Noami Sakr points out, between 2000 and 2010, there were no fewer than four changes of management under six different prime ministers (2015: 28), thwarting continuity, progress, and expectations for JRTVC's administrative independence. From 2010 until March 2019, Jordan has had seven prime ministers, with only one lasting four years, and eight different boards of directors of JRTVC.

The JRTVC 2000 law still stipulates that its budget is allocated by the government, using part of the revenue collected from commercial income and the one JD fee (≈US $1.41) attached to households' monthly electricity bills. Although JRTVC is given a competitive advantage vis-à-vis privately owned media outlets in that it does not have to pay a broadcast licensing fee, financial strain has been a persistent concern for this state-owned enterprise. In 2001, AFP reported that JRTVC was attempting to restructure its operations with "dismissal of 308 employees, despite workers' protestations," to address its US $7 million deficit, more than half of its US $12 million budget at the time. Moreover, most of the budget "aimed mainly at paying salaries" of its 2,200 employees, of whom "more than half were hired in the last five years" (AFP, 2001). The bloating of state institutions through hiring based on *wasta* (personal connections), not need or competence, are an essential fixture of the semi-rentier state. For JRTVC and other state-controlled media, such hiring practices have been a way to secure compliance with the regime's interests, even at the expense of the long-term viability of the institution.

Committed to the process of privatization, yet still under a tight regulatory environment, by 2002, the Jordanian state effectively ended its monopoly of broadcast media, giving way to dozens of new entrances into the domestic audiovisual market. New radio stations quickly emerged, filling a void that had been created by Radio Jordan's limited offerings and reviving the local scene. According to the Oxford Business Group,

> The new stations, offering a wide variety of music, news, and talk shows, proved an instant hit with the country's audiences, and the annual advertisement spending allocated for radio increased from the mere US $400,000 in 2000 to US $11.7 million in 2006.
>
> *(2007: 191)*

Although the initial advertising boom has since declined, by 2015, there were 41 radio stations in Jordan, 17 were owned by public bodies: five by universities, four by Jordan Radio, two by the Jordan Armed Forces, two by municipalities, and four by other public entities. Community radio stations and privately owned commercial channels comprise the rest.

The new radio stations added new and different voices in the public narrative. Live call-in radio talk shows became particularly popular since they tackle social and economic issues facing its listeners. The growth of the radio sector also meant that outlets could move beyond Jordan's capital, where it has been historically concentrated, and out into the governorates, where around 60% of the country's population resides. Several community radio stations were established through support by international institutions and agencies. These were intended to widen the representation of views and topics beyond the top-heavy approach of state-led broadcasts that tends to focus its local news coverage around state officials' activities, such as a visit by a minister to open a new school or hospital in an area outside of Amman. The rise of privately owned and community radio stations also gave new opportunities for women to break into this male-dominated field, where men outnumber women in JRTVC by a ratio of 5:1, according to a study conducted in 2013 (Al Najjar, 2013; see also Zaideh, 2018).

The turn of the 20th century was an important turning point for television broadcasting in Jordan as well. In 2001, Jordan Media City (JMC) was launched next to JRTVC's premises, through an agreement between the government of the Hashemite Kingdom and the privately owned Saudi-based Dallah Production Company. According to its website, JMC was set up with a capital of JD 10 million, as a tax-free establishment, and offers financial incentives to its clients, most of which are non-Jordanian. Equipped to deliver a range of broadcast services, JMC now transmits and retransmits over 500 channels to the MENA region, in an increasingly crowded regional satellite market. With a relatively low licensing fee of JD 5,000, by 2016, there were 45 satellite channels in Jordan, all operating from JMC. Of these, 20 are owned by Jordanians, while the rest is owned by Arab nationals, mainly Saudi and Iraqi. Just two of the 45 channels carried news, which until 2012 required a different and significantly more expensive license.

Also in 2001, JRTVC restructured itself by scrapping its Channel 2, which was popular for its international entertainment shows and foreign news programming. Instead, it introduced a new primary channel, a sports channel, and a third, family entertainment channel established in cooperation with a local private production company on the premises of JMC. In hindsight, the restructuring was a failure and set JRTVC further back in the market, just at the same time as other players were emerging on the scene.

A real test to the declared policy to liberalize the audiovisual sector came when Mohammad Alayyan, founder and owner of the popular independent daily newspaper *Al Ghad*, became involved in establishing ATV, Jordan's first private television station, as there are no laws in Jordan prohibiting media concentration or cross-media ownership for local or foreign companies. Just a few hours before its launch in August 2007, however, its transmission was suspended by the AVC, citing incomplete paperwork. Since that day, a tangled story began to emerge, starting with the fact that "the decision [to halt operations] was issued by the then JRTV Director-General, in his capacity as acting AVC director, thus raising questions over a perceived conflict of interest" (Center for Global Communication Studies, 2011: 47). And although the ownership of the debt-ridden ATV changed hands in 2008, with the talk that the government would buy the facilities in 2010, the station remains dormant (Jordan Business, 2010).

Finally, in 2011, Roya TV, a privately owned local channel, was launched, broadcasting local news, comedies, and dramas as well as political, social, and economic programs. As an independent station with a strong online presence, Roya TV is generally viewed by Jordanians as more polished and interesting than JRTV. Incubated within the JMC, it was able to invest in production and original content, so that within a few years of its launch it surpassed JTV's viewership and became #1 in Jordan. It is also considered controversial and a magnet for public criticism for occasionally touching on social taboos. In one instance in 2015, the Jordan Media Commission suspended a comedy show on Roya TV, saying one episode was "sexually explicit and totally inappropriate and unacceptable. Using this dirty language and explicitly is in violation of norms and laws," and referred the case to the prosecutor general (Ghazal, 2015).

Strict penal codes criminalizing a broad range of what is considered offensive or dangerous speech have had a chilling effect on the media in Jordan. A regular poll conducted by the Center for the Defense and Freedom of Journalists (CDFJ) consistently found high percentages of local journalists practice self-censorship. In 2017, 94% said they practice self-censorship. As the director of the CDFJ explained, "journalists do not want trouble with authorities and do not want to lose their jobs . . . they just want to make ends meet and avoid conflicts" (Ghazal, 2018). At the same time, the Jordanian public's trust in state institutions – with the notable exceptions of the armed forces (90%), police (82%), and courts (73%) – is around or below 50%; with government at 54%, followed by civil services (44%) and banks (41%), according to a recent study (Jordan Strategy Forum, 2018). Trust in the press is significantly lower at 33%, just above trust in the Parliament (21%) and political parties (10%), indicating an erosion of the public's view of democratic political processes and platforms.

An ending or a beginning?

As JRTVC, as well as the rest of the government-backed media sector, faces deep financial problems as well as criticism for its lack of professionalism, independence, or even relevance against a backdrop of a highly competitive regional and international media landscape, the government launched Al Mamlakah, which means "The Kingdom" in Arabic, a 24/7 channel focused on local news. Based in the King Hussein Business Park in West Amman, with a staff of 300 employees, it distinguishes itself with five fully equipped bureaus in governorates across the country as well as a network of well-trained reporters in different capitals of the Middle East region. With an estimated start-up cost of JD 15 million a year, Jordan's first public-service broadcaster, came to be through a 2015 bylaw stipulating that it is government-funded but administratively independent; therefore it is neither state-owned nor commercial. It is worth noting that its board of directors is appointed by Royal Decree. At this stage, Al Mamlakah is supposed to replace any plans for JTV to introduce a third public-service channel.

Al Mamlakah TV launched on 16 July 2018, under the slogan "Jordan Is the Subject and We Are the Predicate," heralding a new phase in the kingdom's media development, and invoking the image of Jordan as an island of stability in a sea of chaos and regression. Questions, however, continue to surround the premise and future of the station: will it be able to deliver anything substantively different than its predecessor? Why was the decision made to start a new channel rather than use the funds to revive JRTVC and/or ATV instead? What will become of them? Especially since Al Mamlakeh TV attracted many of the top talents from other local media outlets, should this move be seen as a step forward or backward for the whole country? Will it be able to constructively push the editorial boundaries imposed by the state? Will it be able to recapture local audiences and restore the credibility of local news media? As Jordanian journalist Rana Sweis says,

> The public station broadcaster will face a skeptical audience, but its most immediate challenge is to convince the public that it will perform its duty as a watchdog to protect the public interest. Without that, it's not going to fare any better than JRTV.
>
> *(Sweis, 2015)*

For if it fails that challenge, the real and most important question is, what's next?

References and further reading

Agence France-Presse (2001), Jordan Defends Sackings at State-run JRTVC. *Al Bawaba*. Retrieved from www.albawaba.com/business/jordan-defends-sackings-state-run-jrtvc. Accessed 20 April 2019.

Al Hussein II, A. (2002), *Letter to [Prime Minister] Ali Abul Ragheb on the Establishment of a Higher Media Council*. Retrieved from https://kingabdullah.jo/en/letters/letter-ali-abul-ragheb-establishment-higher-media-council. Accessed 20 April 2019.

Al Najjar, A. (2013), Jordan: Toward Gender Balance in the Newsroom. In C. Byerly (ed.), *The Palgrave International Handbook of Women and Journalism*. London: Palgrave Macmillan.

Al Razzaz, O. (2013), *The Treacherous Path Towards a New Arab Social Contract November*. American University of Beirut. Lebanon: Issam Fares Institute for Public Policy and International Affairs.

Anderson, B. (2005), *Nationalist Voices in Jordan: The Street and the State*. Austin: University of Texas Press.

Brand, L. (1992), Economic and Political Liberalization in a Rentier Economy: The Case of Jordan. In I. Harik and D. Sullivan (eds.), *Privatization and Liberalization in the Middle East*. Bloomington: Indiana University Press.

Brynen, R. (1992), Economic Crisis and Post-Rentier Democratization in the Arab World: The Case of Jordan. *Canadian Journal of Political Science*, XXV(1).

Bookmiller, R. (2001), Jordan. In D. Jones (ed.), *Censorship: A World Encyclopedia*. London: Routledge.

Campagna, J. (1998), *Jordan Reins in the Press*. Committee to Protect Journalists. Retrieved from www.refworld.org/docid/47c567c1c.html. Accessed 20 April 2019.

Center for Global Communication Studies, the Annenberg School for Communication (2011), *Introduction to News Media Law and Policy in Jordan*. 2nd edition. Amman, Jordan: Jordan Media Strengthening Program.

Drbseh, M. (2013), The Spread of the English Language in Jordan. *International Journal of Scientific and Research Publications*, 3(9).

Fanack Chronicle (n.d.), *Jordan: Society, Media, and Culture*. Retrieved from https://fanack.com/jordan/society-media-culture/jordan-media/. Accessed 20 April 2019.

Fariz, Z. (1995), 'The Inside Story' of Covering the Peace Talks. In G. Hawatmeh (ed.), *The Role of Media in a Democracy: The Case of Jordan*. Amman, Jordan: Center for Strategic Studies, University of Jordan.

Ghazal, M. (2015), Media Commission Sues Ro'ya Channel over 'Sexually Explicit' Show. *The Jordan Times*.

Ghazal, M. (2017), Jordan's Second-largest Refugee Host Worldwide – UNHCR. *The Jordan Times*.

Ghazal, M. (2018), Most Media Practice Censorship in Jordan – CDFJ. *The Jordan Times*.

Human Rights Watch (1997), *Jordan Clamping Down on Critics: Human Rights Violations in Advance of the Parliamentary Elections*, 9(12).

Jordan Business (2010), The Death of ATV. *Ammon News*. Retrieved from http://en.ammonnews.net/article.aspx?articleNO=6916#.XJ84ECIzbIU. Accessed 20 April 2019.

Jordan Media City. *About*. Retrieved from www.jordanmediacity.com/en/about-jmc/?ID=305&Link=156&Direct=about-jmc. Accessed 20 April 2019.

Jordan Strategy Forum (2018), *Social Capital in Jordan: What is the Level of Trust in Our Institutions & Why?*. Retrieved from http://jsf.org/sites/default/files/EN%20Social%20Capital%20in%20Jordan.pdf. Accessed 20 April 2019.

Lucas, R. (2003), Press Laws as a Survival Strategy in Jordan, 1989–99. *Middle Eastern Studies*, 39(4).

Mendel, T. (2016), *Analysis of the Press and Publications Law, No. 8 for the Year 1998, as Amended*. Amman, Jordan: UNESCO.

Muasher, M. (2011), *A Decade of Struggling Reform Efforts in Jordan: The Resilience of the Rentier System*. Washington, DC: Carnegie Endowment for International Peace.

Oxford Business Group (2007), *The Report: Emerging Jordan 2007*. Retrieved from https://oxfordbusiness group.com/. Accessed 20 April 2019.

Robinson, G. (1998), Defensive Democratization in Jordan. *International Journal of Middle East Studies*, 30(3).

Sahhab, E. (2004), This is Radio Jerusalem . . . 1936. *Jerusalem Quarterly*, (20).

Saif, I. (2007), *The Process of Economic Reform in Jordan 1990–2005*. University of Jordan, Amman, Jordan: Center for Strategic Studies.

Sakr, N. (2013), 'We Cannot Let it Loose': Geopolitics, Security and Reform in Jordanian Broadcasting. In T. Guaaybess (ed.), *National Broadcasting and State Policy in Arab Countries*. Basingstoke: Palgrave Macmillan.

Sakr, N. (2015), *Good Practice in EU Public Service Media and Contemporary Practice in Jordan: A Comparative Analysis*. Amman, Jordan: UNESCO Amman Office.

Sharbel, G. (1999), *Interview with His Majesty King Abdullah II*. Translated from Arabic. Retrieved from https://kingabdullah.jo/en/interviews/interview-his-majesty-king-abdullah-ii-160. Accessed 20 April 2019.

Sweis, R. (2015), *Plans to Launch 'Public Service' TV Channel in Jordan Raise Eyebrows*. Media Power Monitor. Retrieved from http://mediapowermonitor.com/content/plans-launch-%E2%80%9Cpublic-service%E2%80%9D-tv-channel-jordan-raise-eyebrows. Accessed 20 April 2019.

Taher, G. (1995), Radio and Television: Strongholds for the Government, In G. Hawatmeh (ed.), *The Role of Media in a Democracy: The Case of Jordan*. Amman, Jordan: Center for Strategic Studies, University of Jordan.

Zada, J. (1995), The Official Media and Democracy. In G. Hawatmeh (ed.), *The Role of Media in a Democracy: The Case of Jordan*. Amman, Jordan: Center for Strategic Studies, University of Jordan.

Zaideh, S. (2018), *The Status of Women Journalists in Jordan's Media Institutions*. Retrieved from www.mediasupport.org/publication/the-status-of-women-journalists-in-jordans-media-institutions-arabic-version/. Accessed 20 April 2019.

Kuwait

12

CHRONICLING KUWAIT'S MEDIA EVOLUTION

The politics of technology and regulation

Fahed Al-Sumait, Ali A. Dashti, and Ildiko Kaposi

Introduction

Kuwait is a small constitutional emirate located in the northwestern corner of the Arabian Peninsula. It shares land borders with Iraq and Saudi Arabia, as well as a maritime border with Iran. Despite its small size and powerful neighbors, Kuwait has developed a distinctive political system that has profoundly influenced the development of its media environment. It has a historically robust print media scene and a long tradition with broadcast technologies, and today demonstrates significant adoption rates of digital media technologies (Al-Roomi, 2007; Kaposi, 2015; Mellor, 2005; Salem, 2018). Further, it has consistently ranked amongst the freest media environments in the region (Al-Sumait, 2013). However, following the Arab Uprisings, Kuwait's media freedoms have notably declined as the government struggles to keep up with a changing political landscape and the impacts of emerging media technologies (Alkazemi et al., 2018). This chapter outlines some of the significant social, political, and legal conditions which have contributed to this situation, with an eye toward the possible direction that the country's media may be heading.

To understand Kuwait's contemporary media environment, it is helpful to consider two interconnected aspects of its history: its cosmopolitan composition and its political system. Beginning with the former; as a well-positioned port city, since the late 1700s, the territory has served as a point of transit between the transnational Indian Ocean's maritime trade networks and terrestrial caravan routes that extended to Damascus (Al-Nakib, 2016). This history of immigration and multicultural interaction was further accelerated in the mid-20th century by oil-funded growth. According to the country's first census in 1957, of the 200,000 residents living in the country, about 40% were foreigners. By 1965, expatriates made up approximately two-thirds of the population, a proportion that essentially remains to the present day among its 4.2 million residents (Kuwait Central Statistical Bureau, 2018). The flow of ideas and cultural influences these conditions engender has fueled a market demand for news, information, and entertainment connected to the outside world. Kuwait's media environment largely reflects this situation.

A second historical point of consideration is the development of Kuwait's political system, which has demonstrated a type of liberalization not readily found in other countries of the region (Al-Roomi, 2007; Herb, 1999; Power, 2012; Tetreault, 2011). The commonly circulated origins story used to explain Kuwait's democratic aspirations recounts that in the mid-1700s a council of elders elected the Al-Sabah family to govern the area's settled inhabitants, but only after two other prominent families declined the responsibility for fear it would infringe upon their businesses (Salem, 2008; Tetreault, 2000). This story establishes a contractarian beginning to the ruling family's power – rather than one achieved by force or colonial implant. In 1899, Kuwait became a British protectorate partially as a consequence of its significance to British colonial trade networks and its proximity to the Ottoman Empire's influence. This protectorate status emboldened the territorial ambitions and personal opulence of Kuwait's ruler at the time, Mubarak Al-Sabah, who then ran afoul with the strong merchant families who primarily funded the government's activities. In 1909, some of Kuwait's richest pearl traders led a secession to Bahrain in protest over Mubarak's new price controls and taxes to fund his military campaigns (Crystal, 1990). While the ruler was eventually successful in coaxing them (and their valuable fleets) to return, his concessions opened the door for power-sharing experimentations in the form of two later constituent assemblies, first in 1921 and again in 1938 (Al-Mughni, 2001). Following its independence in 1961, the lessons of those earlier (short-lived) experimentations proved formative for Kuwait's newly elected constituent assembly, which drafted a forward-thinking constitution that was approved by the amir in 1962 (Smith, 1999). The ongoing implications of these political conditions for Kuwait's media environment are discussed later under the laws and regulations section. First, however, it is useful to examine the historical context in which Kuwait has adopted three forms of media technology: print, broadcast, and digital.

Historical background

As with many historic transit points, the flow of people and goods in and out of Kuwait also brought with it various forms of media which were initially uncontrolled by the government. Merchants introduced books and newspapers from places like Iraq, Egypt, Syria, and Lebanon. Later a printing press brought from Iraq in 1947 greatly facilitated local production (Farouq, 2016). From 1928 to 1930, Abdul Aziz Al-Rushaid published the first Kuwaiti magazine, printed in Egypt, called *Mujallat Alkuwait* (Kuwait Magazine) (Jurdi and Dashti, 1994). Then in 1946, Kuwaiti students in Egypt established a magazine called *AlBe'thah*, followed shortly thereafter by their monthly magazine, *Kathmah*, which was published inside Kuwait. Throughout the 1950s, approximately 20 publications started and failed due to various operational issues (Almashikhi, 2008; AlShanoofi, 1999). At the time, the growing Israeli conflict and rise in Arab nationalism fueled a critical press that often published content condemning British colonialism, causing embarrassment for Kuwait's rulers. The government's Publications Department entered the scene in 1954 with its official newspaper called *Kuwait Alyoum* (Kuwait Today)[1] (Al-Hatim, 1962). Two years later Kuwait enacted its first piece of media legislation, thereby attempting to regulate the press five years before the country's own independence.

Following independence in 1961, the new state issued its official press law. Immediately, several privately owned and operated publications emerged which represented different political and economic interests, especially from the merchant class. Within two years, Kuwait had its first weekly newspaper (*Al-Rai Al-Aam*), its first opposition newspaper (*Al-Taleea*), the Gulf region's first English-language newspaper (*Kuwait Times*), and numerous magazines of diverse interest (Alkazemi et al., 2018). As mentioned, Arab nationalism had a strong foothold in Kuwait. Coupled with the country's relatively vibrant media environment, rapid economic growth, as well as conflicts in Lebanon and Palestine, many Arab writers and intellectuals migrated to the country. The experience and skills of these expatriates contributed heavily to Kuwait's print media scene.[2] In response to these influences, the Ministry issued a law mandating that the managing editor of any publication be a Kuwaiti citizen (Farouq, 2016). Despite the government's efforts to maintain its direct influence over the print environment, the situation eventually became too competitive for them. In 1976, it closed most state papers and chose instead to officially communicate through the Kuwait News Agency (KUNA), as well as its broadcast media assets (Alkazemi et al., 2018). For decades, Kuwaiti newspapers have demonstrated a high degree of sophistication and range of orientations relative to their counterparts in most Arab countries (Kazan, 1993). For residents, they also served as an alternative to the country's mainly state-run broadcast environment.

The beginning of the broadcasting media

Government control over Kuwait's broadcast environment was much stronger than with its printed press. Mellor (2005) explains this tendency among Arab governments based on broadcast technology's wider reach,[3] its utility as a purveyor of nationalism, and its potential role in propaganda – on behalf of the state or against it. In Kuwait, the first radio set appears to have sparked only a novel interest in this new technology. The story has two known accounts (Al-Hatim, 1962). The first describes Major Frank Holmes – a former British officer, geologist, and oil concession hunter for American-based Gulf Oil Company – offering a radio set as a gift to then ruler Sheikh Ahmad Al-Jaber Al-Sabah in 1935. An alternative account claims a Kuwaiti trader named Ahmad Al Nakib was the first to bring two radios from Iraq in 1933 as gifts to the same sheikh. Regardless of the number of radio sets owned by the sheikh, it took some time for the government to capitalize on the technology. Distribution rights for selling radio sets went through the hands of multiple merchant families beginning as early as 1935, while control over the domestic airwaves went immediately to the government – which then waited almost 16 years before utilizing them. During that time, a simple low-frequency station based in Dasman Palace used the technology to air music alongside international broadcasts transmitted by London, Bagdad, and Cairo. On 12 May 1951, "Huna Al-Kuwait" (here is Kuwait) was the first phrase broadcast from within the country, signifying the official beginning of state radio (Kuwait News Agency, 2015). For the first decade, radio broadcasts lasted only two hours, later expanding to six in the 1960s with more diversified programming. The state continued controlling domestic radio until 2003 when it then opened licensing to private radio (and television) stations (Ayish, 2011). By 2019, nearly 30 radio stations were either broadcasting or intercepted in Kuwait, representing multiple languages and a variety of content, although the majority remain under government control.

In 1957, as had been the case with print media, television broadcasting started in Kuwait as a private enterprise (Alkazemi et al., 2018). A Kuwaiti merchant, using a 10-kilowatt transmission station and a staff of six people, broadcast cartoons and feature films for two hours per day to help promote sales of RCA TV sets (Jurdi and Dashti, 1994). However, after independence television came under direct government control (Boyd, 1999; Press Reference, 2016). By 1962, black-and-white TV was broadcast for four hours per day, doubling to eight hours per day by 1966. In 1974, Kuwait was one of the first Arab countries to broadcast in color. Over the years, Kuwait TV (KTV) expanded its content and number of channels to the point where it could broadcast around the clock. Early programming included a range of entertainment, educational, and cultural programming heavily reliant on imported content, as well as a rudimentary news service.

As early as 1969, Kuwait had its satellite earth station (the second in the Middle East) (Wheeler, 2006), but it did not start its broadcast network until the government later learned the importance of such an asset (Amin, 2000). During the Iraqi invasion of Kuwait in 1990, Kuwait TV played a role in boosting morale among Kuwaitis both inside and outside of the country as they produced and broadcast a daily message from Saudi Arabia while in exile (Alenizi, 2012). In July of 1992, just over a year after its liberation, Kuwait launched its Satellite Channel (KSC) to expand its reach across the peninsula and into North Africa (Jurdi and Dashti, 1994). By 1997, its satellite broadcasts extended as far as North America (Wheeler, 2006). Once the country opened broadcast licenses to private enterprises in 2003, Al Rai Media Group became the first private organization to offer commercial satellite broadcasting in Arabic from Kuwait (Khayrallah, 2017).

Today, the government maintains half of the 20 satellite stations based in Kuwait. Prior to the controversial closing of four stations associated with the AlWatan Media Group in 2015, private satellite broadcasting outnumbered that of the government. In addition to the locally based satellite broadcasters, numerous international media organizations have offices in Kuwait, which share a rented facility managed by the HNDC Company for their occasional broadcasts. These include pan-Arab organizations (Al Jazeera, Al Arabiya, MBC, etc.), a range of regional broadcasters (e.g., Saudi, Dubai, and Abu Dhabi TV stations), as well as those origi-nating from farther afield (e.g., BBC Arabia, American-based Al Hurra, Sky News Arabia, and CNBC Arabia) (Jamal, 2019). This approach appears to provide ready broadcasting capabilities for a vast range of media organizations without the costs, or political capital, associated with maintaining their own facilities. Nine broadcasting satellites transmit the majority of content for the country.[4]

Increasingly, Kuwait and other governments in the region are turning to sophisticated fund-ing arrangements that blur the lines between public and private media ownership to get their broadcast messages out. Rather than outright ownership or ministerial oversight, this model uses private holding companies with close ties or direct links to governments. Such entities own large media conglomerates that tend to be well-positioned in the market (Pavlik, 2015). An illustrative example is the Orbit Showtime Network (OSN). In 2009, Kuwaiti-owned Show-time Arabia and Saudi-owned Orbit Group merged into OSN. It is currently the most profit-able pay-TV platform in the MENA region, delivering content to 24 countries. OSN is part of the Dubai-based Panther Media Group Limited, 60.5% of which belongs to Kuwait Projects Company (KIPCO) with the remainder held by Al Mawarid Investment Company (Bloomb-erg, 2019). Both companies are closely linked to the governments of Kuwait and Saudi Arabia.[5] The potential politicization of this largely entertainment-oriented service can be illustrated in OSN's immediate dropping of the entire Qatar-based Al Jazeera group of channels within days of the 2017 round of the Saudi–Qatar dispute – a move speculated to have cost Al Jazeera around 25% of its regional subscriber base (Hawkes, 2017).[6] The OSN example is further tell-ing of regional circumstances since, in 2018, KIPCO began looking for a buyer of its shares in the Panther Media Group, citing financial losses due to piracy and competition from streaming services (Hamdan, 2018). Of course, the satellite broadcasting industry is not the only one to be hit by the disruptive effects of digital media technologies, which is the point to which we now turn.

The Internet and digital media

Like many of its counterparts in the Gulf Cooperation Council (GCC), Kuwait ranks high glob-ally on important indicators of information and communications technology (ICT). For exam-ple, a 2018 report by Hootsuite listed GCC countries in four of the top five spots worldwide for

Internet penetration (Kuwait was third) (Kemp, 2018). Internet usage in Kuwait has increased briskly since it was introduced in the 1990s (Kaposi, 2015). In 2000, there were 150,000 Internet users in Kuwait, rising to 900,000 by 2008 and then 4.1 million in 2018 (Internet World Stats, 2018). At the government's instructions, ISPs block access to certain websites on moral or political grounds, though many users easily bypass such restrictions. According to the government's 2019 data, 99.7% of households have Internet access and 98% of the population uses the Internet (Kuwait Communication and Information Technology Regulatory Authority, 2019b). Kuwait has seven main international connectivity cables[7] managing the flow of data through the country and is in the process of upgrading its fiber optic infrastructure, a process that has been hampered by delays since it first began in 2007. There are also three mobile operators[8] providing 4G LTE network coverage to over 97% of the country, as well as robust 5G services. Given the slow growth of fixed-line technology, more than double the number of individuals and organizations access their high-speed connections through mobile network routers instead (Kuwait Central Authority for Information Technology, 2017).

The 2016 World Economic Forum's (WEF) global technology report lists Kuwait as first worldwide for mobile coverage, second for cellular and broadband subscriptions, and 14th for household computer ownership[9] (Baller et al., 2016). While reports vary, data on mobile phone subscription rates are well over 200% according to the WEF (218%) (Baller et al., 2016), the *Arab Social Media Report* (260%) (Salem, 2018), Kuwait's Communication and Information Technology Regulatory Agency (223%) (2019b), and Kuwait's Central Authority for Information Technology (240%) (2017), making it possibly the world's highest ratio of mobile subscriptions per person. Despite the availably of these technologies, the WEF's measures of the impacts of ICT on societal development put Kuwait in the bottom third worldwide. It also ranks media usage rates by individuals as significantly higher than those by businesses or the government (Baller et al., 2016). So while infrastructure provisions and technology adoption rates are high, their application for commerce and governance remains underutilized.

It is further telling to examine some of the existing, though limited, data about how residents in Kuwait currently use digital media. With an estimated 99.7% of households using smartphones, most people access the Internet through their handheld devices (Kuwait Central Authority for Information Technology, 2017). It is therefore not surprising that social media use is pervasive. Given the cosmopolitan nature of the society, it is also understandable that platform usage varies by community. For example, according to the most recent government figures, only Facebook is more popular among expatriates, while WhatsApp, Instagram, Snapchat, and Twitter are all over 70% usage among Kuwaitis (Kuwait Central Authority for Information Technology, 2017). Twitter itself exemplifies much about the social media conditions in the country. The platform was quickly adopted as a vehicle for political news and information, as well as networking between politicians and their constituents (Al-Sumait, 2013). Consequently, per capita, Twitter use in Kuwait has been the highest among all Middle Eastern countries[10] almost since regional data about the platform exists, only falling into joint first place with Bahrain in 2018 (Salem, 2018). Tellingly, after the political tensions exposed during the 2011 Arab Uprisings and then the subsequent media laws introduced by the government in 2015 and 2016, Kuwait has been the only Arab country to show declining numbers of Twitter users since its peak in 2012 (Dubai School of Government, 2014). In the case of Twitter and all of the other media discussed so far, it is the political and legal environment in which they are situated that characterizes Kuwait's distinctiveness within the MENA region. For that reason, the story of its regulatory history is the focus of the next section.

The media in Kuwait's constitution

Adopted in November 1962, less than a year after independence, the Kuwaiti Constitution established the socio-political order of the new State of Kuwait as a democratic amiri regime (*Constitution of Kuwait*, 1962). The Constitution is widely interpreted as the articulation of the quasi-contractarian tradition that has governed Kuwait since the beginning of the rule of the Al-Sabah family in the mid-1700s. A commitment to democracy is articulated throughout the Constitution, starting with Article 6 that states, "Kuwait's system of government is democratic; sovereignty is vested in the Nation as the source of all authority." Part II establishes human rights as the basic foundation of Kuwaiti society, including the declaration that "Justice, freedom, and equality are the pillars of society" (Article 7), while Part IV establishes the system of government "on the basis of separation and cooperation of powers" (Article 50). Finally, Part III guarantees the public's rights of personal liberty, unrestricted freedom of belief, freedoms of association and assembly, freedom to petition, and privacy of letters and telecommunications. All of these have potential relevance for freedom of expression and provide insight into the development of Kuwait's media environment.

Among the freedoms listed in Part III, Articles 36 and 37 provide the guarantees for freedom of opinion, expression of opinions, and freedom of the press and publication. Given the significance of *diwaniyyas*[11] in Kuwait politics and public life, Article 38 states that the inviolability of the home cannot be entered without the dweller's permission. This can also be read as a clause protecting the freedom of publicly relevant discussions. Additional freedoms related to speech and expression are included in Part IV that grants absolute privilege to speech employed by Members of Parliament in debates of the National Assembly, as a further guarantee of the separation of powers (Article 110).

Simultaneously, the limits on democratic freedoms are coded into other provisions in the Constitution. The "democratic amiri regime" structure also relies on stipulations that prevent any questioning of the foundations of government and place the ruler above public criticism, similar to the way countries place prohibitions on the desecration of symbols of the nation.[12] Adding political limitations, Article 49 affirms "the observance of public order and the respect of public morals" as an obligation that applies to all inhabitants of the country.[13] The Kuwaiti Constitution leaves the precise contours of freedom of the press to be drawn by the relevant laws; freedom is guaranteed but subject to "the conditions and stipulations prescribed by Law" (Articles 36 and 37). Historically, this has made press laws a reflection of the power struggles between the government and parliament, or the ruling family and other powerful interest groups in society.[14] Since the state broadcaster remained under the ownership and control of the Ministry of Information, no specific laws were required to regulate its workings. However as already discussed, the press not only predated broadcasting but was also primarily privately owned, and thus necessitated legislation before independence.

Media regulations

Kuwait's first press law was issued in 1956 by amiri decree in response to the state of literal lawlessness that saw print publications launched by anyone interested in this new form of media operating freely as long as they did not offend the government (Jurdi and Dashti, 1994). The need to regulate the press, including the formalization of what constitutes press violations, was codified into the short-lived 1956 law that was soon superseded by the more specifically articulated press law of 1961 (Aldayin, 2003). The law established a system of licensing for the press and listed the types of content that newspapers were prohibited from printing, including criticism of the person of the amir, disparagement of God and the prophets, and information that could hurt the economy, violate national interests, create divisions among people, or tarnish public morals (Sakr, 2006). Most controversially, Article 35 of the 1961 press law authorized the government to suspend offending publications. The law was amended four times, each modification impacting Article 35 and, by implication, the tightness of government control over the press. The ebb and flow of press freedom is reflected in the amendments of the press law: the 1972 modification gave the power to suspend publications to the courts, making control over the press more democratic;[15] the 1976 amendment (issued under the same amir who democratized the procedure in 1972) restored rights of suspension and the revocation of licenses to the executive; while the 1986 amendment occurred at a time the Constitution and parliament were suspended and it institutionalized pre-publication censorship in newspapers – a system which stayed in place until the 1991 liberation of Kuwait from Iraqi occupation (Jurdi and Dashti, 1994).

The inadequacies and anachronisms[16] of the 1961 law made it necessary to introduce a new press law. Following years of negotiations in parliament, Law No. 3 of 2006 Concerning Press & Publication replaced the old press law. Reactions to the 2006 press law were mixed, although the Kuwaiti media and international observers mostly agreed that it helped liberalize the press scene. Key changes from the old law included abolishing pre-publication censorship[17] and shifting supervisory control over the licensing and publication process to the judiciary.[18] The door to licensing new publications was opened, and as a result newspaper titles mushroomed. The law also made it easier to sell imported publications catering to both local and expatriate populations, although these must still be submitted to the Ministry of Information for screening prohibited content.

At the same time, however, the 2006 press law significantly increased the maximum amount of fines for an offensive speech on religion, criticism of the amir, the judiciary, or other "friendly" countries, and an extensive list of additional matters banned from publication.[19] The law also keeps opening the possibility of banning content created by third parties, such as commercial advertising, if a resolution by the competent minister prohibits its publication. Although the press law only lists fines as penalties for the publication of banned content, it sets the penalties "without prejudice to any severer penalty stipulated under any other law," which allows for the possibility of imprisonment for certain offenses under the Penal Code – a condition that the government has utilized previously.

The implications of the 2006 press law go well beyond print media. Regarding licensing conditions, procedures, and content-related prohibitions, the provisions of the 2006 law are repeated in laws introduced in the following decade to regulate content delivered through different media technologies. Law No. 61 of 2007 on Audiovisual Information that regulates terrestrial and satellite broadcasting; Law No. 8 of 2016 Regarding the Regulation of Electronic Media such as web-based publications, electronic news services, news agencies, and websites of newspapers and televisions; and Law No. 63 of 2015 on Combating Information Technology Crimes (the "cybercrimes law") all explicitly reference the content-related provisions laid down in the 2006 press law. Similar to the original 2006 blueprint, subsequent media laws have also attracted criticism for vagueness, as the elastic terminology repeated in the laws often lacks precise legal definitions of offenses and enables overbroad restrictions on freedom of expression.[20]

In an attempt to manage the media environment, Kuwait established a Ministry of Information (MOI)[21] roughly six months after gaining its independence. Among its other powers, the MOI had the authority to grant publishing and broadcast licenses (Mellor, 2005). Today, the Ministry still issues new licenses and renewals, but since Kuwait's 2006 media law, the authority to cancel licenses is vested with the courts. Furthermore, media organizations can also appeal through the judicial system if the Ministry denies them a renewal. Today the MOI continues to run the KTV network and several radio stations, as well as provide support for the government in other forms of promotional communication ranging from tourism to politics (Kuwait Ministry of Information, 2016b). With the increasing convergence of media and telecommunications technologies, Kuwait's Ministry of Information is not the only government entity overseeing the media landscape in the country. The Ministry of Communications, which traditionally managed postal and telecommunication functions, also found itself playing a role in emerging wireless and mobile telephone services. In addition, it was given the responsibility of developing the infrastructure and regulations needed to support the country's growing mobile computing and handheld markets.

To keep up with the technological changes inherent in today's media environment, some of the previous powers held by both ministries have been reallocated to two relatively new agencies. The first, the Central Authority for Information Technology (CAIT), founded in 2014, is the planning body now responsible for coordinating the country's electronic government services and overall governance framework, including an e-government portal, the back-end network for exchanging information between ministries, and digitizing historical archives from five (unnamed) daily newspapers in addition to the only government newspaper in operation and its official gazette, *Kuwait Alyoum* (Kuwait Central Authority for Information Technology, 2019). The second and more active agency is the Communication and Information Technology Regulatory Authority (CITRA). Established in 2014, it is described as an "independent corporate body," which works as a public authority administered under the Minister of State for Cabinet Affairs. As declared on its website, it is responsible for "overseeing the telecommunications sector, [to] monitor and protect the interests of users and service provider[s] and regulate the service of telecommunication networks" (Kuwait Communication and Information Technology Regulatory Authority, 2019a). Its duties range from domain and spectrum management to managing the telecommunication services industry and collecting official data on ICT indicators for the country. Interestingly, Article 21 of Law No. 37 of 2014 on the establishment of CITRA also gives it the right to establish, operate, and manage a public telecommunications network and associated services should it so "decide" (Kuwait National Assembly, 2014). To date, there have been no overtures by the government to nationalize the telecommunications sector.

A final body of significance to Kuwait's media laws is that of the official legislature itself: the National Assembly. Kuwait's parliament is a 50-seat unicameral national assembly established by the constitution. Members are elected every four years unless the parliament is dismissed, which is constitutionally allowed by amiri decree as long as new elections are called within two months. It has been dissolved unconstitutionally twice, in 1976 and 1986 (Tetreault, 2000). Due to reoccurring political impasse, constitutionally allowed dissolutions have been a regular occurrence since the parliament was reinstated in 1992 following Kuwait's liberation from Iraq. As a result, it has held early elections eight times (Herb, 2019), leaving the country in a persistent state of political stutter. In this context, media laws are proposed, debated, rejected, and accepted by the various incarnations of the parliament, making their role in media legislation a somewhat unpredictable, though crucial, function. As official representatives of the public, their power to do so is enshrined in Kuwait's constitution regardless of their performance.

Government control versus market rules

The legal controls policing the boundaries of admissibility in public expression ensure government oversight of the media regardless of ownership. The situation in Kuwait has been summarized as being "a privately owned but officially constrained press scene" (Brown, 2017: 72), where widespread self-censorship ensures the observation of red lines, even in the absence of prior censorship. Journalistic self-censorship is undoubtedly a major force of restriction on the freedom of privately owned media, but it may be more helpful to see the media's situation as a manifestation of underlying socio-structural configurations. Kuwait is a small country, with a population that still forms as a close-knit community despite the dynamic demographic growth of the last decades. The fabric of society continues to be based on dense and cross-cutting networks of familial, tribal, and sectarian affiliations and relations sustained through a system of mutual obligations. The boundaries of the spheres of government, politics, and business are permeable and are crossed with ease by actors, thus making the separation of roles in a Weberian sense inconceivable for citizens. Positing the government and the market as a dichotomous pair is thus not particularly helpful in understanding the Kuwaiti scene, where the two spheres are intertwined through multiple personal ties. Since most Kuwaiti private media outlets are part of larger, usually family-controlled conglomerates, state commissions remain a lucrative opportunity for the owners in their other businesses, considerations which inevitably influence the stances media firms take in relation to the government.

The interconnected nature of relationships also enables an informal system of maintaining balance in terms of media firm expansions.[22] Despite the lack of laws and regulations against concentrations of ownership for content-producing media, no single media owner has attempted to achieve market dominance through takeovers, mergers, acquisitions, or price wars. Of the standard economic arguments in favor of government intervention in the market, tendencies toward monopoly have thus not necessitated structural or behavioral measures by the government. On the other hand, negative externalities as another economic reason for government intervention in media markets are covered extensively in media law prohibitions on content deemed to be harmful to society, as discussed earlier.

Censorship

The Kuwaiti government tends to see its system of controls as a way of enforcing a model of social responsibility in the media.[23] This logic is reflected in the 2006 press law that obliges editors-in-chief to "search for accuracy and truth in everything" before publication (Article 17) and guarantees the right of reply to persons and entities covered in the press. Similarly, fair representation, equal treatment, and unbiased coverage of candidates in the election campaign were prescribed for privately owned media in a decree issued by the Ministry of Interior (Democracy Reporting International and Kuwait Transparency Society, 2008). Furthermore, while "encroaching" on God or the office of the amir is strictly forbidden, "enlightened and learned" public discussion on all other issues is permissible.

The need to exercise "quality control" over public discussions to ensure their socially responsible character is evident in the way the potentially combustible debates over religion are handled. According to the government's official position, and supported by some evidence from court cases and amiri pardons, criminal liability does not apply to the dissemination of critical scholarly works on religion if the criticism is delivered in a "calm and composed manner," "devoid of inflammatory phraseology," and if the scholar is "of proven good faith" (United Nations Human Rights Committee, 2014: 39). Even in generally plaintiff-friendly defamation cases, the right of criticism is guaranteed for writers if they can show that they sought to serve the public interest, demonstrated objectivity in presenting the information, and refrained from malice. As long as the criticism does not constitute personal attacks and remains focused on the official conduct of a public official, it will be considered a legitimate component of public discussion[24] (Alkandari and Ghannam, 2015; Alshehab, 2018).

Given the heterogeneous composition of the Kuwaiti population, the threat of (externally fanned)[25] discord leading to the breakdown of social order is perceived to be persistently hanging over the country. In the face of regional tensions and the examples of disorder that have engulfed other Arab countries, national unity appears to be a value preserved at the expense of free expression. This desire is reflected in the laws aimed at curbing seditious speech, from articles of Law No. 31 of 1970 on National Security, the Penal Code (Law No. 16 of 1960), and the media laws discussed above, to Law No. 19 of 2012 on the Protection of National Unity. The 2012 national unity law was issued as an amiri decree and covers radio, television, publishing, printing, Internet, and social media. Prohibitions include advocating or encouraging hate or disrespect towards any group of society, provoking sectarian or tribal strife, or spreading ideas of superiority over any group in society and inciting violence against them on such basis. The list of prohibitions introduced in the law also specifically mentions the transmission and retransmission of false rumors leading to the above, as if the law was taking pre-emptive measures against the fake news epidemic that erupted on social media in the wake of the 2016 US elections.

Examining court cases filed against the media provides a proxy gauge of how censorship is exercised within the country. For example, a stark contrast exists in the number of court cases filed against the media before and after the implementation of Kuwait's 2015 cybercrime law and 2016 electronic media law, which gave significant new powers to the government. In 2014, the Ministry of Information referred to 384 cases against newspapers and TV stations to the public prosecution, compared to the 104 filed by individuals and other parties (Toumi, 2015). At that time, the provisions of the existing 2006 publication law did now allow the prosecution to look into case files against online sites. Two years later, following the implementation of the 2015 and 2016 laws, the prosecution received 3,143 cases (more than six times the total 2014 number), over 90% of which specifically related to violations of these new laws and most of which targeted content from social media platforms like Instagram and Twitter (Al-Abdullah, 2017). The multiplication of cases filed under Kuwait's latest media laws negatively impacts the degree of freedom exercised by journalists and individuals seeking to express their opinions through any type of media – a point also cautioned against by organizations such as Human Rights Watch (2018) and Amnesty International (2017).

Another way to evaluate relative media freedoms in Kuwait is through longitudinal, independent metrics conducted by organizations such as Reporters Without Borders and Freedom House (Alkazemi et al., 2018). While the methodologies of both organizations differ,[26] their relative rankings across time are revealing. In both cases, Kuwait's measures show an initial increase in freedoms that peak in 2008 and 2009 before starting a drastic and persistent decline. The country's turbulent conditions, coupled with the implementation of new laws to cope with changing political and technological circumstances, help explain the trends documented by both Freedom House and Reporters Without Borders. Such results inevitably raise questions about the direction Kuwait's media freedoms are heading after more than 40 years as one of the Middle East's most politically liberalized countries.

Conclusion: media and social change

As stated, Kuwait's media environment reflects the tenor of national politics, especially pertaining to the interplay between the ruling family and the country's strong merchant (and religious) forces, who perform through the executive and legislative bodies respectively. Constant too is the inherent tension between the pressures to exert strong control over media versus allowing for the greatest possible free-market benefits from emerging media. These tensions and their complexity are likely to be exacerbated as media forms increasingly converge across platforms and integrate further into the growing digital economy promised by such ideas as the Internet of Things and Industry 4.0 (Al-Sumait, 2019; Baller et al., 2016; Salem, 2018). The creation of new government institutions like CAIT and CITRA, in addition to the media laws introduced since 2015, reflects the government's attempt to better manage the combination of infrastructure, regulation, and human activities necessary for a robust digital ecosystem. As well, the government has begun implementing large-scale plans that attempt to rewrite its existing social and economic contracts in ways articulated through its Vision 2035 plan. This vision, also referred to as "New Kuwait," has allocated significant resources toward the development of media and ICT capabilities (Al-Sumait, 2019). Simultaneously, the general population (and the parliamentarians) are deeply immersed in digital media technologies on a scale that in several respects is at the vanguard of today's global possibilities. The myriad ways in which such conditions impact people's social interactions, working environment, leisure time, and political engagement – within the permissibility of technology and legality – is only beginning to emerge. At the time of writing, the government exerts a high degree of control over the media environment, but this may be at the expense of its tradition as a relatively free atmosphere. However, should Kuwait's history be any indication, when it comes to media, most often it is the population led by private enterprise that capitalizes on their benefits ahead of the government – despite the latter's advanced regulatory machinations, as well as political and economic advantages.

As a final point of reflection, a multitude of exigent forces occurring outside of the country's control will continue to affect media developments within its borders. These include – but are certainly not limited to – geopolitical conditions at the regional and global levels, the economic shocks of declining fossil fuel dependencies and volatile oil markets, fickle international public opinion toward the region, security threats such as terrorism and proximate military conflicts, and, of course, the march of technological innovation, which has been further accelerated by the impacts of the COVID-19 pandemic. Each of these factors potentially influences the fluidity of Kuwait's media scene and the range of discourse it engenders, making predictions a somewhat spurious exercise. But perhaps a few, cautious, forward-looking points can be made. To begin with, growth is likely to continue in several important areas, such as the country's technological sophistication, the scope of digital media users, and new platforms that will expand the flow of information and entertainment in the country. Adaptive regulatory measures by the government will inevitably follow in kind. Kuwait's storied newspapers, like those in most of the world, will continue losing readership as younger generations look for news and information elsewhere. However, since many of these papers are driven more by political and social imperatives than economic ones, their decline will probably be slower than the global average, giving them opportunities to potentially adapt their business models to stay relevant. Digital media diffusion rates for exiting technologies may plateau among the public since most populations have already reached a high level of saturation. But as 5G networks and other innovations become more widespread, the private sector and individual users will most likely adopt these quickly. However, for the immediate future, it is safe to assume that freedom of speech and the press will continue their downward spiral until and unless citizens and expatriates alike better understand Kuwait's rich media history and choose to help steer it on an alternative trajectory. Perhaps this chapter is a modest contribution toward that goal.

Notes

1 *Kuwait Alyoum* still operates today as the government's official gazette.
2 These Arab expatriates also played significant roles in areas such as education and public administration.

3 The wider reach of broadcasting is a function of its technological range, free-to-air format, and the fact that media consumption can occur irrespective of literacy rates.

4 These include Arabsat BADR-4 and Arabsat 5C; AsiaSat 5; Eutelsat 8, Eutelsat West B, and Eutelsat Hotbird 13B; Galaxy 19; Hipasat – 30W-5; and Intelsat 8.

5 KIPCO's proximity to the government is in part reflected by the composition of its board of directors, which include Kuwait's former ambassador to the UN and three members of the royal family, one of whom is also the granddaughter of the current amir. The other partner, Al Mawarid, is chaired by Khaled bin Abdullah bin Abdul Rahman Al Saud, a member of the Saudi royal family and first cousin to the (current and past) ruler. Its CEO, Fahd bin Abdullah bin Mohammed Al Saud, is also a member of the House of Saud and a former deputy defense minister.

6 The UAE, Qatar, and Saudi Arabia also dropped the Qatar-based beIN media from operating in their countries, which was a growing and direct competitor for OSN. So in addition to the political message, this was also a welcome business move for OSN.

7 FLAG, FOG, SMW3, SMW4, Falcon, and GBI are all submarine cables connected to Kuwait, while a seventh land cable connects to Saudi Arabia.

8 Kuwait's three mobile operators are Zain, Viva, and Ooredoo. They are owned respectively by Kuwait, Saudi Arabia, and Qatar.

9 The WEF figure puts household computer rates at 87.8%, while the Kuwait government estimates the figure at 99.7%, which if true, would place Kuwait as the world's highest on this measure above current number one, Iceland, with 98.1%.

10 This definition of the Middle East includes comparison among all 22 Arab League countries, plus Iran, Turkey, and Israel.

11 *Duwaniyyas* are family-owned, mainly male-only gathering places that play a central role in Kuwait's social and political networks. They vary considerably in formality, function, frequency, and composition. However, they feature regularly in the daily life for many Kuwaiti men (Al-Sumait, 2011).

12 Article 4 declares Kuwait to be a "hereditary Amirate" ruled by descendants of Mubarak Al-Sabah, while Article 54 stipulates that the head of state is the amir whose person is "safeguarded and inviolable."

13 It is worth noting here that religion is not mentioned in the Constitution as an area where freedom of expression is to be limited. Apart from declaring Islam as the official religion of the state and pledging to maintain Islamic heritage, the founding document of Kuwait treats religion as a factor like race, origin, or language, based on which no unequal treatment of people is allowed (Article 29). Shari'a is declared as one of the main sources of law (Article 2), but it does not enjoy exclusivity in shaping legislation, which allows for an amalgam of influences to emerge in the Kuwaiti legal system.

14 Naomi Sakr (2006) makes a similar point when she refers to media policy as a "litmus test" for political change.

15 The ensuing "relatively greater freedom of expression" is part of what made Kuwait attractive to writers from elsewhere in the Arab world. The influx of Arab expatriate journalistic talent helped the Kuwaiti (and Gulf) press "begin to assert greater influence" (Al-Jaber and Gunter, 2013: 24).

16 For example, the law's definition of publications included "sunlight photos," while circulation included "sticking [the publication] on the wall" (Aldayin, 2003: 84).

17 Article 8 of the law specifies that newspapers shall not be subject to any advance censorship.

18 The law gives the courts the power to cancel a license, suspend a newspaper, or detain a journalist; also, applicants who were denied a license have the right to appeal the ministry's decision in court.

19 Prohibited content in the press includes defamatory, sarcastic, or contemptuous speech on Allah and religious figures (Article 19); criticisms of the amir and attributing statements to him without permission from his office (Article 20); contempt for the Constitution, humiliation or degradation of the judiciary, violation of and instigation to violate public morals, disclosure of official secrets, information affecting the value of the national currency or the confidence in the economy, hateful speech or information that impairs people's reputation or wealth, damaging relations between Kuwait and other Arab or friendly countries, deviation from the purpose the specialized newspaper's license was issued for (Article 21); incitement for a coup d'état and instigation for changing the ruling and economic systems by force or illegal means (Article 28).

20 For example, the press law prohibits "any violation to public morals," and the cybercrimes law prohibits content that would "prejudice public morality," without any attempt to explain how "public morality" is to be understood. Since any citizen can make an official complaint about media content they deem offensive, the standards of offensiveness tend to be established according to the most sensitive person's tastes, instead of relying on a standard that would consider whether the average person, applying contemporary community standards, would find the work offensive.

21 Originally called the "Ministry of Guidance and News" from its establishment in January 1962 until 1979 when it received its current name (Kuwait Ministry of Information, 2016a; Kuwait Ministry of Public Works, 2016).

22 The competitive but also cooperative relations between rival media companies were evident in the way four major newspapers (*Al-Qabas, Al-Rai, Al-Jareeda,* and *Al-Anbaa*) jointly announced their concerted decision to suspend publication of the print editions of their Saturday papers in the face of fierce competition newspapers face from digital and social media (Abu Baker, 2019).

23 The periodic report submitted to the Human Rights Committee of the UN in 2014 talks about Kuwait's "evident desire to support the development of free and responsible media in step with the times" and the state's goal of formulating a strategy that "safeguards freedom of information so that the media's full potential can be harnessed in the service of society as a whole" United Nations Human Rights Committee, 2014: 51.

24 This is dictated by the reasoning that there is a strong public interest in evaluating public services and fighting corruption, which outweighs the need to protect the reputations, social status or emotional welfare of public officials, strongly worded and harsh criticism is permitted. Thus for instance describing a public official as 'ignorant', 'pathetic', or 'cowardly in standing against corruption' is not actionable because the criticism is related to the person's official conduct (Alkandari and Ghannam, 2015).

25 Concerns over foreign powers, including Kuwait's large neighbors, covertly interfering in the country's internal affairs predate independence. A recent example of (WikiLeaks) documented attempts at soft meddling would be the more than $80,000 Saudi Arabia paid in subscription fees to Kuwaiti publications in an effort to promote its ties with the country (Hendawi and Mrooue, 2015).

26 In addition to differences in how and what they measure as media freedoms, they also rank order results using a different total number of countries; Freedom House includes 199 countries and territories while RWB tallies only 180.

References

Abu Baker, M. (2019), *Kuwait Papers Suspend Production to Cut Cost in Face of Growing Digital Media.* Retrieved from www.kuna.net.kw/ArticleDetails.aspx?id=2768481&language=en

Al-Abdullah, H. (2017), Alghamlas lil Aljareda: 3143 guthiya talqtaha neabat 'alam almadhhi minha 2865 jareeda alkuwait (Al-Gamlas for AlJarida: 3143 cases received by the media prosecutor last year, including 2865 electronic crimes). *AlJarida Newspaper,* 31 January. Retrieved from www.aljarida.com/articles/1485796695790498900/

Al-Hatim, A. (1962), *Min huna badaat Al-Kuwait (From Here Kuwait Started).* Damascus, Syria: Almatba'e Alamomiya.

Al-Jaber, K., and Gunter, B. (2013), Evolving News Systems in the Gulf Countries. In B. Gunter and R. Dickinson (eds.), *News Media in the Arab World: A Study of 10 Arab and Muslim Countries.* New York: Bloomsbury Publishing USA.

Al-Mughni, H. (2001), *Women in Kuwait: The Politics of Gender.* London: Saqi.

Al-Nakib, F. (2016), *Kuwait Transformed: A History of Oil and Urban Life.* Stanford, CA: Stanford University Press.

Al-Roomi, S. (2007), Women, Blogs, and Political Power in Kuwait. In P. M. Seib (ed.), *New Media and the New Middle East.* New York: Palgrave Macmillan, pp. 139–155.

Al-Sumait, F. (2013), Communicating Politics in Kuwait In P. N. Howard and M. M. Hussain (eds.), *State Power 2.0: Authoritarian Entrenchment and Political Engagement Worldwide.* Farnham, Surrey and Burlington, Vermont: Ashgate, pp. 99–112.

Al-Sumait, F. (2019), From Tankers to Tablets: Is Kuwait Ready for a Digital Evolution? *Middle East Centre Blog.* Retrieved from https://blogs.lse.ac.uk/mec/2018/08/24/from-tankers-to-tablets-is-kuwait-ready-for-a-digital-evolution/

Al-Sumait, F. Y. (2011), *Contested Discourses on Arab Democratization in the United States and Kuwait.* PhD Dissertation, University of Washington. Retrieved from ProQuest, Abstract: http://gateway.proquest.com/openurl?url_ver=Z39.88-2004&rft_val_fmt=info:ofi/fmt:kev:mtx:dissertation&res_dat=xri:pqm&rft_dat=xri:pqdiss:3472331

Aldayin, A. (2003), Critical Appraisal of Kuwaiti Publications and Publishing Law. In Arab Press Freedom Watch (APFW) (ed.), *The State of the Arab Media 2003: The Fight for Democracy.* London: APFW, pp. 83–89.

Alenizi, M. (2012), *Talvizyoon Alkuwait: 55 aman min alriyadah alealamiya wa alenjzatat aldaramiya*. Retrieved from www.kuna.net.kw/mobile/ArticleDetails.aspx?id=2561182&Language=ar

Alkandari, F., and Ghannam, G. (2015), *Explaining Kuwait Penal Code*. Special Section. Kuwait (in Arabic): Kuwait University.

Alkazemi, M., Dashti, A., Kaposi, I., and Duffy, M. J. (2018), Kuwait In P. Valcke and E. Lievens (eds.), *International Encyclopedia of Laws*. Alphen aan den Rijn, NL: Kluwer Law International.

Almashikhi, M. B. A. (2008), *The Media in the Arab Gulf*. Kuwait: Alfalah Publishing.

Alshanoofi, M. (1999), *Tareekh Ale'elam Fi Alkuwait Wal Khaleej*. Kuwait: Department of Mass Communication.

Alshehab, A. S. (2018), *Free Speech and Defamation in Kuwait and US Law: Historical Dimension of Jurisdictions and Law in a Social Context*. Master of Art, University of South Florida, St. Petersburg, Florida. Retrieved from https://digital.usfsp.edu/cgi/viewcontent.cgi?article=1164&context=masterstheses

Amin, H. Y. (2000), The Current Situation of Satellite Broadcasting in the Middle East. *Transnational Broadcasting Studies Journal*, 5 (Fall).

Amnesty International (2017), *Amnesty International Report 2016/17-Kuwait*. Retrieved from www.ref world.org/docid/58b033e413.html

Ayish, M. I. (2011), Radio Breoadcasting in the Arab World. In N. Mellor, K. Rinnawi, N. Dajani, and M. I. Ayish (eds.), *Arab Media: Globalization and Emerging Media Industries*. Cambridge, UK: Polity.

Baller, S., Dutta, S., and Lanvin, B. (2016), *The Global Information Technology Report 2016: Innovating in the Digital Economy*. Retrieved from Geneva: www.weforum.org/reports/the-global-information-technology-report-2016

Bloomberg (2019), *Company Overview of Panther Media Group Limited*. Retrieved from Bloomberg.com: www.bloomberg.com/research/stocks/private/snapshot.asp?privcapId=111266344. Accessed 10 May 2019.

Boyd, D. A. (1999), *Broadcasting in the Arab World: A Survey of the Electronic Media in the Middle East*. Ames: Iowa State University Press.

Brown, N. J. (2017), *Arguing Islam after the Revival of Arab Politics*. New York: Oxford University Press.

Constitution of Kuwait (1962), Published in *Kuwait Alyoum*. Retrieved from http://www.law.gov.Kw/frameflip/book1/index.html.

Crystal, J. (1990), *Oil and Politics in the Gulf: Rulers and Merchants in Kuwait and Qatar*. Cambridge and New York: Cambridge University Press.

Democracy Reporting International and Kuwait Transparency Society (2008), *Assessment of the Electoral Framework Final Report. Kuwait*. Retrieved from http://democracy-reporting.org/wp-content/uploads/2016/02/dri_kuwait_report_08.pdf

Dubai School of Government (2014), Twitter in the Arab Region. *Arab Social Media Report*. Dubai, UAE: Dubai School of Government.

Farouq, A. (2016), Tareekh alsahafat alarabiat – alkuwait (Hisotry of the Arabic Press – Kuwait). *Al Jazeera Documentary*. Doha, Qatar: Al Jazeera.

Hamdan, L. (2018), OSN Shareholder KIPCO Hires Bankers to Sell 60% Stake. *Arabian Business*. Retrieved from www.arabianbusiness.com/media/408426-osn-shareholder-to-sell-60-stake-after-revenue-drop

Hawkes, R. (2017), Lines in the Sand. *Digital TV Europe*. Retrieved from www.digitaltveurope.com/longread/lines-in-the-sand/

Hendawi, H., and Mrooue, B. (2015), WikiLeaks: Saudi Arabia has Bailed out Failing Middle East Media Organizations in Exchange for Pro-Saudi Coverage. *Business Insider*. Retrieved from www.businessinsider.com/wikileaks-saudi-arabia-has-bailed-out-failing-middle-east-media-organizations-in-exchange-for-pro-saudi-coverage-2015–6

Herb, M. (1999), *All in the Family: Absolutism, Revolution, and Democracy in the Middle Eastern Monarchies*. Albany: State University of New York Press.

Herb, M. (2019), *Kuwait Politics Database from Georgia State University*. Retrieved from www.kuwaitpolitics.org

Human Rights Watch (2018), *Kuwait: Events of 2017*. Retrieved from www.hrw.org/world-report/2018/country-chapters/kuwait

Internet World Stats (2018), *Middle East*. Retrieved from www.Internetworldstats.com/middle.htm#kw

Jamal, H. (2019), *Personal Interview/Interviewer: A. Dashti*.

Jurdi, N. A., and Dashti, A. A. (1994), Communication Policies in the State of Kuwait. *Annals of the Faculty of Arts*, 14(96).

Kaposi, I. (2015), The Culture and Politics of Internet Use among Young People in Kuwait. *Cyberpsychology: Journal of Psychosocial Research on Cyberspace*, 8(3).

Kazan, F. E. (1993), *Mass Media, Modernity, and Development: Arab States of the Gulf*. Westport, CT: Praeger Publishers.

Kemp, S. (2018), *Digital in 2018: World's Internet Users Pass the 4 Billion Mark.* Retrieved from https://digitalreport.wearesocial.com/download

Khayrallah, A. (2017), *The Transformation of Kuwait Television from 1961 to 2015: Current Challenges and Future Opportunities for National Public Service Television to Promote and Arab Public Sphere in the Context of Globalisation.* PhD, Queensland University of Technology, Brisbane, Australia. Retrieved from https://eprints.qut.edu.au/115757/1/Abdullah_Khayrallah_Thesis.pdf

Kuwait Central Authority for Information Technology (2017), *Consolidated Kuwait National ICT Indicators Report 2016.* Retrieved from Kuwait: www.e.gov.kw/sites/kgoArabic/Forms/Final_Consolidated_English_Report_single_Pages.pdf

Kuwait Central Authority for Information Technology (2019), *National Projects.* Retrieved from www.cait.gov.kw/National-Projects/Official-portal-for-the-State-of-Kuwait.aspx

Kuwait Central Statistical Bureau (2018), *Statistical Review 2018–2019* (41). Kuwait. Retrieved from www.csb.gov.kw/Pages/Statistics_en?ID=19&ParentCatID=2.

Kuwait Communication and Information Technology Regulatory Authority (2019a), About *CITRA.* Retrieved from https://citra.gov.kw/sites/en/Pages/Home.aspx

Kuwait Communication and Information Technology Regulatory Authority (2019b), *Kuwait National ICT Figures.* Retrieved from https://citra.gov.kw/sites/en/Pages/ict_indicators.aspx

Kuwait Ministry of Information (2016a), *Nibda Tareeka An Alwazara* (History of the Ministry). Retrieved from www.media.gov.kw/History.aspx

Kuwait Ministry of Information (2016b), *Qadha'at AlWazara* (Sectors of the Ministry). Retrieved from www.media.gov.kw/Sectors.aspx

Kuwait Ministry of Public Works (2016), *Brief History of the Ministry.* Retrieved from www.mpw.gov.kw/sites/en/Pages/MinistryBrief/MinistryHistory.aspx

Kuwait National Assembly (2014), *Law No. 37 of 2014 on the Establishment of Communication and Information Technology Regulatory Authority.* Kuwait. Retrieved from https://citra.gov.kw/sites/en/LawofCITRA/Law%20No.%2037-%202014.pdf.

Kuwait News Agency (2015), *Min huna alkuwait: Kladha hlm adhbahhaqeeqa wa miserat najha lilda'at alkuwait* (Here is Kuwait: The Essence of a Dream has Become a Reality in the Journey of Kuwait Radio). Retrieved from www.kuna.net.kw/ArticlePrintPage.aspx?id=2424378&language=ar.

Mellor, N. (2005), *The Making of Arab News.* Lanham, MD: Rowman & Littlefield.

Pavlik, J. V. (2015), *Digital Technology and the Future of Broadcasting: Global Perspectives.* New York: Routledge.

Power, G. (2012), The Difficult Development of Parliamentary Politics in the Gulf: Parliaments and the Process of Managed Reform in Kuwait, Bahrain and Oman. In D. Held and K. Ulrichsen (eds.), *The Transformation of the Gulf: Politics, Economics and the Global Order.* Abingdon, Oxon and New York: Routledge, pp. 29–46.

Press Reference (2016), *Kuwait.* Retrieved from www.pressreference.com/Gu-Ku/Kuwait.html

Sakr, N. (2006), Media Policy as a Litmus Test of Political Change in the GCC. In A. Khalaf and G. Luciani (eds.), *Constitutional Reform and Political Participation in the Gulf.* Dubai: Gulf Research Center Dubai.

Salem, F. (2018), The Arab World Online 2017: Digital Transformations and Societal Trends in the Age of the 4th Industrial Revolution. doi:10.2139/ssrn.3059445

Salem, P. (2008), Kuwait: Politics in a Participatory Emirate. In M. Ottaway and J. Choucair-Vizoso (eds.), *Beyond the Facade: Political Reform in the Arab World.* Washington, DC: Carnegie Endowment for International Peace, pp. 211–230.

Smith, S. C. (1999), *Kuwait, 1950–1965: Britain, the al-Sabah, and oil.* Oxford and New York: Oxford University Press.

Tetreault, M. A. (2000), *Stories of Democracy: Politics and Society in Contemporary Kuwait.* New York: Columbia University Press.

Tetreault, M. A. (2011), Permanent Interests, Variable Policies. In M. A. Tétreault, G. Okruhlik, and A. Kapiszewski (eds.), *Political Change in the Arab Gulf States: Stuck in Transition.* Boulder, CO: Lynne Rienner Publishers, pp. 247–270.

Toumi, H. (2015), *488 Cases Filed against Media in Kuwait in 2014. Gulf News,* 22 February. Retrieved from https://gulfnews.com/world/gulf/kuwait/488-cases-filed-against-media-in-kuwait-in-2014-1.1460554

United Nations Human Rights Committee (2014), *Consideration of Reports Submitted by States Parties under Article 40 of the Covenant: Third Periodic Reports of States Parties due in 2014 Kuwait.* Retrieved from www.refworld.org/pdfid/5783aa064.pdf

Wheeler, D. L. (2006), *Internet in the Middle East: Global Expectations and Local Imaginations in Kuwait.* Albany: SUNY Press.

Lebanon

13

WHITHER THE LEBANESE PRESS? THE TRIALS AND TRIBULATIONS FACING THE LEBANESE PRINT MEDIA

Sarah El-Richani

Introduction

The Lebanese press has long been revered for its plurality, vibrancy, and relative freedom. Indeed, it is claimed that the pan-Arab leader Jamal Abdul-Nasser started his day with a quick read of contrasting and oftentimes fiery views about the affairs of the region and the world offered by crisp Lebanese newspapers flown in daily from Beirut to Cairo (El-Richani, 2016: 1). Although the Lebanese media landscape, including its press, continues to feature a variety of viewpoints, the Lebanese print media today – much as the country itself – finds itself in dire straits. Newspapers operating in a saturated market long propped up by political money have lost much of their influence due to hyper-competition partly brought about by the advent of the Internet, the economic crisis beleaguering the country, as well as the ongoing dominance of TV. Indeed, TV remains the main source of news for 94% of Lebanese despite a 4% decrease when compared with results in 2017 (Dennis et al., 2017; Dennis et al., 2019). Meanwhile, as the Internet has become more accessible, there has been a significant rise in the percentage of Lebanese who get their news on their smartphone (92% in 2019 as opposed to 76% in 2017) (ibid.). The same survey reveals that only 10% of Lebanese only get their news from printed newspapers (ibid.). With the loss of audiences, advertisers and political backers alike have also regressed significantly in the past five years, leaving folding newspapers in their wake. The shuttering of the prominent *As-Safir* daily in late 2016, which was renowned for its pan-Arab and leftist bent after four decades of operation, is a case in point.[1]

The unprecedented economic and financial crisis in which the country finds itself has also exacerbated matters with companies struggling for survival, slashing their advertising spend by 70%–90%, according to one estimate.[2] This chapter surveys the state of the Lebanese offline and online press from its inception to its current day, shedding light on the legal, economic, and political challenges facing this beleaguered medium. The chapter also assesses the socio-political function of the Lebanese press in Lebanon and the region.

Historical background

The Lebanese press traces its origins back to 1858 when *Hadikat al-Akhbar*, the first popular Arabic newspaper published by Arabs, was printed in Beirut by the poet Khalil el-Khuri

(Dajani, 1992: 22).[3] The newspaper, which carried commercial advertising, would publish regularly till 1911. The emergence of *Hadikat al-Akhbar* heralded the launch of several other weeklies by the *Nahda*[4] literati of the time, including renowned scholar and educator Butrus al-Bustani who launched *Nafeer Souria* (The Call/Clarion of Syria), which was "an impassioned evocation of national history, culture, and welfare" (Sheehi, 1998: 89). This political publication was written anonymously and invoked its readers with "O compatriots" (*ya abna' al-watan*) warning them of sectarianism in the post-1860 sectarian conflict[5] (Makdisi, 2002: 604–605). In 1870, al-Bustani would launch the daily *Al-Janna*, which his son edited. Other newspapers launched at the time included the prominent first pan-Arab newspaper *Al-Jawa'ib* (News) started by linguist and scholar Ahmad Faris Shidiak. Others such as *Barid Paris* (Paris Mail) published by Rachid Dahdah followed, and eventually the first daily newspaper *al-Ahwal* (The Conditions) saw the light in 1894 (Dajani, 1992: 23). Several of these commentary-laden papers often folded with the passing of their publishers and were effectively the fruit of individual labor. Nevertheless, 168 publications, including political dailies, weeklies, magazines, and scholarly journals, were issued in Beirut alone towards the beginning of the Great War in 1914 (Traboulsi, 2007: 62). At the time Lebanon was part of the faltering Ottoman Empire, and topics relating to "the awakening of the Arabs," republics, and even French history were banned for obvious reasons. As a result of this tightened grip, some journalists fled to the more autonomous Egypt where they would establish newspapers such as *Al-Ahram*, which was established by the Taqla brothers and remains a prominent Egyptian daily. Other editors and political commentators, however, stayed put and agitated for independence. Some of those intrepid leaders and writers would later be sent to the gallows by the brutal Ottoman Wali Jamal Pasha, "the bloodshedder," due to their role in calling for independence. Indeed, on 6 May 1916, 16 journalists amongst a cohort of leaders were executed in both Damascus and central Beirut, in what would later be named Martyrs' Square.

The fall of the Ottoman Empire offered a brief respite for Lebanese journalists; however, the period of the French mandate also featured a tightening of press laws and freedoms and the emergence of what Nabil Dajani calls the "practice of bribing journalists" (1992: 32). Despite this development, the Lebanese press is still credited with revealing the corruption of the first regime after independence, which culminated in the resignation of the first president, Bechara El-Khuri, following strikes and protests in 1952. While, in the post-World War II period and particularly during the Israeli–Palestinian conflict, the press of the Arab world embodied the slogan "no voice rises above the voice of the battle," the Lebanese press maintained its vibrancy and diversity. In particular, *An-Nahar*, which played "the role of 'collective intellectual' of the bourgeoisie" published pieces criticizing Nasserism as well as Lebanese President Fu'ad Shihab's attempt at etatisme at the expense of confessionalism (Traboulsi, 2007: 142). The hyper-pluralism would only intensify with the socio-economic crisis in Lebanon and the regional turmoil that came with the establishment of the state of Israel. The civil war years, which spanned nearly 15 years and began in 1975, witnessed the emergence of strident and hateful militia tabloids alongside newspapers representing the entire political spectrum with the support of local, regional, and international forces from Libya and Egypt to Saudi Arabia, the USSR, and the United States. With the end of the civil war and the start of the so-called Pax-Syriana phase, tighter control on the media took root with militia tabloids folding and freedoms restricted. Nevertheless, with the return of commercial activity and advertisers, newspapers cautiously toeing the line prospered at least till the next rupture. The assassination of former Prime Minister Rafik al-Hariri in 2005 unleashed a wave of protests culminating in the withdrawal of Syrian troops from Lebanon. This helped ease the restrictions on free expression, despite the assassinations of fervent anti-Syrian regime historian and *An-Nahar* columnist Samir Kassir followed a few months later by the assassination of *An-Nahar* editor, publisher, and parliamentarian Gebran Tueni. A year later and rising from the ashes of the devastating Israeli July War on Lebanon, *Al-Akhbar*, a strident new daily, entered the scene. The newspaper broke away from reporting protocol news and presented brazen critiques of events, leaders, and policies. The paper was unabashedly critical to the extent that some financiers such as former Prime Minister Najib Mikati, according to a WikiLeaks cable, regretted having financially contributed to the launch of the paper (El-Richani, 2016: 108). As is common with other media operations, the newspaper had a powerful backer, which would protect it. *Al-Akhbar* is close to Hezbollah and the Syrian regime as the civil war in Syria revealed. Indeed, with the start of the Syrian civil war, the newspaper's avenues of freedom tightened and several articles censuring the regime were withheld, leading to the resignation of its leftist co-editor Khaled Saghiyyeh and the departure of Max Blumenthal, who wrote for the fleeting *Al-Akhbar* English site. As his parting shot, Blumenthal would label the paper Asaad apologists (El-Richani, 2016: 108). Furthermore, As'ad Abu Khalil, also known by his sobriquet the Angry Arab, had two of his articles in which he criticized Bashar al-Assad withheld (ibid.). Nevertheless, the paper still offers a rich and avant-garde cultural page and a left-of-center and relatively progressive society and economics page. The news website *Al-Akhbar English*, which launched in August 2011, ceased operation in 2015 due to a lack of funds.[6]

Despite the launch of several new newspapers in the post-Pax-Syriana phase, many of which are only online, several others have folded in recent years or have cut back or even converged to only offering online news service. The few remaining battle it out over a share of the limited advertising market or rely on subsidies provided to them by political backers from across the political spectrum in contravention of the loosely applied Press Law, which shall be discussed next.

Press laws and regulations

Lebanon currently ranks 100 out of 180 countries in Reporters Without Border's World Press Freedom Index,[7] whereas Freedom House categorizes Lebanon as "partly free" due to a growing number of infractions limiting free expression, which shall be discussed further later.[8] Article 13 of the Lebanese constitution[9] and Article 19 of the International Covenant of Civil and Political Rights, which Lebanon has ratified, guarantee freedom of expression within the limits of the law. The Lebanese penal code, as well as the media laws and press laws in particular, however, fall foul of these promises. The penal code's Article 384, for instance, criminalizes insulting the president.

The current press law, the Press Law of 1962, which has been slightly amended at different junctures, is dated, and as many editors would concede is thankfully only loosely applied. In 1977, Decree 104 was introduced barring content that could be deemed offensive to foreign leaders.[10] Another contentious amendment, Decree 74, stipulates that political publications shall not be licensed till the number of political publications drops from 110 to 25. To help limit the number, the Ministry of Information was tasked with withdrawing the licenses granted to publications that have been dormant or have published less than 32 copies per year. However, the Ministry of Information largely refrained from implementing this decree, and owners circuitously circumvented this threshold when needed. As a result, anyone wanting to start a newspaper had to purchase an existing newspaper license from those lucky 110 who had previously been licensed. The prices of the licenses were extortionate and beyond the means of most Lebanese.[11] This hurdle to starting a paper has largely been curtailed by the Internet since a news site is not subject to this condition.

Another clause that is also laxly applied is the Ministry of Information's duty to monitor the accounts of the media to ensure revenue streams are legitimate and flowing from advertising, subscriptions, and sales. The limited size of the advertising market – estimated to have dropped by USD 10 million between 2010 and 2015 and has reached USD 28 million[12] as well as limited sales – not surpassing 60,000 copies a day, according to several stakeholders (El-Richani, 2016: 112) – indicates that the Lebanese media have had to rely on "subsidies" from leaders and states.[13]

Furthermore, the 1962 Press Law also stipulated the formation of the Lebanese Press Association and the Journalists' Association, which together form the rather benign Press Union. The law also stipulates strict conditions on accession to the Journalists' Association. Today the majority of media practitioners are not members and therefore at risk of being tried for "impersonating journalists." However, this does not mean that the law is not implemented at all. On the contrary, publication offenses relating to "false news," "slander and defamation," and "incitement" are often brought before the publications court.

Other articles from the Press Law that are controversial, albeit rarely used, allow for the imprisonment of journalists.[14] As it stands, the penal code and the audiovisual and military justice laws can be used to penalize "press crimes." For almost a decade, campaigners led by the Maharat Foundation have tried to amend the media laws by convening stakeholders ranging from media practitioners and lawyers to parliamentarians. The ensuing draft media law, which sought to decriminalize press offenses, was presented to the Parliamentary Communications Committee; however, ultimately due to a variety of reasons including the political crises that are commonplace in Lebanon, these efforts did not bear fruit.

Meanwhile, with the exception of the E-transactions and Data Protection Law issued in October 2018 (Law No. 81/2018), there is currently no legislation that governs the Internet. The aforementioned recently passed law offers some form of legal security but has fallen short of expectations on data protection. This absence of more wide-reaching legislation regulating the Internet has been viewed as both a boon and a bane for free expression. On the one hand, this has allowed the Lebanese avenues of freedom, on the other, it had meant that freedoms have also been arbitrarily and opaquely curtailed. Indeed, there has been a growing number of arrests made and charges filed because of posts on social media platforms that have been deemed insulting. For instance, in November 2017, a journalist was detained for 13 days for allegedly defaming the president; another was arrested for insulting the Virgin Mary in a Facebook post.[15] The Lebanese NGO Social Media Exchange has launched a website entitled *Muhal*, which documents detentions and arrests relating to expression on the Internet. According to their documentation, there have been 38 summons in 2018 and just over 60 summons in 2019 for posts written on social media and news websites.[16] Amongst those, a 15-year-old was detained for one day for posting a photo on WhatsApp criticizing the president. The teenager was not sentenced but was requested to sign a pledge, which is a common occurrence.[17] Some of these summonses resulted in detentions spanning several days, others have remained open, which could have a chilling effect. Furthermore, the blocking of websites, which now stands at 53 websites including mostly pornographic, gambling, and Israeli websites, has also been carried out without rhyme or reason.[18] A case in point was the blocking of Grindr, a dating app popular amongst homosexuals, in January 2019. There was conflicting information about who ordered the ban, with the Ministry of Telecommunications denying their involvement.[19] While Article 125 of the recently passed E-Transactions and Data Protection Law[20] attempts to remedy this situation by stipulating that such decisions should be sanctioned by the judiciary; this case also points to the importance of assessing both the "de jure" and the "de facto" situation in Lebanon as sometimes – for better or worse – the laws are not implemented.

While civil society has been calling for an overhaul of media laws as well as the slander and defamation penal code articles, campaigns thus far have borne no fruit due to a variety of reasons, including the series of political crises. On the other hand, there have also been several attempts to pass controversial laws that have also failed thanks to the efforts of civil society groups as well as some media. For instance, in 2011, there was an attempt to legalize the seizure of hard drives and computers. In 2012, the then minister of information put forth the Lebanese Internet Regulation Act, which aimed to register all online news websites. This attempt was ridiculed by civil society, the media, and some political leaders and subsequently shelved (Miller, 2016: 10).

Social and political functions of the press

In his "The Myth of Media Freedom in Lebanon," media scholar Nabil Dajani argues that the Lebanese media is free from government control because the state is weak (2013). However, he argues, the media is very much beholden to their owner and political backer, meaning that their freedom is mythical (ibid.). As argued elsewhere (El-Richani, 2016: 77), this is somewhat hyperbolic and dismisses the diverse points of view offered on the Lebanese media landscape as a whole and at times within the same outlet. Indeed, on the level of the media system itself, it is incontrovertible that "external pluralism" or diversity on the level of the media system exists (Hallin and Mancini, 2004: 29). The majority of media outlets and newspapers, in particular, have more or less clear political or religious affiliations, representing the political and religious diversity extant in the nation.

While the major groups and political inclinations are all represented in one form or the other, it is often argued that the Lebanese media outlets exist to serve their owners or patrons more so than the public. This is particularly true with the partisan newspapers which are directly linked to or owned by political parties and movements and primarily serve their partisans. Amongst those is *Al-Mustakbal* (Arabic for the Future), which is part of the media network owned by the Lebanese prime minister's Hariri family Future Movement. *Al-Mustakbal* ceased its print edition and converged completely online in January 2019 two decades after it first launched, citing financial difficulties.[21] Their current news website and app, *Mustaqbalweb*, prioritizes party members and carries a link to the Future Movement website. It is worth noting that this is the only media operation remaining that is connected to the Hariri-led group after Future News TV and Future TV, which before the assassination of Rafik Hariri was popular across the country and the region, ceased operations in 2012 and 2019 respectively. The *Al-Anba'* weekly – owned and run by the Progressive Socialist Party and founded by the late Druze leader Kamal Jumblatt in 1951, has also converged to only digital delivery in 2012.[22] Meanwhile, *Al-Bina'*,[23] a daily owned and run by the Syrian Socialist Nationalist Party, continues to publish in print primarily targeting their partisans. Another of the newspapers directly owned by a politician is *Al-Jumhouriya*, which belongs to former Minister of Defence Elias al-Murr. The paper relaunched in 2011 and is closely affiliated to the Christian camp in the March 14 coalition, which emerged following the assassination of Rafik Hariri and included parties against Syrian intervention in Lebanese affairs. On the other side of the political spectrum is March 8, a coalition consisting amongst others of Hezbollah and the Amal movement, which represents large swathes of Shiite Muslims and the current president's party the Free Patriotic Movement, which enjoys wide support amongst Lebanese Christians.

The rest of the newspapers occupy a variety of positions on the political spectrum and are not as clear-cut in their affiliation to particular parties or leaders. Indeed, newspapers range from the liberal newspaper *An-Nahar* to the left-oriented and now-defunct *As-Safir*, and more recently *Al-Akhbar*, whose editor's explicit wish is to perturb the American ambassador on a daily basis (El-Richani, 2016: 102).[24] The economic downturn ongoing since the start of the Syrian civil war in 2011 and which reached its pinnacle in 2019/2020 has also made the more independent newspapers open to overtures from patrons as advertising expenditures dwindle.

An-Nahar, which often brings in the highest ad shares and at one point brought in shareholders, including the late Prime Minister Rafik Hariri and the wealthy businessman and former deputy speaker of parliament Issam Fares, has been facing dire straits. In 2009, they fired 50 staff members including the prominent novelist and editor of the culture page Elias Khoury. On 11 October 2018, they published a blank issue in an attempt to bring attention to the financial and economic crisis facing newspapers as well as the nation at large and have since been collecting donations to ensure their continuity.[25] Without a doubt, the newspaper, now in its fourth generation, has also suffered the loss of its renowned publisher Ghassan Tueni, who edited it during its heyday followed by his outspoken son Gebran who was assassinated in 2005, presumably for speaking out against Syrian intervention in Lebanon. Gebran Tueni's daughters, who currently run the paper alongside senior editors, have not been able to slow the descent of the newspaper described by the prickly commentator As'ad AbuKhalil as having "its future well behind it."[26] Although the newspaper continues to claim the lion's share of the advertising market for newspapers, thanks to the strength of its representative, the Choueiri Media Group, in the local and regional advertising market, even this has appeared inadequate particularly in the economic crisis gripping the nation from mid-2019.[27] Still, the daily, which is "struggling [to keep] . . . the newspaper and its legacy alive," as its current publisher put it, claims it continues to sell around 25,000 copies a day and has almost 9,000 paying online subscribers.[28]

Another daily, *Ad-Diyar,* has also been facing financial woes. Its colorful publisher and editor Charles Ayyoub memorably lamented in an editorial the inadequacy of the subsidies coming in from Saudi Arabia, Prime Minister Hariri, Syria, and local politicians, thus compelling him to increase the price of the newspaper (El-Richani, 2016: 103).

Meanwhile, *Al-Akhbar,* mentioned earlier, is closely linked to Hezbollah. Nevertheless, the daily has hosted a variety of voices including columnists and journalists close to current President Michel Aoun's Free Patriotic Movement, as well as leftists such as its founding editor, the late Joseph Semaha, and former co-editor Khaled Saghieh, who departed due to conflicts arising on coverage of the ongoing war in Syria. According to Alexa analytics, the newspaper's website is amongst the top 50 sites visited in Lebanon,[29] well ahead of any other newspapers' digital platforms. This is most likely due to its politically relevant and often strident take on issues ranging from cultural and societal issues to the economy and politics.

Other Lebanese print newspapers with much smaller readerships include *Al-Liwa',* owned by the prominent Salam family, whose editor ran against Prime Minister Saad Hariri in the 2018 parliamentary elections, and *El-Sharq.* Both newspapers are considered to be close to the Gulf regimes. *El-Sharq*'s publisher Awni Kaaki was elected head of the Press Syndicate in 2015 after the death of Mohammad Baalbaki, who spent more than 30 years atop the association.[30]

Furthermore, two foreign-language dailies continue to exist: *L'Orient Le Jour* and *The Daily Star. L'Orient Le Jour* is a French daily with a small, loyal, and affluent readership. While the paper is largely allied to the March 14 coalition, it also includes a variety of voices such as Scarlet Haddad, who is a staunch supporter of President Michel Aoun. The newspaper has several shareholders, including the affluent Pharaon and Edde families as well as the Choueiri family. The Choueiri family are advertising moguls and can thus secure the French daily a sizeable portion of advertisements.[31]

Meanwhile, the English-language daily *The Daily Star* has also undergone some changes in recent years. Established in 1952 by Kamel Mroueh, the founder of *Al-Hayat, The Daily Star* was acquired by Hariri associates and Qatar in 2010 with its former publisher, the founder's son, resignedly conceding, "the consumer has migrated elsewhere" (quoted in El-Richani, 2016: 88). In February 2020, the daily decided to switch to only digital distribution due to a significant drop in advertising in the last quarter of 2019.[32]

Al-Hayat, which was also founded by Kamel Mroueh in 1946, was sold to Saudi Arabian Prince Khaled bin Sultan in the early 1990s and transformed into a pan-Arab newspaper (Mellor, 2007: 133).[33] *Al-Hayat* has also folded in 2020 after downsizing, stopping its print editions and shuttering its Beirut and London offices in June 2018.[34] The daily, which suspended Saudi columnist Jamal Khashoggi by order of its publisher Prince Khaled and his son shortly before the columnist was assassinated, was allegedly sold to Muhammad bin Salman in November 2018.[35]

In addition to newspapers that have for a variety of reasons adopted clear political positions, two newspapers that also ceased operations in 2018 were considered centrist. The first was *Al-Anwar*, founded in 1959 and part of As-Sayad publishers and the second was the commercial and centrist newspaper *Al-Balad*. *Al-Balad*, backed by a Kuwaiti-owned conglomerate Al-Wataniya, launched in late 2003 offering a myriad of prizes to lure subscribers in exchange for largely insipid centrist news and popular society pages. The newspaper also launched a French daily, but that lasted a mere three years, again due to financial reasons.[36] The assassination attempt targeting Minister Marwan Hamadeh, an anti-Syrian politician in late October 2004, followed by the assassination of former Prime Minister Rafik Hariri in February 2005, unleashed polarization and rigorous political debates in the country. As a result, try as it may and despite the support of the Al-Wataniya conglomerate to which the tabloid belonged, the staff was let go and ultimately *Al-Balad* folded, having had little impact.

Finally, and contrary to the trend of folding and converging newspapers and perhaps in a testament to the resilience of this industry, a new daily *Nida' al-Watan* was launched in 2019.[37] The newspaper, which is squarely in the March 14 camp, has already attracted some attention due to its strident criticism of the March 8 affiliated leaders.

As Internet penetration rises (estimated at 78% in 2018 by the ITU) and ever more Lebanese get their news on their smartphones, there has been an increase in newspapers ceasing operations entirely or converging to purely digital distribution. A series of news sites have also emerged offering their news exclusively online. While the Internet has undoubtedly allowed many more Lebanese to access a myriad of viewpoints and also voice their views and form newspapers without the need of a costly license, ultimately and as the brief survey of the most popular news sources online reveals, the patterns of ownership have "filter[ed] ever outwards to the Internet" (Fenton, 2011: 13). Indeed, websites such as Saidaonline, BintJbeil, Lebanon Debates, Lebanon Files, and ElNashra also represent the variety of political stances in the country and are in some cases supported directly or indirectly by the powers that be. ElNashra, for instance, is owned by Arz el-Murr and whilst not overtly partisan, is inclined towards March 14 as are other Murr family media outlets. Lebanon 24, another online news service, meanwhile is owned by former Prime Minister Najib Mikati. Another of the online news sites is Bint Jbeil, which covers news from the southern town and falls under the March 8 umbrella, whereas Kalima Online is close to the president's party, the FPM.

Daraj Media meanwhile is a website founded in 2017 by three veteran journalists in an attempt to offer independent and investigative news content. While it seeks at some point in the future to rely on advertising, subscriptions, or other forms of revenue, it currently relies on funds from European donors, which again raises questions about this project's long-term viability.[38]

While online advertising is growing, the revenue does not always go to the news content providers but the platforms on which these stories are shared. In 2013, online advertising claimed roughly 9.5% of total advertising spending in 2013, whereas newspaper advertising claiming claimed 15.8% having dropped roughly 6% during the period 2009 to 2013 (BankMed, 2014:

20–21).[39] According to one source, digital advertising in the region today is closer to 30%; however, these figures remain difficult to verify and vary greatly from one source to the next.[40]

Nevertheless, while *Al-Akhbar*'s website and other purely online platforms such as ElNashra and Lebanon Files boast large numbers of online visitors, online advertising remains "insufficient" more so now due to the unprecedented economic crisis facing the nation.[41]

The Lebanese media, in general, have been accused of serving the elites who own and finance it rather than the citizens. That may be true to a certain extent in light of the financial subsidies political elites furnish on the media; however, the diversity of platforms that exist and the thirst for local news and commentary on the many crises afflicting this beleaguered nation means that ultimately audiences can select from the plurality of voices existing in a region where free expression is anathema.

Conclusion

The Lebanese press as discussed earlier is undoubtedly facing an existential crisis. For one, the Lebanese market is a small one – in part due to the small size of the state with a population estimated at five million but also due to the economic and financial crisis gripping the nation. This has been further exacerbated by the high number of publications competing for a stake of the market despite the migration of audiences to television and more recently online. As a result of those hardships, some newspapers – including prominent ones such as *As-Safir* – have elected to completely cease operations. Meanwhile, others have suspended only their print editions and have converged online, thereby cutting their printing and distribution costs. As more and more Lebanese resort to the Internet for their news, cutting printing and distribution costs could offer some respite for these content providers. Ultimately, however, and particularly for media practitioners not completely reliant on illicit financial subsidies from local, regional, or international sources, content still matters. Indeed, the Lebanese's thirst for local news delivered in Arabic, which is heightened in times of crisis,[42] places the ball in the content provider's court. The problem, the million-dollar question, is how to monetize these endeavors.

In light of the previous discussion and amidst this fierce battle for eyeballs, it is worthwhile to reiterate the fact that despite the echo chambers which will exist, content that would at times disappoint and effectively at times serve the highest bidder, the vivacity and diversity of the Lebanese media in general and its press, in particular, is undeniable.

APPENDIX

Name	Newspaper affiliation	Status
1 *Ad-Diyar*	Syrian Nationalist Charles Ayoub (1988)	Founded 1944
2 *Al-Anba'*	Partisan weekly, Progressive Socialist Party	Founded 1951 by Kamal Jumblatt Converged 2012
3 *Al-Akhbar*	Hezbollah, Leftist, Aounists	Founded 2006 *Al-Akhbar* English folded 2015
4 *Al-Balad*	Al–Wataniya	Founded 2003 Folded 2018
5 *Al-Bina'*	Syrian Socialist Nationalist Party	Founded in 1958
6 *Al-Jumhouriyya*	Former Minister of Defense Elias Murr March 14	Relaunched in 2011
7 *Al-Liwa'*	Salam Family, close to Hariri and the Gulf states	Founded 1963
8 *Al-Mustakbal*	Future Movement (Hariri)	Founded 1999 Converged 2018
9 *An-Nahar*	Liberal, Tueni Family, Hariri family and associates, Issam Fares, other shareholders	Founded 1933
10 *As-Safir*	Leftist, pan–Arab Talal Salman and family Jamal Daniel (2014)	Founded in 1974 by Talal Salman Folded 2016
11 *El-Sharq*	Awni al-Kaaki	Founded in 1958
12 *L'orient le jour*	Edde, Choueiri, and Pharaon families	Founded 1971 after the merging of *L'Orient* founded in 1924 and *Le Jour* in 1934.
13 *Nida' al-Watan*	Michel Mkataf, former Phalange member March 14	Founded 2019
14 *The Daily Star*	Hariri associates and Qatar	Founded in 1952 by Kamel Mroueh Converged 2020

Figure 7.1 List of Lebanese newspapers, including those which folded or converged to online

Notes

1 "Lebanese newspaper As-Safir to stop publishing after 40 years," 9 December 2016, Annahar staff. Retrieved from https://en.annahar.com/article/507839-lebanese-newspaper-assafir-to-stop-publishing-after-40-years (last accessed on March 29, 2019).

2 "Lebanon: Advertising in a Time of Crisis," *Arab Ad*, February 18, 2020. Retrieved from https://infoweb-newsbank-com.libproxy.aucegypt.edu/apps/news/document-view?p=AWNB&t=pubname%3ALAL5%21ArabAd%2B%2528Lebanon%2529/year%3A2020%212020/mody%3A0218%21February%2B18&action=browse&format=text&docref=news/1792F024D75D8970 (last accessed on March 14, 2020).

3 While *Al-Waka'eh*, which was published in Cairo by the Ottoman Khedive (viceroy) Mohammad Ali Basha, is sometimes considered the first Arab newspaper, it was in fact akin to an official gazette that was distributed primarily to officials.

4 The term *Nahḍa* refers to the Arab literary-cultural renaissance that began in the late 19th century.

5 The civil wars of 1860 began in Mount Lebanon and culminated in a massacre in Damascus. The conflict was largely sectarian in nature.

6 The Daily Star, "Al-Akhbar Pulls Plug on English Site," *The Daily Star*, March 6, 2015. Retrieved from www.dailystar.com.lb/News/Lebanon-News/2015/Mar-06/289891-al-akhbar-pulls-plug-on-english-site.ashx (last accessed on April 7, 2019).

7 "Highly politicized media, free speech under attack," 2018, Reporters Sans Frontieres. Retrieved from https://rsf.org/en/lebanon (last accessed on April 14, 2019).

8 Freedom House. Freedom in the World 2019. Retrieved from https://freedomhouse.org/report/freedom-world/2019/lebanon (last accessed on April 14, 2019).

9 The Lebanese Constitution. Retrieved from www.ministryinfo.gov.lb/en/sub/Lebanon/LebaneseConstitution.aspx (last accessed on April 3, 2019).

10 A copy of all press laws and relevant decrees can be found using the following link: http://ministryinfo.gov.lb/main/MediaLaws/ActNo.382.aspx.

11 The prices varied depending on the name but ranged from $200,000 to $500,000 according to a Press Union board member who revealed these figures in an interview with the author.

12 Media Ownership Monitor Lebanon, *Reporters Without Borders/The Samir Kassir Foundation*. Retrieved from https://lebanon.mom-rsf.org/en/media/print/ (last accessed on April 14, 2019).

13 Author's interview with Nizar Saghieh, lawyer and activist, conducted on 19 October 2010.

14 Articles 16, 20–23, and 25 of the Lebanese Press Law.

15 Human Rights Watch, "Lebanon: Patterns of Prosecutions for Free Speech," *Human Rights Watch*, January 31, 2018. Retrieved from www.hrw.org/news/2018/01/31/lebanon-pattern-prosecutions-free-speech (last accessed on March 31, 2019).

16 Muhal, Observatory for Freedom of Expression. Retrieved from http://muhal.org/en/about/ (last accessed on April 3, 2019).

17 Lebanese army intelligence arrested Yousef Abdullah for criticizing the Lebanese president. Retrieved from http://muhal.org/en/cases/recukqbkfwsvukhxy/ (last accessed on April 3, 2019).

18 For a list of blocked websites cf. https://docs.google.com/spreadsheets/d/1khbB20bo15L41j7ruYZLkJEOaSrNGU8gSOJuiy_RsHM/edit#gid=0 (last accessed on April 5, 2019).

19 Statement: Block of Grindr App in Lebanon, *SMEX*, January 23, 2019. Retrieved from https://smex.org/statement-block-of-grindr-app-in-lebanon/ (last accessed on April 5, 2019).

20 Chedid, E., G. Salame and K. Tymburski, "New Lebanese Law on E-transactions and Data Protection," *JDSUPRA*, January 21, 2019. Retrieved from www.jdsupra.com/legalnews/new-lebanese-law-on-e-transactions-and-97004/ (last accessed on April 5, 2019).

21 McDowall, A., "Newspaper Owned by Lebanon's Hariri Prints Last Edition," *Reuters*. January 31, 2019. Retrieved from https://news.yahoo.com/newspaper-owned-lebanons-hariri-prints-last-edition-151332492.html (last accessed on April 9, 2019).

22 Al-Anba', About us. Retrieved from https://anbaaonline.com/about (last accessed on April 7, 2019).

23 "The newspaper is considered an official spokesman of the opposition, the resistance and Hezbollah," said its then editor-in-chief Kamil Khalil. Author's interview with Khalil conducted on January 24, 2011.

24 Worth, R. F., "Rarity in Region, Lebanese Paper Dares to Provoke," *The New York Times*, December 28, 2010. Retrieved from www.nytimes.com/2010/12/29/world/middleeast/29beirut.html (last accessed on September 3, 2014).

25 The Daily Star Staff, "An-Nahar Raises Red Flag over Lebanon's Woes in Blank Issue," *The Daily Star,* October 11, 2018. Retrieved from www.dailystar.com.lb/News/Lebanon-News/2018/Oct-11/466026-local-daily-an-nahar-publishes-blank-newspaper.ashx (last accessed on April 6, 2019).

26 AbuKhalil, A., "Margalit Fox on Ghassan Tuwayni," *The Angry Arab News Service,* June 13, 2012. Retrieved from https://angryarab.blogspot.com/2012/06/margalit-fox-on-ghassan-tuwayni.html (last accessed on April 6, 2019).

27 The Choueiri Media Group dominates the Arab ad market and represents major media outlets in the Arab world.

28 Akerman, I., "Nayla Tueni: We Have to Be the Voice of the People," *ArabAd,* January 3, 2020. Retrieved from https://infoweb-newsbank-com.libproxy.aucegypt.edu/apps/news/document-view?p=AWNB&t=pubname%3ALAL5%21ArabAd%2B%2528Lebanon%2529/year%3A2020%212020/mody%3A0103%21January%2B03&action=browse&format=text&docref=news/1783C6D981B32A58 (last accessed on March 13, 2020).

29 The top 50 websites in Lebanon. Retrieved from www.alexa.com/topsites/countries/LB (last accessed on March 13, 2020).

30 The newspaper *Al-Bayrak* and publications owned by the long-serving former head of the Editor's Union Melhem Karam folded in 2011 following his death.

31 Media Ownership Monitor Lebanon *Reporters Without Borders/The Samir Kassir Foundation.* Retrieved from http://lebanon.mom-rsf.org/en/media/detail/outlet/lorient-le-jour/ (last accessed on April 14, 2019).

32 Spencer, R., "Daily Star, Owned by the Family of the Former Lebanese Prime Minister Saad Hariri, Switches to Online Publishing," *The Times,* February 5, 2020. Retrieved from www.thetimes.co.uk/article/daily-star-owned-by-the-family-of-the-former-lebanese-prime-minister-saad-hariri-switches-to-online-publishing-d9wdg5gnz (last accessed on March 13, 2020).

33 *Al-Hayat* as well as LBC – a leading Lebanese private TV channel – reveals the Saudi–Lebanese nexus where Saudi moguls finance the media operated or launched by Lebanese media practitioners (Kraidy, 2012: 185).

34 MEE and agencies. Pan-Arab newspaper al-Hayat closes office in birthplace Beirut. *Middle East Eye,* June 30, 2018. Retrieved from www.middleeasteye.net/news/pan-arab-newspaper-al-hayat-closes-office-birthplace-beirut (last accessed on April 9, 2019).

35 A number of sources have reported this although none are conclusive.

36 The end of the French Al-Balad. Skeyes Media. Retrieved from www.skeyesmedia.org/en/News/Lebanon/The-End-of-the-French-Al-Balad (last accessed on April 14, 2019).

37 Ayyi, G., "Nida' al Watan, a New Daily for Lebanon," *Arab Ad Magazine,* March 27, 2019. Retrieved from http://arabadonline.com/details/industry-talk/nida-al-watan-a-new-daily-for-lebanon (last accessed on April 9, 2019).

38 Daraj, *Who we are.* Retrieved from https://daraj.com/en/who-we-are/ (last accessed on March 15, 2019).

39 BankMed. Analysis of Lebanon's Media and Advertising Sector, May 2014. Retrieved from www.databank.com.lb/docs/advertising.pdf (last accessed on April 13, 2019).

40 Akerman, I., "Eli Khouri, CEO of Omnicom Media, Questions Regional Adspend Figures Released by Ipsos," *Arab Ad,* June 10, 2019.

41 Author's interview with Joseph Semaan, ElNashra online, editor-in-chief, conducted on 9 June 2011, cited in El-Richani, 2016: 103.

42 Crisis was identified in my monograph *The Lebanese Media: Anatomy of a System in Perpetual Crisis* (2016: 181–183) as a salient factor impacting the Lebanese media system in a variety of ways. First, the audiences' interest in local news heightens during any crisis. Second, if the conflict is internal, usually the media would suspend commercial logic and fall into their communal trenches and play the role expected of them by their financiers.

References and further reading

BankMed (2014, May), *Analysis of Lebanon's Media and Advertising Sector.* Retrieved from www.databank.com.lb/docs/advertising.pdf. Accessed 13 April 2019.

Dajani, N. (1992), *Disoriented Media in a Fragmented Society: The Lebanese Experience.* Beirut: American University of Beirut Press.

Dajani, N. (2013), The Myth of Media Freedom in Lebanon. *Arab Media and Society,* 18(Summer). Retrieved from www.arabmediasociety.com/?article=833.

Dennis, E. E., Martin, J. D., and Hassan, F. (2019), *Media Use in the Middle East, 2019: A Seven-nation Survey*. Northwestern University in Qatar. Retrieved from www.mideastmedia.org/survey/2019.

Dennis, E. E., Martin, J. D., and Wood, R. (2017), *Middle Use in the Middle East, 2017: A Six-nation Survey*. Northwestern University in Qatar. Retrieved from www.mediaeastmedia.org/survey/2017. Accessed 7 April 2019.

El-Richani, S. (2016), *The Lebanese Media: Anatomy of a System in Perpetual Crisis*. New York: Palgrave Macmillan.

Fenton, N. (Ed.) (2011), *New Media, Old News: Journalism and Democracy in the Digital Age* (Repr). Los Angeles: Sage.

Hallin, D. C., and Mancini, P. (2004), *Comparing Media Systems: Three Models of Media and Politics*. Cambridge: Cambridge University Press.

Kraidy, M. M. (2012), The Rise of Transnational Media Systems: Implications of pan-Arab Media for Comparative Research. In D. C. Hallin and P. Mancini (eds.), *Comparing Media Systems Beyond the Western World*. Cambridge: Cambridge University Press, pp. 177–200. Retrieved from http://ebookcentral. proquest.com/lib/aucegypt/detail.action?docID=824469.

Makdisi, U. (2002), *After 1860: Debating Religion, Reform, and Nationalism in the Ottoman Empire*. International Journal of Middle East Studies, 34(4) (November), pp. 601–617.

Mellor, N. (2007), *Modern Arab Journalism: Problems and Prospects*. Edinburgh: Edinburgh University Press.

Miller, A. L. (2016), Digital Rights and Online Expression in Lebanon. *Skeyes Media*. Retrieved from www.skeyesmedia.org/extensions/pdf/Digital_Rights_in_Lebanon.pdf. Accessed 3 April 2019.

Sheehi, S. (1998), Unpacking Modern Arab Subjectivity: Reading al-Mu'allim Butrus al-Bustani's "Nafir Suriya." *The Arab Studies Journal*, 6(1) (Spring), pp. 87–99.

Traboulsi, F. (2007), *History of Modern Lebanon*. Pluto Press: London. ProQuest Ebook Central. Retrieved from http://ebookcentral.proquest.com/lib/aucegypt/detail.action?docID=3386375. Accessed 7 April 2019.

14

LEBANESE BROADCASTING

Small country, influential media

Natalie Khazaal

Introduction

Lebanon is one of the smallest Arab states with a territory of 10,452 km^2 (4,036 sq. mi) and an estimated population of six million inhabitants for 2016. It was established as a modern state in 1920 under the French protectorate and as an independent state in 1943. Two main watersheds in its modern history were the shorter civil conflict in 1958 and the longer civil war of 1975–1991. As a nation entirely comprised of religious and ethnic minorities (12 Christian sects, five Muslim sects, other religions, 3.3% atheists, as well as different nationalities including Armenian, Palestinian, Syrian, Iraqi, among others), it is organized politically as a consociational democracy. A country of immigration – host to close to two million refugees – and emigration – with a diaspora estimated between eight and 18 million, Lebanon prides itself on its leading role in the areas of media, culture, and education across the Arab world. This chapter discusses the development of the radio and television industries in Lebanon, their main players and current issues, and how the country's unique geography and social makeup have affected those industries. The chapter also discusses broadcast policy and journalist censorship in the country.

Lebanese radio

The first radio station in Lebanon – now called Radio Lebanon – was established in 1937 as a French operation, which served the Vichy government to counter Nazi propaganda in the region (Boyd, 1999). Radio Lebanon's brand is irrevocably linked to Lebanese national history, starting with a landmark broadcast in November 1946 during which renowned poet Said Akel announced Lebanon's independence. After independence, the station was handed over to the Lebanese Ministry of Interior, which didn't immediately grasp the medium's importance. Like radio in the rest of the Arab world, the station is financed by the government and doesn't allow advertising. However, when several pirate partisan radio stations appeared during the brief 1958 civil war, the government quickly decided to increase coverage and expand programming even though it shut down all pirate stations (Boyd, 1991). In the early 1960s, Radio Lebanon moved to the new building of the Ministries of Information and Tourism where it built six studios. Embarking on educational, informational, and cultural projects that depicted Lebanon as a unified nation with rich national folklore allowed Radio Lebanon to become a platform for Lebanon's poets, writers, and musicians. Yet, in the public eye, it continued to represent the government and deny other political groups access to the airwaves.

When the 1975 war erupted, Radio Lebanon adopted a deliberate policy to pursue neutrality. However, this policy created "a peace bubble" – the overt or subtle occlusion of the hostilities in broadcast media, which often focused on peace initiatives and reran the pre-war golden archive that portrayed Lebanon as a peaceful cosmopolitan nation (Khazaal, 2018). As a result of the bubble, the Lebanese public didn't get regular news about the war or warnings about danger zones. To overcome the bubble, listeners tuned in to international radio like The Voice of America, Radio Monte Carlo, and the BBC. In the early days of the conflict, listeners also followed Sharif al-Akhawi, a traffic report host, who became famous for airing information about safe roads around the clock until Radio Lebanon's headquarters and its Amsheet transmitter were taken over by opposing warring factions and split in 1976 (Khazaal, 2018). The radio service was reunified in December the same year, but a host of pirate stations (some from the dormant 1958 facilities) quickly filled the airwaves with sectarian propaganda on unregistered frequencies (Boyd, 1991). While their sectarian owners used them as another weapon, most stations claimed neutrality and ownership of Lebanon, as we can see from the names of the three of the most successful ones: The Voice of Lebanon, The Voice of Arab Lebanon, and Free Lebanon Radio. Radio transmitters were not affected as badly as television was by the bombing and shelling because each warring faction protected the transmitter it erected on its territory. Nonetheless, losses in transmission, equipment damage, and the pirate partisan voices turned wartime radio into an intermittent, prolific, and divisive medium.

Partisan radio fundamentally changed the structure of Lebanese broadcasting. On one hand, the several hundred new voices infused the previously univocal ether with diverse, eristic viewpoints (local newspapers had long served this purpose, but they had lesser reach). On the other hand, pirate radio practically ended government monopoly, creating the world's most sectarian broadcasting system. The new diversity only reflected the views of the faction's leader, while suppressing internal polemics (Kraidy, 1998). Second, pirate radio created an antagonistic post-war mediascape that challenged the government's attempts to re-establish its authority after years of weakness and debility. Sectarian radio almost decimated Radio Lebanon's listener base, and currently, the station seeks to rehabilitate its service by revamping its brand as the station of Lebanese national heritage and coexistence (Gharib, 2019). Its 83-year-old archive, unmatched in most of the Arab world, allows the station to celebrate its unifying national value by showcasing its former achievements. For instance, in November 2015, the station dedicated one whole day of programming to celebrating Fayrouz's 80th birthday; the diva singer Fayrouz became popular on Radio Lebanon, one of its seven studios is named after her, and her songs and musical theater could be heard there often as they are one essential pillar of legitimacy for the station.

Main radio stations and current issues

Radio stations in Lebanon, around 40 in number, may broadcast political programs if they have a license for that; otherwise, they are licensed to air non-political programs. They fall under one of four categories: sectarian (sectarian-commercial), non-sectarian (government-owned or independent), religious, and English-language entertainment stations, as the following explains.

Sectarian: Sawt Lubnan (The Voice of Lebanon; est. 1958) is the first private Lebanese radio. It was launched during the short 1958 civil conflict as a pirate Maronite station but closed down after a few months until reopening again in 1975 when the long civil war erupted. The Voice of Lebanon became a respected, commercial station with good organization and local and international correspondents, that according to contemporaneous research boasted 20% of the local radio market (Associated Business Consultants, 1978). As its brand was based on providing news bulletins and political shows, the station's existence was threatened when the 1994 media law banned broadcasters from airing news programming. After a public outcry and ensuing demonstrations, The Voice of Lebanon like other broadcasters was allowed to resume political programming. Idha'at Lubnan al-Hurr (Free Lebanon Radio; est. 1978) was first launched from a couple of rooms in a monastery in Kesrwan during the 100-day war between the Syrian army and the right-wing Christian militia – The Lebanese Forces (LF) – on the orders of LF's leader Bashir Gemayel. A mouthpiece for LF, the station struggled after the end of the war when LF was banned and its current leader Samir Geagea was imprisoned until the Syrian army left Lebanon in 2005. Idha'at al-Sharq (Radio Orient; est. 1982) first launched from Paris. In 1994, Sunnite Rafik Hariri bought the station when he was Lebanon's prime minister and immediately issued it a license to operate in Lebanon. Idha'at al-Nur (Nur Radio; est. 1988) is affiliated with Hizbollah. It espouses religious values and airs a diverse bouquet of political, economic, social, cultural, entertainment, and religious programming, 95% of which is made in house. Sawt Van (The Voice of Van; est. 1988) is affiliated with the Lebanese Armenian community. It airs political and entertainment programing primarily in Armenian. Sawt al-Ghad (The Voice of Tomorrow; est. 1997) was launched by former LF member Elie Hobeika. Although it is licensed to air political programing, today it's a general appeal station with hourly news bulletins and a range of political, cultural, social, and sports programs. Sawt al-Mada (The Voice of Space; est. 2009) was launched by the Free Patriotic Movement party, which supports current Maronite President Michel Aoun and has an overwhelmingly Christian base.

Non-sectarian: Idha'at Lubnan (Radio Lebanon; est. 1937 under French owners, Lebanese government-owned since 1946) had branded itself as the "national unity" station, and before the 1975 war was a platform for poetic and musical talent, as well as for creating most television stars. Sawt al-Sha'b (The Voice of the People; est. 1978, see "In the Spotlight" section later).

Religious: Idha'at Sawt al-Mahabba (The Voice of Charity Radio; est. 1984) is a Maronite Christian station with religious programs. Idha'at al-Basha'ir (Tidings; est. 1987) is a Shiite-based station launched by famous cleric Muhammad Hussein Fadlallah that currently employs 37 people. Idha'at al-Qur'an al-Karim min Lubnan (Holy Quran Radio of Lebanon; est. 1997) was launched by the Sunnite Dar al-Fatwa to air various religious programs produced in house or donated from other stations and famous preachers.

English-language entertainment: Radio One FM (owned by Raymond and Roger Gaspar; est. 1983) airs English-language and international music 24/7. Virgin Radio (part of the international Virgin label owned by Richard Branson; est. 2013) was launched after the success of Virgin Radio UAE. Both stations are enormously popular with younger audiences.

Audience reach and financing are the two main issues that face Lebanese radio today, in the context of global and local developments. Global access to free digital media that provide instantly updated news and interactive entertainment have picked up a large chunk of radio's market shares. Besides, radio program consumption has been reduced to car commutes.

Locally, the industry's sectarian structure slices the market into small enclaves of dedicated listeners. In addition, intra-sectarian feuds over ownership have rocked the industry. The case of The Voice of Lebanon illustrates the complicated nature of sectarian ownership in Lebanese broadcasting. The strongest commercial radio in Lebanon, the station split in 2010 because of a legal dispute over ownership between two rival factions of its Phalangist owners. After Phalange leader Amine Gemayel refused to renew the lease on the station's name and headquarters, a faction formed under the leadership of Rose Zamel – director of political programming and advertising – who refused to hand over the station. The opposition faction later opened an independent branch in Dbaiye. In the aftermath of the split, both stations experienced internal shake-ups and resignations. Other local issues in radio stem from technical challenges, in particular in providing total and reliable coverage of Lebanon's challenging mountainous terrain. Understanding local audience consumption is another issue. Since audience research organizations in Lebanon – STAT IPSOS, COMTRAX, and GFK – poll more substantively eight major television stations than radio outlets, there is insufficient reliable independent information about market shares, program popularity, and cultural influence. Often, show hosts themselves decide when it's time to tweak the format or retire the show (Gharib, 2019). This has affected most significantly non-partisan stations that don't have a guaranteed sectarian listener base. Their focus on Arabic language information and social programming has cost them young audiences, who flock to English-language music entertainment stations. Two Beirut-based international stations provide mainly entertainment, in contrast to the news coverage that the Lebanese sought from international radio during the war years.

In the spotlight: how Sawt al-Shaʻb illustrates audience reach issues in Lebanese radio broadcasting

Established in 1978, following a period of intense fighting, the station aimed to stand up for workers and, since 1982, for the anti-Israeli resistance. Although it has clear leftist leanings, Sawt al-Shaʻb, or Voice of the People (VoP) brands itself as a secular antidote to sectarianism, because it's not owned or affiliated with a particular sect. One of the strongest stations during the war, as a non-commercial brand, it has since suffered long periods of financial trouble, including occasional inability to pay its employees. Still, it survived the 1994 licensing crisis (see later) without interrupting service. Today, it focuses on news broadcasts and numerous information-heavy programs that discuss daily concerns like unemployment, the environment, and poverty, as well as political issues like security conditions and the Palestinian cause (e.g., in its "The Voice of Palestine" program).

Most problems VoP faces are typical for Lebanese radio. Lebanese households no longer own radio sets and people listen to the radio only in their cars. Even that is not guaranteed because covering the mountainous Lebanese terrain remains a challenging task for the terrestrial technology radio stations use. Social media also causes the already saturated local broadcast advertising market to shrink further. Other problems are more unique. Whereas sectarian or the bigger, more successful hybrid sectarian-commercial stations may have a dedicated audience from their sect, more independent secular stations like VoP are losing audiences with the defeat of leftist movements and the onslaught of neoliberalism. Besides, as a critic of big business and a defender of the working class, VoP finds attracting advertisements challenging especially at a time when funding for leftist establishments has dried up.

Lamenting the split in the leftist intellectual circles and the onslaught of social media, VoP's management nonetheless understands that any station that wants to survive needs to develop with the times. To solve these burning issues, stations like VoP have turned to the Internet and to diversifying funding. Since 2016, VoP has had its app and a presence on Facebook and on the popular WhatsApp from where listeners can tune in and call or text the station. Facebook provides VoP with simpler, cheaper, and more inclusive coverage – a clear advantage over terrestrial technology. Making radio services available through social media solves another problem – the disappearance of radio sets and the shrinking listening time. This solution, however, hasn't helped VoP to revamp its best studio, which remains empty after decades of producing excellent recordings of famous Lebanese musicians. Yet, VoP is hopeful for the future for one important reason – since Lebanon is a country constantly rocked by political changes, demand for news coverage daily, especially from more independent, non-sectarian sources, will continue.

The government-owned Radio Lebanon is dealing with similar issues. Newly elected director Muhammad Gharib has vowed to turn the dilapidated station around and make it relevant again. He aims at turning Radio Lebanon into a smart medium through a well-developed website, an app that is already superior to those of the other Lebanese radio stations in its functionality and available content, and live broadcasts through Facebook. In addition, Radio Lebanon is exploring cooperating with private radio (Gharib, 2019); recently it signed an agreement to air on Cablevision's MVDS platform free of charge.

Whereas all radio stations have diversified their methods of coverage (terrestrial, satellite, and electronic), diversifying funding is a solution sought mostly by commercial stations at the moment. For instance, Radio One FM, which has one of the most popular sites in Lebanon (5,000 hits per day), is a success story when it comes to funding. It has incorporated income from entertainment services like web entertainment, concert production and recording, DJ services, and restaurant music services.

Lebanese television

Lebanese television history can be roughly separated into four main periods: *early television* (1959–1968) during which television established itself as a legitimate medium due to its novelty as a technological miracle, *first golden age* (1968–1975) that saw the professionalization and increasing sophistication of the medium, a *wartime "peace bubble"* (1975–1990) that witnessed, like radio, the deliberate and unconscious occlusion of the war, and a *post-war period* that includes a second golden age (mid-1990s), the spread of satellite technology, and the incorporation of multimedia.

The country's first two television stations – CLT and Télé Orient – launched as a commercial enterprise in 1959 and 1962 with a license to operate two Arabic and one French channel without securing a monopoly from the government (Dajani, 1992). The young entrepreneurs who started them attracted some capital from local businesses; however, international financial and management support (from the French government, Time-Life broadcasting corporation, the American Broadcast Corporation, and the Thomson Organization) was indispensable in the industry's first decade because of the heavy monetary burden. The two stations struggled to make a profit, yet they created the foundations of the national television industry as a commercial medium in their efforts to outcompete each other. Competition forced them to overinvest in grand infrastructure and high-tech equipment, steal each other's cadre, play dirty tricks, engage in bluffing campaigns, and conduct secret negotiations to coordinate their operations (Boulos, 1995). In this period, television became a symbol of Lebanon's modernity. Lebanon was among the first adopters of the medium in the world, as well as of color television, and also saw itself as a transmitter of modernity to the rest of the Arab world. As a national institution, television modernized public space, becoming a geographical landmark and the first medium that truly constituted a mass audience. Despite mediating between the audience and the political machine of the newly independent nation-state, television triggered fears in intellectual and traditional elites. The elites maligned the manipulative nature of advertising and fumed that the most popular genres – music, game, and variety shows – would damage public morality (Khazaal, 2018).

By the arrival of its first golden age, Lebanese television had reshaped what was considered vulgar and low class into a mass culture that threatened the radio's authority (Kouyoumdjian, 2015). The period boasted television's financial stability, a boom in local entertainment production, and the first wave of professionalization. Now an established industry (75% of Lebanese households owned a set by 1974 as TV sets became the fastest-selling appliance after fridges; Kouyoumdjian, 2015), television resolved its two serious issues – its dependence on foreign aid and the unsustainable competition between CLT and Télé Orient (Khazaal, 2018). The two stations merged their advertising budgets through Telemanagement – a new company they equally owned, coordinated their programming grids, and chose Télé Orient as the only station to produce news bulletins (Dajani, 1992). In addition, they developed a specialization in entertainment – local drama and comedy in Lebanese dialect for CLT and series in standard Arabic or Bedouin dialect exported to the regional market for Télé Orient, which became the second-largest exporter of television programming in the region. A professionalized industry, television ditched the earlier, cheaper genres for mature, higher-quality productions that reflected better the increasingly more sophisticated Lebanese tastes. The 13-episode drama in a variety of subgenres came to dominate the period (Kouyoumdjian, 2015), no less served by the creation of Lebanon's first private production companies. In 1974, when it was time for CLT to renew its license, the government institutionalized its control over informational programing, stipulating that two censors should be stationed at the outlet and the government should prepare a daily informational program (Boulos, 1995). At the same time, though, daring political talk shows embarked on open discussions of censored topics with previously blacklisted guests (Kouyoumdjian, 2015). Television represented Lebanon's collective experience; however, it tended to depict the multicultural nation as an idyllic modern land of harmony, prosperity, and cosmopolitanism, covering up its many classist and sectarian issues (Khazaal, 2018).

The 1975 civil war ended the golden age of television. Advertising revenue plummeted, local production almost disappeared, while regular power blackouts and infrastructure damage left whole areas with no coverage (those resorted to watching neighboring outlets from Syria, Jordan, Cyprus, Israel, and Egypt; Dajani, 1992). Things got so bad that the government had to bail out the two stations, which were facing bankruptcy. It purchased 50% of their shares and merged them into a new station – Télé Liban – with the total capital of 30 million LL. Licensed for 25 years with monopoly until 2012, Télé Liban was managed by a 12-member board of directors, whose chair was proposed by the ministers of information and finance (ibid.). The government's main role in the merger was to provide liquidity and help with rebuilding damaged transmitters, while the two outlets – now formally branches – continued to function as two independent cultures. Between 1976 and 1977, and again in 1984, each branch was taken over by an opposing faction and began supporting that faction in its political messaging, even if the branches continued to coordinate their entertainment programming (ibid.).

In addition to losing managerial control over its branches, Télé Liban faced another problem. Like Radio Lebanon, it deliberately occluded the ongoing violence, which convinced the audiences that it was unresponsive to their needs and damaged the television-audience relationship (Khazaal, 2018). Seasoned actors and long-time production staff left the industry or the country for better opportunities. Television's strained relationship with its employees led to frequent strikes as the budget provided by the government couldn't cover salaries, production, piling interest on bank loans, and infrastructure repairs. Télé Liban's capital had to be raised to cover up the difference, but that hardly helped to address the real issue that the funding it was receiving from the government was inadequate.

Television broadcasting technology had gotten so cheap by the mid-1980s that a political faction was soon bound to venture into a pirate transmission, given the weak government control. The first to challenge Télé Liban's monopoly was LBC, an outlet launched by the right-wing Christian militia Lebanese Forces. It began operating Arabic- and French-language channels in 1985, but in 1991 was facing two challengers of its own – al-Mashreq TV and New TV (al-Jadeed, owned by the Lebanese Communist Party). LBC's launch changed the dysfunctional television-audience relationship (Khazaal, 2018). Within months, the station conquered much of Télé Liban's market with uncensored risqué movies, a proud and openly Christian identity, and fresh, bold local programming that challenged the government's take on ongoing events, broached taboo topics, and put the audience at the center of attention. With LBC's arrival, television regained the upper hand after radio had enjoyed 15% larger audiences than television in the late 1970s and early 1980s when Télé Liban reigned. Another development during this period was the professionalization of television writing, which raised the profile of screenwriters. LBC's advent and the revolution in writing ended television's crisis of legitimacy and by the war's end television transformed into an exciting medium, which entered into its second golden age during the 1990s.

In the post-war period (1991–), 54 sectarian-affiliated stations launched following LBC's example. While a small number became bigger, commercial stations, the majority remained small enterprises run by members of the sect or its leader's family. Despite cheaper production costs, their tiny budgets didn't allow them to compete with Télé Liban or LBC (which could produce three hours of local drama series a week). As a result, most showed Egyptian films – incidentally also available in local video rentals – for which the press dubbed these stations "video stores with antennae" (Khazaal, 2018). However, since the government didn't want to recognize their existence officially, they could broadcast news without any censorship, reflecting the viewpoint of their sectarian leader (El Richani, 2013). In 1994, the government stepped in and closed many of them, yet such political parallelism, or influence, over television embedded sectarian divisions further in the industry, which continues to be the world's most sectarian broadcast industry until this day.

During this period, Lebanese television made many important contributions to the regional television industry and Arab culture. It started the first satellite broadcast from the Arab world, served as a dubbing and distribution capital for foreign productions to the Arab world, and introduced to the region genres like anime, the Latin American telenovela, and reality television (in particular singing talent competitions), among others. Its most important stations have been supported with Gulf capital, while the forging of international corporate ventures and mergers have allowed Lebanese television access to the lucrative Saudi market (Kraidy and Khalil, 2009). Lebanese light entertainment formats, which are shaped by relatively liberal values on gender relations, have affected the region's culture and its social taboos more than any other Arab television (Kraidy, 2010). Beirut became one of the major Arab media cities, attracting television corporations with financial incentives and a liberal political climate.

Main television channels and current issues

Like radio, the 22 Lebanese television stations fall under four categories: sectarian (sectarian-commercial), non-sectarian (government and independent), religious, and international stations.

Sectarian: LBC (est. 1985, see later). Al-Jadeed (New TV; est. 1991) brands itself as a non-sectarian station, envisioned by The Voice of the People radio. However, it was bought by Sunni businessman Tahseen Khayyat (a fierce Hariri rival). The station strongly criticized the Hariri government, which closed it in 1996 for four years by denying it license under the pretext of the 1994 audiovisual law. Al-Jadeed survived as a production company before reopening after winning a legal battle and a license to broadcast (El Halabi, 2019). MTV (est. 1991) is a mixed news-entertainment channel affiliated with the Greek Orthodox Murr family. It was shut down by the government in 2002 because it led the resistance against the Syrian military presence in Lebanon. In 2005, after the Syrians left, Parliament legalized the station and it relaunched in 2009. Al-Manar (Lighthouse TV; est. 1991) is a Hizbollah-owned station financed from advertising and Iranian funding. It is a role model for aspiring radical, religiously based, mixed programming stations because of its successful use of programming as a weapon against Israel during military crises (when it ranks #10 regionally), such as in promotional music videos that feature martyrs, the Palestinian intifada, and Muslim suffering (Kraidy and Khalil, 2009). Future TV (est. 1993) is a station affiliated with the Hariri family and their Sunni supporters. It was Lebanon's number two station in the 1990s but has since fallen behind after the assassination of Rafik Hariri. NBN (est. 1996) is Lebanon's first all-news television station; it's affiliated with Shiite Speaker Nabih Berri and the Amal movement. OTV (est. 2007) is Lebanon's first publicly traded television station. It's affiliated with Lebanon's current Maronite President Michel Aoun and his supporters from the National Patriotic Movement.

Non-sectarian: Télé Liban (see earlier). Arab Woman TV, previously Heya TV (She TV; est. 2002) is a successful channel that reflects the industry trend of segmenting audiences into niche markets. Run by 70% female staff, Heya TV both promotes feminist agendas and focuses on shopping, fashion, and the beauty industry (Kraidy and Khalil, 2009).

Religious: Télé Lumier (est. 1991) was launched as a non-profit by the Assembly of Catholic Patriarchs and Bishops in Lebanon and currently broadcasts without a license on frequencies from Télé Liban. Since 2003, it has launched also a satellite service called Noursat.

International stations: al-Mayadeen (est. 2012) is a pan-Arab, pro-Hizbollah news station headquartered in Beirut.

After two decades of private and a decade of government ownership, since the mid-1980s Lebanese television has operated under a regime of sectarian affiliation with important positive and negative consequences. Lebanese television enjoys great journalistic freedom and political diversity. There is also some internal pluralism due to efforts at each station to reach out to audiences from other sects and create a variety of non-political programs. Nonetheless, the sectarian broadcast regime mirrors and reinforces the country's political and social fragmentation and benefits the elites (El Richani, 2013). Pluralism is mostly present on the level of the system, but each station is internally muzzled. Political money – funding coming from political groups and interests – are essential for the survival of the sectarian broadcast system, as the small and saturated advertising market in Lebanon is inadequate to support the high number of television stations that currently operate in the tiny country. The sectarian stations are often used as political or election campaign weapons; for instance, in the mid-2000s, different stations incited their supporters to descend on the streets and stage pro- or anti-Syrian demonstrations related to the ongoing election campaigns. OTV has played a role in Michel Aoun's bid for the presidency, which he won in 2016.

The second negative consequence of the sectarian broadcast regime is its devastating effect on Lebanon's government-owned television station (Boulos, 2007). Like pirate radio, pirate television ended government monopoly. According to television doyen Jean-Claude Boulos, who was appointed Télé Liban's CEO between 1993 and 1996, during that period Prime Minister Hariri demanded that the post of government sensor at Télé Liban be given to one of Hariri's loyal Sunni supporters. This move angered Shi'a Speaker Nabih Berri and started a rivalry over whose political hack to install. As of 2019, Télé Liban has had no CEO or board of directors for two years because of similar bickering among the sects over installing their political hacks.

Third, the sectarian television system has produced a far larger number of stations that the advertising market of the tiny country can support (hence the importance of political money). The shrinking advertising market due to the rise of electronic and social media has further stressed the industry. The cheap prices viewers pay to get about a 200-channel bouquet (as low as $10) also affect television income and production capabilities (El Halabi, 2019). To survive, Lebanese stations have begun exploring multi-channel ventures; they have also joined a conversation about a Lebanese multi-channel bouquet that would help with countering the effects of the shrinking advertising market and boost the stations' revenues (ibid.).

In the spotlight: how LBC illustrates the impact of Lebanese television on the Arab region

Its sectarian beginnings notwithstanding, LBC quickly adopted commercial strategies to capture the Lebanese local market and in 1996 transitioned into a successful regional satellite station. Its US-educated CEO, Pierre Daher, claims that in 1992 he bought the station from LF, when the government outlawed LF, and in 2019 he prevailed in a lawsuit over ownership filed by LF in 2007. Much more important than news channels for shaping the regional industry, LBC has pioneered one of the three television models that are the most widely imitated in the region (Kraidy and Khalil, 2009). LBC's model is based on general entertainment supported by advertisements and product placement, which reflects the rise of American-style television and later the fusion of different genres. LBC owes its vast regional success to two main strategies (ibid.). The first is LBC's focus on light entertainment, including music videos, game shows, and reality television with prizes. These genres thrive on branding attractive women in revealing clothes as a key marketing tool. Despite its liberated sexuality, the station has been able to get away with the backlash from conservative Muslim circles because it's Christian-owned and located in relatively liberal Lebanon. LBC's second strategy is founding multi-channel conglomerates like LBC Holding and LBC-Rotana. By integrating with Rotana, owned by Saudi mogul al-Waleed b. Talal, LBC received substantial investments and access to Saudi viewers – the region's most lucrative television market – where it consistently ranked #5 most-watched channel in the 2000s. In addition to financial benefits, this strategy has also granted LBC political protection, which has come in handy after the hostile climate some Lebanese media had faced during the post-war Syrian presence (1991–2005, when LBC was part of the anti-Syrian resistance and some of its show hosts like May Chidiac were bombed).

Recently, LBC pioneered another major regional trend. As financing is a critical issue for the industry, LBC began tapping into new, interactive revenue sources outside of advertising, such as mobile phones, social media, and digital applications (ibid.). The station integrated these sources into its iconic controversial and mostly live-streamed reality shows (e.g., *Star Academy*, *Mission Fashion*), which attract a massive young audience. LBC's remarkable reputation as the trendsetter of Arab entertainment, however, has hurt it in at least one way – its merging venture with the Saudi-owned *al-Hayat* political newspaper (2002–2010) de facto failed because LBC was not seen as a legitimate player in the field of news.

Broadcasting policies and journalists' censorship

After the war ended in 1991, the government was finally able to address the many issues in television, which were inadequately tackled by the 1962 Press Law that covered it. Some of the issues included the existence of multiple private channels that were unlicensed and not held accountable, their status as symbols of wartime sectarian segregation and a weak Lebanese state, and the danger to air traffic the media anarchy caused. In an attempt to find a solution, in 1994, Rafik Hariri's reconstruction government passed Audio-Visual Law 382 to great backlash from the industry. The main reason for discontent was that the government licensed only six big stations affiliated with major political players and forcefully shut down the rest (El Richani, 2013). The law, coupled with Syrian meddling, caused several political crises, e.g., over raiding or closing channels like NTV and MTV or overrestricting, for a period, news bulletins aired by private broadcasters.

The law had two major effects. First, it institutionalized television's sectarian character. Second, it sabotaged the national channel. The latter means that Télé Liban's CEOs were incapable of convincing the government to ensure the adequate and steady budget for the station because elected government officials and parliament members, who hold Télé Liban's purse, are affiliated with different sects, just like the private channels against whom it competes. According to Boulos, in the 1990s Télé Liban spent $24 million annually and only made $6 million in advertisements, which left a gap of $18 million. However, his proposal that the Ministry of Information allocate from its budget an amount that would cover the gap fell on deaf ears, even though other government-owned businesses like the army and transportation receive adequate budgets from their respective ministries (Boulos, 1995). As a result of long-term underfunding, Télé Liban closed down for six months and when it reopened only ran at 25% capacity, with its Hazmiyeh branch remaining unused for years (Shaqqur, 2017). Télé Liban's and Radio Lebanon's ownership has been a frequently discussed issue, given the low financial support they receive and the resulting underperformance and loss of market shares in a highly competitive, saturated market. Until 2018, privatizing these stations has been unsuccessful. In 2018, Prime Minister Saad Hariri approved a new privatization plan for 50% of Télé Liban's and Radio Lebanon's shares, which caretaker Information Minister Melhem Riachi argued would cut down government spending and curb mismanagement. In addition, attempts to fill the post of government monitor at Télé Liban with political hacks and meddle with the station's running have caused constant rivalry among the top three political offices. For instance, in the mid-1990s, Information Minister Farouk Mikari, who was close to Hariri, handed Télé Liban's CEO a list of Télé Liban's best employees, demanding that they be fired so they can be then hired at Future TV – Hariri's own private station (Boulos, 1995). In another example, a 2009 plan for restructuring the government-owned station was scrapped out of fear that it would damage the interests of the private channels.

Finally, in 2016 the government began deliberations on a new media bill that would cover digital-era media as well, which currently are covered by the 1962 Publications Law (based in part on older, Ottoman regulations). The television and radio stations in the country participated in workshops with the government agencies to explore how to change the existing law. The main concerns are that, first, the current media law causes various problems because it's not consolidated but depends on two different sets of laws from 1962 and 1994. Second, it excludes electronic media; and third, it rests on a cumbersome bureaucratic process where the National Council of Information only has an advisory role to the minister of information, who reports violations to Parliament, which takes action. In the new bill, the Council would deal with violations directly.

While this bill proposes to cut down bureaucracy and unify regulatory frameworks, it would also have negative effects. For instance, it proposes to double the annual dues that stations have to pay the government. The higher dues may in practice cause independent struggling outlets such as The Voice of the People radio to go out of business. As this radio station isn't in the business of making a profit and only receives income from advertising accidentally, the proposed law would in effect force its closure on financial grounds and silence its signature critiques of big business as well as its championing of the interests of workers and struggling families, even if some of that may be lip service. Second, the law retains provisions that allow the government to imprison and fine journalists for expressing their opinion freely. Even though imprisonment is rare, journalists are sometimes pressured into silence in other ways. Last, the new bill doesn't effectively protect local stations as it only takes dues from the eight licensed local stations but not from other players that operate in Lebanon like multinational channels al-Mayadeen, US-owned al-Hurra, or Qatari-owned Al Jazeera. This may incentivize international players but it also places an undue burden on local players to operate from Beirut even though they employ thousands of Lebanese households and create a market for production companies and other satellite businesses (El Halabi, 2019).

Conclusion

One of Lebanon's main contributions in broadcasting is developing a highly qualified cadre of managerial, technical, and presentational professionals, many of whom became the driving force behind the establishment of broadcasting outlets in the rest of the Arab world. Another contribution is its role as an industry pioneer – from establishing the first commercial broadcasting stations to adopting color television, to introducing the first legal frameworks for commercial television and social media. It's also a trendsetter that has served as a model for entertainment television for the rest of the Arab world and as a gateway that has translated Western models into viable local successes, consumed and imitated in the region. It has produced numerous high-quality programs, especially in the entertainment genres, and received many regional and international awards. For decades, Beirut has been a top media city, successful in selling the Lebanese dream and its liberal freedoms to the rest of the Arab world.

On the other hand, even though Lebanon boasts the first regulatory systems for broadcasting in the Arab world, regulation has not often translated into enforcement, which leaves an open door for sectarian and government abuse and lack of accountability. In addition, some of the flaws that plague regional broadcasting industries also take a toll on Lebanon. For instance, new technologies are regularly subsumed under older technology laws with no specific provisions about the different circumstances they face; overlapping jurisdictions and rivalries over jurisdiction among the top three political posts give rise to abuse and lack of transparency and accountability; ambiguously phrased laws have led to direct repression (Kraidy and Khalil, 2009).

Today, the main challenges Lebanese broadcasting faces come from the intense competition with other media, the legal, financial, and protectionist aspects of the 2016 bill, the shrinking advertising market, the changing habits of its users, and the entrenchment of the sectarian broadcast regime. To meet them, Lebanese radio is transitioning to broadcasting from social media and apps to reach bigger audiences and ensure access in all regions of the country, while television explores controversial programming, counts on its citizens' regular interest in local news to guarantee advertising sales, and prepares to engage the future regular viewers – teenagers starting at age 12.

Despite its eventful history that spans through a widening and shrinking accordion of stations, international awards, childish antics, government raids, the bombing of journalists, lawsuits over ownership, and more than a 40-year-long sectarian formula, Lebanese broadcasting has had a significant influence in the country and the region and hopes to be a model of coexistence and modernity in a turbulent region. After all, unlike other Arab countries, where audiences prefer pan-Arab channels, Lebanese viewers watch local channels first and foremost.

References

Associated Business Consultants (1978), *Extracts*, Part V.

Boulos, Jean–Claude (1995), *Al-Televizion: Tarikh wa Qisas*. Beirut: Sharikat al-Tab' wa-l-Nashr al-Lubnaninyyah.

Boulos, Jean–Claude (2007), *Al-Televizion: Rihla ila al-Jahim*. Beirut: Dar al-Nahar li-l-Nasir.

Boyd, Douglas (1991), Lebanese Broadcasting: Unofficial Electronic Media during a Prolonged Civil War. *Journal of Broadcasting & Electronic Media*, 35(3), pp. 269–287.

Boyd, Douglas (1999), *Broadcasting in the Arab World. A Survey of the Electronic Media in the Middle East*. Ames: Iowa State University Press.

Dajani, Nabil (1992), *Disoriented Media in a Fragmented Society: The Lebanese Experience*. Beirut: American University of Beirut.

El Halabi, Ibrahim (2019), Head of Administrative and PR, al-Jadid TV. Interview by author, Beirut, May.

El Richani, Sarah (2013), The Lebanese Broadcasting System: A Battle between Political Parallelism, Commercialization, and De-facto Liberalism. In Tourya Guaaybess (ed.), *National Broadcasting and State Policy in Arab Countries*. London: Palgrave Macmillan, pp. 69–82.

Gharib, Mohammad (2019), CEO of Radio Lebanon. Interview by author, Beirut, May.

Khazaal, Natalie (2018), *Pretty Liar: Television, Language, and Gender in Wartime Lebanon*. Syracuse: Syracuse University Press.

Kouyoumdjian, Zaven (2015), *Lebanon on Screen: The Greatest Moments of Lebanese Television and Pop Culture*. Beirut: Hachette Antoine.

Kraidy, Marwan (1998), Broadcasting Regulation and Civil Society in Postwar Lebanon. *Journal of Broadcasting & Electronic Media*, 42(3), pp. 387–400.

Kraidy, Marwan (2010), *Reality Television and Arab Politics: Contention in Public Life*. New York: Cambridge University Press.

Kraidy, Marwan, and Joe, Khalil (2009), *Arab Television Industries*. London: Palgrave Macmillan.

Shaqqur, Hassan. Director of Programming at Télé Liban. Interview by author, Beirut, July 2017.

Libya

15

MEDIA AND SOCIAL CHANGE IN LIBYA

Mokhtar Elareshi

Historical background

The Libyan media, like most Arab media, have been affected by government censorship since their beginnings. They have to follow official government policies and regulations (El Issawi, 2013a; Rugh, 2004). In terms of the press, because of high illiteracy rates and low income, readership has been very low and development very slow (El-Zilitni, 1981). There was no Arab-owned press media before 1951 (Rugh, 2004). The press, therefore, struggled, although several political parties/groups published several daily and weekly papers reflecting their allegiance to different ideologies such as communism, capitalism, or Nasserism (referring to the Egyptian president, Gamal Abdel Nasser) and also to conservative and religious standards. After 1951, the government restricted the press and newspapers were published only in Tripoli and Benghazi (Musa, 2018). The post-independence period consisted of two different eras that affected the development of the local press. The first period is the era of Muammar Gaddafi who set the political, economic, and social structures of Libya. The former king's existing press rules were renewed, based on the *Green Book*[1] (1980: 34) which stated that "the press is a means of expression for society and is not a means of expression of a natural or a corporate person. Therefore, logically and democratically, the press should not belong to either one of them." The official name of the country became the Great Socialist People's Libyan Arab Jamahiriya.[2] This was reflected in the media outlets that the state ran and managed via its institutions governed by the People's Committees (El Issawi, 2013b; Watch, 2006).

From 1969 to 2010, there were four main newspapers run by the state (via the General Press Corporation [GPC]), including *Al-Shams* (The Sun; a 12-page daily) (1962), which was launched by Gaddafi when he was a student at high school, although it was later closed in 1962. After the revolution, it was republished by the GPC. *Al-fajr al-Jadeed* (The New Dawn) (1972) was an eight-page daily newspaper. It was also published in English in 2000. *Al-Jamahiriya* (1980) was a 16-page daily. *Al-Zahf al-Akhder* (Green Marsh) (1980) (a six-page daily) was an ideological newspaper that followed the *Green Book*. It was run by Libya's Revolutionary Committees Movement. Most of these newspapers had a circulation of approximately 10,000 copies daily. There were also a few very popular local and regional dailies such as *Kul al-funun* (All the Arts) (2002), a bi-monthly newspaper, *Akhbar Benghazi* (Benghazi News), and *Akhbar Tobrouk*. *Al-Jamahiriya Al-Youm* (Al Jamahiriya Today) (2003) was the first electronic newspaper published in Libya, issued by the GPC. These newspapers had very similar headlines and content as they focused on government activities.

In 2003, Libya returned to the international community after the economic sanctions of 1993 when Libya was accused of planning the 1988 Lockerbie bombing. This had huge effects on the country's economy and media and widely changed the Libyan political scene (Reporters Without Borders, 2008). For example, several newspapers were established as semi-state media – the newspapers *Oea* (Tripoli in Greek) and *Quryna* (Benghazi in Greek and online only) were the most obvious manifestations of this change. These were established in 2007 and were hailed as Libya's first foray into liberal media (IREX, 2006). They were owned by the Al-Ghad Media Corporation (GMC) (supported by Saif al-Islam, Gaddafi's son). They followed a new liberal line that focused on the development of new media (Elareshi, 2013). Since 2011, many new newspapers have been launched which are now circulated in different cities and towns, and some of these still exist as online-only publications. Despite this number, it seems that these new newspapers have not been a major step forward for the Libyan press as they look unprofessional and lack any sense of national mission or vision (Musa, 2018).

Libyan radio

Radio has mostly been operated and managed by the government. The Gaddafi governance devoted a high level of attention to radio broadcasting, endorsing its expansion so that it was utilized as a political tool in the "al Jamahiriya era" (Ghejam, 1990: 324). Radio broadcasting started with a single medium-wave service in the Tripoli, Benghazi, and Sebha areas (Boyd, 1982) with a short-wave service and a limited broadcasting staff. A minimum of two hours' programming in Arabic was provided. In the evening, a radio station in Tripoli and Benghazi provided two hours of programs in English and French (Boyd, 1982). There were two other radio stations in Tripoli, Radio Voice of the Koran and Voice of the Arab Homeland. The latter was renamed several times due to the changeable political situation and is currently known as the Voice of Africa.

Internationally, Voice of the Arab Homeland was an ideological station which broadcast programs to neighboring countries and aimed at dealing with Arab issues (El-Zilitni, 1981; Vandewalle, 2006), although the station usually criticized Arab government systems. It included a specific program known as *Voice of Friendship and Solidarity* (Boyd, 1982: 191), which encouraged Arabs to hold the authorities to account for their decisions.

As of 2006, the government started to allow local radio stations (FM) that provided local news and social activities. However, no investment was allowed in radio and all expenses were covered by the Libyan Jamahiriya Broadcasting Corporation (LJBC) (1969–2011). Interestingly, the number of local radio stations has risen sharply since 2011, and now most cities and large towns have several public and private radio stations, with most of these providing local news and information, such as morning shows/talks and entertainment, and they are very popular among locals. However, some are already struggling financially and are starting to look for outside revenue, such as advertising (Musa, 2018).

Libyan television

TV in Libya was founded in the mid-1950s when the monarchy started to provide a television transmission service, although it was predominantly in English and Italian and the programs were transmitted from British, US, or Italian military bases (Al-Asfar, 2002; Elfotaysi, 1996;

Musa, 2018). In 1968, the first national Libyan TV was founded and started broadcasting in Tripoli, administered by French technicians (Boyd, 1982; Elfotaysi, 1996), with non-local programs. Viewers were also able to receive a few TV channels from neighboring countries, mainly Tunisia and Egypt (Boyd, 1982). Initially, television broadcasting covered just the Tripoli and Benghazi areas. Five to six transmissions operated between Tripoli and Benghazi, but owing to the large area and poor transmitters, most Libyans were not able to watch the channel's programs (Elfotaysi, 1996). After 1969, television was mobilized, and according to *al Jamahiriya*, the mass media were an important platform that was used only to support society by enlightening and informing people about the state's policies.

Libyan TV (later known as Al-Jamahiriya) became the main Libyan channel (Boyd, 1982; El-Zilitni, 1981). Due to a lack of staff, almost its entire broadcasting schedule was composed of programs featuring extracts from the Qur'an, as well as newscasts and some Libyan national songs. Although the channel broadcast a range of different programs, it was seen as being boring, low quality, and unattractive (Al-Asfar, 2002; Elareshi, 2013). All broadcasting expenses were covered by state subsidies from the LJBC.

Since 1995, Arab media have undergone major changes, moving from analog TV to satellite broadcasting, then to digital channels and now the Internet. The development of these changes has had an impact on the local media industry, although satellite dishes were very expensive and limited to the wealthy Libyan elite until the late 1990s. Since 2000, several technological and economic changes (such as the ending of international sanctions against Libya) made it possible for local people to own satellite dishes. Moreover, the demand for accessing more satellite TV channels resulted in the public being allowed to watch unlimited free-to-air TV programs (Al-Asfar, 2015; Elareshi, 2013). After this, competition from abroad forced Libyan TV broadcasting to modernize and become more liberal with several Libyan satellite TV channels going on air, but few are still broadcasting regularly as a result of fluctuations in their financial sustainability. This was the point when the government allowed some advertising on television as a revenue source and this was seen as a new development in Libyan TV in late 2000.

Under Gaddafi's governance, TV was managed by the LJBC and a range of terrestrial and satellite channels, including Al-Jamahiriya TV (terrestrial) and other satellite stations such as Al-Manawa (The Diversity) (1995), the main national TV Al-Jamahiriya (1996) (rebranded Alwatnya in 2012), Al-Nadi (The Club) (1998), Al Badeel (Alternative) (2007), Al Shbabiya (The Youth) (2007), Al Hedaya (2008), Al Jamahiriya Sport 1 (2008), Libya Educational 1 (2008), and Al-Tanasoh (The Hypnosis) (2009). In 2007, Libya experienced a slight pluralization of media with the establishment of GMC which managed Al-Libiya TV (Libyan) alongside two newspapers.

As of 2010, other non-state satellite TV followed, such as Al-Mutawassit TV (The Average) (2010), Al-Nabaa TV (The News) (2011), Al-Aseemah TV (The Capital) (2011), Libya al-Ahrar TV (The Free) (2011), Misrata TV (2011), Libya al-Hurra TV (Free Libya) (2011), Libya TV (2011), Tobactes TV (2011), Libya Awalan TV (The Motherland) (2011), Libya One TV (2011), Benghazi TV (2012), Fezzan TV (2012), Dardaneel TV (2012), Al-Zintan TV (2012), Al-Khadrya TV (The Green) (2012), Libyan International Channel (2014), Al-Qabael TV (2014), Libya 24 TV (2014), and 218TV Channel and News (2015). Others may be being established as we write. In terms of viewership, Libyans are addicted to watching different satellite channels, but they preferred more non-local TV at least until 2011. Now viewers are split as the country is led by different governments and the situation is still unfolding (to be discussed later).

Business models for TV and radio broadcasting and the press

The Libyan media industry was exclusively state-owned and unstable and limited in its legislation (Al-Asfar, 2015; Ziani et al., 2017). There is no clear business model yet in Libyan media as the situation has been unstable ever since the media first began. However, two periods are highlighted here: pre-2011 and post-2011. The former represents a period when the Libyan media were run by the government (in terms of legalization, regulation, and revenue) with limited competition. This meant that all the media productions were regulated and completely financially supported by the government and that advertising was not the main revenue source (El Issawi, 2013b).

Libyan consumers only had to pay for the sets required to receive the television and radio signals since subscription had not yet been introduced, although some Libyans did buy satellite TV packages to watch events (e.g., European football matches). As a result, advertisements during this period were very primitive and the state considered the media a critical part of the community (Gaddafi, 1980). Financially, during the early 1970s, the Libyan media sector spent approximately US $3.5 million to establish basic mass-media facilities (Boyd, 1982). Moreover, nearly US $50 million were allocated to continue the construction of the media's requirements in the late 1970s (Al-Asfar, 2002). In the late 1990s, another US $33 million was spent to improve media services. During the early 2000s, the state flourished and constructed several new media facilities by importing new technologies, training staff, and enrolling new graduate media students. This was an indication that other revenue sources were not needed and the concept of advertising was unfamiliar to Libyan media businesses.

Post-2011, the Libyan political scene has witnessed a raging conflict between three parties claiming to be the legitimate party of the national government.[3] To cover running costs, some media now broadcast and publish online (e.g., Facebook/YouTube). Most media staff employed (5,000) during Gaddafi's era continue working in the same field. However, there have been some changes to the leadership of these media, as several employees have left to join non-state media that offered better pay packages. Salaries in state media are very low, usually in the range of US $700–1,400, and payments are received several months late. Conversely, the non-state platforms pay much higher, more competitive salaries, ranging between US $2,000 and US $10,000 (Musa, 2018).

It is fair to say that because of the nature of the Libyan media scene, it is not ready to be formulated into any business model (because of the chaotic situation). The main indicator is that Libyans are not able to subscribe to paid-for TV and radio stations as there are still free-to-air channels and television marketing in Libya is not yet being considered. This is because, although some television channels have appeared since 2009, there is no level of competition between them, nor are they applying any business models. The marketing evolution within the television sector, for example, lacks the development of identity policies that would attract Libyan audiences and promote TV channels' positions to attract advertisers. Despite the existence of some good TV channels, reflecting some improvement in programs and talk shows that target Libyans, orientation towards the advertising market is not a central business concern. Reliance on subsidies from the state or individuals eliminates the need to attract advertising. However, some Libyan media use advertisements during the Muslim holy month of Ramadan when their consumption is at its peak.

In comparing state and independent media, they both have pros and cons. For example, although the state media were known for poor quality and unattractive productions, they were *honest*, provided local content, and fostered local unity. Now, however, there are several independent media, but they are *distrusted* and spread hate speech and discrimination among Libyans, as reported by RSF (2018). Because most Libyan media are owned by parties and businesses, advertisements are still very new phenomena, although some media can understand the importance of generating revenues for their businesses to survive in the new media environment.

Audience share and market competition

As stated earlier, Libyan media were largely exploited for political mobilization, which affected their quality. As of 2006, several changes were made to develop the media sector and provide more attractive and quality media productions (IREX, 2006, 2009). One non-state company (GMC) started to run media and competed with state media to gain local interest, improving media quality with a little revenue generated from advertisements, especially during Ramadan.

Since 2011, a handful of non-state media outlets are now well acknowledged by the Libyan audience, although these providers suffer from a lack of branding, as consumers remain unable to name and distinguish their favorite media supplier(s) (Musa, 2018). This is because these media are shaped according to political trends rather than audiences' interests. They do not follow professional pluralism as they only follow their parties' and funders' views, especially those related to the Islamist camp, and they have become mouthpieces for political parties, tribes, or cities (Abou-Khalil and Hargreaves, 2015), suffering from bias and a lack of fair competition.

Furthermore, Abou-Khalil and Hargreaves (2015), for example, indicate that there are three types of TV channels demanded by Libyan viewers: relatively popular local ones, such as Misrata, Tobactes, Benghazi, and Fezzan, which are usually linked to supporting and mobilizing local political and military forces; national ones that have progressively turned to support competing political parties openly, such as Libya Al-Ahrar, Al-Nabaa, and Libya Awnlayn (online); and finally non-local channels which support only their interests and agendas, such as Al Jazeera TV and Al-Arabiya TV.

Regarding audience share, most Libyans name frequently consumed satellite TV programs (especially non-local) and the Internet as their important sources of information, as opposed to newspapers and radio, with the latter only used for information and entertainment, especially morning shows. Currently, the Libyan media market is filled with media targeting a wide spectrum of consumers. The Internet has become more accessible – especially social media – and Libyans go online to satisfy their thirst for local and national news and information (Lynch, 2015). In terms of media preference, Libyans prefer news television (e.g., Alwatnya TV) as the content is more customized to their political inclinations. Local radio stations are thriving within each city and town and are getting more popular because of their focus on local content, while print media are less consumed.

Laws and regulations

The Libyan media emerged under the Publishing Law No. 11 of 1951. Following the 1969 revolution, the media, including journalists, editors, and directors, were directly appointed by the authorities, ensuring their loyalty (this is known as the Journalism Law 1971). In 1993, the government issued a new law to restructure the media and place them under the management of the National Press Organization (NPO). This law was known as Decree No. 246. The NPO was formed by the People's General Committee and was renamed the General Press Corporation in 2001, under Decree No. 180, and linked to the Information Ministry in Tripoli. The main GPC aimed to raise public awareness of the contemporary world, and Arabic and African issues, and to enlighten public opinion on different world ideologies in a way that helped to achieve the objectives of Libyan revolutionary ideas, highlighting the 1969 revolution's achievements on both the state and international fronts. In this way, the aim was to create an intellectual and spiritual bond between the Arab people and the African continent, reflecting the true reality of Libyan society and emphasizing its international, African, and Arabic historical context.

Article No. 13 of 1969 states, "freedom of opinion is guaranteed within the limits of public interest and the principles of the revolution." This meant that freedom of expression was placed within the limits of the public interest and the revolution's principles, as stated by the Publications Act No. 76 (1972) and declared by the Declaration of the People's Authority (1977), the Green Charter for Human Rights (1988), and Law No. 20 on Enhancing Freedom (1991). The law states:

> every citizen has the right to express and publicly proclaim his opinions and ideas to the people's congresses and the media of the Jamahiriya. No citizen shall be answerable for his exercise of this right unless he exploits it to detract from the people's authority, or for personal ends.

At this stage, the Libyan radio station was launched after the merger of the Tripoli and Benghazi stations in 1975, and this was followed by the establishment of the Radio and Publications Authority in 1985, which witnessed an increase in the number of newspapers and magazines. Independent civil society organizations were prohibited by law in Libya (IREX, 2009) and the press union was state-run (1969–2011). Two main bodies were used to control the media in Libya before 2011: the GPC for press media and the LJBC for broadcasting media. There was a lack of enforcement of the laws that made ownership of media possible, as stated in Article 12 of the Publications Law No. 76 of 1972.

Challenges of how to regulate after the "Arab Spring" revolutions

As of 2011, some new laws and regulations have emerged, aimed at liberating the media, but these are still just proposals. The lack of clear laws and regulations has made the situation worse, as it is difficult to know how to manage all these media in the new chaotic environment. For example, the media sector has observed a significant change in its structure and media discourse (post-2011). The media are no longer controlled by Gaddafi's legislation, regulations, and political directives, which had obstructed them (BBC News, 2016). To launch any medium, no authorized statement is needed. In addition, the Constitutional Declaration, issued by the National Transitional Council (NTC) after the political change, gave the right of freedom of expression, communication, and ownership, based on Article 14 of 2011 (Al-Asfar, 2013).

This guarantees freedom of opinion of the individual and of collective expression, communication, the media, and printing and publishing. The consequence has been an excessive increase in the number of newspapers, satellite channels, and other media outlets without taking into consideration society's needs or its ability to absorb this huge increase in media. The state is now unable to manage all these media as they are run and supported by local and non-local bodies, especially those appearing on online formats such as Facebook and YouTube channels. This means that most news outlets are bankrolled by private entities and business interests. The majority of Libyans, however, wish to receive less politicized, more localized, and unbiased news.

The Internet and social media use

Libyans first accessed the Internet around the mid-1990s, but access was limited to elites and wealthy bodies until the early 2000s (El Issawi, 2013b). With the only provider being Libyan

Telecom (LT), Internet users were closely monitored (1996–2010). Because of a lack of broadband at home, people used to access the Internet via café shops. In 2009, the LT established WiMax coverage in most cities, offering a wireless service that enabled locals to access and interact with others. As of 2011, there has been a rapid increase in the number of online users in Libya, despite the lack of electronic power and the ongoing conflict. Online activists on social media are reported to constitute 61% of the population, with social media reaching more than 4,000,000 users in 2019 (DRI, 2019) and those users divided between politics and entertainment.

The Internet started to provide tech-savvy Libyans with another way to consume information as a multitude of Libyan news sites and blogs emerged. Therefore, the Internet has become an important source of independent news for Libyans. Dozens of sites now provide massive amounts of news and information. However, to make matters worse, after the 2011 unrest, an unprecedented amount of news and media outlets sprang up across the country and are now well acknowledged by Libyans, with 57% of Libyans using social media as their primary source of information, especially during the 2011 unrest (Khan, 2018). However, these media have become more polarized and entrenched in the hands of radicalized factions (since 2014). They are now driven by polarized narratives and views of different ideological and ethnically based alliances and rivalries. This has driven many users to migrate towards social media for news and updates as social media enable users to document their news and stories. However, social media have also become a platform used by politicians and militias for "propaganda" purposes or to fuel armed conflict (Abou-Khalil and Hargreaves, 2015; DRI, 2019). This includes delivering false information aimed at misdirecting people and creating confusion (Gatnash and Dahan, 2019).

Social and political functions of broadcasting

In Gaddafi's era, media content was used as a propaganda tool, delivering the official line and imposing certain ideologies, leading public opinion, and mobilizing the public to support the state's political views. In February 2011, the social and political functions of broadcasting changed after the UN and the so-called Friends of Libya[4] mandated NATO airstrikes, which led to the death of Gaddafi, and the country descended into an ongoing civil war (Gatnash and Dahan, 2019; Moore, 2015). Politically, the country has been governed by different governments since then, from the NTC in March 2011 to the General National Congress (GNC) in August 2012 (Barbour et al., 2016). Militias and Islamists adopted a political isolation bill to prevent officials who worked under Gaddafi's government from participating in politics, including the former prime minister, Ali Zidan (2012–2014), and the National Congress president, Mohamed El Magariaf (2012–2013), as well as judges, police, army officers, and members of the boards of oil companies and banks (Clément and Salah, 2014; El Issawi, 2013b).

There is a disagreement between the House of Representatives (HR) in Tobruk (which was formed following the June 2014 elections) and its supporters, the GNC in Tripoli and its supporters, and various jihadists and tribal elements controlling different parts of the country, including ISIS-affiliated jihadist groups in Sirte and Derna. The GNC was supposed to hand power to the unicameral HR. However, the former refused to step down and give up its mandate and continued as the GNC, a now largely unrecognized rival parliament based in Tripoli (European Forum, 2016). The war has proved, on balance, to be a disaster and has turned the country into the model of a "failed state" (Kedze, 2015; Ronen, 2016; Shaoul, 2016). As a result, most Libyans do not trust local or non-local media outlets and alternatively choose to express themselves freely on social media.

Censorship

The media scene has been controlled exclusively either by the state (1969–2011) or by individuals and groups (post-2011). In the 1970s and 1980s, Libyan media developed an intense form of state censorship (Musa, 2018). Media generally served as a platform for controlling information and mobilizing citizens, and its content was heavily monitored by the security apparatus. The government monopolized and nationalized the media and increased censorship policies, with news and information provided by one agency, the Libya News Agency (LAN), founded in 1964 by the Information Ministry and supported by UNESCO. It used to have two offices (in Tripoli and Benghazi) and aimed to collect news to serve the public, as well as collaborate with different agencies. In 1977, the LAN was renamed the Jamahiriya Arab News Agency (JANA) (El-Zilitni, 1981) and then became the Jamahiriya News Agency (JNA). This meant that the media sector was unstable, with low-quality productions, a lack of media discourse, and an inability to confront the information revolution and satellite broadcasting. As a result, Libyans relied on non-local sources of information, such as the Voice of America or BBC radio stations, for news and information. As of 2001, news and information were hard to control with the arrival of more satellite TV services and the Internet (Elareshi, 2013).

As of 2011, media legislation remains frozen and has not evolved to support freedom of expression or the rights of journalists. As reported by the RSF (2018), press freedom in Libya and the seriousness of the situation facing journalists is said to have increased with violations being regularly committed against media staff. Libya is thus ranked 162 out of 180 countries.

Audiences and media as spaces of free speech

Libyan media were affected by the new wave of satellite television established in the mid-1990s, led by MBC TV and Al Jazeera TV (Elareshi, 2013; Miladi, 2011). These new media brought critical news and information and political debates to the public and led to the 2011 Libyan uprising. They, however, misled and fabricated news, creating "fake news," even though there had been hopes for real change (Lynch, 2015).

Among the charges made against Gaddafi in 2011 was "suppression of freedom of expression and the press." Although the reality of the press in Libya under Gaddafi's governance was not ideal, and it is impossible to deny the existence of absolute state control over the media and harsh laws of publication and distribution, what is certain is that this "repression" and "oppression" were concentrated in the hands of the state and its security apparatus, something which changed greatly after 2011. With the end of Gaddafi's governance, the situation became more complex and there has been an increase in repression of journalists and press freedom and freedom of expression (RSF, 2018). Militant groups, mostly jihadists, were the first line of attack in the battle against freedom. For example, Moftah Bouzid, a well-known editor-in-chief of the *Berenig Newspaper*, was killed in Benghazi in 2014. He was known for his rejection of these groups and had called for the building of a civil state and institutions. Moreover, the Libyan political conflict is strongly reflected in the media sense as political groups are employing media outlets to pass on their projects and agendas. For example, the Muslim Brotherhood is one of the most vital political groups in Libya because of its long history and its organizational rigidity, and it has declared different projects that have created conflicts and political wars in Libya. Such groups are controlling the media to a large extent in an attempt to direct public opinion.

These media do not comply with professional standards and media ethics and have become tools of fighting, discrimination, and disrespect for human rights and the dissemination of the principles of justice and equality. This chaos has led to several assassinations, and kidnappings and attacks on local and non-local media institutions in various areas of Libya have increased. For example, several cases have been documented by national and international human rights and media bodies, including the RSF, the International Organization for Human Rights (IHRF), and the Libyan Press and Freedom Centre in their reports.[5] The Libyan state and its successive governments have not been able to protect journalists and the public or take the necessary means to ensure their safety.

The media landscape in Libya mirrors the division and factionalism seen in the current conflict, reflecting broadly pro- and anti-Islamist lines and the propaganda of armed groups such as Fajer Libya and al-Karama.[6] As a result, Libyan media outlets, especially TV, have become a focus for factional violence (Gatnash and Dahan, 2019; Kedze, 2015). Opposing fighting groups and militias have targeted several TV stations and their staff in Benghazi and Tripoli. For example, Libya Alwatnya was attacked and taken by pro-Islamist militias in 2014 and Al-Rasmiya TV had been controlled by a pro-Islamist militia for almost a year before both were taken off the air by the authorities in Tobruk.

Conclusion

This chapter has discussed media and social change in Libya. The media have always been run and managed by different bodies and groups. Several TV and radio stations and several newspapers have been launched; some of these started as private media before being brought under state control (Musa, 2018). The chapter describes the fact that Libyan media were affected by the government's policies for promoting political, religious, and cultural life according to the *Green Book* (1975–2010).

Media serve as important sources of information for most Libyans about events that occur around the world every day. Given the nature of Libyan media, some interesting changes were made following 2011 when nongovernmental bodies were allowed to own media. Moreover, because they had different directions and ownerships, some of these media faced major obstacles put in place by the government, the militias, and other radical groups, as well as a lack of funding and a lack of quality, which resulted in some being shut down (El Issawi, 2013b). Despite all these new Libyan media, the broadcasting or publishing of outspoken criticism can now lead to violent recriminations and killings (al-Amiri, 2017; Dowson-Zeidan et al., 2014; Pargeter, 2013).

Libyan media now reflect the wider circumstances of the state, with journalists, media employees, and consumers being frustrated and poorly served (al-Amiri, 2017; Gaub, 2014). Thus, instead of stimulating debates on political and social issues, Libyan media have become mouthpieces for political parties, tribes, and cities (Al-Asfar, 2016; BBC News, 2016). It has been observed that Libyan transitional bodies have no clear vision of how to deal with post-2011 media outlets as they do not have sufficient power to manage or implement decisions to improve the local media legacy. This is because of disagreement between the transitional bodies themselves. Extensive media legislation is still lacking, and existing vilification and defamation laws allow a local right to take up civil claims. As a result, the discussion around a media business model for dealing with the media sector is still very much in its early stages as the focus is now on the high media council – which is already powerless – which is supposed to support and oversee the sector instead of a body such as a ministry of information (El Issawi, 2013b). The absence of transparent funding models (state vs. private funds) has led to unsustainable business models and a lack of newsroom structure and has resulted in chaos.

These media have become involved in local warfare, and they fuel the conflict by supporting one group over another. This is the case for both local and non-local media outlets. The battle between pro-liberal and pro-Islamic interests is also reflected in the Libyan media landscape. For example, Libya al-Hurra TV is the main voice of the Muslim Brotherhood in Libya and is accused of bias over its coverage, while Al-Rasmiya TV is perceived as a liberal (anti-religion) voice. On the other hand, Al Jazeera considers the Libyan Shield Force and the Libyan Revolutionaries Operations Room (LROR) to be the Libyan National Army (LNA) and both the Zintani Brigades and the LNA, General Haftar's forces, to be illegal groups attempting a coup against democratic institutions. Meanwhile, Al-Arabiya considers Haftar to be a representative of the LNA, and strenuously promotes Operation al-Karama (El Issawi, 2013b). Lynch (2015: 91) states that Al Jazeera TV, for example, "went from a primary source for news across ideological lines to an outlet that catered to Islamists, while being shunned by their enemies." This has led to further fragmentation of these media, which have now been mistrusted by Libyans for a long time as they are not able to tackle polemic national issues, suggesting that the responsibility is on the Libyan government to show greater awareness of the nature and importance of media, especially considering the lack of professionalism, the lack of funding, and the lack of transparency.

Notes

1 The Book (1973–2010) contains a compilation of perspectives on the political system (Chapter I), the economic system (Chapter II), and social issues (Chapter III).
2 The Libyan political system was a combination of socialism and Islam, derived in part from ethnic practices. The *Green Book* represented the constitution of the country alongside Islamic law (1973–2010). In this system, the General People's Congress, whose members were elected by universal and obligatory suffrage across a pyramid of people's committees and local government, guided the country. The government's purpose was to serve as the intermediary between the masses and the leadership.
3 These are the Government of Tobruk in the east, which emanates from the Libyan Parliament; the Rescue Government, which emanates from the General National Congress in Tripoli; and the National Reconciliation Government, led by Fayez Sarraj, which is supported by the United Nations. This conflict has had an impact not only on civil peace and public security, but also on public freedoms in the country, especially press and media freedom.
4 This was a group established as an international collective to support the NTC in 2011 in their efforts to overthrow Gaddafi.
5 In 2014–15, 15 journalists were killed and there have been 38 cases of attempted murder, 43 cases of abduction and torture, 44 cases of beatings, and also prevention of the work of journalists and correspondents, in addition to 76 cases of attacks against media organizations. In 2018, 186 journalists were kidnapped, and there were 143 cases of abduction and torture and 34 attacks.
6 *Fajer Libya* (Libyan Dawn) is an operation launched by a group of armed militias – mainly supported by Misrata – after the announcement of the Libyan Parliament election in 2014 and the failure of the Islam Wing party to get seats in Parliament. These militias have attacked all areas and institutions under the jurisdiction of Parliament, including Tripoli International Airport, and have burned some of the oil-storage tanks in south Tripoli. In contrast, *al-Karama* (Dignity) is a major military operation, launched in May 2014 and led by the principal commander, Khalifa Hafter, against Islamist militants and extremist Islamic movements in Benghazi and eastern Libya.

References and further reading

Abou-Khalil, Naji, and Hargreaves, Laurence (2015), *Libyan Television and its Influence on the Security Sector.* United States Institute of Peace, Washington, DC, SR364-The-Role-of-Media-in-Shaping-Libya?s-Security-Sector-Narratives.pdf. Accessed 2 July 2018.

Al-Amiri, S. al-D. (2017), The Reality of Libyan Media: Frightening Figures, Weak Organizations and a Mysterious. *European Journalism Observatory.* Retrieved from https://en.ejo.ch/. Accessed 7 December 2018.

Al-Asfar, Mohamed (2002), *Direct Satellite Broadcasting Its Impact on the Audiences for Local Television Channels in Tripoli Libya.* PhD thesis, University of Manchester, Manchester, UK.

Al-Asfar, Mohamed (2013), Freedom of Expression and Information Circulation in Libya between the Legislator and Authority Orders. *Azzatouyna University Journal*, 8, pp. 29–50.

Al-Asfar, Mohamed (2015), Libyan Satellite Television and its Role in the Military and Political Conflict [الفضائيات الليبية ودورها في الصراع السياسي العسكري]. *Aljazeera.net*. Retrieved from http://studies.aljazeera.net/ar/mediastudies/2015/02/201528113223744200. Accessed 10 September 2016.

Al-Asfar, Mohamed (2016), The Structural and Legal Reform of the Media Sector in Libya [الإصلاح الهيكلي والقانوني لقطاع الإعلام في ليبيا]', *Libya al-Mostakbal.org*. Retrieved from http://bit.ly/2et3UOT. Accessed 19 October 2016 and 10 September 2018.

Barbour, Nevill., Brown, Carl L., Cordell, Dennis D., Fowler, Gary L., and Buru, Mukthar (2016), Libya. *Encyclopaedia Britannica*. Retrieved from www.britannica.com/place/Libya/Government-and-society. Accessed 21 September 2016.

BBC News (2016), Libya Profile. *BBC News Site*. Retrieved from www.bbc.co.uk/news/world-africa-13754900. Accessed 12 September 2016.

Boyd, Douglas (1982), *Broadcasting in the Arab World: A Survey of Radio and Television in the Middle East*. Philadelphia: Temple University Press.

Clément, Françoise, and Salah, Ahmed (2014), Post-uprising Libyan Associations and Democracy Building in Urban Libya. *Built Environment*, 40(1), pp. 118–127.

Dowson-Zeidan, Najla., Eation, Tim., and Wespieser, Karen (2014), After the Revolution: Libyan and Tunisian Media through the People's Eyes. *BBC Media Action*. Retrieved from http://downloads.bbc.co.uk/rmhttp/mediaaction/pdf/research/libya_tunisia_media.pdf. Accessed 13 September 2016.

DRI (2019), *Libya Social Media Monitoring Report*. Democracy Reporting International. Retrieved from www.democracy-reporting.org/libya-social-media-report/january/pdfs/Libya-Social-Media-Monitoring-Report-Jan-2019.pdf. Accessed 16 October 2019.

El Issawi, Fatima (2013a), Is Libyan Media More Free after the Revolution? *Polis Blog*. Retrieved from http://eprints.lse.ac.uk/59913/. Accessed 20 September 2016.

El Issawi, Fatima (2013b), *Libya Media Transition: Heading to the Unknown, LSE Eprints, Westminster*. Retrieved from http://eprints.lse.ac.uk/59906/1/El-Issawi_Libya-media-transition_2013_pub.pdf. Accessed 10 December 2018.

El Zilitni, Abdulsalam (1981), *Mass Media for Literacy in Libya: A Feasibility Study*. PhD thesis, University of Ohio State, OH, USA.

Elareshi, Mokhtar (2013), *News Consumption in Libya: A Study of University Student*. Newcastle: Cambridge Scholars Publishing.

Elfotaysi, Jouma (1996), *The Development and Structure of Libyan Television Broadcasting 1968–1995*. PhD thesis, University of Leeds, Leeds, UK.

European Forum (2016), *Libya. The European Forum for Democracy and Solidarity*. Retrieved from www.europeanforum.net/country/libya#top. Accessed 20 September 2016.

Gaddafi, Muammar (1980), *The Green Book*. Tripoli: Green Book World Centre for Research and Study.

Gatnash, Ahmed, and Dahan, Nadine (2019), In Libya, Traditional and Social Media are Used to Fuel War. *Arab Tyrant Manual*. Retrieved from https://arabtyrantmanual.com/in-libya-traditional-and-social-media-are-used-to-fuel-war/. Accessed 24 October 2019.

Gaub, Florence (2014), A Libyan Recipe for Disaster. *Global Politics and Strategy*, 56(1), pp. 101–120.

Ghejam, Ali (1990), Mass Communication in the Libyan Jamahiriya. *Journal of Black Studies, Culture, Communication, and Development in Africa*, 20(3), pp. 324–334.

Human Rights Watch (2006), *Libya: Events of 2006*. Retrieved from http://hrw.org/english wr2k7/docs/2007/01/11/libya14712.htm.

IREX (2006), Media Sustainability Index 2005: The Development of Sustainable Independent Media in the Middle East and North Africa. *IREX*. Retrieved from www.irex.org/programs/MSI_MENA/2006/MSIMENA06_Libya.asp. Accessed 23 February 2016.

IREX (2009), Media Sustainability Index 2009 Libya. *IREX*. Retrieved from www.irex.org/sites/default/files/pdf/media-sustainability-index-middle-east-north-africa-2009-libya.pdf. Accessed 21 December 2018.

Kedze, Dia Tumkezee (2015), The 2011 Libyan Crisis: Would the African Solution have been Preferred? *Conflict Trends ACCORD*, 1, pp. 18–24.

Khan, Arianna (2018), *The Impact of Social and Digital Media on Traditional Agenda-setting Theory in Relation to the Arab Spring Revolutions*. FIU Graduate Research, 1, Florida, US. Retrieved from https://digitalcommons.fiu.edu/graduate-research/1. Accessed 24 October 2019.

Lynch, Marc (2015), How the Media Trashed the Transitions after the Arab Spring. *Journal of Democracy*, 26(4), pp. 90–99.

Miladi, Noureddine (2011), New Media and the Arab Revolution: Citizen Reporters and Social Activism. *Journal of Arab & Muslim Media Research*, 4(2–3), pp. 113–119.

Moore, Candice (2015), Four Years after the Fall of Gaddafi: The Role of the International Community in Stabilizing a Fractured Libya. *Conflict Trends*, 1, pp. 50–56.

Musa, Rami (2018), Libya – Media Landscape. *European Journalism Centre*. Retrieved from https://media landscapes.org/country/pdf/libya. Accessed 17 December 2018.

Pargeter, A. (2013), Libya: The Rise and Fall of Qaddafi. *Journal of Islamic Studies*, 24(3), pp. 398–400.

Reporters Without Borders (2008), Violations of Press Freedom Barometer. *Reporters with Borders*. Retrieved from https://rsf.org/en/barometre. Accessed 7 December 2018.

Ronen, Yehudit (2016), Libya's Descent into Chaos. *Middle East Quarterly*, 23(1), pp. 1–8.

Rugh, William (2004), *Arab Mass Media: Newspapers, Radio, and Television in Arab Politics*. London: Praeger Publishers.

Shaoul, Jean (2016), UK Parliamentary Report Criticizes Libya War but Conceals its Geostrategic Aims. *World Socialist Web Site*. Retrieved from www.wsws.org/en/articles/2016/09/21/liby-s20-s21.html. Accessed 20 September 2016.

Vandewalle, Dirk (2006), *A History of Modern Libya*. Cambridge: Cambridge University Press.

Ziani, Abudlkriam, Elareshi, Mokhtar, and Al-Jaber, Khalid (2017), News Media Exposure and Political Communication among Libyan Elites at the Time of war. *Mediterranean Journal of Social Sciences*, 8(1), pp. 330–339.

Mauritania

16

MEDIA IN MAURITANIA

Challenges and development

Mohammed Al-Sheikh

Introduction

This chapter aims at identifying the most significant stages that the Mauritanian press has gone through since its establishment. It also sheds light on the turning points such media have witnessed and how it has evolved from being in a suppressive role to becoming an instrument that facilitates people's freedom of speech, to the extent that the Mauritanian press has been internationally classified as a "free press" in the Arab region. Rather than detailing the beginning of Mauritanian journalism and the troubled development of many initiatives, the chapter will focus on pre-independence newspapers as well as those which emerged after the country gained independence from French colonization in 1960.

As far as pre-independence newspapers are concerned, the first Mauritanian newspapers were launched by political parties in Senegal, which mainly served as bulletins circulated by the parties to the revolutionists. One example of these newspapers was the *Mauritania Paris*, which was issued by the Mauritanian Party of Understanding led by Ahmed Ould Harma Ould Babana. It was a bi-monthly newspaper whose first issue was produced on 15 July 1949. Another example was *L'Éclair Mauritania* which was issued monthly in French and Arabic and first appeared in February 1957. Moreover, there were other bulletins issued by the French Propaganda Department from 1944 to 1949. The maturing of journalism at that period was demonstrated in the emergence of the *Mauritania Nouvelle* newspaper in 1957 directed by Abdel Wahab Achiker and later run by the Mauritanian People's Party.

Post-independence, Mauritanian journalism has been volatile. After the 1959 constitution, journalists expressed a different viewpoint from the one adopted by the regime. It was an attempt to break up the centrality of opinion and unilateralism, possibly due to the measures granted by the 1959 constitution and the 1961 constitution. The publishing law of 1963, which stipulates freedom of publication, allowed the emergence of several newspapers. Through these media platforms, various political parties were able to express views that were actually or seemingly different from those of the regime. They sometimes aspire to exercise a watchdog role by criticizing what they saw as errors and wrong policies of the regime.

However, this type of journalism did not last long, for various reasons. For instance, the legal framework that used to regulate the practice of such journalism ended when the regime exerted its influence on various political and civil organizations. In addition, several constitutional amendments were enforced by the regime between 1961 and 1965 to restrict the activity of journalism. Nonetheless, this was not enough to suppress opposition, especially after the political turmoil that swept the country and reached its climax in the 1966 events. Opposition groups, coming from various left-wing movements, were brought together by their absolute rejection of the existing system. This was reflected in the secret press[1] (Ould Abdel Kader, 1982) in the late 1960s and early 1970s, which took the form of occasional bulletins at one time and regular periodicals at another (such as *Oppressed Voice*, *Unity*, and *Young Mauritania*). Secret journalism was an expression of the rejection and anger of people and served as evidence of tensions at that time. Underground newspapers were the only choice left after all other means of expression were blocked. Although they operated illegally, they reached a good segment of readers who opposed the authority.

This period can be regarded as the first stage in the story of the Mauritanian press. Yet it was born in Senegal and France, since newspapers were printed in those two countries before independence and continued to be printed there for six years after independence. This was because of the lack of basic printing technology in Mauritania at the time. The political administration which allowed for limited pluralism in the 1959 and 1961 constitutions and the Publishing Act of 1963 could not find suitable grounds to effectively apply such policies. However, when the infrastructure became relatively available to start publishing newspapers in Mauritania, and with the National Printing Press established in 1968, newspapers were forbidden by law from practicing their activity. The government at that time used the mass media mainly for mobilization campaigns to strengthen the influence of the newly born state, highlighting the new challenges and eliminating doubts about political independence. At this point, the regime was not ready to allow for the existence of a press that did not agree with it on the fundamental principles, including the establishment of the state itself. After that phase, the private press was in hibernation, especially after the Publishing Act was practically suspended. It was not until the late 1980s that a private press emerged, relying on the Publishing Act of 1963 and its several subsequent amendments.

Media pluralism: emergence and early challenges

The main goal of successive military regimes was to enhance development rather than gain support. After consolidating the pillars of independence, the press faced new challenges that contributed to delaying its development. The state was fully engaged in fulfilling citizens' basic needs of livelihood and was focused upon achieving economic growth. In the 1980s, there was a political will to enforce the Publishing Act of 1963, licensing for the expression of opposing voices and engaging the public in the political process. As a result, several newspapers appeared in Arabic and French (*Mauritania Tomorrow*, *The Mirror*, and *Chinguit*). However, the real media boom occurred after the declaration of political pluralism, which entailed media pluralism according to the Publishing Act of 1991. This act, which included promising provisions and was based on a liberal approach, allowed for the establishment of hundreds of newspapers and many professional press institutions. That, in return, meant greater participation in the media process and a better chance for marginalized audiences to express their thoughts and opinions freely. This great leap was reinforced by numerous measures, which aimed at backing up the newly incepted press through securing financial support and investment.

Because of the aforementioned measures, journalism thrived, and various newspapers were launched. For instance, the well-known journalist Habib Mahfouz founded *le Calame Newspaper* in June 1993, which was widely circulated and famous for Mahfouz's weekly column "Mauritanide." His writings were characterized by notable criticism that reflected the great change pluralism implied. However, making comparisons between the Mauritanian experience and other examples from well-established democracies without considering the local context will be misleading. In any case, it can be argued that the short experience of independent media in Mauritania sets a good example of pluralism. It has improved slowly but steadily without ignoring the challenges surrounding its birth or represented by the gap between ideal legislation and its actual application: "The duration of this experience has not been long enough for the elimination of drawbacks caused by the fact that democracy has not been fully-fledged in the society" (Abou El Maaly, 2008a).

Public and private media

The Mauritanian media can be divided into two categories: government-run media and independent media. The history of government-run media can be illustrated by the experiences of official radio and television as well as the Mauritanian News Agency, which issues *The People* and *Horison* newspapers. *Horison* is the French version of *The People*, and they both express the voice of the regime and were the first daily newspapers in the country since 1975. Based in Saint-Louis city in Senegal, the first radio broadcast appeared in the late 1950s, just one year before independence, and was mainly devoted to broadcasting bulletins and a few entertainment programs. Despite its simple program scheduling, radio broadcasting was widely popular among Mauritanians, who viewed it as an unprecedented technological and media event. This radio service had an official character in the first place. It was the mouthpiece of the government where official announcements and speeches of the president were broadcast to the citizens, in addition to some other functions which aimed to preserve the cultural heritage. Later, the purposes of the radio included the modernization and development of Mauritania, which were manifest in the later decades of the rural radio services.

Radio and TV broadcasting

The establishment of the National Radio dates to 27 June 1959. With its simple equipment and limited broadcasting capacity, it became the national radio instead of the one which was broadcasting from Saint-Louis N'Dar, known for its colonial architecture, under the French administration (Mauritanian Development Gateway, 2020). This radio service was inaugurated by President Moctar Ould Dadah in Nouakchott in 1959. It was not more than a symbolic radio with a single kilowatt transmitter installed in a car. The station was only heard on the outskirts of Nouakchott.

Despite all the difficulties at the time, radio broadcasting made great strides along the path of development and modernization, initially using a medium wave transmitter with a capacity of 1 kilowatt, progressing to a transmitter of the same wavelength, with a capacity of 50 kW, and moving from a shortwave transmitter with a capacity of 4 kW to another with a capacity of 250 kW, and later on broadcasting on FM in 24 cities – covering the whole country, as well as now broadcasting by satellite and Internet to all parts of the world. Regarding its headquarters, the radio station has been transformed from a studio in a truck and a small apartment opposite the National Museum to a modern building with all equipment and sophisticated studios. In terms of broadcasting, it has also moved from broadcasting four hours a day, at its inception, to eight hours a day on its first and second channels and its four stations in cities such as Nouadhibou, Rosso, and Aleg.

Today, Mauritania Radio is considered a free platform that addresses all national issues and an effective medium to combat corruption in all its manifestations. It has preserved the country's heritage since the earliest days of independence and embraced its culture in its diversity, richness, authenticity, and openness, as well as contributing to strengthening national cohesion and safeguarding independence.

As for television broadcasting, supported by Iraqi funding, the Mauritanian TV service was launched in 1980 as a project and was officially inaugurated in September 1982 as a national public channel of the Mauritanian government to start its trial broadcast (Mauritanian TV 2020). The program production had started from the studios of the Mauritanian Radio and Television Corporation. It began broadcasting mainly in Arabic, then French, as well as in other local languages.

From the beginning of 2002, Mauritanian television began broadcasting on the Arabsat 2A, and in the following year it was allowed to broadcast to the Badr 4 of Arabsat, to make its outreach more widespread. Before 1984, the channel was broadcasting from the radio studios and later moved to the current headquarters after it was equipped with all necessary infrastructure. The channel remained the only television broadcasting from within the country officially licensed until 2011, when the law on the liberalization of radio and TV broadcasting was passed and made it possible for private channels to operate from within the country.

In 2007, a second channel was launched, and recently more channels have been licensed such as the "Cultural Channel" and the "Parliamentary Channel," which offer programs closer to Mauritanians. Mauritanian television became a public institution of commercial nature in 1990 after its separation from radio. In 1991, it moved to the status of a public institution of an administrative nature, aiming to inform and entertain the public.

Constraints affecting the development of journalism

Following partisan pluralism and the developmental project of the military regime, the contribution of the successive period lay in press pluralism. However, this pluralism has encountered various obstacles. The sustainability of the free press was a major issue, especially in the absence of guarantees to ensure the sustainability of the newspaper market. There were also other problems at the legal, organizational, and ethical levels. For example, several legal and illegal measures, based on the interpretation of Article 11 of the Publishing Act, resulted in the prohibition and hampering of press activities. Furthermore, other issues were raised by the violation of Article 9 of the same law, which led to changing legal depositing into a distribution license.

In accordance with Article 11, the minister of the interior is entitled to issue a decision to prohibit the circulation or sale of newspapers if they (1) are sympathetic to or coming from foreign states, (2) are detrimental to the principles of Islam and the credibility of the state, or (3) may cause harm to the public interest or disturb public order or security. Such a decision can be enforced if the newspaper, regardless of its language, is issued in the territory of the Islamic Republic of Mauritania. This article gave powers to the government, represented by the Ministry of the Interior, to seize every newspaper that is considered involved in one of the "prohibited" practices. The bottom line is that these measures made the press vulnerable to all kinds of restrictions based on personal interpretation of this article. This provision was considered arbitrarily and reflects the bias of the Ministry of the Interior. Instead of practicing its supervisory role, it adopted a suppressive one, so that any news article that hinted at the mobilization of public opinion against the ruling regime or explicitly took an opposite side was seized in one way or another.

However, despite the aforementioned, the picture is not all bleak since there was always room for free speech. For instance, the late journalist Habib Ould Mahfouz managed to get his opinion respected by everyone. It is argued that former President Maaouya Ould Sidi Ahmed

Taya, despite his dissatisfaction with the writings of Ould Mahfouz, was keen to read his column and had a special ritual for that. He used to send his chief of protocol to bring *le Calame News-paper*, then he would sit thoughtfully in his office, smoking "Dunhill" cigarettes and sipping coffee. As he read Ould Mahfouz's articles, he would frown for some time and burst into laughter at another, wishing the article would have been longer. Ould Mahfouz's column "Mauritanide" often criticized Ould Taya in a funny and sarcastic way (Al-Sheikh, 2008).

However, this boom in the number of newspaper media sources was not accompanied by an increase in the number of printing presses. There is only one printing press – the National Printing Press, which was founded in the late 1960s. It deals with the free press very carelessly, most likely because it was originally founded to provide its services to the state-run newspapers, particularly *The People* newspaper in its Arabic and French versions, which is the mouthpiece of the ruling regime and issued by the Mauritanian News Agency. Consequently, this has led to increasing costs of printing, resulting in suspensions of newspaper publishing. Perhaps the latest example happened on the 26 December 2009, when independent newspapers ceased to appear, in protest at the high prices of printing imposed by the National Printing Press.

The following is a list of the most important newspapers issued in Mauritania in the last 20 years:

1 *Al-Seraj*
2 *Al-Safeer*
3 *Al-Fajr*
4 *Al-Elm*
5 *Al-Amal*
6 *L'Authentique*
7 *Nouakchott News*
8 *Nouakchott Info*
9 *Rénovateur*
10 *La Tribune*
11 *Tahalil*
12 *Le Calame*
13 *l'Eveil Hebdo*
14 *Al-Huriya*
15 *Le Véridique*
16 *Al-Saheefa*
17 *Maghreb Quotidien*
18 *Biladi*
19 *Le Quotidien de Nouakchott*
20 *Al-Akhbar*
21 *Al-Badeel Al-Thaleth*
22 *Eshtari*

Journalism and publishing laws

Complaints against Mauritanian newspapers emerge every time they try to criticize public affairs. Judges deal with such complaints with unprecedented vigor, and sometimes with exaggeration. The new press law issued by the transitional government, which ousted the rule of President Maaouya Ould Taya on 3 August 2005 and took power on the same date, includes punitive measures against the journalism industry.

The new law regulating press freedoms in Mauritania approves the adoption of a permit system for issuance in lieu of the licensing system that prevailed over the past period. The new law also puts an end to the seizure penalty and repeals the subordination of the press to the Ministry of Interior and changes it to the Ministry of Justice. It also abolished the requirement to deposit copies of the printed newspapers prior to their distribution to be replaced by the condition of depositing one copy to the Censorship Authority at the Department of Public Prosecutor before or after distribution. In addition, one of the most prominent points in this law is the approval of media rights and press freedom for all citizens. Article (3) states that it is the right of the journalist to "protect his sources in all cases, except in cases provided by law for the necessity of combating crimes and misdemeanors, particularly terrorism and acts endangering national security."

However, this law has not protected journalists from prosecution and imprisonment. For example, Mauritanian journalist Hanafi Ould Dehah was jailed for six months for being critical to the regime in his online newspaper. The Mauritanian authorities considered him a danger to national security. A complaint was filed against him and used as evidence to arrest him. There were also threats to close any website or press institution talking about the security and military of the country (Ould Abdel Aziz, 2009). A recent development was the establishment for the first time of a High Authority for Press and Audiovisual Media. It came to existence based on a law that considers freedom of the press and audiovisual media as a right guaranteed by the Mauritanian Constitution. This right encompasses respect to the values of Islam, human dignity, the freedom and property of others, the pluralistic nature of the expression of thoughts and opinions, and protection of public order, national unity, and territorial integrity.

The law defines the powers of this regulatory body in various areas, the most important of which are public and private press and audiovisual communication, as well as advertising through the printed press and audiovisual media. The law also stipulates that the powers of this Authority cover all forms of international media broadcast from Mauritania. Moreover, the High Authority for Press and Audiovisual Media is responsible for ensuring that the laws relating to press and audiovisual communication are applied objectively, transparently, and without discrimination. The Authority also seeks to make sure that the ethics of the profession are adhered to by companies, public and private radio and television broadcasting institutions, public and private newspapers, and periodicals to guarantee equality between all actors in the field of communication (Ahmed Salem, 2020).

The High Authority for Press and Audiovisual Media is required to make annual reports about its activities and the application of laws and regulations. Its first grand task was to supervise the content of campaigns of candidates for the municipal, parliamentary, and presidential elections. A report by Reporters Without Borders (RSF) in 2008 praised progress in press freedom that has been achieved in Mauritania since 3 August 2005. The report confirmed that Mauritania had ascended from point 138 at the bottom of the scale to 77, an important leap given the dire situation of press freedoms under the rule of former President Muawiya Ould Taya.

Liberalization of the audiovisual media

The 3rd of July 2010 marks a milestone for the Mauritanian media, as the National Assembly passed Law No. 045–2010 to liberalize the audiovisual media, end the state monopoly over radio and television broadcasting, and transform the state-owned media into "public media." The process of passing the act, at the time, triggered political controversy between the ruling majority and opposition parties regarding the legitimacy of the law. This political controversy revealed the importance of institutionalizing the new press sector by means of restructuring its legal, organizational, and professional system and detaching it from the political system. It is also important to ensure the independence of the press sector, its freedom, and political, cultural, spatial, and social pluralism so that it can perform its role in responding to the democratic and cultural needs of the country. Thus, five radio stations and five television channels were licensed, and the High Authority for Press and Audiovisual Media, in its capacity as a regulatory body, supervises the activities of these institutions and spares no effort to implement legislations related to the communication sector.[2]

Owing to these developments in the media scene, Mauritania has been at the top of the Arab states regarding the freedom of press ranking for the fourth year (Atlas, 2015). Yet, the institutionalization of the press sector and transformation of the state-owned media into public outlets did not, during the past five years, yield fruitful results and did not garner a consensus among journalists, union members, activists, politicians, and the Mauritanian community elites in general. This indicates that the problem, in essence, was not related to the extent of freedom. For the state media, the policy of liberalizing the audiovisual media and public service is part of the regime's vision. That is to say, it has a connection with the regime and its intellectual and cultural system in terms of its notion of authority, the ways of managing public affairs and running public institutions, and their interaction with the public televised broadcast services.

Regardless of the conflicting views of the Mauritanian community elites on the law of liberalization of the audiovisual media, the country went through the first transitional period governed by a military council. The second transitional period was governed by President Sidi Mohammed Ould Cheikh Abdallahi (Mauritanian uprising). Such political transitions paved the way for establishing a recent democratic state prior to the Arab uprisings that started in Tunisia on 14 January 2011. This highlights the importance of the legitimizing of the press sector of Mauritania that was formed during those stages and its role in institutionalizing communication or mutual negotiation between citizens and actors in search of the public interest. The question, however, remains: have the Arab Spring revolutions influenced the outcomes of this legal formation and communication via public media outlets and private audiovisual media?

Outcomes of liberalizing the audiovisual media

Although the Mauritanian elites have conflicting views on the law liberalizing broadcasting, they agree on demonstrating respect for diversity and pluralism as one of the most important values for democracy. This value acts as the primary inspiration for the liberalization of the press sector. This philosophy arises from the nature of society, which is not fully homogenous due to cultural and sociological factors. This requires the recognition of intellectual, cultural, religious, and political diversity. Few consider the importance of media pluralism in Mauritania as a key principle to democratic openness, which has provided the political opposition and others with various media outlets they have never dreamt of. Through radio and television broadcasting, political groups can demonstrate their views and engage in various debates on how to reform the country. This transformation has been considered a milestone achievement over the past five years (Erraji, 2015).

The following list demonstrates the increasing number of radio and television stations licensed in 2011 and 2013: Sahara Media FM, Radio Kouben, Mauritanid FM Radio, Al-Tanweer Radio, Radio Nouakchott Libre, Sahel TV, Al-Watania TV, Chinguit TV, Elmourabiton TV, and Dava TV.

Few community elites in Mauritanian society acknowledge the gains of pluralism, which is a fundamental pillar for the values of a prosperous society. However, there is room for criticizing such an approach, its mechanism, and its outcomes. For them, it remains incomplete pluralism in terms of granting enough spaces to opposition and dissenting opinion. Although certain private channels host opposition voices, they remain under the state's control (Erraji, 2015). According to them, this is due to political constraints on granting licenses to certain radio stations and television channels and not to others. As argued by Al-Ghabid (2008), pluralism has brought actors who belong to the majority of regime supporters. They belong to the families that are close to President Mohammed Ould Abdulaziz. They have been granted licenses to manipulate TV channels. Except for Elmourabitoun TV (voice of the opposition), the rest of the TV channels are owned by the supporters of the president, who control the ceiling of liberalization. The High Authority for Press and Audiovisual Media strongly denies this account. In its view, free media is the major driver of pluralism. The existence of democracy itself requires free media.

Current challenges of Mauritanian media

The Mauritanian press has experienced chronic difficulties and problems, including lack of financial support, non-availability of experienced journalists, censorship, and absence of a trade union. Such problems have led to the demise of scores of newspapers and obstruction of others. The media scene is still monopolized by the state. Although the Military Council, after the change of power on 3 August 2005, pledged to the Europeans that they would liberalize the audiovisual sector, the only real outcomes were the emergence of new press law and the establishment of the Higher Audiovisual Committee.

The second feature of the current situation is the weakness of the partisan press in Mauritania. Few critics attribute this to the weakness of the political parties, although a few of them managed to establish online news websites or publish irregular newsletters.

Thirdly, Arabic and French bilingualism has created differing media realities. While the national Francophone newspapers enjoy a regularity and institutional level of stability due to the support of few Western embassies in Nouakchott, Arabic independent newspapers are afflicted with serious financial problems, insufficient dissemination, and poor connection with the Arabic reader. This is reflected in their low revenues and weak distribution which remains limited to the capital city. For instance, the independent Arabic newspapers *Eshtar* distributes around 1,500 copies while *Al-Hurriyya* distributes around 2,000 copies.

Fourthly, on the technological side, the Mauritanian press still suffers from lack of equipment and printing means as well as relying on the modest resources at the National Printing Press. This tends to impede the national press development and makes it outdated (not coping with the color image printing and the revolution of fifth-generation communication). Rather, such newspapers use poor-quality paper with sizes contrary to the media's recognized classification of newspapers and journals.

Nevertheless, the previous analysis would remain incomplete unless one highlights the most visible challenges facing the national media as well as ways to overcome them:

a   Challenges related to the media structure, in light of the rapid development of communication technology and, post-revolution, of fifth-generation communication (for instance, the spread of electronic press, image media, and satellite channels). Mauritanian media has either to keep up with such rapid advances or sink into the abyss of stagnation and deterioration. In this context, the prevalence of illiteracy is perhaps the most eloquent challenge. That is to say, more than half of the population suffers from this deficit, causing more than two-thirds of the citizens to have nothing to do with such media writings. The effects of this factor are exacerbated by the absence of an established professional tradition governing the presswork, or what might be called a lack of professional scruples.

b   Challenges related to material aspects such as a lack of press-allocated funding, advertising clutter, and non-standardized financial support. About 90 million ouguiya was allocated in the 2008 budget, the lion's share of which was directed to the National Printing Press. There is a weakness in the distribution of national newspapers in general, and Arabic ones in particular. The distribution rate rarely reaches 80% while most Arabic daily newspapers are content with printing only 1,000 copies.

c   Challenges related to journalism staff due to lack of experience, limited training opportunities, and the absence of skilled media professionals. Media studies as a discipline is still excluded from the University of Nouakchott programs.

d   In the legal and institutional aspects, it is necessary to note the flexibility of new laws governing the press, with weaknesses in including the trade union's press aspects and absence of a clear vision of the national press objectives.

In sum, for the media outlets to properly thrive in Mauritania they need to be freed from government monopoly and transformed into public service institutions. Also, such media outlets should improve their editorial policies by embracing diversity, encouraging local media production, and promoting investment in the audiovisual sector.

Sheikh (2003), a former BBC correspondent and prominent Mauritanian journalist, responded to a question about the developments of the Press Law by arguing,

> What is needed is a radical change in the mindsets of the officials of public affairs and security agencies. Above all, there should be a revolution in the mindsets of media workers, most of whom are below the qualification level while practicing unrelated professions."

These concerns are also echoed by Mauritanian journalist and parliamentarian Salik Ould Sidi Mahmoud, in a seminar organized by the Mauritanian *Al-Rayah* newspaper:

> The Mauritanian press suffered a twin crisis that stemmed and originated from the excessive presence of censorship as well as excessive absences of two types of control. That is to say, the excessive presence of censorship means the regime's control over words and freedoms of people. Our regime does not allow people to express themselves freely. It interprets the law as it pleases and does not tolerate other views expressed in the press. Journalism is a means to convey the social interactions, political developments, people's unpleasant comments and criticism on the regime, reflecting the realities which the regime wants to make equivocal and covered with false claims. The regime bears the primary responsibility in this regard.
>
> *(Ould Sidi Mahmoud, 2003)*

Various journalists and media critics in Mauritania voiced their concerns regarding the status of journalism. Ahmed Al-Wadiaah, editor-in-chief of *Al-Rayah* argues,

> The talk of Mauritanian media problems has many aspects. First, the media in Mauritania is new, dating back less than 10 years. Then, it developed in an environment that is not encouraging for creating fully-fledged press. Thirdly, the media is mostly run by individuals who lack experience, efficiency, and sometimes, honesty and commitment.
>
> *(cited in Al-Sheikh, 2008)*

Others consider that part of the problem of independent journalism in Mauritania to be the French-speaking newspapers. Ould Ahmed Al-Hadi (2001) argues, "They have benefitted from the support of the French-speaking organizations regarding constitutional set-up, training, and equipment. This support is sponsored by France and other organizations to encourage the French culture in Mauritania." However, as part of the solution to improve free speech in the country, Abou El Maaly (2008b) argues,

> The government should protect free speech and admit that the press is indispensable for raising political awareness in the country, establishing public freedoms and letting citizens perceive their responsibilities. The press exerts efforts to raise awareness as part of its official responsibility not only for the support of freedom but also for the support of society's development and education.

Conclusion

The general context of liberalizing broadcasting media in Mauritania shows that the process required a political will that was developed into an institutional action (Adoption of Decree 045–2010 by the National Assembly) thanks to various national and international contributions. This acknowledgment could discard the subjective feature whereby credit is attributed to the president/leader instead of the institution. This also stresses that the outcomes of this political strategy were subject to negotiations that brought together various stakeholders whose level of participation was different with regard to determining or specifying the value of the decree.

Public media have been open to the components of political parties and civil society and its various institutions, pushing towards the representation of political, cultural, and ideological diversity in the Mauritanian society. This makes the public media, to a certain extent, cope with the issues that affect the daily lives of citizens. One may argue that the private and government media today make greater efforts to respond to the democratic and cultural needs of citizens. Despite this, and after eight years since it was transformed into "public media," the media continue to act sometimes like a propaganda tool, reflecting the tone of those in power.

Moreover, despite all previously mentioned progress regarding diversity in the media, the president acts as a guard over broadcasting and the printed press. He is even considered by some as the real chief editor of Mauritanian TV, giving direct orders to stop programs and direct the newsroom.

In contrast, private media attempt to create free space for news reporting and critical debates. They have managed to provide an alternative sphere through involving the public in open discussions on government policies, government programs, and the activities of the political elite as well as civil society initiatives. This is in spite of the fact that a few commercial media outlets have been accused of being created by the state authority to serve its agenda and weaken the opposition, as was done by the regime of former President Maaouya Ould Taya in the late 1990s. This last granted licenses to newspapers and news websites so that other independent media platforms lose their audience and influence.

Thus, broadcasting media have been facing different and multiple professional, structural, legal, and financial challenges. These challenges put limits on their effective contributions to develop communication between citizens and actors at the lowest levels of community and the more organized, collective areas where discussions take place. In addition, such challenges diminish the contribution of the media in widening the public domain that provides the central mechanism for the democratic organization of society.

Notes

1 This term refers to bulletins which were distributed by the left-wing movements to their supporters to stimulate them to revolt and give them instructions (Ould Abdel Kader, A. 1982).
2 The High Authority for Press and Audiovisual Media was established as per Decree 034–2006 and the 026–2008 Act, which laid down the basic control principles and powers over commitment to work ethics, elevation of free and sound competition within the press sector, measures to guarantee freedom of the press, evaluation of requests to license radio and television stations, respect for the national unity and cultural identity, and measures to secure that access to public media outlets is open to all actors.

References

Abou El Maaly, M. M. (2008a), *Glimpse of the Press Freedom Reality in Mauritania*. Arab Press Organization. Retrieved from www.arabpressfreedom.com. Accessed 19 February 2019.

Abou El Maaly, M. M. (2008b), Editor-in-Chief, AlAkhbar Newspaper, Personal Interview, Nouakchott.

Ahmed Salem, S. A. (2020), The Beginnings of Political Pluralism, Special Files. *Al-Jazeera Net*. Retrieved from www.aljazeera.net/specialfiles/pages/7629517d-4d4b-459e-b027-95d456524348. Accessed 23 April 2020.

Al-Ghabid, M. (2008), Director of El-Mourabitoun TV, Personal Interview, Nouakchott.

Al-Sheikh, M. (2008), *Mauritanian Media and its Role in Political Mobilization*. Unpublished M.A. thesis, Waad Alnil University, Atbara.

Atlas (2015), Retrieved from https://bit.ly/353Qfbe. Accessed 24 October 2015.

Erraji, M. (2015), *Audiovisual Media in Mauritania: The Structure of Authority and Society*. Al-Jazeera Studies Center, Doha, Qatar. Retrieved from https://studies.aljazeera.net/ar/mediastudies/2015/11/2015111 790258911.html. Accessed 22 April 2020.

Mauritanian Development Gateway (2020), *The Mauritanian Radio Celebrates 49 Years since its Launch*. Retrieved from https://bit.ly/2S6vy9b. Accessed 23 April 2020.

Mauritanian TV (2020), *About the Institution*. Retrieved from http://tvm.mr/ar/%d8%b9%d9%86-%d8%a 7%d9%84%d9%85%d8%a4%d8%b3%d8%b3%d8%a9/. Accessed 23 April 2020.

Ould Abdel Aziz, President M. (2009), *Speech in City of Rosso*.

Ould Abdel Kader, A. (1982), *One Night at the Gendarmerie, Asda'a Al-Remal*. Tunis: Almanar p. 19.

Ould Ahmed Al-Hadi, R. (2001), Interview with the editor-in-chief of Le Calame Newspaper, Nouakchott.

Ould Sidi Mahmoud, S. (2003), Seminar Organized by the Mauritanian Raya Newspaper. Nouakchott, 19 January 2003.

Sheikh, B. (2003), Personal Interview, Nouakchott (19 January 2003).

Morocco

17

THE MOROCCAN PRESS

Challenges and development

*Bouziane Zaid, Abdelmalek El Kadoussi,
and Mohammed Ibahrine*

Introduction

Morocco was a protectorate of France and Spain from 1912 to 1956. The colonial powers introduced print press in its modern form, and Spain played an important role in establishing several publications in the northern cities of Morocco, namely Sebta, Tangiers, and Tetouan, as early as 1820 when the Spanish periodical *El Liberal Africano* was published in Sebta (Sami 1990: 23). Other publications included French papers such as *As-Saada* in 1905 and English papers such as *Times of Morocco* in Tangier in 1882 (Sami, 1990). The French and Spanish colonial powers also published in Arabic to help propagate their ideologies.

Unlike radio, which was controlled by foreign powers from 1928 till the independence in 1956, print media was a site of political struggle. Moroccan nationalists published their first Arabic papers *Lisan Al-Maghrib* and *Sinan Al-Qalam* in 1907 to promote nationalist ideas among Moroccan educated elite as tools of liberation (Sami, 1990: 26). The French colonialists responded by introducing several press codes to administer and regulate the nationalist newspapers. The first legislation was the Dahir (decree) of April 1912, followed by a series of decrees that demanded prior authorizations and allowed the colonial powers to shut down publications deemed too critical (Alami, 1985: 37; Sami, 1990: 60). After independence in 1956, the print press remained a tool at the heart of politics (Zaid, 2017).

Like many countries in the early post-colonial era, Morocco perceived the role of media as a nation-building project (Mowlana, 1985). Morocco was a proponent of the modernization theory which conceived development in terms of industrialization, transfer of technology and innovations, and economic growth. State-controlled media was therefore mandated with a role in modernizing the economy, serving as an instrument for education and social change (Ibahrine, 2007), and ensuring political stability.

Until the mid-1990s, the culture of media in Morocco was authoritarian, administrative, and partisan (Zaid, 2017). It was authoritarian and administrative in that the state controlled the financing, regulation, production, and distribution of broadcast media, which was considered the most powerful media. It was partisan in that print media was mainly controlled by political parties. In a country with low literacy rates, the state maintained complete control over broadcasting, which is perceived as a powerful media. Print media, however, was not seen as a great threat to the regime. Print media became since the independence a site of political tensions between the opposition political parties and the monarchy (Zaid, 2018). Opposition leaders used newspapers and magazines as chief weapons of political agitation, and the margins of freedom, though with consequences, were more significant compared to government-owned and -controlled TV and radio.

The dawn of independence (1956) marked the issuing of the first press code in 1958 and the politicization of the Moroccan press. Political parties launched newspapers to express their ideologies and political aspirations. The principal actors were the already established Al Istiklal/ The Independence Party (IP) which started *Al Alam* in 1946 and The National Union of Popular Forces (NUPF) which started *Almoharir* 1959. Both newspapers had frictions with the monarchical institution, particularly with the heir to the throne at that time Hassan II, who did not seem to tolerate much of the discourse of political parties (Lakmahri, 2012).

During the nearly four-decade reign of King Hassan II (1961–1999), state surveillance of the partisan press prevailed and instances of repression multiplied. Successive retributions of journalists and closures of publications characterized a period of seminal socio-political upheavals spanning from the beginning of the 1960s to the late 1980s. The major junctures of this period were the 1963 plot, the state of exception after momentous riots in Casablanca in 1965, the massive protests of 1968, the state of exception in 1970, and mainly the 1971 and 1972 failed coup attempts after which waves of arbitrary arrest, imprisonment, and disappearance of political and military dissidents took place (Zaid, 2016; El Kadoussi, 2016). Although the Green March in 1975 managed to rally all political and social factions behind the palace as the principal guarantor of national sovereignty and territorial integrity, consensus would not last long.

Before his death in 1999, Hassan II was keen on repairing Morocco's image outside and introducing it to the international community (mainly to the European Union) as a potential economic partner. To do so, he had to alleviate socio-political tension inside by initiating a series of significant opening measures. Effectively, between 1991 and 1994, most political prisoners were released and the infamous detention camp Tazmamart was closed. More important were the constitutional revisions of 1992–1996 which included, among other advanced provisions, respect of public freedoms and the principles of human rights as they were universally recognized. Moreover, the monarch opened a genuine dialogue with the opposition which culminated in convincing historical opposition leaders to take part in the alternation government in 1998 (El Kadoussi, 2018).

Mohamed VI's reign is referred to, in Moroccan mainstream public discourse, as "The New Era," which means a categorical breach with his father's contentious past and the initiation of genuine reform and modernization measures (Zaid, 2010; Zaid and Ibahrine, 2011). One of the first major pro-human-rights measures under Mohamed VI was the 2003 creation of the Equity and Reconciliation Commission (ERC), which investigated human rights violations from the years of leadership to establish the truth. The Commission organized public forums in 2004 in which victims voiced their pain and suffering under the old regime. These forums were broadcast live on television and marked an important moment in Moroccan history. Another major initiative was the Family Status Law, or *Moudawana*, decreed in 2003 to protect the rights of women. To safeguard and promote Amazigh language and culture, Mohammed VI created the Royal Institute of Amazigh Culture (L'Institut Royal de la Culture Amazighe, IRCAM). The Amazigh constitute a large ethnic group, but their culture was undermined for decades (Zaid, 2010; Zaid and Ibahrine, 2011).

Further, an advanced press code was introduced in 2002 encouraging entrepreneurship and diversification of the press product. The press code provided a relatively clearer definition of the journalistic profession and facilitated access to information. The media benefited a great deal from these reform measures. All sectors – print, broadcast, and digital – witnessed significant growth during the period. Under the impact of the rise of Arab satellite broadcasting, the partial liberalization and modernization of the audiovisual sector allowed new commercial radio and TV stations to emerge. The new private radio stations, which increased from two in 2005 to 16 in 2009, reinvigorated the broadcast landscape especially through their live debate shows and news programs. Government restrictions on print media also eased. A new generation of young journalists pushed the boundaries of the comfort zone of mainstream media and society at large. Many taboos were broken, from reporting on the king's salary to reporting on the arrest of high officials close to the palace. Morocco was also spared from the draconian measures used in other authoritarian countries against the Internet such as the blocking of social media platforms or web content. Moroccan citizens can create websites and write for blogs without any registration requirements imposed by the government.

However, while the ERC, the *Moudawana*, and the IRCAM are positive developments, they do not constitute serious opportunities for challenging the status quo in Morocco. The state continues to use legal and financial penalties to keep the most critical outlets in line. A record number of libel and defamation suits were filed against print media. Powerful business entities, such as the three telecommunication companies, are known to adhere to state pressure to withdraw advertising money from news outlets that run counter to the state-sanctioned media narrative. The state rewards consenting media outlets by granting them access to the main advertisers and punishes other media for their dissent.

Main players

Current regulatory practices aim to reduce concentration, but they fail to encourage pluralism in media ownership. According to the Press and Publications Code, any media organization in the broadcast industry cannot hold an investment in the capital of more than one print media company. Any person owning 30% or more of a newspaper company must declare it to the National Press Council, as must any newspaper or magazine that owns 10% or more in the capital of another newspaper or magazine. Internet service providers (ISPs) cannot own part of the capital of another ISP (Le Desk and Reporters Without Borders, 2017). In Morocco, the absence of concentration does not necessarily imply an increase in pluralism. Private ownership of print media consists primarily of pro-government business figures (Le Desk and Reporters Without Borders, 2017). The list includes businessmen such as Othman Benjelloun and Moulay Hafid El Alami; members of the administrative (pro-government) political party such as Abdelaziz Akhenouch and Mouncif Belkhayat; and former employees of the state-owned TV and radio stations such as Kamal Lahlou. Aside from state control over broadcasting, only a handful of media companies owned by key pro-government political players, such as the Caractères Media Group, EcoMedias Group, and Maroc Soir Group, control a few media outlets in print, online, and broadcasting. No single company has control over a significant audience share.

A few of Morocco's billionaires such as Moulay Hafid Elalamy, Aziz Akhannouch, Othman Benjelloun, and Meriem Bensaleh Chaqroun have stakes in five of the nine French-language publications, including *Aujourd'hui Le Maroc*, *La Vie Eco*, *Les Inspirations Eco*, *La Nouvelle Tribune*, and *L'Economiste*. Currently, two of them are also ministers (Le Desk and Reporters Without Borders, 2017). The publications are editorially pro-government, and they benefit from advertising despite their limited circulation. This close relationship between economic power and the French-language media is creating an unhealthy media market because these newspapers receive advertising budgets regardless of their primary circulation and readership. This promotes a culture of clientelism, which is harmful to media transparency and professionalism. Ostensibly, media in Morocco has been strongly controlled by political and economic clientelism. These political leaders need these publications for reputation management, to play down corruption scandals, and to ensure electoral campaign success (Benchenna et al., 2017). This clientelism is also a manifestation of the rentier state in Morocco threatening the freedom of the press for which independence from government interference and big money is vital.

Business models and audience share

Morocco's media system consists of a mix of public and private ownership and allows the government's intervention to ensure public service. Moroccan media outlets use three main financing models. The first is advertising: the media firms expose audiences to advertising messages in exchange for free content. This is the dominant business model in Morocco's media, which permeates both private and partisan print media. The second is the subsidy: the government pays media firms in return for some form of public service. This applies to both private and political party newspapers. The aim, as stated by the government, is to help these media firms be more independent and distanced from all vested economic interests. The third is subscriptions: consumers access media content in return for a monthly or annual fee. This is the case for news websites such as *Le Desk* and *Telquel*.

Regarding audience share, television remains the primary media of information and entertainment given the high rates of illiteracy, lack of local digital content creation, and shortage of digital literacy skills. The second most used source of news is news websites. In 2010, the country's top 10 most visited websites did not include any Moroccan news sites. By 2018, the list included six Moroccan websites – three news sites, two classified ad platforms (*Avito* and *Jumia*), and one sports site. In 2020, the country's top 10 most visited websites included six Moroccan websites, four news sites, and two sports news websites. The remaining four are Google, Facebook, YouTube, and google.co.ma. Chouftv and Hespress surpassed Facebook to rank third and fourth respectively (Alexa.com, 2020). For print newspapers, circulation has always been modest, but the excessive practice of self-censorship has drained the Moroccan press from its substance and eventually from its readership. Readership at its best has been estimated at 350,000; less than 1% of the population reads a newspaper every day. Before the Coronavirus crisis, less than 150,000 papers were sold per day (OJD, 2019), which is a strong indication that the press has lost the luster it once had. Moroccan readers have converted to online venues and platforms for less censored and less self-censored news. Today, with the total shutdown imposed by the Covid-19 pandemic for over two months, media practitioners are seriously anxious that the pandemic could be the final *coup de grace* of traditional print press.

The Coronavirus pandemic has deeply impacted press institutions' information-processing practices and people's information-seeking choices and orientations. With the high uncertainty that surrounds the situation, Moroccans have become more avid for information and orientation than ever before. In addition to public television, news websites and social networks constitute the primary sources of news. Moroccans turn to television mainly for updates and related news. Meanwhile, news websites have become more dynamic than ever. *Hespress*, for example, has known a dramatic increase in monthly visits from 12 million in February 2020 to more than 25 million in March 2020 (similarweb.com, 2020). As for social networks, Facebook and WhatsApp maintain their superiority as sources of news, entertainment, and interaction. Facebook has witnessed an unprecedented increase in monthly visits from 21.3 billion in February to 25.7 billion in March, while visits of WhatsApp have risen from 1.4 billion in February to 1.9 billion in March (similarweb.com, 2020).

Advertising market

The advertising industry cannot support sustainable media business models. In addition to the deteriorating advertising market, an estimated 70% to 80% of Moroccan advertisers use global online platforms such as Google and Facebook, whose market share will continue to grow at the expense of local websites. According to the Group of Moroccan Advertisers, the total advertising market stood at US $596 million in 2017, US $18 million more than in 2016. In 2018, the big advertisers, the telecom operators, banks, and the food sector, lowered their advertising budgets by 14.6%, 14.7%, and 10%, respectively. The most significant decreases happened in print media with a loss of 23.7% and TV with 14.2% of their advertising income. Digital media and radio perform well with an increase of 10.3% and 9.5% respectively. TV lost US $330,000 of advertising revenue, yet it continues to capture 35% of the total media advertising budget.

The advertising budget is distributed not based on professional standardized and transparent criteria, but on who is close to the center of power. Advertising revenue provided by the government or government-linked companies is not split fairly between independent and pro-government publications. In a recent example, the Office Chérifien des Phosphates (OCP) and Caisse de Dépôt et de Gestion (CDG), two state-owned companies that do not offer any particular products to Moroccan consumers, buy advertising time and space. This move is meant to secure advertising funding the state can use to reward obedience.

Laws and regulations

In addition to the Constitution, the Press and Publication Law, the Penal Code, and the Anti-Terrorism Law contain provisions that regulate print media in Morocco. Article 25 of the Moroccan 2011 Constitution guarantees all citizens "freedom of opinion and expression in all its forms" (Constitution of the Kingdom of Morocco, 2011). However, before the 2011 Constitution, the Moroccan legislature adopted an array of laws that limited freedom of expression, such as the Penal Code, the Press and Publication law, and the Anti-Terrorism Law.

The 2016 Press and Publication Law

The new press law brought about many positive advances compared to its earlier versions (1959, 1963, 1973, 2002), but a close look at the text shows that the oppressive nature of the legal environment in the country has not significantly changed. The positive adjustments include the elimination of jail sentences for journalists and the establishment of a self-regulatory body, the National Press Council. The law also carries specific provisions to regulate digital media. However, the three taboo topics, monarchy, Western Sahara, and Islam, were preserved in the new code and jail sentences were replaced by steep fines; failure to pay the fines can lead to jail time. In the meantime, the Penal Code still stipulates jail sentences for any offense against taboo topics, so journalists can always be charged using the Penal Code and not the Press and Publication Law.

The Anti-Terrorism Law

Passed in 2003 after the May 16 terrorist attacks in Casablanca, this law gave the government sweeping legal powers to control the media content that is deemed to "disrupt public order by intimidation, force, violence, fear or terror." Ostensibly intended to combat terrorism, the authorities have wide latitude in defining vague terms such as "national security" and "public order," opening the door for abuse. The law broadly defines terrorism and considers it as "the involvement in organized groups or congregations with the intent of committing an act of terrorism," and critically, "the promulgation and dissemination of propaganda or advertisement in support of the above-mentioned acts" (HRW, 2005). This latter clause enables the state to conflate reporting with inciting while denying the right of citizens to know. In 2003, three journalists were convicted of "justifying acts of terrorism via a publication" and sentenced to jail time for publishing articles that included commentary by alleged terrorist organizations.

In the most publicized case, Ali Anouzla, journalist and editor-in-chief of the Arabic-language *Lakome* online news site, was arrested in September 2013 on charges of supporting and advocating terrorism four days after publishing an article on extremists' calls for holy war against the state. The article included a link to the site of Spanish news outlet *El Pais*, which in turn had embedded the extremists' video in its article on the same subject. Anouzla is a recognized journalist and his positions against terrorism are known to the public, prompting many to view the charges as an attempt to silence dissent. He was released on bail on 25 October 2013, and while he still faces these charges, his trial has been continually postponed.

The National Press Council (NPC)

Ratified in 2018, the NPC was effectively established as a self-regulatory body with the self-proclaimed aims to contribute to the development of the journalistic profession, to defend freedom of expression, and to promote journalism ethics. It considered ethical conduct and freedom of speech to be two sides of the same coin. The NPC mediates in case of professional disputes within the industry as well as monitors media organizations for complying with journalistic ethics. More significantly, it issues press cards for professional journalists in compliance with the requirements stated in the Decree Law on the Status of Professional Journalists.

NPC's self-proclaimed philosophy is self-organization by media professionals based on the values of democracy, independence, and ethics. Overall, it provides consultancy to the formation of laws and decrees relating to the media. The NPC is responsible for educating journalists on the importance of media ethics and in building trust in the quality of news, especially in the context of digital platforms. The NPC is a manifestation of these concerted endeavors toward instituting more media accountability.

The NPC is composed of 21 members who serve a four-year term, with 14 members elected by publishers, journalists, and civil society organizations (Ibahrine, 2019). The first and current president of the NPC is Younes M'jahed, who is also the general secretary of the Moroccan journalists' union, *Syndicat National de la Presse Marocaine* (SNPM). It is worth mentioning that Younes M'jahed is a pro-government media personality. His record of defending the freedom of expression in Morocco is debatable. He acted in many instances as an apologist to the state in cases where journalists were victims of state repression (Interviews with Aboubakr Jamai and Driss Ksikes, 2017).

Social and political functions of the press: interplay between state and media

Morocco's political regime can be best characterized as a competitive authoritarian regime. Competitive authoritarian regimes use elements of democracy to ensure domination over the other opposition forces in the country. Levitsky and Way (2002) defined competitive authoritarianism as civilian regimes in which "formal democratic institutions are widely viewed as the primary means of gaining power, but in which fraud, civil liberties violations, and abuse of state and media resources so skew the playing field that the regime cannot be labeled democratic" (p. 4). These regimes are competitive in the sense that the democratic institutions are real and that "opposition forces can use legal channels to seriously contest for (and occasionally win) power; but they are authoritarian in that opposition forces are handicapped by a highly uneven – and even dangerous – playing field. Competition is thus real but unfair" (p. 4). Competitive authoritarian regimes are characterized by the presence of some democratic institutions and some democratic practices such as elections, a multiparty system, and, in this case, a self-proclaimed independent media regulator and a new press law. We argue that Morocco's media reforms are in line with this vision of governance, whereby the state creates democratic institutions to use as a site of struggle with opposition forces while steadfastly maintaining control by establishing an uneven playing field.

Morocco's media system offers a good illustration of the complex process of media reforms during political transitions. As a competitive authoritarian regime, the state uses democratic institutions to reform its media system, while entrenching these institutions via authoritarian laws. Morocco has witnessed periods of tight authoritarian control and periods of reformist tendencies. This cyclical fluctuation has resulted in significant progress in media structure and performance and, at the same time, in the state maintaining its control over the media landscape through various mechanisms of repression.

The private press represents a good site to show this cyclical fluctuation in state media relations. The atmosphere of economic liberalization and media deregulation of the 1990s facilitated the rise of the private press which promised a resurgence of newsy, critical, and investigative reporting to serve society and citizens rather than parties and politicians. That meant getting into a confrontation with the political establishment and its corporate associates. The new trend appealed to Moroccan middle-class readers who found its language simple and meaningful unlike the blunt language of partisan papers. They noticed also that it represented the society at large instead of representing political parties' ideologies. Further, they were exposed to stories never told before, dossiers of human rights violations, political and cultural taboos, and, above all, investigations of most powerful institutions and persons. However, the authorities did not tolerate a critical press.

The four phases of press development

We propose to divide the history of the Moroccan private press into four phases: Uncertain Beginnings (1991–1998), Free Retrospection (1999–2005), Confrontation and Censorship (2006 2011), and Normalization and Self-censorship (2011–2020). This periodization is buttressed by the consideration of six fundamental factors: (1) political environment, (2) media environment, (3) main titles, (4) editorial features, (5) ratings, and (6) censorship.

Uncertain beginnings (1991–1998)

Historians refer to this period as the most determinant in Moroccan postmodern history (Maghraoui, 2001; El Hachimi, 2007; Darif, 2012). Though historically situated in the last years of the "Old Era," it represents the real beginnings of reform in Moroccan politics, economy, society, and media. At the political level, Hassan II proposed two important constitutional revisions (1992–1996) and launched a serious dialogue with the opposition for a participatory articulation of politics, responsible interaction among political institutions, and smooth transition of monarchical power. The human rights issue was crucial in this period, as well. The creation of a Ministry of Human Rights in 1991, the release of political prisoners, and the closure of torture camps were indicators of a considerable openness in this regard.

So far, the media environment had been under the strict control of the state and political parties with the first controlling audiovisual outlets and an important part of the print and the latter controlling the other part of print media. Still, in terms of policy and regulation, the state maintained absolute control over publications through prior censorship at times, and post-publication retributive measures of critical newspapers at other times. Consequently, introducing non-partisan outlets in this environment was not an easy thing.

Hesitation characterized the few pioneering private papers. Some of them quickly disappeared after failing to elude the authorities. After several bans, for example, the progressive newspaper *Almouatine* had to appear under four different titles and, after several bans, had to leave the scene eventually. However, the real first steps of the non-partisan trend took an economic orientation. The first license was attributed to a French press patron Schreiber who bought *La Vie Economique* in 1994. This transaction ushered the press into an era of socio-economic investigation which published meticulous reports and statistics about serious socio-economic issues. Benefiting from considerable margins of freedom, *La Vie Economique* relied on national and international reports to publish the first alarming realities concerning poverty, illiteracy, unemployment, rural and urban disparities, and the situation of women.

The new political environment encouraged more private outlets to emerge. These included *Maroc Hebdo* (1991), *L'Economiste* (1991), *La Nouvelle Tribune* (1996), *La Gazette du Maroc* (1997), *Le Journal* (1997), *Le Reporter* (1998), and *Assahifa* (1998). These new dailies and weeklies started to report about current affairs and political and rights issues. They initiated a novel public discourse which, true, was less assertive mainly towards powerful institutions, but which would be more investigative and critical to these institutions in the following years.

Free retrospection (1999–2005)

The second phase coincided with three crucial political historical developments: (1) a year after the alternation experience, (2) the end of Hassan II's era, and (3) the beginning of Mohammed VI's era. Also, the media environment was arguably less tense than before. These major factors encouraged the press to truck interesting news stories. So far, two untold stories were the atrocities of the "Old Era" and the inefficacies of the new left-wing-led government.

First, "while it remained illegal to criticize the [current] monarchy and the king in person," Storm (2007) noticed, "the media . . . and intellectuals have been allowed to criticize former king . . . Hassan II." Until then, no one dared investigate the thousands of arbitrary imprisonments, disappearances, displacements, tortures, and murders of opposition figures and military dissidents during the reign of Hassan II. Second, the alternation experience was supposed to attract more praise than criticism. It was supposed to consolidate consensus between the state and political parties domestically and rally international plaudits for what was perceived as unequaled political audacity. Yet, the press was keen on keeping an eye on El Youssoufi's government and exposing its flaws to the public. For these two huge dossiers to be tracked, the private press needed a *carte blanche*, which was arguably granted by the new monarchy institution via its intelligence and home affairs departments (Naji et al., 2006).

During the second phase, new titles emerged and swiftly became popular. The principal ones were *Tel Quel* launched in 2001, *Le Journal* in 1997 before it was banned in 2000 and reissued as *Le Journal Hebdomadaire* in 2001, its Arabic version *Assaheefa* in 1998, banned in 2000 and reappeared as *Assahifa Alosbouia* in 2001, *Le Reporteur* in 1998, and *Alahdath Almaghribia* in 1998. Benchemsi, founder of the weekly magazine *Tel Quel* testifies:

> Unlike the party journalists, ossified by decades of self-censorship and political cal-
> culations, we were young, independent, uninhibited, and craving for freedom. We
> quickly waded into hot territories, thoroughly exposing the king Hassan II's "years
> of lead", past secret police abuses, and the corruption of top officials. . . . As our sales
> boomed, the new king and his advisors took advantage of our audacity, waving it in
> the face of the Western observers as early proof of Morocco's democratization.
>
> *(Benchemsi, 2011: 46)*

This double-directional free retrospection was ascribed to the new monarchical institution's determination to break with the past. The first goal of the young king was to gain popular legitimacy (Darif, 2012) which, for Moroccans and outsiders alike, required Mohammed VI to pass the test of difference with his father (ibid.). For this purpose, all national mainstream outlets precipitated to depict him as "King of the Poor," as a democrat and liberal monarch, as a reformer, and as the visionary savior of Moroccans from long decades of oppression and dictatorship.

Though press readership occasionally increased during the partisan phase, it was until the beginning of the new century that ratings became important and consistent. The readers were exposed to stories about core issues such as (past) monarchical despotism, official injustice, and human rights violations. Nevertheless, the upbeat provisions of the 2002 press law quickly regressed on the aftermath of the Casablanca terrorist attacks on 16 May 2003 and the implementation of the anti-terrorism law in the same year. While anti-terrorism law does not include articles addressing journalists directly, it gives the authorities sweeping legal power to filter or block content deemed disruptive to public order (Freedom House 2004).

Overall, the second phase of the private press was characterized by increased audacity and criticism. For the first time in the history of Moroccan journalism, political taboos were broken, inside-palace and high officials' stories were divulged, atrocities of the past "years of lead" were told in detail, government leaders were interrogated, and readership revived. Still, suspicions accompanied the editorial flow of the press during this period, especially with regard to its unequivocal unleashed critical retrospection of the past era and its heavy surveillance of the alternation government.

Confrontation and censorship (2006–2011)

This period was arguably the most momentous as far as the relationship between the press and the authorities is concerned. As journalists pushed more red lines and investigated institutional corruption, the authorities responded by enforcing heavy lawsuits at times and applied economic sanctions at others.

Important socio-political developments underpinned the general mood of this phase. At the political level, the predominant feature was a political stalemate (Monjib, 2011) which was mainly due to the absence of real opposition in the Moroccan political scene (El Hachimi, 2007). The failure of traditional socialists in the socialist party-led alternation experience (1998–2002) made them lose much of their social legitimacy. The meager voter turnout (37%) of the 2007 elections showed how citizens had lost trust in politics. This is added to an array of alarming indices in human development and civil liberties with Morocco classifying near the bottom of MENA countries in terms of education, employment, and freedom of expression and the press (World Bank, 2008; Gallup Report: Morocco, 2009).

During this period, Benchemsi states, "having exhausted the vein of the old regime's flaws, [the press] started investigating those of the new one" (2011: 46). This statement points to an important but hazardous shift in editorial lines from covering the atrocities of the Old Era to covering the deficiencies of the New Era. As new influential outlets ushered the media scene, Moroccans were exposed to more sensitive dossiers like the salary of the current king, the budget of the palace, the inside stories of the royal family, prostitution and homosexuality in Morocco, corruption in military and judiciary institutions, interviews with controversial figures, and so on.

That is when the trouble began, according to Benchemsi. The curve of official repression measures took a sharp ascent in both intensity and frequency. A longitudinal look at the annual reports of national and global media freedom watchdogs shows that the years 2005, 2006, and 2007, for instance, recorded the highest number of lawsuits against journalists. They were also the years in which journalists were subjected to extra-legal retributions and unprecedented economic sanctions. In 2006, two of the most outspoken press outlets were created: *Nichan*, the Arabic version of *Tel Quel*, and *Almassae*. Both managed, in a short time, to appeal to Moroccan readers for their simple (sometimes dialectical) language and critical tone.

Ratings were at their best during this phase. A year after its inception in 2006, *Almassae*, for example, reached the highest circulation ever, 200,000; that is almost 50% of sales nationwide (OJD, 2007) and has, since then, maintained an aggregate 30% of total readership (OJD, 2013). During the three last years of this phase, however, *Almassae* and other critical papers had to face heavy lawsuits and exorbitant fines. While some newspapers pleaded for public support for survival, others closed after bankruptcy.

Normalization and self-censorship (2011–2020)

The year 2011 and its aftermath brought about seminal socio-political developments that dramatically affected the Moroccan media environment. The 20 February Movement (Moroccan version of the Arab Spring) demanded "comprehensive and fundamental constitutional and political reforms" (Darif, 2012: 9). The palace promptly promised important constitutional and political reforms, unprecedented restrictions of traditional monarchical prerogatives in addition to more opening and liberties. Whereas the first wave of the Arab Spring toppled presidents and changed regimes in some Arab countries and ushered others into civil war, the Moroccan authorities prided themselves for anticipating reform and alleviating social tension. The media environment was already grim by then. Previously flamboyant pages were closed by judicial rulings, bankrupted, or driven to adopt softer editorial lines as the price of survival. Many press pioneers quit and left the country, leaving behind an increasingly subdued media landscape (Benchemsi, 2011).

Four years after the approval of an advanced press code in July 2016, the situation is not vastly different. With less penalizing postulations, more insurance of safety against physical coercion, and more recognition of digital media, the new press legislation was supposed to release Moroccan journalists from the complications and ambiguities of the previous code of 2002. Nevertheless, media content is still likely to be sifted and critical journalists may still be harassed and muted. How media dealt with the long *Rif* riots known among Moroccans as *Hirak Rif*, for instance, bears witness to this.

For seven long months, while the whole northern region was in turmoil, there was an utter blackout on the press. Apart from sporadic citizen content that managed to break into the digital sphere, mainstream outlets could not mention a word about it. It was until regional and international networks and rights organisms released unfavorable reports that all national outlets at once started to talk about it. It was clear that they had been waiting for the green light from above. And once they had it, their reports did not diverge from official narratives and their analyses most often lacked balance. And when they had to be critical, they addressed minor centers and peripheral officials and avoided real holders of executive power. The very few journalists who dared diverge from mainstream coverage were sentenced to prison. Reporters Without Borders documented several assaults against journalists during the riots. After arresting over 170 dissidents including dissent leaders, the authorities chased bloggers and journalists. One of them, El Mehdaoui, the director of *Badeel* news website, is still in prison after appeal court extended his initial three-month sentenced to one year, and then to three years. His principal accusation is "undermining public order by inciting people to riot."

A further muting strategy implemented by the authorities against critical journalists is surveillance of their private lives. In September 2019, a female journalist, Hajar Raissouni, was sentenced to one-year prison on premarital sex and abortion charges. After her arrest triggered a wave of condemnation among national and international rights organisms, the journalist benefited from a royal pardon in October 2019. Before she left prison, Raissouni stated that the purpose of her arrest was vengeance against her activities as a journalist and that her coverage of *Hirak Rif* had put her in the crosshairs of the state.

Since 2012, the Ministry of Communication has published annual reports, supported by quantitative indicators, on the efforts to improve freedom of the press in Morocco. The reports mentioned, for example, categorical absence of prior censorship, confiscation or ban or suspension of any publication, closure of any electronic outlet, or imprisonment or torture of any journalist (Ministry of Communication, 2016–2018). Taken at their face value, these official narratives may imply a favorable media environment. Nevertheless, global media watchdog organizations reported the situation as alarming. The 2014 report of Freedom House, for example, placed Morocco among the "not free" countries with an alarming rank of 145 out of 191 countries (Freedom House, 2014). The 2019 report of Reporters Without Borders ranks Morocco 135 globally (Reporters Without Borders, 2019). This disparity between official and watchdog narratives reflects serious methodological disparities concerning the measurability of press freedom in general and the validity of its indicators in Morocco.

Ratings during the fourth phase point to a dramatic regression. *Almassae*, for example, which reached 130,000 copies a day in 2007 (about 32% of the total circulation) and an average circulation of 110,000 until 2012, hardly reached 48,000 in 2016 and 27,400 in 2019. Also, the weekly *Tel Quel*, which maintained top sales of news magazines between 2005 and 2011 with over 20,000 copies, has made a decrease of 54% (OJD, 2019). With less than 0.5% readership, according to the latest reports from the *Organisme de Justification de la Diffusion* (OJD), the press seems to be in its dying phase.

The decrease in press readership may be ascribed to the exponential expansion of digital information through far-reaching and timely news websites and social networks, and it also relates to the unsubstantial content quality of newspapers in recent years. As the digital world is relatively less controlled, its content is likely to be more diverse, better documented, and above all more critical, and therefore, more appealing to readers. If the third phase was arguably a period of administrative and economic censorship, the fourth phase is that of self-censorship. Journalists self-censor by avoiding sensitive stories, glossing over them, decentralizing and displacing criticism, or conforming with the official narratives.

On 19 February 2020, due to the Covid-19 pandemic, the Moroccan authorities issued an order to close all print media outlets. As the lockdown situation heads through its second month without signs of light, Moroccan people, uncertain and anxious, are now more glued to their TVs and social networks for news updates and connection. People's information-seeking habits after the pandemic will undoubtedly not be as they were before it. The Coronavirus pandemic is a real test to the validity and functionality of media old and new. The old configuration of the press will not work anymore; only outlets with reinvigorated structural and functional potential will sustain a place in the fast-paced competitive digital media space.

Conclusion

McQuail (1994) points out that the media are both a product and a reflection of the history of their host society. From the nationalist movement's struggle with colonization and opposition political parties' struggle with Hassan II's regime to the post-1999 era, Morocco witnessed periods of authoritarian control and periods of reformist tendencies. This cyclical fluctuation resulted in both significant progress being made in the media's structure and performance and, at the same time, the state maintaining control over the media landscape through various mechanisms of repression.

Today, Moroccan news media face three main challenges: quality media content, economic sustainability, and disruptive technologies. The rise of sponsored content, misinformation, sensationalism, and poor-quality journalism have raised serious concerns about the quality of information Moroccan audiences receive. Entertainment and celebrity stories have increased at the expense of news on national affairs. This dismal picture is the result of several factors, including the fierce competition over audience attention, the logic of algorithm-driven platforms, and the integration of the editorial, marketing, and analytics functions in the digital news industry. The value of news stories is no longer based on the standard quality but a range of metrics, including the number of visits, hits, and views.

Another factor that negatively affects the quality of content is the journalists' education and training. Journalism seems to have become the profession of those who have no profession. In January 2019, a journalist at *Al-Ayam* newspaper interviewed an orphaned 7-year-old girl about her experience of her mother's murder. Both events triggered a vast wave of criticism from social media users and activists who denounced the unethical practices of the journalists.

In terms of economic sustainability, clientelism and the unfair distribution of advertising money continue to represent a threat to media business models. In January 2018, the government placed an additional financial burden on the fragile media sector by imposing a 5% tax on digital advertising. To enhance the level of attractiveness in a highly competitive media content market, digital news content providers are called to personalize their news content over multi-cross platforms and different devices. Rather than targeting readers, news and content providers (media organizations) will realize that real value is in the market of one reader/consumer. The emerging world of media has become more personal than ever before, where readers access their news and media content through their personal and mobile devices. The personalization of news and media content is likely to take another dimension when the superfast 5G enters the Moroccan telecom market.

Finally, disrupting technologies are aggravating the fragility of the business models of the print media, despite the government subsidies. Moroccan websites depend on revenue streams built on the commercialization of media platforms such as Google, Facebook, Twitter, and other global tech companies. Reliance on social media platforms has created a major structural shift in news production, distribution, and monetization. The tech giants deprive local news websites of vital revenue streams and sources. Digitalization has been making the profession of a journalist in Morocco more volatile and insecure.

Moroccan policymakers should, therefore, direct their attention to designing flexible regulatory frameworks to protect Moroccan readers and their data, and such a framework should be based on innovative business models.

References

Alami, M. D. (1985), Réquisitoire pour un Droit de l'information. In M. Amzazi (ed.), *Le Parlement et la Pratique legislative au Maroc.* Casablanca: Les Editions Toubkal.

Alexa stats (2020), *Top Sites in Morocco.* Retrieved from https://www.alexa.com/topsites/countries/MA. Accessed 27 April 2020.

Benchemsi, A. R. (2011), Morocco and Press Freedom: A Complicated Relationship. *Arab News*, Nieman Reports, pp. 46–58.

Benchenna, A., Ksikes, D., and Marchetti, D. (2017), The Media in Morocco: A Highly Political Economy, the Case of the Paper and On-line Press since the Early 1990s. *The Journal of North African Studies,* 22(3), pp. 386–410.

Constitution of the Kingdom of Morocco (2011), Retrieved from www.maroc.ma/en/system/files/documents_page/bo_5964bis_fr_3.pdf. Accessed 27 April 2020.

Darif, M. (2012), Morocco: A Reformist Monarchy? *The Journal of the Middle Eastern and Africa,* 3, pp. 82–103.

El Hachimi, M. (2007), The Independent Press as Political Opposition. *Alhiwar Almoutamaddin.* Issue 1918. (Researcher's Translation of Title From Arabic)

El Kadoussi, A. (2016), The Moroccan 'Independent' Press: Issues of Independence and Political Opposition. *International Journal of Social Science and Humanities Research,* 4(4), pp. 299–306.

El Kadoussi, A. (2018), Four Phases in the History of the Moroccan Private Press. *The Journal of North African Studies,* 23(4). doi:10.1080/13629387.2018.1434510

Freedom House (2003, 2004, 2006, 2007, 2012, 2014), *Freedom of the Press.* Retrieved from www.freedomhouse.org. Accessed 22 April 2020.

Gallup Report: Morocco (2009), Retrieved from www.gallup.com/topic/country_mar.aspx.

Hespress (2018), *Advertising Budgets in Morocco Decline* (in Arabic), 14 November. Retrieved from www.hespress.com/economie/412277.html. Accessed 22 April 2020.

Ibahrine, M. (2007), *The Internet and Politics in Morocco: The Political Use of the Internet by Islam Oriented Political Movements.* Berlin: VDM Verlag.

Ibahrine, M. (2019), The Emergence of a News Website Ecosystem: An Exploratory Study of Hespress. *Journalism Practice.* doi:10.1080/17512786.2019.1679037

Lakmahri, S. (2012), La Saga de la Presse Marocaine. *Zamane.*

Le Desk and Reporters Without Borders (2017), *Media Ownership Monitor: Morocco.* Retrieved from http://maroc.mom-rsf.org/en/. Accessed 22 April 2020.

Levitsky, Steven, and Way, L. (2002), Elections without Democracy: The Rise of Competitive Authoritarianism. *Journal of Democracy,* 13(2), pp. 51–65.

Maghraoui, A. M. (2001), Monarchy and Political Reform in Morocco. *Journal of Democracy,* 12(1), pp. 73–86.

McQuail, D. (1994), *Mass Communication Theory: An Introduction.* London: Sage.

Ministry of Communication (2016–2018), *Annual Report on Press Freedom in Morocco.* Retrieved from www.mincom.gov.ma. Accessed 22 April 2020.

Monjib, M. (2011), The 'Democratization' Process in Morocco: Progress, Obstacles, and the Impact of the Islamist-Secularist Divide. *SABAN Centre for Middle East Policy.* BROOKINGS 1775 Massachusetts Ave., NW Washington, DC 20036–2103.

Mowlana, H. (1985), *International Flow of Information: A Global Report and Analysis.* Paris: UNESCO.

OJD Maroc (2007, 2012, 2013, 2014, 2015, 2019), Retrieved from www.ojd.com.

Reporters Without Borders (2019), *Data of Press Freedom Ranking 2019.* Retrieved from https://rsf.org/en/ranking_table. Accessed 20 April 2020.

Sami, A. (1990), *Presse, Etat et Société au Maroc.* Rabat: University of Rabat.

Similarweb (2020), *Top News and Media Websites in Morocco.* Retrieved from https://www.similarweb.com/top-websites/morocco/category/news-and-media/.

Storm, L. (2007), *Democratization in Morocco: The Political Elite and Struggles for Power in the Post-Independence State.* Oxon: Routledge. OX144RN.

World Bank Report: Morocco (2008), Retrieved from www.worldbank.org. Accessed 22 April 2020.

Zaid, B. (2010), *Public Service Television Policy and National Development in Morocco: Contents, Production, and Audiences*. Saarbrück, Germany: VDM Verlag.

Zaid, B. (2016), Internet and Democracy: A Force for Change or an Instrument of Repression. *Global Media and Communication Journal*, 12(1), pp. 49–66.

Zaid, B. (2017), The Authoritarian Trap in State/Media Structures in Morocco's Political Transition. *The Journal of North African Studies*, 22(3), pp. 340–360.

Zaid, B. (2018), Comparative Study of Broadcast Regulators in the Arab World. *International Journal of Communication*, 12, pp. 4401–4420.

Zaid, B., and Ibahrine, M. (2011), *Mapping Digital Media: Morocco*. New York: The Open Society Foundations.

18

MEDIA CONFIGURATION IN MOROCCO

Sam Cherribi, Akshatha Achar, Drew Siegal, and Patrick Harris

Introduction

Ever since Morocco's independence from France in 1956, the media sector in Morocco, a field of competition between different societal forces shaped by institutions, media outlets, markets, individuals, and groups, was dominated by the state's strong presence. Three major transformations best characterize this relatively polarized media field, the first of which marked the transition from state monopoly to free market; the second transformation was the struggle to find a viable business model; and the third transformation was caused by global competition in the digital media sphere that resulted in the emergence of new modes of media consumption and audience fragmentation.

This chapter elaborates upon each of these transformations while providing a brief historical perspective centered on the main parties in the broadcasting sector. This perspective will, in turn, offer a conduit to the assessment of the evolving role of politics, media economics, audiences, and the state's control mechanisms on the media outlets. The chapter also sheds light on the extent of autonomy in the broadcasting sector and the role of media as a propaganda tool.

Historical background

Morocco is uniquely pluralistic in its contemporaneous African, Arab, Berber, and European influences (Khatibi, 2002). The manifestation of this historic plurality can be best attributed to the multilingual nature of the past and contemporary media landscape. Morocco has been described as a "composite society," in which tradition, religion, rurality, and urban life synthesize and leave a tremendous impact on the social behavior of the populace (Pascon, 2002). The relationship between faith and tradition remains central to the Moroccan ethos and greatly impacts the media in the present day.

Morocco has shown a degree of self-confidence, alluding to its stability and its people's comparatively muted participation in the Arab Spring. Beyond the clichés of the blockbuster film *Casablanca*, which has immortalized Morocco, government officials and media executives alike never waste an opportunity to flaunt and flourish Morocco's close historical diplomatic relationship with the United States of America. It was the first country that recognized the independence of the United States of America, evidenced by the Moroccan–American Treaty of Friendship 1786. Morocco is also the only country in the Arab world that had never been occupied by the Ottoman Empire, a fact heavily utilized to convey Morocco's historical self-determination and strong national identity.

It is imperative to note that much of the stability of the monarchy is because of the emphasis placed on tradition and the notion that the monarchy has served as a constant stabilizing force for the kingdom. The former Islamist prime minister, Abelilah Benkirane, has argued the importance of preserving and bolstering this 12-century-old dynasty, exasperated by the state's fear of the Arab Spring thrusting its domino effect onto Morocco. This argument has been articulated in the past by numerous scholars long before the Arab Spring changed the rules of the game, so to speak (Laroui, 1977; Boudoudou, 2004; Arkoun, 2007; Tozy, 2008; Khatibi, 1999; Bentahar, 2002; Boukhars, 2011).

The Moroccan sociologist Abdelkebir Khatibi (2002) argues that, since Morocco's independence, the monarchy has mastered the art of subjecting the population to accepting the political status quo.

Background and contextualization – Moroccan broadcasting sector

Radio

In 1907, the Moroccan government stated its determination to lay sole claim to the broadcasting sector, in the form of Sultan Hassan's issuance of a royal decree, which states, "the use of the wired and wireless telegraph system shall remain a state monopoly throughout the Chérifien Empire."

Under the auspices of the protectorate, radio broadcasting was introduced in Morocco and was noticeably reflective of the prevailing state monopoly zeitgeist (especially in European countries). In 1928, Radio Maroc was launched as a public utility service, operating under the regulation of the Moroccan Post and Telecommunications. With the arrival of television in 1962, Radio Maroc evolved into RTM or Radio Television Marocaine. After Morocco's independence, the state's monopoly further cemented itself with the issuance of the 1959 *dahir* (royal decree) on the decolonization of the media. This monopoly was unabashedly weaponized in the hands of the state by means of a relentless string of legislative texts; as such, the government's unwavering commitment to control information grew disconcertingly evident.

The Moroccan authorities' power further consolidated in the 1970s, to the degree in which state control was partially enforced over the print media (such as Maghreb Arabe Presse news agency) and almost entirely over the broadcasting sector. As such, freedom of expression sharply deteriorated in public political circles. Here, the paradox lies in the fact that the same period witnessed the birth of the iconoclastic movement for the current modernization and liberalization of the media. The 1980s bore witness to the initiation of a movement, the sole purpose of which was to initiate legal and institutional reform of this sector. A remarkable offshoot of this movement was the creation of the radio station Medi 1 in the 1980s, which was markedly a legal anomaly, as the law categorically banned such creations in principle. This led to several replications; one notable example of such blatant derogation to the law of monopoly being the creation of the television channel 2M in 1989. In a national symposium in 1993, Infocom, an exhaustive set of proposals for the reform of the sector, was elucidated. The recommendations provided by the symposium laid the foundation of what would later become the very guidelines of the reform of the broadcasting sector.

When a new government ascended to power in 1998, the reform process was initiated. While a plethora of guidelines specifically about the restructuring of the Moroccan broadcasting sector was successfully passed into law, it was not until 2002 that the High Authority for Audio-visual Communication (HACA) was created to herald the termination of the state monopoly. Consequently, in 2005, the law pertaining to broadcasting communication was publicized.

In 2005, the NGO Reporters Without Borders classified the condition of the Moroccan media as "difficult," the second lowest of five categories. However, they welcomed the reform of the Moroccan broadcasting sector and were vocal on the belief that the empowerment and liberation of the Moroccan audiovisual landscape were imperative. In their 2005 annual report, they expressed that this would be a "first for broadcasting in North Africa unless the government cheats on this test of democracy" (Reporters Without Borders, 2005). This viewpoint, a tempered amalgam of caution, is mirrored by most of the Moroccan civil society, as they expressed a wish to see tangible progress before endorsing this reform.

The total state monopoly over the radio came to an end in 2006; the zeitgeist was characterized by the blossoming private media companies. The entire domain started to organize itself in terms of companies; however, the largest share of the market is held by the state-owned company Société Nationale de Radiodiffusion et de Télévision (SNRT). The major private-public company is known as SOREAD. The shift in radio began in 2002 when HACA was created by royal decree to oversee the media. A major role of HACA and specifically the General Directorate of Audiovisual Communication – nominated by the king – is to review license applications and grant distribution rights to media companies. HACA issued the first license for a radio station in the Arab world (Hidass, 2010: 30, 31).

The process of liberalization in radio took place in two stages; the first phase in 2006, when six radio stations and two groups of local radio stations were granted broadcasting frequencies. The second stage was in 2009 when many small radio entities were added. Only Midi-Un radio, which was created in 1980, and 2M radio were granted licenses in 2004, as part of a private-public partnership through SOREAD. This process of liberalization meant that many individuals became major players overnight in the infotainment style of radio, broadcasting in Arabic, French, Dericha, Berber, and Spanish. High illiteracy rates continue to contribute to the staggering Moroccan audience, 15 million strong, who, on average, listen to 2 hours and 52 minutes of radio during the week; 6.5 million of this audience listening from 6 am to 10 am. Partly driven by affordability, as of 2010, there is one radio for every two Moroccans (Journal of Arab and Muslim Media Research; Radio and Television in Morocco: New Regulation and Licensing for Private Channels, 23).

The two largest corporations, SNRT and SOREAD, represent a total of 32.35% of the state's radio audience, and other privately owned radio stations reach 64.23% of this audience (SNRT. 2017). The reach of privately owned radio stations indicates that the transition from state to market control, in terms of audiences, has been relatively successful. Other significant stations include the Quran-station known as the Mohamed VI of the Saint Quran, which has a share of 14.66% of the audience; Med-Radio, which has a share of 12.34%; and the Berber radio Al-Edia Amazighia, which holds a 4.93% share of the market. While the bilingual Midi-Un station was formally the main competition to the national radio, the station today holds only 6.62% of the listenership and is destined to the Maghreb audience (SNRT. 2017).

The following chronology briefly sums up the main stages of developing the broadcasting sector in Morocco:

- 1928: Creation of Moroccan radio
- 1946: Creation of Radio Tangier
- 1978: Creation of regional radio stations: Tangier, Oujda, Fes, Casablanca, Laaypune, Marrakech, amongst others

- 1980: Creation of Médi1 Radio
- 2004: Creation of Radio 2M in January
- 2004: Creation of Radio Mohammed VI of the Holy Quran
- 2006–2019: Liberalization of the airwaves, along with the licensing of private radio stations to Atlantic Radio, Hit Radio, Aswat, Chada FM

Several radio stations have hosted talk shows since 2011, serving as mediators between state institutions and their publics. These talk shows and call-in radio shows made it possible to receive calls from citizens on specific topics such as tax advice, family problems, and matters of general interest. In 2011, these shows became receptacles for various societal and personal problems. The person who receives the call (often referred to as the "doctor") draws upon the religious and homeopathic register to explain and justify people's problems and provide them with solutions. Radio stations such as Chada FM and Med Radio have made this type of broadcast their signature programming. Roqya Shar'iya (Muslim exorcisms) have also been featured in these programs recently (H24 info).

Television

Though private-sector television licenses were granted in 2006 and 2008, the liberalization of the television sector lies exponentially behind the accelerated privatization of the radio sector, with eight television channels directly belonging to the state (Naji, 2011: 191). The public broadcaster Société Nationale de Radiodiffusion et de Television (SNTR), broadcasting primarily in French and Arabic, is an important source for news and information in Morocco. Two other major stations in the country are Al-Aoula, operated by SNTR, and the state-owned 2M. These stations' newscasts capture 37.6% and 48.2% of news viewership respectively and require an aerial antenna to be received. The domestic television audience in Morocco, which was approximately five million homes in 2015, spends, on average, 3 hours and 8 minutes a week watching television (Naji, 2011: 191).

A characteristic of the Moroccan media field is the race for politicians to procure television airtime. According to HACA, the government and its political parties receive double the airtime as that allocated to the opposition parties. This potentially results from the saturation and ubiquity of state-owned broadcasters. This point is echoed by Reda Benjelloun (2014), who reported that he has been contacted by politicians who complained that their junior colleagues were given more airtime than they were. Similarly, *TelQuel* published a flattering survey on the popularity of King Mohamed VI, in which the king had an approval rating of more than 90% (Tourabi, 2014). However, the authorities censored that issue. Abdellah Tourabi argues that if this were to happen in France, the president would send flowers to the newspaper instead of the bailiff (ibid.)

The foreign competition presents a noticeably challenging environment for Moroccan broadcast business models, due to domestic taxes and the rising budgets of foreign stations. The Moroccan media is subject to a stamp duty of 5% on its advertising revenue, but this is not imposed on foreign stations. Further complicating the financial situation is the budget disparity between Moroccan broadcasters and major competitors, including Al Jazeera, which alone captures 53.3% of domestic Moroccan viewership. The budget of Al Jazeera is $450 million, whereas the budget of the entirety of the Moroccan audiovisual landscape is still under $300 million (Naji, 2011: 194). Moroccan broadcasters also underperform, when compared to the BBC, TV5, and TV Andalusia, because of the Moroccan broadcasters' comparatively low budgets.

The openness of Moroccan audiences to consume both Arab and Western satellite television is compounded by the frailty of both the public and private Moroccan media sectors (Naji, 2011: 194). For comparison, the public sector in France spends more than US $1.9 billion on drama alone, while in Morocco the public sector spends only US $32 million (Naji, 2011: 194). The resulting reluctance to spend on quality programing has driven local audiences to hover between 40% and 45% (Naji, 2011: 195). This figure is not expected to increase, as many European media projects are being prepared for launch to compete with the Moroccan state and private media. Moreover, many Gulf countries, especially Saudi Arabian companies, are launching television programming destined solely for the Moroccan market, which, in turn, has caused the authorities to become quite nervous, especially after the tensions that recently arose between Qatar and Saudi Arabia. Moroccan media has written extensively about this fear.

In addition to the fact that Morocco has a huge diaspora in Europe, the linguistic diversity in Morocco opens it to different international influences, including Spanish and French. In some international cities, such as Marrakesh, during the World Cup, people were able to watch football in the popular cafés in German, French, English, and Arabic. This multilingual aspect of the society is often overlooked by authors and academics who focus their work on Morocco, which leads to the derivation of fallacious inferences, such as that Moroccans are perhaps too French, or too Berber-oriented. It is the cultural and linguistic plurality of Morocco that makes it a nation open to the various influences of global television. In this vein, Médi1 TV, which is attempting to transform itself into a continuous news channel, has decided to turn to the news coverage of West Africa and to dedicate a special channel, headquartered in Dakar, with correspondents in Abidjan, Bamako, Libreville, and other African capitals.

In sum, the following timeline sums up the important dates in the history of Moroccan Television:

- 1954–1955: TELMA
- 1962: TELMA relaunched as TVM
- 1972: TVM goes on air for the first time
- 1989: 2M was born
- 2006: Médi1 TV launched
- 2015: On 17 June, Morocco turned off all its analog signals and switched to TNT, in which the SNRT (formerly TVM) offers a wide range of thematic channels, such as Al-Oula, Arrabiaa, Assadissa, and Arriyadya
- 2017: Creation of Télé Maroc, a satellite channel broadcast from Spain

Notable developments in media configuration and the process of liberalization

Research on Morocco's media usually centers on three main themes: the state control of media, the liberalization and the relative privatization of the media sector, and the transformations in the global and regional media sectors with the advent of Arabic and Western satellite television and the corresponding proliferation of the Internet. This multicultural competition, paired with the changing behavior of Internet media audiences, has led to the fragmentation of the Moroccan media landscape, an inability to compete with foreign media outlets, and a lack of a viable business model.

After King Hassan II died in 1999, Morocco embarked upon a new period of promising social reforms and established reconciliation efforts with the political detainees who had populated many a Moroccan prison. Social reforms were introduced in the first national conference,

Infocom, in 1993, and the later 2002 reforms formalized the relative liberalization of the media field. These changes drastically altered the framework created by the French-inspired *dahir* of 15 November 1958, which had laid the first framework for the domination and domestication of all the outlets and forces involved in the production and circulation of media content (Naji, 2011: 15–16).

Some cite Morocco as an archetype of authoritarianism with the state regulation of the media sector during the past 60 years. Several domains are taboo for the Moroccan news media to cover. For example, the media is censured in its coverage of the king, Islam, and national sovereignty, especially pertaining to Western Sahara; another problem is the limited scope of provincial media, especially the print media. Many news outlets, especially in television broadcasting, are still owned by the state, even after liberalization. This unprecedented censure led Mohamed Naimi (2016) to pose the argument that media outlets in Morocco do not reflect the diversification of content. Omar Radi (2017) also argues that investigative journalism is simply too costly, in terms of money and potential repression; another social ramification is that most journalists eventually become armchair journalists.

The first decade of the 21st century heralded in the liberalization of the Moroccan broadcasting sector, coinciding with the first 10 years of King Mohammed VI's reign. This liberalization process of the media and political spheres started, albeit in a timid way, in 1992, when King Hassan II included the Socialist Union of Popular Forces (USFP) in the political process. For years, the USFP formed the backbone of the government, until they lost credibility. Abdelwahed Radi, a prominent member of the Socialist Party since 1962, argues that the organization paid the price of trying to govern a country that simply did not have many of the necessary democratic prerequisites (Radi, 2017). At the same time, there were rumors that the king had blocked several ministers from the Islamist party, PJD, and other coalition partners. Newspapers, along with other media sources, pointed to a potential power struggle between the palace and the new cabinet.

The response to the Arab Spring and the ousting of President Zein Elabidine Ben Ali of Tunisia on 14 January 2011 led the monarchy to seriously contemplate further media reorganization and reform. The era of Mohamed VI has been characterized by relative freedom of the press and political parties being given the freedom to criticize the government. This lies in stark contrast to the state's earlier control of the media and public opinion out of fear of political anarchy (Smith and Loudiy, 2005). With the continual rise of both the Internet and satellite television, mainly Al Jazeera, Mehdi Chaibi (2016) states that the majority of discussions in the Moroccan public sphere, since the beginning of the Arab uprisings, have revolved around the constitutional monarchy, the title of the king as "Commander of the Faithful," the protocols of the palace, the budget of the palace, and the friends of the palace. The social protest of Al-Hoceima in 2017, which followed a gruesome accident in which a fishmonger was crushed to death, and the subsequent trial of some journalists who covered the said protests and of protesters themselves, brought back the image of the Makhzen (the state) wanting to control both the media and political fields simultaneously.

The nature of journalism in Morocco has changed profoundly in recent years. A survey among 402 Moroccan journalists reveals the generational differences; the older journalists generally focus on political issues, whereas younger journalists focus on economic issues (HCP, 2006). Interestingly, the majority of journalists concurred that the future of journalism would be largely electronic, replacing paper-based journalism. Moroccan journalists have different opinions about the future of Morocco. They can be placed into three rather broad categories: optimists, moderates, and pessimists. More than one-third, or 38%, of journalists are optimistic about the systemic progress made at the level of governance. The rest are either moderates or pessimistic about the chances of governmental reform.

Given the rough division between optimistic and pessimistic journalists, it is clear why there is simply no unified agenda for social change in Morocco. The infrastructure for social media already exists in the country, as the number of Internet users in Morocco is the second highest of all Arab countries, second only to Egypt. The percentage of partisan journalists has declined to 14%, meaning that the partisan print media has lost its ideological pillars (Bakkali, 2018). Social media has allowed youth to bypass traditional media and publish their blogs and tweets online, expressing their political and economic frustration.

Legal framework and regulations of the media landscape in Morocco

A set of regulatory texts govern the entirety of the broadcasting sector in Morocco, the most conspicuous of which is the Moroccan Constitution. Article 9 of the Constitution addresses both the freedom of opinion and the freedom of expression. According to this article, the roots of this freedom and the checks to be applied to the state monopoly are embedded in primary law. Article 15 corroborates this by guaranteeing all citizens the freedom of enterprise – which is certainly germane to the right to invest in the broadcasting field. Issiali (2010) contends, "maintaining state monopoly over the broadcasting communication sector would be an anachronism in relation to freedom of enterprise."

The galvanizing wave of political liberalization in the 2000s brought further media reforms to the nation. In 2002, a new Press Code was enacted to usurp the outlandishly repressive 1976 Press Code, and in 2016, a further updated version, inclusive of provisions for digital media regulation, was ordained with parliament approval. The High Authority for Audiovisual Communication (*Haut Autorité de la Communication Audiovisuelle*, commonly known as HACA) was created in 2002, with the objectives of mandating the establishment of a legal framework for the liberalization of the audiovisual sector and of overseeing a public service broadcasting division. In November 2004, the Parliament adopted the Audiovisual Communication Law, in a landmark move, formally terminating the state's monopolization of broadcasting management. In April 2005, Radiodiffusion et Télévision Marocaine, the institution that previously managed state TV and radio, metamorphosed from a mere subsidiary of the Ministry of Communication to a self-standing body, the National Company of Radio and Television (*la Société Nationale de Radiodiffusion et de Télévision* – SNRT). Between 2006 and 2014, new licenses were granted by HACA to nine public television stations, 16 private radio stations, and one private television station; "Thus, the structure of Morocco's media was redefined, a new print and online media law promulgated, a broadcast regulator set up, and a framework for private broadcasting was created" (Farmanfarmaian, 2017).

Established as an independent administrative authority, HACA has a huge advantage, as it is theoretically a "fully impartial institution" whilst under the tutelary protection of the king. HACA is responsible for providing a legislative service that prescribes both technical and legal standards be employed in operationalizing the audience of broadcasting media. Ideologically, it is responsible for laying down the rules to safeguard the pluralistic expression of thought and thorough equity in access to airtime.

Furthermore, HACA is the authority that is responsible for processing applications for the creation and day-to-day functionality of broadcasting communication companies, delivering frequency-usage licenses and approving specification sheets of operators meant to monitor the activities. Monitoring compliance with the sector's stringent set of principles is another one of

HACA's tasks, as is addressing complaints concerning damages suffered as a result of the dissemination of prejudicial and warped information.

A duality in access to information exists in Morocco. While the laws do indeed allow access to information; journalists have a difficult time practicing that right. For instance, journalist Omar Radi published a list of all the beneficiaries of cheap land distribution in Morocco, as he was able to obtain a login to a government database via an anonymous source, but other journalists experienced great difficulties in accessing information from the government's website (Radi, 2017). The government has become a well-built citadel, making it rather difficult for reporters to verify and fact check, let alone conduct quality investigative journalism.

The roadmap of the Parliament of Morocco has reported that the global community-at-large is on the road to an unstable revolution in the media sector. Therefore, the only solution to this impending crisis is the freedom of the media and to be connected to the new global digital configuration (Naji, 2011: 22). The report presents the case that the economic logic of globalization fails to take into consideration the religious, ideological, cultural, and political ethics that define quality journalism. Hence, the report requests keeping in mind that the national model of journalism should be the ideal goal (Naji, 2011: 24). The report, in essence, sums up the crisis between the media and the state as being caused by the confrontation between the private media and the state apparatuses, mainly the judicial system and the police, which seeks to exercise its usual tactics of manipulation and infeudation.

The report concludes that the state apparatuses assume that the freedom of expression could diminish state authority and credibility in the eyes of the people and that there is an intention to make the media dependent on the state (Naji, 2011: 45–46).

The report also argues that many players have different strategies to domesticate the media, including the new owners of media outlets and digital platforms, and different individuals who adhere to the dominant agenda (Naji, 2011: 46). The report argues that the democratic option had been underlined by the king during his historic discourse at the time of the Arab Spring, when he dissolved the Parliament, called for new elections, and nominated a constituent assembly to revise the Moroccan Constitution.

The platform for the national dialogue in the media, and in society, had one strategic goal, which is to normalize and police the role of the media within Moroccan society, to achieve freedom of expression in a democratic setting. Four specific goals were mentioned:

1 To institutionalize a permanent dialogue between media outlets and democratic institutions, including Parliament, and the judicial system.
2 To legitimize and give credibility to the media outlets in society, based on the metrics of professionalism and ethics.
3 To create a new legislative arsenal, to regulate the media in a modern manner, based on the principles of liberty and democracy.
4 To create a national media environment that can survive various financial and economical upheavals, to reach a business model that can benefit the society-at-large (Naji, 2011: 51).

This national dialogue has had modest implications on media legislation, according to several journalists we spoke with in Morocco.

Whereas news outlets are generally reserved in their coverage of controversial issues to evade financial ramifications and sanctioning, 2M opened the floor to the 20 February Movement during the Arab Spring. Despite this coverage, Benjelloun (2014) notes that protesters were chanting, "down with the channel." This slogan is highly reminiscent of the Tunisians' "down with Ben Ali." The underlying truth here is that the conflict between the public and the media is on the account of a deep-seated divergence.

Voices of content producers: advertising and competition

The most daunting problem for media content producers is the attainment of funding. It is especially difficult for the media, because there is, in fact, less advertising space. To elaborate, established media outlets have complained about the strings attached to sources of funding. For example, the case of Moroccan television channel 2M is considerably more complicated than the general wisdom already surrounding the television service. Reda Benjelloun (2014) poses the aforementioned argument during his visit to Paris in 1997. At this same time, King Hassan II discovered Canal Plus, a private channel that requires a subscription, and a box that decodes television content, in his hotel suite. Before the liberalization of the media field, the king announced the launch of 2M, using the Canal Plus model. The launch quickly came to an impasse after Moroccans hacked into the decoder to watch the channel for free. The word *derb ghalef* in Casablanca refers to "hacking Mecca," even for European decoders or ones in the Gulf region. At that point, 2M decided to become a part of public funding as a private-public entity. The people were, generally speaking, under the impression that they were now not only paying for their utilities but also for 2M. Benjelloun (2014) contends, "the reality of the matter is that advertising is the major source of our revenue." Indeed, 95% of 2M's budget comes from advertising revenues. For print outlets, such as *TelQuel*, 80% of their budget comes from advertising revenue.

Abdellah Tourabi (2014) of *TelQuel* argues that it is indeed sometimes quite difficult to strike a balance between the critical editorial line and the needs of advertisers, who desire certain, specific angles. One of the largest challenges for Moroccan news outlets is their lack of audience, due to their major competitors, such as France 24 (available in French and Arabic), BBC World, BBC Arabic, BBC French, and Russia Today (available in Arabic). Additional competitors are Arabic infotainment stations, such as Rotana, MBC, news stations Al Jazeera, Al Arabiyya, and Al Mayadin, in addition to the hundreds of religious televangelists in Arabic.

These international stations draw a significant percentage of viewership simply because of the sheer inadequacy of Moroccan news. Moroccan media outlets struggle to pay salaries of reporters and cannot afford to send correspondents to international locations (Chaibi, 2016). Moroccan news outlets also have, subjectively speaking, the weakest international news segments. Furthermore, advertisers are increasingly wary of potentially being paired with marginal political debates and controversial topics. As a result, the news station 2M faces great difficulties in programming political debates on prime-time television.

The field of advertising has indeed experienced major transformations. In the 1970s and the 1980s, most of Morocco's advertisements focused on food products and other necessities. Advertisements were limited to the national public broadcaster RTM, Médi1 Radio, and newspapers *Le Matin* and *La Vie Economique*. Then, in the 1990s, the professionalization of the advertisement sector became a reality (Naji, 2011: 261). In the early 2000s, the magazine *TelQuel* opened the field of competition to other Arabic and English magazines (Naji, 2011: 262). The structure of the advertising market in Morocco primarily comprises two distinct characteristics. First, the majority of advertising is carried out through media outlets. To elaborate, in 2005, 53.2% of the total advertisement in Morocco was through media outlets. The outlets that hold a larger share of the media commonly have a team dedicated to bolstering the structure and hierarchy of advertisement and exercising aggressive strategies to acquire optimal business (Naji, 2011: 264).

Conclusion

The state, as the main player, sets the rules and dictates the logic of the game. The weak link in the Moroccan regulatory system appears to be a strategic state-devised roadmap that provides the "role players" with a categorical set of directions on how to reconfigure the media landscape in line with a set of indicators and benchmarks.

Thus far, elements, such as technological convergence and the shift from analog to digital broadcasting, coordination, and synergies between stakeholders are conspicuously missing in Morocco. To that end, such inadequacies and incongruities within the national media field must be promptly dealt with, adhering to transparent and democratic procedures. The roadmap stipulates that it is imperative that Morocco parts company with the paradoxes that characterize the media systems in MENA region, and instead consorts with the North American and Western European liberal models.

Acknowledgments

We want to thank Omar Radi, Mehdi Chaibi, Wafa Belarbi, Abdellah Tourabi, Reda Benjelloun, and HACA for their input.

References

Arkoun, Mohammed (2007), *Abc de l'islam: pour sortir des clôtures dogmatiques*. Grancher, Paris.

Bakkali, Mohammed (2018), Media Landscape in Morocco. *Al Alam Daily*, 5 June.

Benjelloun, Reda (2014), *Issues and Challenges of the Media in Morocco*. Institute of the Arab World (Paris) in Partnership with Telquel, BM, and TV 2M October 2.

Bentahar, Mekki (2002), *Le Maroc Contemporain: Immuable et Changeant*. Faculté de lettres, Rabat.

Boudoudou, Mohammed (2004), Changement Social et Problematique Identitaire au Maroc. *Bulletin Economique et Social du Maroc. Rapport du Social*. Rabat: Okad.

Boukhars, Anton (2011), *Politics in Morocco. Executive Monarchy and Enlightened Authoritarianism*. London and New York: Routledge.

Chaibi, Mehdi (2016), *Au Maroc, les Chaînes de Télévision Privées N'ont pas Droit de Cité*. Retrieved from www.huffpostmaghreb.com/2016/01/13/teles-privees-maroc_n_8967334.html. Accessed 10 August 2019.

Cherribi, Sam, and Diez-Nicolás, Juan (2007), World Values Survey for Morocco. *WVS*.

Farmanfarmaian, Roxane (2017), Introduction. *Journal of North African Studies: Special Section: Medias in Morocco*, 22, pp. 335–339.

Grotti, Laetitia, and Goldstein, Eric (2005), Morocco's Truth Commission Honoring Past Victims during an Uncertain Present. *Human Rights Watch*, 17(11(E)) (November). Retrieved from www.hrw.org/sites/default/files/reports/morocco1105wcover.pdf.

H24 info. Retrieved from www.h24info.ma/culture/radio-haca-epingle-emission-religieuse-incitation-a-violence/. Accessed 24July 2019.

HCP (2006), Prospective Maroc 2030. In *Les Perceptions de L'avenir Enquête Auprès des Journalists*. Rabat: le Haut Commissariat au Plan.

Hidass, Ahmed (2010), Radio and Television in Morocco: New Regulation and Licensing for Private Channels. *Journal of Arab and Muslim Media Research*, pp. 19–36.

Issiali, Aarab (2010), La regulation de l'audiovisuel au Maroc: un choix irreversible ou un alibi? *Horizons Maghrebins- Le Droit à la Mémoire*, 62, pp. 48–57.

Khatibi, Abdelkebir (1999), *L'Alternance et les Partis politiques*. Casablanca: Eddif.

Khatibi, Abdelkebir (2002), *Chemins de Travers. Essais de Sociologie*. Rabat: Okad.

Laroui, Abdallah (1977), *The History of the Maghrib: An Interpretive Essay*. Princeton: Princeton University Press.

Morocco (2016), Freedom House.

Morocco (2017), Freedom House.

Morocco (2019), Freedom House.

Naimi, Mohamed (2016), Liberté de presse écrite au Maroc: l'évolution au regard de l'évaluation. *L'Année du Maghre*, 15.

Naji, Jamal-Eddine (ed.) (2011), *Dialogue National*. Maroc: Livre Blanc.

Radi, Omar (2017), Omar Radi on Inspiration, Lessons, & Investigative Journalism. *YouTube,* 21 October.

Reporters Without Borders (2005), *Reporters Without Borders Annual Report 2005 – Morrocco, 2005.* Retrieved from https://refworld.org/docid46e690e5c.html. Accessed 4 August 2020.

Smith, Andrew R., and Loudiy, Fadoua (2005), Testing the Red Lines: On the Liberalization of Speech in Morocco. *Human Rights Quarterly,* 27(3), pp. 1069–1119. doi:10.1353/hrq.2005.0042. The Johns Hopkins University Press.

SNRT (2017), Performances des chaînes TV de la SNRT, Performances des Radios de la SNRT, Performances de la SNRT sur le Digital. In *Rapport d'activité*. SNRT.

Tourabi, Abdellah (2014), *Issues and Challenges of the Media in Morocco*. Institute of the Arab World (Paris) in Partnership with Telquel, BM, and TV 2M, 2 October.

Tozy, Mohamed (2008), Islamists, Technocrats and the Palace. *Journal of Democracy*, 19(1), pp. 34–41.

19

THE NEW AND SOCIAL MEDIA IN MOROCCO

Aziz Douai and Mohamed Ben Moussa

Introduction

The Internet and social media were hailed as harbingers and facilitators of the wave of social and political change sweeping the region during the "Arab Spring" uprisings. While those assertions should by no means dispute the indispensable role of collective action and social mobilization undertaken by disaffected populations who protested stagnating economic conditions and entrenched authoritarianism, we argue that social media's unique role in these social and political upheavals lies in creating a new space for activism that abridges the offline/online divide. In other terms, the current chapter adopts a social constructivist approach that transcends the classic dichotomy between online and offline spaces, arguing that online activism has shaped and is in turn being shaped by offline politics. After Mohamed Bouazizi set himself on fire, Tunisian citizens appalled at the incident took to blogs and other social media to protest the authoritarian excesses of and eventually bring down Zein Elabidine Ben Ali's regime. The Facebook page "We Are All Khaled Said," commemorating an Egyptian blogger killed by police, generated public attention, and Egyptians quickly mobilized to protest the corruption of Hosni Mubarak's regime. Perhaps a continuation of the "Moroccan Spring," videos of the gruesome death of Mohcine Fikri, a fish vendor in the northern region of Morocco known as Al-Rif, were widely shared on social media platforms, sparking outrage and massive protests (called Hirak al-Rif) in 2016 and 2017 (Spadola, 2017). Social media evolved from an organizational tool for the Hirak activists into an arena for waging information warfare and a fierce struggle against the state and its allies accusing activists of treason and separatism. These events demonstrate that the Internet and social media platforms have become reliable public vehicles for video-sharing, publicizing police clampdowns, and grassroots organizing, as well as exposing the fuzzy/blurry boundaries between offline and online politics in the region.

This chapter provides a comprehensive outlook on new media developments and discusses the complex historical, economic, and legal infrastructure enabling the rise of networked activism and civil society in Morocco. We first shed light on the Moroccan state's liberalization policy underpinning successive "digital" plans over the last two decades that are meant to fast track the country into the era of the "information society." We then turn to examine the political and social ramifications of the Internet and social media in the aftermath of the "Arab Spring." The chapter presents recent cases of social protest in the country to illuminate both the promise of and the obstacles facing digital activists in Morocco and the broader region. We argue that mediated and digital activism in Morocco continues to thrive, taking advantage of high levels of penetration and relative ease of access to the Internet in the country, and a new wave of online activists have used social media tools to educate and mobilize the public on a variety of social issues.

Historical background

Morocco is one of the first countries in Africa that adopted the Internet at a mass level so much so that the country has now one of the highest penetration rates in the continent with more than 22 million users, representing 61.6% of the population (Internet Stats, 2018). While the Internet in the country has been available since 1995, its usage on such a large scale did not kick off until a few years ago when 3G mobile telephony became available. The development of the Internet and information and communications technology (ICT) sector generally in the country gained real momentum after 1997, when a landmark Post Office and Telecommuni-cation Act (Law 24–96) was passed that provided for the liberalization of the telecommunica-tion industry and set up an independent regulatory agency, the National Telecom Regulatory Agency. Two years later, the government awarded the second mobile phone operator license to Médi Télécom (Méditel) through an international tender for US $1.1 billion – the most lucra-tive award for a Global System for Mobile communications (GSM) license ever in a develop-ing nation by then (Willis, 2006). The liberalization process continued when the government sold 35% of Maroc Telecom to the French group Vivendi Universal for US $2.11 billion. In 1999, another telecommunication company, WANA Corporate (formerly Maroc Connect), was established and later marketed its Internet services under the brand name Wanadoo. The company was initially affiliated with France Télécom, but is now controlled by the Moroccan conglomerate Omnium Nord-Africain (ONA) (Hlasny, 2014).

In 2008, the company won the third mobile license, and, through marketing its third-generation (3G) mobile system, it controls less than 2% of the mobile market in Morocco (Agence Nationale de Reglementation des Telecommunication ANRT, 2018). Morocco was also one of the first countries in the region to introduce mobile broadband in 2007, and three years later the country launched the first commercial Internet Protocol Television (IPTV) ser-vice in the continent that was followed also in the same year by the first mobile payment service (Mobicash) in the country (Hlasny, 2014: 12). So far, the telecommunication market is shared between three operators, namely Maroc Telecom, Medi Telecom (Orange Maroc), and Wana/ Inwi. The three operators control 42.25%, 29.64%, and 28.11% of the market respectively and their total income represents more than 75% of total industry revenue (Amaoui, 2017). The majority of mobile subscribers in the country (95%) are using the prepaid option compared to only 5% to postpaid (Directorate of Studies & Financial Forecasts DSFF, 2014). Until 2010, the majority of Moroccans accessed the Internet through public spaces, notably cybercafés whose number was estimated to be between 2,000 and 3,000 and employing some 5,000 people, thus contributing to the reduction of both poverty and illiteracy among the youth (Open Arab Internet, 2009). Wheeler (2009) contends that cybercafés in North African countries, including Morocco, played an important role in diffusing IT skills and Internet use, as well as in building civic culture and social networks:

> In most cases, these café users have subsequently taught a friend, family, or community member to use the Internet, thus demonstrating a form of civic engagement whereby knowledge once attained is shared with others through informal networks. Moreover,

many became Internet users to reduce the costs and increase the likelihood of staying in touch with friends and family members, especially when individuals in their kin and care networks are abroad.

(p. 316)

A key factor that contributed to the spread of cybercafés in the country has been the low fixed telephone penetration, which increased only from 5.5% in 2002 to 8.9% in 2013 (Data Reportal, 2019). The advance of mobile telephony has been a turning point in this trend since a large number of users shifted to 3G mobile access. The mobile market grew between 2000 and 2013 from 2.52 to 43.76 million with a penetration of 120% in 2019, one of the highest in the world, although smartphone penetration constitutes only 57% of the population (Data Reportal, 2019). The prepaid subscription constitutes the majority of them with more than 95% of subscribers. The growth of 3G mobile Internet was due to multiple factors such as the falling prices of mobile telephones and tablets, 3G flash drives, and the introduction of competitive offers for mobile data (DSFF, 2014). Compared to the strong growth in 3G mobile penetration, the penetration of fixed telephony remains weak with nearly 9% of the population – placing Morocco 93rd out of 142 countries (DSFF, 2014) – and this rate has been decreasing by 1% every year during the last decade (ANRT, 2017). The fast development of mobile Internet was at the expense of fixed telephony as the country failed to invest adequately to boost its landline infrastructure (Constant, 2011). The introduction of ADSL technology in 2003 helped to improve the quality of Internet streaming, which was ranked the best in the North African region by 2007 (Hlasny, 2014: 12). But this improvement remains severely hindered by the fact that the rate of penetration of computers (desktops and laptops) in the country is estimated at only 25% of the population since the majority of users rely on smartphones for connection (Data Reportal, 2019).

Despite formidable economic and social challenges facing the country, Morocco has made considerable progress in the domain of ICTs. Though having the region's lowest GDP per capita, Morocco liberalized telecom environment has allowed it to take the region's lead in the mobile sector (Gray, 2002). Within Moroccan official discourse, the liberalization of the communication sector is often described as a vital step towards wider societal adoption of new technologies that can accelerate economic and social development. This is why, and similarly to the rest of the developing world, the information revolution is viewed as a highly political affair and not as a technical challenge (Wilson, 2004).

Politics of "digital" Morocco and information society

Since the mid-1990s, Morocco's telecommunication sector went through various stages corresponding to strategic plans adopted by the state. The first one, between 1994 and 2000, laid down the foundations of the country's ICT policy and began with the liberalization of the telecommunication industry, the creation of the ANRT (National Telecom Regulatory Agency) along with the first private telecommunications company (Ittissalt Al-Maghrib/IAM). Whilst Morocco's national domain name, —.ma, was handled before by Maroc Telecom, it has since become the responsibility of the ANRT, which declares it is now offering users the possibility of registering their domain names in Arabic under the national name of "المغرب" (Morocco) instead of —.ma (ANRT, 2008). The second stage ran between 2000 and 2008 and was marked by the launch of the e-Maroc strategy that set to address some of the key shortcomings in the previous phase and set forward to achieve the following main goals: enforcing more business transparency on the operators, reinforcing the telecoms network coverage and speed through the optical fiber, ADSL high speed and GSM and landline connectivity, enhancing local content such as e-government and a national portal, and ensuring access to services to all, especially in rural and remote areas.

The third stage covers the period between 2009 and 2013 and was marked with the launch of the second national ICT program Maroc Numeric 2013 [Digital Morocco 2013], which was financed by a World Bank loan. Building on the objectives of the previous stage, the program defined four strategic priorities, namely boosting the rate of PC penetration and use among individuals and businesses, enhancing e-government and good governance, helping the computerization of small and medium companies, and boosting Moroccan ICT industries and businesses (Kettani, 2015). Recently, the country has launched the new strategic initiative dubbed "Digital Morocco 2020" that aims to address some of the limitations in the previous plans and consolidate their key achievements. The new strategy rotates on four main axes, namely the reinforcement of the position of the country as a regional digital hub, the use of the ICT sector as a vehicle for economic and social development, reduction of the digital gap within society and boosting citizen digital engagement, and enhancement of e-government and e-governance (UNESCO, 2018). The government, for instance, launched first the national open data portal of Morocco (www.data.gov.ma) in 2011 that was upgraded in 2014 using the SCAN software, and it has committed itself to deliver at least 50% of all public services online by 2020 (Organization for Economic Cooperation and Development, 2018).

The country's ICT strategy over the last two decades has yielded important results in terms of expanding usage, enhancing competitiveness, and diversifying the economy. According to Constant (2011: 10), the country was ahead over its neighbors in "establishing an independent regulating authority" and also in "instituting competitive markets in both the fixed and mobile industry as well as the launch of third-generation (3G) mobile services." Morocco is ranked second in Africa on the e-readiness index (behind only South Africa), and it is better placed than other neighboring countries such as Algeria and Tunisia with higher human development index and income levels (World Economic Forum, 2016). The country enjoys one of the highest broadband penetrations in Africa and the MENA region (Kettani, 2015). It also boasts a highly dynamic and competitive ICT market and infrastructure supply, with half of the employees at least using a PC and connected to the Internet (Constant, 2011). More importantly, investment in the ICT sector and the liberalization reforms have boosted the telecommunication industry in general and its share in the country's economy, which according to official reports, accounted for more than 3% of Moroccan GDP, 12% of government fiscal revenues, and 1% of jobs (World Bank Group, 2016).

Morocco's relative success in the telecommunication domain has been widely framed as a success story to be emulated in the developing world. In an enthusiastic article entitled "Morocco – Leaving the Others Behind," Vanessa Gray (2002) suggested that Morocco's impressive telecommunication breakthrough is an excellent example of today's worldwide liberalization and transformation process (para. 1); similarly, Sutherland (2007: 8) contended that the country is one of the telecommunications successes of Africa. These highly positive assessments adhere, in fact, to a global discourse on a technology whose ascension to prominence in the last few decades is intrinsically linked to a neoliberal economic system. Fisher (2010) points out several aspects that distinguish the articulation between what he calls the narrative of the digital discourse and the —network of capitalism:

> [t]he withdrawal of the state from the planning, management, and regulation of the economy and its welfare obligations; the move from national protective economy to a

globalized, deregulated, and unitary market; the privatization of work; the eradication of work and the working class as viable social categories.

(p. 3)

The development of the telecommunication sector in Morocco spearheaded a very aggressive economic liberalization policy, under the supervision of international monetary institutions, which saw the privatization of key state-owned companies and sectors. While these policies have led to the fast diffusion and adoption of ICTs such as the mobile phone and more recently the Internet, they have also, paradoxically, aggravated existing social and economic inequalities between regions, social classes, and genders. Despite introducing 3G Internet as early as 2007 and 4G in 2015, the broadband service and market remain restricted to the main urban centers and expensive to the majority of the population due to failure of investment in infrastructure, insufficient regulations, and lack of competition (World Bank Group, 2016). Development in this area has stalled in recent years, and many neighboring countries are overtaking Morocco because broadband service is limited to ADSL and 3G (Constant, 2011). Additionally, though Morocco has the highest number of users per capita in North Africa, high illiteracy rates and low performance in human development prevent the country from benefiting from this numerical growth. Gray (2002) points out, for instance, that Morocco is in advance of other countries in the region in terms of ICT access and use; however, it trails these countries in ICT skills. These discrepancies explain, in part, the growing digital divides that characterize Internet adoption and use between big cities and peripheries, urban centers and rural areas, rich and poor, and gender and generations. The still high level of illiteracy was estimated at 30% in 2017, and this rate is even higher among women and girls (OECD, 2018). The government has also failed to compel the major telecommunication operators to invest more in infrastructure and adopt transparent practices in line with ANRT and International Telecommunications Union (ITU) standards (Zaid, 2016). This explains why "urban dwellers are more likely to have internet access than rural inhabitants, with penetration at 67 percent versus 43 percent, respectively" (Freedom House, 2017).

Legal infrastructure: Internet and cyber laws

Several legal regulations and structures have been set up related to the protection of privacy and cybersecurity in the last decade. These include a cybersecurity strategy, a National Information Systems Security Detective, as well as new regulations for personal data protection, electronic data exchange, cyber consumer, and cybercrime (OECD, 2018: 19). Two regulatory bodies are overseeing ICT policy in the country. The first one is the Ministry of Industry, Commerce, Investment, and the Digital Economy, which has supervised the various digital plans the government has launched over two decades. The second one is the Ministry for Administrative Reform and Public Service, which is responsible for civil service policies modernization and reform, and administrative simplification and rationalization (OECD, 2018: 50). In 2013, the Moroccan government tried to pass a new code that would allow authorities to closely monitor the cyberspace and impose severe restrictions on freedom of expression, according to its detractors. The project drew harsh criticism from a broad coalition of activists who launched what they called "an electronic disobedience" campaign on Facebook and other social media that eventually compelled the government to withdraw the project code (AlRimi, 2013).

Morocco adopted in 2016 a new Press and Publication Code that eliminates prison time as a punishment but maintains fines and court-ordered suspensions of publications and websites. The code, however, maintains imprisonment in case the fine, which can be very hefty, was not paid.

The new law is a step forward in comparison with the previous code that imposed prison as a punishment for offenses to the monarchy, Islam, or territorial integrity (Human Rights Watch, 2017). The code was the first time where online and print media have been addressed jointly in the same legal document. The code stipulates that blocking any online news site has to be mandated by judicial order and that the blockage should not exceed one month. Moreover, any definitive closure of the news site can be implemented solely through a court decision. However, the offenses that are punished by fines and suspension are framed in broad and vague terms, providing the state with vast discretional authority that can be misused (Luengos and Thieux, 2017). Moreover, journalists can still be persecuted through the penal code that "continues to punish with prison a range of nonviolent speech offenses" (Human Rights Watch, 2017). The new code also prohibits news organizations, both print and online, from receiving any funds from foreign governments or international organizations alike. In 2018, Moroccan authorities have condemned the editor of the independent daily *Akhbar Alyaoum*, Taoufik Bouachrine, for 12 years in jail on the ground of sexual charges. He was later also fined 1.4 million dirhams in libel damages in a trial that was deemed by numerous international bodies and observers to be violating due process (Human Rights Watch, 2019a). The United Nation's Working Group on Arbitrary Detention has lambasted his imprisonment, which it described as "arbitrary detention" and "judicial harassment" (Le Figaro, 2019). A year later, one of the daily's most critical journalists, Hajar Raissouni, was condemned for one year in prison on charges of having an illegal abortion and premarital sex, which was described by Human Rights Watch as a violation of "her rights to privacy, liberty, and numerous other rights" (Human Rights Watch, 2019b). Her persecution prompted Reporters Without Borders to state that "Sex-related charges are often used in Morocco to harass individuals who annoy the authorities" (Reporters Without Borders, 2019a).

According to the Ministry of Communication, there are around 400 news sites in Morocco that are distributed all over the kingdom. Moreover, the number of journalists working in online news sites and who hold professional press passes issued by their media institutions have increased from 89 in 2015 to 265 in 2016, 66 of whom are women. Most of the licensed journalists, however, are concentrated in a few of the leading online newspapers such as *Hespress* and *Hibapress*. Moreover, dozens of existing online news sites are believed to have been created by Moroccan authorities to counterbalance and attack the news organizations and sites that criticize the government or state. These online sites try to enlist high profile personalities to enhance their legitimacy and often resort to defamation and propaganda to silence journalists who criticize the state (Luengos and Thieux, 2017). With the crackdown on independent and critical newspapers and journalists intensifying in the last years, Morocco's news industry has been dominated, more than ever, by news outlets that are either owned by the government or close to its vast political and financial clientele network. This applies equally to online professional news as well, where the top-ranked news sites are either close to the sphere of power or follow a type of journalism marked by sensationalism and populism, such as ChoufTV.com (Alexa.com, 2019). These new players in the news-scape have benefitted, in fact, not only from the persecution of independent newspapers that forced many of them either to shut down or "toe the line," but also from an already weak and vulnerable print news industry that has only worsened with the mass adoption of the Internet. In a country where the leading newspaper's circulation does not exceed 37,000 (l'Organisme de justification de la diffusion, OJD, 2018), online news sites have emerged as the de facto news source for the majority of citizens.

The capacity of the state to control free speech online, however, is constantly challenged by the expanding importance of social media and citizen journalism, with Facebook and WhatsApp being the most used applications in the country (Salem, 2017). It is estimated that more than 17 million (47% of the country population) have been active on at least one social media platform by January 2019 (Data Reportal, 2019). WhatsApp is the most popular social media platform in the country with an estimated total of 81% of social media users, followed by Facebook with 76% and YouTube (60%). Unlike many other countries in the MENA region, Twitter's use remains limited with only 17% of online users (Data Reportal, 2019). While the popularity of WhatsApp is due to its use as a cheap and alternative communication tool to mobile voice calls and SMS, Facebook remains the most vibrant platform for connecting, sharing, and public debates in the country. If the vast majority of social media users in the country are young people between 18 and 34 years, the gender gap remains very wide, since women constitute only 27% of this age group compared to 45% for men (Data Reportal, 2019). The gender digital gap only reflects other forms of gendered disparities in the country, as illiteracy is still very high among women who constitute more than 60% of illiterate people in rural areas (Freedom House, 2018).

Social and political functions of social media

Social media platforms have played a significant role in Morocco, akin to the wider Arab world, including the mobilization of social networks, building of coalitions, decentralized/non-hierarchical social movements, and bridging of the online/offline political divide. Commenting on the role of social media in the "Arab Spring" uprisings, Howard and Hussain (2011: 35–36) observed that activists and other people used digital technologies to build

> extensive networks, create social capital, and organize political action with a speed and on a scale never seen before. Thanks to these technologies, virtual networks materialized in the streets. Digital media became the tool that allowed social movements to reach once-unachievable goals, even as authoritarian forces moved with a dismaying speed of their own to devise both high- and low-tech countermeasures.

In the same fashion, social media enabled the airing of political and economic grievances and subsequent organization and mobilization of Moroccan activists who protested against the government and demanded genuine political reforms, known as the "20 February Movement." Naming their movement after the first big demonstration on 20 February 2011, young activists sparked a public discussion about political reforms, demanding genuine democratization, on the le Mouvement de 20 Février, or M20, "Mouvement du 20 Février – Maroc - فبراير 20 حركة" Facebook page and ushered in the "Moroccan Spring" (Emiljanowicz, 2017). In addition to the dissemination of public grievances, social media became an indispensable tool to unite the nodes of the social protest network given the leaderless, "decentralized character" of the movement. Social media connected autonomous groups in cities around the country. Moreover, the 20 February Movement did not align itself with the country's mainstream political parties and instead sought to build coalitions among ideological factions from across the political spectrum – Islamists from "Al Adl wal Ihsan" and secularists, Berber/Amazigh language rights and other human rights activists. Their social media posts and videos called for nationwide rallies exhorting other citizens to join their cause and demand a "Morocco of dignity and freedom" and challenging "fear and oppression" (Maroc 20 Fev. 2011). The protests forced King Mohamed VI to overhaul the constitution, reaffirm the government's commitment to "democratic principles," formally recognize Amazigh language rights, and consolidate the rule of law, among other reform measures (Entelis and Chomiak, 2011).

The power of social media in Morocco sparked a social movement that wielded new communication tools to elevate local issues to global concerns and connect online activism to offline politics. Regardless of its inability to bring about a major political transformation, the 20 February Movement demonstrates the critical role of social media to highlight authorities' repression of young activists. The regime's repression did not go unnoticed on social media as repression of activists brought new networks of solidarity and led to renewed pro-democracy protests beyond what has been described as "the first movers," activists "who often came from families that had been punished for opposing the regime in the past" (Lawrence, 2017). Moreover, social media connected the pro-democracy protests in Morocco to the transformations occurring in the wider Arab world and beyond. In seeking to mobilize other citizens to join their cause, for example, the 20 February Movement's activists openly declared that the country has to "seize the moment of social change" sweeping the Arab world. They deliberately connected their struggle to global social movements such as that of the Occupy Wall Street movement, attempting to organize demonstrations and sit-ins with banners of "We are the 99%" (Diouwer and Bartels, 2014).

Traditional state clampdown on free speech in Morocco has been met with innovative digital activism, which takes advantage of high levels of access and Internet penetration, as well as other affordances of the web such as anonymity and non-hierarchical and leaderless organization. The anonymously led consumer boycott launched on 20 April 2018, for example, an anonymous Facebook page of more than two million users, backed boycotting goods in protest of high price and market manipulation and monopolization (*Middle East Monitor*, 2018). The anonymous boycott movement deployed the language of digital activism, including the use of effective and popular Arabic hashtags, roughly translated as "Let_it_spoil" and "SayNotoHigh-Prices," to initially target three prominent businesses, Afriquia Gasoline, a gas company owned by the powerful and rich businessman and minister of agriculture, Aziz Akhennouch; Sidi Ali, a bottled mineral water company owned by the chairwoman of enterprises in Morocco, Meriem Bensaleh; and French-owned dairy company Centrale Danone (Ben Saga, 2018) The boycott expanded to other sectors of the economy, such as utilities and fish, and led to enormous financial losses for the affected businesses, including loss of market share that eventually forced Danon to reduce its prices. Aside from its economic and political overtones in decrying the confluence of big business in political life, the significance of this digital movement lies in using social media to (1) evade state repression in deciding not to take to the streets and focusing on boycotting these goods; (2) ensure the mobilization of large segments and thus be more inclusive of citizens living in both rural and urban areas; and (3) avoid co-optation from both the state and a failed/inept political party system as the boycotting movement eschewed clear/conventional leadership structure (Gillien, 2018).

Freedom of speech online

Access to and use of the Internet in Morocco has benefitted from a considerable margin of freedom, although in the last few years after the "Arab Spring" uprisings the state has tried to control access to particular websites, and crackdowns on online journalists and digital activists have increased (Freedom House, 2017). Many observers have noted that Internet users enjoy a level of freedom that is relatively unmatched in most Arab countries. For instance, in its report on Morocco, the Initiative for an OpenArab Internet (2009) affirms that – though in Morocco the Internet is largely free of filtering – bloggers and forum participants generally avoid "red lines" topics such as Western Sahara, defamation of the royal authority, and defamation of Islam (Douai, 2009). The 2018 Freedom House report (2017) affirms that the Internet in Morocco is "partly free," as Tunisia is the only MENA country that enjoyed more online freedom on the index. Nonetheless, the Freedom House report also outlines three areas where Internet freedom is still threatened in the country, namely the use of pro-government commentators to manipulate online discussion, the incarceration of bloggers or ICT users, and technical attacks against government critics or human right organizations.

It is doubtful that the country's relative leniency towards online expression stems from a policy of free speech tolerance, since the country is ranked 135th out of 180 in the World Press Freedom Index (Reporters Without Borders, 2019b). Goldsmith and Wu (2006: 49) argue that governments can indeed control the Internet at three levels, the level of users or recipients, the level of websites, and the level of intermediaries or transmitters. The Moroccan state has tried repeatedly to place controls over the Internet by selectively blocking undesirable sites or IP addresses, but it has failed since users can usually access the same content on other websites. Moreover, setting up a comprehensive and intelligent filtering system, as applied in other countries like China, requires many resources that the state cannot afford. As Sadiki (2004: 75) notes about the potential for online free speech and the practice of Internet censorship in Arab countries, the capacity to monopolize loyalty in these countries is being enfeebled by the deluge of the multipolar flow of information made possible by the new information and communication technologies, such as the Internet, that either defy official censorship or cannot be scrutinized without imposing a burden on the public funding.

The success of the 2018 consumer goods boycott movement discussed earlier came also in response to the government's frequent attempts to persecute Internet users and bloggers deemed to have transgressed the red lines, in what seems to be a bid not to silence all criticism online, but to increase self-censorship. Before "the Arab Spring" uprisings, government repression of online speech was infrequent despite some high-profile persecution cases of bloggers and online journalists. For example, Moroccan blogger Mohamed Erraji was convicted in September 2008 of disrespecting/insulting the king after an article for Moroccan Arabic-language news website Hespress. com and was sentenced to serve two years in prison (Reporters Without Borders, 2008). Another blogger, El Bachir Hazzam, was sentenced to four months in prison after he was accused of posting false information online about human rights abuses in the country (Global Voices, 2019). In the aftermath of the "Arab Spring," Internet freedom has declined as the government increases its scrutiny for online expression and actively prosecutes online journalists and activists alike. Stiff jail sentences have threatened prominent journalists, such as Ali Anouzla, editor-in-chief of the online news website Lakome, who faced terrorism charges related to a 2013 article that focused on jihadist threats facing the kingdom and linking to a Spanish website featuring a jihadist video. He was arrested and prosecuted in September 2013 for "advocacy of acts amounting to terrorism offenses" and "providing assistance to perpetrators or accomplices of acts of terrorism," although his trial has been repeatedly postponed (Freedom House, 2017) Hamid Mahdaoui, editor-in-chief of the news site Badil, has faced been arrested and jailed for his outspoken critiques of the government and also his support of the Hirak protest movement that rocked the northern region of the country in 2017.

Internet surveillance and manipulation of social media provide the government with another tool of repression and curtailing freedom of speech online. Online activists have faced state surveillance as international media reports exposed Morocco's and other governments' hiring the services of what RSF describes as "digital mercenaries" to hack into activists' online accounts after infecting them with highly sophisticated spyware. For instance, a 2016 exposé in *Foreign Policy* revealed that the Supreme Council of National Defense in charge of the country's security agencies was behind highly sophisticated surveillance attacks on the pro-democracy website Mamfakinch, "rendering Tor, or any other encryption software, useless. . . [and allowing Morocco's] spooks. . . [to] read the Mamfakinch team's emails, steal their passwords, log their keystrokes, turn on their webcams and microphones" (Kushner, 2016). In addition to the use of malware products, such as those purchased from the Italian company Hacking Team, the government resorts to other tactics to suppress online speech and target activists including social media attacks, derogatory comments, publishing private/personal information, and intimidation from anonymous and pro-government social media accounts. These direct and indirect surveillance tactics are designed to induce self-policing and self-censorship in cyberspace, and thereby inhibit overall freedom of speech and online activism. The risk of turning the Internet into an "instrument of repression" becomes too real to ignore.

Civil society development

Social media platforms and Internet-enabled communications have expanded participatory spaces for citizens, primarily the young, urban, and educated, to engage in civic life and bolstered the development of Morocco's civil society and a vibrant public sphere. Discussing the historical development of civil society, John Sater explains,

> In its modern sense and especially in Morocco, civil society is associated with the presence of NGOs outside the direct influence of the state and its institutions. Consequently, in Morocco, the notion of civil society and NGOs is not politically neutral. It has a connotation that is related to political contestation and the legitimate expression of the Moroccan people in the absence of real democratic representation.
>
> *(Sater, 2002: 103)*

That is why the liberal model of civil society and democracy where political participation in the public sphere, in the Habermasian sense, runs in parallel with consensus building, may not apply to the experience of Morocco (Ben Moussa, 2016). After decades of contestation, where the public sphere expanded and retracted via cycles of openings and closure, civil society finds itself, once again, marred in political stagnation where the monarchy and its network of power (Makhzen) is the real and, perhaps, the only source of power. In this sense, Chantal Mouffe's (2005) notion of "agonistic public sphere" provides a better framework to understand Moroccan politics because it places the issues of power and adversarial relationship at the center of political participation:

> While antagonism is we/they relation in which the two sides are enemies who do not share any common ground, agonism is we/they relation where the conflicting parties, although acknowledging that there is no rational solution to their conflict, nevertheless recognize the legitimacy of their opponents. They are adversaries, not enemies.
>
> *(p. 20)*

Throughout the post-independence era, the Moroccan state's willingness to cede space for genuine political participation becomes possible only when its legitimacy is seriously challenged, as in the aftermath of the Arab Spring. Although the state usually tries to regain full control afterward, it is compelled to assimilate "subversive" claims and agendas into its discourse and, consequently, legitimize new groups and movements (Sater, 2002). For instance, in the aftermaths of the Arab Spring and to quell the growing unrests that threatened the monarchy's grip over power, the state was forced to accommodate the first government led by an Islamic-oriented party, namely the Justice and Development Party. In the last two decades, we have witnessed the gradual withering of traditional civil society players that have long marked Moroccan politics, such as leftist and secular political parties and trade unions, and the ascension into prominence of new movements and groups. Some of the most important and active civil society organizations to emerge from the relative liberalization that Morocco experienced in the 1990s focused on gender equity, human rights, and Berber/Amazigh language rights, such as the Association Democratique des Femmes du Maroc (ADFM), the Union of Feminine Action, and the Association Marocaine des Droits de l'Homme, that successfully campaigned for the reform of family law, the Mudawana, in 2004 (Salime, 2012).

The ascendancy of the Internet and social media as new communicative spaces has facilitated a new engagement among the youth with gender equity, human rights, and Amazigh/Berber rights issues. Discussing the role of female activists in the 20 February Movement, for example, Salime (2012) argues that a "new feminism" of gender "parity" – instead of the traditional feminist focus on "equality" – has emerged outside the purview of traditional feminist organizations. Women activists made sure to have a say and be represented in the leadership and day-to-day operations. The YouTube video that called for public demonstrations started with a young woman, Amina Boughalbi, who confidently articulated the reason for taking to the streets: "I am Moroccan and I will march on February 20th because I want freedom and equality for all Moroccans" (Boughalbi, 2011). Beyond the political protest movement, young activists have used social media, such as Twitter, Facebook, and YouTube, to shine more light on gender-based violence and sexual harassment. One such anti-harassment campaign, Woman-Choufouch, used their Facebook page to invite Moroccan men and women to join the public debate about the difference between "flirting" and "harassment," "rape," and other forms of violence against women (WomanChoufouch, n.d.). In interviews with Woman-Choufouch founders, Skalli observes that these activists are fluent in the language of human rights' discourses and they savvily use social media as a platform for collecting and circulating reports documenting the brutal impact of sexual harassment, testimonies from victims of sexual harassment, and a variety of online publications (Skalli, 2014). Moroccan cyber activists wielded social media platforms to publicize the case of Amina Filali, a young woman who committed suicide after being forced to marry her rapist, and galvanize the public, highlighting the anachronous nature of family laws addressing gender-based violence (Abadi, 2014). Women's access to the Internet, taking advantage of the affordances of cyberspace such as anonymity and other social media activism tools, should signal growing confidence, greater visibility, and participation in the Moroccan public sphere. In the words of feminist scholars, "women's cyberactivism, their citizen journalism, and their self-organization both contribute to and reflect the social and political changes that have occurred in the region" (Gheytanchi and Moghadam, 2014: 3).

Conclusion

The chapter has provided a historical overview of the development of the Internet and ICTs in Morocco and highlighted the role of the state and industry in the diffusion and adoption of the new communication technologies. It then examined the implications of the new communication technologies for political participation and democratic transition in the North African country. The liberalization of the telecommunication industry in the late 1990s enabled ICTs to develop quickly, especially after the introduction of the 3G mobile phones. Nonetheless, due to institutional weaknesses and endemic social and economic gaps, the country has not been able to take full advantage of the potential of ICTs to build a competitive economy and usher the country into the age of "information society." Likewise, Moroccan civil society has, initially, benefited enormously from the fast adoption and expansion of ICTs in the country, prompting real hopes for long chased democratic transition in the country.

Our critical assessment of the development of social media and Internet-enabled communication situates these communication innovations in the social and political turmoil shaking up the Middle East and North Africa region within which Morocco exists. The chapter demonstrates the complex role the Moroccan state played in spearheading the diffusion of these communication technologies through investments in the burgeoning ICT sector, followed by a frantic scramble to "police" the new networked spaces created by the new technologies. The intensification of repression against independent journalism and freedom of speech in the last decade has also been met with the development of new social movements that transcend traditional actors that have shaped the country's political sphere since independence, and have adopted the Internet and social media in novel forms that blend online and offline activism, artistic expression, and everyday life politics with popular protests against economic and social marginality. The disillusionment with the traditional civil society actors in the country in the aftermath of the Arab Spring, and the aggressive attempts by the state to regain full control over the public sphere, have all but dissipated hopes for a smooth political transformation. From a social-constructivist perspective, the Moroccan experience with the Internet in the last two decades sheds light on the dialectic between technology and society, as it reflects a tale of fast growth and stagnation, huge potential and disillusionment, and dominant conservative powers and continuous popular struggle. It is unlikely that the Internet alone will determine the outcome of these social-political struggles. Nonetheless, the spread of digital literacy and culture coupled with the expansion of affordable connectivity and multilayered networking are already transforming how new generations are shaping alternative representations and discourses in a way that seriously challenge the status quo.

References

Abadi, H. (2014), Gendering the February 20th Movement: Moroccan Women Redefining: Boundaries, Identities, and Resistances. *Digital Islam*, 8(1). Retrieved from www.digitalislam.eu/article.do?articleId=8817. Accessed 12 September 2019.

Agence nationale de réglementation des télécommunication (ANRT) (2008), *Annual Report*. Retrieved from www.anrt.ma/publications/rapport-annuel. Accessed 10 October 2018.

Agence nationale de réglementation des telecommunication (ANRT) (2017), *Annual Report*. Retrieved from www.anrt.ma/publications/rapport-annuel. Accessed 15 October 2018.

Alexa.com (2019), *Top Sites in Morocco*. Retrieved from www.alexa.com/topsites/countries/MA. Accessed 15 September 2018.

AlRimi, A. (2013), *Electronic Disobedience' in Morocco Forced the Government to Withdraw a Publication Law*, December. Retrieved from www.dw.com/ar/عصيان-إلكتروني-في-المغرب-سقط-قانونا-للنشر-على-الانترنت/a-17325468. Accessed 17 September 2018.

Amaoui, R. (2017), *Opérateurs et Télécoms au Maroc*. Tic Maroc Technologies. Retrieved from www.tic-maroc.com/p/operateurs-telecom.html. Accessed 18 October 2018.

Ben Moussa, M. (2016), Evolution not Revolution: A Longitudinal Study of the Role of the Internet in Morocco's "Third Way". *Journal of Middle East Media*, 12, pp. 1–39.

Ben Saga, A. (2018), *It's Been a Bumpy Ride: A Recap of the Moroccan Boycott*, May. Retrieved from www.moroccoworldnews.com/2018/05/246931/prices-economy-moroccan-boycott. Accessed 15 September 2019.

Boughalbi, A. (2011), *I am Moroccan Video*, 16 February. Retrieved from www.youtube.com/watch?v=mZm750joM0U&list=FLey8yasfl0GQIGJp01t1SLA&index=2. Accessed 11 November 2019.

Brouwer, L., and Bartels, E. (2014), Arab Spring in Morocco: Social Media and the 20 February Movement. *Afrika Focus*, 27(2), pp. 9–22.

Constant, S. M. (2011), *Broadband in Morocco: Political will Meets Socio-economic Reality*. Washington, DC: infoDev/World Bank. Retrieved from www.broadband-toolkit.org/. Accessed 11 October 2018.

Data Reportal (2019), *Digital 2019: Morocco*. Retrieved from https://datareportal.com/reports/digital-2019-morocco. Accessed 10 October 2018.

Directorate of Studies & Financial Forecasts (2014), *Deployment of the 4th Generation of Mobile Phones (4G) in Morocco: Opportunities and Challenge*. Retrieved from www.finances.gov.ma/Docs/2014/DEPF/4g_study.pdf. Accessed 16 October 2018.

Douai, A. (2009), In Democracy's Shadow: The 'New' Independent Press and the Limits of Media Reform in Morocco. *Westminster Papers in Communication & Culture*, 6(1).

Emiljanowicz, P. (2017), Facebook, Mamfakinch, and the February 20 Movement in Morocco. *Participedia*. Retrieved from https://participedia.net/de/node/4961. Accessed 24 October 2018.

Entelis, J. P., and Chomiak, L. (2011), The Making of North Africa's Intifadas. *Middle East Report*, 259 (Summer). Retrieved from www.academia.edu/1253059/The_making_of_North_Africas_Intifadas. Accessed 17 September 2018.

Fisher, E. (2010), *Media and New Capitalism in the Digital Age: The Spirit of Networks*. New York: Palgrave Macmillan.

Freedom House (2017), *Freedom on the Net 2007: Morocco*. Retrieved from https://freedomhouse.org/report/freedom-net/2017/morocco. Accessed 20 October 2018.

Freedom House (2018), *Morocco Profile*. Retrieved from https://freedomhouse.org/report/freedom-world/2018/morocco. Accessed 18 October 2018.

Gheytanchi, E., and Moghadam, V. N. (2014), Women, Social Protests, and the New Media Activism in the Middle East and North Africa. *International Review of Modern Sociology*, 1–26.

Gillien, M. (2018), Is Morocco's Boycott the Future of Political Resistance in North Africa? *The Middle East Eye*, 12 June. Retrieved from www.middleeasteye.net/columns/morocco-s-boycott-future-resistance-north-africa-1353240629. Accessed 17 October 2018.

Global Voices (2019), *Moroccan Blogger, Internet Cafe Owner, Sentenced*, December 15. Retrieved from https://advox.globalvoices.org/2009/12/15/moroccan-blogger-internet-cafe-owner-sentenced. Accessed 08 August 2020.

Goldsmith, J., and Wu, T. (2006), *Who Controls the Internet? Illusions of a Borderless World*. New York: Oxford University Press.

Gray, V. (2002), *Morocco – Leaving the Others behind*. Retrieved from www.itu.int/ITUD/ict/cs/letters/morocco.html. Accessed 5 September 2018.

Hlasny, V. (2014), *Understanding the Competitive Landscape in Morocco's Telecommunication and Its Socio-Economic Implications*. Universitas Gadjah Mada – Institute of Intl. Studies policy paper. Retrieved from SSRN: https://ssrn.com/abstract=2838911. Accessed 15 September 2018.

Howard, P. N., and Hussain, M. (2011), The Upheavals in Egypt and Tunisia: The Role of Digital Media. *Journal of Democracy*, 22(3), pp. 35–48. doi:10.1353/jod.2011.0041

Human Right Watch (2017), *The Red Lines Stay Red Morocco's Reforms of its Speech Laws*. Retrieved from www.hrw.org/report/2017/05/04/red-lines-stay-red/moroccos-reforms-its-speech-laws. Accessed 20 September 2018.

Human Rights Watch (2019a), *Morocco: Jailed Journalist Stuck in Abusive Solitary*. Retrieved from www.hrw.org/news/2019/04/12/morocco-jailed-journalist-stuck-abusive-solitary. Accessed 15 September 2018.

Human Rights Watch (2019b), *Morocco: Trial Over Private Life Allegation: Jailed Journalist Accused of Non-Marital Sex, Abortion*. Retrieved from www.hrw.org/news/2019/09/09/morocco-trial-over-private-life-allegations. Accessed 10 August 2018.

Internet Stats (2018), *Internet Users Statistics for Africa*. Retrieved from www.Internetworldstats.com/africa.htm#ma. Accessed 23 July 2018.

Kettani, D. (2015), *Broadbands in Morocco: Political will Meets Socio-economic Reality*. The International Bank for Reconstruction and Development. Retrieved from www.infodev.org/articles/broadband-morocco-political-will-meets-socio-economic-reality. Accessed 18 September 2018.

Kushner, D. (2016), Fear this Man. *Foreign Policy*, April. Retrieved from https://foreignpolicy.com/2016/04/26/fear-this-man-cyber-warfare-hacking-team-david-vincenzetti/#. Accessed 10 October 2018.

Lawrence, A. K. (2017), Repression and Activism among the Arab Spring's First Movers: Evidence from Morocco's February 20th Movement. *British Journal of Political Science*, 47(3), pp. 699–718.

Le Figaro (2019), *Maroc: appel à la libération de Taoufik Bouachrine (Amnesty)*. Retrieved from www.lefigaro.fr/flash-actu/2019/02/26/97001-20190226FILWWW00185-maroc-appel-a-la-liberation-de-taoufik-bouachrine-amnesty.php. Accessed 05 November 2019.

l'Organisme de justification de la diffusion (2018), *Chiffres*. Retrieved from www.ojd.ma/Chiffres. Accessed 11 October 2018.

Luengos, J. G., and Thieux, L. (2017), *Les Medias en ligne au Maroc et le journalisme citoyen: analyse des principals limites a un environment favorable*. International Institute for Non-Violent Action. Retrieved from https://novact.org/wpcontent/uploads/2017/09/OSF-Finale.pdf. Accessed 13 September 2018.

Maroc 20 Fév (2011), شباب حركة 20 فبراير المغربية المطالبة بالتغيير. Retrieved from www.youtube.com/watch?v=FmHVWk37TSo. Accessed 5 November 2018.

Middle East Monitor (2018), Morocco: Consumer Boycott Campaign Proving to be Successful against Political Elites. *The Middle East Monitor*, 2 June. Retrieved from www.middleeastmonitor.com/20180602-morocco-consumer-boycott-campaign-proving-to-be-successful-against-political-elites/

Mouffe, C. (2005), *The Democratic Paradox*. London: Verso.

Open Arab Internet (2009), *Morocco: High Price for Freedom*. Retrieved from www.openarab.net/en/node/364. Accessed 19 November 2018.

Organization for Economic Cooperation & Development (2018), *Digital Government Review of Morocco: Laying the Foundations for the Digital Transformation of the Public Sector in Morocco*. OECD Digital Government Studies. Paris: OECD Publishing. doi:10.1787/9789264298729-en

Reporters Without Borders (2008), *Appeal Court Overturns Blogger's Conviction*. Retrieved from https://rsf.org/en/news/appeal-court-overturns-bloggers-conviction. Accessed 08 August 2020.

Reporters Without Borders (2019a), *Another Moroccan Journalist Subjected to Judicial Persecution*. Retrieved from https://rsf.org/en/news/another-moroccan-journalist-subjected-judicial-persecution. Accessed 11 November 2019.

Reporters Without Borders (2019b), *Growing Judicial Harassment*. Retrieved from https://rsf.org/en/morocco-western-sahara. Accessed 13 November 2019.

Sadiki, L. (2004), *The Search for Arab Democracy: Discourses and Counter-discourses*. New York: Columbia University Press.

Salem, F. (2017), Social Media and the Internet of Things: Towards Data-driven Policymaking in the Arab World. *Arab Social Media Report*. Retrieved from www.mbrsg.ae/getattachment/1383b88a-6eb9-476a-bae4-61903688099b/Arab-Social-Media-Report-2017. Accessed 27 November 2018.

Salime, Z. (2012), A New Feminism? Gender Dynamics in Morocco's February 20th Movement. *Journal of International Women's Studies*, 13(5), pp. 101–114. Retrieved from http://vc.bridgew.edu/jiws/vol13/iss5/11. Accessed 13 October 2018.

Sater, J. (2002), The Dynamics of State and Civil Society in Morocco. *The Journal of North African Studies*, 7(3), pp. 101–118 doi:10.1080/13629380208718476

Skalli, L. H. (2014), Young Women and Social Media against Sexual Harassment in North Africa. *The Journal of North African Studies*, 19(2), pp. 244–258. doi:10.1080/13629387.2013.858034

Spadola, E. (2017), Justice and/or Development: The Rif Protest Movement and the Neoliberal Promise. *Third World Resurgence*, (326/327) (October/November), pp. 60–63. Retrieved from www.twn.my/title2/resurgence/2017/326-327/world5.htm. Accessed 14 October 2018.

Sutherland, E. (2007), *Unbundling Local Loops: Global Experiences*. Learning Information Networking and Knowledge Centre (LINK). Retrieved from http://link.wits.ac.za/papers/LINK.pdf. Accessed 10 September 2018.

The United Nations Educational, Scientific and Cultural Organization (UNESCO) (2018), *Stratégie Maroc Digital 2020*. Retrieved from https://en.unesco.org/creativity/periodic-reports/measures/strategie-maroc-digital-2020. Accessed 16 September 2019.

Wheeler, D. (2009), Internet Use and Political Identity in the Arab World. In A. Chadwick and P. Howard (eds.), *Routledge Handbook of Internet Politics*. Oxford and New York: Routledge, pp. 305–320.

Willis, M. (2006), Containing Radicalism through the Political Process in North Africa. *Mediterranean Politics*, 11(2), pp. 137–150. doi:10.1080/13629390600682859

Wilson, E. (2004), *The Information Revolution, and Developing Countries*. Cambridge, MA: MIT Press.

WomanChoufouch, Premier mouvement féministe contre le harcèlement sexuel au Maroc (n.d.), Retrieved from www.facebook.com/WomanChoufouch-105487879580033. Accessed 2 October 2018.

World Bank Group (2016), *Broadband: The Platform of the Digital Economy and a Critical Development Challenge for Morocco*. Retrieved from http://documents.worldbank.org/curated/en/547301493384118940/Broadband-the-platform-of-the-digital-economy-and-a-critical-development-challenge-for-Morocco. Accessed 25 October 2018.

World Economic Forum (2016), *The Global Information Technology Report 2016: Innovating in the Digital Economy*. The World Economic Forum and INSEAD, Geneva. Retrieved from http://www3.weforum.org/docs/GITR2016/WEF_GITR_Full_Report.pdf

Zaid, B. (2016), Internet and Democracy in Morocco: A Force for Change and an Instrument for Repression. *Global Media & Communication*, 1(18), pp. 1–19. doi:10.1177/1742766515626826

Oman

20

MASS MEDIA FOR DEVELOPMENT – THE MEDIA IN THE SULTANATE OF OMAN

Abdullah K. Al-Kindi

Introduction

Oman is located in the southwestern part of the Arabian Peninsula, and it has land borders with the United Arab Emirates on the northwest, with Saudi Arabia from the west, and with the Republic of Yemen from the southwest. It has maritime borders with the Republic of Pakistan and the Islamic Republic of Iran. The total area of the Sultanate is 309.9 square kilometers. The sultanate is also geographically characterized by a long coastline reaching approximately 1,700 kilometers (Economic Demographic Atlas, 2018).

This geopolitical status of the sultanate in the contemporary period is very much related and linked to historical heritage and civilization. Some historians assert that the reference to Oman first appeared in Roman sources between the third century BC and the second century AD and was referred to as OMANA (Ministry of Heritage and Culture, 2013: 2557–2568). Its geographic position enabled Oman to engage from the third century BC with several countries and civilizations, most notably Persia, Mesopotamia, Greece, the Romans, China, India, and several neighboring Arab countries (Ministry of Heritage and Culture, 2013: 2566–2568).

In the 18th century, the Omani state grew to encompass an empire that included countries and regions from the Indian peninsula and East and Central Africa. Starting in 1835 during the rule of Sayyid Said bin Sultan (1797–1856), the Omani empire had two capitals: Muscat and Zanzibar (Marefa.org, 2019a). After the death of Sayyid Said in 1856, the empire began to split mainly because of European colonial rivalry on management and resources (Al-Qasimi, 2015).

The contemporary Omani renaissance is linked to the beginning of the rule of Sultan Qaboos bin Said starting on 23 July 1970, succeeding his father Sultan Said bin Taimur (1910–1972), who ruled the sultanate from 1932 to 1970 (Marefa.org, 2019b). Sultan Qaboos (1940–2020) worked since the beginning of his rule on a comprehensive development project in accordance with specific plans drawn up by various institutions, with new plans created every five years, starting from 1976.

In 1996, the sultanate announced its "Oman Vision 2020" with the main objective and slogan "transforming into a sustainable and diversified economy." In early 2020, a new long-term vision will be implemented – "Oman Vision 2040" – focusing on national priorities such as education and research, health, citizenship and identity, social protection, economic diversification, financial sustainability, private sector, investment, and international cooperation, and other priorities (Supreme Council for Planning, 2019).

Another important development in contemporary Oman was the emergence and development of parliament institutions starting with an establishment of the Advisory Council in 1981. The Omani parliament gradually evolved when the Shura Council established in 1991, whose members are fully elected by the people. On 27 October 2019, a total of 87 members of the Shura Council were fully elected for the ninth Shura term. The other parliamentary body under the Oman Council is the State Council, in which members are appointed by the government. In parliamentary life, municipal councils have existed since 2011 in various governorates of the sultanate. Half the members of these councils are elected, while the other half represent state institutions.

The language of the state is Arabic, but English is widely used in the private sector and in international schools. Oman is culturally diverse; its citizens use several languages. Some residents of northern Oman, especially in the capital Muscat, speak the Swahili language they inherited from their ancestors and relatives who lived in East Africa, especially in Zanzibar. Some residents in several areas of northern Oman also speak Baluchi, which entered Oman as a result of Oman's presence in Asia and the Indian Ocean since the 17th and 18th centuries, as well as other languages such as Zadjali and Sindhi (Al-Balushi, 2015: 9). People in Musandam Governorate speak the Shihi language. In the south of Oman, the population speaks other languages in addition to Arabic, such as Shahriyah, Jabaliya, Harsusia, and Btahriya (Al-Mashani, 2003). According to the latest statistics by the National Centre for Statistics and Information, the population of Oman is 4,676,161, of whom 53.3% are Omanis and 42.7% are foreigners (National Centre for Statistics & Information, 2019).

Contemporary Oman faces a political challenge in maintaining its stability and non-interference of regional and global powers in its internal affairs, especially as it is located in a region that was and is still politically inflamed for both internal and external reasons. It is enough to recall some of the direct conflicts in this region such as the Iraq–Iran war 1980–1988, the civil war in Yemen 1994, the liberation of Kuwait 1990–1991, the US–British campaign on Iraq 2003, and the war on Yemen from 2015 until today. This is in addition to the power struggles between some countries in this region and several world powers.

The emergence of Omani mass media

Omanis have practiced press journalism since the early 20th century; in 1911 the Omani writer, poet, and journalist Nasser bin Salim bin Adeem Al-Rawahi founded *Al-Najah* newspaper on the island of Zanzibar. The newspaper was an intellectual reflection of the Omani presence in East Africa and Zanzibar in particular. Omani early migrations to East Africa dated back to the 7th century when some Omani families and groups began to migrate to these areas (Qasim, 2000: 322). After *Al-Najah* newspaper, the Arab Association in Zanzibar founded *Al-Falaq* newspaper in 1929, to become the means of the association and its media arm in that island. The Arab Society in Zanzibar was a socio-political institution founded by Omani Arabs on the island in 1926 to achieve their political, social, and cultural goals.

Another Omani figure, Ahmad Bain Saif Al Kharousi, founded *Al-Murshid* newspaper in 1942. Then, Omani journalist Sayyid Saif bin Hamoud Al Said established *Al-Nahda* newspaper in 1951. In its first issue, the newspaper published a large picture of Sultan Said bin Taimur, who ruled Oman from 1932 to 1970, as a testimony to the relationship of Arab newspapers and journalists in Zanzibar and the Sultanate of Oman (Al-Kindi, 2004b: 72).

These newspapers consistently covered Omani affairs in that they published news from Oman, articles, and pictures that commented on issues and events occurring in Oman. One study pointed out that *Al-Falaq* and *Al-Nahda* newspapers reported heavily on Omani issues and topics in the period from 1939 to 1962, and Oman came third in the list of countries covered by the press in those two newspapers (Al-Kindi, 2004a: 86–88). Some of these newspapers continued to be published until the end of the Arab rule of the island of Zanzibar, which ended on 12 January 1964 (Qasim, 2000: 367).

On 30 July 1970, the first Omani radio station went on air, and shortly after, other mass media outlets such as newspapers, magazines, and television were launched gradually, as this chapter will show. The Omani press in contemporary Oman was launched on 28 January 1971 with the establishment of *Al-Watan*, the first Omani daily newspaper, owned by the private sector and still published today. The newspaper and other private magazines were printed at that time outside the sultanate because of the lack of printing possibilities available in that period. In 1972, *Oman* newspaper was founded as a government-owned daily newspaper with its printing facility, and in 1975, Oman's first English-language daily newspaper, *The Times of Oman*, was established. Official reports by the Omani Ministry of Information show that nearly 80 publications are published today in Oman, and governmental institutions own more than 50% of these publications, of which several are public relations publications (Ministry of Information, 2018: Unpublished Report). In total, there are seven daily newspapers published in Oman today, namely *Al-Watan* (1971), *Oman* (1972), *Times of Oman* in English (1975), *Oman Daily Observer* in English (1981), *Al-Shabiba* (1993), *Muscat Daily* in English (2009), and *Al-Roya* (2009). Only *Oman* and *Oman Daily Observer* are government-owned.

As for the broadcasting sector, it emerged in the 1970s. Radio broadcasting began on 30 July 1970, and the start was modest, with only 1 kilowatt of power and broadcasting to some areas of the capital Muscat (Al-Mashiaki, 2015: 32). The government was the sole investor and owner of this radio sector, but today the sector is witnessing tangible developments in terms of the number of radio stations, ownership patterns, and hours of broadcasting. As of 2019, there are 12 radio stations in Oman, of which four are English stations and one is bilingual (English and Arabic), while the rest provide programs only in Arabic. The oldest of these stations is General Radio Station 1 (set up in 1970) offering programs in Arabic and General Radio Station 2 (set up in 1975) which offers English-language content. The rest of stations were set up between 2003 and 2018, such as Youth Station (2003), Holy Quran (2006), Hala FM (2007), Hi FM in English (2008), Classic Music in Arabic and English (2010), Al-Wesaal Radio (2011), Merge Radio in English (2011), Muscat Radio (2017), Shabiba FM (2018), and Virgin Oman in English (2018). Of these, only General Radio 1 and 2, Youth Radio, Holy Quran, and Classic Music are governmentally owned, whereas the rest are privately owned. Thus, the private sector outperforms the government in the number of radio channels it owns. The private radio stations emerged as a result of the reforms of the Private Radio and Television Establishments Law of 2004. Private stations tend to offer features and general affairs content to attract the largest audiences.

Television broadcasting began in Oman in 1974, and the start was modest in terms of television coverage, broadcasting hours, and program quality. As of 2019, there are six TV channels in the sultanate: Oman TV (1974), Majan TV (2009), Sports TV (2013), Oman TV Live (2014), Culture TV (2015), and Al-Istiqama (2015), which is the only channel broadcasting in Arabic, Swahili, and Amazigh. Of these channels, only Majan TV and Al-Istiqama are privately owned, and they operate from outside Oman as, to our knowledge, they have not obtained a license to operate and broadcast from within the sultanate. Generally, private investors are reluctant to invest in new television channels due to the high operations costs required compared to the investments needed to set up radio stations.

As for the Internet and its related applications, it is today the most influential medium in the sultanate. Internet public usage began in Oman in 1997. According to some international statistics, the number of users was only 90,000 in 2000. In contrast, there were 3.7 million users in 2019, representing 77% of the total population of the sultanate. Facebook is very popular in Oman in terms of the number of users, with about 1.8 million users in 2019 (Digital, 2019).

Censorship and self-censorship

The mass media in the Sultanate of Oman can be described as allying with the government in content and orientation. The government controls media contents, and there is limited space for media to criticize public policies, official entities, or government projects. Any criticism by any media outlet may lead to direct or indirect penalties, including suspension. Media outlets can also receive instructions by various governmental entities to refrain from covering certain topics, and one recent example is "*Al-Zaman* Case" recorded in 2017, in which a daily newspaper launched an investigation entitled "Corruption in the Judiciary Sector." In 2016, *Al-Zaman* newspaper was suspended after publishing an article investigating an allegation of corruption among senior officials. Then, the case escalated in May 2017, when the Omani authorities blocked the website of the online magazine *Mowaten*, affiliated with *Al-Zaman* after the magazine moved to Britain to avoid the government's censorship. The public prosecutor brought charges against the daily newspaper, which ended with the Supreme Court ruling to permanently shut down the newspaper in October 2017 (Freedom House, 2018).

Official control over media content is not confined to state-owned media but can also be imposed on private outlets. To avoid clashes with the authorities, private outlets usually resort to self-censorship and they usually follow and adopt the practices of government-owned media. Thus, all media outlets tend to avoid covering certain topics that are deemed sensitive and which might cause negative reactions by that authority, which means Omani media are not wholly autonomous.

In terms of ownership, private outlets tend to outnumber the state-owned outlets, but the latter tend to provide specialized content; generally, state-owned media total 43 publications from the total of 80 publications in Oman (Ministry of Information, 2018), while the private sector owns more radio stations, or the total of seven, compared to five state-owned stations operated and supervised by the Omani General Authority for Radio and Television. As for the number of television stations, the state owns four channels, compared to only two privately owned, which means that there is still a huge potential for private investments in the broadcasting sector in Oman. The government's tight grip on the media sector extends to the journalism profession with strict regulations imposed on Omani and other foreign journalists in Oman. On the other hand, privately owned media have limited initiatives and investments in upgrading professional journalists' skills.

Regarding media policies, Omani media is regulated by a set of laws and regulations which will be discussed later in this chapter. On the other hand, there are no official media strategies and policies that could be considered a point of reference for media professionals in Oman, explaining the aims, principles, values, and mission of media strategy in the country. One positive initiative was the adoption of the Media Code of Conduct in 2017 by the Omani Journalists Association; this code aims to contribute to the development of the journalistic practices and environment while enhancing the journalists' and other media professionals' capabilities to equip them to produce better content. The practice of investigative journalism, however, is absent in Oman due to the aforementioned restrictions on media production.

Working in tandem with the state

The mass media in Oman are aligned to the policies and objectives of the political system, which is not a unique situation, as many other Arab countries suffer from similar restrictions. Traditionally, since the early beginnings of mass media in contemporary Oman, the government has supported the establishment of these media, both financially and morally, which ensured the continuity of those outlets. On the other hand, the state also controlled the media, directly and indirectly, to ensure that the media are aligned with the state's declared development goals. In conjunction with these goals, the Omani media are characterized as "development media," whose main function and purpose are to serve the state's development project and to emphasize their significance and the plan of action to reach those developmental goals.

Generally, governments of developing countries tend to use their media to promote their policies and consolidate their power. As such, media outlets, whether private or public, tend to cover public policies and projects positively. In Oman, media outlets are aligned to the state objectives as they tend to praise and positively cover the state's projects. The problem is not in the focus on developmental projects or the positive coverage of developmental policies per se; rather, the main concern here is how development is understood, interpreted, and promoted, whether in Oman or other developing countries.

In my view, there are two types of developmental media: one-sided developmental media and critical developmental media. In the first type, the focus is mainly on the governmental and official perspectives and their achievements in various fields, while the space given to comment on or criticize these achievements and activities is almost totally absent or allowed only to a very limited extent. In contrast, critical media dedicate more space to discuss development projects and the governments' achievements, offering ample opportunities, platform, and space to debate these projects and criticize them.

Different media theoretical frameworks are offering different typologies on media systems across the world, focusing on the media's alignment with the state policies, ownership patterns, and censorship, among other factors. There is, for instance, the classical "four theories of the press" written by Fred Siebert, Theodore Peterson, and Wilbur Schramm in 1963; these scholars identified four models of the press worldwide, namely (1) authoritarian, (2) libertarian, (3) social responsibility, and (4) Soviet-totalitarian (Nerone, 2018: 1). One more recent typology was published by Hallin and Mancini (2004) and covered 18 countries in North America and Europe, based on three types of media systems, namely (1) liberal model, (2) democratic-corporatist model, and (3) polarized-pluralist model (Hallin and Mancini, 2004: 11). In the Arab world, Farouk Abu Zeid (1986) presented an extensive study on media systems based on media laws and regulations in 16 Arab countries, including Oman. Abu Zeid's typology is based on three press systems, namely (1) authoritarian, (2) liberal, and (3) socialist. For Abu Zeid, although the media in the Arab world seem to fall under the authoritarian type, there was no clearly defined Arab press system; instead, there are mixed media systems in terms of practices and traits, or a blend of authoritarian, socialist, and sometimes liberal systems (Abu Zaid, 1986: 67).

In Oman, the mass media have been performing multiple political, social, and cultural functions, which in turn affect the relationship with the government upon which many outlets depend for their financial development and sustainability. At the beginning of the new political era in 1970, the first mass media, particularly radio, newspapers, and magazines, devoted most of their space and content to encourage citizens to embrace the new political system and support it because it was seen as totally different from and much more advanced than the previous regime and therefore was worth supporting and sustaining.

In addition, the Omani media have served as a political tool for the new political system in its war against the "communist" movement in the southern province of Dhofar, which was officially started on 9 June 1965 and ended in December 1975 (El-Rayyes, 2002: 122). Omani radio and the first Omani newspapers and magazines from 1970 to 1975 harnessed much of their potential to present the new political system's stance on the movement. In that early period, the media also focused on inviting Omanis living abroad to return home and use their potentials to serve their country.

The mass media in Oman continued such political functions, focusing mainly on supporting the political system and explaining the state's stance and policies on key internal and external issues. Oman's foreign policy principles also underpin this political function of Omani media as there are usually restrictions regarding certain political issues. Usually, the media evade debating certain political topics – especially regional ones – according to one of Oman's foreign policy principles, which stipulates non-interference in the others' internal affairs (Ministry of Foreign Affairs, Foreign Policy: 2019). Recently, for example, the mass media in Oman have been avoiding covering the developments of the Gulf Crisis and Qatar Boycott that officially started on 5 June 2017. Moreover, nearly all Omani media avoid providing details about the war on Yemen which began on 25 March 2015. One can argue that evading or ignoring such regional events goes beyond the idea of adhering to the entrenched principles of Omani foreign policy of non-interference because the long-term effect here is that media jeopardize their credibility and may lose the trust of their audiences as they continue to evade certain political issues.

From a social perspective, the mass media in Oman dedicated much coverage to social issues related to education and health. The Omani mass media called for the need to invest in education at various stages. As for health issues, the media have always been involved, from its inception, in various awareness campaigns related to infectious and chronic diseases and in many other campaigns related to reproductive health, among many others. The Omani mass media also see their role as supporting Omani businesses, particularly the small and mid-size enterprises, and the media usually reiterate the official policy calling for economic diversification, innovation, and new means to attracting international investment and encouraging local industries. Sports activities have also been covered extensively in Oman, especially regional activities. However, as mentioned earlier, the state's tight grip on the various media policies means that the space for criticizing, let alone debating, state policies is rather limited. Instead, Omani media see its primary function as providing positive coverage of the various state developmental projects, avoiding discussing any of these projects critically. One can argue that both media institutions and the state are culpable because media institutions have not taken the initiative to claim their autonomy and declare a vision of their sector as independent of the state's control, able to provide more balanced coverage of local and regional affairs.

With the emergence of new media, the Internet, and social media platforms, this one-sided coverage has been challenged. Social media, in particular, have enabled ordinary individuals to present their views and positions on various local and regional issues, in clear defiance of the one-sided coverage of mass media inside the country. It is common now to read social media posts reflecting a variety of views about many political, social, cultural, health, and economic issues relevant to Oman. This should prompt Omani media outlets, whether public or private, to review their missions in this era of digitalization with its increased individualization and the emergence of amateur media content on social media platforms.

This is particularly important as 70% of Omani citizens are under the age of 30, and those young people do test the limit of their freedoms online despite the authorities' legal restrictions (Windecker, 2016: 166).

In conjunction with the World Press Freedom on 7 May 2012, Oman had its first online newspaper, *Al-Balad* Oman, owned by Turki Al-Balushi, but on 30 October 2016, *Al-Balad* Online announced on its website that it would close down (GCHR, 2016). It was known that *Al-Balad* showed solidarity with colleagues in *Al-Zaman*.

Media rules and regulations in Oman

The State Basic Law of Oman 1996, or the Constitution, includes several articles about journalism and the role of media. The constitution affirmed several fundamental freedoms and rights in the "Public Rights and Duties" chapter. Article (29) of the Constitution affirms that "freedom of opinion and speech expression by writing and other means of expression is guaranteed within the limits of the law."

Article 31 of the Constitution guarantees press and publication freedom as it stipulates, "freedom of the press, printing, and publishing is guaranteed under the conditions laid down by law and prohibits acts that lead to sedition, prejudice the security of the state or offend human dignity and rights." Despite this guarantee, however, it can be argued that these rules still need to be revisited and reviewed when drafting future laws governing journalism and media in Oman, especially as some laws regulating journalism were dated even before the constitution.

The Ministry of Information is the key official entity in regulating journalism and media in Oman. It organizes and supervises public and private publications, as well as state and private radio stations and television channels. The ministry also owns and operates two daily newspapers; *Oman Daily* and *Oman Daily Observer*, a cultural quarterly magazine, *Nizwa*, as well as Oman News Agency (ONA), which is the official news agency and news source in Oman. ONA was set up on 29 May 1986. It is regarded as the main source of domestic news, and most of its staff are Omanis. In 1997, ONA, *Oman* newspaper, and *Oman Daily Observer* were run under single management renamed as Oman Establishment for Press, Publication, and Advertising (OEPPA) (Al-Hasani, 2003: 59). OEPPA was founded by a Royal Decree and is considered one of the largest media houses in Oman.

The Ministry of Information works within the framework of two main pieces of legislation, namely the Press and Publications Law (1984) and the Private Radio and Television Establishments Law (2004). The Press and Publications Law 1984 consists of six sections: Licenses, Supervision and Liability, Censorship, Prohibitions, Penalties, and the Periodicals and Publications Committee. It can be said that the section on the prohibitions is one of the most important sections of this law. In this section, several topics are identified and the press and media cannot tackle, debate, or discuss them; these topics include criticism of the sultan or any of the royal family members, state internal or external security affairs, damage to the national currency or influencing the economic policies of the state, investigations, and prosecutions deemed harmful to individuals' reputation, secrets of private or family affairs, and misleading or unauthorized advertisements by any entity.

If seen from a positive perspective, such prohibitions may help journalists and media professionals avoid dealing with such topics, but conversely, many of those topics covered by the press and other media outlets overlap with the prohibited topics, and therefore journalists and media professionals are always cautious to ensure that they avoid covering prohibited themes, even if it is sometimes difficult to discern these themes. In addition to those prohibitions, there is another important and problematic article which states that the mass media should avoid publishing about any additional topic prohibited specifically by the minister of information. This means that the Ministry of Information generally, and the minister of information specifically, has unlimited power to control media coverage in the sultanate. Thus, the law imposes censorship on media professionals, while the latter may resort to self-censorship to avoid being subjected to state penalties in the name of public interest. Such penalties and prohibitions are usually justified by the need to maintain the political status quo and hence stability, maintaining the public order, protecting the principles of Islam, protecting national security, as well as protecting personal and family life and avoiding disinformation and propaganda.

The state monitoring can apply its censorship in any of the following three stages of media practice: firstly, there is the pre-print stage where Article (10) of the Press and Publications Law stipulates that, before the print, the press must deposit five copies of the publication with the Ministry of Information. Then there is the after-print stage, as the law stipulates that once a newspaper or publication has been published, five copies of it should be deposited with the Ministry of Information (Article 50 of the Press and Publications Law, 1984). The third stage relates to the distribution and circulation of publications within the sultanate; Article (20) of the Press and Publications Law indicates that each publishing house should deposit five copies from the publication, including imported titles, to the Ministry of Information, and Article (21) of the same law prohibits importing of any publications that are deemed to violate the public morals, as well as prohibiting its circulation in the sultanate.

Mass media in Oman is under administrative and legal supervision, led mainly by the Ministry of Information through a set of laws, as well as several administrative instructions and guidelines dealing with the press and media content, of both private and state-owned media. From an administrative perspective, the Ministry of Information in the Sultanate of Oman depends on its daily supervision of journalism and media content via several committees and directorates affiliated to the ministry such as the Committee of Periodicals and Publication, as stipulated in the Press and Publications Law, and the General Directorate of Information. The General Directorate of Information conducts daily monitoring of the press and broadcasting media content to ensure that they comply with the said laws and regulations. According to the Press and Publications Law of 1984, the Committee of Periodicals and Publication handles all matters relating to journalists, journalism practices, and, in principle, it guarantees the journalists' rights and freedoms. The law states the following roles for this committee: firstly, it should protect the journalistic work; secondly, it should ensure journalists' rights; it should also hold journalists accountable while imposing penalties in cases of legal breaches; it should coordinate between different press institutions and assist such institutions to regularly improve their professional standards.

The Ministry of Information uses the "Instructions and Guidelines" as an administrative tool for exercising censorship of media contents. The Ministry continuously sends such instructions and guidelines to media outlets identifying topics that should not be addressed or exposed to media coverage. A previous study examined the impact of these instructions on the journalistic work in Oman and it summarized it as follows,

> these instructions give all or most official institutions and government entities, a chance to monitor the press materials that are published about them, and then constantly control their images that are presented by the local media. Such opportunity helps official institutions and authorities to impose their conditions and perceptions on the media.
> *(Al-Kindi, 2004a: 142)*

It can be argued that most of these administrative instructions negatively affect the work of the press and broadcasting media as they promote negative self-censorship, where the journalists avoid dealing with topics prohibited by such administrative instructions and guidelines, to avoid any administrative or legal penalty. The existence of these instructions and guidelines deprives the work of journalists and media professionals of taking new initiatives in their coverage or attempt to debate acute problems. Indeed, the law grants the Committee of Periodicals and Publications the right to punish any journalist or media establishment. However, as this law has become outdated and impractical, many journalists and media outlets have recently challenged it and raised the matters in courts.

The restrictions imposed by the 1984 Press and Publications Law do not only hamper journalists' initiatives and need for autonomy, but they also open the door for many international institutions and media think tanks to criticize the government in Oman and/or the Omani media practices, as well as media policies. Therefore, keeping such laws or even parts of them that are no longer effective will only increase the criticism leveled at the government of Oman when it comes to the state's record of ensuring media freedoms.

Finally, another important law in regulating the media in Oman is the Private Radio and Television Establishments Law issued in 2004. This law opened the way for the private sector to invest in the broadcasting sector of radio in Oman, which was previously monopolized by the government. The law consists of six chapters, and some of its most important articles stipulate that journalists and media outlets can contest decisions related to violations of the law in Omani courts. This is in contrast to the 1984 law which imposed penalties through administrative entities and which were not to be contested later in courts. The Private Radio and Television Establishments Law in Oman 2004 stressed the need for radio and television establishments to be formed as shareholding companies owned by Omani citizens. The law also referred to several media policies that should be observed and adhered to by private radio and television channels, including the respect of individual privacy, maintaining public order and morals, highlighting the Omani heritage, ensuring compatibility of broadcasting programs with the specific age groups targeted by their content, avoiding any incitement for violence or sectarianism, keeping pace with the scientific and artistic developments in Oman, and respecting intellectual property rights.

Conclusion

This chapter provided a panoramic overview of the history and development of the mass media in Oman, focusing on the contemporary period, which commenced in 1970. The media was – and still is – an integral part of the political system and one of its tools aiming to serve the state's developmental projects. Media always promotes and documents such projects and calls for maintaining this pace of development for the benefit of both the present and future generations. The Omani media, therefore, refrain from debating or criticizing any such projects, focusing instead on their benefits.

The mass media in Oman then adopts a unilateral approach in meeting their responsibilities towards the audiences. This approach is directed and influenced by the government's regulations and policies, not to mention that the government owns, operates, manages, and supervises several media institutions. Although private media ownership is granted, such private outlets hardly disagree with or defy the media policies stipulated by the state.

On a positive note, the new and social media have opened the way for the Omani audiences to provide amateur content different from that provided by the mass media. Such amateur content does not follow state regulations or policies, which may push the limits of mass media outlets in the future.

References

Abu Zaid, Farooq (1986), *Press Systems in the Arab World*. Cairo: Book World.

Al-Balushi, Khalid (2015), *Multiculturalism in Oman: Its Foundations and Problems*. Nizwa Book, No. 28. Oman Institution for Press, Publishing and Advertisement, Ministry of Information: Muscat.

Al-Hasani, Abdulmonam (2003), *Influences on Media Content: Domestic News Production Processes at Four Omani Print News Organisations*. Unpublished PhD thesis submitted at the University of Leicester, UK.

Al-Kindi, Abdullah (2004a), Freedom of Mass Communication in Oman: Analysis of Publication Laws and Media Instructions. *Journal of Human Sciences*, University of Bahrain, (9), pp. 112, 177.

Al-Kindi, Abdullah (2004b), The Beginnings of the Omani Press in Zanzibar. *The Arab Journal of Human Sciences*. Kuwait University, (88) (Fall), pp. 47–110.

Al-Mashani, Mohammed (2003), *Dhofar Hemiari Contemporary Tongue: Survey Comparison Study*. Muscat: Oman Studies Center, Sultan Qaboos University, p. 55.

Al-Mashiaki, Mohammed (2015), *Media in the Gulf: Current and Future*. Al-Ain, UAE: Al-Falah Books for Publishing and Circulation.

Al-Qasimi, S. (2015), *Dividing the Omani Empire 1856–1862*. 6th edition. Al-Sharjah, UAE: Al-Qasimi Publications.

Digital 2019: Oman (2019), Retrieved from https://datareportal.com/reports/digital-2019-oman. Accessed 15 September 2019.

Economic Demographic Atlas (2018), Retrieved from https://ncsi.gov.om/Elibrary/LibraryContentDoc/bar_Economic demographic atlas. pdf. Accessed 15 September 2019.

El-Rayyes, Riad (2002), *Dhofar The Political & Military Struggle in the Gulf (1970–1976)*. Riad El-Rayyes Books: Beirut.

Freedom House (2018), *Oman*. Washington, DC: Freedom House. Retrieved from https://freedomhouse.org/print/50102

GCHR (2016), Oman: "Al-Balad" says Farewell to Readers and Stops Publishing. *The Gulf Centre for Human Rights (GCHR)*, 31 October. Retrieved from www.gc4hr.org/news/view/1413

Hallin, D. C., and Mancini, P. (2004), *Comparing Media Systems*. Cambridge: Cambridge University Press.

Marefa (2019a), *Said bin Sultan*. Retrieved from www.marefa.org. Accessed 20 September 2019.

Marefa (2019b), *Said bin Taimur*. Retrieved from www.marefa.org. Accessed 20 September 2019.

Ministry of Foreign Affairs (2019), *Foreign Policy*. Retrieved from www.mofa.gov.om/. Accessed 20 October 2019.

Ministry of Heritage and Culture (2013), *The Omani Encyclopedia*. Vol. VII. Muscat: Ministry of Heritage and Culture.

Ministry of Information (1984), *Press and Publications Law*. Retrieved from www.omaninfo.om/files/Rules/2.pdf. Accessed 10 November 2019.

Ministry of Information (2004), *Private Radio and Television Institutions Law*. Retrieved from www.oman info.om/files/Rules/3.pdf. Accessed 10 November 2019.

Ministry of Information (2018), *List of Periodicals in the Sultanate of Oman*. Unpublished report. Muscat: Sultanate of Oman.

National Center for Statistics & Information (2019), *Population Clock*. Retrieved from https://ncsi.gov.om. Accessed 25 October 2019.

Nerone, John (2018), Four Theories of the Press. In *Oxford Research Encyclopaedia of Communication*. Oxford: Oxford University Press.

Supreme Council for Planning (2019), *Oman Vision 2040*. Retrieved from https://www/scp.gov.om

Windecker, Gidon (2016), Virtual Space and the Rise of the Public Sphere: Social Media in the Sultanate of Oman. A published conference paper, Gulf Research Meeting 2016, Cambridge, United Kingdom, 15–19 August. doi:10.3929/ethz-b-000339875

Zakariya, Qasim (2000), *Albosaid State from its Establishment to the End of its Rule in Zanzibar and the Beginning of its New Era in Oman (1741–1970)*. Abu Dhabi, UAE: Zayed Centre for Heritage and History.

Palestine

21

PALESTINIAN MEDIA BETWEEN PARTISANSHIP AND PROPAGANDA

Ibrahim Natil and Bahjat Abuzanouna

The development of the Palestinian press

During the early decades of the 20th century, there were a few newspapers in major urban areas such as Jerusalem and Jaffa, including *Filisteen, al-Karmel*, and *al-Difaa*; during that time, Palestinian newspapers reached other Arab countries and the newspapers from neighboring countries were also available in Palestine (Jamal, 2009: 40). Under the British Mandate (1920–1948), there were 41 publications in Arabic such as *al-Ittihad* set up in 1944 as the voice of the Communist Party (Arrar, 2016: 20). In the wake of the 1948 war, however, the Palestinians lost their cultural institutions and many newspapers ceased publication, except *al-Ittihad*, which had a limited influence (Jamal, 2009: 40–41).

The Israeli authorities, such as the Arab Unit in the General Federation of Labor, set up various media projects to reach out to the Palestinian population such as the daily *al-Youm* (in 1948) out of the offices of the daily *Filisteen* after it ceased publication. Other outlets included the biweekly *al-Youm* for children, and *al-Hadaf* (monthly) and *Liqaa* (quarterly). The Arab Unit and the Information Center at the prime minister's office invested the money of the Islamic Endowment (Waqf) in such publications in Arabic as "services to the community" (Jamal, 2009: 42–43). Another outlet set up by the Israeli authorities was *al-Anbaa*, which closed down in 1968 (Arrar, 2016: 26–27).

Between the wars of 1948 and 1967, the Palestinian press witnessed a notable revival thanks to the increasing number of literate Palestinians; during that time, the West Bank was part of Jordan while Gaza was administered by Egypt (Arrar, 2016: 23–25). Outlets launched at that time included *al-Jihad* and *al-Manar* in addition to 18 other publications in Jerusalem, Ramallah, and Amman, but the Jordanian authorities closed down most of the Palestinian newspapers in 1966 and merged them in two of its official press houses, *al-Quds* and *Addostour*. Meanwhile, in Gaza, several outlets were also launched such as the weeklies *Gaza* set up by Kamal Eddin Abu Shaban and which ran from 1950 until 1964, in addition to *al-Saraha* (ran between 1952 and 1963) and the first daily *al-Tahrir* (1958) (Abdelal, 2016: 33). Other newspapers launched by Palestinians included *al-Shaab* (1970), *al-Fajr* (1972), *al-Darb* (1985), and *al-Wahda* (1982), and they were concentrated in the West Bank (Arrar, 2016: 27). In Gaza, however, there were limited press activities and most of the publications were affiliated to the Islamic university and professional syndicates (Arrar, 2016: 160). The partisan press flourished since the late 1980s and formed a strong competition to *al-Ittihad* and the subsequent influence of the Communist Party in the Palestinian society while increasing the influence of the Islamic and national movements which backed the new publications (Jamal and Awaisi, 2011: 19). Other outlets included the weeklies *Assennara* (1983), *Kul al-Arab* (1987), *Panorama* (1988), *al-Midan* (1994), *al-Ain* (1999), and *al-Akhbar*, set up in 2001 (Jamal, 2009: 65–70). Most of those publications were private enterprises, but many of them did not last long due to limited circulation (Jamal, 2009: 69). Other outlets included partisan newspapers such as *al-Watan*, set up in 1985 by the Progressive List of Peace, which ceased in 1993, mainly because the PLP failed to enter the Knesset in the 1992 elections (Jamal, 2009: 66). Generally, Palestinians employed the press as a strategy of struggle against the Israeli military, which was chiefly responsible for enforcing these restrictions and closely resembled the pre-democratic authoritarian model from 1967 to 1993 (Nossek and Rinnawi, 2003: 184).

Moreover, several Palestinian publications appeared outside Palestine, based primarily in other Arab countries, and some were also founded in Cyprus, London, and Paris. Needless to say, those based in Arab countries such as Jordan, Syria, and Libya faced the risk of closure when they published views opposing the ruling regimes; moreover, divisions within the Palestinian groups were reflected in each group's coverage of the Palestinian issue and how they saw it and the solution to their problem (Abdelal, 2016: 36). Also, between 1948 and 1967, individual Palestinian journalists had to leave Palestine and work abroad. Between the 1970s and 1990s, however, it was noted that many Palestinian outlets moved altogether outside Palestine and chose to be based in Europe, particularly Cyprus, London, and Paris (Abu Zeid, 1993: 271). One such outlet was *Sho'un al-Saa'*, set up in 1979 in London as a political Arab magazine; it published articles defending the Palestinian Liberation Organization (PLO) against the Arab regimes' policies, which led several Arab countries to ban the magazine from circulation inside their territories (ibid.: 273). Another outlet was *al-Ofouq* set up in 1981 in Cyprus and which also defended the PLO, in addition to the weekly *al-Bilad* and *al-Arab* magazine, both set up in 1984 in Cyprus. Perhaps the most famous Palestinian émigré outlet was *al-Quds al-Arabi*, set up in London in April 1989, as the international edition of *al-Quds* issued in Jerusalem in 1951. The émigré paper was led by Abdel Bari Atwan, who used to work for the Saudi-funded *al-Sharq al-Awsat* also based in London; Atwan argued that *al-Quds al-Arabi* began as a Palestinian outlet expressing Palestinian views but ended up being a pan-Arab paper focusing on pan-Arab issues, "the Palestinian readers would prefer to read about Palestine in an Arab newspaper, not a Palestinian one," he said (cited in Abu Zeid, 1993: 283). Atwan also argued that *al-Quds al-Arabi* was an objective outlet, at least when he was its editor-in-chief, evidenced, as he said, by the various invitations he received from Western news media for him to appear as an expert commenting on important Arab events (Abu Zeid, 1993: 284). This implies that the yardstick of measuring objectivity is based on Western criteria in identifying the messages and guests to comment on the news, or it may also indicate an implicit hierarchy of media institutions in which the top places are occupied by most Western institutions, whose claimed credibility extends to the pundits appearing in their coverage (Mellor, 2007: 68).

Following the Oslo Accords and the establishment of the Palestinian Authority (PA), several new outlets emerged, including dailies such as *al-Watan*, which is affiliated with Hamas, and *al-Istiqlal* (1995), affiliated with the Islamic Jihad (Arrar, 2016: 29). Under the PA, the Palestinian media have been used as a tool for state building with new dailies launched in 1994, namely *al-Hayat al-Jadida* (New Life) and *al-Ayyam* newspapers. The former served as the official voice of the PA and the late President Yasser Arafat, and it was led by the Fatah leader Nabil Amro; the latter daily was a semi-official daily headed by Akram Haniya (Abdelal, 2016: 40). Another daily, *Filisteen*, was launched as an independent newspaper, and one of its editors confirmed that it belonged to a private enterprise called Al-Wasat for Media and Publishing; as such, the daily's editors refused to classify the newspaper as part of Hamas's media (Abdelal, 2016: 147). The Israeli authorities classify *Filisteen* as part of Hamas's media, referring to the 50 staff members who were "counted as Hamas" (ibid.). The daily's discourse is characterized by its acceptance of Hamas's government in Gaza, so it hardly referred to it as an illegitimate government or a de facto one; nor does it refer to it as "Hamas government"; the daily is banned in the PA in the West Bank and in return Hamas banned in Gaza the three dailies belonging to Fatah and the PA (Abdelal, 2016: 147).

The development of Palestinian broadcasting

Broadcasting began in Palestine prior to the establishment of the state of Israel. For several decades, the Palestinian media suffered from various forms of control and mandates in which suppression and repression were the main characteristics. After Palestine became a British Mandate, the British tried to allow some freedom of expression manifested in the realms of education and culture. However, after the outbreak of the Second World War in 1939, Britain found itself obliged to establish a government-run radio station in 1940 to publicize its policies; they named it *Al-Sharq Al-Adna* (Near East Radio) and appointed a British officer as its director (Abu Shanab, 2001).

The station started broadcasting in 1941 from Jenin (in the West Bank) and subsequently moved to Jaffa. Among its tasks was to re-establish the Palestinian–British relationship which had been spoilt because of the government repression of the Palestinians as a reaction to the disturbances in 1939. The radio also worked on enhancing Palestinian confidence in the government and its commitment to the development of Palestinian society. The government adopted Arabic as an official language for broadcasting and appointed Palestinian journalists in various posts. Cultural programs were given prominence in the station, granting a platform for poets, writers, and artists to introduce their work to the Palestinian people (Suleiman, 2009). However, with the outbreak of the 1948 war between Jewish and Arab Palestinians, the station had to stop broadcasting. According to Abu Shanab (2001), the establishment of radio in Gaza city was a mark of the influential political struggle against the newly formed state of Israel. Broadcasting equipment was brought from Egypt and installed in Gaza city, but by the 1967 war, these attempts had been unsuccessful. By that time, Gazan villagers were gathering in coffee shops or homes to listen to international radio broadcasts.

In 1936, the radio station, Jerusalem Calling, started broadcasting from Jerusalem. The famous Palestinian poet Ibrahim Toqan was the manager of the station and was later replaced by the Palestinian politician Ajaj Nwaihed, who was instrumental in providing a powerful platform for many Arab writers and artists. The station broadcasted a news bulletin in Arabic, English, and Hebrew, in addition to other programs. During the 1948 war between Israel and Arab Palestinians when Israel occupied West Jerusalem, the station was attacked several times, forcing it to move its office from Jerusalem to Ramallah (in the West Bank). It continued to broadcast there until Jordan annexed the West Bank and the station moved to Jordan (Abu Shanab, 2001). Moreover, the Egyptian "Voice of the Arabs" radio broadcasts were available to Palestinians, but with the decline of Nasserism, Jordanian broadcasting (radio and television) became the primary Arab source of programming to Palestinians (Jamal, 2009: 53). In the 1950s, attempts were made to establish Eza'at Falastin station (Palestinian Broadcast) and to be related to Voice of the Arabs radio station in Egypt, but it was later replaced by the Palestine Radio Program broadcast daily from Cairo through the Egyptian Voice of the Arabs station. Radio was a particularly effective tool for communication with the Palestinian population – most of whom were illiterate. The medium also contributed to the consolidation of the Palestinian national heritage until the Israeli occupation. On 7 June 1967, Israel occupied the remaining 22% of historical Palestine, areas known today as the Gaza Strip and the West Bank, which includes Jerusalem. Although the Israeli military administration exercised military control over the population, it allowed Palestinians to exercise their religious rights (Natil, 2014).

A shifting political landscape, however, emerged and developed after the Oslo interim agreement signed between Israel and the PLO, which led to the establishment of a Palestinian Authority in the Gaza Strip and the West Bank. This led to a new relationship between the PA, civil society, and media while adopting new regulations, rules, and laws, operating within PA's jurisdiction (Najjar, 1997). During the Oslo period (1993–2000), several broadcasting outlets were set up by small businesses, while the PA set up Voice of Palestine radio station and Palestine TV in 1994. Western donors also provided funding for new outlets and media content (Bishara, 2010).

Post-1994, a few radio stations and an official Palestinian Broadcasting Corporation (PBC) were also launched (Jamal, 2004: 130). Among the radio stations, there are Gaza FM, Palestine Radio, Wattan FM, Al Quds Radio, Al Aqsa Radio, Houria FM, and Radio Bethlehem. The PBC, controlled by the PA in the West Bank, operates Voice of Palestine, while Hamas controls Al Aqsa radio in Gaza. As for television, the PBC controls Palestine TV, while Hamas controls Al-Aqsa TV; private channels include Al Quds Educational TV and Watan TV. Moreover, Palestine News Agency (Wafa) is the official agency providing news in Arabic, English, French, and Hebrew; in addition to Maan News Agency, which is a private agency set up with Dutch and Danish funding (BBC, 2018).

This political landscape, with all its complexity, has impacted on the broadcasting sector in the OPT as the relationship between the state, political groups, and civil society actors are entirely controlled by surveillance, monitoring, intimidation and violence, and even manipulation on the part of Israel, while the PA declares its aim to employ broadcasting as a tool to promote the Palestinian cause to end the Israeli occupation and contribute to "state building" by engaging the following actors.

The state

In 1994, the PA was established in the OPT according to the interim Oslo agreement, signed between Israel and PLO in September 1993. The Palestinian leader, Yasser Arafat, became the head of PA and started to establish national institutions in the Gaza Strip and the West Bank (Natil, 2015). In July 1994, Arafat established the PBC, operating mainly the Palestine TV channel and Palestine Radio to communicate the PA's political ideologies to the Palestinian citizens in the OPT. The PBC aimed at spreading the message of solidarity and creating harmony among the Palestinian citizens ahead of establishing a Palestinian state.

The PBC was directed and centralized in the hands of the state leaders. Arafat and his close loyalists controlled all official Palestinian institutions, prevailing over every level of decision-making by appointing people loyal to him in central and sensitive positions. Arafat was aware of the influence of the mass media; for example, he hired Radwan Abu Ayyash, a Fatah activist who was the head of the Palestinian Journalist Association in the West Bank, to run the public radio station, "Voice of Palestine," in July 1994 (Abuzanouna, 2012: 46). Technically the PBC has been the mouthpiece of the PA and PLO, influenced by Arafat, who appointed the chief of operation, located at his compound in the Gaza Strip. In 1996, the television station started broadcasting and was run by Hisham Micki, another Arafat loyalist (Abuzanouna, 2012).

The current "broadcasting system" in the OPT is always challenged by a high level of political complexity, owing to the shifting landscape after the Oslo agreement in 1993. The Israeli occupation, however, still imposes its full control by implementing its military laws and procedures over the PA and the entire Palestinian population. The PBC followed "the developmental model" during the transitional phase in the nation-building process (McQuail, 1994), as is the case in many developing countries. This means that the PBC is expected to promote the declared national goals identified by the PA leadership, aiming to unify the Palestinian society. The PA maintains the right to intervene and directly control the broadcasting sector, which includes applying a mixed policy of censorship and subsidies (Caspi and Limor, 1999). There has been, however, a boom in the satellite television and radio stations outside the control of the PA media sector compounded with the challenge of several Palestinian groups establishing their local stations to express their views.

The third sector "NGOs"

The shifting political landscape created in response to the Oslo agreement has allowed numerous foreign donors to channel their donations to engage with and contribute to the Palestinian civil society and nongovernmental organizations (NGOs) promoting independent media (Abuzanouna, 2012). Numerous Palestinian elites established NGOs to cooperate with international organizations to promote the concepts of independent media based on the values of freedom of speech, free press, and protection of journalists. This sector, however, is dependent on international foreign aid. The capacity-building component is always given a top priority by both Palestinian and international NGOs. The NGO sector also cooperates with the private sector to promote these values, an integral part of state building (Natil, 2014). Society Voice Foundation (SVF), a Gaza-based NGO, for example, has contracted with Radio Alwan to run a weekly radio program since 2004; NGOs like SVF announce their mission as promoting the values of freedom of speech, despite the limitation and intervention imposed by the existing authorities (Amer, 2019).

Private sector

The shifting political landscape has also allowed the private sector to engage in the media market despite the very complex political and economic challenges in the OPT generally and the Gaza Strip particularly (Nossek and Rinnawi, 2003: 189). The first private channel was set up in Nablus in 1994, and it was followed by several other stations, of which some were illegal, driven by financial profit and depending on pirated content such as Egyptian movies and Syrian series (Tawil-Souri, 2007: 9). By 1996, there were 17 illegal stations and by 2000, there were 30 television stations; the West Bank, moreover, listed over 40 private stations in 2005, and many such stations depended on commercials for their revenues, but the second intifada (2000–2005) caused many economic damages and plummeting advertising revenues (Tawil-Souri, 2007: 14–18).

This sector has expanded in the West Bank, but it is nonexistent in the Gaza Strip, except for one radio station, called "Alwan" after the closure of "Ramttan Agency," which was involved in a subcontract to provide media services to Al Jazeera in the Gaza Strip. Several local NGOs cooperate with the private sector to produce and broadcast their programs about different issues including human rights, community peacebuilding, and women's empowerment.

The current large number of private television and radio stations may be seen as a reflection of the freedom of expression granted to the Palestinians under the PA, as the Ministry of

Information in OPT stated that these media outlets allow "people to express themselves in matters concerning their daily life. The authority should not monopolize information about cultural, intellectual, and political activities to deepen democracy and the public freedom and creates a large space for argumentation between different ideas" (Al-Bayader Assiyasi, 1997: 54). The reality, however, is that the PA controls most of the media sector, with the media functioning as a mouthpiece of the PA elite, who use and abuse it to present their views and defend their political agenda (Jamal, 2001).

Non-state broadcasting

This sector has emerged during the second Palestinian uprising when the peace process negotiation between the PA and Israel had failed in the summer of 2000. Since the second Palestinian uprising, this sector has been growing against the PA's political will and outside of its media control as more Palestinian political groups have established their radio and satellite television stations to spread their political ideologies while employing their loyalists. The weakness of the PA has encouraged groups like Hamas in particular to establish its broadcasting sector, including the launch of its own Al Aqsa Radio station. During the second uprising (2000–2004), Al Aqsa Radio station operated mainly to communicate Hamas's political ideology against the PA's policies and PA's security cooperation with Israel. To gain public support, the Islamic movement, Hamas, also launched its Al-Aqsa TV station in Gaza City in January 2006 (Abuzanouna, 2012: 46). This launch came a few days before the Palestinian legislative elections. The station reflected Hamas's views and it focuses only on the positive messages of the movement, which is listed as a terrorist organization by the US and Israel. Three weeks after the launch, the PA closed the station because it did not have the proper license to broadcast. The head of the station, Raed Abu Dayer, admitted to the Palestinian Centre for Human Rights that the station could not have the license because the Ministry of Information did not accept its application (PCHR, 2004). Hamas, however, has been a main political, business, and media rival to the PA until Hamas defeated the PA in the Palestinian elections on 20 January 2006, and it subsequently hurled its full military takeover of the Gaza Strip on 14 June 2007 (Natil, 2015).

Subsequently, Hamas controlled and closed down the PBC's offices in the Gaza Strip until October 2014. Hamas has already controlled the Gaza broadcasting sector and imposed its monitoring policy since June 2007. Consequently, the tensions have risen to the level of an armed conflict during which Hamas took over the PA's institutions in the Gaza Strip. This political conflict between Fatah and Hamas has also affected freedom of expression. Many Palestinian journalists and media entities in the Gaza Strip and the West Bank have been subjected to assault, and several radio and television stations as well as newspapers were attacked and saw their equipment confiscated (MADA, 2009).

The dispute between the two factions led the PA in the West Bank to ban Hamas's newspapers and radio stations; meanwhile, Hamas prohibited Fatah's newspapers and radio stations from operating in Gaza City. In addition, Hamas raided Palestine Television and confiscated its equipment. The Palestine Television office in Gaza city was taken over, while the Al-Aqsa television station continued broadcasting. This tension imposes a real opposition and threat to the PA's political ideology and communication strategy, and it contributes to deepening the Palestinian division between both entities in the Gaza Strip and the West Bank politically and geographically under different rules, laws, and regulations. Hamas's local broadcasting sector also permits the operations of other TV and radio stations that are not aligned to the PA's policy.

Laws and regulations

In a report published in 1999, the Committee to Protect Journalists (CPJ) concluded that the censorship and arrest of Palestinian journalists were practiced by Arafat and his allies (Bishara, 2010: 69–70). This is despite the fact that the Palestinian Basic Law, which was amended in 2003, ensures freedom of expression.

Despite the large number of private television and radio stations in the OPT, there were no broadcasting laws to manage its operations. There were plans to issue such laws, but they never materialized. The question of the spectrum and radio frequencies for the Palestinian territories is still negotiated between the PA and Israel. However, a small number of frequencies have been granted to the PA (Sakr, 2007). The other parties which condemned the negotiations with Israel are the Islamic parties, led by Hamas and Islamic Jihad, and these parties sought to own the media to mobilize the public and gain their support (Jamal, 2005).

The Palestinians usually watch TV via satellite dishes, which have become affordable despite the political battle over control of the airwaves. Indeed, even before the PA's advent and the establishment of television and radio stations, Palestinians were watching Jordanian, Israeli, and Egyptian programs (Kuttab, 1993). The PA barely established a public broadcasting service as the Israeli occupation restricted TV and radio stations during its occupation of the Palestinian territories, and restrictions were about the content allowed to be broadcast. Palestinian media were obliged to support the Oslo agreement to stabilize the relationship between the PA and Israel. Palestinian politicians took advantage of the growing media sector to promote their interests, particularly with the launch of media content supporting the Fatah party.

According to Abuzanouna (2012), human rights activists and organizations are aware of the two governments' control and negative action against journalists. They also argue that the two factions used their television channels to target human rights activists, and there have been attacks on several independent media outlets. They conclude that a review of Palestinian Press Law is acutely needed, and the government should ensure that the free flow of information to support democracy is safeguarded by the law. Legislation should be enacted to encourage media pluralism and prevent the concentration of media ownership by the government. Finally, the government should encourage media diversity to safeguard the public interest, as democracy and state building can only be achieved if the two political parties, Fatah and Hamas, end the internal division and stop using their media outlets as propaganda tools.

Since the PA is controlled by Fatah, and Fatah elites control Palestine Television as a governmental channel, this outlet can be regarded as a partisan channel. Fatah elites use the channel to respond to Hamas's actions, and they tend to show Hamas as the party which has betrayed the Palestinian cause by pursuing the power to further their ideological interests. On the other hand, Hamas depicts Fatah and the PA as the party that is selling out the Palestinian cause to Israel. The other smaller political parties have also tried to establish their media to provide an alternative source of information, but the two governments have been exerting control over these channels via censorship. In the times when the national television channel fails to provide the platform for diverse opinions, provide information for the public, or act as a watchdog to protect the public interests, then opposition media may be seen as a partial solution.

In summary, despite restrictions by the PA, Palestinian businessmen, political factions, and other groups were able to launch their TV and radio stations. Some of these stations were used as a platform to oppose the Oslo agreement and criticize the PA practices, while the PA sought to close many unauthorized stations. After the start of the second intifada in 2000, the PBC served as a tool of struggle against the Israeli occupation, offering extensive coverage of the Israeli invasion and attacks on Palestinians, which eventually led to the Israeli attack on the PBC and its correspondents (PCHR, 2002). Moreover, the emergence of satellite television broadcasting in the Arab region since the late 1990s, which has been accessible to the Palestinians, helped strengthen the Palestinian and Arab identity among Palestinians, although they remain equally connected to the Israeli media sphere (Jamal, 2009: 2). It is claimed that by the end of 2006, there were 33 TV stations and 32 radio stations in the West Bank as well as 12 radio stations and one TV station in Gaza (InterNews, 2006: 4). Usually, there are generally huge differences between the Palestinian journalists working in local outlets versus those working in satellite channels, in terms of income and working conditions, not to mention that those working in satellite channels had better access to information than did those working in local outlets (Jamal and Awaisi, 2011: 87).

Social and political functions of broadcasting

Both the PA and Hamas control the information disseminated by the media in their regions. Both authorities have the right to grant broadcasting licenses, and there is no independent system for media regulation (Jamal, 2003). The PA's control has curtailed the Palestinian media; the Palestinian president has the power over all public institutions, including mass media, and especially broadcasting. The control is manifested in the appointment of loyalists such as the head of the Palestinian Broadcasting Corporation, and even locating the PBC building within the compound of the president's office (Jamal, 2001). According to Jamal (2003), there is a clear relationship between the Palestinian elites and the media sector, where the elites not only control the process of state formation but also control the media messages geared to promote their interests and goals. Moreover, Jamal (2001) affirmed that even the Palestinian president has played a major role in constructing a bureaucratic regime, and he managed to intervene in all Palestinian institutions; in some respects, this situation is not dissimilar to the dynamics between media and the state in other Arab countries, many of which have authoritarian regimes (Lynch, 2006).

The two television channels, Palestine TV managed by the PA and Al-Aqsa TV managed by Hamas in the Gaza Strip, broadcast political talk shows, served to further the political agendas of the two groups so that the channels in effect function as a mouthpiece for the two movements. Al-Aqsa TV does not have an article referring to its being owned by Hamas, but it is generally known that the station is the main voice of Hamas; the deputy director of al-Aqsa, Mohammed Thuraiya, said in an interview that the channel "considers itself as the voice of resistance and its project" and that it was owned by Hamas and is based at the "geographical heart of the resistance," referring to the Gaza Strip (cited in Abdelal, 2016: 132). Needless to say, Al-Aqsa discourse usually aims to mobilize public opinion in Palestine for the idea of resistance (ibid.).

These television channels are not autonomous, as they avoid critiquing the local policies. The rise of private television has provided an opportunity, however limited, to the Palestinians to express their views, but the private and partisan television channels are not able to function as a fourth estate, and they do not provide credible information or promote democracy by encouraging tolerance among Palestinians, nor are they protecting human rights including freedom of expression. Instead, they tend to promote division and partisanship in Palestinian society. Originally, the private televisions channels aimed to promote the democratization process by functioning as a fourth estate monitoring the government, but, in reality, they contribute to the instability of OPT by providing a one-sided coverage. The two political factions are trying to manipulate the public and conceal information that could impact their influence. As a result, the political divisions have further polarized Palestinian public opinion. Thus, the internal division coupled with the Israeli occupation has disrupted any attempt to establish a democratic sphere in Palestine. Also, the factions' control of the two television channels, together with the censorship of other media channels, has resulted in the deterioration of performance by the Palestinian media. Moreover, it is difficult to practice independent journalism in the Palestinian territories as media institutions and journalists have to work under strict censorship coupled with other means of state harassment, especially when covering human rights violations. The conflict between journalists and the two governments over access to information has compromised the role of the media in providing the basis for democratic communication and participation in the political process. The television channels representing the two authorities – Hamas in the Gaza Strip and PLO in the West Bank – are not enabling the development of democracy in Palestine.

The audience survey conducted by Abuzanouna (2012) showed that Palestinians tend to favor Hamas strategy in the Gaza Strip while those who live in Fatah-controlled areas tend to favor Fatah policies in the West Bank; other groups criticized both governments. The same study, which included interviews with journalists, political analysts, human rights activists, and academics, argued that the political divisions and the lack of security arising from the Israeli occupation have made it difficult for journalists to practice their profession efficiently and effectively, not to mention that they have to endure censorship and self-censorship. In addition, the Israeli occupation and its operations have already prevented journalists from working freely, especially when covering violations committed against Palestinians. Moreover, the Israeli blockade prevents journalists from participating in international conferences and training opportunities. As Shahin (2010) argues, if the main television two channels were independent, it would benefit Palestinian communal interest, not just the factions' interest, and they would play a pivotal role in reconciliation and in reducing the Palestinian divisions.

There are around 300 journalism graduates each year, of which 50% are female, but such journalism programs usually lack resources and adequate textbooks; moreover, there are differences in terms of quality of programs and courses between universities which do not offer postgraduate programs save for the Islamic University in the Gaza Strip (UNESCO, 2014). The original Palestinian Journalists' Syndicate split into two sections: one in the West Bank and the other one in Gaza (UNESCO, 2014: 16). In Gaza, there is also the Palestinian press agency SAFA, led by Yasser Abu Heen, who refused to attribute the agency to Hamas, arguing that it was an independent institution, although the Israeli authorities claim that SAFA was created by Hamas (Abdelal, 2016: 148).

To sum up, the Palestinian media present an example of partisan media with the two television channels providing limited functions of democratic communication to their audiences. The PA treats Al-Aqsa television channel as opposition media, considering it to be the cause of discontent and disunity among Palestinians. In addition, they believe that the criticism it makes of the Palestinian Authority and Fatah threatens political stability. On the other hand, Al-Aqsa's supporters believe that the existence of the television channel is their only guarantee of freedom and democracy (Abuhashish, 2010). They think that it would be impossible to have democracy without such an opposition media channel, providing a platform for critics of the PA. The Palestinian authorities, in the West Bank and Gaza, do not promote community media either, but there is, however, a few radio stations catering to marginalized groups (UNESCO, 2014).

Conclusion

Since the Israeli occupation of the Palestinian territories, Israeli authorities have been imposing restrictions on journalists, censoring those who report anti-Israeli stories and arresting the ones who violate the occupation laws. Although the Palestinian media had played an important role in raising the Palestinian cause among other Arab nations, and indeed internationally, in its domestic context, it contributes to fueling the internal conflict and to the drift into a spiral of political division.

Despite the fragile political situation in the Palestinian territories, Al-Aqsa television declares its mission to act as a watchdog, monitoring and exposing the Palestinian Authority in relation to violations against human rights and freedoms, especially that Palestine Television as a governmental institution operates under a range of restrictions. In this ideological battle for power and privilege, the official and opposition media in Palestine reflect their respective party's position and broadcast partisan, and sometimes inflammatory, material rather than disseminate information and opinion, which would create a culture of tolerance and promote democratic pluralism. Such a partisan media environment blocks the establishment of democracy in an already fragile and fragmented polity.

It is also argued that this tension between the two main television channels can also ensure that each channel acts as a watchdog of their rival faction, and thus between them sufficient information is made accessible and the two platforms are sufficient for the public to express their views against each local government. Media in Palestine are either controlled directly by the two governments or indirectly via censorship. The law has also proved unable to safeguard their independence or the safety of journalists. The key factors required for independent media to flourish are not present, as in many transitional and post-conflict countries, leaving it vulnerable to power elites. In situations such as Palestine, where there is strong political control and little democracy, international NGOs have played an important role in promoting independent media and professional journalism by providing resources and training courses to build capacity and skills. The role of the Internet is also important as an alternative space or public sphere as a source of independent information. Projects supporting media development such as those of UNESCO or the Swedish International Development Cooperation Agency (SIDA) collaboration with Birzeit University have played a role in the Palestinian territories, which lack the basic tools to sustain a robust public sphere.

Instead, it was the perception that Palestine Television had been used as a tool for political manipulation and to mislead the public. In addition, because of its partiality, it was not upholding proper journalistic ethics, which meant it had no credibility and therefore could not function as a fourth estate. The media discourse used during times of political tension has further incited for conflict leading to violence and deepening internal divisions while completely ignoring professional journalism ethics. Such an adversarial discourse is negatively affecting the process of state building and progress towards democracy.

The lack of freedom of expression and access to information has prevented the establishment of a democratic space essential to create a coherent political system and on which to base a democratic society that respects human rights. The success of the Palestinian state depends on political unity and an effective media system that can perform the function of serving as a forum for critique and information.

References

Abdelal, Wael (2016), *Hamas and the Media*. London and New York: Routledge.

Abu Shanab, H. (2001), *Palestinian Media: Experiences and Challenges*. Palestine: Al Qadeseya Library.

Abu Zeid, Farouk (1993), *Arab Émigré Press* (in Arabic). Cairo: Alam Al Kotub.

Abuhashish, H. (2010), *Palestinian Authority and Hamas Government: Dispute over Palestinian Media*. [Interview] Gaza, 24 March 2010.

Abuzanouna, B. (2012), *Enhancing Democratic Communication? Television and Partisan Politics in Palestine*. Germany: LAP Lambert.

Al-Bayader Assiyasi (1997), *Violations of Palestinian Journalist's Rights*. Ramallah: Alayyam.

Amer, F. (2019), Society Voice Foundation Director, Interview, *Gaza*, 21 April.

Arrar, Mohi Eddin A Hussein (2016), *al-Sahafa al-Falistiniyya*. Amman, Jordan: Dar al-I'ssar al-Ilmi.

BBC (2018), *Palestinian Territories Profile – Media*, 30 January. Retrieved from www.bbc.co.uk/news/world-middle-east-14631745

Bishara, Amahl (2010), New Media and Political Change in the Occupied Palestinian Territories: Assembling Media Worlds and Cultivating Networks of Care. *Middle East Journal of Culture and Communication*, 3, pp. 63–81.

Caspi, D., and Limor, Y. (1999), *The In/Outsiders: The Media in Israel*. Cresskill, NJ: Hampton Press.

InterNews (2006), *Palestinians and the Media: Usage, Trust, and Effectiveness*. Retrieved from https://internews.org/resource/palestinians-and-media-usage-trust-and-effectiveness

Jamal, A. (2001), State-building and Media Regime: Censoring the Emerging Public Sphere in Palestine. *International Communication Gazette*, 63(2–3), pp. 263–282.

Jamal, Amal (2003), *State Formation and Media Regime in Palestine*. Israel: The Tami Steinmetz Centre for Peace Research.

Jamal, Amal (2004), Feminist Media Discourse in Palestine and the Predicament of Politics. *Feminist Media Studies*, 4(2), pp. 129–146.

Jamal, Amal (2005), *Media Politics and Democracy in Palestine: Political Culture, Pluralism, and the Palestinian Authority*. Brighton: Sussex Academic Press.

Jamal, Amal (2009), *The Arab Public Sphere in Israel. Media Space and Cultural Resistance*. Bloomington: Indiana University Press.

Jamal, Amal, and Awaisi, Rana (2011), *The Challenges to Journalistic Professionalism: Between Independence and Difficult Work Conditions*. Nazareth: ILAM – Media Center for Arab Palestinians in Israel.

Kuttab, D. (1993), Palestinian Diaries: Grassroots TV Production in the Occupied Territories. In D. Tony (ed.), *Channels of Resistance: Global Television and Local Empowerment*. London: BFI.

Lynch, Marc (2006), *Voices of the New Arab Public: Iraq, Al-Jazeera, and Middle East Politics Today*. New York: Columbia University Press.

MADA (2009), *Violations of Media Freedoms in the Occupied Palestinian Territories*. Ramallah: MADA Centre.

McQuail, Denis (1994), *Mass Communication Theory*. 3rd edition. London: Sage.

Mellor, Noha (2007), *Modern Arab Journalism*. Edinburgh: Edinburgh University Press.

Najjar, O. (1997), The 1995 Palestinian Press Law: A Comparative Study. *Communication Law and Policy*, 2, pp. 41–103.

Natil, Ibrahim (2014), A Shifting Political Landscape: NGOs' Civic Activism and Response in the Gaza Strip, 1967–2014. *Journal of Peacebuilding and Development*, 9(3), pp. 82–87. doi:10.1080/15423166.2014.983369

Natil, Ibrahim (2015), *Hamas Transformation: Opportunities and Challenges*. Newcastle: Cambridge Scholars.

Nossek, H., and Rinnawi, K. (2003), Censorship and Freedom of the Press Under Changing Political Regimes: Palestinian Media from Israeli Occupation to the Palestinian Authority. *Gazette (Leiden, Netherlands)*, 65(2), pp. 183–202. doi:10.1177/0016549203065002005

PCHR (2002), *Silencing the Press: A Report on Israeli Attacks Against Journalists*. Gaza: PCHR.

PCHR (2004), *The Right to Freedom of Opinion and Expression and the Right to Peaceful Assembly*. Gaza: PCHR.

Sakr, Naomi (2007), *Arab Television Today*. London: I.B. Tauris.

Shahin, L. (2010), *Independent Media in Palestine*. [Interview] Gaza, 19 January.

Suleiman, M. (2009), *British Laws and the Development of Palestinian Press* (in Arabic). Ramallah: Ministry of Information.

Tawil-Souri, Helga (2007), Global and Local Forces for a Nation-State Yet to be Born: The Paradoxes of Palestinian Television Policies. *Westminster Papers in Communication and Culture* (University of Westminster, London), 4(3), pp. 4–25.

UNESCO (2014), *Assessment of Media Development – Palestine*. Paris: UNESCO. Retrieved from www.unesco.org/new/en/communication-and-information/resources/publications-and-communication-materials/publications/full-list/assessment-of-media-development-in-palestine/

22

PALESTINIAN NEW MEDIA

Nahed Eltantawy

Introduction

The Internet today is a significant tool in the Palestinian resistance against Israeli occupation. However, it took years for Palestinians to gain access to new media. Although Palestinians today enjoy access to new media via the services of two main service providers, Jawwal and Watanyia Mobile Palestine, Palestinians face many challenges in terms of lack of access to the latest telecommunications technologies, illegal Israeli provider competition, as well as Israeli government hindrances and censorship. All of this has caused the country's new media technology to lag behind the other countries in the region.

According to the United Nation's ICT Development Index, an index that ranks countries based on a variety of information and telecommunication technology indicators, Israel ranked one of the top countries at 23 for 2017, while Palestine ranked very low at 123 out of 176 countries (ICT Development Index, 2017). "This anomaly is a direct result of Israel's occupation and control of Palestinians, and the severe technological gap is just another example of how Israel dominates and restricts almost all aspects of Palestinian life" (Mohamed, 2017: para. 4).

As of 2017, Palestinians in the West Bank and Gaza Strip totaled close to five million, while Palestinians in the Occupied Territories totaled 8.4 million. For Palestinians in the West Bank and Gaza Strip, Internet users totaled 61% of the population while 79% of the population in the West Bank and Gaza Strip were using the Internet (Jaddeh, 2017). Average Internet speed is significantly different for Palestinians in the West Bank and Gaza Strip, at 9 Mbps (landline) and 0.3 Mbps (mobile) compared to 43 Mbps for Palestinians in the Occupied Territories (landline) and 22 Mbps (mobile) (Jaddeh, 2017; the statistics for Internet speed for the West Bank and Gaza Strip do not include 3G service). This chapter follows the development of new media in the Palestinian territories, shedding light on issues of regulations, censorship, and competition in this sector.

Historical background

Israel first connected to the Internet in 1990, with commercial Internet service providers (ISPs) beginning operation in 1992 (Najjar, 2007). Palestinians relied on Israel for telephone services until 1995, after which Israel transferred about 80,000 telephone lines to the Palestinian Authority (PA) (Decoster et al., 2016). One of the major achievements for Palestinians was the 1997 launch of the Palestine Telecommunications Company, Paltel, as a public shareholding company (Najjar, 2007; The Portland Trust, 2012). Paltel was awarded by the PA an exclusive license to build Palestine's telecommunications network for 20 years and operate it for 10 years, with the Ministry of Telecommunications and Information Technology (MTIT) regulating service prices and quality (Dhaher, 2010). The telecom infrastructure of the West Bank and Gaza Strip had only 77,000 telephone lines for the region's 2.5 million inhabitants at the time Paltel was established. Nearly 200,000 other users were on a waiting list, and this demand worked in Paltel's favor, contributing to its rapid growth (Najjar, 2007). Paltel started offering fixed phone services in 1997, and, in 1999, its subsidiary Jawwal began offering mobile services. Jawwal had been awarded an exclusive license to provide mobile services between 1997 and 2004, but only started operations in 1999 once it was able to secure frequencies from Israel (Dhaher, 2010).

Palestinians have not been able to gain their promised independent telecommunications sector due to Israel's tight control. According to the Oslo Accords, which are a set of agreements between Israel and the Palestinian Liberation Organization (PLO) that started in 1993, Israel agreed that the Palestinians had the right to create and manage their independent communication and infrastructures, including their own telecommunications networks. However, the Oslo agreement principles with regards to telecommunications are not applied. "This is presenting enormous challenges for Palestinian telecom operators, a clear detriment to the Palestinian consumer, a fiscal loss for the Palestinian Authority, and an overall delay for the sector development" (Decoster et al., 2016: 6).

Main players: key outlets

Palestine today has two main cellular communication providers, Jawwal, operated by Paltel Group, and Wataniya, which was granted a license to operate 2G and 3G services in Palestine in 2007 but was not allowed to serve Palestinians in the West Bank until 2009. Wataniya currently has about 786,000 customers in the West Bank. The company was serving Palestinians in the West Bank only, as Israel prevented it from importing its equipment to the Gaza Strip until 2017. On 24 October 2017, Israel finally granted Wataniya the right to launch its services to Gaza Strip customers, ending Jawwal's 18-year monopoly over the telecommunications sector (AbuShanab, 2018b).

Business models and competition

Today, Paltel Group is a multi-company operation that provides Palestinian users with a wide array of services, such as domestic and international telephony services, data communications, mobile services, as well as Internet ("About PalTel Group" 2019). Paltel Group owns four main subsidiaries: Jawwal, Hadara, Reach, and the Paltel Group Foundation for Community Development. Jawwal was created in 1999 and is Palestine's first mobile operator and 3G provider. By April 2019, Jawwal had nearly three million subscribers (Najjar, 2007; "About PalTel Group" 2019). Hadara was founded in 2005 and is an Internet service provider with over 125,000 subscribers, while Reach, launched in 2009, is a specialized communication center that offers services via multi-communication channels ("About Paltel Group" 2019). Established in 2008, the Paltel Group Foundation for Community Development is a non-profit organization that caters to the needs of the Palestinian society ("About PalTel Group" 2019).

Wataniya, which was created in 2007 as a joint partnership between the Kuwaiti Wataniya Group (57%) and the Palestine Investment Fund (43%), was successfully publicly traded on the Palestine Exchange in 2011. Today, the international communications company, Ooredoo Group, has majority ownership and control over Wataniya through the Wataniya Group. Wataniya's name was recently changed to Ooredoo Palestine. The company launched cellular services in the West Bank in November 2009 and was finally allowed to enter the Gaza Strip in January 2018, following an Israeli boycott that lasted for over 10 years (Ooredoo Palestine Website, 2019).

According to Decoster et al. (2016), between 2013 and 2015 alone, Palestinian mobile operators lost over $1 billion due to Israeli restrictions, while unauthorized Israeli operators that offer 3G and 4G capabilities without receiving proper authorization from the PA can sell their services to Palestinians at a lower cost.

Internet usage for Palestinians in Israel

According to the 2017 Palestinian Digital Activism Report, published by 7amleh organization, 1,110,582 Palestinians were using the Internet in Israel in 2017. The Israeli Central Bureau of Statistics adds that, in 2016, 65% of Israeli Palestinians who used the Internet were over the age of 20 (872,300 out of 1,797,300 Palestinians in Israel in 2016) (AbuShanab, 2018a: 8). The Palestinian Digital Activism Report for 2017 breaks down Palestinians' Internet usage by the following: 25.8% of users used the Internet for studies; 21.6% used it for work, 57.8% used it daily, 61.6% accessed the Internet via their mobile phones, while 43.4% accessed the Internet on a computer (AbuShanab, 2018a: 8).

The 2017 Palestinian Digital Activism Report states that 60.5% of Palestinians in the West Bank and Gaza Strip (the Occupied Territories) were using the Internet in 2017 (3,018,770 out of 4,985,506 Palestinians). Out of these users, about 1.6 million were active on social media, with 1.4 million accessing social media on their mobile phones. Facebook and WhatsApp were the most commonly used social media platforms for users in the West Bank and Gaza Strip, followed by Instagram and YouTube (AbuShanab, 2018a: 9).

Israeli competition

Palestine's two cellular providers, Jawwal and Wataniya, are not only competing against each other, but the two companies also face strong competition from Israeli service providers. The companies also face many hindrances and challenges due to Israeli government control (Decoster et al., 2016). In fact, in November 2002, Jawwal's CEO, Hakam Kanafani, published a message to Jawwal customers expressing frustration at some of the challenges his company was facing. "For over a year, the Israeli authorities have detained our network radio stations (towers and cellular equipment)," Kanafani wrote (2002). "These are the towers needed to expand our network and increase the capacity to allow our subscribers to make more calls. Those towers are Jawwal's private property and they fully conform to all international (and Israeli) communication standards" (para. 2). In addition, Kanafani said that the Israeli army destroyed 14 of Jawwal's towers and two of their showrooms and raided Jawwal's headquarters. The CEO also accused Israel of blocking 7.5 tons of imported cellular stations. Kanafani added that Jawwal also faced illegal Israeli competition. "To Israeli operators, Palestinian subscribers are extremely profitable since the Israeli market is now fully saturated and each new Israeli subscriber entails a high acquisition cost," he said (Kanafani, 2002: para. 6).

Laws and regulations

Under the Oslo agreements between Israel and the PLO, the Palestinian Authority was given rights to construct and operate telecommunications networks in the areas under its control in the West Bank and Gaza Strip. The agreement also stipulated that any issues relating to spectrum allocation and international connectivity should remain under Israeli control (Dhaher, 2010). Then in 1996, a telecommunications law was signed by the PA president to oversee the development of the sector by private sector operators. This 1996 telecommunications law, which remains in effect today, gave the MTIT the role of establishing the telecommunications sector policies and regulatory activities (Dhaher, 2010). However, according to Decoster et al. (2016), the Palestinian telecommunications industry has been limited in its progress since 2008 on several issues that include:

- Palestinian cellular operators face a competitive disadvantage to their Israeli counterparts, due to limited mobile broadband services. In 2007, Palestinian operators requested to introduce mobile broadband, and it was only in November 2015 that an agreement was finally signed to allow the limited release of frequencies that allow Palestinian operators to launch 3G services to their customers (Decoster et al., 2016). Palestinian operators, however, were only allowed to offer 3G services, beginning in January 2018, and only in the West Bank and not in the Gaza Strip ("Palestinians get 3G Internet. . .," 2018). Palestine was one of four countries worldwide in 2016 with no access to mobile broadband (Mohamed, 2017). This puts Palestinian operators at a disadvantage, compared to their Israeli counterparts, who have had 3G capabilities since 2004 and 4G capabilities since 2015, and are, therefore, able to attract more customers (Decoster et al., 2016).
- The second Palestinian operator, Wataniya, has been unable to operate to its full capacity. Due to Israeli restrictions in releasing the spectrum, Watanyia endured a two-year delay. The company currently faces spectrum and civil material import restrictions, hindering its operations for Gaza consumers (Decoster et al., 2016).
- Palestinian operators face unfair competition due to the widespread presence of Israeli operators with unauthorized activity in the West Bank. These operators offer 3G and 4G capabilities, allowing them to control about 30% of the West Bank market, in addition to their likelihood of capturing high value-added Palestinian customers (Decoster et al., 2016).

Additionally, a December 2018 report by 7amleh – The Arab Center for the Advancement of Social Media – lists several challenges that hinder the full development of Palestinian telecommunications companies in the region:

- Control of Palestinian ICT infrastructure by Israel: Israel took full control of the ICT sector following its 1967 occupation. Then, in 1995, as part of the Oslo Accords, Israel transferred partial control of ICT infrastructure in the Gaza Strip and the West Bank (except for East Jerusalem) to the PA. Israel has full control of ICT infrastructure in East Jerusalem, and Palestinian service providers are not allowed to operate in this area.
- Control under the Oslo Accords: Even though, under the accords, Israel recognized Palestinians' right to build and operate an independent telecommunications system, it continues to control Palestine's telecommunication infrastructure and service deployment in most Palestinian-controlled areas.

- Limited access to frequencies and technologies: Israel consistently denies Palestinians' requests for updated ICT technologies. As the world is ready for 5G frequencies, Palestinians only started enjoying 3G frequencies in early 2018, while Israelis enjoy 4G services. Additionally, Israel denied Palestinians from introducing WiMax systems that provide access to wireless broadband networks and enable high-speed data transmission. Such hindrances to technological advancement have economically impacted Palestinian telecommunication operators who are unable to compete with Israeli operators' services (AbuShanab, 2018b).
- Limited access to global technologies: ICT infrastructure development for Palestinians is controlled by Israel. Palestinian providers must apply for permits to build infrastructure. Israel to this date has only approved 3G systems. All of this results in fragmented networks for the Palestinian providers, which causes them to lose customers to their Israeli competitors who have stronger and more updated networks.
- Restricted imports of necessary equipment: Palestinians face many restrictions when importing telecom equipment, although the Oslo Accords clearly state that Palestinians have the right to make imports to build an independent network and that Israel has to abide by this. Israel also imposes challenging conditions for Palestinian importers of ICT materials that burden them with a long and tedious bureaucratic process that involves multiple request submissions to various Israeli authorities (AbuShanab, 2018b).

The contemporary regulatory environment

MTIT is the main regulatory body in the telecommunications sector. Twice, telecommunication laws aimed at liberalizing and regulating the sector have been rejected, once in 2006 and a second time in 2009. The telecommunications law was rejected in 2006 due to "technicalities and formalities" (Daher, 2010). In 2009, the PA approved the establishment of a telecommunications law that would include the creation of the Palestinian Telecommunications regulatory Authority (PTRA). The goal was to establish a regulatory system to advance consumer interests, handle market-related disputes, as well as provide a non-political market referee and offer a fair environment to encourage investors. The law was again rejected in early 2010 because the Palestinian territories are still under occupation (Dhaher, 2010; "The ICT sector in the Palestinian Territory," 2012). This means that the Ministry of Telecommunications and Information Technology is the main regulator of telecommunications in Palestine, in charge of everything from licenses to operational issues to pricing ("The ICT sector in the Palestinian Territory" 2012).

State media versus independent media

According to Najjar (2007), Palestinian media is largely dependent on outside funding. This reliance on outside capital, in addition to the presence of a weak Palestinian National Authority, and the Israeli occupation have all led to negative as well as positive consequences for the Palestinian media (Najjar, 2007). On the positive side, external funding has allowed Palestinian media to develop away from government bureaucracy, which has resulted in a speedier process. The occupation also encouraged the establishment of independent Palestinian media, to compete with Israeli journalists on who has the right to tell the Palestinian story (Najjar, 2007). Today, Palestinians make up the majority of correspondents for the major Arab satellite networks in Gaza and the West Bank. These include networks, such as Al Jazeera, Abu Dhabi Media, as well as Al-Arabiya (Najjar, 2007). The Internet also enabled Palestinians to get in touch with social media enthusiasts and activists around the world (Najjar, 2007).

The spread of the Internet among Palestinians has encouraged the establishment of a number of independent online media outlets that give voice to Palestinians and that strive to provide an alternative side to stories posted by mainstream Israeli media (Steele, 2014). Among the most prominent of these is *The Electronic Intifada*, which is an independent, privately funded online news outlet that was established in 2001. According to the official Intifada website, the news outlet is an "online news publication and educational resource focusing on Palestine, its people, politics, culture, and place in the world" (Electronic Intifada website, 2019). Another prominent news outlet is the Ma'an News Agency (MNA) that was launched in 2005. MNA is part of the Ma'an Network, "a non-profit media organization founded in 2002 to strengthen professional independent media in Palestine, build links between local, regional and international media, and consolidate freedom of expression and media pluralism as keys to promoting democracy and human rights" (MNA website, 2019). *The Palestinian Chronicle* is another prominent independent online newspaper that was established in 1999. The newspaper's mission is to "educate the general public by providing a forum that strives to highlight issues of relevance to human rights, national struggles, freedom, and democracy in the form of daily news, commentary, features, book reviews, photos, art, and more" (The Palestine Chronicle website, 2019).

On the state side, there are several media outlets that are active online. These include the official PA newspaper, *Al Hayat al Jadida*, which is published out of Ramallah. Wafa agency, also known as the Palestinian News and Information Agency, is another media outlet affiliated with the PA.

According to Jaddeh (2017), the most visited online news sites for Palestinians in 2017 include *Al-Quds*, one of Palestine's oldest and most popular political daily newspapers that was established in 1951; Donia Al-Watan, an independent news website that focuses on local Palestinian news, as well as regional and global issues; *Al-Ayyam*, another daily independent news outlet, and Zamn Press, a Palestinian non-profit media outlet established in 2010.

Censorship

When it comes to social media activity, Palestinians face censorship from three different sources: the Israeli government, the Palestinian Authority, and Hamas authorities (AbuShanab, 2018a). The most heavily targeted social network for 2017 was Facebook, with Israel arresting nearly 300 Palestinians from the West Bank for Facebook-related charges. Also, in 2017, the PA and Hamas both arrested political activists, journalists as well as dissidents, in the Gaza Strip for social media-related activity. Additionally, nearly 530 violations against media freedom were reported in the Occupied Territories. These include 376 Israeli violations and 154 attacks by Palestinian factions (AbuShanab, 2018a). From the Israeli side, authorities continued their monitoring and censorship of social media activity, especially Facebook-related activity. In 2017, the Israeli cyber unit reported that 85% of government requests to remove Facebook and Twitter content deemed "harmful or dangerous" were accepted (AbuShanab, 2018b, p. 5). The PA's most noteworthy violations against media freedom for 2017 included blocking West Bank websites and adopting a cybercrime law in 2017 that allows the PA to justify political arrests (AbuShanab, 2018b). According to the Palestinian Center for Development and Media Freedoms (MADA), Palestinian authorities forced service providers in the West Bank to block access to 29 websites that belong to political parties, opposition as well as media outlets ("Mada: 51 violations of media freedoms in Palestine during June 2017," 2019).

In August 2017, Amnesty International released an online news release titled "Palestine: Dangerous Escalation in Attacks on Freedom of Expression." The human rights organization stated that Palestinian authorities in the West Bank, and the Hamas administration in Gaza, were detaining and interrogating journalists from opposition media outlets as a way to pressure their political opponents ("Palestine: Dangerous escalation in attacks on freedom of expression." 2017). Amnesty International added in the news release that President Mahmoud Abbas adopted an Electronic Crimes Law in July 2017 that "violates citizens' rights to privacy and freedom of expression and blatantly flouts the State of Palestine's obligations under international law" (para. 5). Under this newly adopted law, journalists and whistleblowers face heavy fines and arbitrary detention if they post online criticism of Palestinian authorities. Additionally, anyone sharing such news online could also be targeted by authorities. "Anyone who is deemed to have disturbed 'public order', 'national unity' or 'social peace' could be sentenced to imprisonment and up to 15 years hard labor" ("Palestine: Dangerous escalation in attacks on freedom of expression." 2017: para. 6). The appendix lists several social media-related arrests made by Israeli, Palestinian Authority, and Hamas government and security forces.

Social and political functions of this medium

Many Palestinian activists utilize social media as a political tool to launch campaigns and raise awareness on Palestinian-related issues. In 2017, there were a number of such prominent campaigns, such as #LightsOnGaza, launched on 10 August 2017, by 7amleh organization, partnering with Oxfam, to "raise awareness of the Gaza electricity crisis and its terrible consequences on the Palestinians living there" ("#LightsOnGaza," 2017). #BoycottHyundai was another prominent campaign that was launched on 7 February 2017 by the Boycott, Divestment, and Sanctions Committee of Palestinian Citizens of Israel (BDS48). The campaign called for the boycott of all Hyundai products and called on Hyundai to "end its involvement in Israel's 'ethnic cleansing of Palestinian communities in Jerusalem and the Naqab'" (AbuShanab, 2018a). This campaign was launched because Israel was using Hyundai machinery in its demolitions of Palestinian homes (AbuShanab, 2018a).

In 2017, the Women Media and Development Center in the West Bank launched a 16-day campaign, partnering with the Palestinian Basketball Federation. The campaign, titled "No to dropping the personal right in crimes of femicide," was part of Palestinian activists' engagement with the United Nations' 16-day campaigns that aim to bring attention to the November 25th International Day for the Elimination of Violence Against Women, and the December 10th Human Rights Day (AbuShanab, 2018a). The Women's Affairs center in Gaza launched their campaign, titled "No to violence . . . Our lives are better without violence." This was part of a larger initiative to end violence against women and girls in Gaza (AbuShanab, 2018a).

Social media activism was also important for the LGBT community in Palestine in 2017. AlQaws for Sexual & Gender Diversity in Palestinian Society partnered with 7amleh Arab Center for Social Media Advancement in their social media campaign, "Difference never justifies violence," aimed at bringing attention to violence against LGBT individuals in Palestine. According to alQaws's website, the campaign garnered over half a million Facebook views and 300,000 YouTube views for one of the campaign videos ("Social media campaign marks a new milestone in Palestinian Queer Organizing" 2018).

On the political side, Palestinian activists have also launched campaigns to raise awareness on the PA's Cybercrimes Law and digital security awareness. Following the adoption of the Cybercrime Law in July 2017, the PA made several arrests of journalists in the West Bank. According to 7amleh (2018), the PA and Hamas authorities use these arrests as a bargaining chip, negotiating the release of their journalists by one side as a condition to release journalists from the other side (AbuShanab, 2018a). Activists protesting these arrests used multiple hashtags online to bring attention to this problem. These hashtags include #Where_are_the_journalists and

#Journalism_is_not_a_crime (AbuShanab, 2018a). Activists were also joined by members of the National Coordination Committee for the Defense of Freedoms in October of 2017. The committee called for a sit-in, demanding that the PA government repeal the law. The committee also launched a digital campaign, with the hashtags #Jail_Us and #Cybercrime_Law_is_a_Crime (AbuShanab, 2018a). Additionally, in their battle against censorship, 7amleh launched an Arab social media campaign that aimed to raise awareness on digital security, following the increased censorship and arrests by Israeli, Palestinian Authority, and Hamas government and security forces (AbuShanab, 2018a).

Conclusion

Overall, Palestinians have come a long way in terms of access to social media and telecommunications technologies. With their recent access to 3G technologies, Jawwal and Wataniya, or Ooredoo Palestine, the two service providers, are gradually increasing their customer base and enabling the spread of Internet services across Palestine. Yet, many challenges impede the success of these two companies, most prominent of which is how Israel, despite Oslo agreement stipulations, continues to hinder and delay telecommunications infrastructure development for Palestinians, among other challenges. From the customers' side, there are also challenges that social media users are increasingly facing. With a new cybercrime law in place, the PA has increased its harassment and arrest of journalists and activists alike, while Israeli and Hamas authorities have also continued their crackdown on social media activists.

References and further reading

#LightsOnGaza (2017), *7amleh.org*, 10 August. Retrieved from http://7amleh.org/2017/08/10/lightsongaza/

About Paltel Group (2019), *Paltelgroup.com*, 11 April. Retrieved from www.paltelgroup.ps/#about

AbuShanab, A. (2018a), Hashtag Palestine 2017: Palestinian Digital Activism Report. *7amleh – Arab Center for Social Media Activism*. Retrieved from http://7amleh.org/wp-content/uploads/2018/04/Palestine-2017-English-final.pdf

AbuShanab, A. (2018b), Connection Interrupted: Israel's Control of the Palestinian ICT Infrastructure and its Impact on Digital Rights. *7amleh – Arab Center for Social Media Activism*. Retrieved from https://7amleh.org/wp-content/uploads/2019/01/Report_7amleh_English_final.pdf

Decoster, X., Rossotto, C., and Lewin, A. (2016), *The Telecommunication Sector in the Palestinian Territories: A Missed Opportunity for Economic Development*. World Bank Group. Retrieved from www.academia.edu/34565176/The_Telecommunication_Sector_in_the_Palestinian_Territories_A_Missed_Opportunity_for_Economic_Development

Dhaher, Omar (2010), Independence of the Telecommunications Regulatory Authority in Palestine: Institutional Challenges. *21st European Regional ITS Conference*, Copenhagen 2010, ITS Europe, Berlin.

ICT Development Index (2017), Retrieved from www.itu.int/net4/ITU-D/idi/2017/index.html

Jaddeh, H. (2017), *Digital and Social Media Report in Palestine. Social Studio Me*. Retrieved from https://socialstudio.me/wp-content/uploads/2018/04/SMRP2017EnglishFinal.pdf

Kanafani, H. (2002), A Message from the CEO of Palestine's Cellular Company (Jawwal). *Saltfilms.net*, November. Retrieved from www.saltfilms.net/zababdeh/nov02/jawwal.html

Ma'an News Agency (2019), Retrieved from www.maannews.com/About.aspx

Mada: 51 Violations of Media Freedoms in Palestine during June 2017 (2017), *Palestinian Center for Development & Media Freedoms*, June. Retrieved from www.madacenter.org/report.php?lang=1&id=1719&category_id=13&year=2017

Mohamed, M. (2017), How Israel Represses the Internet in Palestine. *Mondoweiss*, 13 December. Retrieved from https://mondoweiss.net/2017/12/represses-Internet-palestine/

Najjar, O. A. (2007), New Palestinian Media and Democratization from Below. In P. Seib (ed.), *New Media and the New Middle East*. Palgrave Macmillan Series in International Political Communication. New York: Palgrave Macmillan, pp. 191–212.

Ooredoo Palestine Website (2019), Retrieved from www.ooredoo.ps/en

Palestine: Dangerous Escalation in Attacks on Freedom of Expression (2017), *Amnesty International,* 23 August. Retrieved from www.amnesty.org/en/latest/news/2017/08/palestine-dangerous-escalation-in-attacks-on-freedom-of-expression/

Palestinians get 3G Internet after Decade-long Row (2018), *AFP*, 23 January. Retrieved from www.timesofisrael.com/palestinians-get-3g-Internet-after-decade-long-row/

Steele, K. (2014), Palestinian-Arab Media Frames and Stereotypes of Israeli-Jews. *Elon Journal of Undergraduate Research in Communications*, 5(1), pp. 43–56.

Social Media Campaign Marks a New Milestone in Palestinian Queer Organizing (2018), *alQaws Online*, 4 June. Retrieved from www.alqaws.org/news/Social-Media-Campaign-Marks-New-Milestone-in-Palestinian-Queer-Organizing?category_id=0

The Electronic Intifada Website (2019), Retrieved from https://electronicintifada.net/content/about-electronic-intifada/10159

The ICT Sector in the Palestinian Territory (2011), *The Portland Trust*, August. Retrieved from https://portlandtrust.org/sites/default/files/pubs/ict_special_aug_2012.pdf

The Palestine Chronicle Website (2019), Retrieved from www.palestinechronicle.com/about/

Internet

Appendix 1

2017 ICT DEVELOPMENT INDEX BY COUNTRY

Table BM.1 IDI country comparison 2017 for Israel and Palestine

ICT Development Index (IDI) country comparison 2017

Indicator	Israel	Palestine
IDI 2017 Rank	23	123
IDI 2016 Rank	22	122
IDI 2017 Value	7.88	3.55
IDI 2016 Value	7.71	3.42
IDI ACCESS SUB-INDEX	8.17	3.35
Fixed–telephone subscriptions per 100 inhabitants	41.61	9.26
Mobile-cellular telephone subscriptions per 100 inhabitants	131.67	76.81
International Internet bandwidth per Internet user (Bit/s)	158696.29	0
Percentage of households with a computer	81.14	70.42
Percentage of households with Internet access	75.71	56.54
IDI USE SUB-INDEX	7.34	2.42
Percentage of individuals using the Internet	79.78	61.18
Fixed (wired)–broadband subscriptions per 100 inhabitants	28.13	6.87
Active mobile-broadband subscriptions per 100 inhabitants	93.42	0
IDI SKILLS SUB-INDEX	8.38	6.22
Mean years of schooling	12.8	8.9
Secondary gross enrollment ratio	101.86	83
Tertiary gross enrollment ratio	66.18	44.28

Data Source: IDI Website www.itu.int/net4/ITU-D/idi/2017/index.html#idi2017comparison-tab

Appendix 2

PARTIAL LIST OF SOCIAL MEDIA-RELATED ARRESTS BY ISRAELI AND PALESTINIAN AUTHORITIES IN 2017

Name	Location	Arresting Authority
Mohammad Khalaf	Tamra	Israeli Police
Loay Azeri	Beersheba	Israeli Police
Sami al-Hazel	Negev	Israeli Police
Nour Issa	East Jerusalem	Israeli Forces
Ahmed Sa'ida	East Jerusalem	Israeli Forces
Ahed Tamimi	Ramallah	Israeli Forces
Ibrahim Abu Snina	East Jerusalem	Israeli Forces
Ahmed al-Shawesh	East Jerusalem	Israeli Forces
Saleh al-Zghari	East Jerusalem	Israeli Forces
Ibrahim Abu Nea	East Jerusalem	Israeli Forces
Ahmed Aweisat	East Jerusalem	Israeli Forces
Thaher Al-Shmali	Ramallah	Palestinian Authority Security Forces
Nassar Jaradat	Ramallah	Palestinian Authority Security Forces
Issa Amro Palestinian	Hebron	Authority Security Forces
Mohammad Al-Haj	Ramallah	Palestinian Authority Security Forces
Mashaal al-Kouk	Ramallah	Palestinian Authority Security Forces
Baraa al-Qadi	Ramallah	Palestinian Authority Security Forces
Baha al-Jayyousi	Tulkarem	Palestinian Authority Security Forces
Abdelmohsen Shalaldeh	Hebron	Palestinian Authority Security Forces
Baraa al-Amer	Nablus	Palestinian Authority Security Forces
Tareq Abu Zaid	Nablus	Palestinian Authority Security Forces
Amer Abu Arfeh	Hebron	Palestinian Authority Security Forces
Mamdouh Hamamra	Bethlehem	Palestinian Authority Security Forces
Qutiba Qasim	Bethlehem	Palestinian Authority Security Forces
Ahmed Haliqa	Hebron	Palestinian Authority Security Forces
Oroba Abu Arfeh	Hebron	Palestinian Authority Security Forces
Ahmed Abdel Aziz	Nablus	Palestinian Authority Security Forces
Shadi Krakra	Ramallah	Palestinian Authority Security Forces
Loay Shlalada	Hebron	Palestinian Authority Security Forces
Salam al-Atrash	Ramallah	Palestinian Authority Security Forces
Alaa al-Teiti	Bethlehem	Palestinian Authority Security Forces

Name	Location	Arresting Authority
Mosab Qafesha	Hebron	Palestinian Authority Security Forces
Jamal al-Swaiti	Hebron	Palestinian Authority Security Forces
Ameer Abu Aram	Ramallah	Palestinian Authority Security Forces
Ashraf Abu Aram	Ramallah	Palestinian Authority Security Forces
Fadi al-Arouri	Ramallah	Palestinian Authority Security Forces
Ayman al-Qawasmeh	Hebron	Palestinian Authority Security Forces
Diaa Hroub	Ramallah	Palestinian Authority Security Forces
Thaer al-Fakhouri	Hebron	Palestinian Authority Security Forces
Ismael al-Bazam	Gaza	Hamas Authorities Security Forces
Adel Meshoukhi	Gaza	Hamas Authorities Security Forces
Amer Baalousha	Gaza	Hamas Authorities Security Forces
Mohammad Lafi	Gaza	Hamas Authorities Security Forces
Mohammad Othman	Gaza	Hamas Authorities Security Forces
Hazem Madi	Gaza	Hamas Authorities Security Forces
Nasir Abu Ful	Gaza	Hamas Authorities Security Forces
Ayman al-Qawasmeh	Hebron	Palestinian Authority Security Forces
Shukri Abu Oun	Gaza	Hamas Authorities Security Forces
Mohammad Sawali	Gaza	Hamas Authorities Security Forces
Ahmed Qadeh	Gaza	Hamas Authorities Security Forces
Mohammad al-Bar'ai	Gaza	Hamas Authorities Security Forces
Khaled Hammad	Gaza	Hamas Authorities Security Forces
Khader Mehjar	Gaza	Hamas Authorities Security Forces

Source: Table courtesy of 7amleh, April 2019, pp. 30–31. See http://7amleh.org/wp-content/uploads/2018/04/Palestine-2017-English-final.pdf

Qatar

23

MEDIA DEVELOPMENTS IN QATAR

Khalid Al-Jaber

Introduction

The emergence of a prominent media apparatus in Qatar parallels the country's rise in prosperity and its growing expertise in various fields. In some specialties, the media industry in Qatar is considered among the most influential and effective in the region and internationally, particularly through the global news giant Al Jazeera. Media organizations have grown and evolved to serve their audience in a way that resonates with Qatari society's internal and external messaging priorities. This chapter analyzes the media landscape in Qatar and how Qatar benefited from the experiences of other leading organizations. The discussion also involves different types of media including the Qatari press, radio and television broadcasting services, and digital media. The chapter explores the laws and regulations enacted related to different forms of media. The last part of the chapter looks at the social and political power of media and how it is being used to reach a wider audience in today's world.

The media landscape in Qatar

In comparison to other Arab countries, the emergence of visual, audio, and print media in the Gulf states in general (and Qatar in particular) arrived later than in their Western counterparts as a result of several factors, including low population, weak formal education, widespread illiteracy, and low penetration of standardized Arabic. Additionally, economic factors (such as the recession in the first half of the 20th century experienced by the Gulf states following the collapse of the pearl trade) suppressed the ability of a formalized media apparatus to emerge due to a weak market (Al-Jaber and Gunter, 2013).

Prior to the discovery of oil, Qatar experienced difficult economic and living conditions. The nation's livelihood relied entirely on sea resources, mainly diving for pearls, fishing, limited maritime trade, shipbuilding, and fish-net making. Oil was discovered in Qatar for the first time in 1939; however, the extraction of this wealth came later due to the circumstances of World War II (1939–1945). Even after the war ended, Qatar continued to experience a deterioration in economic conditions that did not end until 1951.

A reversal in economic fortunes occurred in the mid-50s as a result of the big boom that emerged after major investments were made in oil exploration, production, and export (Ismail,

2004). This relative prosperity led to improved living conditions in all aspects of life and helped build the modern state and its associated economic, cultural, and social institutions. Trade activities accelerated and individual incomes increased, two factors that also positively affected living conditions. As a result, the state services provided to citizens improved as well. By 1971, Qatar had discovered that its coastline overlooked the largest natural gas field in the world, which led to perhaps the most significant transformation that has allowed Qatar to become one of the globe's richest countries (Al-Jaber and Gunter, 2013).

As in many other nations, print media arrived on the scene before audiovisual media. Several daily and weekly newspapers, as well as literary and cultural magazines, began publication in Qatar. Today, many of these same newspapers and magazines retain Arabic digital publications. Some of them publish sister newspapers in English in addition to various foreign languages. Since its inception, the media in Qatar has learned from the successes and failures of media in other Arab countries, and from this has forged its path to accommodate the specific conditions of Qatari development at the community and media levels.

Qatar has also benefited from the experiences and successes of other leading media organizations. The tiny emirate has attracted leading journalistic and cultural talent from the Arab region and the world, especially from Egypt, Lebanon, and the Maghreb, known for having developed press industries, in addition to those in Europe and the United States.

The media journey of Qatar has been influenced by various political conditions in the surrounding region, including growing post-World War tensions in the Middle East, the Arab–Israeli conflict, the Iranian revolution, the Iraq–Iran war, and the establishment of the Gulf Cooperation Council (GCC). Each of these factors has had an impact on the press and media in Qatar, providing emerging media outlets with opportunities to explore these issues through discussion and analysis.

Historically, the State of Qatar has been involved in printing and publishing books since the advent of printing in the surrounding region. The founder of the State of Qatar, Sheikh Jassim bin Mohammed bin Thani, contributed to the printing of one of the first books in the Gulf Arab countries when he ordered the printing of his book *Message in Nabati Poetry*, from the Mustafawiya Press in Mumbai, India, in 1907.

This poetry diwan, or collection of Sheikh Thani, was considered an important reference for the study of the historical and social conditions of the State of Qatar in the early 20th century, as well as a record of important events in the region during the past four centuries. Additionally, it includes poems of Sheikh Thani and other contemporary poets.

From 2000 to 2007, Internet usage in the Arab world increased significantly in conjunction with the release of the second generation of the Internet, Web 2.0. This allowed Internet penetration rates in the Arab world to reach 11%. During the same period, this rate reached 26.6% in Qatar (Al-Jaber and Gunter, 2013). An electronic press, regional and international news websites (which have received support from Qatar since their launch and proliferation), have contributed to shaping the Arab world's new public domain. These outlets (such as Al Jazeera) provided new space for unprecedented public debate by raising the ceiling on freedom of expression and introducing new issues that had not been known or made available through traditional media. Online forms of media increased the level of interaction and disseminated ideas to a wider audience (Miladi, 2018).

Qatari Press

Printed media began in Qatar with the publication of an official government gazette in 1961 that contained the laws and decrees of the emir. In 1969, Qatar established the Department of Information, which released *Doha Magazine* in the same year (Ismail, 2004). Moreover, the Ministry of Education began issuing *Education* magazine one year later. Also in 1979, *Al Urooba Press* and *Gulf News* (a bimonthly English language magazine) were launched as the first private press publications in Qatar (Auter and Al-Jaber, 2003).

Currently, there are three daily newspapers in Qatar: *Al-Raya*, *Al-Sharq*, and *Al-Watan*. Prior to these newspapers, there was a publication titled *Al-Arab*, which was first printed in 1971, temporarily ceasing publication in 1996, only to be resumed in 2008 (GCC Publications, 2004). The oldest of the other three publications is *Al-Sharq*, which had its first issue released in September 1978, followed by *Al-Raya* in May 1979 and finally by *Al-Watan* in September 1995. In addition to Arabic, Al-Raya Press also publishes *Gulf Times*, an English-language newspaper. *Gulf Times* was first published in December 1978. This was followed by *Al-Sharq*'s English edition, *The Peninsula*, which was first issued in 2001. Al-Watan Press's English-language iteration, the *Qatar Tribune*, was not published until September 2006. *Al-Arabi Al-Jadeed* was established in 2014 and *Lusail* in 2016. Outside of these newspapers, additional magazines in Qatar are published and cover many subjects including politics, business, society, finance, health, art, and entertainment. The total circulation of these newspapers is estimated to be around 145,000 copies (Al Mashikhi, 2014). See the Appendix for an overview of newspaper circulation.

The Qatari government began providing financial support to local newspapers and presses upon the establishment of the Ministry of Information in 1979. However, this practice was stopped in 1995 when Law No. 5 of 1995 abolished the Ministry of Information and Culture and delegated its responsibilities to various independent bodies. In its wake, the National Council for Culture, Arts, and Heritage was established (Rugh, 2004). This left the press and media essentially free from government interference, allowing many national and international newspapers and magazines to appear on the Qatari market, such as the *New York Times*, the *Washington Post*, *Time*, *Financial Times*, and *Alquds Alarabi* (Auter et al., 2005).

On 26 September 2018, the Qatari cabinet approved the establishment of Media City and referred the bill to the Shura Council for approval. In December of that same year, after nearly three months of deliberations, the body approved a draft law establishing Media City. An ambitious project, Qatar's Media City will be a benefit to local media while also attracting international media by providing the necessary services for them to perform their work. Details concerning the selection of media companies have yet to be announced, but it is known that specific standards will be applied to ensure that approved outlets take into consideration the nature and traditions of Qatar. Still, despite these Qatari specificities, the standards are expected to be guided and inspired by international precedents from around the world.

The Qatari government is expected to offer incentives to attract companies and institutions as investors for the city. The proposed inducements to invest in the project include exemptions to taxes and customs, as well as offering an attractive environment for international media. Even though it is a free zone, the laws of the state will apply to all institutions located in the city. The media institutions targeted by the draft law are nongovernmental organizations, and therefore do not require oversight by the Audit Bureau. The aim of Media City is to achieve the economic and professional integration of various state projects while encouraging investment funds for projects in the realms of digital media, technology, and film and television production.

Radio broadcasting services in Qatar

The first radio broadcast in Qatar began in the early 1960s. Pioneering this field was Mosque Radio, which reached audiences in the Doha capital area. In June 1968, Qatar Radio acquired Mosque Radio's transmission facilities. The Qatar Broadcasting Service (QBS) began airing radio programming in Arabic. English, Urdu, and French programming were added to the lineup in 1971, 1980, and 1985 respectively. In Qatar, there is no private, non-state-run radio. However, international radio stations such as the British Broadcasting Corporation (BBC), Voice of America, and Radio Sawa (which is publicly funded by the Broadcasting Board of Governors and the US Congress) have been made available (Auter and Al-Jaber, 2003).

The Voice of the Gulf Radio, an affiliate of the Qatar Media Foundation, is keen on documenting Gulf and Arab heritage. The station was launched from Doha and since its establishment in 2002 has broadcast thousands of exclusive songs from over 70 artists and poets from the Gulf, Arabian Peninsula, and around the world. Since its beginning, The Voice of the Gulf has hosted the Doha Music Festival and provides full coverage for the event. In addition to its arts programming, the station also broadcasts local and regional sporting competitions.

Television broadcasting services

Qatar Television began broadcasting in 1970. However, transmissions were initially confined to black-and-white programming broadcasted during afternoons from 3 pm to 7 pm. Upon the advent of color television in 1974, the transmission was extended to nine hours per day. This pattern continued to develop until 1982 when Channel 2 in English was launched to broadcast cultural programs, sporting events, and other important happenings. In 1998, satellite transmissions were introduced to Qatar, allowing for broadcasting to occur for more than 18 hours per day (ACRPS, 2014). All television channels were government-owned except for the Al Jazeera satellite news channel, which was introduced in 1996 (Zayani and Ayish, 2006). Al Jazeera TV is considered a private entity even though it was originally financed by the Qatari government (Lynch, 2006; Zayani, 2005).

Al Rayan Satellite Channel was established on 23 May 2012, by Al Rayyan Media and Marketing Company, with diverse content. The channel targets Qatari society as a primary audience and takes into account the specificity of their national identity and aspirations. Its vision is based on the adoption of the Qatar National Vision (2030), to help in achieving sustainable development through three main functions: "development, awareness and entertainment," which are translated into a programmatic mix representing its media strategy.

Digital media in Qatar

In recent years, online media has greatly influenced the global communication scene. Digital media platforms have fundamentally shifted how various activities and tasks are executed, in addition to making available a variety of previously impossible enterprises.

The use of the Internet in Qatar has grown significantly over the past five years, jumping from 85% in 2013 to 95% in half a decade (Elareshi and Al-Jaber, 2016). The study divided the rates of those using the Internet in Qatar into different brackets based on age. The findings showed that the 25 to 34 age group used the Internet at a rate of 100%, while the age group from 18 to 24 years used the Internet at a rate of 96%. The age group from 35 to 44 indicated using the Internet at a rate of 97%, a number that decreases to 82% for those over 45. The study found that the consumption of traditional media (television, radio, newspapers, and magazines) experienced a significant decline of 15% among Qataris from 87% in 2013 to 72% in 2017. Reading saw a 34% decline over the last five years, with only 29% of Qataris in 2017 indicating they still read, compared to 67% in 2013. The reading of magazines decreased from 22% in 2013 to only 9% in 2017.

As in other Gulf Cooperation Council states, social media has expanded significantly in Qatar. According to one study, WhatsApp is the most widely used social media platform in the country, with an 82% penetration rate among the sample (Northwestern University Qatar, 2018). WhatsApp has a 96% awareness rate, according to another study. Of all the applications covered by this study, Facebook and WhatsApp were the first to be widely used in Qatar. They both facilitate sharing photos and videos, meeting new people, as well as exchanging views and ideas. More than half of the study's participants and 70% of Qataris considered the possibility of browsing these social media applications via mobile phones as a key driver for their use. Twenty percent indicated that they would be less likely to use any platform that is not available for mobile use. This preference was more prevalent among Qatari women in particular, with 77% expressing the importance of having those applications on cell phones (ACRPS, 2014).

A recent study published in 2017 by Northwestern University in Qatar revealed that Qataris are most connected to digital media and more distinguished in their usage of the technology (Dennis et al., 2017). The study notes that 100% of Qataris use the Internet and spend about 60% more time on the Internet compared to citizens of other countries of the region. The study showed that Qatar has unique patterns in its usage of social media. Some 93% of Qataris use WhatsApp, while 70% use Instagram and 64% use Snapchat. Qatar has the highest utilization rates for Instagram and Snapchat in the world. Qataris spend much more time on the Internet compared to people in other countries. Qataris spent about 44.5 hours a week on the Internet in 2017 compared with 36.9 hours in 2013, the highest in the region (Dennis et al., 2017). Over the past five years, trends concerning the use of social media in Qatar have changed. You-Tube has seen a significant decline among Internet users in Qatar, from 52% in 2015 to 39% in 2017, while usage of the same platform has seemingly remained stable throughout the rest of the region. Instagram has seen steady growth in Qatar consistent with the usage patterns in the greater region since 2015. Qataris have the highest rate of Snapchat usage among citizens of other countries, followed by Twitter (Bar'el, 2016; Dennis et al., 2017).

Social media platforms are considered open spheres that allow Qatari citizens to express their views on politics, society, and religion, among other delicate issues that used to be taboo. This has influenced political, social, and religious speech in most Gulf countries including Qatar since social media has enabled young people to reply or argue with the politicians, religious leaders, executive officials, media professionals, intellectuals, elites, newcomers, and residents (Gunter and Dickinson, 2013). The powerful role social media plays in Qatar is attributed to the fact that it allows a real opportunity for marginalized members of society, particularly women, to express their opinions and mobilize their efforts to address their grievances through initiatives that promote feminist demands for a more equal society. In turn, they can practice independent roles that are more liberating than the traditional roles found in Gulf communities, particularly conservative ones (Al-Jaber, 2017).

Unlike traditional media, the use of social media platforms has assisted in real transformation as it has offered a broad and effective space for discussion, dialogue, argument, and debate. They have changed the rules of the old game and introduced inexperienced players to the world of political communication in Qatar and the Gulf countries in general. The intellectual influence of new media activists in society has far surpassed the influence of the old traditional intellectual elites and mass media (Elareshi and Al-Jaber, 2016). Furthermore, the citizens of these countries have grown used to presenting their ideas outside of the traditional media, including political demands and social taboos. New media allows for the discussion of religious, cultural, intellectual, educational, economic, and health issues in an unprecedented and bold way. Examples include the issue of feminist movements, workers in Qatar, government corruption, and divorce (Dennis et al., 2017; Al-Jaber, 2017).

Laws and regulations on media and journalists

When looking into media and press freedom, it is very important to understand the details of relevant laws and regulations. Press freedom is guaranteed in the Qatari Constitution and other applicable laws. Article 48 of the Qatar Constitution states, "Freedom of press, printing, and publication shall be guaranteed in accordance with the law." Article 48 of the Qatari Press and Publications Law of 1979 regulates the right to work in journalism and the duties and obligations of the journalist, in accordance with the provisions of the Constitution.

However, other parts of the Constitution make promises that seemingly conflict with principles of free expression. For instance, Article 19 states that the government will ensure "security" and "stability." Article 20 declares that the "State shall strive to strengthen the spirit of national unity, cooperation, and fraternity among all citizens." Articles 19 and 20 could effectively permit the government to act against the free expression of individuals as a method to ensure stability and harmony. Officials, for instance, could argue that criticism of the government promotes discord, and therefore should not be tolerated. The balance between creating a harmonious society and allowing for free and open expression permeates all debates on press freedom in the GCC. Other nations of the Arabian Peninsula feature constitutions that also guarantee freedom of expression (e.g., Kuwait, Bahrain, and the UAE). However, the real test for free expression comes not in a given law's documentation, but rather in its enforcement (GCC Publications, 2004).

The rights of journalists are restricted by a set of controls and obligations to be observed while conducting journalistic work in Qatar. Article 46 of the Press and Publication Law states, "the personality of the Emir of Qatar shall not be subject to any criticism and no statement shall be attributed to the Emir without written permission from the manager of his office." Article 47 of the same law provides for a list of prohibitions against calling for violence or the overthrow of the regime. However, the list includes several unreasonable restrictions. For example, journalists should not publish material that causes "any damage to the supreme interests of the country." This article also criminalizes any statement that may cause "confusion with the economic situation in the country." With these provisions, a journalist specializing in these sectors may be penalized if he or she reports on falling economic numbers.

When reading and interpreting these different concepts, it can be inferred that the Qatari Press and Publication Law adopts a broad definition of a journalist. The "press" is not confined to the written press but extends to all forms of media including electronic media. As for the conditions that must be met by journalists under the Qatari Press and Publications Law, a distinction has been made between a Qatari journalist and a foreign journalist. The primary distinction is that Qatari citizens are allowed to exercise their right to practice journalism without receiving prior registration and confirmation, as is the case for foreign journalists. This is stated in Article 11 and is inferred in Article 9 of the Press and Publications Law.

Article 12 of the same law stipulates that foreign journalists must meet all the conditions required for a Qatari journalist, and in addition must acquire a certificate from a recognized journalism institute or college, as well as a resume indicating he or she has practiced journalism at least three years prior at a recognized institution. Additionally, a foreign journalist should be registered in a press or editors union and should hold a press card issued by one of the official authorities of his country. Another important condition for a foreign journalist is that he or she is not allowed to practice any non-media work while performing his or her duties as a journalist in Qatar.

The Qatari Press and Publications Law, however, does not address questions surrounding the legal association between the journalist and the newspaper for which he or she works. The law only stipulates the conditions that must be met by the journalist to practice the craft. The contract between the journalist and the newspaper is the legal basis for the adaptation of journalism work and the terms and conditions related to the obligations and rights of the journalist. This relationship can be described as a relationship governed by the Labor Code, and in other terms may be subject to the provisions of a contract.

As long as the elements of remuneration and subordination are present in the management and supervision of the relationship between the journalist and the newspaper, this is sufficient to consider the association between the journalist and the newspaper as a legal contract of employment subject to the provisions of the Labor Code. This is true of the journalist who is employed regularly and is under the supervision of the newspaper, so long as the work is the source of his or her livelihood. If his or her work is for a fee, an independent journalist can work for more than one newspaper. Such an arrangement is outside the scope of the Labor Code and is legally subject to the provisions of the contract.

In September 2018, the Council of Ministers approved a draft law for regulating printing, publishing, media activities, and the arts. The new law draft incorporated the Press and Publications Law No. 8 for the year 1979 and Decree-Law No. 16 of 1993 regulating the practice of publicity activities, public relations, artistic production, and works of art.

One of the main features of the new draft law is that it adopted some basic amendments concerning the press, in line with Article 19 of the Universal Declaration of Human Rights and Article 19 of the International Covenant on Civil and Political Rights. These are considered important legal protections for free expression. The significance lies in three main aspects: respect for human dignity, the free exchange of ideas and views, and the flow of information.

The new draft provides for freedom of the press in accordance with the Qatari Constitution, the Universal Declaration of Human Rights, and the International Covenant on Civil and Political Rights. The draft law also adopted the establishment of a committee in the Ministry of Culture and Sports for the registration of journalists and media personnel.

The new draft law added provisions related to publications and electronic media. The new draft provides for the granting of cinema and theatre licenses. There is some added text in this regard that regulates the establishment and management of cinemas and theatres. Additionally, the draft created a new chapter for audio and visual broadcasting. In the future, an administrative body will be established for this purpose. The new government entity will be tasked with granting licenses for media activities, organizations, and the circulation of books and various works of art to ensure that cultural diversity and the openness of civilization conforms with Islamic teachings and the values and ethics of Qatari society. The entity will also be responsible for implementing laws and regulations related to the press and publications, studying and issuing the necessary licenses for press publications, and issuing procedures in accordance with the law. The ministry will also be responsible for issuing the necessary licenses for printing presses, publishing houses, commercial libraries, import and export institutions, and licenses to practice the professions of journalism, advertising, public relations, artistic production, and the distribution of licenses to sell related items. In coordination with relevant administrative units, the law will be used to approve the issuance and distribution of publications by diplomatic and consular missions and bodies accredited to Qatar. Local and foreign publications and works of art will also be governed in accordance with this law.

This law comes as Qatar's state legislation begins to modernize its framework in line with technological developments in the fields of the press, publishing, media, and the arts. As part of this goal, the framework is also in line with the principles of free expression and freedom of the press that can be found in Qatar. Provisions within the bill outline specific instructions related to the organization of printing presses and the establishment of publishing houses and cinemas, in addition to art installations, film production, broadcasting, and public relations services (Al-Jaber and Gunter, 2013).

There seems to be no apparent conflict between the draft law and the current laws governing publicity and media, as the private sector will be involved by way of attracting businesspeople to invest in the infrastructure necessary to start operating Media City. Media City is another building block for Qatar and its evolution into a knowledge-based economy, equal in importance to Education City, the Qatar Financial Center, and other leading projects in the country.

Social and political functions of broadcasting

The debate concerning media freedom and democracy is based on the fact that principles of real democracy are represented efficiently within political communication between the majority of people, the authority, and the elite. This principle should be established alongside the protection of free speech, freedom of thought, and freedom of belief. Each of these factors cannot be generated without a full system that maintains a balance between everyone while retaining the ability to supervise, audit, investigate, criticize, and present views and thoughts freely as protected by the rule of law (Dahlgren, 2009; Mutz and Martin, 2001).

This element is equally as important as the freedom to obtain and circulate information, present delicate, crucial, and important issues, as well as initiate a societal dialogue (ACRPS, 2014; Habermas, 2006). People concerned with political, economic, societal, and cultural life need to effectively use communication, with different and numerous media platforms to express their views, thoughts, and perspectives. Therefore, any decrease in freedom of communication, restriction on the media, or the lessening of free speech will subsequently lead to the decline of an effective democracy (Gambill, 2000).

Despite the media changes that have arisen over recent years, the communication scene in Qatar and the rest of the Gulf region is generally characterized by an ill-defined and contentious relationship between the governing authority, state institutions, and the target audience. In the Gulf, there has never been a clear separation between these authorities, a situation further confused by the appearance of mass media emerging as the Gulf's very own "fourth estate" to challenge other bodies (Ayish, 2002b; Kraidy, 2006). The advent of new modes of usage and new platforms of media has helped to reform the political and press communication sphere in the GCC region.

There is also a continuing dialectical relationship in the political system in Qatar between the ruling authority and the press as a fourth authority. The equation is linked to the logic of freedom of information, and power, and a particular concern over who should control knowledge and disseminate it in society. The political authority uses the press as a major tool to reach all segments of the public in promoting its political, economic, and social projects. The press also deals with political systems as an important source of political and economic news adopted by governments to gain the reader's confidence. Thus, they can win the trust of readership, and therefore, more influence in society. Nevertheless, when traditional media and the ruling power engage in confrontation, the latter always wins in a knockout.

Conclusion

The improvement of living conditions in Qatar as a result of the improving economy extended to all aspects of life, including the media landscape. Major political and security events in the region influenced the media journey in Qatar, which started with print media.

However, the electronic press provided a new space for increased public debate and public engagement. Qatar aspires to be a regional hub for media with its plan to establish Media City. The government is expected to provide incentives to attract investment for this ambitious media project.

As is the case in many other countries, social media in Qatar has fundamentally changed the media landscape. Cell phone applications are also important in this regard, as many Qataris link their social media usage to accessibility on their handheld devices. As a result, traditional media consumption in Qatar has significantly declined. WhatsApp and Snapchat are among the most widely used social media platforms among Qataris, and the Internet penetration rate in Qatar is among the highest worldwide.

Despite the development of media and new means of expression, laws and regulations in Qatar still contain provisions and prohibitions that impede the professional and free exchange of opinions and ideas. A new draft law, however, indicates there is some hope for greater press freedom. The new draft provides freedom of the press in accordance with the Qatari Constitution, the Universal Declaration of Human Rights, and the International Covenant on Civil and Political Rights.

One important major transformation in the field of media is the transformation from one-way and homogeneous content to two-way interactive communication via a growing number of applications. The rise of "new media" and "digital media" is reflected in the wider political, social, and economic trends in the wider world, and the Middle East in particular.

Communication and information breakthroughs have contributed to the transformation of the media landscape in the last decade of the 20th century. Media outlets in Qatar have had a variety of responses to the overwhelming impact of this revolution, and have been able to develop their institutions to benefit from opportunities in the so-called new wave media of satellite channels, newspapers, electronic journals, and Internet news sites (Al Mashikhi, 2014).

In light of the transformation and the development of modern media and interactive social media, the traditional media in Qatar are under considerable pressure to maintain their status among the public to compete with new media's ability to report events instantly and facilitate direct audience interaction (Elareshi and Al-Jaber, 2016). Because of this, traditional media outlets are trying to catch up with new media but are impeded by traditional laws and regulations that have not undergone a comparable change. In addition, traditional media outlets have not challenged government decisions and legislation and are not liberated from subordination to capital and advertisers. These factors mean that they perform a lesser role than social media in raising the ceiling of freedoms and providing space for those calling for political, economic, or social reforms (Mellor, 2007).

New media now offers a broad range of ideas based on expression, dialogue, open discussion, the sharing of supportive and opposing views, and the dissemination of news and information (Ayish and Mellor, 2015; Zayani and Ayish, 2006). This can be termed "communication democracy" as it involves widespread participation by the vast majority of people, particularly marginalized segments of society (e.g., women and youth who represent the majority and the future of the GCC region). In spite of this, there have been several obstacles and challenges that have hindered Qatar's efforts to encourage the optimal use of these new communication platforms and applications (Mourtada and Salem, 2012; Saad and Kilany, 2012).

The media landscape in Qatar has witnessed clear developments that make it different from the government-controlled local television stations, radio stations, and newspapers that have typified long-standing repressive and tyrannical regimes throughout the greater Arab world.

References

ACRPS (2014), *Arab Public Opinion Poll Program 2014*. Retrieved from www.dohainstiute.org. Accessed 9 August 2020.

Al-Jaber, K. (2013), Satellite TV and New Media in Supporting the Arab Spring. In *Paper presented at the Media and Democratic Transition in the Arab Spring Countries Conference*. Doha, Qatar: Media Department, University of Qatar.

Al-Jaber, K. (2017), Impact of New Media Platforms on the Gulf Political Communication Landscape: Consumption Patterns and Public Sphere. In Ibrahim Al-Boaz (ed.), *Information and Communication Technology in the Gulf Cooperation Council Countries*. Kuwait: Gulf Development Forum.

Al-Jaber, K., and Al-Sayed, K. (2013), *Arab Media in a Turbulent World*. Doha, Qatar: Al-Sharaq Publishing Ltd.

Al-Jaber, K., and Gunter, B. (2013), Evolving News Systems in the Gulf Countries. In B. Gunter and R. Dickinson (eds.), *News Media in the Arab World: A Study of 10 Arab and Muslim Countries*. New York: Bloomsbury Publishing USA, pp. 21–40.

Al Mashikhi, M. (2014), *Alia'lam fi alkhalij ala'rabi waka'h wmstkblh* (Media in the Arabian Gulf: Reality and Future). 2nd edition. Amman, Jordan: Al-Falah House for Publication and Distribution.

Auter, P., and Al-Jaber, K. (2003), Qatar Media/Al-Jazeera TV. In D. DesJardins (ed.), *World Press Encyclopedia*. Farmington Hills, MI: Gale Group, pp. 759–762.

Auter, P., Arafa, M., and Al-Jaber, K. (2005), Identifying with Arabic Journalists: How Al-Jazeera Tapped Parasocial Interaction Gratifications in the Arab World. *International Communication Gazette*, 67(2), pp. 189–204.

Ayish, M. (2002b), The Impact of Arab Satellite Television on Culture and Value Systems in Arab Countries: Perspectives and Issues. *Transnational Broadcasting Studies*. Retrieved from www.tbsjournal.com/Archives/Fall02/Ayish.html

Ayish, M., and Mellor, N. (2015), *Reporting in the MENA Region: Cyber Engagement and pan-Arab Social Media*. London: Rowman & Littlefield.

Bar'el, Z. (2016), *How Al Jazeera Further Damaged the Fast-deteriorating Egypt-Qatar Relationship*. Retrieved from www.haaretz.com/middle-east-news/.premium-how-al-jazeera-further-damaged-egypt-qatar-relations-1.5472766. Accessed 9 September 2018.

Dahlgren, P. (2009), *Media and Political Engagement*. Cambridge, MA: Cambridge University Press.

Dennis, E., Martin, J., and Wood, R. (2017), *Media Use in the Middle East: A Seven-nation Survey*. Retrieved from http://mideastmedia.org/survey/2017/. Accessed 23 January 2018.

Elareshi, M., and Al-Jaber, K. (2016), The New Media as Alternative Medium in the GCC Region: The Growing Influence of Social Networks. In B. Gunter, M. Elareshi, and K. Al-Jaber (eds.), *Social Media in the Arab World: Communication and Public Opinion in the Gulf States*. London: I.B. Tauris, pp. 157–178.

Gambill, G. C. (2000), Qatar's Al-Jazeera TV: The Power of Free Speech. *Middle East Intelligence Bulletin*, 2(5), p. 1.

GCC Publications (2004), *Media Institutions in the Arab Countries of the Gulf Cooperation Council (GCC): Radio, TV, and News Agencies*. Riyadh, Saudi Arabia: Secretariat General.

Gunter, B., and Dickinson, R. (eds.) (2013), *News Media in the Arab World*. New York: Bloomsbury.

Habermas, J. (2006), Political Communication in Media Society: Does Democracy still Enjoy an Epistemic Dimension? The Impact of Normative Theory on Empirical Research. *Communication Theory*, 16(4), pp. 411–426.

Ismail, I. I. (2004), *Arab Daily Press in Qatar*. Doha, Qatar: National Council for Culture, Arts, and Heritage.

Kraidy, M. (2006), Reality Television and Politics in the Arab World: Preliminary Observations. *Transnational Broadcasting Studie*, 15. Retrieved from https://repository.upenn.edu/cgi/viewcontent.cgi?article=1311&context=asc_papers

Lynch, M. (2006), *Voices of the new Arab Public: Iraq, Al-Jazeera, and Middle East Politics Today*. New York: Columbia University Press.

Mellor, N. (2007), *Modern Arab Journalism: Problems and Prospects*. Edinburgh: Edinburgh University Press.

Miladi, N. (2018), *AlJazeera and the Arab Revolution: Public Opinion, Diplomacy, and Political Change*. Bristol: Intellect Books.

Mourtada, R., and Salem, F. (2012), Social Media, Employment, and Entrepreneurship: New Frontiers for the Economic Empowerment of Arab Youth? In *Dubai School of Governance*. Retrieved from www.researchgate.net/publication/233759686%0D

Mutz, D. C., and Martin, P. (2001), Facilitating Communication across Lines of Political Difference: The Role of Mass Media. *American Political Science Association*, 95(1), pp. 97–114.

Rugh, W. (2004), *Arab Mass Media: Newspapers, Radio, and Television in Arab Politics*. London: Praeger Publishers.

Saad, A., and Kilany, N. (2012), *Kuwaiti Women and their Green Chair Struggle*. Retrieved from www.skynewsarabia.com/web/article/56899/. Accessed 15 February 2013.

Sakr, N. (2007), *Arab Media and Political Renewal: Community, Legitimacy, and Public Life*. London: I.B.Tauris.

Zayani, M. (2005), *The Al-Jazeera Phenomenon: Critical Perspectives on New Arab Media*. London: Pluto Press.

Zayani, M., and Ayish, M. (2006), Arab Satellite Television and Crisis Reporting. *International Communication Gazette*, 68(5–6), pp. 473–497. doi:10.1177/1748048506068724

Appendix
NEWSPAPER USAGE IN QATAR

Newspaper Name	Establishment Date	Circulation	Language	Publisher
Al Jareedah Al Rasmeyah	1961	5,000	Arabic	Information Department – Doha
Al Arab	1972	20,000	Arabic	Dar Al-Ouruba Printing and Publishing
Al Sharq	1987	22,000	Arabic	Dar Al Sharq Printing
Gulf Times	1978	20,000	English	Gulf Publishing and Printing Co.
Al Rayyah	1979	18,000	Arabic	Gulf Publishing and Printing Co.
Al Watan	1995	25,000	Arabic	Dar Al Watan Printing
The Peninsula	1996	10,000	English	Dar Al Sharq Printing
Al-Arabi Al-Jadeed	2014	5,000	Arabic	Fadaat Media Group
Qatar Tribune	2006	10,000	English	Qatar Information & Marketing
Lusail	2016	10,000	Arabic	Dar Al Sharq Printing
		Circulation Total 145,000		

Source: Al Mashikhi, 2014; Rugh, 2004.

24

AL JAZEERA NETWORK AND THE TRANSFORMATIONS IN THE GLOBAL COMMUNICATION FLOW

Noureddine Miladi

Introduction

During the last couple of decades, satellite technology has fundamentally transformed the flow of information and provided unprecedented opportunities for global news reporting (Thussu, 2018). The impact of ensuing digital technologies on modern society circumvents mere changes in journalism practices. The unparalleled transformations encompass a paradigm shift in the dissemination and reception of news. Traditional gatekeepers, be they ruling regimes or old-style global media conglomerates, have arguably lost control of their traditional privilege of information control (Castells, 2012).

The Al Jazeera network has been at the heart of these global changes. With controversial news reporting at times, which resulted in fierce criticism from governments in the Arab region and beyond, Al Jazeera's editorial line has earned it attention since its inception. The Arabic channel (Al Jazeera Arabic), which was inaugurated in 1996 as a niche TV service targeting Arab viewers in the Arab world and in diaspora, has been transformed into a media network of a global reach. After gaining fame and influence in the region, its effects on the international media and political scenes have been unmissable. On a global level, everyone realizes that its news and current affairs programs are challenging and different. To many, the network has enduringly reshaped the landscape of global news reporting in a short time (Zayani, 2005; Miladi, 2006; Tatham, 2006; Miles, 2009; Abdelmoula, 2015).

This chapter attempts to provide an overview of the Al Jazeera phenomenon. It analyzes its atypical news culture from the perspective of paradigm change in the global communication flow. It traces the key transformations attributed to Al Jazeera network and the key characteristics of its phenomenal success. The Al Jazeera effect is obviously contested. As much as the network has received praise the world over, it has also faced fierce criticism, and sometimes its journalists were subject to repetitive incarceration. Its perceived popularity has also been arguably followed by a "decline in its viewership" (Mellor, 2016). This decline, they contend, should be understood in the context of "Arab mediascape where media and politics are unremittingly intertwined, making it often difficult for news media to achieve full professional independence" (Mellor, 2016: 349). Therefore, this chapter also discusses the challenges it has faced both in the Arab region and beyond, marred by myriad criticism and sometimes contempt. However, to understand these successes, challenges, and sometime hostile responses to its inimitable journalism practice, it is worth discussing aspects of Arab media practice before the Al Jazeera age.

Arab broadcasting before the Al Jazeera revolution

For decades and after the popularity of Voice of the Arabs, a radio broadcasting service launched by the then Egyptian president Gamal Abdel Nasser in 1953, a pan-Arab voice quasi appealing to Arab audiences across the Arab world had been an anomaly. Generations of Arab listeners, especially educated people looking for balanced and critical analysis of news and current affairs, tended to flock to Western reputable radio broadcasters such as BBC World Service, Voice of America, Radio Monte Carlo, and Deutsche Welle (Boyd, 1999). A symbolic example, which typified that era, was that the assassination of former Egyptian president Muhammad Anwar El-Sadat (serving from 1970 to 1981) had been immediately announced by Western radio broadcasters in the morning of 6 October 1981, while the Egyptian media at the time confirmed his death very late that evening. A few decades later, the advent of satellite TV also meant, as was the case in many parts of the world, that BBC World and CNN became the prime sources of live TV news coverage in the Arab region.

Against the backdrop of this vacuum in the Arab news media market, it was not very hard for Al Jazeera to dominate Arab broadcasting in news and current affairs soon after its inception in 1996. Arab media outlets remained far from being able to compete with the professionalism standards of Western media outlets. Namely, before the fast growth of Arab satellite TV across the region and in diaspora, TV and radio broadcasting in the Arab region used to be state controlled, and much of its content was pure government propaganda (Ben Messaoud, 2019). Critical investigative journalism was unaccounted for in their journalism culture.

In most of the Arab countries, public as well as private media were tools for public opinion control. National TV and radio channels served as propaganda tools directly controlled from presidential palaces. Managers of state media institutions, news editors, and sometimes key journalists were appointed through a president's/king's decree. Across all media platforms, total censorship on critical voices has always been the norm (Boyd, 1999; Rugh, 2004). Human rights abuses, freedom of speech, presidents' and kings' personal affairs along with their families and entourages, in addition to issues related to poverty, unemployment, corruption, and underdevelopment, were among the taboos that all media and critics tended to refrain from.

Amidst this environment of Arab regimes' tight media control, Al Jazeera had emerged. Breaking all taboos concerning political corruption and human rights abuses and providing a voice for political opposition figures was a breakthrough to the Arab media's stringent censorship (Zayani, 2005; Miladi, 2016). It was not hard, then, for the Arabic channel, the first brand of Al Jazeera's network, to slowly carve its name in both regional and global broadcasting scenes. It seems also evident to historically situate the channel as inaugurating a new era in Arab broadcasting. The benchmark it set and the professionalism norms and news values it epitomizes have been unchallenged. The burgeoning digital media and satellite technologies have aided its impact. Its brand name has become a recognizable trademark associated with free speech, daring news reporting, and support of the suppressed (Tatham, 2006; Miles, 2009).

To diasporic Arabs, Al Jazeera was of a particular importance. Initially through satellite broadcasting, Al Jazeera Arabic succeeded in appealing to Arabs in Europe and the USA. With the commercialization of Arabic television in the 1990s and the growth of satellite broadcasting, a pan-Arab audience has emerged and changed the way that media programmers, advertisers, and politicians conceived of Arab audiences (Mellor, 2008). The multi-channel environment via satellite that followed Al Jazeera has expanded the choice of Arab viewers despite tight

Arab governmental control on what can be broadcast on local terrestrial services. News from their home countries, which used to be read the next day in Arab newspapers or discussed in cafés, mosques, churches, or community centers became live broadcasting through Al Jazeera's airwaves.

The September 11, 2001, attacks in the USA, the war in Afghanistan 2001, and the war on Iraq 2003 marked defining moments for Arab audiences where satellite TV became central. Diasporic communities found also in Al Jazeera a refuge for what they saw as alternative news reporting compared to the narrative of Western media outlets. Tatham (2006) and Miladi (2006) argued that it was mainly the advent of Al Jazeera's alternative approach to news coverage that led to increased awareness among the Arab diaspora and their interest in news. It also led to their ability to compare news output from various international sources.

Reporting the world differently: Al Jazeera's stance

Part of what distinguishes Al Jazeera is its atypical editorial line in reporting the world. Defining impartiality and objectivity in news reporting differently from the existing norms at the time was a major leap. In its pursuit for impartiality, Al Jazeera guaranteed a large room of independence from the government of Qatar, although its critics would argue that it systematically steers away from criticizing Qatari government affairs or foreign policy (Seib, 2016).

In what follows, I will analyze examples from Al Jazeera's challenging news reporting, which has over the years distinguished it from other global news networks. Two cases in point were the war in Afghanistan in 2001 and the invasion of Iraq in 2003. In both instances one may argue that the channel stood as one of the biggest challenges for the American administration in these foreign-led wars, which in the absence of Al Jazeera would have been easily sold to the Western public as well as people in the Middle East. For instance, the plethora of information, exclusive footage, and interviews coming from Al Jazeera's reports emphasized a dominant paradigm that the war in Afghanistan and the invasion of Iraq were never just wars. The Al Jazeera narrative on the Iraq War was that the strategic aim of the war was not to free the Iraqi people from a dictator (Saddam Hussain) and save the region from the weapons of mass destruction he amassed but to control the oil fields and build further military bases in the Middle East.

Moreover, the early existence of Al Jazeera's offices in Afghanistan helped it report the invasion of Afghanistan 2001, in a manner Western audiences did not experience on CNN or the BBC. Al Jazeera's reporters in Kabul secured exclusive interviews with Al Qaida leaders (Osama bin Laden and Ayman Aldawahiri), who voiced starch criticism about the American administration. Live footage kept relaying on Al Jazeera's airwaves the scale of destruction the USA army's air raids in Afghanistan caused. Also, the scale of the casualties and destruction of Afghanis' livelihoods changed the discourse of the war. The American government media machine found itself always on the defensive and hence in a challenging position to win the hearts and minds of Muslim publics around the world (Tatham, 2006).

Similarly, Al Jazeera's early existence in Baghdad gave it an advantageous edge over other international channels in providing exclusive reports about the course of events on the ground. During the outbreak of the war on Iraq (March 2003), Al Jazeera was concretely the eyes and ears of the world. One may argue that all of the aforementioned conflicts would not have been known to the world the way we know them if it was not for the camera of Al Jazeera. This form of exclusive reporting also brought Al Jazeera to the world stage when the Tunisian revolution broke out on 14 January 2011.

Another aspect of Al Jazeera's distinctive reporting is related to the language of news. Terminology and choice of vocabulary in newsmaking is a sophisticated bundle of debates in the core of the ethics and values of journalism practice. An integral component of Al Jazeera's reporting is the unique choice of culturally specific vocabulary when reporting, for instance, from various parts of the Middle East. The alternative value that underlies its news coverage is therefore a commitment to the local voices it aims to represent while embedded in their daily reality.

The vocabulary of news reporting is a tricky area related to measuring bias or accuracy in the news. The terms "terrorism"/"terrorist," for instance, have become one of the very controversial terminologies employed by the media in their news reporting. A longitudinal analysis of Al Jazeera's news reporting of the past 20 years tells that it is not hard to notice that the channel has always steered away from adopting such labels to describe rebel groups, freedom fighters, or even groups who use violence as a means for social change like Al Qaida and Daesh (ISIS/IS). In news stories as well as other documentary or discussion programs, the editorial line sticks to the name by which any given group is known or presents itself. Instead of saying, for example, "*tandheem al Qaida al irhabi*" (Al Qaida terrorist group) or "*Tandheem al dawla al Islamia al irhabi*" (the Islamic State terrorist group), Al Jazeera would call them "Al Qaida" or "The Islamic State group." In the same way and in covering the Palestinian–Israeli conflict, Al Jazeera does not associate the various Palestinian groups such as *Hamas*, *Al Jihad Al Islami* (Islamic Jihad), *Fatah*, *Kataib Al Qassam* (the Al Qassam Brigades), and *Al Jibha Al Sha'bia* (the Popular Front) with terrorism. Such groups are always reported as legitimate Palestinian freedom fighter groups who are struggling against the Israeli colonization of the Palestinian land.

Finally, a significant aspect of Al Jazeera's distinctive news reporting is its obvious strategic approach in capitalizing on native reporters. In its various offices around the world, Al Jazeera tends to employ locals who understand the language and dialect as well as cultural specificities of the region they report from. But, more importantly, those local reporters understand well the target audience of Al Jazeera and their concerns. Often global broadcasters are criticized for what a few call "parachute" journalism (Yusha'u 2015), in which reporters simply come from the metropolis of global centers and report about a land they little know about. News reporting of the war in Afghanistan since 2001, the invasion of Iraq in 2003, and the Palestinian–Israeli conflict are cases in point (Miladi, 2006). For instance, various journalists working for global news channels tend to report the Palestinian–Israeli conflict from their comfort zones in a hotel somewhere in Jerusalem or Tel Aviv. The Israeli wars on Gaza in 2009 and 2014 were examples in which scores of Western journalists had never been to Gaza while they reported daily news on the day-to-day aerial bombardment and the destruction of the city by the Israeli air force. The incursion of the Israeli army artillery used to be remotely reported from tens of miles away on global channels like CNN, BBC World, MSNBC, and Sky News, among many others (Philo and Berry, 2004).

The Arab Spring revolutions: Al Jazeera's galvanizing effect

The political unrests known as "Arab Spring revolutions" became emblematic with both social media networks (namely Facebook) and Al Jazeera. When the protests started in Tunisia on 17 December 2010, the Al Jazeera network dedicated its leading satellite and digital platforms to 24-hour rolling coverage of the events. Al Jazeera Arabic, Al Jazeera English, and Al Jazeera Mubasher (which means Al Jazeera live), as well as its digital platforms (AJ+ Arabic and AJ+ English), all had full commitment to the minute-by-minute development of events on the ground (Norris, 2017).

The ever-evolving new digital technologies have kept Al Jazeera's live content incessantly in flux. In addition to the earlier mentioned platforms, Al Jazeera Mubasher Egypt was launched in January 2011, a live streaming channel dedicated to reporting news and analysis from Egypt.

The channel was available both on satellite and online via http://mubasher.aljazeera.net. While the content was mainly news and current affairs coverage, the channel reported other live events like conferences, debates, key speeches or press conferences, demonstrations, vigils, or any other deemed newsworthy content.

As noted earlier, the Arab Spring revolutions have been pivotal historical moments that popularized Al Jazeera, but they were also times to test the integrity of the network. Although its various channels have received mounting criticism regarding the evident support for protesters against the regimes of Tunisia, Egypt, Libya, Yemen, and Syria (Bakr, 2014), Al Jazeera Arabic as well as its sister channels were decisive in promoting people's struggle for democracy and freedom in those countries. It was clear since the beginning of the unrests in Tunisia, for example, that Al Jazeera sided with the Arab public who have been yearning for regime change for decades under the rule of Zein Elabidine Ben Ali. The same goes regarding the regimes of Muammar Gaddafi in Libya, Hosni Mubarak in Egypt, Abdallah Saleh in Yemen, and later Bashar Alassad in Syria. The airwaves remained open to members of the public and political and human rights activists from across the Arab world to voice their wrath in criticizing corrupt regimes and their poor performance.

Wadah Kanfar (former director general of the Al Jazeera network) unveiled how during those events the camera was a crucial tool for protecting the protesters in Tahrir Square in Egypt. Whether in Tunisia, Egypt, Libya, or Yemen, he argued,

> Al Jazeera explicitly associates its news reporting to fighting for democracy and free speech in those countries. The network sees itself as the voice of the voiceless and a platform of free speech for those who have none. The revolt in Libya was topping the news and it was described as civil war. In Gaddafi's view, the West was using humanitarianism as a cover to seize control of Libya's oil wealth. Hassan Al Jaber (Al Jazeera's camera operator) killed in Libya – likely a targeted killing. Beliefs have been circulating among Al Jazeera staff that Gaddafi put out a bounty on their heads.
>
> *(Khanfar, 2015)*

Building on that analysis, the Al Jazeera snowball effect on the Arab Spring events was unmistakable. The galvanizing impact was further aided by providing exposure to social media activists. The camera-bearing citizen or the citizen journalist has become the witness and sometimes the maker of the history of our time. During the events leading to the Tunisian revolution, for instance, there was obvious synchronization between Al Jazeera news reports and social media networks. User-generated material from activists in the field was gathered, sifted, and selected to support its news coverage. Namely, where the network did not have regular reporters, it capitalized on social media networks' content and videos sent to its newsrooms by citizen journalists. Such news scoops were amplified by Al Jazeera news channels and turned into credible news stories that attract attention from around the world (Hassan and Elmasry, 2018).

During the Tunisian revolution, Facebook groups increased exponentially in number. These platforms served as valuable sources of news for Al Jazeera's channels. Groups like "Tunis" and "Tunisia" had over 600,000 people subscribing at the time. Activists used to wait for *Hasaad Al-Yawm* (Al Jazeera's flagship evening news program) and *Al-Hasaad A-Magharibi* (which was a special evening news program reporting about the Maghreb countries [Tunisia, Libya, Algeria, and Morocco]). Al Jazeera further encouraged direct engagement with activists in the field by promoting a dedicated page (yourmedia.aljazeera.net) to gather more news stories. This space proved significant in gathering crude information with no cost in terms of logistics or personnel to Al Jazeera. This space was also treasurable for activists as it facilitated broadcasting their reports.

Consequently, the opening up of social media platforms as a residue of diverse narratives about the Arab revolutions presented a multiplicity of perspectives. Through bringing these different voices coming from within the Arab region and beyond both in its news and documentary programs, Al Jazeera symbolized a unifying platform for these voices and a fusing mechanism that made sense of all of the divergent narratives. All of this process was efficiently achieved in Al Jazeera's newsrooms aided by an army of editors and researchers in its offices around the world. Al Jazeera has been adapting with this fast-developing socio-political atmosphere in the region and responding to the fast-growing "eco-media" reality overwhelmed by social media networks.

It is worth noting that Al Jazeera has gained trust not only from millions of viewers from around the world but also journalists who appreciate its daring journalism. On 25 February 2011, journalists of Tunisia TV went on strike, and the main news program at 8 pm was not broadcast for the first time. One of the journalists was interviewed on *Al-Hasaad Al-Magharibi* (news program at 10:50 pm on Al Jazeera) to express her disappointment of the way the TV was run and its continuation of what she called the same culture of dictatorial control. Khalid Nejah, the then news editor, tendered his resignation and sent it to the Al Jazeera Arabic channel to be broadcast to the public. This marked a very significant event symbolizing the continuous lack of confidence in the Tunisian main public service broadcaster at the time.

In the midst of Algerian and Sudanese social activism: Al Jazeera's bustling public sphere

Bold support of the Arab public's peaceful protests against their corrupt regimes did not stop with the Arab Spring events. The resumption of what can be called the Arab public's second awakening was another opportunity not to be missed by the Al Jazeera network. During the Sudanese political unrests in February–April 2019, the network was again reporting the news differently from the Sudanese official TV channel. This led the regime to arrest its bureau chief in Khartoum and a couple of other journalists in a bid to silence the Sudanese opposition voices who find in Al Jazeera a platform for blatant criticism.

Early in the morning of 11 April 2019, the Sudanese army staged a coup, ousting president Omar Albashir from power. From early hours in the morning, Al Jazeera stopped all other scheduled programs and kept a live broadcast of events from the scene. Its journalists joined the crowds and kept for hours reporting from in front of the army headquarters, interviewing scores of activists and political analysts. The Al Jazeera camera kept being fixated on the celebrating Sudanese crowds who streamed in by the thousands to join the sit-ins. From early that morning, it reported that the army got control of the radio and TV headquarters. The official Sudanese TV kept displaying a still image of the army logo for about nine and a half hours with military songs as background sound. From 6 am that morning and for most of the day until the declaration of the coup, no reporting about the protests in the capital or any other content could be watched on the official TV. It was only later in the afternoon that day that the official Sudanese TV broadcast the first coup announcement by the self-declared interim president (Awadh ben Ouf).

Al Jazeera channel, instead, provided a free platform for activists of all types. It kept echoing people's responses vis-à-vis that historical moment, their concerns about what would happen next, and their aspirations for the future. Al Jazeera also kept showing a split screen: on the left was a frozen image from the official Sudan TV and on the right live reporting of the protests from in front of the army headquarters in Khartoum. Journalists, political activists, and academics were interviewed via satellite or over the phone and some were even flown to Al Jazeera's studios in Doha to comment on the events. Commentators were speculating about what they expected. Other analysts gave suggestions about what the army should do in case the regime of General Omar Albashir fell.

Parallel to the coverage of the coup in Sudan, on Friday 12 April 2019, one day after the coup on Omar Albashir and while protests started to calm down, Al Jazeera turned its focus to the evolving events in Algeria. The Arabic channel kept airing live streaming from the capital Alger and opened the airwaves to various commentators to discuss responses to the political developments. Al Jazeera anchors discussed with members of the public as well as analysts what should be done next. For most of the daily live broadcasting, the channel kept its platforms resembling virtual public spaces where Algerians discussed amongst each other their responses and aspirations regarding the agenda for a way forward.

While such live exchanges took place between various political analysts, academics, and activists, Al Jazeera kept a rolling stream of footage from protests that Friday across Algeria. A panoramic split screen showed constant updates from various cities such as the capital Alger, Wahran, Tilimsan, Bjaya, Annaba, and Jijle, among others. These unremitting discussions turned the Al Jazeera airwaves into uncensored space through which Algerians could listen to each other and probably for the first time express themselves without fear of arrest or incarceration. Also via the never-ending people's interventions, Al Jazeera reflected a unanimous public urge for regime change. All of the aforementioned unbroken news coverage by Al Jazeera Arabic, Al Jazeera English, and Al Jazeera Mubashir took place for many hours of the day while the national Algerian TV had a total blackout on what was happening on the ground.

War on Al Jazeera's daring journalism

The earlier analysis regarding aspects of Al Jazeera's atypical journalism will undoubtedly explain the mixed responses it has received since its inception as a single Arabic-speaking satellite channel in 1996. Initially, Al Jazeera was praised by Western powers as a beacon of hope and free speech in the region. Its appearance was overwhelmingly welcomed by various policymakers from Europe as well as the USA who knew how suppressed the media in the Arab world had been. However, the tone of those who praised it started to change when Al Jazeera became the embodiment of a challenging form of journalism and reporting of news events unfamiliar on Western TV screens.

This explains why Al Jazeera's journalists in the field and in various conflict zones faced harassment, arrests, and even targeted killing. Al Jazeera had its offices closed in various Arab capitals and its broadcasting signal cancelled from the Egyptian Nilesat.[1] For many years, the network remained banned from news reporting in Tunisia, Algeria, Libya, Saudi Arabia, Bahrain, UAE, Sudan, Syria, and the occupied Palestinian territories, among others. For instance, before the revolution of 14 January 2011, the regime of Zein Elabidine Ben Ali in Tunisia waged wars against all critical voices both inside and outside Tunisia (Marzouki, 2013: 12). Al Jazeera channel was on top of the list of targeted media outlets.

The American administration also had its own rough relationship with the network. Al Jazeera's anti-occupation discourse about the war in Afghanistan (2001) and in Iraq (200) and the ability of Al Jazeera to appeal to Arabs' hearts and minds were of serious concern to the Bush administration at the time. The frustration of his administration was frequently expressed over Al Jazeera's bold coverage. In 2003, Foreign Secretary Colin Powell made an official complaint to the Qatar government about the Arabic channel. Powell's main criticism was that Al Jazeera "has fabricated stories about American abuses in Iraq, inflaming Arab anger against the occupation." The channel also was "accused of giving Osama bin Laden a platform to spread his hate, by broadcasting a succession of videos from the al-Qaida leader since September 11, 2001" (O'Carroll (2004). US Defense Secretary Donald Rumsfeld put it that Al Jazeera's coverage was "inaccurate and inexcusable" (Miles, 2009).

Reporting the Palestinian–Israeli conflict is another cause for concern that Al Jazeera keeps receiving. The Israeli government had frequently condemned Al Jazeera for arguably supporting Hamas or being biased and anti-Semitic in its reporting of events, especially during major conflicts like the 2009 or 2014 Israeli attacks on Gaza, the Israeli settlers' attacks on Palestinians or confiscation of their land, among others. However, worthy of a mention is that Al Jazeera was the first Arab channel since its inception in 1996 to provide a platform for the Israeli cabinet members to air their views and address Arab audiences directly. This major move in Arab news reporting was a taboo until Al Jazeera broke it. As regarded by many, "This move was a major departure from past practices and truly shocked the Arab public" (Miles, 2009). Therefore, the contention that Al Jazeera is sympathetic towards Palestinians is no more than saying CNN or the BBC are sympathetic towards the Israelis. Also, claiming that the network was critical towards the American war in Iraq is similarly equal to arguing that CNN was fully supportive of the American invasion of Baghdad in 2003 and the BBC was in full support of the British troops, "our boys," in their military involvement in the same war.

However, this international attention has always been of great service to Al Jazeera. The criticisms and sometimes direct targeting of the channel and its journalists has increased global attention. Its exclusive reports were of significant financial benefits too. Namely when reporting from war zones, the network reported to have signed sharing agreements for footage and news reports with major global news networks such BBC World, CNN, NBC, Japan's NHK, and Germany's ZDF, among others.

In sum, although Al Jazeera's news values as explained in its code of journalistic ethics[2] have little dissimilarity with major global broadcasters, in practice Al Jazeera's news reporting is plentifully different. Any analysis of a news broadcast by Al Jazeera compared to that of CNN or the BBC, for instance, will find ample discrepancies, to the extent that sometimes it may be thought that what was reported in the three channels was a completely different event in a different context (Miladi, 2006; Barkho, 2011). However, the fact that Al Jazeera provided a platform for Bin Laden and other Al Qaida leaders to voice their opinion does not make it "Bin Laden's mouthpiece," nor does giving voice to opposition leaders make it an attempt to destabilize Arab regimes. In the same way, we assume that giving former American president George W. Bush and his administration ample air time to explain their rationale for the invasion of Iraq in 2003 does not make the channel a mouthpiece of the American administration or one that condones the American foreign policy in Iraq. Nor does it make any other channel a tool for the Israeli government or Hamas when key figures from both sides appear on its screen defending their viewpoints. In fact this is what makes Al Jazeera's editorial line challenging, namely in covering wars and conflicts.

Conclusion

Al Jazeera's motto, "The opinion and the other opinion," bears a simple message but in fact sums it all. Simply put, it is the raison d'être of the network. Since its inception, Al Jazeera sees itself as siding with the Arab public. It provides a platform for those publics who do not have access to media controlled by Arab regimes. Being amid the day-to-day concerns and struggles of those publics gave Al Jazeera a rooted acceptance and turned it into a household name. Proponents of this contentious approach in the region argue that Al Jazeera unleashed the potential of the Arab public sphere and has given it a new life (Abdelmoula, 2015). Being the voice of the voiceless in the Arab world meant a channel providing large room for freedom of opinion to its audiences; a channel that represents the concerns and aspirations and reflects the struggle that the Arab public go through in their daily lives. Its discussion programs turned into virtual alternative spaces to coffee houses, clubs, community centers, and other social environments which have been until recently tightly controlled by ruling regimes' apparatuses.

Moreover, Al Jazeera's news culture in reporting the world has become significantly influential internationally first through Al Jazeera Arabic and then its sister Al Jazeera International (later named Al Jazeera English) (Carpenter, 2017). However, its arguably biased reporting at times during the Egyptian and Syrian conflicts (2011–2016) affected its credibility among some. Moreover, political changes in the Arab Spring countries have meant complete change of course in the media scene through the emergence of scores of independent satellite channels. Tunisia, Libya, Yemen, Syria, Algeria, and Sudan constitute significant cases of countries which have been witnessing substantial transformation in their media environment. This new reality has led Arab audiences to flock back to their national/independent TV channels for local news and current affairs instead of to Al Jazeera.

In order to keep itself afloat, and like other competitive global and national media players, Al Jazeera network has developed new digital platforms for an interactive involvement of its viewers. Its online provision of news content has also been equally important and has been developing side by side with the speedy technological developments in terms of diverse Internet platforms. The Digital Division AJ+ has attracted international attention through its short current affairs pieces and AJ Shorts. Also Al Jazeera Arabic (the original news outlet of Al Jazeera network) has harnessed online technologies to the full. Its obvious success to break the barriers of censorship, especially in countries where the channels did not have offices or their signal was barred, meant a new chapter of influence had opened for the nascent Arab media outlet. As argued by Kaul (2012: 3),

> Today, media companies are investing huge sums of money in non-traditional media delivery options, start-ups are innovating and redefining how the content industry works, and consumers are demanding and expecting access to virtually any content on any device at any time.

Al Jazeera managed for more than two decades to keep abreast of rapid technological developments. With the fast introduction of public service media in a few Arab countries and a growing market of independent media outlets, the network has been arguably losing ground. The future of this market will remain problematic to decipher given the current climate. The Arab world is slowly moving towards more free market in the media and growth in the provision of a variety content that will be competitive with what Al Jazeera has been providing. The question now is how the Al Jazeera network, which has dominated the Arab media scene for the last two decades at least in news and current affairs programs, will manage to survive a growing media free market that may characterize the region in the next decade or two.

Notes

1 Nilesat is an Egyptian Satellite company, based in 6th of October City, in the outskirts of Cairo and was launched in 1998. In addition to its various telecommunication services, Nilesat provides uplink services for various Arab satellite TV channels.
2 Al Jazeera, *Code of Ethics*. Retrieved from: https://network.aljazeera.net/about-us/our-values/code-ethics (last accessed on August 9, 2020).

References

Abdelmoula, E. (2015), *Al Jazeera and Democratization: The Rise of the Arab Public Sphere*. London: Routledge.

Al-Jazeera English (2019), Al Jazeera Wins Record Prize Haul at New York Awards Festival. *Aljazeera.et*. Retrieved from www.aljazeera.com/news/2019/04/al-jazeera-wins-record-prize-haul-york-awards-festival-190409165343744.html. Accessed 10 April 2019.

Bakr, A. (2014), Defiant Al Jazeera Faces Conservative Backlash after Arab Spring. *Reuters*, 2 July. Retrieved from www.reuters.com/article/us-qatar-jazeera-media/defiant-al-jazeera-faces-conservative-backlash-after-arab-spring-idUSKBN0F70F120140702. Accessed 21 April 2019.

Barkho, L. (2011), The Discursive and Social Paradigm of Al-Jazeera English in Comparison and Parallel with the BBC. *Communication Studies*, 62(1), pp. 23–40. London: Routledge.

Ben Messaoud, M. (2019), Media and Communication and the Democratic Transition in Tunisia. In J. Zran and N. Miladi (eds.), *Media and the Democratic Transition in the Arab World*. Tunis: Sotumedias & AMCN, pp. 283–316.

Boyd, D. (1999), *Broadcasting in the Arab World*. Ames: Iowa State University Press.

Carpenter, J. C. (2017), Creating English as a Language of Global News Contraflow: Al Jazeera at the Intersection of Language, Globalization and Journalism. *Journal of Arab & Muslim Media Research*, 10(1), pp. 65–83.

Castells, M. (2012), *Networks of Outrage and Hope: Social Movements in the Internet Age*. Cambridge: Polity.

Hassan, M. M., and Elmasry, M. H. (2018), Convergence Between Platforms in the Newsroom: An Applied Study of Al-Jazeera Mubasher. *Journalism Practice,* 13(4), pp. 476–492.

Kaul, V. (2012), Changing Paradigms of Media Landscape in the Digital Age. *Mass Communication Journalism*, 2(110).

Khanfar, W. (2015), *Wadah Khanfar: A Historic Moment in the Arab World*. Keynote speech delivered at TED Conference, 18 July. Retrieved from www.youtube.com/watch?v=2XiDdnDCD34. Accessed 25 March 2020.

Marzouki, M. (2013), *The Black Book: Propaganda Machine under the Rule of Ben Ali (in Arabic)*, Tunis: Media and Communication Unit, Tunisian President's Office.

Mellor, N. (2008), *The Making of Arab News*. Lanham, MD: Rowman & Littlefield.

Mellor, N. (2016), A New Era of Public Broadcasting in the Arab World. In A. Ezzeddine and N. Miladi (eds.), *Mapping the Al Jazeera Phenomenon 20 Years On*. Doha, Qatar: Al Jazeera Centre for Studies, pp. 349–366.

Miladi, N. (2006), Satellite TV News and the Arab Diaspora in Britain: Comparing Al Jazeera, the BBC and CNN. *Journal of Ethnic and Migration Studies (JEMS)*, 32, p. 6. London: Routledge.

Miladi, N. (2016), Reporting News in a Turbulent World: Is Al Jazeera re-writing the Rules of Global Journalism? In A. Ezzeddine and N. Miladi (eds.), *Mapping the Al Jazeera Phenomenon 20 Years On*. Doha, Qatar: Al Jazeera Centre for Studies.

Miles, H. (2009), Think Again: Al Jazeera. *Foreign Policy*, 19 October. Retrieved from https://foreignpolicy.com/2009/10/19/think-again-al-jazeera/. Accessed 12 April 2019.

Norris, A. (2017), A Look at AJ+ – Al Jazeera's Unique Approach to Engaging with Millennials. *FIPP*, 26 January. Retrieved from www.fipp.com/news/features/a-look-at-al-jazeeras-unique-approach-millennials. Accessed 13 April 2019.

O'Carroll, L. (2004), US Makes Al-Jazeera Complaint. *The Guardian*, 28 April. Retrieved from www.theguardian.com/media/2004/apr/28/iraq.iraqandthemedia. Accessed 12 April 2019.

Philo, G., and Berry, M. (2004), *Bad News from Israel*. London: Pluto.

Rugh, A. W. (2004), *Arab Mass Media: Newspapers, Radio, and Television in Arab Politics*. Westport, CT: Praeger Publishers.

Seib, P. (2016), The Future of Al Jazeera and Arab News Media. In E. Abdelmoula and N. Miladi (eds.), *Mapping the Al Jazeera Phenomenon 20 Years On*. Doha, Qatar: Al Jazeera Centre for Studies, pp. 33–348.

Tatham, S. (2006), *Losing Arab Hearts and Minds: The Coalition, Al Jazeera and Muslim Public Opinion*. London: C. Hurst and Co.

Thussu, D. K. (2018), *International Communication: Continuity and Change*. London: Bloomsbury Publishing USA.

Yusha'u, M. J. (2015), Extremism or Terrorism: Communicating Islamophobia on YouTube in the Norwegian Attacks. *Journal of Arab & Muslim Media Research*, 8(2), pp. 171–191.

Zayani, M. (2005), *Al Jazeera Phenomenon: Critical Perspectives on New Arab Media*. London: Routledge.

Saudi Arabia

25

THE SAUDI PRESS – THE COMBINED POWER OF WEALTH AND RELIGION

Noha Mellor

Introduction

The history of the Saudi press, and media generally, is very much tied to the combination of Wahhabism and the massive oil wealth accumulated in the country since the second half of the 20th century.

The history of the Kingdom of Saudi Arabia (KSA), as its name suggests, is very much linked to the history of the Saud family. Members of this family ruled an area called al-Dir'iyya, part of Nejd province in Arabia, in the early 18th century. The Saudi leader Mohammad ibn Saud allied with the cleric Mohammad ibn Abdel Wahhab in 1744, calling for what was to be known as "Wahhabism,", a puritanical form of Islamic teaching. The Saudi family, aided by the Wahhabi adherents, invaded other parts of Arabia, such as Mecca in 1803 and Medina in 1805, until the Ottomans recovered the lost territories from the Saudis in 1816, ending the first Saudi theocratic state. However, Turki ibn Saud marshaled his troops to reinvade Hijaz in 1824, and he ruled the Emirate of Nejd until 1891 when it was defeated by the al-Rashid dynasty; in 1902, Abdul Aziz ibn Saud captured Riyadh and continued his invasion across Arabia. An agreement was reached with Britain in 1927 acknowledging his rule over the Hijaz and Nejd regions. In 1932, the third modern state was proclaimed, and it encompassed most of the Arabian Peninsula.

In 1938, oil was discovered in the new kingdom, which is said to encompass one-quarter of the world's oil reserves. This discovery transformed the lives of its rulers and inhabitants, and it has done so until today. The growing prosperity also attracted waves of immigration by non-Saudis seeking lucrative work opportunities in the oil fields (Al-Ahmed, 1987: 60) and throughout the country's expanding economy. It can be argued that the Saudi wealth combined with its religious status among the Muslim-majority countries have played a pivotal role in the development of the Saudi media, including the press. Moreover, the staggering oil wealth has made it possible for the Saudi rulers to spread their influence across the world via a large network of international Islamic organizations and funding mosques across the world, particularly in Western cities, to attract diaspora Muslim communities, as well as academic chairs for Islamic studies in the USA and Europe. Pilgrimage revenue not only added to the Saudi wealth but also appointed the KSA ruler as "the Custodian of the Two Holy Mosques," a title that was embraced by the late King Fahd (d. 2005) when he became the KSA's ruler in 1982. Moreover,

Saudi wealth and expat communities helped fund the kingdom's growing printing industry. The subsequent sections follow the development of the Saudi press, from a modest local start to an international media empire that seeks to influence regional and international public opinion.

The beginnings of the Saudi press

The first newspaper established by the Saud family was *Um al-Qura*, launched in Mecca in 1924. As the official Saudi newspaper, it focused on news about the Saudi ruler and his trips, speeches, and directives. However, one of the main reasons behind launching *Um al-Qura* was a series of negative articles targeting the Saudi ruler in the Egyptian *al-Muqattam* newspaper that prompted the Saudi ruler to establish his newspaper to counteract the Egyptian propaganda (Al-Ahmed, 1987: 483). An important function of *Um al-Qura* was to repudiate foreign reports and news about the kingdom; for instance, on 25 November 1955, it published a press release by the Directorate of Press and Broadcasting dismissing news published by the British *The Times* newspaper, about possible tension between KSA and Egypt, and rebellious movements within the KSA, claiming, "the aim of these rumors is to break up and sow discord among the Arab nation and countries" (*Um al-Qura*, 1955). The paper also served as the voice of the ruler, celebrating him as the guardian, not only of KSA but of all the Muslim-majority countries; for instance, on the occasion of the 21st anniversary of King Abdulaziz's accession to the throne, the paper reported,

> the memory of this happy ascension brings back to mind the era of the righteous Salaf, the era of justice and the era of Islam in its best era, when the supreme word was that of the true law, the era of equality and the covenant to work by the Book of Allah and the Sunnah of His Messenger.
>
> *(Um al-Qura, 1946: 2)*

During the early 1950s, several publications were printed outside the kingdom due to the lack of printing facilities in major cities and lack of professional labor to staff those few facilities. For instance, the late Saudi journalist Hamad al-Jasem (Al-Arab, 1991: 2) recalled the difficulty in printing his publication inside the kingdom due to lack of professional labor, which made him arrange for his publication to be printed in Beirut. This meant that many newspapers could not publish daily. Censorship by the ruling family also meant that news was not prioritized; instead, religion, arts, and literature were the main themes of the circulated periodicals and magazines (Al-Ahmed, 1987: 152).

Ownership was granted to individuals (usually males) who would personally apply for permission from the palace (Al-Ahmed, 1987: 152). *Al-Yamamah* magazine, for example, was set up in 1952 by the prominent Saudi journalist Hamad Al-Jasser (d. 2000) as a monthly magazine, printed in Cairo; and *al-Jazirah* magazine was launched in 1960 from Riyadh as a literary magazine (ibid.). Printing facilities began to improve from the early 1960s, allowing several outlets to follow suit, such as *al-Arab* (launched by Hamed al-Jasser) and *al-Faisal*, which aimed to promote Islamic culture. *Al-Arab* magazine was launched in November 1966 as a monthly magazine. It was printed for seven years, until 1973, when it faced printing problems due to the high costs of publishing it inside the kingdom combined with the lack of professional labor. The owner and license holder was forced to produce it as a bimonthly and to print parts of it in Beirut, Cairo, and Riyadh (*al-Arab*, 1982: 2–5). Its founder and editor, Hamad Al-Jasser, worked as a teacher, judge, and journalist. He founded *al-Yamama* magazine (in 1952) as well as *al-Riyadh* newspaper and *al-Arab* magazine. He moved to Cairo briefly to study at the Faculty of Arts at Cairo

University but never completed his degree and had to return to Saudi Arabia, where he worked in the education sector before setting up his bookshop and printing house (*al-Arab*, 1985: 1–5).

Individuals were free to establish their publications, and use printing facilities abroad, until about 1963 when the Saudi government turned the General Directorate of Broadcasting, Press, and Publication into the Ministry of Media and assigned it the task of regulating press ownership. One can argue that the decision was triggered, inter alia, by Nasser's move in Yemen supporting those who opposed the monarchical rule in Yemen. The government then decided to limit newspaper ownership to organizations, leaving the government the right to license publications and appoint editors-in-chief (Mellor, 2005: 31). Available statistics confirm that there were around five dailies in the kingdom in 1970, which increased to 13 by 1986 (Al-Jammal, 2001: 94).

Thus, in terms of ownership in the first three decades of the modern Saudi state (1932 to 1963), a mixed model of government and individual ownership of publications was allowed. Following the 1963 decrees, ministries and organizations of more than 15 members (now the number is 30) could establish publications after seeking government permission; this included oil companies who produced their PR materials and magazines (Al-Ahmed, 1987: 171–172).

As part of the kingdom's media plan, the Saudi Press Agency (SPA) was set up in 1971 in Riyadh, and it marked its first year by its massive coverage of the Hajj season. The agency aimed at not only spreading the news about the Saudi government but also to

> inform the international public opinion about the Kingdom's views regarding Islamic issues relevant for the Kingdom and other Islamic countries, in addition to raising the awareness of the Islamic world, cultivating the people in this world, informing them of their homeland, and keeping abreast of new inventions and scientific achievements in the world, and opening their eyes to atheist conspiracies targeting Muslims and the imported values disseminated by the enemies of Islam.
>
> *(Ezzat, 1983: 138)*

SPA claims to have a staff of around 500 employees broadcasting bulletins in Arabic, English, and French. In addition, the KSA together with the other Gulf states and Iraq set up the Gulf News Agency in 1976, with headquarters in Bahrain, and later became a department within Bahrain Radio and Television News in 1988.

Media conglomerates

Following the restructuring of the Saudi media market in 1963, several Saudi businessmen launched their media ventures abroad. London proved a favorable headquarters for many such ventures including *al-Sharq al-Awsat* newspaper, launched by two Saudi brothers, Hesham and Mohamed Hafez, in 1978. The two brothers bought the British Central Press Photo building in central London as the headquarters for their newspaper, thus mirroring the success of the *International Herald Tribune*. Most of its writers are Saudi, Egyptian, Lebanese, or Palestinian. The newspaper is published simultaneously in several Western and Arab cities, such as Cairo, Beirut, Frankfurt, New York, and Marseilles. It claims the largest circulation among pan-Arab dailies and includes a large number of advertisements (Mellor, 2007: 94). The newspaper is said to adopt the official Saudi views, although the owners have argued that their publications are based in London to ensure a neutral view on Arab issues (Mellor, 2007: 134–135). The newspaper is part of a large portfolio of publications owned by the Saudi Research and Marketing Group (SRG), which also includes the following publications from London: *al-Majjallah* magazine (launched in 1980), *al-Rajul* men's magazine (1992), and the following women's magazines: *Sayydati* (launched in 1981), *Heya* (1992), and *al-Jamila* (1994). SGR produces the following titles from its offices in Jeddah: *Arab News* (launched in 1975), *al-Jadida* (1986), *Basem* (1987), *Urdu News* (1994), and *Urdu* magazine (1999). It launched *al-Riyaddiyya* sports newspaper in 1987 from its offices in Riyadh and *al-Iqtisadiyya* economic newspaper (launched in 1992). SRG also owns the Saudi Distribution Company, a subsidiary company based in Jeddah, with branches across the Gulf states, servicing thousands of outlets via 180 distribution lines across the KSA. It competes with Al-Watania Distribution Company, jointly owned by several leading Saudi publishers, such as *Al Yamamah, Okaz*, and *al-Jazirah* (Shoult, 2006: 279).

There are two other large publishing houses in the KSA: al-Yamama and Okaz. The former owns titles such as *al-Riyadh* newspaper and *al-Yamama* magazine, while Okaz Press and Publications own *Okaz* newspaper and *Saudi Gazette* (in English). *Okaz*, based in Jeddah, is the mainstream newspaper in the western province of Saudi Arabia. Assir Press and Publishing, owned by the governor of Assir Province, Prince Khaled al-Faisal, released *al-Watan* newspaper in 2000, which was considered a bold publication daring to tackle controversial topics (IREX, 2005: 23). All publications benefit from government subsidies in the form of daily bulk sales of thousands of copies to the government for distribution to ministries and government offices (Shoult, 2006: 273). *Al-Riyadh* and *Okaz* newspapers, for example, print up to 170,000 copies daily, half of which are subscribed to by ministries and government institutions (IREX, 2009: 185).

There were 10 daily newspapers by 2005, with a combined circulation of about 763,000. *Al-Riyadh* is claimed to be the largest newspaper, rivaling the official paper, *Um al-Qura*, as the source of government information. According to Mideast.org,[1] there are now around 17 titles and a total circulation of 2.1 million copies annually. *Al-Sharq al-Awsat* and *al-Hayat* are claimed to have the highest circulation of 235,000 and 166,000 respectively, followed by *al-Riyadh* daily (150,000 copies), *Okaz* (110,000), *al-Riyadiyya* (110,000), *al-Jazirah* (110,000), *Arab News* (110,000), and *al-Iqtisadiyya* (77,000) (Shoult, 2006: 274). There are no reliable circulation figures, however, as other sources (e.g. BuMetea, n.d.: 22) claim that the circulation of *Arab News* was no more than 21,000, while that of *al-Hayat* is the largest among all Saudi titles of about 270,000 copies.

The magazine market is dominated by lifestyle and women's magazines, representing 75% of the total circulation in the whole pan-Arab market, particularly in Saudi Arabia; the top-selling of those are said to be *Sayydati, Zahrat al-Khaleej, Laha*, and *Heya* (Arab Media Outlook, 2012: 30–31). Subscription rates are generally rather low, and it is said that around 88% of the people in Saudi Arabia do not subscribe to any magazines (ibid.).

The advertising spending concerning the press is mainly concentrated on the three leading Arabic daily newspapers, namely *Asharq Al-Awsat, Al-Riyadh*, and *Okaz*, although an estimated 20% of this spending is in the Saudi-English language daily press. A lower level of advertising spend is allocated to the other regional titles, e.g., *al-Yaum, al-Madinah, al-Jazirah, al-Bilad*, and *Al-Nadwa*. Many well-educated newspaper readers in Saudi Arabia read more than one title, typically subscribing to a local pan-Arab title, such as *al-Hayat*, and perhaps a business and economics daily, such as *al-Alam al-Youm* (Shoult, 2006: 271).

Journalism education and practice

There are around 10 communications colleges in the KSA, where students can receive training in communications and journalism; chief among them is the Communications Department in the Faculty of Arts and Humanities at King Saud University, which opened in Riyadh in 1972 as the first academic department in the Gulf region. Other universities offering journalism education, for both men and women, are the Imam University (Riyadh), King Abdulaziz University (Jeddah), and Um al-Qura University (Mecca). Freelance contributors are paid by the article, but there are not enough guidelines as to how much a writer should expect to receive at the end of each month: it depends on "the mood of the editor and his relationship with the writer" (IREX, 2009: 183). The government changed the laws in 2000, to allow the establishment of professional journalism societies and the publication of foreign newspapers in the country; however, the same rules applied in terms of allowing state censorship of content that is deemed to defame Islam or harm the public interest (IREX, 2005: 226).

Forms of censorship

The press was used to being sanctioned by the Shura Council, set up in 1929. The laws changed again in 1959, when the General Directorate of Publication, part of the Saudi Ministry of Media, issued new rules for the press to follow. A Higher Media Council was established in 1967, led by the minister of information; but, in 1981, the responsibility to oversee this council was moved to the minister of interior. The council has the power to approve new Saudi editors, penalize publications, and oversee the overall implementation of the Saudi printing laws. It is generally prohibited from disseminating information that is deemed to harm the royal family, the government, or Islam (Almaghlooth, 2013). The directorate also prohibits the sale of foreign publications without its prior review and approval. This means that foreign magazines, such as *The Times*, may be sold in the Saudi market after removing some of its pages or pictures if those are deemed to be harmful or indecent.

There are numerous cases of journalists who have been arrested or banned from writing, following the publications of articles criticizing the government. The editors of *Dharan News* and *al-Fajr al-Jadid*, for instance, were arrested and their newspapers closed down because one of them criticized the government's educational policies, which were not geared to help alleviate girls' illiteracy; the other editor was punished for criticizing the government's delayed support to farmers (Almaghlooth, 2013: 60). Other newspapers and editors could disappear for no clear reasons. Saad al-Bawardi, who established *al-Eshaa'* newspaper in 1955, for instance, was ordered to abandon his publishing activities, which led to the closure of his newspaper only three years after launching it. The editor-in-chief of *al-Riyadh* newspaper was suspended for three months in 1977, after calling the Saudi minister of information a "minister of denial" (Almaghlooth, 2013: 62). The Lebanese Jihad al-Khazen, who used to edit *al-Sharq al-Awsat* (1978–1986) and later *al-Hayat*, between 1988 and 1998, also admitted that Arab news media were generally expected to praise Arab rulers or face the penalties of information ministries. In 1977, a large number of international outlets published the story of the 19-year-old Saudi princess Masha'el bin Fahd al-Saud, who was publicly executed for allegedly committing adultery. A TV documentary entitled *Death of a Princess* was jointly produced by US and UK companies. The film unleashed an unprecedented angry reaction from the Saudi government: the then British ambassador, James Craig, was asked to leave KSA; visa restrictions were placed on British businessmen; and the US government was also asked to censor its broadcasting. When Iraq invaded Kuwait in 1990, posing a threat to neighboring Saudi Arabia, the Saudi newspapers were banned from reporting on the event; the then editor of *Arab News* wrote that he "received direction from the ministry to not publish any news about the invasion" (Almaghlooth, 2013: 63).

Journalists often resort to self-censorship to avoid conflicts with the Saudi ruling family. They could run the risk of losing lucrative advertising contracts from Saudi corporations or even face a ban on Saudi territories. Jihad Khazen admitted that self-censorship is prevalent to prevent stirring up any national conflicts in Saudi Arabia, where the newspaper cannot afford to be banned or they "stand to lose tens of thousands of dollars in advertising revenue" (Khazen, 1999). Hazim Saghiya, another prominent Lebanese journalist, also warned that the "media investment is a field that is left to the regimes and those close to them who believe that preserving the status quo is a prerequisite for the continuity of their concessions and interests" (Saghiya, 2006: 565).

Private ownership is allowed in the KSA, although Saudi businessmen still need the support of the ruling family, and are, therefore, unlikely to allow the printing of criticism of the royal family or the system of governance. A former columnist in the daily *Okaz*, Hussein Shobokshi, for instance, once wrote a column calling for democratic governance, which led to blacklisting him from the Saudi press and canceling his contract with a Saudi TV channel to host a talk show (Campagna, 2006).

The Saudi press is thus subject to direct government censorship in addition to self-censorship practiced by editors and journalists alike to avoid falling out of favor with the government or the ruling family whose direct subsidies supported various news outlets. The king supported *al-Nadwa* national newspaper in 2007, for instance, with a grant of ca. $199,000 during the outlet's financial hardship (Almaghlooth, 2013: 63). Religious leaders also exerted considerable influence on the Saudi press.

Clerics as censors

Religious leaders (or *Ulama*) have historically played a critical role in the political and cultural scene in Saudi Arabia, and their support, or lack of it, can sway political power and public opinion. The Committee for Propagating Virtue and Preventing Vice (CPVPV), which oversees the *Mutaween* or the religious police, is another authority that has exercised significant power in Saudi society. Editors-in-chief can face tremendous pressure from the CPVPV to reduce the amount of coverage and pictures of women in their reporting. The Saudi government stripped the religious police of its power to arrest in 2016, and the current king curbed CPVPV power: it can no longer protest against new regulations such as granting women the right to drive.

Religious authorities used to oppose the press and other media forms, particularly television; they often called for subjecting editors and journalists to religious trials. The prominent Saudi journalist Hamad Al-Jasser (d. 2000), for instance, told of his ordeal with the religious authorities in the 1950s for publishing an article commenting on Indian Prime Minister Nehru's visit to Saudi Arabia, calling Nehru "Messenger of Peace." Religious groups charged Jasser for giving Nehru such a title which, for them, was confined only to Prophet Mohammed. The government granted him mercy but warned him to exercise caution in the future (Al-Ahmed, 1987: 162).

The CPVPV exerts much pressure on editors-in-chief if their outlets publish articles criticizing religious authorities in the news or pictures of women in their news coverage because they deemed such images as indicators of moral corruption (Almaghlooth, 2013: 162). However, in March 2002, a fire broke out at the girls' school in Mecca in March 2002, killing 15 students, because the religious police had reportedly slowed rescue operations on the ground that the girls inside the burning building were not wearing their black over-garments/abaya, and stopped the girls from leaving the blazing building. The incident prompted several newspapers such as *al-Watan*, *Okaz*, and *al-Riyadh* to criticize the religious police for its prejudice against women (BBC, 2002). Later, in 2006, a group of Islamists disrupted a panel at a book fair in Riyadh that was discussing censorship in the KSA. The group called for a religious trial of all panelists, including the editor of *al-Riyadh* newspaper, Turki al-Sudeiri (Campagna, 2006).

Online press

It can be argued that the electronic press in Saudi Arabia began in 1995 when *al-Sharq al-Awsat* announced that it would launch its electronic archive; the e-version of the newspaper was simply PDF files of the printed papers. The Saudi-owned *Al-Hayat* began to publish an edition on CD-ROM in the same year. The first online-only newspaper was the Saudi *Elaph*, launched in 2001 (no paper copy), followed later by other ventures such as *al-Wefaq* and *Bab* that closed a few years after their launch. *Elaph* is based in London and claims to have well over one million users every month. Its editor-in-chief and owner is Othman al-Omair, a Saudi journalist who used to be the editor of *al-Sharq al-Awsat*. When he initiated *Elaph*, al-Omair remembered that his online project became the "laughing stock" of many in the profession in the Middle East; he said, "At the time, everyone was laughing at me, thinking it was a crazy idea, saying that people are not going to read news from a machine. People had no idea that the new media would be the solution" (Flanagan, 2017). It is worth noting that *al-Hayat* newspaper announced on 1 June 2018 that it would no longer be printed in the UK, Lebanon, or Egypt; instead, a PDF copy of the newspaper would be available online.

Al-Weeam online was launched in 2006, the same year in which the short-lived paper *al-Wefaq* was closed down. *Al-Weeam* focused on Saudi affairs and marked itself as a daring voice by discussing controversial issues such as the powers granted to the religious police (Alotaibi, 2016: 149). *Sabq* online was launched in 2007 by a Saudi journalist who used to be affiliated with *al-Wefaq* until its closure. Many of *Sabq*'s journalists worked from home but they managed to produce popular content or "scoops" that attracted the Saudi public. The online newspaper used modern technology, drawing on solid financial resources, a large database of subscribers, and advertising income to become the most visited site by Saudi users (Alotaibi, 2016: 150). In 2007, *Ajel* online was launched in the al-Wassim region, but it did not have to match financial or human resources to compete with other outlets such as *Sabq*; similarly, *Anaween* online was launched in 2009, followed by *Sada*. This online site had a crew of 20 journalists, who depended heavily on translating news from international agencies into Arabic; by 2005, *Sada* was the third most favorite online newspapers in the KSA (Alotaibi, 2016: 151–153).

The rising number of Saudi online users meant that Saudi news sites and forums needed new tools to moderate these online forums and debates on their sites; in fact, moderation tools have been used by Western and Arab news outlets alike, which proves that news professionals still have some power in monitoring users' comments online (Ayish and Mellor, 2015). *Sabq* online outlet, for instance, has a team of comment controllers who monitor the comments sections on the website. The newspaper's editor-in-chief confirms that religion is the most important topic for moderation, as the newspaper does not "allow anyone to scoff at religion," and religion still contributes to the "high number of hits" received by *Sabq* (cited in Almaghlooth, 2013: 180).

Saudi ministry of media

Saudi media policy has consistently reflected a dedication to the spread of Islamic messages through the drawing up of formal information policies and guidelines since the establishment of the Higher Committee of Information in 1977. It has usually emphasized the function of the media in spreading Islamic values and practices (Tash, 1983: 58f). The current media policy was revised in 1981 and revisited in 2013. The declared aims are the establishment of the faith (Islam) in the hearts of people, the obedience of the rulers, and the commitment to what is in the public interest; this implies refraining from what is deemed "sinful" (Saudi Ministry of Media, 2018).

The Saudi Ministry of Media is assigned with the power to grant licenses to new press foundations and approval of new editors. A press foundation is defined as an establishment by a group of Saudi citizens of no fewer than 30, managed by a director who must be Saudi, over the age of 30, who has a university qualification or the relevant media experience of a period of not less than five years. To apply for a license for a newspaper, an initial capital of at least $350,000 is required and the license holder must be a Saudi national who holds an adequate degree (IREX, 2005: 226). The license is granted by the Ministry of Media, which also reserves the right to suspend the appointment of the director if he (usually a male) is deemed not to meet any of the requirements. Editors should also be Saudi citizens, have a relevant university education and/or journalistic experience, and receive approval by the ministry. According to the ministry's published regulations, it is prohibited to publish material that is deemed "contrary to the provisions of Islamic law, calls for the breach of security of KSA, serves foreign interest[s] that conflict with the national interest, defame the Grand Mufti of the KSA or the *Ulama* and other state officials" (Saudi Ministry of Media, 2018).

If an editor crosses a line by publishing news critical of or unfavorable to certain royal family members, he will be relieved of his duties or forced to resign. The late Saudi journalist Jamal Khashoggi, who was later killed inside the Saudi consulate in Istanbul in October 2018, was relieved of his job as editor of *al-Watan* newspaper in 2003. The reason given was that he was critical of the religious authorities and their strict religious teachings. In his view, these led to the terrorist attacks in 2003, when two major bombings occurred in residential areas in Riyadh, killing 39 people; they were attributed to Islamic extremists who were said to be protesting the presence of US troops in the KSA. Editors and journalists who are forced to resign are usually able to write for other outlets; however, in a few cases, they may face harsher penalties. For instance, Hamzah al-Muzeini's opinion articles angered the religious court, which sentenced him to four months in prison and 200 lashes in 2005 (IREX, 2005: 225–226).

The press has also been utilized in the blockade against Qatar, since 2017, with the Saudi press publishing opinion articles as well as cartoons accusing Qatar of inciting against the kingdom in the wake of Khashoggi's murder in October 2018 (Meital, 2018).

As part of the "2030 vision" launched by the crown prince, Mohmad bin Salman, the king issued a decree in 2018 establishing the Ministry of Culture, as a new entity to work separately from the Ministry of Media, responsible for preserving the unique Saudi national identity and culture.

The (un)declared mission of the press

Mass communication, since its emergence in the Arabian Peninsula, has been seen to center on propagating Islamic preaching (Tash, 1983: 34); even the first publications were characterized as literary, thus carrying little non-political content, which further enhanced the political stability in the region (p. 39f). This tendency was intensified during the 1950s and 1960s with the spread of socialist Nasserism and Nasser's attack on the Arab monarchies. It can be argued that the main functions of the media in the KSA are to spread favorable coverage of the Saudi rulers as the custodians of the Islamic faith and holy sites and to disseminate the Saudi-based Islamic teachings as the most correct version of Islamic practice. To achieve this goal, the Saudi royal family have extended their control over media outlets inside and outside KSA via a unique carrot-and-stick policy, to ensure positive or at least neutral coverage of Saudi affairs.

According to WikiLeaks' *Saudi Cables*, the KSA controls its image by buying loyalties from leading media outlets across the world, including North America, Australia, and Europe. Those outlets comprise local Arab and regional pan-Arab outlets, and the Saudi control usually takes the reward and punishment approach or what the documents call "neutralization and containment," in which the former strategy refers to buying out loyalties of international outlets so that they become "neutralized" or refrain from publishing negative news or criticism about the Arabian kingdom. The containment approach refers to buying out journalists' loyalty so that they praise the kingdom and are ready to attack critics of KSA. To facilitate this strategy, the KSA purchases hundreds or even thousands of subscriptions in selected publications in return for praise or refrain from attacking KSA. An example cited in the "Saudi cables" was when the Egyptian ONTV station, owned by the Egyptian Sawiris, hosted the Saudi opposition figure Saad al-Faqih in November 2011. That episode prompted the Saudi embassy in Egypt to intervene and investigate the case with Sawiris. He "scolded the channel director" and offered the Saudi ambassador the opportunity to appear on the same show as a guest. Buying loyalty can cost any amount, ranging from a few thousand US dollars for a small outlet in a developing country, for instance, to millions of dollars, depending on the outlet and its outreach and status.

The KSA is also said to exercise direct pressure and even confrontation: it issued a royal decree in January 2010 to remove Iran's Arabic-language news network, al-Alam, from the Riyadh-based regional satellite operator, ArabSat. The plan failed, and the Saudi government resorted instead to weakening the signal of al-Alam (WikiLeaks, 2015). Al-Mayadeen news network, based in Beirut and claimed to provide counter-propaganda to Saudi-controlled pan-Arab media, announced in 2015 that it faced suspension from ArabSat because it covered the humanitarian crisis as being a direct result of the Saudi-led war on Yemen. Al-Mayadeen director Ghassan bin Jeddou said that the news network was asked to refrain from covering the war on Yemen and the strikes on Yemeni civilians (PressTV, 2015).

According to WikiLeaks (2015), the Lebanese Prime Minister Saad al-Hariri once complained about the critical coverage targeting him in the Saudi outlets *al-Hayat* and *al-Sharq al-Awsat*, which resulted in a directive by the Saudi foreign ministry to stop broadcasting these types of articles. A further example of the extent of Saudi control resurfaced in the wake of the ensuing tensions between KSA and Qatar in 2017: the former simply blocked several Qatari websites, including Al Jazeera network and hundreds of sites which were classified as "indecent" (Eid, 2017: 17).

The Egyptian human rights activist and lawyer Gamal Eid stated in his report "The Princes' Media" (2017) that Egyptian editors-in-chief of privately owned as well as state media refrained from publishing any news that might even slightly defame KSA lest they lose "pilgrimage visas." He also discovered that the Saudi Ministry of Media hosted many editors, journalists, and TV presenters − whom he called "friends of KSA" − every year, offering them free visas, accommodation, and transportation during the Hajj season (Eid, 2017: 6). According to WikiLeaks, several Egyptian public figures and institutions were on the KSA payroll in the kingdom, such as the TV presenter and parliamentarian Mustafa Bakri as well as the TV preacher Amr Khaled. KSA also paid thousands of US dollars to the Egyptian press institution *Dar al-Helal* in 2012, as a reward for publishing a series about the KSA's achievements during the previous year's Hajj season (Eid, 2017: 7). The Egyptian journalist Khaled Dawood, leader of the Constitution Party of Egypt, and a journalist for *Al-Ahram Weekly* since 1996, published an article in 2015 entitled "Hajj paid for by KSA" in which he revealed his shock to learn that the Egyptian media could criticize anyone in the government, including the president himself, but were not permitted, or did not dare, to do the same with KSA and its rulers. The Hajj rewards were the incentives for journalists, but the KSA rulers could also exercise significant economic pressures by banning any Egyptian outlets from distributing in the kingdom or diverting KSA advertising money elsewhere (Eid, 2017: 7).

Although private ownership of media institutions is allowed, most outlets are owned by royal family members who ensure the containment of any negative coverage of the KSA (WikiLeaks, 2009). SRG, for example, the largest publisher in the country, claims a global readership of 180 million. The institution is chaired by Prince Faisal bin Salman, the son of the current king, who also owns 7% of the company; his late brother owned 3%, and Prince al-Waleed bin Talal owns 35%; the rest is owned by private Saudi businessmen. Editors nevertheless usually refer to SRG as owned by King Salman, and the company and its subsidiaries have been the hub for recruiting a new generation of well-educated, pro-US Saudi editors (WikiLeaks, 2009).

Conclusion

Oil and the holy sites are the two factors that have played the greatest role in shaping the modern Saudi state, and it can be argued that both factors have also played a pivotal role in the shaping and development of the modern Saudi press. The holy sites entitled the KSA to claim a leading role among the Muslim-majority countries, while the oil wealth helped fund the Saudi press ventures around the world, whether initiated directly by a member of the royal family or close business allies. Combined with a staggering network of worldwide, international Islamic organizations and activities, the Saudi influence has grown massively, especially with the web of investments in international outlets, in the form of advertising or benefits to non-Saudi journalists, such as granting Hajj permission to Arab journalists. The staggering wealth accumulated by Saudi business tycoons has enabled the expansion of their media investments including pan-Arab press with Saudi titles, such as *al-Sharq al-Awsat*, claiming the largest circulation among pan-Arab dailies and a major share of press advertising money.

Restrictions still prevail in KSA, however; they continue to grant the Saudi authorities the right to approve or revoke press licenses, which compel many journalists to resort to self-censorship to avoid being out of favor with the authorities, including the religious leaders. The media have thus been regarded as a powerful tool, both in shaping Saudi public opinion in the Arabian kingdom and in disseminating favorable coverage of the Saudi rulers overseas.

Note

1 www.mideastmedia.org/industry/2016/newspapers/#s32

References

Al-Ahmed, Mohammed S. (1987), *The six Normative Theories and the Role of Social, Political, and Economic Forces in Shaping Media Institutions and Content: Saudi Arabia – a Case Study*. Unpublished PhD thesis, Leicester University, UK.

Al-Arab (1991), Editorial, 26(1 & 2) (January/February 1991), pp. 1–5.

Al-Arab Magazine (1970), 5(1) (September 1970); 17(1 & 2) (May/June 1982), pp. 2–5; 26(1 & 2) (January/February 1991), p. 5; 2(1–2) (May 1985), pp. 1–5.

Al-Jammal, Rasem M. (2001), *al-Ittisal wal ilam fil watan al-arabi*. 2nd edition. Beirut: Center for Arab Unity Studies.

Almaghlooth, Abdullah (2013), *The Relevance of Gatekeeping in the Process of Contemporary News Creation and Circulation in Saudi Arabia*. Unpublished PhD thesis, Salford University.

Alotaibi, Naif Mutlaq (2016), *Online News: A Study of 'Credibility' in the Context of the Saudi News Media*. Unpublished PhD dissertation, Sussex University, UK.

Arab Media Outlook (2012), Forecasts and Analysis of Traditional and Digital Media in the Arab World, 2011–2015. Dubai: Dubai Press Club.

Ayish, Mohammad, and Mellor, Noha (2015), *Reporting the MENA Region*. Lanham, MD: Rowman & Littlefield.

BBC (2002), *Saudi Police Stopped Fire Rescue*, 15 March. Retrieved from http://news.bbc.co.uk/1/hi/world/middle_east/1874471.stm.

BuMetea, Adnan Jasim (n.d.), *The Media Landscape in the Arab Gulf Countries*. Retrieved from www.researchgate.net/publication/237388387_The_Media_Landscape_in_the_Arab_Gulf_Countries

Campagna, Joel (2006), *Saudi Arabia Report: Princes, Clerics, and Censors. Committee to Protect Journalists*. Retrieved from http://cpj.org/reports/2006/05/saudi-06.php.

Eid, Gamal (2017), *The Princes' Media (I'lam al-umraa)*. Cairo: The Arabic Network for Human Rights Information (ANHRI).

Ezzat, Mohamed Farid (1983), *News Agency in the Arab World (Wekalat al-Anbaa fi al-Alam al-Arabi)*. Jeddah: Maktabat el-Elm.

Flanagan, Ben (2017), Othman Al-Omeir: A Legend in Arab International Journalism. *Arab News,* 2 May.

IREX (2005), *Media Sustainability Index – the Middle East and North Africa*. Washington, DC: IREX.

IREX (2009), *Media Sustainability Index – the Middle East and North Africa, 2008*. Washington, DC: IREX.

Khazen, Jihad (1999), Censorship and State Control of the Press in the Arab World. *The Harvard International Journal of Press Politics*, 4(3), pp. 87–92.

Meital, C. (2018), Qatari, Saudi Press Wage Cartoon War Over Khashoggi Affair. *MEMRI*, analysis no. 1422, 29 October. Retrieved from www.memri.org/reports/qatari-saudi-press-wage-cartoon-war-over-khashoggi-affair

Mellor, Noha (2005), *The Making of Arab News*. Lanham, MD: Rowman & Littlefield.

Mellor, Noha (2007), *Modern Arab Journalism. Problems & Prospects*. Edinburgh: Edinburgh University Press.

PressTV (2015), *Arabsat Suspends Services to Lebanese al-Mayadeen*, 6 November. Retrieved from www.presstv.com/Detail/2015/11/06/436550/Al-Mayadeen-Arabsat

Saghiya, Hazim (2006), The Arab Press and Various Sources of Repression. In *Arab Media in the Information Age*. Dubai: The Emirates Center for Strategic Studies and Research.

Saudi Ministry of Media (2018), *Regulations*. Retrieved from www.media.gov.sa/en/page/ministry regulations

Shoult, Anthony (ed.) (2006), *Doing Business with Saudi Arabia*. 3rd edition. London: GMB Publishing.

Tash, Adbulkader (1983), *A Profile of Professional Journalists Working in the Saudi Arabian Daily Press*. An unpublished PhD dissertation, Southern Illinois University.

Um al-Qura, 22(1088) (11 January 1946) and 32(1592) (25 November 1955).

WikiLeaks (2009), *Saudi Cables*. Retrieved from https://wikileaks.org/plusd/cables/09RIYADH651_a.html

WikiLeaks (2015), *Buying Silence: How the Saudi Foreign Ministry Controls Arab Media*. Retrieved from https://wikileaks.org/saudi-cables/buying-silence

26

SAUDI BROADCASTING MEDIA – A TOOL FOR REGIONAL INFLUENCE

Andrew Hammond

Introduction

This chapter presents an overview of the Saudi broadcasting sector, which began in the Arabian Kingdom with the first radio station launched in 1949 and with the developmental aims of combating illiteracy and promoting the modernization of the kingdom, drawing on the growing oil wealth. Broadcasting was also used to promote the kingdom's religious ideology partially to assuage the growing criticism by the Wahhabi clerics and partially to increase the influence of the kingdom as the representative of Sunni Islam, thanks to its hosting of two holy sites. This was facilitated by the fact that the first television broadcast coincided with the Hajj season and so it was a means to promote the pilgrims' experience. Finally, another aim of establishing the broadcasting sector was to protect the Saudi against what was deemed as hostile coverage of the kingdom by foreign media (such as the BBC Arabic) or other regional media (such as the Egyptian Voice of the Arabs).

After reviewing the main historical milestones in the development of the Saudi broadcasting sector, the chapter looks closely at the proliferation of Saudi-funded pan-Arab television and radio channels based outside the kingdom to increase the Saudi influence regionally and even internationally. The owners of those channels, members or allies of the royal family, faced their major crisis in 2017–2018 when the Saudi crown prince, using the pretext of combating corruption, detained several of them to transfer the ownership and management of several outlets. The chapter also follows the development of the Saudi broadcasting regulations, which have become even more challenging post-2011 and with the introduction of the anti-terrorism laws initiated in 2014 and amended in 2017.

Historical background

Broadcasting began in the kingdom with a Mecca radio station established in 1949 by royal decree in Jeddah, placing the enterprise under the responsibility of his son Faysal. The motivation was largely to help combat illiteracy and make basic steps towards modernization, but the need for radio was framed in religious terms to assuage criticism from conservative quarters (Al-Garni, 2000). The argument advanced by the government was that modern media was a means to propagate the word of God, so it could not of itself be harmful, and the first broadcasts were planned to coincide with the Hajj season to be a means of advising and enhancing the pilgrim's experience (Al-Badawi, 2018). In 1953, King Saud established the first mass media regulatory agency, the General Directorate of Broadcasting, Printing, and Publishing, which in 1963 became the Ministry of Information. This paved the way for national television in 1965.

Saudi radio was conceived, as was its television, as a protective wall against hostile coverage from outside, be it London (BBC Arabic) or Egypt (Sawt al-Arab), which were viewed as dangerous in the 1950s and early 1960s when secular Arab nationalist sentiment was spreading through the labor movement at the oil giant Aramco in the Eastern Province. In addition to the state-run Saudi Radio, which has several foreign language iterations and local versions such as Mecca Radio, there is MBC FM managed from Dubai and the private station Mix FM.

The first domestic television in the kingdom was the US Air Force's local channel AJL-TV launched in 1955, on which Aramco employees in the Eastern Province had been able to watch American comedy and drama. This led to the first Arabic-language television broadcasting in the kingdom a year later with Aramco's Dhahran television station aimed specifically at Saudis. Its first film was an American-directed drama about Abd al-Aziz called *Jazirat al-Arab*, which it was hoped would wean Saudis away from Egyptian propaganda on Voice of the Arabs, which targeted King Saud and Aramco as the vanguard of American imperialism in the region. In 1961 government officials sympathetic to the secular pan-Arab cause used Aramco TV to lobby for changes to the Saudi state's revenue arrangement with Aramco, which was US-owned throughout this period. Establishing a national television was one of the policy aims of the government following Faysal's coup against Ibn Saud in 1964 (Vitalis, 2007: 123, 183–184, 223, 230, 242, 248), but Faysal was careful to make sure that media and education would not lead to the creation of the kind of technocrat intelligentsia of Egypt and other urban Arab states.

Plans for national television were first laid in 1962 and carried in close coordination with the United States as the technical facilitator of the project. The US Army Corps of Engineers was responsible for training technicians and operation of stations in Riyadh and Jeddah in their early stages. The first shows were simple affairs – music and Mickey Mouse cartoons – but the new entertainment quickly became hugely popular and American, European, and Japanese TV sets flooded the markets and shops. In 1968, three more television stations equipped with the latest technical facilities were built at Madmali, Qassim, and Dammam, and the government installed numerous microwave relay stations around the country. In 1972, two satellite ground stations were completed in Jeddah and Riyadh and linked to the Intelsat system; in 1976, Saudi television started broadcasting in color; in 1977, new broadcasting studios were opened in Abha; and in 1983, television was centralized through the Riyadh Central Television Complex, which was at the time the largest and most advanced television facility in the region. To assuage the religious establishment, programming was largely focused on the discussion of Islamic issues and women were restricted to presenting and guesting on children's and women's shows, observing a strict dress code (Al Garni, 2000: 150).

Clerics against television

Communications had been a subject of bitter dispute during the *Ikhwan* or Brotherhood rebellion of 1928–1929, when rebel leader Faysal al-Duwaysh objected to the introduction of the telegraph as a form of sorcery. The *Ikhwan* were the Wahhabi armed group that originally supported the reign of the Saudi rulers. When Faysal became king in 1964, he embarked on a new round of modernization, including national television in which women would appear. This provoked opposition from the religious scholars who staged protests against television in 1965 in which Faysal's nephew Prince Khalid bin Musa'id ibn Abd al-Aziz was shot dead (it was his brother who assassinated Faysal in 1975, apparently in revenge). The clerics were pacified on the one hand with the argument that television was a means to spread Islam and on the other with their integration as state functionaries in Islamic universities, the Ministry of Justice established in 1970, as well as other authorities (Al-Rasheed, 2002: 123–125). State television has remained a staunch bastion of state and religious propaganda since then, playing an important role during crises such as the 1979 insurrection in Mecca by Wahhabi activists denouncing modernization as un-Islamic and the Gulf crisis of 1990–1991, after which popular clerics Salman al-Awda and Safar al-Hawali led their supporters in a protest movement for reforms that would lift what they perceived as restrictions on the role of the religious establishment in many areas of state policy and public life. This included broadcast media which was giving concessions to liberals such as women whose faces were uncovered, although a ban on Western films and television shows was introduced on Channel 1 following the Mecca incident, and non-Arabic material was shown only on the English-language Channel 2, and a Censorship Committee was established to vet foreign material in particular (Fandy, 1999: 58–9; Al-Garni, 2000: 151, 155). State media also played an important role in propagandistic events such as the centennial celebrations of the modern Saudi state's founding in 1999, managed by the Ministry of Information.

Saudi-funded pan-Arab television

The development of Saudi televisual media is the story of the evolution of pan-Arab television and Saudi efforts to dominate the sphere since the early 1990s when the cable and satellite revolution began. The main Saudi projects have often taken place in collaboration with Kuwait or Emirati government and businessmen, and they have involved news, religion, and entertainment media, in both cases with an underlying political motive at play. The development of the Saudi broadcast media has also been characterized by keen competition with Qatar since it launched Al Jazeera in 1996. Competition with Arab media from Egypt or Lebanon has been far less intense since their governments were broadly aligned with Saudi policy. The main channels in question are Al Arabiya news channel, MBC entertainment channels, Rotana music, and Wesal religious channel, though this configuration has changed over the years owing to changing ownership and merging of channels. Saudi terrestrial television should be considered a separate category, with different programming and socio-political aims. The pan-Arab satellite carrier Arabsat is used by Arab states as a means of shutting out any channels that are deemed as a threat. Although it is owned by a consortium of Arab governments, Saudi Arabia is the largest shareholder and hosts its operations in Riyadh. Channels can be removed for political reasons, such as the Iranian Al Alam which moved to the Eutelsat's Hotbird satellite network where the Saudi London-based dissident Saad al-Fagih's al-Islah channel also aired.

The business model of the Saudi satellite channels is political in that budgets are never made public, but it is well-known that advertising is an important element. The Saudi television market, particularly during the fasting month of Ramadan, is the prize target audience of advertisers around the region. Comedy programming, in particular, is made on a cycle that fits with Ramadan and the captive audience sought by advertisers. Gulf actors and actresses from Kuwait and Bahrain are drafted to play Saudis in shows that are aimed at Saudi audiences but made in Dubai, Manama, or Kuwait. Advertising is weaponized too: Saudi and many other Gulf advertisers avoid Al Jazeera for fear of retribution from the Saudi authorities, such as banning them from airing on MBC. Qatar's response was an aggressive policy of domination in the fields of sports television, transforming its Al Jazeera Sport channel into beIN Media Group in 2014 with a range of subsidiaries that won rights to a host of international sports events. With the political rivalry between Qatar and Saudi Arabia intensifying in 2017 with Saudi Arabia and the

UAE imposing a form of a blockade on Qatar, beIN channels were jammed in Saudi Arabia to prevent access.

The initial impulse to expand into pan-Arab televisual media came with the Gulf War of 1991. The crisis had two serious consequences for Arab media generally: weakened by war and international sanctions, Iraq drew back its funding of Arab media outlets, and alarmed at the dissent which the crisis had unleashed, Saudi Arabia decided to upgrade its presence. The war and Saudi Arabia's backing for it posed questions of image and legitimacy for Saudi Arabia both domestically and in other Arab and Muslim countries. Using their financial resources, the royal family and its allies acted to drown out secular-nationalist and Islamist opposition critical of the kingdom. Like other regimes in the region, the leadership perceived satellite television as a threat, and while the religious establishment would make its war on the phenomenon of domestic viewership – with the religious police confiscating satellite dishes throughout the 1990s – the government realized it could not hope to hold back the tide in the long run. When Iraqi forces rolled into Kuwait in 1991, Riyadh kept the Saudi population in the dark for three days; but most Saudis had got the news anyway from CNN. The solution was to dominate the expanding airwaves with political propaganda and innocuous entertainment that would shut out subversive material and occupy minds with lighter matters.

Thus, Walid al-Ibrahim, a Saudi businessman married to a sister of King Fahd, launched the Middle East Broadcasting Center (MBC) with Kuwaiti businessmen in 1991. It began as a news channel billed as the Arab CNN in an attempt to frame political events in the Arabic language from a Saudi leadership perspective and create a Saudi discourse for the Arab world but expanded to include daytime television in the American format that was becoming popular at the time. In 1994 the satellite entertainment network Orbit was launched by Prince Khaled bin Abdullah bin Abdel-Rahman (via Mawarid Holdings) and the cable entertainment network ART (Arab Radio and Television) was launched the same year by businessman Saleh Kamel with funding from Prince Alwaleed bin Talal. In 1995 Orbit shelved a project to carry BBC World Service Arabic television after the domestic terrestrial channel BBC1 aired a program about the Saudi justice system. This incident led to the exodus of several BBC Arabic radio presenters who were involved in the project to Al Jazeera, giving the Qatari channel professional strength from the beginning that it may not have otherwise enjoyed, and it also delayed BBC Arabic's television launch by over a decade. In 2009 Orbit merged with Kuwait Showtime Arabia to form OSN (Orbit Showtime Network), with a 50% stake held by Kuwait investment firm KIPCO, which is linked to the ruling Al Sabah. In 2003 Alwaleed bought the 49% stake ART's Kamel had acquired in Lebanon's LBC International entertainment network on satellite television, and in 2008 he raised his stake to around 85%. In 2009, ART sold its sports channels that broadcast the FIFA world to Al Jazeera's beIN sports and its remaining channels to OSN. Both OSN and MBC are based in Dubai.

Saudi Arabia's delayed response to Al Jazeera came in 2003 with 24-hour news broadcaster Al Arabiya. Part of the MBC network, Al Arabiya was launched in the wake of the September 11 attacks of 2001 and only weeks before the Iraq invasion in 2003. As with the 1990–1991 Gulf crisis, the Saudi government again sensed that its voice needed propagandizing in the Arab public sphere at a sensitive time when its pro-West policies faced considerable criticism on channels such as Al Jazeera, which had led Riyadh to withdraw its ambassador from Doha in 2002. The channel was under the effective control of King Fahd's favorite son Abdulaziz, with its editorial output managed by Abd al-Rahman al-Rashid, a liberal writer from Jeddah.

In 2002, MBC1 launched an Arab version of *The View*, called *Kalam al-Nawa'im* (Women's Talk) featuring a changing lineup from across the Arab world. ART acquired ownership rights of a large number of Egyptian movies during the 1990s. Reality TV and talent shows were also popularized in the Arab region through the Saudi channels. In 2004, an Arabic version of the Big Brother franchise was launched on MBC such as *al-Ra'is* (The Boss), featuring a pan-Arab cast on an island in Bahrain, but was ended after three months because of objections in Saudi religious quarters to unmarried men and women living in the same house. Similar shows on MBC were mainly held in Beirut. MBC has aired *Arabs Got Talent*, *Arab Idol*, and *Ahla Sawt* (The Voice), all of which led to a raft of national talent shows on terrestrial networks around the region, and in 2017 *Star Academy Arab World*, which has young Arabs living together in a Beirut house for four months as they train for musical or acting stardom, moved to MBC from LBC. In 2011, MTV Arabia was launched by MTV International as a free-to-air channel featuring a range of US entertainment shows and Arabic and Western music videos. In 2015, it changed its name to MTV Live HD via the pay-per-view model on OSN with options for watching shows from its website. The channel came after the entry of Fox movie and drama channels bringing more American television to the Arabic audiences. Fox was itself following in the footsteps of MBC and the UAE's Dubai One, which pioneered bringing American entertainment comedy and drama to the Middle East in the early 2000s (such as *Oprah*, *The Sopranos*, *Friends*, *Frasier*, among others).

Saudi Arabia has staked an important position in Arabic religious television. The major Saudi religious channels are Majd, Risala, Saha, and Wesal. Wesal became the most prominent among them as a propaganda outlet against the Syrian government during the Syrian civil war and has been at the forefront of anti-Shi'a sectarian discourse. The minister of information and culture was forced to resign in 2014 after the channel aired opinions in support of Islamic State's attacks on Shi'a communities in Saudi Arabia, but the channel remained up and running, indicating that it has support from the government despite its private ownership. It launched an Urdu version in 2016.

Important changes in ownership and control of Saudi media took place in 2017–2018. The Saudi government launched a major anti-corruption drive that in 2017 led to the detention of dozens of businessmen and princes involved in Saudi media and arrangements to transfer ownership and management of several outlets. These changes had the ulterior motive of bringing important vehicles of economic and political power in the hands of Saudi princes under the control of the Crown Prince Mohammed bin Salman, removing potential sources of rivalry to his political power. Unofficial reports said the Saudi government took a 60% stake in MBC, leaving its founder Waleed al-Ibrahim with 40%. In 2015, al-Ibrahim had rejected a government offer as too low. Following the seizure, the state-run Saudi Telecom struck a $1.8 billion agreement with MBC for exclusive rights to broadcast professional soccer matches in Saudi Arabia. The MBC Group has risen to become a powerful media juggernaut: it now includes 11 channels with an estimated daily viewership of 140 million people daily across the region. No changes took place in the ownership of Al-Waleed's Rotana network of music, cinema, religion, news, and drama channels.

The fluidity of broadcasting regulations

Saudi media regulation since the Arab uprisings of 2011 has generally treated social and traditional media together as one threat, and tightened regulations were also seen in Kuwait, Bahrain, and the UAE during that period. Media laws were amended twice in the space of a few months: in January after Tunisia President Zein Elabidine Ben Ali fled the country (taking refuge in Saudi Arabia) and in April after the Egyptian president was also forced to resign and protests spread in Libya, Syria, Yemen, Bahrain, Morocco, Oman, and Kuwait. In March 2011, the late King Abdullah issued decrees dispensing large amounts of money to various sectors of the population, including the army, religious scholars and other government employees and Grand Mufti Abd al-Aziz Al al-Shaykh issued a fatwa deeming expression of opposition via street protest or petitioning the country's rulers as impermissible. Another decree in April 2011 banned the publication in any format of information deemed to be contradictory to sharia law, disruptive to state security, serving foreign interests, stirring sectarian discontent, or slanderous of the senior religious scholars or any other government figures. The terms were vague, but the punishments were severe – a fine of 500,000 riyals ($133,000) which could be doubled in the case of recurring violations, the closure of outlets that published the violation, and banning the journalist from any work (Hammond, 2012: 204).

Anti-terrorism laws also have implications for broadcast and other media. A counter-terrorism law promulgated in 2014 was amended in 2017 to include definitions of specific acts of terrorism and their corresponding sentencing guidelines. It includes criminal penalties of 5 to 10 years in prison for portraying the king or crown prince, directly or indirectly, "in a manner that brings religion or justice into disrepute" and criminalizes a wide range of peaceful acts that bear no relation to terrorism. The new law does not restrict the definition of terrorism to violent acts. as the definition of terrorism includes "disturbing public order," "shaking the security of the community and the stability of the State," "exposing its national unity to danger," and "suspending the basic laws of governance," as well as violence which "forces a government or international organization to carry out or prevent it from carrying out an action." Article 30 allows prosecutors to limit the right to free expression by designating criticism of the king and the crown prince that "brings religion or justice into disrepute" as a terrorist act. Article 34 provides a prison term of three to eight years for anyone who supports, promotes, sympathizes with, or incites terrorism, and Article 35 stipulates a sentence of no less than 15 years for anyone who "misuses their status in any way either academic or social status or media influence to promote terrorism." Article 19 allows the public prosecution to hold a suspect in pretrial detention for up to 12 months, with unlimited extension upon court order, and Article 20 allows suspects to be held for up to 90 days in incommunicado detention. Both laws put writers, bloggers, and journalists at risk and were criticized by the UN Special Rapporteur on Human Rights (HRW, 2017). Further laws enacted in 2019 give prosecutors the right to "request records or documents from a suspicious institution" (Al-Kinani, 2019).

Domestic terrestrial channels face pervasive censorship. The state-run Saudi Broadcasting Authority operates almost all domestic broadcasting outlets. The minister of culture and information chairs the body which oversees radio and TV. Presenters whose guests veer into criticism of state policy in any area are liable to be removed from air for several weeks in punishment or held under house arrest or detention. In one case in 2008, disgruntled callers on a live show on Al-Ikhbariya news channel complained about inflation, government salaries, and some officials. The information minister at the time, Iyad Madani, fired the network's director, Muhammad Al-Tunsi, as a result, and introduced a temporary suspension of live broadcasts on state TV channels. In 2018, Reporters Without Borders ranked Saudi Arabia 169th out of 180 countries for freedom of the press across all media.

Cultural gatekeeping

The construction of a Saudi media empire with headquarters located partly inside the kingdom and partly outside fulfilled a number of political functions, one that kept the threat of liberal political and social values sectioned off to allow them to be piped into the Saudi domestic arena in a controlled manner. The underlying principle has been the same as that which drove the launch of MBC in 1992 – if outside actors are going to air content that impacts the stability of the Saudi regime, questions its policies and the balance of power between the royal family and the Wahhabi religious establishment, it would be better to have a Saudi version that protects the inner sanctum from the worst of it and forms a discourse that challenges criticism. The target audience for Saudi satellite television is then firstly Saudi, secondly Gulf, and thirdly pan-Arab. The more dominant Saudi Arabia became in satellite media, the more successful this approach was. The Wahhabi clerics accepted the trade-off with liberalism that the government had negotiated. In the era of King Abdullah (2005–2015), liberal social values were also sectioned off from society through the concept of economic cities – liberal zones where unrelated men and women would mix in public space, women could drive, and cinemas and café culture would thrive (Hammond, 2009: 35–38).

This approach belied an unresolved conflict in Saudi society since the 1980s between Islamic and liberal forces, a conflict in which liberals began to see gradual gains during Abdullah's reign in the early 2000s. This was in part due to the association of Wahhabism with radical movements which had become a threat to the Saudi state: 15 of the 19 September 11 attackers were Saudis, members of a group led by Saudi citizen Osama bin Laden, and the al-Qaeda insurrection that lasted from 2003 to 2006 demonstrated that a significant number of the Wahhabi religious establishment sympathized with the movement. Under King Salman, the government tipped the scales further towards liberal social values, allowing women to drive, music concerts, and cinemas while restricting the remit of the religious police force (or the so-called *Hay'at al-Amr bi-l-Ma'ruf wa-l-Nahi 'an al-Munkar* – Authority of promoting virtue and denouncing vice) to maintain the Wahhabi moral code, and this shift was made possible by the controlled entry of liberal values through the Saudi television empire.

Saudi popular comedy shows that aired during Ramadan such as *Tash Ma Tash* were moved from Saudi Channel 1 to MBC in 2006 during Abdullah's reign because their social criticism, particularly of the religious establishment, provoked outrage among conservative constituencies. The show ran from 1992 to 2011, making stars of its two lead actors Nasser Al-Qasabi and Abdullah Al-Sadhan. In one episode of the 2006 series, would-be revolutionaries attended a school for training and indoctrination named the Terrorism Academy, mimicking the popular talent show. The revolutionaries were depicted as simpletons robotically repeating language about infidels. In another episode, a religious police officer argued at a local council meeting that the town should have separate secondary schools for boys and girls, located so that prevailing winds do not carry the smell of the girls in the direction of the boys. Other episodes satirized the dual social worlds in which many Saudis move, of piety at home and dissolution abroad.

In terms of politics, Al Arabiya news channel has formed a strong counter-narrative to Al Jazeera, although it is widely understood across the Arab region to be not much more than a propaganda outlet. Domestic news channel Al-Ikhbariya was initially conceived as the Saudi response to Al Jazeera and suffered from underfunding once Al Arabiya proved the success of its offshore model. The US State Department viewed Al Arabiya favorably as a channel countering anti-Americanism following the 2003 Iraq War and the Saudi policy of blitzing audiences with American entertainment was also seen as effective in that regard. In a WikiLeaks cable from May 2009, one unidentified Saudi media figure tells a US diplomat:

> It's still all about the War of Ideas here, and the American programming on MBC and Rotana is winning over ordinary Saudis in a way that Al Hurra and other US propaganda never could. Saudis are now very interested in the outside world, and everybody wants to study in the US if they can. They are fascinated by US culture in a way they never were before;

Al-Arabiya is referred to by the author, chargé d'affaires David Rundell, as moderate in relation to Al Jazeera (WikiLeaks, 2010). The Al Arabiya editorial line was broadly anti-terrorism and pro-American, highlighting the human rights abuses of Saddam Hussein, depicting Hizbullah as the aggressor during the 2006 war with Israel, and condemning Turkish championing of Palestinians. In 2004, President Bush chose Al Arabiya over Al Jazeera for an Arab media interview to answer charges of torture of Iraqi detainees at Abu Ghraib prison, and President Obama turned to Al Arabiya for the first interview with Arab media after his election in 2008. Since 2011, it has played a central role in the Saudi narrative against the revolution in the Arab region, demonizing Islamist political parties as a terrorist threat to Gulf monarchies and Iran as a sectarian imperialist threat to Sunni Arabs.

Saudi pan-Arab entertainment television was weaponized in the early period of the Arab uprisings to direct an anti-insurrectionist message. In the first Ramadan of the Arab Spring era, which fell in August 2011, the first show that ran after sundown on the Saudi MBC1 channel was *Khawatir* (Thoughts), in which a popular preacher in Western clothes travels to different countries to show how Muslims can improve their societies. The theme of the *Khatawir* shows that year dealt directly with the slogan of the uprisings "the people want to bring down the regime" (*al-sha'b yurid isqat al-nizam*). *Khawatir* tried to co-opt the subversive slogan and transform it into something less threatening. The opening section of every episode began with the sounds of crowds chanting "the people want," then a graphic of the word for regime with a bold red cross over it on placards carried protesting crowds and a second crowd bearing placards saying "no corruption" in the Islamically approved color of green. The closing song appealed to Muslims to endeavor their revolution in behavior and lifestyle rather than rebellion in any political sense. This reflected the message throughout the shows, that Muslims must change their social values, not their governments. For example, in one episode, the presenter visited Finland to compare its teaching methods to those of Saudi Arabia where even the harsh school bell was the target of his criticism. In *Tash Ma Tash* too, the uprisings in Egypt and Tunisia were ridiculed as the work of children goaded by foreigners and foreign ideology into rebelling against their father.

The fate of the hugely popular show *Al-Bernameg* (The Program) bluntly demonstrates the limits of political satire. Based on Jon Stewart's *The Daily Show*, *Al-Bernameg* began as the personal YouTube project of the Egyptian surgeon Bassem Youssef, managed from his laundry room with a table, chair, one camera, and mural of photos from Tahrir Square. Calling it *The B+ Show*, Youssef began uploading five-minute episodes in May 2011, skewering the official Egyptian media's coverage of the news. Business tycoon Naguib Sawiris, the then owner of the Egyptian channel ONTV, came to him with an offer of a TV show. Known as *Al-Bernameg*, it ran from 2011 to 2014, shifting from various Egyptian channels to MBC. During the Muslim Brotherhood's year in power in Egypt, the show made a name for itself lampooning the Islamist government and its president Mohammed Mursi, but in the atmosphere of repression following the military coup in 2013, Youssef couldn't make similar humor of interim leader and later president Abdelfattah al-Sisi. Had he not treated the new leadership in the same irreverent manner, his integrity would have been lost. In April 2014, MBC said it would suspend the show until the end of May to avoid influencing voters ahead of presidential elections, but in June 2014, Youssef said unspecified pressure had become too great to bear and the show would not return. He subsequently left Egypt for the United States. The pressure was reported to have been from Saudi Arabia, the main backer of the Sisi government. The show had been revolutionary; during its second season, it moved to a live studio format, the first time this was done in Arab television. Meanwhile, an Arabic version of *Saturday Night Live* began airing on pay-to-view OSN in February 2016 from Cairo but it goes nowhere near Arab politics.

As political freedoms shrank dramatically following the initial success of the Arab uprisings, YouTube became an alternative outlet for Saudi creative talent, particularly humor. Riyadh-based video production company Telfaz used YouTube to launch its *Temsahly* comedy show featuring a puppet crocodile who interviews celebrities. The show has more than 100 million views. When the crocodile spoke to a Gulf actress in February 2013, the actress Amal Awadhiah was careful to say "welcome to Kuwait" to suggest she was located outside the country, since terrestrial television culture would not accept the notion of a Saudi actress. *Khambala* (Bumming Around) and *La Yekthar* (Enough) are other popular YouTube comedy shows. Saudis who choose to engage in critical political satire have had to do so from London. Saudi comedian Ghanem al-Dosari publishes the *Ghanem Show* on YouTube, though he was attacked in the streets of London by two Saudi men in 2018 (Dearden, 2018). Other popular Internet TV shows include *EyshElly* (What Is It That?), *Sa7i Channel* (Awake Channel), *Al Temsah* (The Crocodile), *Lumink* (a cartoon channel), *Takki*, and *Ala Al-Tayer* (Quickly). Some shows have moved from the margins to the mainstream: Joshua Van Alstine, an American of Turkish descent, moved from YouTube to MBC with his soft sendups of elements of Saudi culture and a message that Americans should do more to understand Islam. The role of such online shows will be discussed in detail in the following chapter.

Conclusion

The development of Saudi broadcast media since the 1960s has passed through a number of major social, economic, and political transformations. Media played a limited role in the model of modernization adopted by the state since Faysal took over in 1964, but the growth of media outlets in the West and among regional rivals such as Qatar prompted the kingdom to stake its place in the pan-Arab public sphere expanding since the 1990s, carving out a formidable role for the kingdom in influencing discourse in domestic, Gulf, and Arab media more broadly. This was critical in managing the domestic political conflict between liberal and Islamic constituencies and warding off foreign policy challenges from regional rivals such as Iran, Turkey, and Islamist political forces. Media plays a critical role in Saudi Arabia's post-Arab Spring strategy of supporting a network of allied governments to counter the perceived threat to domestic stability from Iran, Qatar, and Turkey.

Under Abdullah's and Salman's rule, Saudi media has been a mirror of the shifting narrative of Saudi identity from an emphasis on Islam towards the notion of a Saudi ethnic nationalism. In this process, the religious establishment has lost ground in the policing of conservative public morality yet remains critical to the state's political model. The crown prince's Vision 2030 reform is concerned with sweeping changes in the social and economic profile of the kingdom but not in its political structure, so it is the Wahhabi establishment that is required to confer legitimacy upon the system in the absence of electoral democracy and restrictions on expression. The Saudi media empire fulfills an important function in this strategy too.

References

Al-Badawi, Umar (2018), al-Idha'a al-Sa'udiyya Intalaqat ma'a Ta'sis al-Dawla wa-ma Zal al-Athir Hafilan. *al-Hayat*, 13 February.

Al-Garni, Ali Dhafer (2000), *Broadcasting in Saudi Arabia in the Era of Globalization: A Study of Local Constraints on Television Development*. Unpublished PhD thesis, Stirling University.

Al-Kinani, Mohammed (2019), Counterterrorism Law Comes into Effect in Saudi Arabia. *Arab News*, 28 January.

Al-Rasheed, Madawi (2002), *A History of Saudi Arabia*. Cambridge: Cambridge University Press.

Dearden, Lizzie (2018), Saudi Human Rights Activist Attacked by Men 'Shouting about Crown Prince Mohammed bin Salman' in London. *The Independent*, 16 September.

Fandy, Mamoun (1999), *Saudi Arabia and the Politics of Dissent*. London: Palgrave Macmillan.

Hammond, Andrew (2009), Liberal Enclaves: A Royal Attempt to Bypass Clerical Power. In *The Kingdom of Saudi Arabia, 1979–2009: Evolution of a Pivotal State*. Washington, DC: The Middle East Institute.

Hammond, Andrew (2012), *The Islamic Utopia: The Illusion of Reform in Saudi Arabia*. London: Pluto, pp. 184–209.

Human Rights Watch (HRW) (2017), *Saudi Arabia: New Counterterrorism Law Enables Abuse*, 3 November.

Vitalis, Robert (2007), *America's Kingdom: Mythmaking on the Saudi Oil Frontier*. Stanford, CA: Stanford University Press.

WikiLeaks (2010), *Cable from Riyadh,* 11 May. Retrieved from www.wikileaks.org/plusd/cables/ 09RIYADH651_a.html. Accessed 7 December 2010.

27

THE JANUS-FACED NEW MEDIA IN SAUDI ARABIA

Deborah L. Wheeler

Introduction

Saudi Arabia was one of the last countries in the Middle East to allow public access to the Internet in 1999. In 1998, Saudi government officials explained that continued "delays in opening the Internet to public access" was a result of the state searching "for a system by which authorities could block the flow of 'undesirable' information" (Human Rights Watch, 1999). Given this slow start, it is surprising that Saudi Arabia now leads the region, and in some cases, the world, in social media access and use. For example, Saudi Arabia's Internet penetration rate reached 93.3% as of 2018 for the 10–74 years age group (CITC, 2018). The country is fifth in the region for Internet connectivity (Internet World Stats, 2020). Given the geographic largess of the country (12th largest state geographically in the world), Saudi Arabia's Internet penetration rates are even more significant. All of the Middle Eastern countries that beat Saudi Arabia in Internet connectivity are the size of a Saudi city (Bahrain, Qatar, Kuwait) or province (UAE, Lebanon). A drive throughout the kingdom reveals cell and electricity towers in even the most remote locations (based on the author's fieldwork insight in 2018), which means one is rarely without access to new/social media apps including Twitter, WhatsApp, Google Maps, Facebook, and Instagram. What explains this dramatic shift in the country's digital footprint?

This chapter provides insights into the scope and impact of Saudi Arabia's social media transformation. It highlights processes of change, linked in part with the use of social media tools, and it reflects on the uneven responses of the status quo to a more liberal and digital kingdom. The main argument is that scholars should not underestimate the serious transformations in communications, government policies, and social behaviors sweeping the kingdom. Access to digital tools means that Saudi citizens are often more wired and cosmopolitan in pockets of everyday life. At the same time, political space for dissent is shrinking, especially online, and there are increasingly real costs for activism or any behavior determined to shed a negative light on the country, its citizens, its allies, and its rulers. The fluidity of the regime's red lines makes resistance or any kind of oppositional discourse potentially dangerous in the public sphere. Self-censorship is on the rise at the same time that daily surprises about "what is allowed" in the kingdom shape a new, more relaxed and fluid Saudi public culture – including, for example, women driving and flying as pilots for the Saudi national airline (Alfaisal, 2019) and a Jeddah aquarium equipped with Western classical music to enhance the viewing of fish swimming.

Sorting through these digital, political, cultural, and economic changes in an increasingly wired kingdom occurs in the pages that follow. Two months of fieldwork in Saudi Arabia, including visits to Riyadh, Ha'il, Jubba, Jeddah, Taif, Baha, Bisha'a, Abha, and Qunfudha, in the summer of 2018 provide ethnographic insights into these transformations.

Historical background

Saudi Arabia is wired for the 21st century. Under the Vision 2030 plan, the kingdom has worked collectively to make Internet access and mobile service available to each citizen and visitor. Low-cost sim cards and free Wi-Fi are available throughout the country; the latter is especially ubiquitous at coffee shops and malls, even in remote locations. Impressively, Saudi Arabia has 9% of the world's Snapchat users (Jaffrey, 2018). Saudi Arabia also leads the Middle East in Instagram accounts (GMI_blogger, 2019) and Twitter accounts (Mideastmedia.org, 2019). For Instagram, the most popular topics are travel, fashion, fitness, and foodies (Kell, 2018); for Twitter, the leading hashtag for 29 April 2019 with 32,000 tweets is #GameofThrones (http://tweeplers.com/hashtags/?cc=SA, which is updated every 75 minutes). Saudi Arabia also leads the world in per capita social media users who access video content online (95%) and who access video content daily (64%) (*Statista*, 2018a).

What explains this rapid growth in social media use? One Saudi Twitter user explains the popularity of social media in the kingdom by the boredom effect. In other words, people in Saudi Arabia turn to social media because "There are no entertainment places, no cinemas, no parks, nothing" (Hebblethwaite, 2014). This explanation, however, no longer describes Saudi Arabia under the influence of Crown Prince Muhammad bin Salman. During summer fieldwork in 2018, evidence revealed that the Saudi government is increasingly promoting entertainment options throughout the kingdom, including live theater, cinemas, concerts, art shows, coffee house culture, tourism, and shopping festivals. Even a "Big Red Bus" tour of popular cities visited by foreigners has been launched in the kingdom. Interestingly, as of summer 2018, the only way to order tickets to attend a movie theater is through an online portal and downloading the QR code to your smartphone in place of a paper ticket. The growing social media footprint in the kingdom is also linked with the rise of the crown prince and his Vision 2030 plan (Shiloh, 2016). Another explanation is linked with the youthfulness of the Saudi population (Fadaak and Roberts, 2019; Alkhalisi, 2017; Murphy, 2013). With more than 70% of the population in Saudi Arabia under the age of 30, and with nearly all of these youths having Internet access from birth or early childhood, new media use has become a ubiquitous feature of everyday life (Stratfor, 2018).

The following sections shed light on the country's social media footprint and its impact on politics and social practices in the kingdom. I argue that social media use in Saudi Arabia is embedded in polarizing forces for change, including overt processes of liberalization which confront and are potentially sanctioned by enhanced state surveillance and repression. This study is supported by insights collected via fieldwork in Saudi Arabia in 2013 and the summer of 2018. The differences between everyday life and new media use in 2013 and 2018 were stark, as were transformations in social, cultural, and political practices, including social/media practices in non-urban centers, as discussed in subsequent sections.

New media vs. social media

For this analysis, social media is defined as "forms of electronic communication (such as websites for social networking and microblogging) through which users create communities to share information, ideas, personal messages, and other content (such as videos)" (Meriam Webster, 2019). New media is digital media that relies on the Internet for distribution. As such, social media is a subset of new media, and what makes it distinct is its social aspect – social media texts create a network of interactions and support a community of viewers who can like, share, alter (memes, for example), and comment on digital media texts (Penn, 2016). For example, a meme was distributed in Saudi Arabia via Twitter on the occasion of the 2017 announcement that women would be allowed to drive legally in the kingdom, with the subtitle "dreams come true"; the meme was then reprinted in *Arab News* (Farid, 2017). What makes this meme "social media" is the sharing and commenting process on Twitter. What makes this text "new media" is its digital distribution through *Arab News'* website (www.arabnews.com). So, the meme on Twitter is social media, while the meme distributed via *Arab News* online is new media. As soon as someone posts a comment on the *Arab News'* distributed meme, tweets the article link, shares the article on Facebook or Reddit, or posts the image on Instagram, the text becomes social media, especially as comments and likes and reposts grow into networks of distributed communication acts. Such practices build virtual communities, and they are the embodiment of what makes media "social." A text can be new media (digital) without being social (no network or comments attached to it); but a social media text is always new media, as is any text distributed digitally.

This chapter focuses on social media as a more granular approach to understanding the new media landscape and transformations occurring in Saudi Arabia. Moreover, the social component of social media reflects society's participation in the creation, distribution, and meaning of new media texts. Windows on forces for change in Saudi Arabia are embedded in social media practices, the analysis of which provides glimpses of participatory culture (and enhanced state repression) in the making. The Saudi state's desire to regulate and control social media practices when red lines are breached provides glimpses of what the crown prince fears, in his efforts to preserve his emerging power and the status quo. As discussed in the pages that follow, in this contest between state and society, some things change while others remain deeply entrenched. For example, linked with the meme discussed earlier, as of 24 June 2018 women can now legally drive, but those women who started a new media-distributed "pink" revolution (Oriti and Newton, 2018) to demand this right were imprisoned by the state (Tsujigami, 2018) or exiled (Al-Sharif, 2017) for their subversive behavior. While three high-profile right-to-drive activists arrested in May 2018 have been temporarily released from prison (March 2019), after their bail hearing, in April 2019, a new wave of arrests occurred, including the son of one of the right-to-drive activists, who is now out on bail, with some activists nabbed for challenging the regime's human rights record (Yee and Kirkpatrick, 2019). Often their only crime is publicly voicing support for the imprisoned women's right-to-drive activists (Romo, 2019). The use of social media to promote women's rights while simultaneously being used by the state to crack down on women's rights activists and their supporters highlights the Janus-faced nature of change in the kingdom.

A Saudi social media snapshot: users and key social media outlets

As of 2018, Saudi Arabia is estimated to have a social media growth rate of 32%, among the highest in the world (McDonald, 2018). Hours spent online per day in Saudi Arabia are just under seven hours a day, placing the country in the top 20 countries worldwide (Mcdonald, 2018).

Digital media saturation in Saudi Arabia has occurred despite (or perhaps because of) conservative social values. For example, until the spring and summer of 2018, movie theaters were not allowed, which might explain why, as of 2015, an estimated 96% of Saudi Internet users watch videos on YouTube, and seven million have uploaded video content (The Social Clinic, 2015). Saudi Arabia has the largest social media footprint in the Middle East. An estimated 71% of the population has a social media account, and of those accounts, 54% are accessed via a mobile device (Global Media Insights, 2018). The top five social media platforms in Saudi Arabia are as follows:

1   WhatsApp (founded in the US in 2009); with 24.27 million users in Saudi Arabia; 73% of the Saudi population uses this platform.
2   YouTube (founded in the US in 2005); with 23.6 million users in Saudi Arabia; 71% of the Saudi population uses this platform.
3   Facebook (founded in the US in 2004); with 21.95 million users in Saudi Arabia; 66% of the Saudi population uses this platform.
4   Instagram (founded in the US in 2010); with 17.96 million users in Saudi Arabia; 54% of the Saudi population uses this platform. (The top 10 Instagram influencers in Saudi Arabia can be viewed here, https://bit.ly/2D55aof.)
5   Twitter (founded in the US in 2006); with 17.29 million users in Saudi Arabia; 52% of the Saudi population uses this platform (Global Media Insights, 2018).

Social media use profiles – YouTube and Twitter

To get a better understanding of what draws Saudi audiences to social media, the following section takes a closer look at YouTube and Twitter use in the kingdom. The top three YouTube channels in Saudi Arabia (2019) include a family-based comedy, a youth-focused variety and entertainment show, and a children's channel:

1   In first place with the most subscribers is The Moshaaya Family YouTube channel.[1] This YouTube channel features a Saudi Vlogger, Mohamed Moshaya, who has amassed nearly 11 million subscribers. Mr. Moshaaya is the most popular vlogger in the Middle East. The channel features family comedy episodes with the actor and his three children, Yusif, Anas, and Iman. According to Mr. Moshaaya, "through our videos, followers get a glimpse of how a family is living in Saudi Arabia and what they do on their travels" (Mansor, 2017). Skits include pranks which the children play on their father, including stealing his food when he's not looking or giving the dad catsup when he is in the shower and asking for shampoo. The skits are suitable for all audiences and are quite entertaining. Mr. Moshaaya attributes his success to "avoiding religious topics." He argues that his show is about entertainment, not religion. If people want religious programming, they can view the many religious YouTube channels online (Mansor, 2017).
2   Sa7i. Sa7i (pronounced Sahi)[2] is one of the top 10 Saudi comedy channels on YouTube (Istizāda, 2018). With 3.3 million subscribers and more than 755 million views (Socialblade, 2019a), this show features Saudi youth covering social and cultural topics of interest. For example, on 25 April 2019, Sa7i featured a 13-minute show with nearly 51,000 views and 6.5 thousand likes, in the first three days it was posted. This segment was on the new *Avengers* film which was shown in May 2019 at the Vox Cinema in Riyadh.[3]
3   The Canary TV Channel is a family targeted Islamic values station with nearly 1.1 million subscribers and more than 692 million views (Socialblade, 2019b). In the segment titled "I Need You"[4] (with English translation), social and environmental commentary is presented with a plea for people to turn to the Prophet's example with the message "how we need you today" to heal our planet and divisive community.

All three of these YouTube channels provide windows on social media use and Saudi culture. Saudi Arabia is the biggest YouTube user per capita in the world (Kagel, 2013). Using the three most visited YouTube channels as profiled earlier, we can conclude that the country enjoys family-friendly entertainment and video content which sometimes promotes Islamic values and at other times just seeks to entertain and to give voice and image to everyday life in the kingdom beyond the global media stereotypes. We see an intensification of the Canary Channel's objectives to spread moderate Islam in "the most followed" Twitter accounts in the following section.

In terms of Twitter, the top three Twitter accounts in Saudi Arabia by followers according to social media marketing firm Social Bakers (2019) are all Islamic modernists, two of whom are currently in prison on death row:

1 Dr. Awad Al Qarni, with 18.4 million followers, is a popular sheikh with sermon podcasts widely available via his Twitter account and on YouTube. He is the author of the pop-psychology text *Don't Be Sad*, written in 2002. He was arrested in Saudi Arabia in 2017 and was given a death sentence in September 2018 for supposedly criticizing the Saudi blockade of Qatar (Middle East Eye, 2018). He was charged in 2010 by an Egyptian court in absentia for funding the Muslim Brotherhood (*The New Arab*, 2017).
2 Ahmad Al Shugairi, is a TV host and activist with 17.9 Twitter followers. Called in 2009 by the *New York Times* a "Satellite Sheikh preaching modern and moderate Islam," Shugairi claims that Islam "is an excellent product in need of better packaging" (Worth, 2009). In 2016, BBC Trending featured a video by Al Shugairi in which he explained the causes of Islamic radicalization (BBC, 2016) and his desire for moderate Islam. According to the BBC, Ahmad Al Shugairi is a "cool Muslim preacher" (BBC, 2016).
3 Salman Alaoudh is a prominent Saudi Sheikh who was arrested in 2017 and in 2018 was charged with the death penalty for 37 counts including "incitement against the ruler and spreading discord" (Al Jazeera, 2018). Alaoudh is an Islamic reformist who was critical of the Saudi blockade of Qatar. According to Awda's son, a Georgetown professor, his father was arrested for calling for an independent judiciary and political and social reform, and for being critical of Crown Prince Salman (Alaoudh, 2019).

The Saudi public has an appetite for Islamic messaging and guidance, and social media is one of the most significant platforms for spreading such awareness, at least according to the Twitter data given earlier. Given the current political climate in Saudi Arabia, crackdowns on Islamist behavior and voices that challenge the crown prince's vision of a new "modern" and "open for investment" Saudi Arabia are common. Raising one's voice on Twitter, in the name of Islam, can be dangerous. YouTube use for entertainment that avoids religion to reach a wider audience and to promote relaxation contrasts with the most followed Twitter accounts, where Saudis turn for religious advice and inspiration. The fact that owners of the two of the most followed Twitter accounts (Dr. Awad Al Qarni and Salman Alaoudh) are on death row for challenging the regime illustrate the conflicting forms of change emerging in the kingdom. Social media can promote liberal behavior which encourages cosmopolitanism in the kingdom, while the same platforms can be used by the state to promote authoritarianism and human rights violations. Likewise, the same social media tools that celebrate movies, concerts, and Western-style entertainment options can also be used to promote Islamic conservatism. Through these multi-layered images, voices, and power struggles, we see a more complete view of the kingdom, a kingdom of contradictions – a new Saudi Arabia being birthed by social media enabled state-society contests for change.

Governing the net

According to the 2018 "Freedom on the Net" report by Freedom House, Saudi Arabia's Internet freedom score is waning, because of "an escalating intolerance for all forms of political, social and religious dissent" (Freedom House, 2018: 2). Part of this decline in Internet freedom comes from a new 2017 anti-terrorism law that has been employed by the state to crack down on dissent and to punish oppositional acts, including social media activities. In 2014, Saudis explained the success of Twitter in the kingdom by its promotion of freedom, including claims that Twitter "provides a space for freedom without censorship" and that "people need an outlet to express themselves, to start to disclose what's hidden and drop the masks, without fear or commands, or censorship from anyone" (Hebblethwaite, 2014). Five years later, and with dozens of arrests, we see that Saudi social media practices are "not free," not "anonymous," and not protected by law. As the murder of journalist Jamal Khashoggi illustrates, there can be increasingly high prices paid for social media activism and any form of criticism of the regime.

During my fieldwork, even before the Khashoggi murder, concerns about regime repression for digital expression were amplified by public crackdowns on Saudis and foreigners alike whose social media practices were considered a violation of Saudi culture, values, and law. Examples include the imprisonment of Saudi right-to-drive activists, who dared to post videos of themselves driving around the kingdom before the rules were changed. The distribution of their videos drew international attention to their activism and to the fact that Saudi Arabia was the only country in the world where women could not drive. The state responded by withholding three well-known right-to-drive activists in prison for more than a year. The women cited abuse while incarcerated, and one even tried to commit suicide. Public prosecution of activists deters future activists who increasingly fear the unpredictability of the state. Knowing where and what the "red lines" are is difficult with the ascension of the crown prince. Other Saudi citizens who have been punished for their social media posts include three Saudi women who made a music video poking fun at the treatment of women in the kingdom and a young woman who dared to post a video of herself without hijab and wearing a mini skirt and was subsequently arrested for indecent exposure (Taylor, 2017). Another Saudi woman was arrested for posting a video of herself wearing shorts and a midriff top doing the Kiki challenge from a moving vehicle (Lemon, 2018). All these arrests for social media acts have at least five things in common: they all feature women activists, they all went viral on social media, they all resulted in arrests, they all represent norm-violating behavior; and they all illustrate the potential costs of challenging norms and laws governing "proper" public behavior – from dress to dancing to criticisms of patriarchy, especially when such acts are publicly distributed on social media.

Social and political functions of social media

The sweeping changes happening in the kingdom at least since 2017 with the rise of the crown prince are in part attributable to his Vision 2030 plan for the kingdom. Opening movie theaters for the first time in decades, allowing women to drive, and opening the kingdom to expanded tourism opportunities all correspond with increasingly open and wired communication environments in Saudi Arabia, and all these changes are discussed as goals in the Vision 2030 plan. At the same time, the expansion of state repression and the use of social media texts to charge dissidents with crimes against national security indicate contradictory trends in Saudi openness to change in the political realm. So, while there is increased freedom of expression culturally and enhanced entrepreneurialism economically, the red lines for political participation and opposition are more tightly conscribed, with overt exercises of state power as evidence for breaching them – from arrests to financial shakedowns, to imprisonment, torture, and even murder.

The contrasts between the new and old Saudi Arabia are observable most perceptively in a recent film (2016) made in Saudi Arabia, *Baraka Meets Baraka*. This is the first romantic comedy ever produced in the kingdom. It was Saudi Arabia's submission for the Academy Awards for best foreign-language film. While the film did not win the Oscar, it did garner several other film festival awards and honors. *Baraka Meets Baraka* has a 100% rating on Rotten Tomatoes and is available for streaming on Netflix. In the film, Bibi, the female lead, (short for Baraka) is a fashion icon/Instagram star, with millions of followers. The idea that a Saudi filmmaker is in the romance and comedy business and is examining the fragility of tradition, while challenging the rules governing public space and dating and providing clear representations of cultural transformation and social media use, indicates the power of youth and media to craft new ways of engaging socially and artistically in the kingdom. The fact that one can watch this new vessel of Saudi culture and meaning on Netflix is a sign of how globalized and accessible this new Saudi Arabia is.

A culture of increased liberalism, from women driving to opening movie theaters and sponsoring rock concerts (Toby Keith performed in the capital) and plays, competes with an environment of enhanced state repression for political activism in the kingdom. The arrest of women driving activists, their torture and flimsy trial for being "enemies of the state," the brutal murder of journalist Jamal Khashoggi, the execution of a Shi'i sheikh charged with sedition, and the arrest and financial shakedown of ruling family members who might challenge the ascension of Crown Prince Muhammad bin Salman and their 2017 detention at the Ritz Carlton Hotel are all examples of how potential freedom of voice, enabled by social media technologies, are risky to use for political change.

Why all the changes in Saudi Arabia? Are social media diffusion and use causing cultures of change and openness and enabling government crackdowns, or are the transformations currently taking place in the kingdom linked with the new leadership of the youthful crown prince? Or is some other factor driving such transformations? One argument is that increased openness and an expanding digital footprint in Saudi Arabia are linked with declining oil prices (Liao, 2017). The argument is that "as oil prices plummet," the kingdom "is looking to the internet for more sources of revenue" (Liao, 2017). This makes good business sense because, given the youthfulness of the population, Saudi Arabia is "hyper-social and hyper-digital" (Liao, 2017). At the same time, not all the web is an open-access forum, "extremist, pornographic, and gambling-related websites" are censored (Liao, 2017). In searching the Vision 2030 document, we see a link between social media and entrepreneurialism when the policy plan states:

> Our productive families now enjoy vast marketing opportunities through social media and digital platforms. We will facilitate access to these channels, enable microfinance, and motivate the non-profit sector to build the capabilities of our productive families and fund their initiatives. Vision 2030[5]

In other words, part of Vision 2030's goal is to stimulate new business opportunities, especially for small and medium-sized family-owned enterprises, and the vehicle through which marketing and growth opportunities will flow are social media platforms. The Saudi government commits to "facilitate access to these channels" as a part of its economic restructuring beyond oil. The most widespread use of social media is for entertainment. The government plays a big role in social media use, and the smallest, most dangerous form of social media use (the aspect that makes the most headline news) is activist use of the tool.

Social media uses beyond activism

According to Nigel Stanger, Noorah Alnaghaimshi, and Erika Pearson, studies of social media use and impact in the Middle East are rare, and those which do exist tend to focus on political uses of the technology by activists, rather than the general use by the public in everyday life (Stanger et al., 2017: 1). With a focus on political uses of social media, especially in the post-Arab Spring context, the widespread use of social media in the practice of everyday life by non-activists and the state can be overlooked (Wheeler, 2017). Surprising uses of social media apps in Saudi society illustrate the technology's pervasiveness and importance beyond activism. For example, the General Authority of Meteorology and Environmental Protection uses text messaging services to provide public service announcements about weather-related hazards, such as sandstorms and fog (Arab News, 2018). Social media is also used to spread public health awareness. For example, a 2018 study conducted in Dammam Saudi Arabia used Snapchat to spread breast cancer awareness among female students (Alanzi, Alobrah, Alhumaidi, and Aloraifi, 2018). Education, health and public safety, marketing, and entertainment are all contributors to the Saudi social media footprint. Moreover, when the tools are used for activism, the most publicized forms of digital resistance are those linked with struggles for women's rights. Resistance to promote human rights, Islamic observance, and a more equitable livelihood for Saudis, however, are all represented in the digital public sphere. For example, "The salary is not enough" movement triggered 17.5 million tweets in approximately four months and called attention to the kingdom's working poor. The movement demanded that the government raise Saudi purchasing power via higher public sector salaries (Boghardt, 2013). In a 2015 study of Saudi social media practices, using the Twittersphere as a case study, Helmi Noman, Robert Faris, and John Kelly observe,

> The Saudi Twittersphere contains a wide spectrum of opinions and activities, including political and social commentary; political dissidence and criticism of the monarchy; media professionals discussing and promoting their products; religious preachers spreading Islamic messages; Syrian revolution supporters; sports officials and fans tweeting about local soccer teams; users relying heavily on pre-selected content tweeting automation tools; and users tweeting popular quotes, banal messages, and observations of daily life.
>
> *(Noman et al., 2015: 1)*

Of all the competing topics in the Saudi social media environment, Noman, Faris, and Kelly find that "Religion, football, and politics are the topics that draw the most attention" (Noman et al., 2015: 1). Digital discussions of religion and politics are the two topics that are the most likely to get you noticed by the regime, and engaging in behavior which is norm-violating of these two topics is risky. Wearing revealing clothing, challenging patriarchy, dancing in public, challenging the crown prince's Vision 2030 reforms, especially those which bring Western entertainment and allow for the mixing of genders in public life, including on highways by allowing women to drive, and sending these messages of opposition over social media can get people arrested, or even killed, in this high-risk environment of inconsistent change. People are encouraged to watch a movie or attend Western pop stars' performances, as long as they do not tweet criticism of the regime for promoting these practices. Women can wear *abaya* open, and even take off the hijab if they wish, but they should not wear a mini skirt or roller skate while challenging patriarchy online. Throughout my field research, I was told by Saudis that they are encouraged by certain changes but are fearful of others. They like having wider entertainment options and increased public freedoms in choosing how to dress, but they are also uncertain about what the limits of change are, and thus they self-censor and wait for the new normal to be better defined.

Conclusion

This chapter on social media use in Saudi Arabia contributes to an emerging conversation on culture, communication, and the practice of everyday life in the Middle East (Wheeler, 2017; Shirazi, 2013; Hofheinz, 2011). It highlights how social media is embedded in polarizing forces for change, by supporting the process of liberalization (which compete with and are often shaped by Islamist cultural remnants) in the kingdom, while also enabling enhanced forms of state repression (which pits state against society in increasingly transparent expressions of conflict).

Globally, Saudi Arabia's reputation is dominated by images of "terrorism, oil and poor human rights" (Muyidi, 2015, p. iii). Other representations of the country are more nuanced, yet equally limiting. The desert kingdom is known as being among the most conservative Islamic countries in the world, the birthplace and center of Islam (Devji, 2018), a country with strict sharia laws and public executions (Calamur, 2018). Saudi Arabia is associated with hosting the Hajj and *Umra* (two forms of pilgrimages) and the controversies that accompany them (Bianchi, 2017) and conservative/repressive social mores, including constraints on the dress, dating, and public events where genders might mix (Fahmy, 2018). Saudi Arabia is ranked 85th in the world on the Social Progress Index (www.socialprogress.org), despite its wealth; a fourth-tier nation, outranked by Fiji and El Salvador.

Media representations matter. Negative or limiting news coverage "prepare the public mind" and can influence how a country is treated in the international community (Wanta et al., 2004: 34; Alsultany, 2012; and Qutub, 2013: 139). Social media platforms, however, give local and global audiences a voice with which to challenge narrow stereotypes. With images of conservatism and restrictiveness characterizing the country, Saudi Arabia's growing engagement with new media provides competing images of the country. For example, while movie theaters were banned from the 1980s until 2018 (Radwan, 2019), Saudi Arabia has the highest global percentage of social media users who access video content online – 95% – and the highest percentage of social media users who access video content daily – 64% (*Statista*, 2018b). In part, widespread new media use in Saudi Arabia is shaped by the country's demographics. An estimated 75% of the population in Saudi Arabia is under the age of 30, and this youthful population has grown up with Internet access, making use of the technology a regular part of everyday life; just over 90% of Saudi society has access to the Internet (Kemp, 2018).

Access to new media, a crown prince determined via his Vision 2030 plan to transform the country's image, and openness/accessibility to the global market are having deep impacts on Saudi society and media practices. While narratives and practices of enhanced state repression compete with images, voices, and acts of liberalism and change, this chapter explained the puzzles that emerge in this contest between state power and social (media) forces for change. Through an analysis of the evolution of social media use and impact in Saudi Arabia, we see how increased voice and citizen representation on platforms like YouTube and Instagram do not necessarily equate with enhanced agency and opportunity for creating political change. In other words, we may see surprisingly overt evidence of changing gender relations and dress in

Saudi Arabia but do not necessarily see these same processes of liberalization accompanied by increases in political rights and protections for citizens. Sometimes, as in the case of women driving, we see major shifts in digital representations and voice, even changes in legislation, but less significant transformations in actual social practice and behavior offline (Wheeler, 2020). It is possible that digital transformations could pave the way to new forms of "normal" public behavior by enabling risk-taking in imagined and digital communities online. Social media can be a testing ground for what may be perceived as risky behavior, but with replication in social media practices, becomes more acceptable – such as women showing their faces in Instagram posts – whereas previously it was considered a violation of women's privacy and modesty for face shots, and thus an ear, or a close-up of some other non-distinct body part or an inanimate object was posted as an identifier instead.

Finally, we may also see overt state punishments for violating red lines online, through increased state policing of digital media space, and more overt and stringent punishments for violators, designed to encourage self-censorship. The political environment in Saudi Arabia has become more oppressive with the rise of Crown Prince Mohammad bin Salman in spite of, or perhaps because of, increased access to social media tools in the kingdom. Exploring the curious relationship between enhanced social media use, forms of social liberalization, and an uptick in political repression, in part enabled by digital spying by the state, is the main contribution of this chapter.

Notes

1 https://bit.ly/2KHpJLF
2 www.youtube.com/user/sa7iChannel
3 www.youtube.com/watch?v=iK4tLErlW7Q
4 https://youtu.be/jrsLzIhw62k
5 https://vision2030.gov.sa/download/file/fid/417

References

Al-Sharif, Manal (2017), *Daring to Drive*. New York: Simon and Schuster.

Alanzi, Turki M. al Alanoud al Obrah, Alhumaidi, Reem, and Aloraifi, Shahad (2018), Evaluation of the SnapChat Mobile Social Networking Application for Breast Cancer Awareness among Saudi Students in the Dammam Region of the Kingdom of Saudi Arabia. *Breast Cancer Targets and Therapy*, 10, pp. 113–119. Retrieved from www.ncbi.nlm.nih.gov/pmc/articles/PMC6047612/

Alaoudh, Abdullah (2019), My Father Faces the Death Penalty. This is Justice in Saudi Arabia. *New York Times*, 13 February. Retrieved from www.nytimes.com/2019/02/13/opinion/saudi-arabia-judiciary.html

Alfaisal, Leen (2019), Yasmeen Al-Maimani First Female Pilot in Saudi Commercial Airlines. *Saudi Gazette*, 15 June. Retrieved from http://saudigazette.com.sa/article/568936/SAUDI%20ARABIA

Aljazeera (2018), Saudi 'Seeks Death Penalty' for Muslim Scholar Salman al-Awdah, 5 September. Retrieved from www.aljazeera.com/news/2018/09/saudi-seeks-death-penalty-muslim-scholar-salman-al-awdah-180905055754018.html

Alkhalisi, Zahraa (2017), Saudi Arabia's Crown Prince Has Youth on His Side. *CNN Business*, 20 November. Retrieved from https://money.cnn.com/2017/11/20/news/economy/saudi-crown-prince-young-people/index.html

Alsultany, Evelyn (2012), *Arabs and Muslims in the Media: Race and Representation after 9/11*. New York: New York University Press.

Arab News (2018), *Flood Warning as Cyclone Nears Saudi Arabia*, 26 May. Retrieved from www.arabnews.com/node/1309796/saudi-arabia

BBC (2016), *BBC Trending: Meet Saudi Arabia's Stars of Social Media*, 3 March. Retrieved from www.bbc.com/news/blogs-trending-35609249

Bianchi, Robert (2017), Reimagining the Hajj. *Social Sciences*, 6(2), pp. 36. doi:10.3390/socsci6020036. Retrieved from www.mdpi.com/2076-0760/6/2/36/htm

Boghardt, Lori P. (2013), Insight: Saudi Arabia's War on Twitter. *Middle East Voice, Voice of America News*, 12 December. Retrieved from https://middleeastvoices.voanews.com/2013/12/insight-saudi-arabias-war-on-twitter-79407/

Calamur, Krishnadev (2018), Saudi Arabia Rejects Human-Rights Criticism, Then Crucifies Someone. *The Atlantic*, 9 August. Retrieved from www.theatlantic.com/international/archive/2018/08/saudi-crucifixion/567128/

Communication and Information Technology Commission (CITCA), Saudi Arabia (2018), *ICT Performance Indicators: Fourth Quarter Report*. Retrieved from www.citc.gov.sa/en/indicators/Pages/CIT-CICTIndicators.aspx and www.citc.gov.sa/en/indicators/Indicators%20of%20Communications%20and%20Information%20Techn/ICTIndicators-Q42019En.pdf

Devji, Faisal (2018), Will Saudi Arabia Cease to Be the Center of Islam? *New York Times*, 7 September. Retrieved from www.nytimes.com/2018/09/07/opinion/saudi-arabia-islam-mbs.html

Fadaak, Talha, and Roberts, Ken (2019), *Youth in Saudi Arabia*. New York: Palgrave Macmillan.

Fahmy, Dalia (2018), *5 Facts about Religion in Saudi Arabia*. Pew Research Center, 12 April. Retrieved from https://pewrsr.ch/2HvADkX

Farid, Aisha (2017), Hashtags, Memes, and GIFs: Social Media Celebrates Saudi Women Driving. *Arab News*, 27 September. Retrieved from www.arabnews.com/node/1168191/saudi-arabia

Freedom House (2018), *Saudi Arabia Country Report Freedom on the Net 2018*. Retrieved from https://freedomhouse.org/report/freedom-net/2018/saudi-arabia

Global Media Insights (2018), *Saudi Arabia Social Media Statistics 2018*, 28 May. Retrieved from www.globalmediainsight.com/blog/saudi-arabia-social-media-statistics/

GMI_blogger (2019), Saudi Arabia Social Media Statistics 2019, 29 October. Retrieved from https://www.globalmediainsight.com/blog/saudi-arabia-social-media-statistics/

Hebblethwaite, Cordelia (2014), Why Twitter Is So Big in Saudi Arabia. *#BBC Trending*, 23 January. Retrieved from www.bbc.com/news/blogs-trending-25864558

Hofheinz, Albrecht (2011), The Arab Spring/Nextopia? Beyond Revolution 2.0. *International Journal of Communication*, 5, pp. 1417–1434. Retrieved from https://ijoc.org/index.php/ijoc/article/view/1186

Human Rights Watch (1999), *The Internet in the Middle East and North Africa: Free Expression and Censorship*. Retrieved from www.hrw.org/legacy/advocacy/Internet/mena/int-mena.htm

Internet World Stats Usage and Population Statistics (2020), Middle Eastern Internet Users, Population and Facebook Statistics 2020. *Interneworldstats.com*. Retrieved from https://www.internetworldstats.com/stats5.htm#me

Istizāda (2018), *Top 10 Arab Comedy Channels on YouTube*. Retrieved from https://bit.ly/37rhVYk

Jaffery, Rabiya (2018), Is Saudi Arabia Addicted to Social Media? *Culture Trip*, 27 June. Retrieved from https://theculturetrip.com/middle-east/articles/is-saudi-arabia-addicted-to-social-media/

Kagel, Jenna (2013), The World's Most Avid YouTube Viewers Are in Saudi Arabia. *Fast Company*, 18 November. Retrieved from www.fastcompany.com/3021832/the-worlds-most-avid-youtube-viewers-are-in-saudi-arabia

Kell, Laura Andrea (2018), This Is the Most Active Country in the Region on Social Media: Surprised? *ITP Live*, 4 September. Retrieved from https://itp.live/content/saudi-arabia-social-media

Kemp, Simon (2018), *Digital 2018: Saudi Arabia*. Datareportal, 1 February. Retrieved from https://datareportal.com/reports/digital-2018-saudi-arabia.

Lemon, Jason (2018), Kiki Challenge: Saudi Arabia Arrests Woman for Jumping Out of Car and Dancing To Drake Song. *Newsweek*, 1 August. Retrieved from www.newsweek.com/kiki-challenge-saudi-arabia-arrests-woman-jumping-out-car-dancing-drake-song-1053233

Liao, Shannon (2017), Saudi Arabia Lifts Ban on Skype, WhatsApp, and Other Messaging Apps. *The Verge*, 20 September. Retrieved from www.theverge.com/2017/9/20/16340342/saudi-arabia-skype-whatsapp-snapchat-censorship-ban-lift

Mansour, Karim (2017), From Full Time Job to Full Time Family Man: Saudi Vlogger Mohamed Moshaya's Journey. *My Salaam*, 15 February. Retrieved from www.mysalaam.com/en/story/from-full-time-job-to-full-time-family-man-saudi-vlogger-mohamed-moshayas-journey/SALAAM15022017061745

McDonald, Nathan (2018), Special Report: Digital in 2018. *We Are Social*, 30 January. Retrieved from https://wearesocial.com/us/blog/2018/01/global-digital-report-2018

Meriam-Webster (2019), *Social Media*. Retrieved from www.merriam-webster.com/dictionary/social%20media

Middle East Eye (2018), Saudi Prosecutor Demands Death Penalty for Cleric Awad al-Qarni, 6 September. Retrieved from www.middleeasteye.net/news/saudi-prosecutor-demands-death-penalty-cleric-awad-al-qarni

Mideastmedia.org (2019), *Social Media Use 2019*, Northwestern University Qatar. Retrieved from http://www.mideastmedia.org/survey/2019/chapter/social-media/

Murphy, Caryle (2013), *A Kingdom's Future: Saudi Arabia Through the Eyes of its Twentysomethings.* Washington, DC: The Wilson Center. Retrieved from www.wilsoncenter.org/sites/default/files/kingdoms_future_saudi_arabia_through_the_eyes_twentysomethings_0.pdf

Muyidi, Ahmed (2015), *American Students Perception Toward Saudi Arabian Coverage in the U.S. Media.* Unpublished MA dissertation, University of Kansas. ProQuest Dissertations Publishing.

Noman, Helmi, Faris, Rob, and Kelly, John (2015), *Openness and Restraint: Structure, Discourse, and Contention in Saudi Twitter.* The Berkman Klein Center for Internet & Society Research Publication No. 2015–16. Retrieved from https://dash.harvard.edu/bitstream/handle/1/28552580/SSRN-id2700944.pdf?sequence=1&isAllowed=y. Accessed 27 August 2019.

Oriti, Thomas, and Newton, Laura Brierley (2018), Saudi Women Have a Long Way to Go in Order to Be Free Says Manal al-Sharif. *ABC News Australia,* 11 February. Retrieved from www.abc.net.au/news/2018-02-08/saudi-women-revolution-has-a-long-way-to-go-says-manal-al-sharif/9396306

Penn, Christopher (2016), What's the Difference between Social Media and New Media? *The Medium,* 7 October. Retrieved from https://medium.com/@cspenn/whats-the-difference-between-social-media-and-new-media-71f7f5ae1eea

Qutub, Afnan (2013), Harem Girls, and Terrorist Men: Media Misrepresentations of Middle Eastern Cultures. *Colloquy,* 9(Fall), pp. 139–155.

Radwan, Rawan (2019), Saudi Mother's First Cinema Trip with Daughter Revives Happy Memories. *Arab News,* 18 April. Retrieved from www.arabnews.com/node/1484161/saudi-arabia

Romo, Vanessa (2019), Saudi Arabia Releases 3 Women's Rights Activists from Prison. *NPR,* 28 March. Retrieved from https://www.npr.org/2019/03/28/707722564/saudi-arabia-releases-3-womens-rights-activists-from-prison-others-still-held

Shiloh, Nachum (2016), Saudi Vision 2030: One Vision, Many Views. *The Bee Hive: Middle East Social Media.* Moshe Dayan Center for Middle East Studies, 31 May. Retrieved from https://dayan.org/content/saudi-vision-2030-one-vision-many-views

Shirazi, Farid (2013), Social Media and the Social Movements in the Middle East and North Africa: A Critical Discourse Analysis. *Information Technology and People,* 26(1), pp. 28–49. doi:10.1108/09593841311307123

Social Bakers (2019), *Twitter Statistics for Saudi Arabia,* April. Retrieved from www.socialbakers.com/statistics/twitter/profiles/saudi-arabia/

Socialblade (2019a), *sa7i Channel Statistics.* Retrieved from https://socialblade.com/youtube/user/sa7ichannel

Socialblade (2019b), *The Canary TV Channel Statistics.* Retrieved from https://socialblade.com/youtube/user/cannnarytv

Statista (2018a), *Percentage of Internet Users in Selected Countries Who Watch On-Line Video Content Every Day as of January 2018.* Retrieved from www.statista.com/statistics/272835/share-of-Internet-users-who-watch-online-videos/.

Statista (2018b), *Percentage of Internet Users Who Watch Online Video Content on Any Device as of January 2018 by Country.* Retrieved from www.statista.com/statistics/272835/share-of-Internet-users-who-watch-online-videos/

Stratfor (2018), Riyadh Revisits Its Relationship with Religion. *Stratfor.com,* 2 May. Retrieved from https://bit.ly/2qstX3c

Taylor, Adam (2017), Saudi Arabia Says a Woman Arrested for Wearing Skirt in Viral Video has been Released. *Washington Post,* 19 July. Retrieved from www.washingtonpost.com/news/worldviews/wp/2017/07/18/a-video-of-a-woman-in-a-skirt-sparks-outrage-in-saudi-arabia/

The New Arab (2017), *Popular Saudi Cleric Awad al Qarni Banned from Twitter,* 17 March. Retrieved from www.alaraby.co.uk/english/society/2017/3/17/popular-saudi-cleric-awad-al-qarni-banned-from-twitter

The Social Clinic (2015), *The State of Social Media in Saudi Arabia.* Vol. 3, March. Retrieved from www.thesocialclinic.com/the-state-of-social-media-in-saudi-arabia-vol-3/

Stanger, Nigel, Alnaghaimshi, Noorah, and Pearson, Erika. (2017), How Do Saudi Youth Engage with Social Media? *First Monday* (3 April). Retrieved from https://firstmonday.org/ojs/index.php/fm/article/view/7102/6101

Tsujigami, N. (2018), Stealth Revolution: Saudi Women's Ongoing Social Battles. In S. Khamis and A. Mili (eds.), *Arab Women's Activism and Socio-Political Transformation.* Cham, Switzerland: Palgrave Macmillan.

Wanta, W., Golan, G., and Lee, C. (2004), Agenda Setting and International News: Media Influence on Public Perceptions of Foreign Nations. *Journalism & Mass Communication Quarterly*, 81(2), pp. 364–377. doi:10.1177/107769900408100209

Wheeler, Deborah (2017), *Digital Resistance in the Middle East: New Media Activism in Everyday Life*. Edinburgh: Edinburgh University Press.

Wheeler, Deborah L. (2020), Saudi Women Driving Change? Rebranding, Resistance, and the Kingdom of Change. *The Journal of the Middle East and Africa*, 11(1), pp. 87–109. doi:10.1080/21520844.2020.1733865

Worth, Robert (2009), Preaching Moderate Islam and Becoming a TV Star. *New York Times,* 2 January. Retrieved from www.nytimes.com/2009/01/03/world/middleeast/03preacher.html

Yee, Vivian, and Kirkpatrick, David D. (2019), Saudis Escalate Crackdown on Dissent, Arresting Nine and Risking U.S. Ire. *New York Times,* 5 April. Retrieved from www.nytimes.com/2019/04/05/world/middleeast/american-detainees-saudi-arabia.html?login=email&auth=login-email

Somalia

28

MASS MEDIA DEVELOPMENT IN SOMALIA

Ismail Sheikh Yusuf Ahmed

Introduction

This chapter provides an overview of Somali media and its role in society and media education. Somalis generally have been described as having an oral society (Jama, 1994; Issa-Salwe, 2008) that emphasizes receiving and preserving knowledge, wisdom, poetry, history, and art through spoken communication. Poetry was and still is one of the most powerful tools in Somalis' political and social life, playing a major role in disseminating news and information and creating awareness about a given phenomenon (Jama, 1994). Furthermore, the Somali societal structure mainly is shaped by nomadic pastoralism (Haydarov et al., 2016), in which people are governed by their need for water and grass. When Somalia gained independence in the early 1960s, the government implemented literacy campaigns among the nomadic and rural communities.

Since the nation became independent, several civil and military regimes that allowed differing degrees of freedom have ruled the country. From 1960 to 1969, two civil governments came to power through elections and represented different ethnic clans. Freedom of expression and freedom of the press was practiced extensively during this period, until a military regime led by General Siad Barre came to power through a white coup in October 1969 and put an end to the nation's constitution and regulatory boards. It also suppressed all kinds of freedoms, including a free press. This regime ruled the nation for over 20 years until armed rebel factions ousted it in 1991, but political and social disintegration followed throughout the 1990s. Somaliland, Somalia's northwestern region, declared unilateral independence from the rest of the country in May 1991, but the world at large has not recognized this declaration (Osman, 2017).

After the Barre regime was overthrown, the country plunged into a civil war that left its mark on all aspects of life, affecting all citizens: Thousands were killed, and more than one million fled the country, leaving behind their property, loved ones, and land (Human Rights Watch, 1995; Osman, 2017). After Barre was ousted from the capital, the war entered a phase that Lidwien Kapteijns describes as a "clan cleansing" (Kapteijns, 2013), in which civilians of certain clans became targets of armed militias. Nationwide, various clan-based factions (such as the United Somali Congress [USC], Somali Democratic Movement [SDM], Somali National Front [SNF] and Somali National Movement [SNM], among others), who all participated in the overthrow of the Barre regime, began a new stage in their struggle for power (Kapteijns,

2013; Haji Ingiriis, 2017). The USC, which took control of the capital, splintered into two rival groups. Due to the USC's intense fight for power and to the growing humanitarian issues in the country, the United Nations launched its operation in Somalia in early 1992 to restore peace and hope, as well as facilitate aid deliveries (Human Rights Watch, 1995). Most of the nation's infrastructure, including state-owned media outlets and the only telecommunications company, was destroyed in the war. However, the Somali conflict is not confined to clan warfare but is also fueled by other factors, including international community involvement, unequal access to resources, and poverty (Osman, 2017).

To end the enduring civil war and conflict, several reconciliation conferences were organized with the help of the international community, most of which failed to make any lasting impacts, but at least one, the Embakasi Reconciliation Conference (named after a city in Kenya), paved the way for the current federal system (Gilkes, 1999; Kapteijns, 2013). Under the concept of federalism, each state would have semi-independence in managing its resources and local administration. Since the beginning of this century, and after 10 years with no formal government structure, several transitional governments were formed, with varying degrees of challenges. In 2000, the transitional national government (TNG) was formed at a national conference in Djibouti, which was attended by clan elders, civil society organizations, and some of the fighting warlords. However, the TNG failed to restore governance structure due to limited capacity, resources, and law enforcement. A second attempt at restoring governance structure was made at another conference held in Kenya in 2004, resulting in the transitional federal government (TFG) (Osman, 2017). Although the TFG faced similar challenges, it was able to accommodate most warlords and the Islamic Courts Council in 2009, resulting in a new, inclusive government. The interim periods ended in 2012 when the first permanent federal government was established since 1991.

The current Somali federal structure comprises six geopolitical regions: Hirshabelle, Galmudug, Puntland, Jubbaland, Southwest, and Somaliland (despite its aforementioned independence claim, it receives a federal budget allocation). Each federal state has local representation from each tribe and ethnic group in that state. However, some international community organizations and scholars prefer to describe the nation as comprising three regions: South-Central, Puntland, and Somaliland. The current federal government is the product of the aforementioned Embakasi conference. Thanks to the international community's efforts, led by the United Nations (UN) and the African Union, Somalia is now on a development track. Recently, the UN's Somalia envoy described the nation as "transforming itself from a failed state to a recovering state" (Citizen TV, 2015).

This chapter discusses the country's media landscape history and development. Even though the landscape comprises radio and TV stations, newspapers, online-based news portals, and local and diasporic media, the chapter only discusses the history of the nation's mass media platforms, namely newspaper, radio, and TV platforms, followed by a discussion of the role of these platforms in society as well as media education and its contribution to the media industry.

Newspapers

The emergence of Somali print media coincided with the emergence of political movements in the 1940s, with the first newspaper being the *Couriera Della Somala*, which translates to "Somali Courier" (Ministry of Information and National Guidance, MING, 1977). The Italian colonial administration established and operated the paper, circulated in Italian and English, to counter rising political movements and liberation aspirations among the Somali people. The *Talro News*, established by a labor union in Djibouti, was the second newspaper to emerge in the Somali territories. The paper focused on defending labor rights, as well as documenting and opposing violations and restrictions of these rights by the French colonial protectorate.

Although journalistic activities existed during the colonial era, as well as under Italian trusteeship administration and civil governments after independence, the readership was confined to educated individuals and political elites who had mastered foreign languages. A rapid newspaper proliferation and increases in readership were observed during the military regime (1969–1991). Following the writing of Somali script, *The October Star* was established on 21 January 1973, marking a new chapter in the nation's print media history. Being the official regime newspaper, it was published in four languages: Somali, Arabic, English, and Italian (MING, 1977; Whitehead et al., 2011; Gaas et al., 2012; Ahmed, 2020).

The military regime controlled the media landscape, including newspapers, through the Ministry of Information, with journalists given limited press freedom and the public afforded limited free speech. During this period, another two government-owned and -operated newspapers emerged. *The Heegan* was published in English twice a week in the 1970s, while the *Ogaal* newspaper was established in the 1980s to become the official mouthpiece for the ruling military regime's Somali Socialist Revolutionary Party (SSRP). The first privately owned newspaper that emerged during this era was *Aldaleeca*, which was published only in Arabic (Gaas et al., 2012).

As contended by Gaas and colleagues (2012), the *Ogaal* paper was exceptional in this highly censored media environment. Edited by young, educated members of the SSRP, the paper sometimes was critical of government policies, garnering wider respect and trust among the Somali public. However, this critical approach towards government officials and policies eventually led to the government terminating it in 1988.

Following the overthrow of the military regime, all the aforementioned newspapers collapsed and ceased operations. More than a quarter of new daily or weekly newspapers that emerged between 1991 and 2000 nationwide published news and information mostly related to the politics and conflict between fighting political factions. However, a few focused on sports, fiction stories, women's rights, development issues, general social affairs, and short stories. Most of these papers stopped publishing due to various technical, economic, and security reasons. Overall, sensational journalism was the norm during this period (Gaas et al., 2012; Geedi, 2015).

International organizations' interventions, led by the US and UN, in their efforts to restore the nation's peace and stability, partly influenced these newspapers' proliferation. Newspaper circulation increased sharply in south-central regions, where many aid organizations had a huge physical presence. Generally, low circulation, poor quality, unprofessional journalism, bias, and partisanship characterized the era's print media practices. Newspapers published news, articles, and caricatures that incited violence and conflict, usually siding with certain warlords or their clans against rival warlords and clans. Many newspapers either were allied with or owned by the warlords, acting as these warlords' official mouthpieces to counter their rival clans and factions' rhetoric. However, the newspapers sometimes were forced to show support for the warlords controlling their operating areas, under threat of physical harm (Gaas et al., 2012; Ahmed, 2020).

At the turn of the new millennium, print media declined due to several contributing factors. First, the warlords' power and control significantly had diminished, resulting in substantial decreases in conflicts and violence. Second, many diaspora returnees made huge investments in numerous sectors, including the radio industry, creating a huge media market rival for print media. Third, increasing illiteracy rates due to deteriorating education systems affected the print media industry. Finally, the introduction of affordable and competitively priced mobile phone services, as well as cheap Internet services, also contributed to print's decline, particularly in south-central regions. In addition, print media readership is low among most Somalis in the diaspora because the strong oral tradition is still dominant among Somalis, even when they move to Western societies (Gaas et al., 2012; Geedi, 2015).

In the capital city alone, seven daily, weekly, and monthly newspapers were available to readers as of 2015, while no federal government papers exist, unlike electronic media, which include government-run Radio Mogadishu and Somali National Television (SNTV). In an interview with Turkey's Anadolu News Agency, Abdi Adam Guuleed, editor-in-chief of the *Xog-Ogaal* newspaper, contended that print media currently faces many challenges that threaten its sustainability and continued performance amid the Internet's globalization. However, he argued that despite all these challenges of economic and technical media development, the print media industry is determined to survive (Geedi, 2015).

In the Puntland regions, two newspapers were in circulation as of 2011, compared with 11 in Somaliland. Even though both regions are relatively stable politically compared with the south-central regions, the larger number of newspapers in Somaliland may be related to the area's radio restrictions, in that only Radio Hargeisa exists (a state-owned station). Therefore, newspapers may act as alternative channels for public discourse. As a result, Somaliland newspapers are more profitable economically and of higher quality than those in Puntland and south-central regions (Gaas et al., 2012).

Radio

In many poor countries, radio is the most appropriate medium for delivering news and information. Radio in Somalia has been and remains a dominant mass media channel. This dominance is in line with the country's strong oral tradition, where word of mouth plays a greater role in both urban and rural societies' daily activities (Abdi et al., 2011). Other reasons include its poor economy, where most of the populace cannot afford a TV or Internet service, and its high illiteracy rates (LandInfo, 2016). Radios are as cheap as USD 5 each, and some people access radio stations through their mobile phones (USAID, 2019). Radio provides news and information, and it continues to play an integral role in today's political and social arenas. However, today's TV and online news platforms pose a greater challenge to the radio's dominance.

The country's radio history and development can be divided into four stages: the colonial era, the civil government era, the military government era, and the post-military era. Colonial powers first introduced Somalia to radio in the northern region, under British occupation, while the southern region was under Italian occupation. The British colonial administration established a radio station, KUDO, in Hargeisa (northwest Somalia) in 1943 (Adam, 2001; LandInfo, 2016). Its prime objectives were to provide war propaganda and persuade Somalis to accept British rule, as well as deliver news to soldiers and allies. KUDO later was renamed Radio Somalia and increased its transmitting power from just 100 watts in 1943 to 1 kilowatt in 1945, which helped increase its reach (Adam, 2001). The station initially was located in a small building comprising one studio, a small observation room, and an administrative office. The news was picked up from BBC Radio and edited by a British employee.

The southern part of Somalia (previously known as Italian Somaliland) had no radio station during the 1940s. When the British took over the entire nation during World War II, news from the south was collected and sent to KUDO to broadcast once a week. As Adam (2001) has argued, the British administration was reluctant to establish a radio station in the south, considering "the fact that British rule (there) was only *ad interim* – the fate of the country was being decided by the United Nations" (p. 16). The Italian trusteeship administration established the southern region's first radio station, Experimental Radio of Mogadishu, in 1951, operating in a small section of the Ministry of Information building. It initially had a 200-watt transmitter, but later boosted its power to 4 kilowatts. However, transmission quality was poor, often leading to the station going off the air intermittently.

However, remarkable developments in radio were introduced immediately after independence in 1960. Radio Hargeisa and Radio Mogadishu merged, and the new station was named Radio Mogadishu, under the management of the newly established government's Ministry of Information. A radio development project supported by the Soviet Union funded a modern transmitter with 50 kilowatts of power, extending the station's reach beyond the nation's borders. In addition, the Federal Republic of Germany funded this project. The funds were utilized to build a new sound-proof, air-conditioned studio, as well as four news recording offices and an independent electricity station used for emergencies (MING, 1977; Adam, 2001).

It should be noted that these radio developments were not confined to equipment and offices, but also included program quality. Following the recruitment of Mohamed Abshir Yusuf in 1965 from BBC Somali Service to be head of programs at Radio Mogadishu, several essential programs were introduced, including *Public Opinion*, in which people aired their views on government services, and *Somali History*, which aimed to educate the public on the nation's history (Adam, 2001). However, these programs were abandoned over budget constraints within a few months of its launch.

Other noteworthy improvements included the quality of the radio's staff (both broadcasters and technicians). In 1966, a group of UNESCO-trained broadcasters joined the station, which boosted programming quality. To increase coverage and listeners, station management established listening centers around Mogadishu so that residents could listen while in public places.

The third stage began in 1969 when a military coup led by Major General Mohamed Siad Barre seized the nation. In July 1976, two new transmitters with 75 kilowatts each were added to the station, increasing its reach on regular medium and short waves. In addition, the Hargeisa transmitter was increased from 10 kilowatts to 25 kilowatts, facilitating short-wave broadcasts (MING, 1977).

During the military regime, the radio station was under government control and served its agenda. Media freedom, including radio, was restricted, and no dissenting opinions were allowed over the radio. Dissent opinion was possible only from outside the country (Abdi et al., 2011). Radio Mogadishu's role was viewed as controversial, as some perceived it as a government propaganda mouthpiece, while others felt it was part of developing the nation and shaping its national identity (LandInfo, 2016; Stremlau et al., 2016). Radio Mogadishu, with two transmitters in Mogadishu and Hargeisa, had been the only radio station widely available in the country from the colonial era until 1999. However, political opponents were able to reach international listeners, beyond government censors' control (e.g., BBC Somali service, which provided equal access to both government officials and their opponents), or establish their own radio. For instance, Radio Halgan was established by SNM during its rebellion, as it tried to take over the northwestern region (Stremlau et al., 2016).

The nation's radio history entered its final stage with the downfall of Barre's military regime, after which radio contributed to the civil war, as it "became part of the terrain of war as warlords sought to establish and control radio to reflect their interests" (Abdi et al., 2011: 4). Both Radio Mogadishu transmitters were subjected to various political regimes with different approaches and ideologies. For example, SNM, which participated in the overthrow of Barre's regime, took over the Hargeisa station and renamed it "Radio Hargeisa: The voice of Somaliland," and some referred to it as "Radio SNM" (Kapteijns, 2013). In Mogadishu, USC, which also participated in the overthrow of the Barre regime, seized the Mogadishu station and used it to promote its political agenda. Radio propaganda was aired against other factions, including songs and poems to generate violence and hatred (Kapteijns, 2013). However, during this era, the station lacked the human resources to succeed, as the previous staff fled the country.

Warlords maintained control over the radio in the country for several years, but business-motivated radio stations challenged them. After eight years of armed conflict and civil war, private radio stations boomed. The first FM-based radio station was Radio HornAfrik, established by three diaspora returnees. The station ceased broadcasting in April 2011 after the Al-Shabaab group seized its equipment. Numerous private stations also were established and left their mark on the nation's social and political fabric (Abdi et al., 2011; INFOASAID, 2012). As of 2019, more than 60 radio stations were reported to exist in Somalia (USAID, 2019). Popular radio stations include Radio Mogadishu, a federal state-run station; Radio Shabelle; Radio Dalsan; Radio Goobjoog; and Radio Kulmiye, all with comparatively large audiences. In addition, international radio stations broadcast to Somali-inhabited territories in East Africa, including BBC Somali Service and Voice of America's (VOA) Somali service. Specifically, the BBC has a long history with Somali audiences, as the BBC Somali Service was established three years before independence (Gaas et al., 2012). However, VOA is viewed as providing a more comprehensive analysis and better approaches to programs than the BBC (LandInfo, 2016).

In addition, some radio stations either were established or funded by international organizations to support their operations in Somalia, including Bar-Kulan (established by the UN Support Office in Somalia [UNSOS]) and Radio Ergo (principally funded by Scandinavian countries, i.e., Norway, Sweden, and Denmark) (Abdi et al., 2011; LandInfo, 2016; Stremlau et al., 2016; USAID, 2019). Moreover, five radio stations were established and operated by Somalis in the diaspora, based outside the country: Radio Halgan (based in Ethiopia), Radio Ogaal (based in Canada), Star FM (based in Kenya), Radio Horyaal (based in Belgium), and Radio Hormuud (based in Denmark) (Whitehead et al., 2011).

Therefore, Somali radio is viewed as an important medium for obtaining news, entertainment, and information, as well as engaging the public in campaigns or other programs promoted by local or international organizations. Most people in urban areas and rural communities (84%) obtain their news and information from the radio every week (BBG, 2013). Although most radio stations are for-profit enterprises, are linked with political factions, or have clan affiliations, private stations are considered trustworthy and effective (Abdi et al., 2011).

Television

The history of television in Somalia is new compared with other electronic media, particularly radio. In 1983, Barre's military regime established the nation's first TV stations (Ismail, 2006). Satellite and domestic TV has begun to flourish recently, becoming an essential medium in all six geopolitical regions, utilized for news, entertainment, and promotional services. No official and accurate statistics on the number of purchased TV sets, existing stations, or viewership patterns currently are available, but recent studies (USAID, 2019) reported that 21 stations are available across all six regions, compared with nine stations in 2011, as reported by a BBC World Service Trust (WST) study (Abdi et al., 2011). Three types of TV access are available to Somali audiences: satellite, terrestrial, and Internet-based.

Private stations, as well as state-owned stations, currently exist. Each of the six geopolitical regions' governments owns and operates at least one TV station; a federal station also exists: Somaliland National TV, Puntland TV, Galmudug TV, South West TV, Jubbaland TV, and Hirshabelle TV at the state level and Somali National Television at the federal level. As of 2011, nine stations operated across all regions, two of which are state-owned (Whitehead et al., 2011).

Numerous privately owned TV stations operate in these regions for local audiences. The Somali Broadcasting Corporation (SBC) and Eastern Television Network (both terrestrial-based) operate in Puntland, along with state-owned Puntland TV. Three private stations operate in Somaliland – Horn Cable, Space Channel, and Bulsho – of which the latter two are terrestrial. In south-central regions, private TV dates back to 1999, when two privately owned TV stations were established in the capital city of Mogadishu: HornAfrik TV and Somali Tele-Media Network. Other popular TV stations include Universal, Somali Channel, and Goobjoog. Most TV stations have radio and website affiliates, offering varying coverage, and broadcast through satellites, allowing them to reach wider audiences (Abdi et al., 2011; Whitehead et al., 2011; INFOASAID, 2012; USAID, 2019).

Most private stations are based outside the country, mostly in London, England. The most common content that these stations broadcast comprises news; political and social debate and discussion programs on matters related to society, politics and the economy; music; entertainment; and commercials. Moreover, other international TV channels are popular among Somali audiences, including BBC, CNN, and Qatar-based Al Jazeera.

Somalis in the diaspora have played a greater role in the nation's TV industry. Their contributions include financial investments, as well as technical knowledge and professional practice. Those who live in the diaspora actively engage in the country's political and other related discourses, with most actively using media, including TV (Osman, 2017). Recent reports suggest that three in 10 Somali households own a TV, with one-third of them saying they had watched TV in the past week (BBG, 2013). Similar results were reported in the BBC WST study concerning Mogadishu residents, who said they watched TV at least once in the previous week (Abdi et al., 2011).

TV viewership in the country remains limited; Somalis in the diaspora and those in major cities can use the TV. TV-related expenses include electricity, fees for TV package subscriptions, and equipment purchases, presenting economic challenges that tend to limit wider TV access in Somalia (Ismail, 2006; Abdi et al., 2011). The TV industry itself deals with a lack of well-trained professionals and its financial constraints, among other challenges (Ahmed, 2020).

Media education

Somali National University's Department of Political Science and Journalism provided the country's media education until 1990, offering a two-year journalism degree. However, the university's infrastructure was destroyed during the civil war. No university-offered journalism and communication degrees were available during the early years of the civil war. In 2000, Mogadishu University launched a four-year journalism degree program (Mogadishu University, 2017). Requiring 164 credit hours to graduate, the program's language of instruction was Arabic; thus, prospective students were those who graduated from Arabic schools.

Indian Ocean University, established during the early years of the civil war in Mogadishu, offers two majors in mass communication (journalism and public relations) (Indian Ocean University, 2017). In Somaliland, the University of Hargeisa once offered a journalism certificate that was launched in cooperation with Africa Virtual University, but this program was converted to a bachelor's degree in mass communication in 2006, with two specializations for print media and electronic media (Ismail, 2006; Skjerdal and Ngugi, 2007; University of Hargeisa, 2017). Moreover, the University of Hormuud (located in Mogadishu) also offers a mass communication program. Started in 2015, the program comprises two specializations (public relations and mass communication) (Hormuud University, 2017). However, the current media education curriculum lacks consistency in finding qualified educators who can teach the syllabus, with very few of current media professionals holding university degrees (Whitehead et al., 2011). Most who teach at these universities hold either master's degrees in communication or a degree in another field of social sciences.

A recent report by the Heritage Institute for Policy Studies (2013) found that enrollment in communication studies is much lower than other specializations, with only 0.3% specializing in communication studies. The institute's report surveyed 44 universities across all six geopolitical regions, comprising more than 50,000 students as of 2013. In other words, media education's contribution (universities and colleges) towards the media industry is significantly negligible. As a result, no relationship exists between the unparalleled explosion in media houses and enrollment in communication studies nationwide.

A recently enacted media law poses a critical challenge to the nation's media industry. Specifically, the main challenges related to media education for professionals. The law, put into force in January 2016, requires media professionals to have university degrees in communication. The consequence of this requirement is that many professionals would lose their jobs and be enforced to return to school (Koronto, 2016), but the law was not strictly enforced. In addition, various local customs and mechanisms previously used to settle disputes in this area (Stremlau, 2012, 2018) pose an additional layer of challenge to the new law, which applies to diaspora-run media as well. Somalis in the diaspora operate more than 1,000 new platforms, with most working in offices or as reporters inside the country.

The low enrollment in media education nationwide possibly can be attributed to four factors. First, no university or college education, or even any form of formal education, is required to enter the media industry. Most segments of the industry employ unskilled, inexperienced youths (Osman, 2017); thus, degree holders are reluctant to join the industry.

Second, the public mostly views journalism as a hobby rather than a field of study. A distorted image of media professionals also exists, in which the public views them as corrupt people with a thirst for cheap propaganda.

Third, the low enrollment in communication studies also may be related to practitioners' attitudes, in that most think that pursuing journalism does not require spending years in college or at university. For instance, a Mogadishu University representative interviewed by BBC WST explained that "practicing journalists don't show any interest in pursuing the courses [communication studies] although the university heavily subsidizes the cost" (Whitehead et al., 2011: 63).

Finally, a large number of electronic media platforms (radio and TV) encourages the emergence of a new variety of so-called journalists who have no proper necessary expertise and professional ethics. What makes the media environment even worse than before is that many qualified professionals have fled the country due to the ensuing conflict or death threats or attacks on their media workplaces.

Even though communication studies enrollment is limited, this chapter is not alleging that no high-quality journalism practices or professional ethics can be found in Somalia. Many of its media professionals have attended training courses funded by international media organizations, while others learned the profession through experience or were trained by qualified Somali media professionals who recently returned to the country (IREX, 2010). For instance, Free Press Unlimited (FPU) has provided short-term training courses to media professionals in the country since 2011. Focusing on radio reporters, FPU's training is an experience-based education in which participants immediately apply the knowledge acquired from the training, as well as share that knowledge with their colleagues (Free Press Unlimited, 2014). To ensure that the gained knowledge is in practice, a trainer from FPU visits participants at their radio stations for additional coaching on the job.

BBC WST is one of the leading international organizations that vehemently support media capacity-building initiatives. From 2001 to 2006, it has conducted all-inclusive journalism training sessions for 250 media professionals in four large cities (Mogadishu, Hargeisa, Garowe, and Bosaso) (Whitehead et al., 2011).

Other actively engaged international media organizations include the Finnish Foundation for Media and Development (Vikes), which mainly is funded by the Ministry of Foreign Affairs of Finland. Since 2014, the foundation has executed numerous projects to support the Somali media, particularly in helping the country realize the "transformation of Somalia's state media towards public service broadcasting" (Stenius, 2018: 3). Vikes has implemented 26 training sessions nationwide, comprising over 600 participants, between 2014 and 2017. It has partnered with national and regional journalist associations and the SNTV, and has engaged with Somali Finnish diaspora in projects to overcome cultural barriers. Vikes's approach entailed peer learning and expert-to-expert exchanges throughout the training courses (Stenius, 2018).

While the aforementioned interventions by international media organizations through short-term courses are important, helping to instill basic skills and awareness, they have not satisfied the media industry's long-term needs. In light of the recently adopted media law's requirements, local institutions (particularly universities) have a great responsibility to change their attitude that no one is interested in communication degrees. They should make visible contributions to the media industry by providing the labor market with qualified graduates.

Role of mass media in society

The military regime (1969–1991) dominated media markets, which were used to promote the government's ideology and controversial policies. Political factions also utilized the media, particularly radio, in their struggle to overthrow the regime. Backed by some neighboring countries, these factions launched over a decade's worth of propaganda and psychological warfare against the regime before they eventually overthrew it.

Following the state's collapse, Somali media arguably could be viewed as having played a part in the civil war, used by fighting factions as a tool to disseminate propaganda and biased news. In particular, Radio Mogadishu, the state-owned radio station that the USC captured, was used to broadcast songs and programs that incited hate and delivered death threats to opposing factions. The Hargeisa station, captured by SNM, was used to disseminate secessionist ideology that SNM promoted, and the station is still operating in northwestern regions (Somaliland) (Kapteijns, 2013).

Some scholars (Ahmed, 2016; Stremlau et al., 2016; Stremlau, 2018) argue that Somali media, especially radio, has a long history in the conflict, as this platform "became intertwined with the conflict and has continuously served as a key weapon in regional struggles . . . to advance competing ideological perspectives on the nature and constitution of the Somali state" (Stremlau et al., 2016: 47). Ahmed (2016) suggested that the adoption of development journalism in Somalia might serve "as a catalyst for a positive change in Somalia" (p. 448), emphasizing positive reports and ideas, rather than negative ones.

Newspapers also have impacted society negatively, contributing to conflict by siding with certain clans or warlords against others. They published news, opinion articles, and caricatures that fueled enduring hostilities and fighting among political factions (Gaas et al., 2012; Osman, 2017). Furthermore, print media "[were] largely controlled by or attached to a warlord and contained clannish attitudes and hostilities, further fuelling conflict" (Gaas et al., 2012: 14). As a result, the public had no trust in the media industry, and media credibility has dropped significantly. However, recent studies show growing trust in media, particularly state-owned platforms, across geopolitical regions, with Mogadishu having the highest rate of trust (Robertson et al., 2017). In a recent survey, Ahmed (2018) found a moderate level of trust in the media among youths in Somalia's Benadir region. He also found that education level negatively predicted judgment of news media credibility, indicating that highly educated young people are skeptical about the media. Following warlords' fading political power and most private media's detachment (particularly radio) from pursuing clan interests in the late 1990s, the media industry came to be described as a source of moderation (Whitehead et al., 2011; Deane, 2013).

Even though the media industry's negative impacts are greatly noticeable, the industry also exerted a positive impact and played a great role in society. Radio Mogadishu made some significant contributions to society through its major involvement in nation-building through various projects, such as literacy campaigns and self-sufficiency initiatives that the military regime promoted (Stremlau et al., 2016). Moreover, the media kept the public informed about reconciliation efforts and peace-restoring conferences held inside and outside the country. Call-in programs and political debates have become very popular during hot political climates, such as election seasons (federal or state level) and during peace-building conferences.

As Somalis are described as an oral society, electronic media have played an essential role in informing the public about news and current affairs, as well as providing entertainment and commercials. Furthermore, the emergence of the Internet and online news platforms has exposed the public to diverse views, opinions, and narratives on the same story.

Conclusion

Before the collapse of the Somali state in 1991, the Ministry of Information and National Guidance monitored state-owned media outlets, such as newspapers, radio and TV stations, and news agencies. Press freedom and freedom of expression were reserved only for those who marched in lockstep with the government's narratives and discourses. However, the media were granted unlimited freedom and worked in an unregulated environment from 1991 until recently. In addition, sensational journalism was the norm during the 1990s, particularly at the height of the civil war, when most newspapers and radio stations either were linked to or owned by political factions that used them to fuel violence and conflict. Even though most media outlets were established as profit-making ventures, many were established for political gain or associated with certain political leaders and factions.

By the late 1990s, relative stability took hold, particularly in the south-central regions following the warlords' declining control and increasing societal awareness about the conflicts that these warlords promote for their political gain. As a result, private media outlets emerged and coincided with the national reconciliation conference in Djibouti in 2000. These outlets were established and funded by the Somali diaspora. Diaspora returnees impacted key sectors – such as telecommunications, banking systems, and remittances – but significantly affected the media sector as early investors in private radio stations and online portals.

Radio has played a huge role in this society as a medium in line with society's strong oral culture. Most radio stations nationwide are privately owned (69%), followed by those owned and operated by Somalis in the diaspora (23%), while states (regional and federal) own about 8%. Newspaper readership is quite limited, with very few newspapers published in the south-central regions. However, this medium is very popular and well-established in Somaliland. The underlying factors behind newspapers' success in Somaliland lie beyond this chapter's scope. Second to the radio, TV stations in Somalia are gaining in popularity and wider geographical coverage in most major cities. Most of these channels are headquartered either outside the country or operated and funded by the Somali diaspora.

Even though hundreds of media platforms (print, electronic, and online) currently exist in the country, enrollment in communication studies remains limited nationwide. Most practicing journalists do not have university degrees in the field. A new media law enacted recently requires media practitioners to have at least a university degree to practice the profession, but the law has not been strictly enforced.

Following the 2006 Ethiopian military intervention (based on an invitation by the former TFG and Alshabaab's fight with the TFG and its Ethiopian allies), all these groups targeted the media industry. As a result, many experienced media professionals fled the country amid intimidation tactics, including death threats. Therefore, many junior journalists emerged to fill the gap. Anyone with an outspoken voice can pursue a journalism career in the country.

While local and international organizations have delivered numerous short-term training courses, the need for well-structured media education curricula is needed the most. International organizations should support local-based curricula that accommodate and satisfy the industry's long-term needs. In addition, the federal government also needs to take greater responsibility towards media education development, protection of media freedom, and fair treatment of private media practitioners compared with their peers working in state-owned outlets. On the practitioners' side, they should be equipped with the necessary skills, expertise, and knowledge that the profession demands. They also should comply with regulations in place to promote a competitive and well-balanced media environment.

References

Abdi, J. et al. (2011), *The Media of Somalia: A Force for Moderation?* London: BBC World Service Trust.

Adam, S. M. (2001), *Gather Round the Speakers: A History of the First Quarter-century of Somali Broadcasting: 1941–1966.* London: Haan Associates.

Ahmed, I. S. Y. (2016), Development Journalism and its Political Contribution to the State-building: The Case of Somalia. *Malaysian Journal of Communication*, 32(1), pp. 437–454.

Ahmed, I. S. Y. (2018), *Determining Public Perceptions on News Media Credibility.* In 7th ICSSR International Conference. Melaka, Malaysia.

Ahmed, I. S. Y. (2020), Somalia. In D. L. Merskin (ed.), *The SAGE International Encyclopedia of Mass Media and Society.* Thousand Oaks, CA: Sage. doi:10.4135/9781483375519.

BBG (2013), *Global Hotspots: Media Use in Mali and Somalia.* Retrieved from www.bbg.gov/2013/09/18/global-hotspots-media-use-in-mali-and-somalia/. Accessed 24 March 2019.

Citizen TV (2015), *Somalia Now a Recovering State – UN.* Retrieved from https://citizentv.co.ke/news/somalia-now-a-recovering-state-un-105861/. Accessed 13 April 2017.

Deane, J. (2013), Fragile States: The Role of Media and Communication. *BBC Media Action.* Retrieved from https://internews.org/sites/default/files/resources/BBC_MediaAction_fragile_states_policy_briefing_2013-11.pdf. Accessed 20 January 2017.

Free Press Unlimited (2014), *Training Journalists in Somalia.* Retrieved from https://reports.freepressunlimited.org/2014/cases/training-journalists-in-somalia. Accessed 20 January 2017.

Gaas, M. H., Hansen, S. J., and Berry, D. (2012), *Mapping the Somali Media : An Overview.* Noragric Report No. 65, Department of Environmental and Development Studies, Norwegian University of Life Sciences. Retrieved from www.umb.no/statisk/noragric/publications/reports/noragric_report_no._65cover.pdf. Accessed 20 January 2017.

Geedi, N. (2015), *Alshafh almktwbh balswmal thtdr amam zhf altqnyh* (Arabic). The Print Media in Somalia is Dying in front of the Advance of Technology. Retrieved from www.alquds.co.uk/?p=416696. Accessed 15 February 2017.

Gilkes, P. (1999), Briefing: Somalia. *African Affairs*, 98(393), pp. 571–577.

Haji Ingiriis, M. (2017), From Clan Cleansing to Galaal Cleansing: Lidwien Kapteijns' False and Fabrications. *Méthod(e)s: African Review of Social Sciences Methodology*, 2(1–2), pp. 178–194.

Haydarov, R. et al. (2016), Evidence-Based Engagement of the Somali Pastoralists of the Horn of Africa in Polio Immunization: Overview of Tracking, Cross-Border, Operations, and Communication Strategies. *Global Health Communication*, 2(1), pp. 11–18.

Heritage Institute for Policy Studies (2013), *The State of Higher Education in Somalia: Privatization, Rapid Growth, and the Need for Regulation*. Retrieved from www.heritageinstitute.org/wp- content/ uploads/2013/08/HIPS_Higher_Education_ENGLISH.pdf. Accessed 16 May 2016.

Hormuud University (2017), *Faculty of Arts and Social Sciences*. Retrieved from http://hu.edu.so/deans-message-3/. Accessed 20 May 2017.

Human Rights Watch (1995), *Somalia Faces the Future: Human Rights in a Fragmented Society*. Retrieved from www.hrw.org/reports/1995/somalia/. Accessed 12 April 2018.

Indian Ocean University (2017), *Journalism*. Retrieved from www.iou.edu.so/journalism.html. Accessed 28 April 2017.

INFOASAID (2012), *Somalia Media and Telecoms Landscape Guide*. Retrieved from www.internews.org/resource/somalia-media-and-telecoms-landscape-guide. Accessed 23 March 2019.

IREX (2010), *Media Sustainability Index: Somalia*. Retrieved from www.irex.org/media-sustainability-index-archived-reports. Accessed 23 March 2019.

Ismail, J. A. (2006), *Somalia: Research Findings and Conclusion*. London: BBC World Service Trust Report.

Issa-Salwe, A. (2008), The Internet and the Somali Diaspora: The Web as a Means of Expression. *Bildhaan: An International Journal of Somali Studies*, 6, pp. 54–67.

Jama, Z. M. (1994), Silent Voices : The Role of Somali Women' s Poetry in Social and Political Life. *Oral Tradition*, 9(1), pp. 185–202.

Kapteijns, L. (2013), *Clan Cleansing in Somalia. The Ruinous Legacy of 1991*. Philadelphia: University of Pennsylvania Press.

Koronto, A. (2016), *Back to School for Somalia's Journalists?* Retrieved from www.bbc.com/news/world-africa-35303220. Accessed 2 May 2017.

LandInfo (2016), *Somalia: Media and Journalism*. Retrieved from www.landinfo.no/asset/3568/1/35681.pdf. Accessed 2 May 2017.

MING (1977), *Wsail al-i'lam fi khidmat al-jumhour* (Mass Media for the Public Service). Mogadishu, Somalia: Government Printing House.

Mogadishu University (2017), *Mogadishu University*. Retrieved from http://mutst.com/ar/program/bach elor-degree-in-journalism-information/. Accessed 15 May 2017.

Osman, I. (2017), *Media, Diaspora and the Somali Conflict*. Cham, Switzerland: Palgrave Macmillan.

Robertson, L., Malla, L., and Oing, L. (2017), *Somali Perception Survey, Part 1: The Emerging Federal States, Mogadishu and Puntland*. Retrieved from http://somaliangoconsortium.org/download/58c7e22834e32/. Accessed 15 May 2017.

Skjerdal, T. S., and Ngugi, C. M. (2007), Institutional and Governmental Challenges for Journalism Education in East Africa. *Ecquid Novi: African Journalism Studies*, 28(1–2), pp. 176–190.

Stenius, N. (2018), *Evaluation of Media Support in Somalia*. Retrieved from https://vikes.fi/wp-content/uploads/2018/08/Evaluation-of-media-support-in-Somalia-2014-2017.pdf. Accessed 13 January 2019.

Stremlau, N. (2012), Somalia: Media law in the Absence of a State. *International Journal of Media & Cultural Politics*, 8(2/3), pp. 159–174.

Stremlau, N. (2018), Law and Innovation in the Somali Territories. In B. Mutsvairo (ed.), *The Palgrave Handbook of Media and Communication Research in Africa*. Cham, Switzerland: Palgrave Macmillan, pp. 297–309.

Stremlau, N., Fantini, E., and Osman, R. M. (2016), The Political Economy of the Media in the Somali Conflict. *Review of African Political Economy*, 43(147), pp. 43–57.

University of Hargeisa (2017), *Background*. Retrieved from http://uoh-edu.net/college-of-social-science-and-humanities/. Accessed 28 April 2017.

USAID (2019), *Somali Media Mapping and Landscape Survey*. Retrieved from https://issuu.com/ste veturner1010/docs/mog022_final_report__email_file. Accessed 11 October 2019.

Whitehead, S. et al. (2011), *An Analysis of the Somali Media Environment*. Retrieved from http://down loads.bbc.co.uk/rmhttp/mediaaction/pdf/AnAnalysisOfTheSomaliMediaEnvironment.pdf. Accessed 11 October 2019.

29

INTERNET AND SOCIAL MEDIA DEVELOPMENT IN SOMALIA

Ismail Sheikh Yusuf Ahmed

Introduction

With a relatively young population and the second-longest coastline in Africa, Somalia is currently recovering from a prolonged civil war (Citizen TV, 2015), having experienced its first peaceful transition of political power in 2004. Since the collapse of the central government and overthrow of the military regime in 1991, the country has experienced a chaotic situation of armed violence and conflict, political instability, and periodic natural disasters such as floods and droughts, as well as migration in large numbers, including human capital. All have had the effect of situating the country among the less-developed nations and the lowest ranking on international organizations' various political, economic, development, and social indicators (Sheikh and Healy, 2009; UNDP, 2014). Many challenges still exist, though the country's recent efforts are promising (Hammond, 2013). It has witnessed four consecutive power transitions since 2004. In recent years, regional states have been created to apply the federalism structure adopted in the 2004 conference held in Kenya. Other positive signs can also be observed, such as the recent attention of the international community and the peoples' earnestness in finding durable solutions to prolonged conflicts.

Another positive aspect is diaspora members' engagement in Somali politics, the establishment of new businesses, and bringing of expertise and investment to various sectors, including the media and telecommunication industries. Many leaders at the federal level, including the president and prime minister, are returnees from the diaspora. The apparent political progress also has advanced in line with the development of telecommunications and the Internet in the country, with the involved companies playing an essential role in the political, economic, and social domains of Somali life. Some common topics heard throughout the media, both local and international, include extremist groups, suicide bombs, famine, and corruption. More rarely reported are positive topics. For example, compared to many politically stable countries on the African continent, Somalia enjoys the more affordable and competitively priced telecommunication services, including mobile money transfer applications, which are efficient and fast (INFOASAID, 2012; Osman, 2013; Stremlau, 2018).

Following the country's independence from Great Britain and Italy in the early 1960s, the Somali media ecology experienced dramatic development and enjoyed much freedom. It contributed to developmental projects as well as to the political diversity that the country enjoyed at the time. However, freedom of the press was abolished by the military regime (1969–1991). Print and electronic media operated under the supervision of the regime, where the pro-government voices are the most frequently promoted. The post-1991 media ecology, on the other hand, has been granted unconstrained freedom and works in an unregulated atmosphere. Though no longer controlled by the government, the media outlets, particularly newspapers and radios, were long exploited by warring factions for propaganda and mobilization, fueling civil conflict (Kapteijns, 2013; Osman, 2017).

Numerous telecommunication companies provide telephone, mobile phones, and Internet access services. Recently, the country's telecom and media sectors have been thriving, attracting huge investments and skills from the Somali diaspora (Osman, 2017). As a result, the country's Internet connectivity has significantly improved in terms of quality and accessibility in various regions and towns. The Internet is no longer merely a tool for entertainment and communication with business associates, relatives, and friends abroad. It has become an integral part of daily life for many Somalis (Ahmed, 2018). For instance, various service sectors, such as remittances, media, telecoms, and banks, depend mainly on the Internet for their daily activities. Internet usage among students and youth have also dramatically increased for both utilitarian and hedonic purposes (Gaas et al., 2012; Dhaha and Igale, 2013, 2014; Ahmed, 2018), and many universities in the country now offer Internet access through computers.

Recently, social media platforms such as WhatsApp, Facebook, Twitter, YouTube, and blogs have received massive attention from both home and diaspora Somalis. They have been employed for free speech and information circulation, in addition to various other motives. Unlike other media platforms, such as print and electronic media, accounts on these platforms can rarely be blocked, monitored, or shut down by the regional and federal governments. Despite their many negative aspects, social media platforms enable the expression of a plurality of opinions and allow the public to engage in open discussions and debates on various issues. Accordingly, the notion of the electronic public sphere is prevalent among Somalis, particularly diaspora communities (Gaas et al., 2012).

Pursued through secondary sources and structured interviews with four media professionals and scholars, the prime objective of this chapter, which is organized into four sections, is to trace Internet and social media developments in a post-conflict country (Somalia). The first section presents contextualizing background information on the telecommunication sector in the country, in recognition of the emergence of the Internet and social media from the telecom revolution. The second part presents an in-depth discussion of the core players, service providers, and fundamental statistics related to the Internet and social media platforms. The third part presents the existing laws and regulations that govern the telecommunication industry, the Internet, and social media, while the final part discusses the social and political functions of social media in the country. This work will generate a fresh insight into the Internet and social media phenomena and their political and social impacts on both society and various sectors.

The telecommunication sector

At the time Somalia gained independence (July 1960), the country hosted one state-owned telecommunication company, the National Telecommunication Company (NTC), which collapsed following the overthrow of the military regime by armed factions in 1991. Numerous privately owned telecoms then filled this gap, but access to telecommunications services was difficult for most Somalis before and during the civil war that broke out in the early 1990s. The majority of, if not all, telephone lines and infrastructure was destroyed during the ensuing chaos, and people most often depended on military radios to communicate between the cities and towns (Mohamed and Childress, 2018). When the first private telecom company was established in 1993, access to telephones was confined to major cities, where a small few fixed lines, each providing to just 1,000 people, were available before the collapse of the central government and the outbreak of civil war (Yuusuf, 2015).

Due to entrepreneurial initiatives and investments by Somali businesspersons, the telecommunication sector in the country has flourished despite a challenging environment that obliterated formal government structures. Numerous private telecommunication companies emerged two years after the outbreak of the civil war. A report by the Center for Global Communication Studies (2014) at the University of Pennsylvania cites the former minister of information, posts, and telecommunications of Somalia as saying that, as of 2012, there were six fixed telephone operators and eight mobile phone operators, with about 1.5 million subscribers. Other reports suggest that these telecoms compete for 1.8 million customers. Major companies include Telecom, Hormuud Telecom, NationLink, Telesom, and Golis. The majority of these telecoms provide multiple services, such as fixed lines, GSM mobile, and Internet services, and compete for a growing market (Telcoma, 2019).

Mobile phone ownership has been rapidly increasing. This technology is suitable for the nomadic and pastoral lifestyle of the majority of the Somali population, due to higher illiteracy rates among rural groups compared to those living in cities and large towns. The mobile phone subscription rate has been estimated to be close to 40% of the population (INFOASAID, 2012). Using a nationwide representative sample of 2,000 participants, the Broadcasting Board of Governors (BBG, 2013) concluded that close to three-quarters of the respondents own personal mobile phones. BBG's study also found some differences in mobile phone penetration in terms of geopolitical regions. The south-central regions were found to have higher penetration, 78.5%, compared to 73.1% and 56.2% in Puntland and Somaliland, respectively. Several uses were reported for mobile phones, including making phone calls, sending and receiving emails and short message service (SMS) texts, listening to the radio, and accessing the Internet and social media. SMS usage is somewhat limited, either because of the high illiteracy rate or because of the general Somali preference for talking due to the influence of their oral culture. In most cases, the use of SMS is confined to sending and receiving money from family, friends, and business associates.

Along with fixed lines, mobile phones, and Internet services, many of these telecommunications operators provide mobile money transfer (MMT) services. For example, Hormuud provides MMT to its customers through EVC Plus technology. Telesom and Golis offer similar technologies, such as Zaad and Sahal in the Somaliland and Puntland regions, respectively. According to a recent report by the World Bank (Randa and Musuku, 2018), MMT services have become vital in both peoples' lives and the economic system. Their penetration is relatively high, used by some 73% of Somalis over 16 years of age. The penetration is much higher in cities (83%). More than 50% of rural residents and 70% of those who live in internally displaced camps (IDCs) also use MMT services. According to this report, more than 150 million transactions are conducted through MMT technologies, accounting for an estimated $2.7 million a month. MMT services have contributed not only to economic growth but also to financial inclusion, as they enable more women and more people in IDCs to perform financial transactions and receive and send money, including receiving remittances from families and relatives in the diaspora (Randa and Musuku, 2018). However, the country lags behind the majority of African nations with regard to "international capacity, national connectivity, and internet take-ups" (World Bank, 2017).

The key players and investors in the telecommunication sector are Somali businesspersons and entrepreneurs, as well as the wealthy Somali diaspora, whose contributions are enhanced by technical expertise from some Chinese and Korean companies. Since the majority of telecom infrastructure, such as the Public Switch Transmission Network, was destroyed during the civil conflict and widespread anarchy, the telecom operators, using their resources, have managed to rebuild the necessary infrastructure (Hare, 2007). They also installed the cell towers that greatly boosted the current mobile network in the country. Unlike many countries in the continent, where multinational telecommunication corporations such as MTN, Vodafone, and Orasccom had hugely invested in and operated these telecoms, the Somalia telecom sector was funded and operated only by Somali businesspersons. This is due to the political instability and lack of regulatory bodies and frameworks in the country, which hinder foreign investments.

Several factors are behind the success of the telecommunication sector in Somalia. The most prominent factor has been the lack of regulatory bodies and frameworks, which were only recently re-established (Osman, 2013; BuddeCOMM, 2019; Somaliland Biz, 2019). The absence of taxes and licenses is among the key boosting factors for the exponential growth of these telecoms. The third factor is the entrepreneurial spirit that characterizes Somali traders. Many Somalis established giant businesses in various African countries after the breakout of civil war, and the majority of these were small entrepreneurs. A fourth factor may be the involvement of members of the Somali diaspora who facilitated access to and engagement with international partners and corporations.

Contrary to these success factors, the sector still faces some challenges. First, the fierce competition among the telecom operators had a somewhat negative impact, particularly a lack of cooperation in terms of interconnectivity, leading to higher prices for consumers and the possibility of a market monopoly. Second, the lack of functioning regulatory bodies creates another layer of challenges. Although the president signed the national communications law in 2017 that aims to provide regulatory frameworks, there have thus far been no tangible actions and efforts, as the regulations are still under draft by the National Communications Authority (NCA, 2019) and have yet to be implemented. The most compelling regulations include the protection of consumer interests and interconnectivity and frequency spectrum matching. Finally, the security issue remains a critical challenge, and telecommunication operators have, on many occasions, been forced to shut down operations or stop some of their products by the Al Shabaab Islamic Group, an Al-Qaeda-linked group in Somalia, usually complying with these demands to preserve their businesses (Garowe Online, 2016).

Main providers and key players

The emergence of the Internet in Somalia dates back to the beginning of the 21st century. Although no reliable and conclusive statistics on Internet penetration in the country exist, contradictory statistics are currently available from international organizations. A report by the Internet World Statistics estimated the number of Somalia's Internet users at around 200 in the year 2000. In more recent years, Internet penetration has experienced exponential growth and is currently at about 8% of the population (1.2 million users). In contrast, reports by the International Telecommunication Union (ITU, 2018) and Internet Live Stats (2016) have estimated Internet users in the country as comprising less than 2% of the population. A more recent statistic (We Are Social and Hootsuite, 2019) shows that the number of users had reached 1.5 million, approximately 10% of the population, as of January 2019.

However, the number of Internet users in Somalia may be greater than those listed previously, as these figures may not be conclusive and representative for a number of reasons. First, World Bank statistics show that more than 40% of the population (six million out of 14 million) use mobile phones, and the majority of them use the Internet through these devices

(World Bank, 2017). Second, more than one million Somalis were estimated to live outside Somalia, with large numbers residing in neighboring countries, mostly in Kenya as refugees, as well as in Western Europe (primarily the UK, Sweden, Norway, the Netherlands, and Italy) and North America (the US and Canada) (Sheikh and Healy, 2009). These large communities of the diaspora, who are well connected to the country politically and economically, are not captured in the aforementioned reports by international organizations. Finally, statistics from some World Bank institutions, such as the International Finance Corporation (IFC), show figures completely different from those of the ITU. A recent report by the IFC concluded that the disruption of Internet service in the country in June 2017 resulted in 6.5 million Somalis losing contact with the rest of the world, a problem believed to have sent them back to the pre-Internet era (IFC, 2018). Based on these reasons, the author argues that the actual Internet penetration is higher than the figures reported by international organizations. He also, however, stresses the need for clear mechanisms to accurately measure and estimate the actual Internet penetration in the country. The main responsibility for this task lies in the hands of the federal government, represented by the Ministry of Posts, Telecommunications, and Technology.

Until recently, the Internet in Somalia has relied on satellite delivery. The country's first access to the Internet via fiber optic cables was delivered by Liquid Telecom (an African fiber optics company based in Mauritius) through a collaborative deal with Hormuud Telecom (one of the largest telecom operators in Somalia) (Reuters, 2013). Thus, Liquid Telecom now provides Internet access to Somalia via both satellite and fiber optic cables. The delay of fiber optic access may be linked to the political anarchy and piracy activities suffered by the country. In June 2017, Somalia experienced a major Internet outage after commercial vessels severed fiber optic cables in the Indian Ocean. This caused a major paralysis in many aspects of life, especially in the southern and central regions, including the capital city of Mogadishu. The disruption of Internet services – which lasted about two weeks – caused the nation to lose about 130 million US dollars (an average of $10 million daily) (BBC, 2018; Guardian, 2018).

While access in Somalia has gone through numerous stages, it can be said that the Somali diaspora communities have pioneered the usage of the Internet. Since 1991, the country has been experiencing a chaotic situation, and hundreds of thousands have fled the country, leaving behind their families and relatives; consequently, a suitable communication channel was sorely needed. With the Internet revolution and the emergence of concepts such as computer-mediated communication, the Somali diaspora have contributed to the establishment of Internet cafés since early 2000. These cafés cater to the ever-increasing need to maintain contact with family and friends overseas. They provided access to the Internet with generally reasonable prices, and the majority of their customers were youth.

The rapid proliferation of websites was observed in the country. Hundreds of websites, the majority owned and managed by Somalis in the diaspora, appeared during the early years of this century. One of the early scholarly studies (Issa-Salwe, 2008) on Internet adoption in Somalia concluded that websites, mostly news portals, provided a wide variety of contents, such as local and international news on business, professions, economics, politics, religion, and social topics including culture and literature. Issa-Salwe (2008) contended that, as of mid-2004, more than 500 Somali websites (news and information portals) existed, most of which have common features. Using content analysis, he divided these platforms into seven groups and found that community and political websites constituted about 39%, followed by personal websites (32%) and professional/business websites (12%).

The main goal of these websites (news portals) was to provide news and information to the Somali diaspora communities as well as their family and friends still in Somalia. Local and international news, along with forums and chat rooms, were among the services provided by these websites. Of particular note, chat rooms associated with these news portals allowed the young generation to engage in various discussions on topics such as sports, religion, and social and political issues. One early-adopted platform was MSN Messenger, which provides instantaneous chatting, allowing families and friends to maintain their ties and update each other on their lives. Recent statistics (We Are Social and Hootsuite, 2019) show that five news-oriented portals (Cassimada.net, BBC.com, Jowhar.com, AllBanadir.org, and Hiiran.com) were among the top 20 most-visited websites in the country as of January 2019.

Using a nationally representative face-to-face survey, BBG (2013) reported that about one-third of their participants access the Internet and that the majority of them receive their news online. About one-quarter of them accessed the Internet and social media platforms through their smartphones, and the same percentage of Somalis in cities have Internet access in their homes (BBG, 2013). Internet usage is predicted by age, education, location of residence, and region. Most of the users tend to be younger, more urban, and better educated than the population at large. More than two-thirds (68.4%) of college degree holders and more than 50% with secondary education access the Internet weekly. Urban dwellers were found to have higher percentages of Internet use than rural residents. With regard to regional differences, the capital city of Mogadishu is leading the Internet penetration, as more than 50% of its residents access the Internet weekly. In addition, Internet penetration is higher in the south-central regions (35%) than in Somaliland (9%) and Puntland (2.7%).

Early social media adoption was fostered by virtual communities and forums, which were associated with the news portals used to maintain social ties, obtain news and information, as well as enjoy leisure and entertainment (Ahmed, 2018). The virtual communities were then replaced by social media platforms, which allow unlimited user-generated content. There were about 1.5 million active users of social media in Somalia as of January 2019, accounting for 9.7% of the population, with the majority of them (1.4 million) accessing social media platforms through smartphones (We Are Social and Hootsuite, 2019). Other reports (Internet World Statistics, 2017) contend that Facebook users in Somalia as of December 2017 reached about 1.2 million (about 7% of the total population).

Facebook and Twitter are among the most widely used social media platforms in Somalia (StatsMonkey, 2015; BBC, 2016). About 8% of the population used Facebook as of June 2017, with an increase of 5% between 2014 and 2017. Half of the 8% are daily active users of the site. Compared to numerous Arab countries, Somalia has a low social media penetration rate. Nevertheless, the nation leads Arab countries in terms of youth usage of social media, as the majority of Facebook users in the country are between 15 and 29 years old (about 83%). There is a noticeable gender imbalance in terms of Facebook usage, with male users accounting for about two-thirds (66%) of the total. For comparison, among the 22 Arab countries, Oman has the highest male dominance in social media usage (79%) and Palestine the lowest (55%) (Salem, 2017).

Twitter penetration has been recently experiencing exponential growth in Somalia, with about 80,000 active users of the platform, of whom 79% are female (We Are Social and Hootsuite, 2019). On average, every Twitter user tweeted about 2.4 times per day as of March 2016 (Salem, 2017). Thus, Somalia has a higher rate of daily tweets than numerous Arab countries, such as Sudan, Jordan, Morocco, and Iraq. Slightly less than two-thirds (64.1%) of these Twitter users use mobile phones for their activities on the site. In addition, Instagram, a photo-sharing platform, is gaining greater popularity in the country, with about 320,000 actively using the site (We Are Social and Hootsuite, 2019). Another emerging social media platform in Somalia is LinkedIn. As of 2017, less than 1% of the population were reported to use LinkedIn (an exclusively career-oriented social media platform) (Salem, 2017), but the penetration of LinkedIn in the country had increased to about 1.2% (90,000 users) as of January 2019 (We Are Social and Hootsuite, 2019).

Taken together, the Internet and social media in Somalia have experienced exponential growth. Numerous telecoms and companies compete to provide services related to the diverse usage of mobile phones and the Internet by both individuals and businesses. Though there are no reliable statistics on market share, Hormuud Telecom, Telecom Somalia, and NationLink are major telecom and Internet providers in the south-central regions and are believed to control about 80% of the market. Golis Telecom Somalia and Telesom are also major telecommunication operators in the Puntland and Somaliland regions, respectively.

Laws and regulations

The fall of the central government in 1991 followed an almost complete collapse of government institutions and the destruction of key infrastructure during the civil war, including the only state-owned telecom company and state-controlled media outlets. Privately owned telecoms and media entities emerged to fill the gap. However, the country's telecom and media sectors were unregulated for almost three decades, as no formal government or independent regulatory bodies existed.

The giant telecom operators benefited enormously from the lack of regulations and, at times, exerted a huge amount of influence on policymakers. However, the lack of governmental guidance and regulations also brings numerous problems (INFOASAID, 2012; World Bank, 2017). First, the telecom operators face challenges related to the coordination and control of the frequency spectrum. In some cases, this lack of control causes risky signal intervention among the competing operators. Second, consumer rights are not guaranteed, since there is no formal regulatory body that they can appeal to in cases of fraud or privacy invasion. Residents of some regions or areas are compelled to use the service of a specific operator, which controls the market by blocking other operators from entering the market through the influence of warlords or clan elders.

Third, interconnections are another major problem faced by the telecommunication sector. Though some level of coordination exists between some operators, the majority of them work according to different standards and incompatible systems, which causes a financial burden on the consumers. Business owners and other individuals usually carry more than one SIM card to gain more flexibility in terms of communication with stakeholders and customers, family, and friends. Fourth, until recently, these telecoms did not pay government taxes, and there have been times when the prices were not reasonable for the quality of the provided services. Finally, all the services provided by these telecoms are priced in US dollars because of the weak currency and lack of governmental support and control of the currency (Somali shilling). With foreign exchange controls also collapsed, businesses, including the telecom sector, typically use US dollars for their transactions.

The transitional governments, which were established following the Djibouti and Kenya reconciliation conferences, attempted to regulate the telecom and media sectors by initiating relevant laws and regulatory frameworks. These efforts failed due to the limited law enforcement capabilities of those governments. In 2012, the transitional period came to an end, and a new federal government structure was formed, backed, and recognized by the international community. Two federal governments have existed since 2012: President Hassan Sheikh Mahmoud (2012–2017) led the first, and the second is currently led by President Mohamed Abdullah Farmajo (2017–2020).

To regulate the telecom sector, a communications act was drafted during the Mahmoud government in 2014. However, this act was halted three times at the stage of parliamentary approval (World Bank, 2017). This occurred due to concerns raised by the telecom operators on a number of issues in the act. Although the giant telecom companies have demonstrated support for the act, they have also tried to undermine it (Stremlau, 2018) through political lobbying. In August 2017, the act was approved by both the upper and lower houses of the federal parliament then signed by the president in December 2017. The NCA was established following the Communications Act of 2017. Its prime objectives include managing radio frequency spectrum allocations, managing interconnectivity, protecting consumers' rights, ensuring fair competition in the sector, licensing, countering cybercrimes, and generating tax and revenue from the broader sector of ICT-related technology such as telecommunications and Internet (Stremlau, 2018; NCA, 2019).

The media sector, on the other hand, is overseen by the Ministry of Information and leads the drafting and oversight of regulations. Following the collapse of the central government, the media sector was regulated according to Somali traditional and customary law (known as Xeer Law) and Sharia law, and many disputes related to media and ICT, in general, were resolved according to these laws (Stremlau, 2012, 2013, 2018).

To formally regulate the media sector, a media law was approved by the parliament of the transitional federal government in 2007. International and local media advocacy groups (i.e., Article 19) and human rights advocacy groups criticized the bill for its primarily control-oriented approach. They cited several issues, including suppression of the freedom of the press, use of vaguely phrased definitions, degree requirements for journalists, heavy fines for violations of the law, licensing and registration procedures, and the media council establishment. To accommodate calls for reform, the federal Ministry of Information called for a consultation meeting that was attended by more than 40 media stakeholders on 18 February 2013 in Mogadishu. The objective of the meeting was to discuss the media law of 2007 and listen to stakeholder concerns over the law. This move was widely welcomed by media professionals and advocacy groups. However, though some positive amendments were incorporated into the newly approved media law by cabinet ministers on 13 July 2017, media and human rights advocacy groups continue to criticize the law and call for a revision before proceeding to the next parliamentary stage (Article 19, 2018; Bader, 2017; NUSOJ, 2017).

The media law also monitors social media and new media generally. Unlike other countries, such as Malaysia, blocking and filtering methods of controlling the Internet are widely practiced in Somalia. Internet censorship and filtering services were provided by a Canadian-based company, Netsweeper, and the Citizen Lab of the University of Toronto questions the company's involvement in providing these filtering services (Citizen Lab, 2014). Their analysis revealed many websites were blocked using Netsweeper's technology, the majority being pornography sites. The Attorney General's office in February 2016 ordered the blockage of 35 websites from access inside the country, including news portals and political news sites. These websites were accused of the defamation of senior officials of the government (Garowe Online, 2015; Radio Dalsan, 2015).

Overall, the laws and regulations that govern the Internet and social media in Somalia are not inclusive and widely implemented. The customary laws mediated by clan elders and religious scholars were predominantly employed to solve disputes and conflicts related broadly to the telecommunication sector. Though these are still active and used on many occasions, official policies are now in place to regulate the sector.

Social and political functions of social media

Across Arab regions, the tremendous growth of social media has been documented (Dennis et al., 2017; Salem, 2017). Communication, self-expression, and freedom of speech have been among the key adoption drivers of these platforms. In the Somali context, their growing popularity has had a remarkable impact on both the social and political aspects of the country. Though the relationship between social media and politics is somewhat complex, the authorities (both federal and regional states) have raised growing concerns regarding the potential effects of social media. Social media has reduced government control over content production and dissemination, enabling anti-government voices to be heard regularly over these platforms. Unlike news portals and political blogs, the authorities are usually unable to block specific social media accounts. These platforms offer the public unrestricted space for freely expressing views and opinions (Nuur, 2019).

The overwhelming presence of politicians, government officials (at both state and federal levels), opposition parties, and members of parliament, as well as other political figures, on social media indicates its power in a country whose majority populace cannot afford to pay for an Internet connection. This situation is more pronounced during crises and election periods. During these events, the types of individuals and groups mentioned earlier employ social media to gain more visibility; to seek the sympathy of the public and criticize opposing politicians, parties and governments, as well as to present themselves as patriotic and caring about public interests, although the public is often skeptical about these portrayals (Webersik et al., 2018). What makes social media so popular, even among non-Internet users, is that the programs on most private radio and television stations frequently discuss what occurs on these platforms, usually regarding the posts and opinions of celebrities, such as political figures, religious scholars, and artists.

According to the Future Center for Advanced Research and Studies, social media has strongly influenced elections in various countries, such as the United States, Algeria, Somalia, Iran, and France, in multiple ways, including affecting voting trends and turnout and disseminating rumors and news (Future Center, 2017). In the context of Somalia, the use of these platforms played an important role in the recent presidential elections of the federal and regional states. The public had not cast votes since the nation gained independence (except Somaliland, a self-declared state), and the candidates utilized these platforms immensely to spread their campaign promises and programs. Social media platforms, along with clan loyalty and financial power, were major players in the federal presidential election of February 2017. Most of the interviewees in this study agreed, with one stating, "huge campaigns were run using these platforms that influenced the parliamentarians" (Haji, 2019). The candidates employed their accounts to run campaigns, while members of the parliament, predominantly the young parliamentarians, used these platforms to conduct opinion polls to identify the public's preferred candidate (Allafrica, 2017; Future Center, 2017; Nuur, 2019; Salaad, 2019). The public and media professionals obtained the candidates' and parliament members' news through their accounts on these platforms. In Somaliland, candidates reached out to the public through social media, particularly those from opposition parties, whose access to mainstream media is limited. They held press conferences through the "Live" feature on Facebook, posted their views and promises, and interacted directly with potential voters (Dualeh, 2017). As one of the interviewees stressed, these platforms became important factors in the political life of the country:

> It is evident that the public closely follows what is going on in social media platforms, albeit their motives are different. Government officials, political think tank centers,

and ordinary citizens usually interact with events discussed on these platforms, particularly Facebook. These platforms became major news sources and led to the creation of lobbying groups whose aim is to influence Somali politics. I believe that the current [federal] government came to power due to social media influence. These platforms also influenced the regional states' elections, although less so than the federal presidential election. Many politicians ran campaigns through these platforms.

(Haji, 2019)

Social media platforms also play a more negative role in Somali political life. As the interviewees contend, there has been a noticeable increase in scams and frauds, as well as fake news and information. These increase particularly during a crisis or when important events are occurring. The platforms are also employed to incite hatred and create hostility among communities and clans. Some use them for conveying information and images that are contrary to society's values and principles (Haji, 2019; Nuur, 2019; Salaad, 2019; Xamaraawi, 2019). This issue is of particularly great importance when vulnerable users are considered. Vulnerability, in this context, refers to those with limited knowledge and understanding of hard topics (politics, economics, finance, security, philosophy, etc.). This is particularly manifest among less- to moderately educated individuals. As one media professional in private television noted, "vulnerable users are sometimes misguided through these platforms" (Haji, 2019).

Social media platforms play a crucial role not only in the political arena but also in social issues. Youth activists have employed social media to promote and advocate for peace in the country and alert their peers to the risks associated with illegal migration and extremism, among other topics (Charmarkeh, 2013; Gotbuam, 2016; AMISOM, 2017). They warn the youth against brainwashing by extremist groups as well as present positive images and stories are that are not often heard in the local and international mainstream media.

Moreover, these platforms sometimes play a role in motivating the youth to illegally migrate to Europe (Haji, 2019). Those who have managed to cross the sea post good-looking photos, which motivate their friends back home to also migrate (Wasuge, 2018; Salaad, 2019). Hundreds of Somalis have died by drowning in the Mediterranean while seeking refuge in Europe. Activists try to raise public awareness on the risks and high costs associated with these dangerous journeys. Among the stories they present are those of individuals who managed to cross the sea and enter Europe but are not living the life they dreamt they would.

The platforms also have contributed to people's social solidarity and support. On many occasions, these platforms have been used to run campaigns to raise money for people injured in explosions by terrorist groups or those who require medical treatment overseas (Nuur, 2019). A social media activist, who is also an anchor at a privately owned media company, gave some of the examples of social causes that are widely popular on these platforms:

> Tracing and searching for people who are lost when explosions occur; blood donation for the injured individuals regardless of their ethnicity and supporting those recently affected by floods in the Shabelle River.
>
> *(Xamaraawi, 2019)*

Other aspects of the social functions of social media include fighting against injustices and offenses against vulnerable segments of society, particularly women and young girls. One recent example is related to rape cases in areas in the central regions. The activists helped contribute to raising awareness about these cases, which eventually led to the culprits being punished by the authorities. There were also protests in the city of Galka'yo, to condemn the rape of a young girl. Moreover, young entrepreneurs have utilized platforms such as Facebook, Instagram, and WhatsApp for online marketing and shopping.

In summary, social media platforms play a critical role in both the political and social life in Somalia. People rely on them for various tasks, such as news-seeking, entertainment, education, online shopping, and keeping up to date on current affairs, particularly in Mogadishu. As one interviewee noted, people do not normally leave their homes without checking social media platforms such as Facebook and WhatsApp to assess potential risks or the locations of new security checkpoints, among other things. Therefore, these platforms have both negative and positive impacts.

Conclusion

Recently, ICT-related technologies and innovations have witnessed a boom in Somalia. The Internet and smartphones have become an integral part of everyday life. Among neighboring nations, the country enjoys the most robust and thriving telecoms, which provide mobile phone subscriptions and telephone and Internet access at competitive prices. Though statistics on current Internet penetration are contradictory, it is clear that access to the Internet and social media platforms has greatly increased and that the thriving telecommunication companies now cover new geographical areas. The Internet has become a necessity for businesses, college, and university students, as well as the public. Various daily transactions occur through the Internet. Recently, the efficiency and affordability of the Internet have increased with the country's new access via fiber optic cables. More than 150 million transactions are conducted daily through mobile money transfer technologies alone.

The Internet and social media are used for various reasons and purposes. The most important and frequently reported purpose is information seeking, whereby users easily find reports of local and world news and events. In addition, connecting with diaspora members is a key determinant of the usage of these platforms. Accessing news and information freely without government control and censorship is another important purpose. Others use the platforms for online shopping and trading and alternatives to expensive phone calls for local and international destinations. Thus, these platforms have had effects not only on the individual but also on the societal level. Along with the mainstream media, these platforms have shaped the space of social activities and politics in the country. The strong presence of political figures and celebrities and their frequent interaction and discussion exemplify the freedom of expression that these platforms offer.

However, these platforms are not without challenges and negative aspects. Among the major challenges is the huge volume of fake news and false information, including some amounting to defamation of public figures, posted on these platforms, most often by young adults pursuing money through advertisements. Vulnerable users are the most likely to be easily misguided by these untruths, as their knowledge and understanding of the world are limited. Although platforms such as Facebook offer features such as filing a report or a complaint about inappropriate behaviors or false information, the simple act of creating awareness around these issues should not be underestimated. Social media activists are making great efforts to raise awareness of the various negative consequences of social media usage. Parents and educational institutions (schools, colleges, and universities) as well as mainstream media can also contribute to raising public awareness about the consequences – positive, negative, or otherwise – of using these platforms.

References

Ahmed, I. S. Y. (2018), *Examining Factors Influencing SNS News Consumption among University Students in Somalia : A Modified Motivational Model*. Unpublished doctoral dissertation, International Islamic University Malaysia, Kuala Lumpur, Malaysia.

Allafrica (2017), *Somalia: How Digital MPs and Social Media Changed the Course of Somali Elections*. Retrieved from http://allafrica.com/stories/201702140240.html. Accessed 3 June 2018.

AMISOM (2017), *Youth Activist Uses Social Media to Advocate for Peace in Somalia*. Retrieved from http://amisom-au.org/2017/09/youth-activist-uses-social-media-to-advocate-for-peace-in-somalia/. Accessed 4 June 2019.

Article 19 (2018), *Somalia: Draft Media Law*. Retrieved from www.article19.org. Accessed 10 May 2019.

Bader, L. (2017), *Review of Somalia's Media Law Falls Short*. Retrieved from www.hrw.org/news/2017/07/18/review-somalias-media-law-falls-short. Accessed 10 May 2019.

BBC (2016), *Somalia Profile-Media*. Retrieved from www.bbc.com/news/world-africa-14094550. Accessed 11 March 2019.

BBC (2018), *Somalia Internet Outage is 'Major Disaster'*. Retrieved from www.bbc.com/news/world-africa-40555122. Accessed 22 March 2019.

BBG (2013), *Global Hotspots: Media Use in Mali and Somalia*. Retrieved from www.bbg.gov/2013/09/18/global-hotspots-media-use-in-mali-and-somalia/. Accessed 24 March 2019.

BuddeCOMM (2019), *Somalia – Telecoms, Mobile and Broadband – Statistics and Analyses*. Retrieved from www.budde.com.au/Research/Somalia-Telecoms-Mobile-and-Broadband-Statistics-and-Analyses. Accessed 29 March 2019.

Center for Global Communication Studies (2014), *Mapping ICTs in Somalia: Policies, Players, and Practices*. Retrieved from www.global.asc.upenn.edu. Accessed 23 March 2019.

Charmarkeh, H. (2013), Social Media Usage, Tahriib (Migration), and Settlement among Somali Refugees in France. *Refuge: Canada's Journal on Refugees*, 29(1), pp. 43–52.

Citizen Lab (2014), *Internet Filtering in a Failed State: The Case of Netsweeper in Somalia*. Retrieved from https://citizenlab.ca/2014/02/Internet-filtering-failed-state-case-netsweeper-somalia/. Accessed 13 April 2017.

Citizen TV (2015), *Somalia now a Recovering State – UN*. Retrieved from https://citizentv.co.ke/news/somalia-now-a-recovering-state-un-105861/. Accessed 13 April 2017.

Dennis, E. E., Martin, J. D., and Wood, R. (2017), *Media Use in the Middle East, 2017: A Seven-nation Survey*. Retrieved from www.mediaeastmedia.org/survey/2017. Accessed 23 March 2019.

Dhaha, I. S. Y., and Igale, A. B. (2013), Facebook Usage among Somali Youth: A Test of Uses and Gratificaitons Approach. *International Journal of Humanities and Social Sciences*, 3(3), pp. 299–313.

Dhaha, I. Y. S., and Igale, A. B. (2014), Motives as Predictors of Facebook Addiction: Empirical Evidence from Somalia. *SEARCH : The Journal of the South East Asia Research Centre*, 6(3), pp. 47–68.

Dualeh, S. (2017), *Social Media has Upended Politics in Somaliland*. Retrieved from https://intpolicydigest.org/2017/11/16/social-media-has-upended-politics-in-somaliland/. Accessed 4 June 2019.

Future Center (2017), *How does Social Media Influence Elections?* Retrieved from https://futureuae.com/m/Mainpage/Item/2807/how-does-social-media-influence-elections. Accessed 5 May 2019.

Gaas, M. H., Hansen, S. J., and Berry, D. (2012), *Mapping the Somali Media : An Overview*. Noragric Report No. 65. Department of Environmental and Development Studies, Norwegian University of Life Sciences.

Garowe Online (2015), *Somalia Blocks Access to 35 Websites*. Retrieved from www.garoweonline.com/en/news/somalia/somalia-blocks-access-to-35-websites. Accessed 10 May 2019.

Garowe Online (2016), *Somalia: Al Shabaab Cuts off Telecommunication Lines in Central Somalia*. Retrieved from www.garoweonline.com/en/news/somalia/somalia-al-shabaab-cuts-off-telecommunication-lines-in-central-somalia. Accessed 29 March 2019.

Gotbuam, R. (2016), *Somali Activists Use Social Media to Warn of the High Costs, and Risks, of Seeking Refuge in Europe*. Retrieved from www.pri.org/stories/2016-04-26/somali-activists-use-social-media-warn-high-costs-and-risks-seeking-refuge-europe. Accessed 4 June 2019.

Guardian (2018), *Somalia Back Online after Entire Country Cut off from Internet for Three Weeks*. Retrieved from www.theguardian.com/world/2017/jul/18/somalia-cut-off-from-Internet-entire-country-three-weeks. Accessed 22 March 2019.

Haji, A. O. (2019, August 9), Personal Interview.

Hammond, L. (2013), Somalia Rising: Things are Starting to Change for the World's Longest Failed State. *Journal of Eastern African Studies*, 7(1), pp. 183–193.

Hare, H. (2007), *ICT in Education in Somalia*. Retrieved from www.infodev.org/infodev-files/resource/InfodevDocuments_428.pdf. Accessed 23 September 2019.

IFC (2018), *Somalia Connects Citizens to a More Prosperous Future*. Retrieved from www.ifc.org/wps/wcm/connect/news_ext_content/ifc_external_corporate_site/news+and+events/news/impact-stories/somalia-connects-citizens-to-a-more-prosperous-future. Accessed 14 March 2019.

INFOASAID (2012), *Somalia Media and Telecoms Landscape Guide*. Retrieved from www.internews.org/resource/somalia-media-and-telecoms-landscape-guide. Accessed 23 March 2019.

Internet Live Stats (2016), *Somalia Internet Users*. Retrieved from www.Internetlivestats.com/Internet-users/somalia/. Accessed 11 March 2019.

Internet World Statistics (2017), *World Statistcs-Africa*. Retrieved from www.Internetworldstats.com/africa.htm#so. Accessed 11 March 2019.

Issa-Salwe, A. (2008), The Internet and the Somali Diaspora: The Web as a Means of Expression. *Bildhaan: An International Journal of Somali Studies*, 6, pp. 54–67.

ITU (2018), *Global and Regional ICT*. Retrieved from www.itu.int/en/ITU-D/Statistics/Pages/stat/default.aspx. Accessed 22 March 2018.

Kapteijns, L. (2013), *Clan Cleansing in Somalia. The Ruinous Legacy of 1991*. Philadelphia: University of Pennsylvania Press.

Mohamed, A., and Childress, S. (2018), *Telecom Firms Thrive in Somalia*. Retrieved from www.wsj.com/articles/SB10001424052748704608104575220570113266984. Accessed 29 March 2019.

NCA (2019), *Regulations, National Communications Authority*. Retrieved from http://nca.gov.so/. Accessed 29 March 2019.

NUSOJ (2017), *2017: Another Grim Year for Journalists and Journalism in Somalia*. Retrieved from https://cms.qut.edu.au/data/assets/pdf_file/0017/631502/2016-annual-report.pdf. Accessed 23 September 2019.

Nuur, A. (2019, August 23), Personal Interview.

Osman, H. M. (2013), *Telecom: Somalia's Success Industry*. Retrieved from www.hoganlovells.com/ . . . /africaseptember2012newslettersomaliatelecoms_pdf. Accessed 13 March 2019.

Osman, I. (2017), *Media, Diaspora and the Somali Conflict*. Cham, Switzerland: Palgrave Macmillan.

Radio Dalsan (2015), *Somali Attorney General Orders the Suspension of 35 Somali News Websites over Allegations of Ethics*. Retrieved from www.radiodalsan.com/somali-attorney-general-orders-the-suspension-of-35-somali-news-websites-over-allegations-of-ethics/. Accessed 21 May 2019.

Randa, J., and Musuku, T. B. (2018), *Rapid Growth in Mobile Money: Stability or Vulnerability?* Retrieved from http://documents.worldbank.org/curated/en/975231536256355812/Rapid-Growth-in-Mobile-Money-Stability-or-Vulnerability. Accessed 28 March 2019.

Reuters (2013), *Somalia Gets First Fiber Optic Link to the World*. Retrieved from www.reuters.com/article/us-somalia-telecoms/somalia-gets-first-fiber-optic-link-to-the-world-idUSBRE9AB0SN20131112. Accessed 29 March 2019.

Salaad, N. (2019, August 20), Personal Interview.

Salem, F. (2017), *The Arab Social Media Report 2017: Social Media and the Internet of Things: Towards Data-driven Policymaking in the Arab World*. Retrieved from www.mbrsg.ae/getattachment/1383b88a-6eb9-476a-bae4-61903688099b/Arab-Social-Media-Report-2017. Accessed 21 April 2018.

Sheikh, H., and Healy, S. (2009), Somalia's Missing Million: The Somali Diaspora and its Role in Development. United Nations Development Program Report.

Somaliland Biz (2019), *Somaliland Telecoms Sector Guide*. Retrieved from www.somalilandbiz.com/sector-guides/telecoms-2/. Accessed 29 March 2019.

StatsMonkey (2015), *Social Network Usage Statistics in Somalia*. Retrieved from www.statsmonkey.com/sunburst/21701-somalia-social-network-usage-statistics-2015.php. Accessed 11 March 2019.

Stremlau, N. (2012), Somalia: Media law in the Absence of a State. *International Journal of Media & Cultural Politics*, 8(2/3), pp. 159–174.

Stremlau, N. (2013), Towards a Diagnostic Approach to Media in Fragile States: Examples from the Somali Territories. *Media, War and Conflict*, 6(3), pp. 279–293.

Stremlau, N. (2018), Law and Innovation in the Somali Territories. In B. Mutsvairo (ed.), *The Palgrave Handbook of Media and Communication Research in Africa*. Cham, Switzerland: Palgrave Macmillan, pp. 297–309.

Telcoma (2019), *List of Mobile Network Operators of Somalia*. Retrieved from www.telcomatraining.com/list-of-mobile-network-operators-of-somalia/. Accessed 29 March 2019.

UNDP (2014), *The UN in Somalia*. Retrieved from www.undp.org/content/dam/unct/somalia/docs/publications/FINAL UN SOMALIA Yearbook Layout.pdf. Accessed 10 September 2019.

Wasuge, M. (2018), *Youth Migration in Somalia: Causes, Concequences and Possible Remedies*. Retrieved from www.heritageinstitute.org/youth-migration-in-somalia/. Accessed 8 July 2019.

We Are Social and Hootsuite (2019), *2018 Global Digital: Essential Insights into Internet, Social Media, Mobile and Ecommerce Use Around the World*. Retrieved from https://datareportal.com/reports/digital-2019-somalia?rq=Somalia. Accessed 29 March 2019.

Webersik, C., Hansen, S. J., and Egal, A. (2018), *Somalia: A Political Economy Analysis*. Retrieved from https://brage.bibsys.no/xmlui/bitstream/handle/11250/2461121/NUPI_rapport_Mozambique_Orre_Ronning.pdf?sequence=1&isAllowed=y. Accessed 22 September 2019.

World Bank (2017), *Legal ICT Framework Is Pivotal Moment for Somalia*. Retrieved from www.worldbank.org/en/news/feature/2017/10/02/legal-ict-framework-is-pivotal-moment-for-somalia. Accessed 30 March 2019.

Xamaraawi, M. (2019), Personal Interview, August 12.

Yuusuf, M. (2015), *Somalia: The Resilience of a People*. Retrieved from www.africanexecutive.com/modules/magazine/article_print.php?article=4693. Accessed 15 March 2019.

Sudan

30

PRESS IN SUDAN

Models, regulatory frameworks, and development

Mohamed Elamin Musa

Introduction

Over a period of 120 years, the Sudanese press experienced several notable landmarks irrespective of the political regime that ruled the country. It has been subjected to shutdowns, bans, confiscation, censorship, restrictions, harassment, and journalists' dismissal. One objective of this chapter is to highlight the central features of the Sudanese press within a political, economic, social, and cultural context, from the colonial era at the end of the 19th century to the present day. The chapter explores the role of the Sudanese press in the transition to democracy for more than a hundred years.

Subsequently, it looks ahead to the Sudanese press in light of the difficulties it faces under restrictions relating to freedom of expression and the challenges associated with the information and communications technology (ICT) revolution. The challenges confronting the Sudanese press include, but are not restricted to, the misuse of power and the restriction of freedom of expression, and recently, the conditions of the press industry in the digital age, as well as the emergence of digital communication spaces which threaten print media distribution.

The emergence of the press

The Anglo-Egyptian Condominium (1898–1956), as a colonial authority, established the first newspapers to serve its purposes. The press then began to play a political role in the struggle against colonialism, misuse of authority in fragile democracies, and national dictatorships from 1930 to date.

The Anglo-Egyptian invasion of Sudan in 1898 resulted in the founding of the first newspaper – in English – named the *Dongola News* (refers to the city of Dongola the capital of the ancient Nubian kingdom). *Dongola News* represented a printed form of communication in Sudanese society whose communicational culture is almost oral (Galander, 2001: 13). Soon after, the newspaper changed its name to the *Sudan Government Gazette*.

The first newspaper aimed at general readership was *Al-Sudan*, established by three journalists: Fares Nimr, Jacob Sarouf, and Shaheen Makarios by Dar al-Moqattam in Cairo in 1903 (Saleh, 1971: 19). Its readers were primarily Syrians and Egyptians working in government and commerce. Dar Al-Moqattam established a printing press in the Sudanese capital Khartoum

(Saleh, 1971: 22). On 25 December 1904, *Al-Sudan* began releasing a short supplement in English, in order to double its distribution, in addition to setting up a library for books, magazines, and foreign newspapers (Sudan Bookshop), as well as benefiting from commercial and governmental advertising (Saleh, 1971: 25–26).

The second outlet was set up in 1911 when two Greeks residing in Sudan established a commercial printing press in Khartoum called the Victoria Press. In 1912, they applied for a semi-weekly English-language newspaper entitled *The Sudan Herald*, followed by an Arabic supplement known as *Raed Al-Sudan* released on 4 January 1913, under the chairmanship of the Syrian writer Abdel Rahim Mustafa Koleilat. This became the second Sudanese newspaper to play a prominent role in the literary and intellectual renaissance of Sudan (Saleh, 1971: 41; Abugarjah, 2014: 463; Deckert, 2012a: 6). It included social criticism by way of addressing harmful social customs. *Raed Al-Sudan* witnessed the emergence of the first Sudanese journalist, Hussein Mohamed Al-khalifa Sharif, who was the editor-in-chief after Abdel Rahim Koleilat before ceasing publication in 1918 (Saleh, 1971: 45–48).

In terms of ownership, editing, and readership, the first fully Sudanese newspaper was *Hadarat Al-Sudan* (Sudan Civilization) which was published on 28 February 1919 and edited by Hussein Mohammed Al-Khalifa Sharif. This paper embodied the first link between politics and the press in Sudan. It was bought out by the leader of the Ansar religious-political group, Abdulrahman al-Mahdi (son of Imam Muhammad Ahmad al-Mahdi, leader of the Mahdist Revolution), and several merchants (Babeker, 1998: 6–11; Saleh, 1971: 49–71).

Al-Nil (The Nile) was the first daily newspaper to be published inside Sudan on 1 August 1935. It was published by the Egyptian journalist Hassan Sobhi and was taken over by Abdul Rahman al-Mahdi, leader of the Ansar sect in 1945 (Babeker, 1998: 14–15). It was the first partisan newspaper in Sudan (Maarouf, 1998: 6–11; Saleh, 1971: 21–22).

The year 1945 witnessed the birth of three newspapers: the first independent daily newspaper in Sudan, *al-Rai Al-Aam*, founded by Isma'il al-Atabani; the first regional newspaper, *Kordofan*, set up by al-Fateh al-Nur, and the *al-Umma* newspaper, the organ of the al-Umma Party, as the first party newspaper in Sudan (Saleh, 1999: 8). The *Al-Alam* newspaper was published on 24 November 1953, as the representative of the National Unionist Party (NUP); followed by *al-Maidan* on 2 December 1954, the organ of the Sudanese Communist Party (Ahmad, 2014: 54–71). In 1946, *Bent al-Wadi* was set up by a Sudanese journalist of Armenian origin, Tkoye Sarksyan, as the first magazine to focus solely on women. This was followed by the magazine *Sawt al-Waha* in 1955 as the mouthpiece of the Sudanese Women's Union (Amin, 2011: 36–38). The only surviving newspaper of those originated in 1945 is the *al-Rai Al-Aam*, although it was suspended on numerous occasions.

One of the major characteristics of the Sudanese press at that time was the short life of outlets. As a consequence, those outlets were unable to grow and maintain accumulated professional traditions and committed readership.

Since independence from British colonial rule on 1 January 1956, six regimes have governed Sudan: three relatively democratic and three military dictatorships maintaining the dualism of democratic–military regimes. The three democratic regimes appeared to be like respites that punctuated the way for the emergence of new military dictatorships. The first democracy that began before independence from 1953 to 1958 was followed by the first dictatorship (1958–1964); and the second democracy (from 1964 to 1969) was followed by the second dictatorship (1969–1985), whilst the third democracy from 1986 to 1989 ended by the third dictatorship which governed from 1989 until 2019.

The instability of the political sphere was one main reason behind the lack of professional developments in the Sudanese press. Military dictatorship deployed press nationalization, thereby ending the natural development that could lead to well-established professional outlets.

Press-politics relationship from 1953 to the 2019 uprising

The first democratic experiment in Sudan began in 1953 under the British–Egyptian rule (1898–1956), taking the form of a legislative authority influenced by the structure of the British parliamentary system. The 1953 Self-Governing Law legislated the formation of the Sudanese parliament from the Senate and the House of Representatives (Abushouk, 2016). The Declaration of Independence was made from the Sudanese Parliament on 19 December 1955 to evacuate the colonial rulers on 1 January 1956.

The first Sudanese parties surfaced under British colonialism to achieve independence and rule the country using a democratic system that had to comprise a partisan press (party-owned or alien). *Al-Nil* was published to be the mouthpiece of the Ansar sect – the supporters of Imam Muhammad Ahmad Al-Mahdi (later becoming the mouthpiece of the Umma Party). *Al-Nil* newspaper pioneered in several ways: it was the first daily, the first with a publishing house, and the first to speak for a socio-political faction of the population (Galander, 2001: 24). Subsequently, a rival religious sect, the Khatmyya, launched its newspaper *Sawt-al-Sudan* in May 1940 (later becoming the mouthpiece of the People's Democratic Party). Next, *Al-Umma* (The Nation) newspaper was published on 15 May 1945 as the representative of the Umma Party. *Al-Alam* newspaper was launched on 24 November 1953 to represent the NUP, and this was followed by *Al-Maidan*, the mouthpiece of the Sudanese Communist Party on 2 December 1954 (Ahmad, 2014: 54–71; Galander, 2001: 24).

With religious sectarianism dominating the Sudanese political scene in the first period of democracy, the sharp polarization resulting from the rivalry between the Ansar and Al-Khatmyya sects and their use of the loyal and affiliated media, the critical press faced complications in continuing and narrowing the margin as regards to freedom of expression. For example, *Al-Saraha* newspaper and its owner, Abdullah Rajab, and the owner of the *Telegraph* newspaper, Saleh Orabi, faced recurrent repression by means of fines, imprisonment, and suspension due to fierce criticism of sectarianism (Galander, 2016: 34–35).

Overall, the Sudanese press in the period of the first democratic experiment was affected by political conflicts based on the dominance of religious sectarianism on the political, electoral, and economic scene, which defeated the intellectual elite's attempts to modernize society so that it could coexist with the values of democracy in its Western form. This situation relating to the partisan press in the first democratic period led to a deterioration in the ethics of the press, which encouraged the military to abandon the democratic experiment and disrupt the party newspapers (Muhisi, 2016: 27–28).

On 17 November 1958, General Ibrahim Abboud took over control of Sudan, and in his first statement, he decided to suspend the newspapers and the news agency, in addition to the printing presses, seeing the press as the root of the conflict between political parties and the source of spreading political chaos in the country (Galander, 2016: 51–52). Aboud's regime adopted a firm stance and ended the publication of partisan newspapers while restricting the freedom of nonpartisan newspapers to the extent that they became loyal newspapers if they wished to continue. The Abboud military regime was more stringent than the colonial system in dealing with the Sudanese press, in its abuse of freedom of expression, which paved the way for the coup against the first democratic system.

The repressive practices of the Abboud military regime led to a revolution in October 1964, marking the birth of the second period of Sudanese democracy. The Sudanese press contributed to the success of the October Revolution through a statement issued by several leading journalists (such as Bashir Muhammad Saeed, Mahjoub Mohammed Saleh [founders of *Al Ayyam*], Ismail Al-Atabani [founder of *Al Rai Al-Am*], and Abdul Rahman Mukhtar), as did the judges, doctors, and lawyers (Galandar, 2016: 41–42). The October Revolution was followed by the general elections in1965 in which the Umma Party won 92 seats and the National Unionist Party 73 seats. This result forced the two main parties to become unwilling allies (Al-Gaddal, 2007; Awad, 2016).

In addition to fueling the conflict between political parties, the Sudanese partisan press undermined the foundations of democracy by calling for the dissolution of the Sudanese Communist Party in response to its newspaper *al-Midan*, calling for the bypassing of the traditional (sectarian) parties as a remnant of colonialism. The attack on the Communist Party was led by the newspaper *al-Mithaq al-Islami*, the mouthpiece of the Islamic Charter Front Party, and *Al-Nil*, the representative of the Ansar sect (Ahmad, 2014: 157–164). This attack resulted in the dissolution of the Sudanese Communist Party and the expulsion of its deputies as well as the suspension of its newspaper *al-Midan* by means of the vote cast by the Constituent Assembly (Parliament) in the session conducted on 19 December 1965 (Ahmad, 2014: 178).

The second dictatorship or the "May regime" started on 25 May 1969, following a military coup led by General Jaafar Muhammad Nimeiri. The May regime resorted to the nationalization of the remaining press institutions and established its outlets such as *al-Ayyam* founded in 1961; the regime also gave media ownership to the Socialist Union as the new ruling party. It formed a committee for the nationalization of newspapers under the name of the "Committee for the Future of the Sudanese Press" (Abdullatif, 1992: 96–101). In addition to the nationalization of existing newspapers, the May regime decided to change the name of the government's newspaper, which was issued by the Ministry of Information in the democratic government, to *al-Ahrar*/The Free (Muhisi, 2016: 48).

In 1970, the regime's *al-Quat al-Musallaha* (the Armed Forces) recruited military personnel, writers, military journalists, and journalists in addition to university graduates who were included to serve as the core for military journalism in Sudan (Galander, 2016: 62). The adoption of the May regime's authoritarianism led to the transformation of the media discourse into propaganda speech, promoting the authority of the tyrannical league as an alternative to pluralistic democracy by way of launching a systematic multiparty attack as a national defeat and betrayal (Muhisi, 2016: 51).

Sudan recognized the third democratic experiment after the people revolted against the dictatorship of the May regime. The uprising of the Sudanese people from 26 March to 6 April 1985 forced the Sudanese army leadership to side with the people in the overthrow of the May regime and the handover of power to civilians one year after the 1986 parliamentary elections.

The transitional government then allowed individuals, parties, associations, and bodies to publish newspapers (Abdullatif, 1992: 117–118). As a consequence of this authorization, the media scene was filled with newspapers and journalists to an almost chaotic level, especially in the context of the conflict between the political components of previous democratic experiences and the nationalization of their media during the period of the May regime.

Regardless of the misuse of the margin of freedom of expression in the era of the third democracy, the Sudanese press criticized the government and the prime minister (Abdullatif, 1992: 120–121). Paradoxically, however, this margin was used to undermine the foundations of the democratic experiment and to pave the way for the third dictatorship. The third dictatorship in Sudan differed from its predecessors in that it came to power through a military takeover supported by a political organization involved in the democratic experiment. The National Islamic Front (NIF), led by Hassan Abdullah al-Turabi, which carried out its coup d'état under the name of the National Salvation Revolution, used its media in the third era of democracy to undermine and question its value to the masses. When it seized power, it feared that the same would happen if left to the press; therefore, it prevented freedom of expression (Galander, 2016: 133).

When National Salvation took power on 30 June 1989, it immediately outlawed all political parties and independent newspapers published during the third democratic era. Less than two months later, the banned newspapers were replaced by *al-Sudan al-Hadeeth* (Modern Sudan) published on 16 August 1989, followed by *al-Inqaz al-Watani* (National Salvation) published on 28 September 1989. This was followed by two political newspapers aligned with the government (Abbas, 2009: 40).

The main characteristics of the National Salvation press were the following: firstly, the National Salvation marginalized the media and replaced it with propaganda that was compatible with the communicative approach and discourse based on rhetoric and slogans instead of facts and information. Secondly, the marginalization of the media extended to the sidelining of the regime's newspapers. National Salvation did not provide its newspapers with the reasons for continuity and success in forming the public opinion, which led to its closure or failure to perform its tasks (*al-Inqaz al-Watani* and *al-Sudan al-Hadith* had been merged into *Al-Anbaa* newspaper). This marginalization extended to Sudan Radio, TV, and the Sudan News Agency. Thirdly, National Salvation exercised all types of censorship that restricted freedom of expression in the newspapers, from the self-censorship required by laws that restricted the margin of freedom of expression and publication, by way of pre-, during and post-censorship by the security apparatus, to the financial sanctions imposed on journalists and publishers. Fourthly, the lack of financial, economic, and developmental support for the press, implicitly acknowledging the role of the press in society, made the press vulnerable to economic pressures leading to bankruptcy and stagnation. Moreover, there were no customs exemptions for press production inputs or direct financial support for newspapers, nor was there any legislation or governmental initiatives that promoted human resources and enabled them to perform their tasks in an appropriate manner, such as securing the financial rights of journalists, training them, enabling them to access information sources, and protecting them. Moreover, extensive negative amendments were added to the laws and regulations governing the press, which had to refrain from criticizing the National Salvation regime by expanding the concepts of "public order" and "national security." Finally, the pressure corrupted the press and dominated its institutions while dominating the editorial policies by bribing editors. Thus, journalistic institutions were kept away from the practice of investigative journalism to reveal the breadth of corruption.

The reality of the Sudanese press during the last three decades reflected on its performance during the uprising of December 2018 that led to the collapse of the National Salvation regime on 11 April 2019. Most Sudanese newspapers deviated from their usual track of defending people's interests to be the regime's outlet. This peculiar situation continued even after the fall of the National Salvation regime. The Sudanese Minister of Information and Culture Faisal Mohamed Salih, a member of the transitional government, stated to *Al-Quds* newspaper on 10 September 2019, "the largest number of newspapers are anti-revolutionary [and so are] their programs and goals" (Majzoob 10 Sep. 2019). Following the December Revolution slogan, "freedom, peace, and justice," the transitional government cannot censor press content, ban it, arrest journalists, or prevent them from practicing the profession.

In its report "Sudan Still Awaits Its Press Freedom Revolution," Reporters Without Borders (RSF) attributed the reasons for the continuation of the situation to the following, stating, "the Sudanese media are still largely controlled or under the influence of the forces that supported Bashir, one of the world's biggest press freedom predators" (RSF 3 Dec. 2019).

On the first anniversary of the December Revolution, the public space in Sudan is characterized by a series of notable attributes: firstly, the majority of Sudanese newspapers are still owned by persons or entities affiliated with the National Salvation regime, which reflected on the obvious resistance to democratic transition led by the December Revolution. Secondly, since publishing lacks financial viability, the December Revolution has failed to publish new papers that can compete with the National Salvation regime papers and pull the rug from under them. Thirdly, the Sudanese press witnessed an improvement in press freedom and freedom of expression after the appointment of the transitional government. Consequently, censorship, confiscation, prevention, and arrest of journalists are no longer the same as before. Finally, the Sudanese Intelligence and Security Service continues to dominate press activity in Sudan through its possession of the most prominent newspapers.

Press business models

The Sudanese printed press has experienced poor distribution in recent years because of a combination of factors, which reinforces the predictions of those who see it as fading. Sudanese newspapers include political, sports, lifestyle, and entertainment papers, and "the number of titles fluctuates: some close down, victims of political or economic pressure and others spring up in their place. Unlike in the past, there are few monthly magazines on the market" (Deckert, 2012b: 16).

According to the annual report issued by the Directorate of Proliferation Control of the National Council for Press and Journalistic Publications in Sudan (NCPP), the general trend was towards a reduced number of printed copies, distributed copies, and daily reading rate (NCPP: 2014–2018). While 47 Sudanese papers printed 120,649,998 and circulated 81,509,174 copies with a distribution percentage of 67.6% and a daily reading rate of 11 copies per one thousand inhabitants in 2014, 37 papers printed 59,954,698 and disseminated 36,424,669 copies with a distribution percentage of 60.8% and a daily reading rate of three copies per one thousand inhabitants in 2018; the number of Sudanese papers, the total printed quantity, and the total distributed quantity was reduced within five years.

Evidence pertaining to the limitation of the spread of the 37 Sudanese papers as described in the *Intishar* report in 2018. According to *Intishar*, the newspapers that distributed more than 10 thousand copies per day were only 7% of the total amount of newspapers, three to seven thousand copies per day were 46% of the total number of newspapers, while newspapers that distributed less than two thousand copies a day were 46% of the total number of newspapers (NCPP, 2018). In 2017, there were 45 Sudanese papers. Newspapers that distributed more than 10 thousand copies per day accounted for only 11% of the total newspapers, five to 10 thousand copies per day were 31% of the total number of newspapers, while newspapers that distributed less than two thousand copies a day were noted to be 58% of the total number of newspapers (NCPP, 2017).

Legal and regulatory frameworks

Sudan is no different from other countries that suffer a lack of democratic values leading to the smooth transfer of power, in terms of the multiplicity of legislation that hinders freedom of expression and makes the practice of professional journalism perilous and liable to abuse by the authorities. The fact that the legislation is too numerous, too chaotic, and poorly interpreted by the authorities to interfere with the spirit on which it is based places Sudan at the bottom of the ranking in the list of some of the world's leading organizations concerned with freedom of expression. This ranking reflects negatively on international policy and investment and creates a negative mental image.

The first press act in Sudan was legislated in the colonial period when the Press and Publications Act was promulgated in 1930 (The Press and Publications Act of 1930), amended in 1948 (The Press and Publications Law of 1948), and replaced by the 1973 act (The Press and Publications Act of 1973). The 1973 act was in turn replaced by the 1985 act (The Press and Publications Law of 1985), which remained for one year and was later replaced by the 1986 act (The Press and Publications Law of 1986). Subsequently, the act has been repealed and replaced on several occasions. It is important to mention that the 2004 act was repealed and replaced by the 2009 act (The Press and Publications Act of 2009), which came after Sudan's Interim Constitution of 2005 when the peace agreement was signed. The 2018 act is in the process of replacing the 2009 act.

There are a few general features of the press and publication laws in Sudan: the strict laws tend to be constant during the colonial period, the first and second democratic regimes, and the first military regime, in contrast with their frequent amendments in the regime that controlled Sudan from 1989 to 2019. Moreover, all Sudanese press and publication laws required prior authorization from the concerned government authorities before publishing (the Administrative Secretary: 1930 act; Minister of Interior: 1948 act; Minister of Culture and Information: 1973 and 1985 acts; Council of Press and Publications: 1986 act; National Council of Press and Publications: 1993 (The Press and Publications Law of 1993), 1996 (The Press and Publications Act of 1996), and 1999 (The Press and Publications Law of 1999) acts; National Council of Press and Press Publications: 2004 and 2009 acts). The acts restrict freedom of expression as a human right, while some countries do not require prior authorization (for example, the 15 November 1958 act in Morocco requires only a declaration in a court of minor jurisdiction containing general information concerning the publication and its responsible director before publication). Also, the authorities that have the right to own press publications have varied according to the ruling political regimes (e.g., the 1930 and 1948 acts did not specify named possessors; Socialist Union/ruling party and individuals were specified in the 1973 act; possessors not specified in the 1985 and 1986 acts; general companies and regional governments specified in the 1993 act; public sector companies (20% was the maximum percentage of ownership by individual or class) in the 1996 act; commercial companies, political parties, social, governmental, or scientific bodies specified in the 1999 act; commercial companies, political parties, social, governmental, scientific, or foreign communities as specified in the 2004 and 2009 acts).

Moreover, 1930, 1948, and 1973 acts did not address the content of the press in terms of subjects that must be published or prohibited, and they were included in the 1985 act under the general rules of compliance (Chapter IV, Article 13). In contrast, topics were specified in the 1993 act of Chapter VI, entitled "Prohibitions of publication and observance of professional ethics"; and in the 1996, 1999, and 2009 acts under "The duties of the journalist." All press acts in Sudan have restricted the freedom of expression, except the 2009 act (established after the Naivasha Agreement between North and South Sudan, which resulted in the 2005 constitution). It explicitly states, in its basic principles in Article 5, the right of journalists to practice freedom of the press in accordance with the Constitution. Generally, the press acts in Sudan have set out criteria for choosing editors which must be met as demonstrated in the 1985 act, Article 6, regarding the nationality, age, and ability to practice the profession. Finally, the Sudanese press acts include the right of reply starting with the 1986 act (Article 18), the 1993 act (Articles 15 and 16), the 1996 act (Article 24), the 1999 act (Article 26), and the 2009 act (Article 27).

Press freedom in Sudan

The media environment in Sudan resembles the tripartite link between the weakness of freedom of expression, the crisis of power and administration, and underdevelopment in various areas. The European Parliament resolution of 10 October 2013 on clashes in Sudan and subsequent media censorship condemned the National Salvation regime according to some freedom of the press violations, stating,

> there have been numerous violations of the freedom of the press, such as disconnection of the internet, the seizing of newspapers, harassment of journalists and the censoring of news websites; while the offices of Al-Arabiya and the Sky News Arabic Service television stations have been closed. Furthermore, daily newspapers such as *Al-Sudani, Al-Meghar, Al Gareeda, Almash'had Alaan, Al-Siyasi,* and the pro-government *Al-Intibaha* were banned from publication on 19 September 2013, and publications of three newspapers, including Al-Intibaha, were seized as they came off the press.
>
> *(European Parliament, 2013: 3, emphasis in original)*

In its report "Sudan: Entrenched Repression: Freedom of Expression and Association under Unprecedented Attack" in 2015, Amnesty International observed several violations pertaining to the freedom of the press and expression by the National Intelligence and Security Service (NISS). The Sudanese print media regularly faced arbitrary confiscation of their publications; the NISS confiscated all editions of 14 newspapers from the printers without explanation and forbade newspapers from critically reporting on the conduct of the security services, armed forces or police, the president, corruption cases, conflict areas, and human rights violations (Amnesty International, 2015: 5).

The classification of Sudan according to institutions interested in freedom of the press highlights its low ranking. The lengthy existence of dictatorial regimes in power shows the extent of the aggravation of the power crisis and Sudan's name among the most underdeveloped countries in various fields of development, in tune with the current crises in the country.

The worldwide press freedom indicators of Reporters Without Borders signifies how far Sudan occupies low levels of freedom of expression. According to the RSF reports from 2002 to 2019, the weight of freedom of expression in Sudan has declined since 2002 from 24.5% (24.5% = Sudan's rank ÷ total number of countries participating in the classification) to 2.8% in 2019 (RSF, 2019). This fact confirms that Sudan is not only failing to improve the level of freedom of the press but is also seeking further restrictions.

Freedom House's ratings on press freedom indicate that Sudan has maintained a rank of more than 75% from 2002 to 2017 as a "non-free" country (Freedom House, 2002–2017). For example, Sudan ranked 87/100 in 2012, 76/100 in 2010, and 86/100 in 2017. The same applies to the freedom of the Internet, which indicates the regular suppression of online journalism and press freedom on digital media platforms. Freedom House classified Sudan as a "not free" in the Internet freedom category for the six years between 2013 and 2018 (Freedom House, 2013–2018). For example, the freedom of the Internet in Sudan was ranked 63/100 in 2013, 64/100 in 2016, and 65/100 in 2018.

Online journalism in Sudan is not immune to restrictions on freedom of expression. Through the new Press Act 2018, the Sudanese government seeks to limit online journalism by including sections that require prior authorization before publishing, and that the online publisher is responsible for publishing it, whether inside or outside the country (Al-Taghyeer, 2017).

The Sudanese Council of Ministers ratified the National Council for Press and Journalistic Publication Act of 2018 on 21 June 2018. The amendments included a set of articles in the 2009 act, most notably the amendment of the interpretation of the term "newspaper" to accommodate online journalism. The organization of online journalism publications also added to the jurisdiction of the Press and Press Council. Article 13, which established how to elect the president of NCPP, was repealed and replaced by a new article guaranteeing the president of the republic the appointment of a full-time president and vice president of NCPP along with the amendment of Article 33, which authorizes the council to impose sanctions by adding new powers to allow it to stop a journalist from writing for the period he or she deems fit and to withdraw his or her temporary license (Sudan View, 2018).

However, the development of online media in the country has been significant in the last few years. This will continue to empower free speech and human rights activists. In a poll on print journalism in Sudan and the impact of online journalism, respondents said that online journalism outperforms print journalism in Sudan for a number of reasons, including rapid deployment, low cost, the prevalence of online journalism among young people, lack of print journalism (lack of videos and sounds), as well as the wide margin of freedom offered by the Internet. Moreover, some concluded that online journalism would prevail over print journalism and may replace it (Yahya, 2017). The first online newspaper in Sudan was known as the "Sudanile" and appeared on 7 January 2001 (Sudanile, 2008). Since 2001, Sudanese online journalism has sought to attract readers accustomed to print journalism based on a group of columnists who contribute to increasing sales through their regular readers. Most Sudanese print papers have neglected their websites because they provide the content free of charge.

Future of the Sudanese Press

As we have seen, the Sudanese press experienced political instability when it was suspended under the changing regimes. It has also suffered interdiction, confiscation, fines, and censorship owing to the narrow margin relating to freedom of expression, besides increasing production costs, weak advertising revenues, and poor distribution. The indicators produced for more than six decades of independence suggest that the future of the Sudanese press is not positive, whether it is the hoped-for role in building and preserving the foundations of democracy or continuing to play its societal and institutional role as a fourth authority capable of supporting governance. The Sudanese press faces a range of challenges that will shape its future. The first and greatest challenge is the lack of freedom of expression or the narrow margin in relation to the degree of violation of professional standards as universally recognized. This challenge is the essence of the other economic, professional, and social challenges. Restrictions on freedom of expression – in the case of Sudan – may take the form of economic conflict against newspapers and their journalists (preventing them from working in any newspaper published in the country). It may prevent the newspaper and the journalist from gathering information, reflecting weakness at the professional level. It may also take the form of a social war through defamation and damage to the social relationships of the newspaper's employees. The sustained restriction of freedom of expression leads to the derailment of the press and turns the media into propaganda and journalists into hypocrites. This threatens to diminish the role of the press as a communication tool in the pursuit of sustainable development. Another challenge is the lack of seriousness in dealing with new media and online journalism as a natural extension of print journalism. Adhering to the economics of print journalism, because of its suitability to the Sudanese reality, prevents the creation of an economic model that makes Sudanese online journalism a genuine alternative for media investors, turning their readership into an interactive audience within the digital environment on the Internet. Thus, it is evident that there is no justification for the cessation of Sudanese print journalism without creating a digital alternative, whether it is a web news portal or an interactive platform that takes advantage of the characteristics of the web in providing authentic media content and to connect current and future generations. A third challenge is the unprofessional performance of the Sudanese press and the weak press institutions in terms of structure, capital, budget, equipment, privileges provided to their members, the (low) number of correspondents, and the overall legal framework. The press is also unable to attract and preserve the right talents, with the latter's preference to pursue better-paid careers outside Sudan. The unprofessional standards can be seen in the neglect of investigative journalism mainly due to the declining freedom of expression. Investigative journalism rarely found within the content of the Sudanese press requires minimum access to information and requires the authorities to enable journalists to do their jobs. The declining professionalism is also seen in the lack of linguistic and informational scrutiny because press organizations are not willing to hire proofreaders. Finally, the press has failed to attract readers with an attractive form and design, because of the modest printing presses available, the high cost of good paper, and the unified style across all outlets (most Sudanese newspapers are published in red headlines on the front page), and few papers provide rich content and a diversity of subjects.

Another challenge facing the Sudanese press is the negative perception of the Sudanese authorities with regard to the media and its role in society. The press is seen as a tool for political action: it is used for political propaganda or it is disrupted and opposed when it is considered a threat to authorities. The press – in this view – is not a mirror of society and must not be allowed to play its role fully, and it is certainly not a fourth estate that can assist the authorities to be efficient, as is the case in some other countries.

The future of the Sudanese press depends on the comprehensiveness of the social dialogue and a compromise between actors to make it become the cornerstone to consolidate the values of democracy and help Sudan in its developmental path. This dialogue should include media actors, political leaders, public opinion leaders, investors, the general public, professional institutions interested in journalism and communication in the country, media training institutions, researchers specialized in different areas of communication, as well as those interested in Sudanese media affairs. Such a dialogue is premised on the degree of awareness of the importance of free and responsible journalism in securing good governance of the state; a legal system supporting the freedom of the press and expression; a new media structure aligned with the global development in digital media; and an economic system capable of achieving the economic and financial viability of journalism institutions. These conditions can then help restore the material and moral value of journalism and preserve and document lessons learned from past experiences.

References

Abbas, H. M. (2009), Human Structure of the Sudanese Press. *Nile Scientific Magazine*, March. Retrieved from http://dglib.nilevalley.edu.sd:8080/xmlui/bitstream/handle/123456789/94/البنية20%البشرية20%للصحافة20%السودانية.pdf?sequence=1. Accessed 18 August 2018.

Abdullatif, S. (1992), *Sudanese Press: History and Documentation*. Cairo: publisher house not unknown.

Abugarjah, M. (2014), *Voices in Sudanese Culture*. Cairo: Safsafa Publishing.

Abushouk, A. I. (2012), *National Elections in Sudan 2010: An Analytical Approach in its Introductions and Results*. Doha, Qatar: Al Jazeera Centre for Studies.

Abushouk, A. I. (2016), The First Democratic Experiment in Sudan (1953–1958) (2): The Basis of the Problem and the Defect? *Sudanile*, 13. Retrieved from www.sudanile.com/index.php?option=com_content&view=article&id=92906:1953-1958-2&catid=177&Itemid=55. Accessed 19 August 2018.

Ahmad, A. D. (2014), *Partisan Journalism and National Unity in Sudan*. Omdurman: Abdulkarim Merghani Cultural Center.

Al-Gaddal, M. S. (2007), Historical Overview: Parliamentary Elections in Sudan (4–3). *Urban Dialogue*, 7 May. Retrieved from www.ahewar.org/debat/show.art.asp?aid=96065. Accessed 20 August 2018.

Al-Taghyeer (2017), Government Procedures to Besiege Online Journalism. *Altaghyeer*, 1 February. Retrieved from www.altaghyeer.info/2017/02/01///تدابير-حكومية-لمحاصرة-الصحافة-الإلكت. Accessed 15 March 2018.

Amin, B. (2011), *Women's Press in Sudan*. Sudan: publisher house not unknown.

Amnesty International (2015), *Sudan: Entrenched Repression, Freedom of Expression and Association under Unprecedented Attack*. Retrieved from https://www.amnesty.org/download/Documents/AFR5413642015ENGLISH.pdf. Accessed January 27, 2019.

Awad, R. (2016), The Role of Political Parties in the Collapse of Democratic Rule after the Revolution of October 1964. *Altaghyeer*, 21 October. Retrieved from www.altaghyeer.info/2016/10/21/دور-الأحزاب-السودانية-في-انهيار-الحكم/. Accessed 20 August 2018.

Babeker, M. A. (1998), The Features of the Emergence and Development of the Sudanese Press: 1919–1935. In A. Dafallah (ed.), *The Birth of the Sudanese Press: Dawn of the Sudanese Press: 1903–1945*. Sudanese National Council for Press and Publications. Khartoum: National Council for Press and Publications.

Deckert, R. (2012a), The History of the Sudanese Press: Background to Conflict. In Jess Smee and Tammi Coles (eds.), *The Sudanese Press after Separation – Contested Identities of Journalism*. Berlin: Media in Cooperation and Transition gGmbH (MICT), pp. 6–15.

Deckert, R. (2012b), The Current State of the Sudanese Press: A Diverse Range of Papers for a Narrow Spectrum of Society. In Jess Smee and Tammi Coles (eds.), *The Sudanese Press after Separation – Contested Identities of Journalism*. Berlin, Germany: Media in Cooperation and Transition gGmbH (MICT), pp. 16–19.

European Parliament (2013), *Clashes in Sudan and Subsequent Media Censorship*, European Parliament Resolution of 10 October 2013 on Clashes in Sudan and Subsequent Media Censorship (2013/2873(RSP)), p. 3. Retrieved from http://www.europarl.europa.eu/document/activities/cont/201310/20131017ATT72981/20131017ATT72981EN.pdf. Accessed 15 February 2019.

Freedom House (2002), *Freedom in the World: The Annual Survey of Political Rights and Civil Liberties 2001–2002*. New York: Freedom House, p. 558.

Freedom House (2003), *Freedom in the World 2003: The Annual Survey of Political Rights and Civil Liberties*. New York: Freedom House, p. 521.

Freedom House (2004), *Freedom in the World 2004: The Annual Survey of Political Rights and Civil Liberties*. New York: Freedom House, p. 533.

Freedom House (2005), *Freedom in the World 2005: The Annual Survey of Political Rights and Civil Liberties*. New York: Freedom House, p. 596.

Freedom House (2006), *Freedom in the World 2006: The Annual Survey of Political Rights and Civil Liberties*. New York: Freedom House, p. 573.

Freedom House (2007), *Freedom in the World 2007: The Annual Survey of Political Rights and Civil Liberties*. New York: Freedom House, p. 755.

Freedom House (2008), *Freedom in the World 2008: The Annual Survey of Political Rights and Civil Liberties*. New York: Freedom House, p. 667.

Freedom House (2009), *Freedom in the World 2009: The Annual Survey of Political Rights and Civil Liberties*. New York: Freedom House, p. 676.

Freedom House (2010), *Freedom of the Press 2010: Sudan*. Retrieved from https://freedomhouse.org/report/freedom-press/2010/sudan. Accessed 20 January 2020.

Freedom House (2011), *Freedom in the World 2011: The Annual Survey of Political Rights and Civil Liberties*. New York: Freedom House, p. 634.

Freedom House (2012), *Freedom of the Press 2012: Sudan*. Retrieved from https://freedomhouse.org/report/freedom-press/2012/sudan. Accessed 20 January 2020.

Freedom House (2013a), *Freedom in the World 2013: The Annual Survey of Political Rights and Civil Liberties*. New York: Freedom House, p. 656.

Freedom House (2013b), *Freedom on the Net 2013: A Global Assessment of Internet and Digital Media*. New York: Freedom House, p. 20.

Freedom House (2014a), *Freedom in the World 2014: The Annual Survey of Political Rights and Civil Liberties*. New York: Freedom House, p. 656.

Freedom House (2014b), *Freedom on the Net 2014: Tightening the Net, Governments Expands Online Controls*. New York: Freedom House, p. 19.

Freedom House (2015a), *Freedom in the World 2015: The Annual Survey of Political Rights and Civil Liberties*. New York: Freedom House, p. 642.

Freedom House (2015b), *Freedom on the Net 2015: Privatizing Censorship, Eroding Privacy*. New York: Freedom House, p. 19.

Freedom House (2016a), *Freedom in the World 2016: The Annual Survey of Political Rights and Civil Liberties*. New York: Freedom House, p. 651.

Freedom House (2016b), *Freedom on the Net 2016, Silencing the Messenger: Communication Apps under Pressure*. Retrieved from https://freedomhouse.org/report/freedom-net/2016/silencing-messenger-communication-apps-under-pressure. Accessed 9 April 2020.

Freedom House (2017a), *Freedom in the World 2017: The Annual Survey of Political Rights and Civil Liberties*. New York: Freedom House, p. 489.

Freedom House (2017b), *Freedom on the Net 2017: Manipulating Social Media to Undermine Democracy*. Retrieved from https://freedomhouse.org/report/freedom-net/2017/manipulating-social-media-undermine-democracy. Accessed 9 April 2020.

Freedom House (2018), *Freedom on the Net 2018: The Rise of Digital Authoritarianism*. Retrieved from https://freedomhouse.org/report/freedom-net/2018/rise-digital-authoritarianism. Accessed 9 April 2020.

Galander, M. (2001), *Mass Media in Sudan: Towards History of Media-Politics Interplay*. Kuala Lumpur: IIUM Press.

Galander, M. (2016), *A Profession in Distress: The Sudanese Press and the Ages of Struggle*. Khartoum: Abdul Karim Merghani Cultural Centre.

Majzoob, N. (2019), Sudanese Minister of Information Faisal Muhammad Saleh told Al-Quds Al-Arabi: The Largest Number of Newspapers are Anti-revolutionary. *Al-Quds Al-Arabi*, 10 September. Retrieved from www.alquds.co.uk/وزير-الإعلام-السوداني-فيصل-محمد-صالح-ل/. Accessed 11 September 2019.

Maarouf, M. S. (1998), The Role of Journalism and the Appearance of the Partisan Press In Al-Nour, Dafallah (eds.), *The Birth of the Sudanese Press: Dawn of the Sudanese Press: 1903–1945*. Khartoum: National Council for Press and Publications.

Marwa, A. (1961), *Arab Journalism: Its Origination and Development*. Beirut: Library of Life Publications.

Muhisi, S. (2016), *The Sudanese Press and the Totalitarian Systems: A Reading in the Biography of Political Tyranny*. Cairo: Civilization for Publishing.

NCPP, *Intishar 2014*. Retrieved from http://ncpp.sd/images/report2014.pdf. Accessed 22 December 2019.

NCPP, *Intishar 2015*. Retrieved from http://ncpp.sd/images/report2015.pdf. Accessed 22 December 2019.

NCPP, *Intishar 2016*. Retrieved from http://ncpp.sd/images/report2016.pdf. Accessed 22 December 2019.

NCPP, *Intishar 2017*. Retrieved from http://ncpp.sd/images/report2017.pdf. Accessed 22 December 2019.

NCPP, *Intishar 2018*. Retrieved from http://ncpp.sd/images/report2018.pdf. Accessed 22 December 2019.

Reporters Without Borders, *Ranking 2002*. Retrieved from https://rsf.org/en/ranking/2002. Accessed 25 January 2020.

Reporters Without Borders, *Ranking 2003*. Retrieved from https://rsf.org/en/ranking/2003. Accessed 25 January 2020.

Reporters Without Borders, *Ranking 2004*. Retrieved from https://rsf.org/en/ranking/2004. Accessed 25 January 2020.

Reporters Without Borders, *Ranking 2005*. Retrieved from https://rsf.org/en/ranking/2005. Accessed 25 January 2020.

Reporters Without Borders, *Ranking 2006*. Retrieved from https://rsf.org/en/ranking/2006. Accessed 25 January 2020.

Reporters Without Borders, *Ranking 2007*. Retrieved from https://rsf.org/en/ranking/2007. Accessed 25 January 2020.

Reporters Without Borders, *Ranking 2008*. Retrieved from https://rsf.org/en/ranking/2008. Accessed 25 January 2020.

Reporters Without Borders, *Ranking 2009*. Retrieved from https://rsf.org/en/ranking/2009. Accessed 25 January 2020.

Reporters Without Borders, *Ranking 2010*. Retrieved from https://rsf.org/en/ranking/2010. Accessed 25 January 2020.

Reporters Without Borders, *Ranking 2011*. Retrieved from https://rsf.org/en/ranking/2011. Accessed 25 January 2020.

Reporters Without Borders, *Ranking 2012*. Retrieved from https://rsf.org/en/ranking/2012. Accessed 25 January 2020.

Reporters Without Borders, *Ranking 2013*. Retrieved from https://rsf.org/en/ranking/2013. Accessed 25 January 2020.

Reporters Without Borders, *Ranking 2014*. Retrieved from https://rsf.org/en/ranking/2014. Accessed 25 January 2020.

Reporters Without Borders, *Ranking 2015*. Retrieved from https://rsf.org/en/ranking/2015. Accessed 25 January 2020.

Reporters Without Borders, *Ranking 2016*. Retrieved from https://rsf.org/en/ranking/2016. Accessed 25 January 2020.

Reporters Without Borders, *Ranking 2017*. Retrieved from https://rsf.org/en/ranking/2017. Accessed 25 January 2020.

Reporters Without Borders, *Ranking 2018*. Retrieved from https://rsf.org/cn/ranking/2018. Accessed 25 January 2020.

Reporters Without Borders, *Ranking 2019*. Retrieved from https://rsf.org/en/ranking/2019. Accessed 25 January 2020.

Reporters Without Borders (2019), Sudan still Awaits its Press Freedom Revolution. *RSF,* 3 December. Retrieved from https://rsf.org/en/news/sudan-still-awaits-its-press-freedom-revolution. Accessed 26 December 2019.

Sudan View (2018), Council of Ministers Authorizes the Press and Publications Law. *Sudan View*, 21 June. Retrieved from https://sudanview.com/2018/06/21/ الصحافة-قانون-مشروع-يجيز-الوزراء-مجلس/. Accessed 27 August 2018.

Sudanile (2008), About Sudanile. *Sudanile*, 19 May. Retrieved from www.sudanile.com/index.php/ سودانايل-عن. Accessed 20 August 2018.

Saleh, M. M. (1971*), Sudanese Press in Half a Century (1903–1953)*, Part I, Khartoum: University of Khartoum.

Saleh, M. M. (1999), The Evolution of the Sudanese Press. In *The Rise of the Sudanese Press: 1945–1969*. Series of Documentaries of Sudanese Press History 2. Khartoum: National Council of Press and Publications.

Saleh, M. Mo. (2016), Introduction. In Mahmoud Qalandar (ed.), *A Profession in the Ordeal: The Sudanese Press and the Ages of the Liver*. Khartoum: Abdulkareem Mirghani Cultural Centre.

NCPP (2017), Summary of the Annual Report on Print and Distribution of Newspapers for the Year 2017. *NCPP*. Retrieved from http://ncpp.sd/images/entshar-2017.pdf. Accessed 15 March 2018.

The Press and Publications Act of 1930. *NCPP*. Retrieved from http://ncpp.sd/images/law1930.pdf. Accessed 15 August 2018.

The Press and Publications Law of 1948. *NCPP*. Retrieved from http://ncpp.sd/images/law1948.pdf. Accessed 15 March 2018.

The Press and Publications Act of 1973. *NCPP*. Retrieved from http://ncpp.sd/images/law1973.pdf. Accessed 15 March 2018.

The Press and Publications Law of 1985. *NCPP*. Retrieved from http://ncpp.sd/images/law1405هـ.pdf. Accessed 15 March 2018.

The Press and Publications Law of 1986. *NCPP*. Retrieved from http://ncpp.sd/images/law1406هـ.pdf. Accessed 15 March 2018.

The Press and Publications Law of 1993. *NCPP*. Retrieved from http://ncpp.sd/images/law1993.pdf. Accessed 15 March 2018.

The Press and Publications Act of 1996. *NCPP*. Retrieved from http://ncpp.sd/images/law1996.pdf. Accessed 15 March 2018.

The Press and Publications Law of 1999. *NCPP*. Retrieved from http://ncpp.sd/images/law%201999.pdf. Accessed 15 March 2018.

The Press and Publications Act of 2009. *NCPP*. Retrieved from http://ncpp.sd/images/law2009.pdf. Accessed 15 March 2018.

Yahya, S. (2017), Journalism and the Effects of the Electronic Tide. *Al-Attibah Newspaper*, 17 and 19 September. Retrieved from http://alintibaha.net/index.php/ المد-وتأثيرات-الورقية-الصحافة9232/-الأخبار. http://alintibaha.net/index.php/2--الإلكتروني-المد-وتأثيرات-الورقية-الصحافة9281/-الأخبار; الالكتروني. Accessed 15 March 2018.

31

RADIO AND TELEVISION BROADCASTING IN SUDAN

Awad Ibrahim Awad

Historical background of radio in Sudan

The British administration established radio services in Sudan in 1940 to be one of the tools of WW2. The reason for that was to exercise a propaganda role for the Allies in their war against the Axis powers led by Germany. Its origins were among several radio stations, which the British established in their colonies in response to German propaganda (Awad, 1990: 62). The British government set three main goals for the radio service it established in Omdurman. The first aim was to broadcast news of the Allied victories in the war. Secondly, they aimed to discredit any news published in the national newspapers against the British administration. Lastly, they wished to embellish the image of the British administration in Sudan due to the hatred that the patriots had for them at that stage.

Thus, the nature of programming was against the patriotic sentiment of the Sudanese, who were hostile to colonialism since the days of the Mahdist revolution in 1882–1885 (Ali Bakhit, 1972: 131). Radio Sudan continued to serve the national cause after the Sudanese leadership took over, upon signing the Cairo Agreement on 13 February 1953, which gave Sudan independence. Before the emergence of radio broadcasting, national newspapers were powerful tools against colonial propaganda (Salih, 1971: 68–70), naturally arising following the Alumni Conference and national uprisings in Atbara, Totti, and Gordon Memorial College. Although the political dimension of newspapers during that time was not clear until after 1935, the literary press was overtly trying to shift national sentiment. So, the British government made sure to use radio to combat this anti-sentiment.

Sudanese radio started its first broadcast at 6 pm on 1 April 1940, from inside a small room in the Omdurman post office. Its name was decided, expectedly, to be Radio Omdurman. The influence of broadcasting was demonstrated through the propaganda of the Allies during what was called the Battle of the Air between the democratic and fascist states. The Axis powers were fortifying their propaganda to discredit everything that was British and to sew hatred among their enemies, especially in Egypt, Sudan, and Palestine (Bashir, 1987: 45). At the same time, they adopted a façade of respect towards Commander Mussolini, who was portrayed as the Messenger of Peace (Ali Bakhit, 1972: 30). The British had established the Arab section of the BBC in January 1938 as the first foreign department to be established for that purpose. Radio Sudan came to follow in these footsteps.

The Sudanese took an interest in this radio since its inception and began listening to it with the few devices that the government provided in public squares. The radio programming used to start with a recitation from the holy Qur'an, followed by news entirely devoted to the war, ending with a traditional Sudanese song. The transmission would end at 6:30 in the evening. However, this radio service almost stopped after the end of the war because the budget for war propaganda was nulled. Concerned about the fate of this new voice, the British ruler Evans made an effort towards its continuation, in which he successfully obtained a detailed budget for the radio. Thus, the budget belonged, for the first time, to the British Government of Sudan. However, the purpose of the radio remained the same – serving colonialism and glorifying its policy in all fields.

The radio operated throughout the first year by volunteers under the presidency of the British Finch Dawson, who was the first and last foreigner to chair it and was succeeded by Metwally Eid. One year later, the first official announcer, Obaid Abdal-Nur, was appointed. Since his appointment, he began to supervise a 50-minute program, presented three times a week, along with a 15-minute program presented during the rest of the week.

When the radio drew the attention of more people, the government distributed a number of large receivers in public places, since individuals were unable to obtain their own devices at the time. After that, the radio moved from the post office building to a small house, which was rented to accommodate the service. This house is located in the western part of the Midwives School, in Al-Mawrada Street in Omdurman (Shummo, 1999: 104). During that period, the programs were broadcast on the medium wave 524 meters with a power of 50 kW. Its transmitter was located in the Al-Ardha district in Omdurman.

Shortly after that, wave 31 was introduced, followed by short waves reaching 25 and 60 meters with a power of 20 kW. In November 1962, a transmitting station launched in the area of Souba in south Khartoum, with two medium waves reaching 312 and 393 meters. The power of each was 100 kilowatts. Subsequently, the short wave 41 was introduced with a power of 120 kW. The culmination of this was that Raiba Station was launched in Sennar Governorate in January 1978, peaking at a medium wave reaching 231 meters and a power of 1,500 kW.

With the beginning of the transitional government led by Ismail Al-Azhari in 1954, the radio began to serve the national government, which continued after the declaration of independence on 1 January 1956. At that stage, the role of the radio was to unify the nation through the Arabic language, which had become Sudan's official language. The patriots resorted to making this decision for cohesive simplicity – there is great variation in the roots of the Sudanese, with 500 tribes each of different ethnicity, language, and culture (Al-Tijani, 1995: 102). Therefore, the issue of unity and identity after Sudan's independence became an obsession among its national leaders (Bashir, 1987: 65). The unity was not an end in itself, but the patriots considered it a way to overcome the reality of national disintegration and heterogeneity, especially since British and Turkish policies before that aimed to consolidate tribal tendencies and dismantle the national unity to fortify their control over the population.

In the early days, Omdurman Radio used to broadcast just half an hour a day. This then evolved to 50 minutes, then an hour, and even developed into four-hour broadcasts in the evening, after which the daily Sudanese music service would begin. Soon after independence in 1956, the volume of radio broadcasts increased to 10 hours. Programs started as early as 6 am, streaming for two-hour periods, with a few intermissions, till as late as 11 pm. A decision was even issued by the Ministry of Information and Radio Administration to extend the morning period to a four-hour broadcast. In March 1962, the transmission reached 17 hours, starting at 6 am and ending at 11 pm. Another hour was then added, allowing it to stop at midnight. These increases flowed into the beginning of 1990, when the radio added another morning hour, to start at 5 am and continue until midnight. In February 1995, the decision was taken to establish 24-hour broadcasting, at long last.

Live and recorded programs

In the beginning, Sudanese radio started broadcasting its programs live without recording. Even the singing was broadcast that way – any performers had to come to the studio and sing on air. This method was not ideal, because any mistakes were simply nationally broadcast. Thankfully, a CD recording system was introduced in 1949, allowing them to record any type of media. However, this was still tiring for technicians because it was rudimentary, and recording was not very clear. It was also difficult to re-record the material onto the record disc (Awad, 1983: 20).

Several divisions were established to produce the programs, the most prominent of them being the news section. It began small, with few reporters, until it became an independent entity after the expansion of news and political services. Naturally, however, with the growth of political competition between parties, specifically the Umma, Islamic Front, and the National Congress, the expansion of news coverage was necessitated. News coverage doubled during the October 1964 government and during the administration of May 1969 (Al-Sudan Alhadeeth, 1991: 1).

In 1971, a worker's union was formed, having registered officially with the Registrar General of Syndicate. Attempts to meet their demands were exemplified by the search for radio specialists and the establishment of legislation to monitor the affairs of radio personnel and their finances.

This was considered a large gain for radio workers, because the workforce had been constantly expanding. In the mid-1970s, the number of radio workers stationed in the service jumped to two hundred people on monthly paychecks and receiving state pensions. Promotions were also escalating generously, creating an administrative problem that was only resolved by inventing new jobs for those promoted.

Leading public opinion

Political concerns in Sudan have varied over the years according to circumstance. These circumstances have sometimes stifled the development of public opinion from one stage to another; for example, radio contributed to the stagnation of public opinion in various stages. Ismail Al-Azhari claimed in a cabinet meeting (10 May 1955),

> It has become clear now that we must direct the energies of the media, especially the radio, to lead the next stage. You may see the danger of these channels in leading and guiding public opinion in our country. If we do not care for this matter from now, things will get out of hand.
>
> *(Abu Al-Aza'im 1994: 6)*

It was clear from that statement that the effort made by the national radio convinced politicians at the time, which made them consider it one of the most important channels in shaping public opinion in the post-independence period. Such a role was especially paramount given the political ruptures in Sudan left by decades of colonialism. This role was defined for the radio in a letter sent by the director of information, Muhammad Aamir Bashir Furawi, commissioned by the minister of information to develop directives for Omdurman Radio. This was formulated around some key points, which will now be discussed.

Preserving the national heritage

The year 1957 saw the most significant expansion of Sudanese radio. Soon it opened its doors to record all that preserves Sudan's national heritage, represented in literature, singing, and popular music. The Sudanese nation is considered to be one of the richest in heritage out of African and Arab countries, due to its unique composition and its location, being adjacent to river beds that historians claim all civilizations originated from (Al-Tijani, 1995: 38). From the beginning, broadcasters were assured that their mission to document and preserve Sudan's national heritage would not be easy but rather arduous for several reasons, including Sudan's vast variety of cultures, tribes, and dialects. Furthermore, the values of artists sometimes differ, therefore it is hard to strike a balance between "popular" music and performances and the principle of modesty. Thus, radio proprietors decided that an appropriate, safe aim would be to unite Sudan without reopening the old wounds that caused cultural fragmentation and tribal rivalry (Al-Khalifa and Hariz, 1982). They also intended to present national heritage in a way that corresponded with popular media across Sudan's history.

Omdurman Radio has established several specialized services, some from within studios in Omdurman and some from various other regions of Sudan. Each radio station was told to achieve a different goal according to the service it was established for. Some were even directed by the radio's founders. The directed radios included the English program, the French program, the Swahili program, Rukn Al-Janoub Radio, National Unity Radio, and The Voice of the Sudanese nation. The Expatriate Radio includes the program for Somalia and the voice of the Eritrean revolution. However, the Department of Specialized Programs has continued to offer material that deviates from directed material; for example, the Holy Qur'an radio, the second program radio, and the Nile Valley radio, joint between Egypt and Sudan.

The Regional Broadcasting Department was established in February 1992, and its leadership was assigned to Salahuddin Al-Fadil, who, after three years of assuming that position, was promoted to general director of the Sudanese radio. He was succeeded by Omar Abdel Moneim, who developed all his radio stations in the different cities of Sudan, followed by Engineer Salah Taha.

If we go beyond the borders of the capital, we find several radio stations that originated in Sudan and provide similar services, showing how each region in Sudan has the autonomy to enjoy its cultural heritage. However, distance has made it difficult for the mother radio to reach these more remote areas, and there was also a need to satisfy the national government, not simply the people. Accordingly, many regional and state radio stations arose, such as Juba Radio (Voice of Peace 1962), Nyala Radio (1983), and Kordofan Radio 1984.

The establishment of Sudanese TV

Perhaps an avid follower of Sudan's TV history would notice that it has two beginnings. The first was on the evening of 23 December 1962 in Studio B of Radio Omdurman, and the second was after it returned to transmit from its 17th building in November 1963. Technology in Studio B was more primitive, as it had been designed for radio, not for television. The TV station came to Sudan as a result of the German Technical Assistance Agreement. It was the Thomson Company that supervised its establishment, and German engineers and technicians continued to train the Sudanese to operate this station until the overall work on the project was completed. Ultimately, Sudanese TV was born in the same city as the radio – Omdurman. Its first experimental transmission was on 23 December 1962 from the National Theater Hotel, where it is still broadcast to this day. The story of the establishment of Sudanese TV is different from the rest of the Arab world since a complete set of broadcasting equipment was gifted to the Sudanese government by Germany. The leader at the time was Lieutenant General Ibrahim Abboud, who ruled Sudan from 17 November 1958 to 21 October 1964.

After the equipment arrived, it was installed by Thomson Company engineers, as agreed between the Ministry of Information and Thomson's management. After installing the devices, an official ceremony held to open the first Sudanese television station on 17 November 1963. This coincided with the fifth anniversary of the government of Lieutenant General Ibrahim Abboud taking power in Sudan, succeeding the liberal administration of Abdullah Khalil. The celebration was simple inside the studio; offices were hastily constructed inside the hotel buildings, including a small studio and a management office.

Since Omdurman Radio, which was established 17 years before television, had played a strong role in uniting the Sudanese nation, the new TV station completed that role in the state's eyes. They considered the media a fundamental tool in forming the image of a strong, independent nation.

Likewise, TV was intended to represent the significance of Sudan's rich cultural heritage. These legacies have become a symbol for Africa, combining singing, dancing, art, literature, and all that encompasses human creativity with national values. Allowing freedom of expression on a local and regional scale was key to achieving this, specifically open dialogue between institutions. Thus, Sudanese TV arose and witnessed development in four main phases, which were founding, qualifying, developing, and identity building.

The founding and qualifying phases extended from 1960 to 1962; however, the previous two years of broadcasting witnessed many moves towards developing a Sudanese "identity" on television. Much, sometimes controversial, dialogue had taken place between the Sudanese and German parties to establish the station. This can be simply attributed to the novelty and uncharted territory that television work was in Africa and the Arab-Islamic world in general. Many voices rejected television in these countries and refused to establish television stations, on the pretext that it would be an extension of colonialism. They believed that citizens prolifically watching European programs would obliterate their national identity and act as a "foreign cultural hegemony."

After the establishment of this station, central transmissions were used for the next 10 years, from 1962 to 1972. They were launched by sending a test signal from a small device with limited power, e.g., 100 watts to a receiver, each with 625 horizontal lines.

The programs started from Studio B in the Sudanese Radio Building next to the TV headquarters. This relatively large studio was set up to be capable of broadcasting TV. Its transmission continued until 24 May 1963, when the operations were moved to the National Theater after the approval of a German delegation. All Sudanese TV programs were broadcast live on air due to the lack of enough recording devices at such an early stage.

Not all people were able to buy television sets at that time. Therefore, the government distributed 300 medium-sized television receivers to public squares in various areas. Some of these devices were subsidized by the Television Department, however. People living in the capital had the largest variety at first – from one newscast per day, some entertainment, and educational programs that included songs, plays, poetry, and dramatic sketches. The transmission lasted for three hours a day, beginning and ending in the evening. The broadcasting area then expanded to cover some areas of Sudan, including the state of Al Jazirah (the area of the service), with its capital Wad Madani, and Atbara, in northern Sudan. The third stage, which was called the regional broadcasting stage, then spanned from 1976 to 1991. This stage was more advanced after the microwave network was established in 1976 and covered vast areas of Sudan.

At that point, several studios were built for television. Studio A, with an area of 35 square meters, was dedicated to presenting live news as well as official interviews. It is now called Ali Shummo Studio, after the first founding director of Sudan TV, Professor Ali Mohamed Shummo, a well-known media expert. Studio B is double the size and specializes in entertainment and drama programs. It is now dedicated to broadcasting Blue Nile programs, which were established jointly with Sudan TV under the Saudi businessman Salih Kamel, owner of ART International TV Network. Likewise, Studio C was established and later called White Nile Studio. Both Studios B and C were opened in 1978.

In the early stages, broadcasting technology consisted of three black-and-white cameras and a telescope with a 16 mm projector and a 35 mm projector. At the time, transmissions were done live, as there were no recorders, on Channel 5. The image appeared on the screen with a power of 600 watts and a frequency of 25,175 MB. The sound was powered at 200 watts with a frequency of 750,180 megacycles for the carrier.

In 1968, the TV station finally introduced a video recording system by importing two Japanese machines valued at $700,191. These devices were installed in the first studio. Programs would be recorded, then broadcast from tapes, which was a far more convenient system. Most materials were recorded inside the studio then aired later, after a manual montage. The ratio of live programs compared to recorded ones quickly declined from 60% to 40%. Similarly, around 50% of programs were recorded as films, while 30% were videos. At this point, broadcasting hours rocketed from three to 40 per week. Moreover, there were five hours dedicated to broadcasting educational programs (Awad, 2019: 40), continuing to air educational programs twice a week, from 8 to 9 am, as they had since July 1964. Despite imports and subsidies, television still suffered from primitive equipment. Video devices were limited, there were only three studio cameras and two telescopes, one 16 mm and the other 35 mm. The development of news footage was largely dependent on the Film Production Department, called the Sudan Film Unit.

On 12 October 1975, the Rural Program Studio was established, becoming the starting point for developing the work after it was officially opened on 28 January 1976. It was supported by several cameras, light bulbs, coolers, and Ampex video machines that operated with a 2-inch tape system and a 1-inch tape system. The studio was also supported by a telescopic device with a 16 mm color display machine from the British company Marconi, measuring 2 mm × 16 mm. A 120-square-meter studio was established, and a central control room was used to broadcast and receive materials sent from outside Sudan. This was done via the satellite station in Umm Harraz in south Khartoum. In addition, another main monitoring room, equipped with videotapes and tele-cinema, was established. It later became a supportive tool for the daily transmission of Sudanese TV.

Broadcasting in color was simultaneously introduced. These new studios brought recording devices to Studio A and Studio B. TIP video equipment was also purchased from the Japanese company AMPX, which operated with 2-inch tape. These devices allowed for a breakthrough in production, and its success was reflected in the quality of performance. Viewers truly felt the evolution of the screen. Naturally, this positive feedback attracted further commercial investment into the television industry. Due to this investment, viewers enjoyed a bountiful variety of foreign programs. Even directors began reviewing their aims, deciding to take advantage of these developments by importing modern materials from abroad. Video recording devices allowed broadcasting companies to massively cut costs because programs could simply be repeated. They also made use of previously exchanged gifts from allied countries.

This technological development opened an avenue for several programs, as well as allowing a new method of presentation and production. Its impact is obvious – television has become a widespread, predominant force in society. At this stage, transmission managed to reach some cities in the west of Saudi Arabia and some parts of North Yemen. Accordingly, the administration made a major update to the format and content of the programs. It also established a number of specialized departments, including announcers, directors, production services, decoration, and makeup. It was decided that these divisions would be under the responsibility of the implementation division. The assistant program manager for planning would manage human resources and adjust the daily program, in consultation with the assistant program director for implementation. As for the News and Politics Department, it is affiliated with the director of television directly because of its importance and privacy. Under such provision, Sudanese TV continued to provide various services, covering entertainment, education, orientation, and news.

Although these goals seem intertwined with each other, each of them has a framework that makes it different from the other. Each program was intended to provide a different use; dramas to evoke emotion and entertain, news to provide international awareness, commercial advertising to perhaps entice spending, and educational programs to awaken the mind. Educational TV programs saw increases during the 1990s, given the aid of more advanced electronic devices. Overall, although the role television played in social change varied depending on the state's circumstance, television undoubtedly became an essential tool in Sudanese society.

As for the International Affairs and Special Programs Unit, it is mainly concerned with documentaries and international events. It also prepares and provides programs for countries that have diplomatic relations with Sudan. They make it possible to cover various political events with only five employees working in the unit. In its early years, Sudan TV had no correspondents at home or abroad. Rather, it used foreign television stations to obtain news, such as CBS, ABC, and NBC, which are all American companies. It also used ATC, Visnews, and BBC, and received news from other companies, such as Reuters and United Service, in addition to cultural programs from other Arab and foreign countries. The material mainly consisted of films and animated cartoons from France, Germany, and former Czechoslovakia.

If we go beyond political material, Sudanese TV and Omdurman Radio played an important role in documenting and publishing Sudanese heritage, as well as its music and folk tales (Bashir, 1987: 60). The music departments in both organizations created for that purpose worked hard to record most of the Sudanese singing in its various languages. The radio formed committees for poems and melodies to authorize artworks before recording them. It also created its own orchestra to perform the songs. The same was done for sports, especially football, where a sports section was established to provide a daily program before the evening bulletin at 3 pm, which was peak time. It also created sections for drama, culture, coordinators, announcers, and directors. Consequently, it had to recruit hundreds of employees to work in these departments. The number of workers exceeded two thousand before radio and television were merged into one body.

In 1991, the devices were provided, and studios were rehabilitated. This development encouraged the station's transition from terrestrial to satellite broadcasting. On 30 June 1995, the president of the republic opened a satellite television station. For the first time, the transmission went international, via the Intelsat and Arab satellites. As a result of this new satellite broadcast, many "dazzling" elements were added to television screens. The coinciding developments in digital technology, combined with increased transmission hours and a viewing range from local to international intensified the whole experience.

The National Radio and Television Corporation

It has been many years since radio and television worked in isolation. Many people began to think of uniting them into one body like the BBC and radio companies in the US, France,

Japan, and other developed countries. The government of Sudan did eventually establish a national radio and television commission. The minister of culture and information formed a committee of specialists to present a study on a potential structure for radio and television services. That committee submitted its report to the minister's office on 7 February 1981.

After studies on that project were completed, on 19 September 1981, the first law was issued for the National Radio and Television Corporation of the Republic of Sudan. According to that law, radio and television became a single administrative and legal body. Subsequently, several regulations were issued clarifying the formation of internal departments and sections. The justification for the merger was the presence of similar services, such as those provided by the Sudan Film Unit, the Radio Training Institute, the Development Media Unit, the Commercial Office, and rural television. A decision was issued by the president of the republic, Jaafar Muhammad Nimeiri, to appoint Al-Fateh Al-Tijani as the first general manager and chairman of the board of directors of the National Radio and Television Corporation.

Powers of the board of directors

The board of directors had the authority over executive action to achieve the goals of the corporation and therefore were entitled to any equipment necessary. They were also responsible for attracting funding and approving the annual budget, provided it was within the Ministry's maximum debt limit. Lastly, they were given control over the movement of workers in and out of the country, ensuring they did not circumvent laws of using foreign expertise in the audio-visual field.

The Corporation's law stipulated that its board of directors meets at least three times a year, as well as attend urgent meetings at the request of the chairman or of two-thirds of the members. According to this law, every radio station established in any region in Sudan is automatically subordinate to the National Radio and Television Corporation. Accordingly, all existing radio services in Sudan were automatically attached to the Corporation, including Juba Radio, Al Jazeera Rural TV, and Atbara TV Station. Thus, the law helped strengthen the relationship between the National Corporation and regional governments. These governments contributed to the construction of regional radio and television buildings and the provision of funding for daily expenses.

Radio broadcasting as an independent body

Ten years after the establishment of that corporation, the vision changed – the Council of Ministers issued a resolution (No. 458, 1992) to once again establish radio and television as separate bodies. Thus, radio now had no administrative connection to television and so decided to establish a new broadcasting organization with its board of directors.

The radio started operating with unprecedented autonomy. The Radio Administration established a separate work structure that included service and program facilities, solidifying into reality after being authorized by the minister of culture and information. The same thing happened to Sudanese TV, which became an independent organization with a similar sense of freedom. The new law provided an opportunity to correct the mistakes that arose out of the old law, allowing a focus on thoroughly training employees, monitoring job promotions properly, and ensuring the well-being of their workers.

A decision was made in 2007 to revise the system which started during the establishment of the Sudanese Radio and Television Corporation. In 2009, it was decided to abolish it and create three new, independent bodies: the General Authority for National Television, the General

Authority for National Radio, and the General Authority of Engineering. Rather than establish an economic sector, its skills were transferred to the advertising departments of these new bodies.

Administrative development of television

Since its establishment in 1962 and until now, Sudan TV has gone through five administrative stages. Through the starting period 1962–1981, television was considered a government department belonging to the Ministry of Culture and Information. Since the company's creation in 1981, the station has become a privatized department of the National Radio and Television Corporation. However, in response to relentless criticism over its administrative failures, it was again nationalized and renamed the General Union of Radio and Television. This union soon deteriorated, however, due to a lack of capability and devices.

From 1991 to 2001, a separate national organization for broadcasting and another for television was established. This separation aimed to compete with other broadcasters and promote performance. Consequently, television became an independent organization called the National Television Commission. From 2001 to 2009, the president of the republic made the decision to merge radio and television once again. The structure included four main sectors: the television sector, the radio sector, the economic sector, and the engineering sector. Each of them had their respective administrative structure within the framework of the general board of directors' plan.

From 2009 to 2015, a new, third structure was announced. It decided to separate the two institutions, reversing the decision to have television centrally managed by the National Television Corporation. The structure included the general manager, the general auditor, the program manager, and the finance department, in addition to some newly established departments. Since 2015, television has been managed by the Sudanese Radio and Television Commission after the Republican decision re-merged the two institutions (for the third time) into one body. At this stage, the powers of the TV director paled in comparison to before, due to the evident erosion of the title. The restructuring phase began with the adoption of a task force system in line with the satellite channel management systems, which became an alternative to the system of departments and divisions.

Planning and program rounds system

Sudan Radio and Television, both in the context of the merger or during the periods of separation, adhered to the annual planning that depended on the introduction of the program courses system. Their attention was consistently focused on four main aspects: entertaining, advertising, disseminating state policy, and educating the people (Awad, 2000: 41). This planning coincided with the establishment of various departments in the two institutions. Both radio and television adopted the "program map" system. The television programs have a half-yearly rotation, while the radio cycle is four months. Each cycle has its structure and goals that change from one to another. In addition to these regular sessions, Sudan Radio and Television continued to hold special, designated programs for the month of Ramadan every year.

Programs percentage

According to the normal schedule of programs, from January through March, 20% of the material is political, 5% are varieties, 4% are cultural, 2% are news, and 1% in sports. There are details that all departments adhere to when offering the proposals, including the title of the program, name of the writer, nature of the program, objective, episode length, time of broadcasting, and replaying of episodes. In a closer look at the structures of the successive years, we find that Omdurman Radio and the channels that emerged from it provided more than a thousand titles through various programs. Each title carried a new idea that had not been introduced before. It also carried new methods of preparation and production techniques. Indeed, every title brings listeners information that may be new to them at times. Perhaps the average person cannot imagine the ordeal any producer goes through in searching for new content or the magnitude of effort exerted by them, the director, and any other person related to the program. Consistent failure to maintain interest or demand may simply mean the end of their career.

Training courses

There were no specialized training centers for broadcasters in Sudan until 1975. However, some intermittent courses were held in which some individuals from the Institute of Public Admin-istration and the Ministry of National Guidance trained the announcers and directors. Overseas training was carried out in some universities and institutes in West Germany, Egypt, Japan, the Netherlands, Britain, and France. After the establishment of the Sudan Academy of Communi-cation Sciences in 1991, training began to continue in it through specialized courses in various radio and TV arts. Since that period, broadcasters, directors, and news editors have found good opportunities. This was not limited to radio and television workers but went beyond this to train a number of state employees working in the radio and television sectors too.

Conclusion

The current state of Sudanese Radio and Television is a result of a myriad of changes across dec-ades. In terms of its future, stringent research has begun, since the overthrow of the government of President Omar Hassan Al-Bashir in 2019, to revolutionize the form and content of radio and television services in Sudan. This change will radically reduce the number of employees to around half. The committee in charge of developing a new radio and television law, however, had a different vision. They predominantly want the freedom of expression to be the basis on which programs operate. Ethnic and tribal diversity in Sudan will be taken into consideration in all services. Fundamentally, the nature of funding will transfer from full state subsidy to an independent economic body, perhaps establishing a more efficient network in the future of Sudanese media.

References

Abu Al-Aza'im, M. (1994), *Al-Sudan Al-Hadith Newspaper*, Saturday, December 31.

Ali Bakhit, J. F. (1972), *British Administration and the National Movement in Sudan 1919–1939*, Henry Riyad (trans.). Beirut: House of Culture.

Al-Khalifa, A. B., and Hariz, S. H. (1982), *Arabic and Local Languages on the Map of the Democratic Republic of Sudan*. Paper Presented in the First Conference for the Arabic Language in Sudan, Khartoum.

Al-Tijani, M. S. (1995), Forming Factors for the Sudanese National Character. *Journal of Sudanese Culture,* 28(May). National Authority for Culture and Arts.

Awad, I. A. (1983), *Political Programs in Radio and Television*. Unpublished Higher Diploma Project. College of Graduate Studies, University of Khartoum.

Awad, I. A. (1990), *Sudanese Radio in Half a Century*. Khartoum: Khartoum Publishing House.

Awad, I. A. (2000), *Language of Broadcasting: An Analytical Study*. Khartoum: University of Khartoum Publishing House.

Awad, I. A. (2019), *Sudan TV through the Years*. Khartoum: Dar Al-Mutman for Publishing and Writing.

Bashir, M. O. (1987), *History of the National Movement in Sudan*. Henry Riyad and others (trans.). 2nd edition. Beirut: Dar Al-Jeel.

Salih, M. S. (1971), *The Sudanese Press in a Half a Century 1903–1953*. Vol. 1. Khartoum: University of Khartoum Publishing House.

Shummo, A. M. (1999), *My Experience with Radio*. 1st edition. Khartoum: University of Medical and Technology Sciences Press.

Syria

32

THE SYRIAN PRESS AND ONLINE MEDIA

A driver of Arabism

Noha Mellor

Introduction

The history of the Syrian press should be chronicled as part of the history of Arabism and its ideology and identity. This is because Syria was the first independent Arab country, formed in the wake of the Arab revolution in 1918, which lasted until the French invasion in 1920. King Faisal (d. 1933) was promoted as the king of Arabs and Syria, and several newspapers were subsequently launched to propagate this Arab unity under his rule (Mrowe, 1961: 306). Before 1920, "Syria" or "Greater Syria" was a label referring to a larger region that encompassed Palestine, Lebanon, Jordan, and parts of Turkey and Iraq (Shoup, 2008). Syria, or what was known as Bilad ASham/Levant, has thus played a pivotal role in shaping the political and cultural context across a large part of what has become known as the Middle East. Modern Syria still has diverse ethnoreligious groups, including Arabs, Kurds, Armenians, and Circassians, who embrace different faiths, including Alawites, Ismailis, Druze, Christians, Yazidis, and Shi'a as well as Sunni Muslims; the latter constitute the majority of the population.

During Ottoman rule, many Syrian journalists from Greater Syria migrated to the center of the Ottoman Empire (Astana) and Egypt. Those who went to the Ottoman center were driven by Sultan Abdel Hamid II, who convinced them to launch newspapers promoting the idea of an Islamic League as a means of controlling the unity of the Arab populations and to combat European threats of agitating Arabs against the Ottomans (Abu Zeid, 1993: 22). Shafiq al-Moiyeed al-Azm set up *al-Ikhaa'* newspaper in January 1909, calling for equality of Turks and Arabs under the Ottoman rule; however, it was suspended after only a few issues (Abu Zeid, 1993: 23).

This chapter reviews the development of the Syrian press and online media, illustrating how these media were deployed mainly to enforce the vision of pan-Arabism and to lead a political struggle in the name of patriotism and later nationalism. The chapter argues that the historical function of the Syrian press was to promote unity in the form of pan-Arabism and, later, social-ism policies as the basis of equality. The Baath rule, since 1963, aimed to enforce a pan-Arab nationalist identity, deploying the press for this purpose. Following the death of Hafez al-Assad in 2000, his son Bashar al-Assad became president in 2001, and he promised media reforms; a few private media outlets were launched shortly after that, but the government resumed its crackdown on journalists, and the private outlets turned into semi-official voices for the government. Post-2011, there were many Syrian regions out of government's control, allowing opposition and anti-government media outlets to proliferate, mainly supported by international and particularly European donors. The chapter argues that Syrians have depended heavily on the Internet since the 2011 uprising, foreign media and social media sites being their main source of information. This is likely to continue in the future, even though the government has regained control of most of the Syrian territories.

The beginnings

Modern Syria was formed in 1916 under the Sykes-Picot agreement, following the collapse of the Ottoman Empire in the First World War, and was thereafter administered by France from 1921. By 1933, Syria had around 48 news outlets based in major Syrian cities (Mrowe, 1961: 314). In 1946, Syria declared independence and went through a series of military coups over 14 years. Three coups occurred in 1949 alone: the first was led by Hosni al-Za'eem, who decided to regulate the press via Decree 149 of 12 April 1949, in which he revoked the subsidies for several newspapers including *al-Balad*, *al-Kefah*, and *al-Arab*. This meant only a few newspapers were left to operate in the wake of the coup, and those included *al-Qabas*, *al-Ayyam*, *al-Shaab*, and *al-Manar*, perhaps due to their declared mission supporting the coup (Ilias, 1983: 73–74).

Another coup followed in August 1949, which prompted yet another decree allowing the newspapers that ceased operating in the previous year to resume their work, resulting in a wave of articles and caricatures attacking the previous coup and its leader al-Za'eem as the embodiment of dictatorship (Ilias, 1983: 75–76). A third coup took place in December of the same year. However, this was yet another disruptive event for the country in general and the press in particular. During the period of successive coups between 1946 and 1949, the Syrian press saw its role as either to praise each coup, to choose to withdraw from the market, or to eventually face closure (Mrowe, 1961: 308).

The Syrian government proposed a new bill to regulate the press in 1954, based on the previous 1949 law, but with some amendments such as penalizing periodicals that called for changing the country's constitution or promoting unconstitutional rule. The bill was opposed by many editors and parliamentarians such as Akram al-Hourani, who was to become one of the main figures in the new al-Baath Party (Mrowe, 1961: 319). The military leader Adib al-Shishkali, who led the third coup, was removed from power by 1954, and, by 1957, the Syrian press had been occupied with one vision – Arab unity – until a union between Egypt and Syria was officially announced in 1958. This was generally endorsed by the press except by the newspapers affiliated with either the Communist Party or the Muslim Brotherhood (Ilias, 1983: 93). The new law of 1958 aimed at reducing the number of media outlets and resulted in the closure of several periodicals; for instance, the total number of newspapers was reduced to only six in Damascus, five in Aleppo, and one in Homs (Mrowe, 1961: 309). One of the outlets closed down as a result of the new law was *al-Qabas*, owned by Najeeb al-Rayyes (Abu Zeid, 1993: 335); al-Rayyes (d. 1952) wrote for several publications in Damascus and Beirut; his *al-Qabas* was affiliated with the national anti-French movement. The reform aimed at dissolving political opposition and the affiliated party's press; the decree of 1958 offered Damascus-based newspaper owners to surrender their licenses in return for financial compensation decided by a special committee. If owners refused such offers, they would have to continue their operations without state subsidy, which meant financial hardships for these outlets. The aim behind that decree was to reduce the number of newspapers, and it was followed by a similar decree in 1960, targeting the newspapers and magazines in other regions of Syria (Ilias, 1983: 95). The union with Egypt was dissolved in 1961, and, two years later, the 8th of March uprising took place, bringing the Socialist Arab Baath Party to power. As one of its first official acts, the party issued a new decree suspending all newspapers in Syria except *al-Baath*, *al-Wahda al-Arabiya*, and *Barda*, and forming the Union/*Wahda* Printing Organization that issued *al-Thawra* newspaper (Ilias, 1983: 105). Hafez al-Assad, a member of the 1963 coup d'état and former prime minister, seized power as the president of Syria in 1971; since then, three main newspapers have remained the voice of the government: *al-Baath* (The Resurrection) established in 1946 as the Baath Party's mouthpiece; *al-Thawra* (The Revolution) in 1963; and *Tishreen* (October) created in 1974 in the wake of the Yom Kippur War.

After Baath

A few Syrian journalists settled overseas and set up newspapers or magazines to criticize the Syrian regime; for instance, in 1973, the Syrian Abdel Wahhab Fattal set up a periodical called *al-Sharq al-Jadid* (The New Orient), which was regarded as one of the first modern ventures of Arab émigré press. The monthly periodical was launched in London, printed on cheap blue paper and with a "primitive layout," which Fattal justified as part of the editorial philosophy to launch a periodical that did not depend on advertising money to ensure the freedom of its editor and contributors (Abu Zeid, 1993: 321). Fattal was a harsh critic of Gamal Abdel Nasser and the Egyptian–Syrian union (1958–1961); to avoid arrest, he fled to Saudi Arabia and lived under the protection of the Saudi King Faisal (d. 1975). It was the Saudi King Faisal who persuaded Fattal to settle in London and set up his periodical there; he provided him with the necessary financial help to establish the project. This explains why Fattal was able to use the periodical to attack all Arab regimes except Saudi Arabia (Abu Zeid, 1993: 323). Fattal believed in reviving Greater Syria, or one nation that included Syria, Lebanon, Iraq, Palestine, Jordan, and part of Cyprus. He therefore avidly defended the Palestinian issue and attacked all Arab regimes if they called for peaceful solutions with Israel (Abu Zeid, 1993: 324).

Fattal's example was followed by several other Syrian journalists who settled in Europe to launch their journalistic ventures attacking Arab policies. Ghassan Zakariyya, for example, set up a weekly called *Suraqia* (a combination of "Syria and Iraq") based on his own belief in Greater Syria (Abu Zeid, 1993: 331). The overseas Syrian press did not have the generous financial resources available to the Saudi or Iraqi press abroad; consequently, its impact was rather limited. This was further compounded by the Lebanese attack on this Syrian émigré press because of Syria's involvement and meddling in Lebanese affairs (Abu Zeid, 1993: 342).

The vision of the socialist Baathist regime was to create a sense of national identity that would unite all religious and ethnic groups; but, in so doing, it sought to force the nation to listen to the voice of the government, which prohibited any other voices of political opposition. The country was placed under emergency laws from the early 1960s up to the 2011 uprising, citing the dormant threats of Israel or different military groups targeting the State of Syria. These laws restricted private gatherings and resulted in human rights violations and the detention of any individual or groups suspected of endangering public security (BBC Media Action, 2012: 4).

In 1987, a Syrian editor said that the whole country had turned into one large intelligence apparatus, and so censorship prevailed; he argued that there were no longer journalists in Syria as "real Syrian journalists are either dead or living in exile, working for other Arab periodicals published in the West or the Middle East" (cited in MERIP, 1987: 42). The problem with the media sector, in general, was there were,

> no guidelines whatsoever for what cannot be included in artistic works. It is all accord-
> ing to someone's whim: the censor, a prominent party member, the president, the
> president's brother, and so on. In some instances, when the authorities like to be
> regarded as "revolutionary", they permit some songs, like those of Shaikh Imam of
> Egypt, or the poetry of the Iraqi, Mudhafar al-Nawab, not permitted anywhere else in
> the region, as long as they are not about the Syrian Baath Party.
>
> *(MERIP, 1987: 43)*

When Hafez al-Assad died in 2000, he was succeeded by his son Bashar al-Assad, who began his rule by promising more media freedom. This allowed the establishment of private media out-lets and the release of hundreds of political prisoners. The government's 1949 General Law of Printed Matter included more than 80 articles regulating all printed materials in Syria, except-ing those issued by state authorities. This law was reviewed in 2001 to allow for private owner-ship of the press and licensed with the prime minister's permission (Panos Institute, 2010: 13). To obtain a license to publish, the owner should be above the age of 25, a Syrian citizen, and a university graduate. The revised law (Law No. 50) ended the state monopoly of the press market, allowing over 150 private publications to be circulated in Syria, of which the majority dealt with economic or cultural affairs (ibid.). Such private outlets included *Al-Iqtissad* (The Economy), the satirical weekly, *al-Doumari*, published by a famous Syrian cartoonist, Ali Farzat, the daily *al-Watan*, the weekly *Abyad wa Aswad*, *Baladna* magazine, as well as private broadcast-ing ventures (IREX, 2005: 124). Those outlets attracted new Syrian talent as aspiring journal-ists, but the lack of healthy competition and adequate recruitment procedures led to overstaffing and a large number of those carrying press cards who had never practiced journalism (Panos Institute, 2010: 22).

It was not long, however, before the government resumed its usual measures of clamping down on civil society and private media, particularly post-2005 (BBC Media Action, 2012: 4). The year 2005 experienced a period of turmoil with the assassination of Lebanese Prime Minister Rafik al-Hariri in February – the Syrian regime being the prime suspect. The assas-sination led to the withdrawal of Syrian troops from Lebanon, after a long military presence since the end of the Lebanese civil war (in 1990). Syria scrutinized many journalists and outlets to filter out any negative depictions of the government or any adverse implications in the wake of al-Hariri's assassination. This scrutiny led to the closing down of several privately owned magazines and the arrest of several journalists (IREX, 2005: 119).

Although the Syrian constitution "guarantees" the freedom of the press (Art. 38), journal-ists and other professionals did not enjoy free speech in Syria, fearing the Emergency Laws permitting the government to detain any individual or group without a fair trial (IREX, 2005: 120). For example, Ibrahim Hamidi, the Damascus correspondent for *Al Hayat*, was detained for five months in 2002, following his report on Iraqi refugees in Syria; Shaaban Abboud, a Damascus-based reporter for the Lebanese newspaper *al-Nahar*, was detained in 2006, follow-ing his report on transfers within the Syrian military. Journalists were also pursued in libel cases under the Printing Law, which could result in prison or a hefty fine (IREX, 2005: 122). The Syrian Union of Journalists was typically unable to protect journalists prior to the 2011 upris-ing; instead, individual journalists would lobby the Syrian courts on behalf of a detained col-league (IREX, 2005: 126).

Post-2011 uprising

The Lebanese veteran Adeeb Mrowe (1961: 254) wrote in 1961 that, unlike the European and American press, the Arab press did not manage to attract investments and therefore remained the work of thinkers and intellectuals. Thus, the total number of Syrian newspapers was limited: going from seven outlets in 1986 (Al-Jammal, 2001: 94) to 10 outlets in 1992 (Singhal and Krishna, 1994: 265), and that was roughly the number of outlets also recorded in 2009 (BBC Media Action, 2012: 4). However, this situation has notably changed post-2011.

Following the uprisings that began in Tunisia in December 2010, which then moved to Egypt by January 2011, protests erupted in Syria in March 2011 in the town of Dera'a, before moving to other hotspots like Homs and Hama (Salama, 2012: 517). The Syrians longed for new outlets to satisfy their need for information regarding the extent of the uprisings, or, as a Syrian journalist put it, "before the [uprising] the media was of no importance to people, now people are reading and discussing the news and commenting on it from all sides" (cited in BBC Media Action, 2012: 2). By 2015, according to a survey of the active media in Syria since 2011, there were 343 active media organizations in Syria, but many of them faced closure due to the withdrawal of donor funding (Free Press Unlimited, 2016: 4); it is generally claimed that only 23% of all publications managed to maintain their services (Dollet, 2015: 4). The main two donors were the Association for the Support of Free Media (ASML) and the Syrian NGO Basma that provided training courses for journalists. Basma was created in 2012 by the Qatari-British company Access Research Knowledge (ARK) and was active until late 2013 (Dollet, 2015: 6). The European Union has also backed several media projects through the European Instrument for Democracy and Human Rights. The EU states have provided support through several international organizations such as CFI, InterNews, Free Press Unlimited, Reporters Without Borders, IREX, Institute for War and Peace Reporting, and International Media Support (Dollet, 2015: 6). It is argued that the lack of transparency of donors' funding strategies resulted in "unhelpful competition between the different newspapers" and it was, therefore, difficult "to foster cohesion and a spirit of solidarity under these conditions" (Dollet, 2015: 13).

The Syrian president approved a new media law in 2011 to establish the National Media Council (NMC) to regulate the media sector and approve the licenses for private media outlets. According to Article 12 of that new regulation, media outlets are prohibited from publishing content that is harmful to religious unity or publishing information relating to the armed forces except that issued by the army itself. Articles 14 and 16 prohibit media organizations to receive money or subsidies from any party, including foreign donors (al-Thawra Online, 2012). The NMC, however, was claimed to lack independence and maintains a strict licensing system to monitor outlets critical of the regime (Trombetta, 2018). The Syrian government endorsed the new constitution in 2012. This was put to a referendum which abolished Article 8 entrenching the political power of the Baath Party. The new constitution grants freedom of expression and prevents the monopoly of the media, but it still gives the state the right to ban media spreading content that is deemed to be harmful to national unity. The government still has the sole right to grant media licenses to organizations operating within the government-controlled areas. The Emergency Law was repealed in the same year and was replaced by the Counter-terrorism Law; this virtually reinstated the state's emergency powers to arrest civilians accused of promoting terrorist activities.

Since 2011, Syrians have depended on foreign news, the Internet, and social media sites as their main sources of information. The government-controlled media, however, remains one main source of news, particularly in the regions controlled by the government (Free Press

Unlimited, 2016: 7). Social media sites such as Facebook hosted several Syrian groups; and although they were not particularly effective as mobilization tools, they could still be used to gather Syrians around some requests (de Angelis, 2011: 105).

Syrians have had access to various news sources including newspapers, online news, and broadcasting channels representing Syrian as well as pan-Arab media outlets. In the government-controlled regions, Syrians tend to favor pro-government news sources, whereas regions that are under opposition control favor other sources (Free Press Unlimited, 2016: 7). In Aleppo, opposition newspapers compete with government ones, while opposition newspapers dominate in other regions such as Idlib (ibid, p. 7); in addition, several outlets are based outside Syria, particularly in the Turkish town of Gaziantep which serves as a hub for such outlets (Dollet, 2015: 2). The editorial content varies across publications, with some of them focusing heavily on politics such as *Koluna Soryyoun*; others focus on human rights such as *Tamaddon* or *Suwar*, or social issues such as *Enab Baladi* or *Souriatna*; some publications are targeted at women such as *Saydet Souria*, or people in the Kurdish region such as *Shar* magazine (Dollet, 2015: 5). One of the successful publications was *Souriatna*, a weekly publication distributed in government and opposition territories. The publication turned to online reporting, however, after a few issues, due to security concerns on the ground, which made it difficult to distribute the print copies (Marrouch, 2014: 10). The publication hosts contributions from a range of young journalists, citizen journalists, and aspiring writers and is edited by a professional journalist.

There are no accurate distribution figures for these publications: they vary between 3,000 and 7,000 copies per issue, with many of them being printed in Turkey before distribution in Northern Syria; others chose to combine the two options of printing in Syria and/or Turkey to maximize their outreach (Dollet, 2015: 8).

The so-called ISIS/ISIL took control over Raqqa by 2014 and expanded the territories under its direct control by forming new media ventures as their official mouthpiece, including a weekly online magazine called *Dabiq* (Marrouch, 2014: 14).

News agencies

The main news agency in Syria was the Syrian Arab News Agency (SANA), set up in 1965 and controlled by the government, before the 2011 uprising. SANA is affiliated with the Ministry of Information and is based in Damascus. It aims to provide news and reports about Syrian affairs; it has offices overseas including in Lebanon, Russia, Jordan, Iran, Egypt, Kuwait, and Turkey, and has more than 43 correspondents across the world; it produces bulletins in English, French, Spanish, Turkish, and Russian.[1]

Post-2011, however, there has been a notable rise in the number of news agencies operated by the opposition and other groups, including citizen journalists. Media networks mushroomed in almost all Syrian territories by sending content to media channels around the world; for instance, Aleppo had 10 media agencies, and, in 2013, the Free Syria News Agency (FSNA) announced that there were more than 39 civilian media offices in the city of Raqqa alone (Dollet, 2015: 2). The Syrian Network for Prints (SNP) was launched in 2014 with support from the French CFI Media Development and the Danish International Media Support. It hosted publications such as *Sada Al-Sham*, *Enab Baladi*, *Tamaddun*, *Koluna Soryyoun*, and *Souriatna*, and later included *'Ayn Al-Madina* and *Zaiton* (Dollet, 2015: 7). A second network was set in December 2014, called Alliance of Light (*Tahaluf al-Daw*), to host magazines such as *Dawda*, *Saydet Souria*, *Henta*, the teen publication *Hentawi*, and the bilingual Kurdish/Arabic magazine *Shar* (Dollet, 2015: 8). Many Western donors provided training workshops which peaked in

2013 and 2014 and were usually held in Turkey or Lebanon for aspiring Syrian journalists and activists coming from areas no longer under government control (Trombetta, 2018).

There were other agencies set up post-2011, including Free News Agency (*al-Wikala al-hurra lilanbaa*); SMART News Agency based in Turkey, supported by CFI Media Development, and the Independent Press Agency/*Ajansa Rojnamevaniya Azad* (ARA), based in the Kurdish region, and set up in 2013; Hawar News Agency (ANHA), which is another online Kurdish news service aligned with the Democratic Union Party or PYD, a Kurdish democratic political party created in 2003; and ANHWA producing news in Arabic, English, Kurdish, Turkish, and Russian. Besides, there was *Aamaq* News Agency, which is affiliated with the so-called Islamic State (Trombetta, 2018).

The main official journalists' syndicate is the *Ittihad al-Sahafiyoun fi Souriya* or the Union of Journalists in Syria (SJU), created in 1974 and regulated by the General Federation of Trade Unions.[2] The then head of Syrian Journalists' Syndicate said in an interview carried out in 2009 that the main aim of the syndicate is not to unite professionals but patriots:

> It is not a professional but a national syndicate. I'm not ready to give any journalist who is not patriotic the card of a contributing or working journalist. If a journalist works inside Syria and criticizes, then there is no problem. But if you work for an external newspaper that fabricates bad news about our nation, I won't protect you nor give you a card.
>
> *(cited in Pies and Madanat, 2011: 7)*

In 2012, however, another union was created, namely, the Syrian Journalists Association (SJA), declaring its mission as "to empower the role of freedom of the press and expression in Syria as well as developing professional skills for the sector and primarily for all members."[3] It is funded by several international organizations including the Swedish International Development Cooperation Agency (SIDA), the International Federation of Journalists (IFJ), Syndicat National des Journalistes (SNJ), and the Accuracy Press Institute (API). There is also the Kurdistan Journalists' Syndicate, which set up its Syrian branch in 2013 defending Kurdish journalists in Syria and Iraq (Trombetta, 2018). The Kurdish Supreme Committee that controls the Kurdish majority areas in Syria set up the Union of Free Media/*Yekîtiya Ragihandina Azad* (YRA) in 2014, to oversee media organizations working in the Rojava area. All news media operating in Kurdish cantons would be requested to apply for permits from the YRA. It is claimed, however, that the Democratic Union Party (PYD) controls the YRA and the news providers in the region, especially those that may be producing content critical of the PYD (Trombetta, 2018).

Syrians in diaspora communities formed their networks on new and social media sites, to circulate news about the situation inside Syria; one Syrian student who fled to Turkey expressed this role of diaspora communities as follows: "Outside Syria, we feel two things: one is that we have the responsibility to show to the world what is going on in Syria, and publish it. The other feeling is that we've left our friends alone there" (cited in Andén-Papadopoulos and Pantti, 2013: 2190). Diaspora Syrians ran several news channels including Shaam News Network (SNN), the Activist News Association, and Ugarit News, distributing citizen-created content captured from inside Syria. SNN was first declared one key source of information about the Syrian conflict when *The Christian Science Monitor* and *The Wall Street Journal* attributed the information to SNN back in April 2011 (Wall and el Zahed, 2014). Shaam Network was claimed to be one of the most reliable services; it passed its information via Skype through a well-organized system with a large network of contributors across the country (Marrouch,

2014: 9). Shaam Network began distributing its first weekly newspaper in February 2013; it was printed in Turkey and distributed across Northern Syria (Wall and el Zahed, 2014).

There were other social media sites such as "the Syrian Revolution 2011" on Facebook and YouTube, administered by three Syrians living in Sweden and claiming to have serviced international outlets such as the BBC, CNN, and Al Jazeera (Andén-Papadopoulos and Pantti, 2013: 2193). Aleppo News Service (ANN), another successful network, launched its Facebook page on 27 March 2011, in addition to other local information services such as the Baba Amro News Network in Homs created on Facebook in 2012 and Lattakia News Network created in June 2011 (Wall and el Zahed, 2014).

New media – from prohibitions to chaos

In 2000, the Internet was forbidden to all except a few high officials, and some sites were blocked, especially those that were critical of the Syrian regime (IREX, 2005: 122). However, access to the Internet improved after 2005, and Syrians, particularly the young generation, were following popular sites like *DamasPost* or *Aljamal* news sites. New online magazines were also launched such as *al-Balad* and *al-Watan*, although still censored by the regime (Marrouch, 2014: 6). A few private online news sites were active in Syria by 2010, such as *Shaku Maku*, owned by Onyxar Group and linked to Sulayman Maaruf, who was the agent for Honda in Syria and also had shares in one of the first private television channels in Syria, al-Dunia. Rami Makhlouf, President Bashar al-Assad's cousin, owned another site called Shaam News, as part of his Ninar group which owned radio Ninar and Shaam FM, and Ninar TV; another site was *Suria al-Ghad* owned by Syriana Group which was headed by the son of a former minister of defense; other websites included *Dpress*, *Cham Press*, and *al-Jamal* (de Angelis, 2011: 113).

According to the International Telecommunication Union, the percentage of Syrians using the Internet has increased significantly over the past decade, going from nearly 8% in 2006 to nearly 32% in 2016.[4] The number of Syrian sites in 2009 was claimed to be 2,500, of which about 140 were information websites (Pies and Madanat, 2011: 10). Syrian bloggers at that time wrote primarily about domestic political issues; most bloggers were men and the majority were in the age bracket of 25–35 years (Etling et al., 2009: 25).

Journalists also used the Internet to express their dissent, but they faced government repression. By the end of 2009, more than 240 sites were banned in Syria, including the blog-hosting platform Blogger.com, as well as social media sites such as Twitter and Facebook. The government then extended the Press Law introduced in 2005, which introduced punitive measures against electronic publications. It also stipulated that these should only be staffed by Syrian nationals, who may not be employed by a foreign government. The proposed 2009 law extended those penalties to include jail sentences. The blogger Karim Arbaji was imprisoned for three years in September 2009; he was charged with undermining national morale (Freedom House, 2010). The government approved a new Internet law in 2010, which would give the authorities the right to raid the offices of online journalists and bloggers and seize materials; bloggers could also face criminal charges if successfully prosecuted (BBC Media Action, 2012: 8). The Syrian government, however, lifted the ban on blocked websites in February 2011 (Pies and Madanat, 2011: 4).

The US government launched the Independent Media in Syria program in 2012. It began under the auspices of the Bureau of Conflict and Stabilization Operations (CSO) and later moved to Near Eastern Affairs, US State Department in 2015, aiming to support the development of independent media, strengthening civil society, and improving accountability; the estimated annual expenditure of the program was US $12–13 million (Issa, 2016: 21–23). There was also support provided by European partners such as the Dutch-based Free Press Unlimited, BBC Media Action, Canal France Internationale, the German-based Media in Cooperation & Transition, and the Italian-based Coordinamento delle Organizzazioni per il Servizio Volontario (Issa, 2016: 22).

The Syrian media landscape was rather chaotic, post-2011, with tens, and later hundreds, of groups reporting on the ground, and developed with external funding into more organized media outlets (Issa, 2016: 5). The number of active media outlets was well over 196, including pro-opposition, independent, pro-regime, and independent Kurdish outlets. The numbers of pro-opposition and pro-regime were nearly equal, at around 71 outlets each (Issa, 2016: 14). Newspapers and radio services flourished in rebel-held areas due to the lack of electricity and access to web-based media services. It is estimated that the majority of independent media (72% out of 39 outlets including press and broadcasting) are classified as traditional media, whereas the majority of pro-opposition media outlets are based online (63%) outside Syria, targeting Syrian diaspora and Syrian refugees abroad (Issa, 2016: 14).

Post-2011, Syria also became one of the most dangerous places for journalists. They faced threats of killing or kidnapping across most of the country. That was especially the case in the territories that used to be controlled by the so-called ISIS and Jabhat Fatah al-Shaam, which were high-risk territories for kidnapping, so foreign journalists used to depend heavily on local counterparts to gather news. Syrian journalists faced more violence than did foreign journalists, according to the Committee to Protect Journalists (CPJ), as the majority of those subjected to kidnapping, violence, or killing were local reporters. Between 2012 and 2014, journalists murdered in Syria outnumbered those in the rest of the world. The number declined in 2015, mainly because fewer journalists were working in Syria, with many of them fleeing into exile (CPJ, 2015).

The Kurdish press has also seen an increase in the number of Kurdish outlets since 2011. The Syrian Kurdish press is said to have begun in 1932 with a bi-monthly magazine called *Hawar* (Cry), launched in Damascus with permission from the government; but it ceased in 1942 and was replaced by the monthly *Ronahi* (Light) in May 1943, which also ceased after only two years. Following the establishment of the Kurdish Democratic Party in 1957, a newspaper, *Danke Kurd* (Voice of the Kurds), was launched around two years later, but the fissure within the party led to its split into different groups, each with its own monthly periodical, mostly in Arabic (Yousef, 2018). There were several Kurdish press ventures launched by the 1990s, albeit operating underground, with many writers using pseudonyms. These lasted until the Qamshili uprising in 2004 and the Syrian army crackdown on Kurdish demonstrators. The events led to the arrest of several Kurdish intellectuals and the burning of their books and bulletins (Yousef, 2018). Following the 2011 uprising, many Kurdish newspapers resurfaced, using the Internet as the new preferred platform. On the other hand, many ventures closed such as *Shar* magazine, created in 2014, *Boweir*/Event magazine, and *Jawan* newspaper, created by the Kurdish Youth movement in July 2015, due to lack of funding (Yousef, 2018).

Conclusion

Syria's history is closely linked to the history of Lebanon, Jordan, Iraq, and Palestine, or what used to be called Greater Syria. Syria has been a melting pot for many cultures, including ethnic and religious groups. The historical function of the Syrian press was to promote unity in the form of pan-Arabism and later, socialism policies as the basis of equality. It was also characterized by its constant struggle to liberate Arab nations from foreign rule (Ottoman reign and later European colonialism). Thus, its main function was to lead a political struggle and not to sell the news. In so doing, the press was not about journalistic practices but patriotism and nationalism (Mrowe, 1961: 255).

The vision of both the Baath regime since 1963 and Hafez al-Assad's accession to power in 1971 was to create a pan-Arab nationalist identity. As part of that vision, political opposition voices were silenced, so that the government's official press would dominate the Syrian media scene. The country was placed under emergency laws between the early 1960s and 2011, which restricted private gatherings on the pretext that such gatherings could compromise public security. Following the death of Hafez al-Assad in 2000, his son Bashar al-Assad became president in 2001 and promised to relax these restrictive laws and allow more media freedom. A few private media outlets were launched shortly after that, but the government resumed its crackdown on journalists, and the private outlets turned into semi-official voices for the government. There were many Syrian regions out of government control by the 2011 uprising, allowing opposition and anti-government media outlets to proliferate, mainly supported by international and particularly European donors. It was estimated that there were more than 340 active media organizations in Syria by 2015; however, many of these outlets have been closed in the past few years due to funding cuts. Syrians have depended heavily on the Internet since the 2011 uprising; foreign media and social media sites being their main source of information. This is likely to continue in the future, even though the government has regained control of most of the Syrian territories.

The sad fact is that the civil and proxy wars have caused immense losses in Syria, both human and financial. The population of Syria was estimated at 22 million in 2010, but that figure declined to about 16 million in 2016 as a consequence of the civil and proxy wars waged on the country since 2011; half of the population was forced to move: seven million have been internally displaced, and between four and five million refugees have fled overseas (*The Economist*, 2015). It is estimated that more than $255 billion is needed to rebuild Syria, which is more than 468% of the country's GDP in 2010 (Issa, 2016: 1). This is going to be the main challenge facing Syria in the future.

Notes

1 www.sana.sy
2 http://journalists-u.org.sy/
3 www.syja.org/en/home
4 www.itu.int/en/ITU-D/Statistics/Pages/stat/default.aspx

References

Abu Zeid, Farouq (1993), *al-Sahafa al-Arabiyya al-Muhajira* (Arab Émigré Press). Cairo: Alam al-Kutub.
Al-Jammal, Rasem Mohammad (2001), *Al-Ittisal wal-'Ilam fil Watan al-Arabi* (Communication and Media in the Arab World). 2nd edition. Beirut: Center for Arab Unity Studies.
Al-Thawra Online (2012), Qanoun al-I'lam fi Souriya (Syria's Media Laws). *al-Thawra*, 24 April. Retrieved from http://thawraonline.sy/index.php/plan-and-update-list/3804-2012-04-24-11-17-39
Andén-Papadopoulos, Kari, and Pantti, Mervi (2013), The Media Work of Syrian Diaspora Activists: Brokering Between the Protest and Mainstream Media. *International Journal of Communication*, 7, pp. 2185–2206.
BBC Media Action (2012), *Country Case Study: Syria – Support to Media Where Media Freedoms and Rights are Constrained*, August. London: BBC Media Action.
CPJ (2015), Journalists Killed, Syria and France Most Deadly Countries for the Press. *The Committee to Protect Journalists*, 29 December. Retrieved from https://cpj.org/reports/2015/12/journalists-killed-syria-france-most-deadly-countries-for-the-press.php

De Angelis, Enrico (2011), Syrian News Websites: A Negotiated Identity. *Oriente Moderno*, Nuova serie, Anno 91, Nr. 1, between Everyday Life and Political Revolution: The Social Web in the Middle East, pp. 105–124.

Dollet, Soazig (2015), *The New Syrian Press. Appraisal, Challenges, and Outlook*. CFI Media Development. Retrieved from www.cfi.fr/sites/default/files/etude_presse_syrienne_EN.pdf

Economist (2015), Syria's Drained Population. *The Economist*, 30 September. Retrieved from www.econo mist.com/graphic-detail/2015/09/30/syrias-drained-population

Etling, Bruce, Kelly, John, Faris, Robert, and Palfrey, John (2009), *Mapping the Arabic Blogosphere: Politics, Culture, and Dissent*. Berkman Center Research Publication No. 2009–06, June.

Free Press Unlimited (2016), *Syria Audience Research 2016*. Retrieved from www.freepressunlimited.org/en/news/syria-audience-research-2016

Freedom House (2010), *Syria Press Report*. Retrieved from https://freedomhouse.org/report/freedom-press/2010/syria

Ilias, Joseph (1983), *Tatouwur al-Sahafa al-Souriya fi mi'at aam: 1865–1965* (The Development of the Syrian Press in 100 Years – 1865–1965). Vol 2. Beirut: Dar al-Nedal.

IREX (2005), *Media Sustainability Index – the Middle East and North Africa*. Washington, DC: IREX

Issa, Antoun (2016), Syria's New Media Landscape – Independent Media Born Out of War. *MEI Policy Paper* 2016–9, December. Washington, DC: Middle East Institute.

Marrouch, Rima (2014), *Syria's Post-uprising Media Outlets: Challenges and Opportunities in Syrian Radio Start-ups*. Oxford: Reuters Institute for the Study of Journalism.

MERIP (1987), A Censor's Testimony: Journalists in Syria are an Extinct Species. *MERIP Middle East Report*, No. 149, Human Rights in the Middle East (November–December), pp. 42–43.

Mrowe, Adeeb (1961), *al-Sahafa al-Arabiya* (The Arab Press). Beirut: Dar al-Hayat (in Arabic).

Panos Institute (2010), *The Syrian Media Environment: A Stability*. Collection Media pour le pluralisme en Méditerranée. Paris: Panos Institute.

Pies, Judith, and Madanat, Philip (2011), *Media Accountability Practices Online in Syria. An Indicator for Changing Perceptions of Journalism*, MediaAcT Working Paper 10/2011. Journalism Research and Development Centre, University of Tampere, Finland.

Salama, Vivian (2012), Covering Syria. *The International Journal of Press/Politics*, 17(4), pp. 516–526.

Shoup, John A. (2008), *Culture and Customs of Syria*. Westport, CT: Greenwood Press.

Singhal, Arvind, and Krishna, Vijay (1994), Syria. In Yahya Kamalipour and Hamid Mowlana (eds.), *Mass Media in the Middle East*. Westport, CT: Greenwood Press.

Trombetta, Lorenzo (2018), Syria – Media Landscape. *The European Journalism Centre (EJC)*. Retrieved from https://medialandscapes.org/country/syria

Wall, Melissa, and el Zahed, Sahar (2014), Syrian Citizen Journalism. *Journalism*, 16(2), pp. 163–180.

Yousef, Emad (2018), Nabza moukhtasara aan waqea' al-sahafa al-kurdiyya (Short Expose about the Kurdish Press). *Rok Online*, 22 April. Retrieved from www.rok-online.com/?p=13417

33

THE "SOFT" POWER OF SYRIAN BROADCASTING

Nour Halabi and Noha Mellor

Introduction

In March 2011, Syrians took to the street to voice their protest against the Baathist regime; their anger was not only directed at the regime but also the national media. They chanted "Syrian media are liars," expressing their frustration with the state media as well as the private media, which was set up by businessmen with close ties to the regime (al-Asi, 2019). The official media narrative has told Syrians that protestors were part of a foreign conspiracy against Syria, and therefore the regime and its cronies set up "an electronic army" to disseminate propaganda online, propagating that official narrative and questioning the integrity of Syrians opposing the regime (al-Asi, 2019). Since then, numerous media ventures have been launched mainly from Turkey and other countries where Syrians have taken refuge.

This chapter sheds light on the development of the Syrian broadcasting sector, entrusted with the main task of promoting a Baathist ideology rather than debating acute social and political problems or developing a unique Syrian journalistic culture. This function is reminiscent of that of the Syrian press, as we saw in the previous chapter. However, the Syrian broadcasting sector has a unique characteristic, in contrast to the press, and this is its success in competing with other Arab broadcasters in producing television drama catering to the pan-Arab satellite channels that have kept sprouting across the region since the mid-1990s.

The chapter is divided into two sections: the first half begins with a short overview of the Syrian broadcasting sector, including recent developments since 2011. The latter half of the chapter is dedicated to a discussion about the development of the Syrian television drama, as a hallmark of the Syrian identity and soft power.

The voice of Arabism

Radio broadcasting began in 1946 when the General Broadcasting Organization was formed, and the Syrian national television was first launched as a joint venture between the Syrian and Egyptian revolutionary unitary governments on 23 July 1960; in fact, both countries shared official television broadcast in July 1960. During the brief period of the union (1958–1961), Syrian broadcasters benefited from the advanced Egyptian broadcasting and technical experience cultivated in the thriving film industry, and many radio employees came from Egypt and Syrian media officials went to Egypt for training. However, the union collapsed in 1961.

From its inception, television broadcasting in Syria was regarded as an important component of the new political alignment of the two nations. The audiovisual transmission was first introduced in Damascus and rolled over to other provinces over time. The earliest television production was completed in studios in neighboring Lebanon, until television production studios were opened throughout the country (Qaddour, 2009). At the time, television broadcasting was restricted to a few hours a day, featuring shows that focused on groups within the Baathist society, such as farmers, workers, students, and Baath youth. By 1967, "television stations across all the major cities of Syria were connected by a microwave link and transmission links were set up in most of the Syrian regions" (Dajani, 2005: 584). In the 1970s, Syria television expanded with the installation of submitters across Syria. By 1992, at least 80% of Syrians owned a TV set to watch the state's two major national channels, and there were 29 transmitters and three million receivers. At the time, Syrian radio programs were produced in a few languages in addition to Arabic, such as Russian, Hebrew, French, and English (Singhal and Krishna, 1994: 264–267).

The broadcasting sector was regulated in 1951 with Decree No. 68 and was directly under the control of the prime minister. Later, the control was transferred to the Ministry of Information, established in 1961. The law was amended several times, such as in 2001 (Decree No. 50) to allow commercial and private ownership of radio and television stations, limited to entertainment shows. The decree came a year after Bashar al-Assad's ascension to power and his announcement of a freer media sphere. The prime minister and the minister of information would still hold the right to issue new licenses or revoke licenses for reasons related to the public interest; subsequently, seven radio FM stations obtained licenses since that amendment (Panos Institute, 2012: 49), including Arabesque, Sham, Mix FM, and al-Madina FM. They were generally prohibited from broadcasting news and political debates, but Sham FM used to broadcast radio shows based on interviews with local officials (Marrouch, 2014: 16). On the other hand, the public stations are controlled by the General Organization for Radio and Television, whose portfolio includes Voice of Youth radio station, Damascus Radio, and Drama Radio, as well as six television channels including two satellite channels. Syrian licensed television channels include al-Oula, al-Thanniyya, Syrian Drama TV, Syria satellite TV, Noor al-Sham, Massaya TV, Sham TV, Arrai TV, Sama TV (which replaced, Addounia TV in 2012 after the latter was dissolved), al-Ikhbariyya (News), and Syrian Educational TV. In addition, Orient TV was set up in 2008 by a Syrian businessman, Ghassan Abboud, who opposed the regime; the channel broadcast from the UAE but had reporters inside Syria. However, the regime closed its office in Damascus in 2010 following the increasing popularity of its talk shows dedicated to discussing acute social, economic, and cultural issues in Syria.

Generally, the state broadcasting media have suffered from decades of bureaucracy, overstaffing, and lack of technical skills, compounded with the regime suppression of critical journalism, which explains why the news bulletins broadcast on national television channels usually lack investigative content (Panos Institute, 2012: 16). The notable increase of pan-Arab satellite channels in the mid-1990s forced Syrian broadcasters to improve their content to appeal not only to local audiences but also to those across the region, particularly with regards to drama production, as we shall discuss later.

The 2011 uprising and the fragmentation of Syrian media

With funding from European donors, at least 100 Syrian media ventures were launched since March 2011, including numerous TV channels and more than 20 radio stations (Marrouch, 2014: 13). Among the numerous radio stations was Souriali, which was funded by PAX Christi, IWPR, British Council, and the Washington-based National Endowment for Democracy;

similarly, Hawa Smart radio received funding from the Asfari Foundation (Marrouch, 2014: 26). Clusters of various media ventures also merged to form networks sharing resources and expertise, and such collaboration was deemed necessary to ensure solidarity in hazardous zones. For instance, the Syrian Media Action Revolution Team (SMART) was launched in 2011 as a network for journalists/activists and later turned into a news agency (Daher, 2017). In 2014, the ABRAJ network of six Syrian radio stations was launched with support from European funders (IMS, 2014). Some of these new media ventures catered for certain audience segments; for instance, the radio station Nasem Souriya produced shows targeting women and conflict; ARTA FM was another community radio in the Kurdish region of al-Hassakah, which ran an academy to train women radio journalists (IMS, 2014). Radio Rozana, launched in 2014, is another independent station broadcasting from outside Syria and targeting Syrian diasporas. The Copenhagen-based International Media Support (IMS) funded Radio Rozana, covering staff salaries, while the French Channel France International (CFI) offered training to Rozana staff (Marrouch, 2014); on its website[1] the outlet lists several other donors, including the Open Society and Asfari Foundation. Moreover, the Kurdish parties – Kurdish Democratic Union Party (PYD) and the Kurdistan Democratic Party of Syria (KDP) – set up a few stations; for instance, there is the PYD-affiliated Ronahi TV set up in 2012, in addition to Radio Arta, Orkes FM, and Hawar News Agency (Daher, 2017). The Kurdish Arta FM was claimed to capture a large share of listeners in 2015, particularly in Aleppo, Idlib, and al-Hassakah (Trombetta, 2018).

Already in 2014, there were more than 20 radio stations set up during various stages of the protests. Activist groups set up their outlets, such as numerous local radio stations inside and outside Syria, including Radio Fresh, set up by Raed Fares in Idlib, Sawt Raya, based in Istanbul and founded by Alisar Hasan, and ANA Radio set up in 2012 by ANA New Media Association; ANA was found by a Syrian-British journalist, Rami Jarrah, who managed to send field reports from inside Syria, and several of his articles to Western media were penned under the name Alexander Page. Many independent media outlets are registered as commercial production companies in Turkey or as NGOs in Europe. However, the numerous outlets meant that there was fierce competition among the newly established radio stations, not to mention that the maintenance of FM transmitters and towers posed a real technical problem to radio stations.

Other media ventures include Halab TV, which primarily covers the situation in Halab/Aleppo and has offices in Turkey and around 30 correspondents in Aleppo. Its staff work for both the television and a radio station carrying the name Halab Today. There is also Deir el-Zor TV, which changed its name to al-Jisr TV broadcasting from Istanbul; it used to focus primarily on news about the Deir el-Zor area in eastern Syria, but it later offered news covering all Syria, although it allegedly did not have a large audience base inside Syria (Marrouch, 2014). Other channels include Syria al-Shaab and Syria al-Ghad; the former operated from Jordan but was closed down due to lack of funding, and the latter operated from Cairo before June 2013 and the toppling of the Muslim Brotherhood's rule. The station was then forced to close down in 2015 (Marrouch, 2014: 12).

In 2011, the government was planning to substitute the satellite dishes with centralized cable TV systems to curb the Syrians' receiving of information from pan-Arab channels such as Al Jazeera and al-Arabiya, but the plan was never materialized. On the other hand, pro-regime outlets were set up by Syria's media conglomerates closely connected to the regime, including Rami Makhlouf, Majd Bahjat Sulayman, Bilal Turkmani, and Ayman Jaber. Makhlouf set up *al-Watan* newspaper already in 2006, while Jaber co-founded Addounia TV, which was later replaced by Sama satellite channel (Daher, 2017). Those businessmen used their outlets to launch a campaign undermining the protesters' demands ever since the beginning of the uprising in 2011. In addition, the Beirut-based, pro-Syrian al-Mayadeen TV, as well as the Russian RT Arabic, allegedly offset the anti-regime campaigns spearheaded by some pan-Arab channels owned by Qatar and Saudi Arabia (Trombetta, 2018). Pro-regime outlets, moreover, have had to face sanctions; for instance, Addounia, owned by several businessmen with close ties to the regime, was subjected to sanctions imposed by the EU, USA, and the Arab League. In 2012, Addounia and other pro-Syrian channels were removed from both Arabsat and Nilesat satellites, but it was later relaunched under the name Sama TV.

There are no reliable audience surveys, but according to a recent report (Free Press Unlimited, 2016), radio stations are followed by roughly half of Syrians included in the report, and the pro-government stations seem to dominate the list of the most followed stations, along with Radio Fresh. Among the most popular television channels are Halab al-Youm and Orient, as well as the pro-government channels Sama TV, al-Ikhbariya, and Syria Satellite TV, especially in the government-held region. Interestingly, pro-government media are also followed by a significant minority in the opposition-held regions (Free Press Unlimited, 2016). Anti-government channels, particularly Halab al-Youm and Orient TV, were also among the most watched in the opposition-held areas but are hardly watched in the government-controlled areas.

Meanwhile, state media have been under immense financial and professional pressures. For instance, in April 2019, the Syrian Ministry of Information published a list of acceptable fees for journalists inside Syria, according to which a reporter can claim only 45 Syrian lira for writing one report, which means 10 reports would amount to less than US $1; a correspondent can claim 375 lira or US $0.70, while a field report can be remunerated for 750 Lira or nearly US $1.50 (al-Sharq al Awsat, 2019). The modest fee structure was revealed following the minister of information's announcement that the 2019 budget would include wage and fee increases for those working in the media sector (al-Alam, 2018). This shows the difficulty which journalists have had to endure to sustain themselves under the current financial lockdown. This was why the regime has reportedly resorted to coercive extortion of money from close allies; for instance, in 2019, Rami Makhlouf, who is Bashar al-Assad's cousin, was arrested and a major part of his assets was seized by the regime. Allegedly, Makhlouf's assets were to be used to pay part of Syria's debt to Russia. Back in 2011, it was estimated that Makhlouf owned 60% of Syria's economy, and he provided the country with hard currency during the civil war (Grinstead, 2019).

Syrian drama – the hallmark of Syrian broadcasting

Like its counterparts throughout most of the Arab world, early television broadcasting in Syria was state owned and run, making it an important national symbol of sovereignty (Wedeen, 1999). Early Arab television was strictly controlled by national governments and functioned more as a political tool to deliver political and developmental messages and status symbols than as an avenue of mass communication with the national public (Dajani, 2005: 582). In the case of Syria, the history of broadcasting is also intertwined with that of the history of the country as an important center of television serials or *musalsalat* production in the region. In 1962, Marwan Shaheen, the artistic director of Syrian National Television, announced the launch of national broadcasting with a detailed broadcast agenda for the coming decade, which would feature local programming. The aim was to encourage Syrian productions that deal with Syrian issues and which would be far more engaging for audiences than any imported shows (Salamandra, 2004). This strategy continued the legacy of earlier successful projects such as Syria's first made-for-television film released in 1960, *The Stranger (al-Gharib)* by director Salim Qataya (Salamandra, forthcoming).

The arrival of satellite television in the late 1960s and 1970s transformed Syrian broadcasting and television production. After witnessing the significant interest of Arab states to join Intelsat following its launch in 1964, the Arab League launched the Arab Satellite Communications Organization – Arabsat – in 1976. Saudi Arabia held 29.9% of shares, followed by Kuwait, Libya, Iraq, and Qatar, and Egypt – the largest producer in the Arab world – at a mere 5.2% (Al-Saadoon, 1990). Egypt, or the then "Hollywood of the Nile" (Amin, 1996), saw no necessity in securing a larger share in Arabsat, banking on the popularity of its productions and the strength of its TV channels. This decision would later prove to be detrimental to both Egyptian TV channels and Egyptian drama. The Syrian satellite broadcasting was limited to eight hours a day in 1996, which meant that it could not compete with several pan-Arab stations beaming from the Gulf region.

Shortly after the creation of Arabsat in 1976, a political and economic embargo of Egypt following the Camp David Peace Treaty with Israel was voted by the Arab states in a summit in Baghdad, Iraq. Egypt was rapidly excluded from Arabsat following the Arab League embargo, and this decision not only affected Egyptian channels, but it also included a concurrent joint agreement by the Arab states to refrain from purchasing productions of the state Egyptian Radio and Television Union. At the same time, the launch of several satellites to cater to the Middle East and North Africa region resulted in the proliferation of Arab-owned satellite channels, as financial barriers to entry of the broadcasting sector declined. The immediate effect of this expansion was a shift in satellite broadcasting demand and supply, and the increase in satellite channels gave rise to a race to secure limited resources to occupy broadcast time (Salamandra, 2005). This rapid expansion had detrimental consequences for television advertising revenues throughout the Middle East, with lasting consequences. This is so because of the rising supply of broadcasters balkanized the audiences among a large pool of satellite channels (Sakr, 2001: 26). The resulting amortization of the Arab audience left broadcasters with low budgets for skein acquisition, as low penetration of individual broadcasting stations disincentivized advertisers from buying airtime or sponsoring shows. The resulting dependence on government support for Arab television broadcasting continues today.

Syrian television generally benefited from the public's early development of discriminating taste, because the initiative to first begin broadcasting from Mount Qassyoun in Damascus went hand in hand with one that developed a wide early audience for the medium. As Muhieddine Al Qabisi recalled to the magazine *Huna Dimashq*, as soon as plans to establish a station were drafted, the government acquired 40,000 television sets from RCA (American) and Phillips (Dutch). The 14-, 17-, and 21-inch televisions were intended to be sold to the Syrian public at wholesale cost, duty-free, with government-supported easy payment plans (Qabisi, July 16, 1960). By 1963, Yaseen Rifa'iya of *Dunia* magazine marveled that the Syrian public had become a highly sophisticated audience. Describing the production process of a made-for-television play, he enumerates the time-consuming steps of screenwriting, casting, rehearsal, and even day-of activities such as makeup, costumes, and other affordances that contribute to the making of the content that Syrian audiences consume.

The earliest period of Syrian television also featured some of the most iconic works of Syrian culture, including *Sah al Nawm* and *Hamam al Hana*. Gradually, the technical expertise theater creatives contributed to Syrian television began to bear fruit for theater as well. In an interview published in *Drama* in 2009, the veteran director Khaldoon al Maleh marveled that the success of *Sah al Nawm*, excitedly recalling, "whenever the show aired, you couldn't find anyone walking in the streets in most Arab cities." He added that the show was so popular in other countries that "when the Kuwaiti television aired it, the broadcaster re-ran the show once again right after the last episode!" This success, in turn, allowed the lead actor, Duraid

Lahham, to achieve unprecedented success on stage in Kassak ya Watan and Ghorba and Dayet Tishreen. Maleh added, "he was allowed to say what no one else could say," attributing this license to the noticeable popularity of Lahham's televised endeavors (Qaddour, 2009: 23). In conjunction with made-for-television plays and short films, Syrian television's strategy emphasized the importance of mixed entertainment programming to complement fictional television, including the Jordanian-produced game show *Fakker Tarbah*. However, the nascent period of Syrian broadcasting was relatively limited, characterized by cross-fertilization between television broadcasting, film, and theater as a strategic response to the still-developing television production techniques and resources. In turn, the success of Syrian made-for-television dramas spread across television stations in the region, establishing itself as a veritable national industry.

In 1985, Syrian National Television launched al-Thaniyya TV (Channel Two), dedicated to entertainment programming, further expanding the need for entertainment content. Drama productions then increased in earnest around 1986 when the government encouraged private producers to film their shows in Syria to promote the country regionally; several companies were created then, although many became dormant after only producing one or a few shows (Dick, 2005). However, the expansion in Syrian private broadcasting was slow, particularly due to the disincentivizing effect of the failure of the first private satellite channel, Sham TV, launched in 2006. Initially, the channel represented the second-largest buyer of television programs in the Middle East region. However, the channel closed down after only a few months, citing the difficulties encountering private broadcasters in Syria, which discouraged future investment in this sector (Al-Zubaidi et al., 2012: 146).

Recognizing the opportunity presented in the growing importance of television production, both as a revenue source and as a harbinger of cultural and political influence in the region, the Syrian government passed a series of economic liberalization reforms in 1991, reversing legislation banning private production companies in Syria (Salamandra, 2005: 5). The liberalization of media production in the early 1990s was also followed by the legalization of private broadcasting stations by Presidential Decree No. 50 in 2001, mentioned earlier.

By the mid-1990s, several Syrian dramas became big hits in the pan-Arab regional market, marking the era of "outpouring of the television drama" or *al-fawra al-dramiyya*, with the production of various genres: from comedy to 19th-century historical epics (Dick, 2005). This outpouring stage of Syrian drama continued between 2000 and 2010 with scores of miniseries produced each Ramadan competing with the Egyptian, and later Gulf, dramas. There was no shortage of screenwriters and novelists as political parties were nonexistent since the 1960s, leading many activists to join the expanding television industry (Joubin, 2013: 26). By the early 2000s, the Syrian television drama industry rivaled Egyptian productions and attracted the attention of the international press (Salamandra, 2005).

In summary, the Syrian regime invested in the growing drama production industry in the 1990s through Sham TV production company, owned by the then vice president, Abdelhalim Khaddam (Al-Ghazzi, 2013: 589), aided by the launch of Syria Drama, a new channel dedicated to the production of drama in 2009 with a staff of 25 people. Arab satellite TV stations, mostly owned by Gulf businessmen, needed new productions, and the Syrian producers filled that demand, especially those with links to the regime.

The transformation of the drama production

The year 2007 brought about a significant turn in the Syrian drama/*musalsalat* industry that came to be known as the 2007 drama crisis. After years of positioning the Syrian drama market towards Arab demand, the 2007 crisis marked the abstention of Gulf broadcasting stations from purchasing Syrian *musalsalat*. There remain three mainstream explanations of this decision. The first explanation points to Syria's political isolation after the Hariri assassination (Birke, 2010). The second explanation cites the financial crisis as the main culprit, lowering the *musalsalat*-purchasing budgets of Gulf broadcasters. The third and predominant explanation within the industry is the "overproduction" explanation put forth by director Muthana Subuh and Laith Hajjo. They explain that 2007 marked a radical increase in production without amelioration of production quality. They add that the technical experts available in the industry such as actors, sound and light engineers, directors, etc. accommodate circa 10 quality productions. Thus, the 40 privately produced productions of 2007 were of poor quality and did not attract purchasers (personal communication, Laith Hajjo, 07/07/2010).

Further deteriorating the financial circumstances of the drama production sector, the national Syrian broadcaster offers minimal prices for Syrian drama. The Syrian National Television, for example, pays around $3,000–$4,000 per episode, roughly 10% of the average production cost per episode of a contemporary urban drama. Syrian productions are marketed to Gulf entities often before production begins, and earnings made in the marketing process are then used to finance the intended productions. The evidence collected in personal research accumulating a production database demonstrates the current crisis of Syrian production companies. An official at the Lajnat Sina'a al Cinema wa al Television (The Commission for Television and Cinema Production) admitted that no production company in Syria today is capable of financing its operations without resorting to investors in Arab states in the Gulf, with the last remaining self-sufficient company, Syria International, opting for Gulf funding in 2009 (personal communication, Ramadan, 19th July 2010). These financial obstacles led to the transformation of the production process, at high costs to Syrian censors.

An official at the Commission for Television and Cinema Production explained the stages of the official production process. In the formal production process, the first step to producing a TV series is submitting a script for approval by the Commission. Following the approval of the script, the project proceeds to the filming stage. With the termination of the filming stage, the end product is resubmitted to the Commission for reapproval to ensure no deviations from the approved script. The second censorship stage, he explains, is necessary to ensure that the end product does not deviate from the approved script with "problematic additions" (personal communication, 19th July 2010). At the end of this process, the series enters the marketing stage.

The past mechanism allowed for stringent monitoring of skein content. Due to rising difficulties of funding skeins, however, the procedure has been transformed since the 1990s. High systematic risk gradually led production companies to devise entirely different production pathways, securing both production funds and broadcasting mediums for their productions.

Most Syrian drama now follows an entirely different pathway from the formal procedure run by the Commission. Firstly, the marketing stage precedes all production stages of a series, sometimes even the creative stage when "concept" discussions take place. There exist two possible production mechanisms. In the first, a script is written and presented to prospective buyers within a "collection" of several scripts; if the script is purchased, it proceeds to the filming and broadcasting stage. Further distribution of the broadcasting commodity is dependent upon the method of sale. In the case of the selling of the rights to a first run, the series may be distributed for reruns after the initial broadcasting stage. On the other hand, when exclusivity rights are sold, rights to the show are passed to the broadcaster, who often chooses to limit distribution.

In the second pathway, dubbed *al-Istiktab*, or commissioning in the drama production industry, a foreign investor (often a broadcaster) commissions a project to a reputable director. The director then becomes a line director, where he or she receives remuneration for directing services and is henceforth released of all risks of the production process. The line director is dictated a creative concept, genre, and historical or social issue. Often the line director is also restricted to a set list of "star" actors, filming locations, and production crew members, according to the broadcaster's chosen strategy. Following the agreement, a script is written that follows the agreed guidelines, and then the filming stage begins.

Although both pathways require that shows are pre-marketed and sold, they differ in the degree of external influence involved in the production stage. While the second production pathway gives complete control of content and production decisions to the purchasing broadcasting station, the first production pathway allows the minimal influence of broadcasters on drama content, as the script is pre-written and bought on a take-it-or-leave-it basis, with the acceptance of minor changes. An example of the first pathway is the production *Zaman al-'Ar*, (*The Time of Shame*), which underwent minor modifications before its purchasing by Dubai Television and Qatar Television. *The Time of Shame*'s realistic illustrations of the corruption of Syrian society and public circles made it a hit with audiences. The first pathway also permits Syrian scripts to bypass the Commission for Television and Cinema Production, as purchasing, broadcasting, and ownership of the series are completed in the Gulf, placing the series under the jurisdiction of Gulf censorship authorities. Notable series that followed this pathway is the banned production *al-Husrum al-Shami*. Examples of the second pathway include Sheikh Mohammed's epic *Struggle on the Sands* and banned productions such as *The Lion of the Jazeera* or *In the Gulf*. It is also important to emphasize that the Gulf investment in Syrian productions has also permitted controversial Gulf productions that would either not have passed Gulf censorship guidelines in the Gulf or not have been accepted by the industry in public.

Thus, regional investment in audiovisual content production had a liberalizing effect on television production in Syria. As the veteran actor Duraid Lahham put it, "if censors can monitor Syrian shows broadcast on Syrian stations, it cannot monitor Syrian shows broadcast in other Arab countries, strict censorship is simply no longer feasible in the satellite era" (personal communication, Lahham, 9th July 2010). Nevertheless, this foreign investment threatened the only vibrant sector of the Syrian media industry. As the director Hani al-Ashi said in an interview, "as long as Syrian production companies are forced to rely solely on Gulf broadcasters to purchase their productions, Syrian TV drama industry will always be hanging at the edge of a cliff" (Alia, 2010).

Drama as a tool of soft power

Since the 1990s, many major Syrian productions tend to look back with nostalgia at the late 19th century and the early 20th century (Reilly, 2018: 88). The state changed the investment laws in the 1990s allowing foreign producers, usually from the Gulf states, to coproduce Syrian dramas. President Bashar al-Assad saw in those television productions a means to develop Syrian soft power in the region (Reilly, 2018: 215). The numerous historical series formed the genre of what is labeled "Damascene milieu" set in a local neighborhood (*hara*) in Damascus, during the late 19th or early 20th centuries when Syria was under the occupation, first of the Ottoman Empire and later of France (Al-Ghazzi, 2013). The most successful series was *Bab al-Hara* (The Neighborhood Gate) broadcast in several successive seasons (Al-Ghazzi, 2013: 587). However, the state kept monitoring the TV productions to ensure the narrative fits its purpose; for instance, in 2007, the scriptwriter of *Bab al-Hara* told the press that he had to change the script once to downplay the anti-colonial struggle against France as depicted in the drama because, at that time, Syria's relations with France was improving (Al-Ghazzi, 2013: 590; Salamandra, 2004).

Following the protests in March 2011, Bashar al-Asad used tropes known in historical series such as *Bab al-Hara*, when he called on the people of the city of Daraa to exhibit the authentic Arabism and demonstrate their "pride, bravery and dignity," echoing the themes of *Bab al-Hara*'s jingle (Al-Ghazzi, 2013: 597). Protestors also repeated the same words when they called for fellow Syrians to continue their street demonstrations, which evinced the political narrative of authenticity and moral values disseminated and consumed via television series (Al-Ghazzi, 2013: 597).

Meanwhile, numerous Syrian actors, producers, and writers moved abroad post-2011, and new TV production companies have been launched since then with the claim to maintain the success of Syrian drama. One such company is Imar al-Sham, founded in 2016 by the businessman Basem Zaitoun, who helped launched a new channel, Lana TV, to broadcast the company's production; another is Sama Art International, founded in 2012, by a member of the People's Council, Mohammad Hamsho (el Kechen, 2018). Other companies were set up outside of Syria in Beirut and the UAE to produce series for the regional market. In return for broadcasting such Syrian drama, however, Arab stations usually demand that the series does not tackle the reality post-2011 (el Kechen, 2018).

In Ramadan 2019, the Syrian state television channels boasted of 26 new series, the largest number since 2011. The Syrian General Organization for Radio and Television produced a few such series, such as two based on love stories, namely *Aan al-Hawa wal-gawa* and *Athar al-Farasha*. Other series were *Daqiqat Samt*, a thriller starring Abed Fahd, the Syrian star, as well as *Salasel al-Zahab* and *Ahla Ayyam*; the latter was filmed in Syria and the UAE. It is known that the Syrian star Abed Fahd left Syria in 2012 but he returned to Syria by the end of 2018 and appeared in several other series during the Ramadan season in 2019. Moreover, the 10th part of the popular series *Bab al-Hara* was also broadcast in 2019 (Salama, 2019). Three new historical epics, *al-Hallaj*, *al-Haramlek*, and *Maqamat al-Ishq*, were also broadcast in Ramadan 2019, thereby reviving the Syrian historical drama productions whose portfolio included series commemorating Islamic figures such as *Khaled bin al-Waleed*, *al-Moutanabbi*, *Haroun al-Rashid*, and *al-Hajjaj* (Al-Ads, 2019). Added to those genres, there were also comedy series, including *Nas min Waraq* with the guest appearance of the veteran actor, Dureid Lahham. Lahham used to be a critic of the regime but surprisingly he endorsed Syrian President Assad during the early stage of the 2011 uprising; for instance, he gave several interviews in May 2011, calling the Syrian uprising a violent rebellion of a minority and warning Syrians not to listen to the defected army officers (Ziter, 2015: 10, 234). Generally, several Syrian actors expressed anti-regime sentiment, while several others appeared on national Syrian television to affirm their support to the regime (Al-Ghazzi, 2013: 598).

Conclusion

The Syrian regime depended on mass media to promote its Baathist agenda, and like other Arab states, it deployed the media to enforce a unique sense of national identity. The broadcasting sector was devoted to promoting the official political narrative and ideas, but the proliferation of satellite television channels has provided the Syrian citizens with numerous new sources of news and entertainment (Wedeen, 1999: 91) At first, the regime announced that owing a satellite dish was prohibited, but then they did not persecute those who owned dishes (Wedeen, 1999: 91), perhaps because the regime, like all Arab regimes, thought that watching television, particularly entertainment and drama, were not harmful, and it was a way to distract citizens from more acute political issues.

True, the regime later granted licenses to selected private broadcasters, but the new media laws still saw broadcasting as a tool for public guidance and to elevate moral standards within society as well as strengthening national identity (Panos Institute, 2012: 49). Meanwhile, the continuous broadcasting of media events arranged at the auspices of the regime, such as local festivals, provided the spectacles that "help replenish the regime's repertoire of symbols while ensuring that citizens through Syrian remain familiar with and able to reproduce the official hagiography" (Wedeen, 1999: 24).

Since 2011, the current Syrian regime no longer has control over the numerous outlets based outside and inside Syria, and Syrian audiences across the world have had access to new media ventures set up by European media donors and independent Syrian activists, or what is called "alternative media." Such media ventures were usually concentrated in Turkey, but since 2017, many such outlets were dissolved due to the lack of funding and suspension of Western support. Currently, those remaining in Turkey are reportedly battling with the strict Turkish regulations to sustain their licenses and obtaining or renewing work permits for their Syrian staff (Khadr, 2019). As television production requires substantial economic and professional resources, it is unlikely for the current set of "independent media" outlets to sustain their operations in the future without considerable investments and a share in the pan-Arab advertising market, usually in the hands of Gulf companies. On the other hand, new technologies now allow for content streaming on the Internet, including web-based shows and video on demand, which means that Syrians can use the Internet and social media to connect with the larger Syrian communities in the diaspora. The future challenge is to create and sustain a sense of cohesion and unity among the swathes of Syrians inside and outside the region, honoring the original chants of March 2011, that "we are all Syrians." Indeed, Syrians' unity and cohesion have borne the brunt of the civil war with the opposition splintering into hundreds of different committees, lacking ideological unity and centralization (Daher, 2019). It is difficult to predict the extent of future efforts by Syrian individuals or groups to experiment with new media content, but it is believed that they will be united in commemorating the uprising as the most significant event in Syria's modern history.

Note

1 www.rozana.fm

References

Al-Alam (2018), Bushra lilameleen fi qitaa al-ilam al-souri. *Al Alam*, 16 November. Retrieved from https://bit.ly/2Nmre3F

Al-Asi (2019), al-Ilam . . . rasasa oula fi sadr al-souriyeen. *Al-Araby*, 15 March. Retrieved from https://bit.ly/2Cli4OQ

Al-Ghazzi, Omar (2013), Nation as Neighborhood: How Bab al-Hara Dramatized Syrian Identity. *Media, Culture & Society*, 35(5), pp. 586–601.

l-Saadoon, Hezab T. (1990), *The Role of ARABSAT in Television Programme Exchange in the Arab World.* Unpublished PhD dissertation, The Ohio State University, USA.

Al-Sharq al-Awsat (2019), *al-Ilam al-souri al-rasmi*, 19 April. Retrieved from https://aawsat.com/home/article/ 1679091 / عشرة-أخبار-بدولار "- الإعلام-السوري-الرسمي

Al-Zubaidi, Layla, Fischer, Susanne, and Abu-Fadil, Magda (2012), *Walking a Tightrope. News Media and Freedom of Expression in the Middle East.* Beirut: Heinrich Böll Stiftung.

Alia, K. (2010), *Al 'Ojoor Fil Drama al-Souriyya* (Actors' Fees in Syrian Drama). *Tishreen Newspaper, Drama Supplement,* pp. 8–9, Sunday 4 April.

Amin, Hussein (1996), Egypt and the Arab World in the Satellite Age. In John Sinclair, Elizabeth Jackay, and Stuart Cunningham (eds.), *New Patterns in Global Television: Peripheral Vision*. Oxford: Oxford University Press, pp. 101–125.

Birke, Sarah (2010), With Ramadan, the Drama Begins. *Global Post,* 11 August. Retrieved from www. globalpost.com/dispatch/middle-east/100810/ramadan-syria-soap-operas?page=0,0

Daher, Joseph (2017), Syria, the Uprising and the Media Scene. *Open Democracy*, 26 October.

Daher, Joseph (2019), *Pluralism Lost in Syria's Uprising*. The Century Foundation, 7 May. Retrieved from https://tcf.org/content/report/pluralism-lost-syrias-uprising/

Dajani, Nabil (2005), Television in the Arab East. In Janet Wasko (ed.), *A Companion to Television*. Oxford: Wiley Blackwell Publishing, pp. 580–601.

Dick, Marlin (2005), The State of the Musalsal: Arab Television Drama and Comedy and the Politics of the Satellite Era. *Arab Media & Society*, 1 September. Retrieved from www.arabmediasociety.com/ the-state-of-the-musalsal-arab-television-drama-and-comedy-and-the-politics-of-the-satellite-era/

el Khechen, Maher (2018), Syrian Serial Drama: There's Hope in Sadness That Challenges War and the "Pennies" of Capitalism. *The Peace Building in Lebanon*, (20) (December), pp. 8–9. Retrieved from https:// reliefweb.int/report/lebanon/peace-building-lebanon-news-supplement-issue-n-20-december-2018-enar

Free Press Unlimited (2016), *Syria Audience Research 2016*. Retrieved from www.freepressunlimited.org/ en/news/syria-audience-research-2016

Grinstead, Nick (2019), Makhlouf no More? Russia is Calling in the Debts in Syria. *OpenDemocracy*, 6 September. Retrieved from www.opendemocracy.net/en/north-africa-west-asia/makhlouf-no-more-russia-calling-debts-syria/

IMS (2014), *Our Work in 2014*. Syria. Retrieved from www.mediasupport.org/annualreport2014/work. html

Joubin, Rebecca (2013), Syrian Drama and The Politics of Dignity, Middle East Report, No. 268, (Fall), pp. 26–29.

Khadr, Abdul Rahman (2019), al-Ilam al-souri al-badeel fi tourkiyya. *Al-Araby*, 5 May. Retrieved from https://bit.ly/2NN9NIx

Marrouch, Rima (2014), *Syria's Post-uprising Media Outlets: Challenges and Opportunities in Syrian Radio Startups*. Oxford: Reuters Institute for the Study of Journalism.

Panos Institute (2012), *Public Service Broadcasting in the MENA Region*, May. Retrieved from http://panos network.org/attachments/article/139/PSB_Brochure_160x240_EN-bd.pdf

Qabisi, Muhieddine (1960), The History of Syrian Television. *Huna Dimashq Magazine*, 16 July.

Qaddour, Hoda (2009), A Session of Memories with Khaldoun al Maleh: Sah al Nawm was a Transformative Moment for Durraid and Nihad. *Drama Magazine*, 30 September.

Reilly, James A. (2018), *Fragile Nation, Shattered Land*. London: I.B. Tauris.

Rifa'iya, Y. (1963), The Audience Judges Several Weeks' Work in 25 Minutes! *Dunya Magazine*, 25 January.

Sakr, Naomi, (2001), *Satellite Realms: Transnational Television, Globalization and the Middle East*. New York: St. Martin's Press, pp. 10–11.

Salama, Sara (2019), Tabashir Mousem 2019- Addrama al-Souriyya tastared afiyatha? *Al-Watan*, 9 January. Retrieved from http://alwatan.sy/archives/182012

Salamandra, Christa (2004), *A New Old Damascus: Authenticity and Distinction in Urban Syria*. Bloomington: Indiana University Press.

Salamandra, Christa (2005), Television and the Ethnographic Endeavor: The Case of Syrian Drama. *Transnational Broadcasting Studies,* (14) (Spring/Summer).

Salamandra, Christa (forthcoming), *Waiting for Light: Syrian Television Drama Producers in the Satellite Era*. Manuscript in Progress.

Singhal, Arvind, and Krishna, Vijay (1994), Syria. In Yahya Kamalipour and Hamid Mowlana (eds.), *Mass Media in the Middle East*. Westport, CT: Greenwood Press.

Trombetta, Lorenzo (2018), Syria – Media Landscape. *The European Journalism Centre (EJC)*. Retrieved from https://medialandscapes.org/country/syria

Wedeen, Lisa (1999), *Ambiguities of Domination: Politics, Rhetoric, and Symbols in Contemporary Syria*. Chicago: The University of Chicago Press.

Ziter, Edward (2015), *Political Performance in Syria From the Six-Day War to the Syrian Uprising*. Basingstoke: Palgrave Macmillan.

Tunisia

34

PRESS IN TUNISIA

From French colonization to post-revolution era

Mongi Mabrouki

Introduction

The emergence of newspapers in Tunisia, and their gradual development over the decades, has been influenced by several factors. The adoption of the printing press, which also spread throughout the Arab region, formed a key factor in this development. But these roots go back to the foundational experiences of journalism in the middle of the 19th century, when the Tunisian kingdom was under the Ottoman Empire, followed by the French colonial phase, by setting the first legislative framework regulating the press in the country.

From the founding stage during the Ottoman era, newspapers witnessed various crisis stages, a form of ebb and flow, which affected its smooth development. Part of the concern at the time was their growth as platforms for public opinion influence. Newspapers were viewed as tools for spreading the Christian faith on the one hand, and on the other as platforms for Western domination.

Although the French colonial control in Tunisia, which had started in 1881, coincided with the growth of the written press industry among the French in particular and European communities in general, it was followed by the involvement of the Jewish community and then the Tunisian elites in establishing a newspaper market that began early in reviving the national spirit and challenging the colonial power. As a consequence, the Tunisian press played a significant role in spearheading the national resistance movement and struggling against the colonial hegemonic attempts in issues related to naturalization and the obliteration of the cultural roots of the country. It has been argued by some (Dabbab, 1973; Al-Arbi, 1995) that the Tunisian press contributed to the development of the first political movement as an effective tool to bring together the Tunisian elite and galvanize their ambitions to resist French exploitation of the Tunisian economic and agricultural riches.

Early stages of press development

The first appearance of the Tunisian press was initiated by the Tunisian authority under the title of *Al-Raid Al-Rasmi*. This newspaper remained the key official outlet since 1860, representing the official viewpoint of the government. This official journal has remained until nowadays under the title of *Alraid Alrasmi of the Republic of Tunisia* (The Official Journal of the Republic of Tunisia). Up until the revolution of 14 January 2011, it symbolized the authoritarian control of news and communication in the country. Perhaps this control enabled the link between the press and the political authority, giving a kind of trusteeship on the printed word.

However, the emergence of the press also coincided on the one hand with the development of the education system and civil societies work within the course of the reform movement that formed the umbrella framework of the Tunisian national movement; on the other hand, it was due to the impact of the two educational institutions, the Zaytouna Mosque (established in 1698) and the Sadiqiyya School (established in 1875), which were involved in the development of the reform tide and fostered the development of the press (*Al-Hadira* 1888–1911) and the birth of associative work headed by the Al-Khaldounia association in 1896. This early educational progress contributed to a large extent in the awakening of a national Tunisian youth movement. Also, the involvement of the Al-Khaldounia association in enabling the students of the Zaytouna Mosque to study modern sciences and expand their intellectual horizons, since its initiative to organize lectures in the fields of history, geography, French language, politics, economy, health, physics, chemistry, and mathematics, represented the cradle of this intellectual awakening.

Against this backdrop, it can be argued that the Tunisian elites contributed to the development of Tunisian patriotism, and the newspaper *Al-Raid Al-Tounisi*, published on 22 July 1860, was one of its manifestations. Also, the publication of Khair al-Din Pasha's book *Akwam al-Masalik fi Ma'rifati Ahwal Al-Mamalik* in 1867 represented another hallmark for this national movement. This also coincided with the publication of the newspaper *Al-Hadira*, after seven years of French protection centering, at the initiative of graduates of the Sadiki School, and with the active participation of Al-Zaytouna graduates such as Salem Bouhajib and Mohamed Al-Senussi, who had experience in the field of journalism. The newspaper's editorials represented constant pressure directed at the French settlers and behind them the French colonial administration and their collaborators (Dabbab, 1973; Rossignol, 1970).

Al-Hadira newspaper was supported by a fringe of liberal figures in the colonial administration during the period of the two general governors, René Millet (1894–1900) and Stephen Pichon (1900–1907), as it drifted into a reformist approach instead of moral resistance. In this context, the lectures of Muhammad al-Bashir Safar, a graduate of the Sadiki School and head of the *Al-Hadira* group that had a real impact on the renewal of Tunisian culture, became popular. His lessons at the Al-Khaldounia Society served as a wake-up call for a cultural renewal among the educated elite (Al-Arbi, 1995: 89). He contributed to the formation of the brightest national journalists, led by Muhammad Al-Ja'ibi (1880–1938), founder of the newspaper *Al-Sawab* in 1904, and the monthly magazine *Khair Al-Din* issued in 1906 (Al-Arbi, 1995: 93).

It is worth noting that the launch of the Tunisian press was no later than it was in the most prominent Arab capitals. If we exclude the early start of the Egyptian press due to Napoleon's invasion of Egypt, then Tunisia was among the countries which set a precedent. The following is a track of the appearance of the early press in the Arab region: The *Alwaqai' Al-Misriya* (Egypt) published in 1828, *Almubashir* (Algeria) published in 1847, *Garden News* (Lebanon) issued in 1858, *Al-Raid Al-Tounisi* (Tunisia) issued in 1860, *Syria* (Syria) issued in 1865, *Tripoli West* (Libya) issued in 1866, *Al-Zawra* (Iraq) issued in 1869, *Sana'a* (Yemen) issued in 1879, *Morocco* (Marrakesh) issued in 1889, *Al-Ghazia Al-Soudania* (Sudan) issued in 1899, and *Hijaz* (Hijaz) issued in 1908 (*Dawatul-Haq,* 2019).

Although most of these newspapers were official publications, there existed private newspapers too. On the one hand, there were public newspapers owned by the state and often expressive of their orientations and editorial line. On the other hand, there existed independent newspapers that gave priority to cultural and historical content, in addition to opinion newspapers that were concerned with current affairs and providing new perspectives. However, newspapers representing the views of political parties did not appear until after the formation of political parties. This coincided with a worsening of colonial grievances, which required new forms of resistance and opposition, in which the written press assumed leading roles.

Impact of the French colonization on the development of the Tunisian press

The experience of the written press during the French colonial period witnessed an ebb and flow depending on the political climate. The suppression of the press depended on the vision of the French resident general, the de facto ruler of the country, his view of the political environment, and the nature of his assignment. On 14 October 1884, the French resident Paul Gambon issued the Press Law in accordance with the French law issued on 29 July 1881 (Karimi, 2011: 28). It aimed at controlling the Tunisians' ambition to use the press as a platform through which they could express their demands. The impact of this law in addition to the financial levy imposed by the colonial authority on all newspapers issued in Tunisia, whether they were in Arabic or European languages, affected their development. It was not until 16 August 1896 that the financial burden was partly canceled, and a number of Tunisian intellectuals were keen to launch various publications, including the comic press (Almahidi, 2010).

To avoid these restrictions, few Tunisian journalists preferred to approach national public opinion through satirical newspapers such as *Abu Qasha* in March 1908. However, these newspapers were only able to last for a few months due to the continuous restrictions on freedom of expression, in addition to the lack of financial resources. The Italian invasion of Libya and the ensuing bloody unrests that spread on Tunisian soil led the French occupation authorities to announce a state of emergency. As a consequence, the publication of the Arabic-speaking Tunisian newspapers was suspended by a decision issued on 8 November 1911, which coincided with the arrests of a few of its journalists and the exile of others (Almahidi, 2010: 226).

Despite the aforementioned restrictions, the Tunisian press managed to remain a source of news and platforms for debates on hot issues. Issues like the legitimacy of the colonial authority, the struggle for independence, negotiations, the demand for a Tunisian parliament, a constitution that regulates the governance, and the creation of parties entrusted with representing Tunisians were part of their digest. Newspapers also addressed various social problems, such as the emancipation of women, travel, hijab, prostitution, drugs, and the rights of workers and peasants. It also defended the Arabic language in education when it was attacked, and the Arab culture when the colonizer attempted to enforce French cultural values in Tunisia.

In sum, as an overview of that period, one may argue that the Tunisian press evolved in terms of form and content, and gradually moved from press opinion to news journalism, and from work based on individual effort to party press based on collective effort. The most prominent manifestation of its development after the First World War was reflecting news stories from around the world as well as internal news supported with pictures.

Soon after 1919, a new era has started for the Tunisian press, in which national newspapers speaking in Arabic or French multiplied, characterized by their courage in dealing with violations of the rights of Tunisians, and the distinction between them and the French and the rest of the other European communities. This period also witnessed the birth of partisan journalism, among which were *Al-Asr Al-Jadid* newspaper 1931–1920, the *Al-Minbar AlArabi* 1920, *Al-Wazir* 1920, *Al-Nadim* 1921, *Almubashir* 1922, *Almuhtal* 1922, *Al-Burhan* 1922, *Al-Haqiqa* 1922, *Al-Nahda* 1923, *Al-Manjaniq* 1923, *Al-Alam Al-Adabi* 1923, *Alzaman* 1929, *Al-Irada* 1929, *Al-Amal* 1935, *Al-Fallah Al-Tunisi* 1932, *A-Shabab* 1935, and *Ifriqia Al-Fatat* 1943.

These newspapers reflected the beginning of the crystallization of a press pluralism expressing the effectiveness of the national movement in all its political and intellectual facets.

In most stages of the colonial era, censorship was applied to all areas of production and intellectual creativity such as the press, books, magazines, cinema, theater, and radio programs; in 1938 and before the outbreak of the Second World War, censorship became a regulated procedure with legal texts (Ben Gafsa, 1972: 25). Censorship did not diminish until the end of the war, as the disruption of the press became subject to organized law. Otherwise, with the Germans occupying Tunisia during 1942–1943, they encouraged the new Constitutional Party to publish the newspapers *Al-Yawm, Ifriqia Al-Fatat,* and *Al-Shabab* as a challenge to the French; however, those newspapers did not survive after the Germans withdrew from Tunisia on 6 May 1943 (Julien, 1985: 119).

Worth noting before closing this historical period before Tunisia's independence is that the number of newspapers issued in Tunisia since the French colonization of Tunisia in 1881 until its independence in 1956 amounted to 338 Arabic-language newspapers and 985 French-speaking and other European language newspapers (Truth and Dignity Commission, 2018). However, the Tunisian press market shrunk during the post-independence period, and freedom of expression was curtailed even more (Al-Arabi, 1998).

Post-independence era: Bourguiba and the press

Habib Bourguiba was the first president of the Republic of Tunisia. He ruled from independence in 1956 to 1987. His era was characterized by a one-party rule where he remained a key figure in the ruling party and head of the state. With all its disadvantages, the colonial era was arguably not as bad as what the press witnessed during the Bourguiba rule. It was understandable for the colonial power to have a systematic policy to control and tame the press so that it did not turn into an effective tool in the hands of the forces of the national movement. But, for Bourguiba's regime to have total control of the media in Tunisia, including the newspapers, was hard for Tunisians to grasp.

Since 1955, the new Constitutional Party resumed the publication of its Arabic newspaper, *Al-Amal*, and its French-speaking newspaper, *Laction.* This coincided with the enactment of the decree on the press in Tunisia on 9 February 1956, a few weeks before the conclusion of the agreement on total independence. However, overall, the newspaper market became weaker and less secure than in colonial times (Karimi, 2011). It became marked by the absence of debate and free expression. The absence of a true democratic atmosphere, freedom of expression, and independent association led scores of intellectuals to leave the country or refuse to return after completing their studies abroad (Truth and Dignity Commission, 2018). A letter revealed by the Truth and Dignity Commission (2018) belonging to Ahmed Al-Tlili (one of the leaders of the Tunisian workers union) revealed the national atmosphere of the time. He headed *Al-Shaab* magazine in 1959, which was the mouthpiece of the Tunisian General Workers union and became one of the significant platforms for critiquing the status quo.

Perhaps the best description of the nature of the media system during the time of President Habib Bourguiba was what he declared at the inauguration of the official Tunisian National TV in 1966, that he was happy with the event because it would allow him to enter Tunisian homes without barriers. In this sense, the concept of public media to him was limited to being a communication tool, that is, a one-way, top-down discourse, from the head of state to the people or public opinion (Kheshana, 2018).

When the African News Agency was established in 1961 to reduce dependency on the French News Agency, it was not part of a vision of a media system based on diversity and professionalism. The report of the Truth and Dignity Commission (2018), entitled "The Propaganda and Misinformation System," highlighted that the media was used to perpetuate the official propaganda of power during the presidencies of Habib Bourguiba and Zein Elabidine Ben Ali, during which time they used the state's capabilities not to produce objective media content but rather to produce a propaganda system that adorned the image of those in power and did not allow any critical approach to their performance. This approach was supported by a stringent legal framework such as the "Press Code" of 1975, which existed to control free speech and silence opposition voices (Truth and Dignity Commission, 2018).

After the recession that dominated the written press in the first two decades of independence, the 1980s witnessed gradual changes in light of the liberal orientation of the government of El Hadi Nouira (1969–1980). This was evident through the licensing of a weekly magazine in French entitled *Dialogue* on 9 September 1974, which was managed by Omar Sahabo and chose to have its editorial line critical and bold. Other weekly newspapers also appeared, including *Al-Ayyam* on 7 December 1970, and *People* on 27 May 1972, which were characterized by diversity in their contents, and they adopted audacity in dealing with political and social issues. However, this window of freedom did not last long. The press code, which appeared under Law No. 32 of 28 April 1975, closed this window of freedom entertained by journalists. In light of these setbacks, human rights demands increased and culminated in the establishment of the Tunisian League for Human Rights on 7 May 1977, and the launch of *Al-Rai* newspaper was issued on 29 December 1977 (Hamden, 1993).

The 1978 general strike in the country had dramatic effects on everything in the country, not the least of which was free speech. This coincided with the suspension of the first issue of the newspaper *Al-Rai* and the seizure of other newspapers such as *Tunis Hebdo* and *Al-Shaab* (Al-Sefi, 2012). In the following year, the wave of harassment included the cessation of *Al-Maarefa* magazine in November 1979, and then *Al-Mujtama* newspaper in December 1979 published by the then known "Islamic Group" (to become called Ennahda in the 1990s).

The era of Prime Minister Mohamed Mezali was distinguished from his predecessor El Hadi Nouira by the gradual acceptance of party and media pluralism. Newspapers such *Altarik Aljadid*, the mouthpiece of the Tunisian Communist Party, resumed publication in April 1983, after a halt at the dawn of independence (Al-Sefi, 2012: 197). The following newspapers also resumed publication: *Unity*, which was the mouthpiece of the Popular Unity Party, the *Stance* belonging to the Progressive Democratic Party, and *Citizens* of the Democratic Bloc for Work and Freedoms. Among the new releases of that era were *Alhaqaik* magazines (in Arabic and French), *The Observer* (in Arabic), and *L'Economiste Magriban* (in French), which covered economic affairs.

Challenges for the newspaper market during the Ben Ali era

As mentioned earlier, the newspaper market witnessed a window of freedom during the late 1970s and the 1980s, due to the pressure of the trade union movement and the beginning of the formation of opposition forces (Ahmed al-Mestiri and his companions). It can be argued that this period represented the "first spring of the Tunisian press," despite the violations and arbitrariness that the sector witnessed. The state of media openness continued until the early 1990s, when the Ben Ali regime took new measures to curb political freedom and the power of the independent media (Al-Jorshi, 2004).

During the rule of Ben Ali, the Tunisian press witnessed a development in the printing industry, by strengthening the press of the ruling party, developing private media, and even the press of "soft opposition" parties. The numbers highlight changes in the newspaper sector, as "the number of professional journalists has increased from 639 journalists in 1990 to more than 1,000 in 2002. The number of newspapers grew from 91 in 1987 to 185 in 1997 and over 210 in 2002" (Middle East Online, 2002).

> [Ben Ali] came with another vision in which he sought to use the financial weapon to domesticate the media scene, and opposition newspapers were deprived of public advertising and approved censorship before, during and after the publication, and put their headquarters, officials and workers in them under security control.
>
> *(Truth and Dignity Association, 2018)*

The policy of restricting and stifling the media expanded to include the entire media system, not just opposition newspapers; all newspapers were subject to censorship, including those classified as independent, and the Ben Ali regime sought to lure them toward loyalty until the binding line for everyone became engagement.

The media has come to live in an atmosphere in which the margin of press freedoms has diminished and workers in the sector have been subject to all kinds of censorship, including self-censorship. The tabloid press (known in Tunisia as yellow press) flourished, all of which were tasked to embellish the image of the regime and defame political opponents (Truth and Dignity Commission, 2018). This effort expanded also to include efforts to vilify and silence dissident voices outside Tunisia. The Tunisian Agency for External Communication was one of the most important tools for controlling the system in the media sector during the rule of Ben Ali, and it was established in the early 1990s to put in place a strict system to monitor the editorial line of local newspapers and to control the communication and advertising market for major public institutions. Its task included buying Arab journalists in the diaspora to propagate a bright image of the Ben Ali regime. Scores of Arab and foreign newspapers have benefited from these funds (Center for the Protection and Freedom of Journalists, 2003).

On the level of legislation, Ben Ali has made amendments to the Press Law of 1975 to reduce its restraining character. The most important amendment that was introduced in 2000 was the removal of the physical penalties stipulated in some of its chapters. The amendment also included the criminalization of disturbing public order due to the ambiguity that this concept carries to accept the expansion of interpretation (Middle East Online, 2002). The Ben Ali system also resorted to other means such as giving oral instructions or threats to newspaper editors without leaving written evidence, as well as fabricating charges or fabricating tapes against targeted journalists. The Ben Ali security apparatus did not have any boundaries in using every possible means to silence critical journalists and political as well as human rights activists.

Although scores of newspapers were voluntary or unwillingly engaged in the propaganda system of Ben Ali, few others did not surrender, and they adhered to their right to an honest, pluralistic, and independent media. They fought long enough to communicate their voices to local as well as international public opinion (Al-Jorshi, 2004).

During his visit to Tunisia for the second information summit in 2005, Secretary-General of the United Nations Kofi Annan considered that Tunisian President Ben Ali should respect the freedom of the media in Tunisia like other countries, especially on the occasion of holding an international summit on the information society. He also called for ensuring freedom of the press, and the United States called on Tunisia to achieve political reforms and respect for human rights. That summit coincided with a parallel summit held by several human rights activists, belonging to Tunisian and international NGOs (Karam, 2005) and the widest spectrum of Tunisian opposition. Through their representatives they organized a mass hunger strike, to draw the world's attention towards the deterioration of freedom of opinion and freedom of expression in Tunisia, a reality that contradicts what the regime wanted to portray to the world at the time.

Lotfi Hajji, the first president of the Tunisian Journalists Syndicate (SJT), which the authority refused to acknowledge, noted that after the World Summit on the Information Society, there was pressure on journalists and they suffered from huge restrictions on the exercise of their work and for the union that the authority refused to recognize. Hajji added it became impossible for journalists to meet. Many of them were forced to work in secrecy. Journalists who supported the press syndicate faced daily harassment as an attempt to discourage them. As a consequence, freedom of expression and freedom of assembly for journalists, and other social and professional organizations, remained subject to severe restrictions, and some critics of the government, including journalists, human rights defenders, and civil society activists, were harassed, threatened, and prosecuted (Amnesty International, 2010: 153). The two decades of incarceration of journalists and control on freedom of expression loosened up with the advent of social media networks in Tunisia. Activists capitalized mainly on Facebook to get their voices heard. The social unrest which started on 17 December 2010 and culminated in the revolution of 14 January 2011 has been recorded as study cases in political science, in which bloggers played an active role in covering these events and providing news channels, especially Al Jazeera, with up-to-date information. Attempts of the Ben Ali regime to silence the revolutionary voices did not work.

A transformed newspaper market post-revolution era

The revolution of 14 January 2011 unleashed freedom of opinion and freedom of expression, which reconfigured the media space. However, the process of reforming the media in Tunisia gave priority to the audiovisual sector in both its private and public aspects. Decree No. 116 of 2 November 2011 states the establishment of the High Authority of Audio Visual (HAICA), but this was not followed by the establishment of a similar regulatory body for the press. From the first few weeks of the Tunisian revolution, scores of newspapers appeared in the market. Several outlets belonging to the opposition parties emerged, like *Al-Fajr*, the mouthpiece of Ennahda. However, many papers could not survive the financial pressures. The director of the *Hakaik* newspaper pinpointed the deteriorating status of the written media in Tunisia, as most newspapers are threatened with bankruptcy, including old newspapers dating back more than 50 years. From over 150 newspapers, only 85 newspapers survived. In contrast, the number of electronic newspapers has grown to 81 newsletters (Wannas, 2019). This is consistent with what Bernard Poulet, the French writer and expert, stated in his book *The End of Newspapers and the Future of the Media* when he considered that "the end of printed newspapers is imminent and it is only a matter of time" (Poulet, 2009: 221).

The emergence of online newspapers has also been constantly increasing as "these newspapers have evolved from being hard copies to news, media and entertainment portals of an independent personality" (Ben Messaoud, 2016). The evolution of the number of electronic newspapers immediately after the Tunisian revolution was due to the freedom of the media from government control and the low cost of electronic media compared to printed ones; however, the number of those newspapers is difficult to list in full.

In sum, the Tunisia newspaper market thrived soon after the ousting of the Ben Ali regime in 2011. However, by 2013, crisis and bankruptcy of scores of newspapers became the norm. This phenomenon is by far not a Tunisia problem only but a global crisis facing the printed press. The decline in economic indicators did not encourage successive governments to adopt options that reduce the weakness of the Tunisian newspapers' economies and devise new ways to develop their market in advertising. One of the main factors hindering the growth of written press resources in the absence of a viable and appropriate plan for distributing public advertising and breaking the system that used to control the advertising market during the Ben Ali era. To maintain press independence and prevent political influences, there has been a call for "the creation of a national agency to distribute advertising, which undertakes the distribution of public advertising in accordance with fair and objective criteria among media institutions" (Ben Murad, 2014).

Countries with long-standing experiences in the field of written journalism have more than one approach to address funding difficulties and ways to rationalize the disposition of advisory resources, but the liberalization of the newspaper market seems to have drastic consequences in Tunisia. This is what Naji Al-Bghouri, secretary-general of the Tunisian Journalists Union, argues, that "there must be a moral charter for the media to be a space for democracy, difference and respect for values, away from violence and hatred, excluding others and violating human rights values" (Wannas, 2019).

It should be noted that journalists who have long been prevented from practicing their profession freely are "at the same time unable to translate this acquired freedom into professional media practices" (Essawi, 2012). That is why there has been a call for establishing an independent press regulator in Tunisia in the same way the TV and radio broadcasting market is regulated by HAICA. In addition to various civil society organizations close to the concerns of public opinion who work as watchdogs on the media, this association has the task of reconciling and mediating between citizens on the one hand and journalists and press institutions on the other. The council would look into complaints of citizens against journalists and handle arbitration. Journalists cannot be professional and respectful of professional ethics and independence, as long as they work in an environment that does not provide them with the basic ingredients that preserve their legal standing and their professional and social role.

It will remain a real challenge for press institutions to adhere to the standards of objective and independent journalism while they are underfunded and under-resourced. A healthy public sphere, as Habermas (2006) argues, entails a free media. In his appeal in 2007 to save the German good press and help it not to become prey to the logic of the market, he demanded that the state save the independent press, because its role is essential for a healthy democracy and because news production is not a free operation.

References

Al-Arabi, Ali (1995), *Al-Hadira*. Tunis: Faculty of Humanities and Social Sciences.

Al-Arabi, Ali (1998), Mafhoum Ilm Al-Tarikh Lada Jamaat 'Al-Hadira'. *Al-Sadiqia,* January, pp. 12–17.

Al-Jorshi, S. (2004), Voices Asking to Remove Restriction on the Press in Tunisia. *Al-Wasat News.* Retrieved from www.alwasatnews.com/news/391882.html. Accessed 27 January 2020.

Al-Sefi, S. (2012), *What Written and Suppressed in the Tunisian Press*. Tunis: Tunisian Book House.

Almahidi, Mohamed Saleh (2010), *History of the Tunisian Arabic Press (1860–1896)*. Tunis: Nukush Arabia.

Amnesty International (2010), *Report on Human Rights in the World*. Retrieved from www.amnesty.org/download/Documents/40000/pol100012010ar.pdf. Accessed 29 January 2020.

Ben Gafsa, Omar (1972), *Adwa Ala AlSahafa Altounisia* (Projections on the Tunisian Press), 1860–1970. Tunis: Dar Bouslama for Printing and Publishing.

Ben Messaoud, M. (2016), *Arab Press Journalism: Struggle for Survival and the Challenges of the Digital Technology*. Retrieved from http://studies.aljazeera.net/ar/mediastudies/2016/12/161206082318636.html. Accessed 18 November 2019.

Ben Murad, M. (2014), *The Written Press is Dying and Post-revolution Governments are Watching*, 21 February. Retrieved from www.turess.com/attounissia/114239. Accessed 21 September 2019.

Center for the Protection and Freedom of Journalists (2003), *Report on Media Freedom in Tunisia*, 3 November. Retrieved from https://bit.ly/3eDpqz1. Accessed 22 December 2019.

Dabbab, Mohamed (1973), *Index des revues et journaux tunisiens de langue française de 1907 à l'indépendance*. Tunis: Cérès.

Dawatul-Haq (2019), *Role of the Arab Press in the Modern Thinking and its Development during the two Wars (1918–1939)*. Retrieved from www.habous.gov.ma/daouat-alhaq/item/1451. Accessed 29 December 2019.

Essawi, F. (2012), *Media in Tunisia in Transition*. Retrieved from https://carnegie-mec.org/2012/07/10/ar-pub-48923, Carnegie Middle East Centre. Accessed 26 January 2020.

Habermas, J. (2006), Political Communication in Media Society: Does Democracy still Enjoy an Epistemic Dimension? The Impact of Normative Theory on Empirical Research. *Communication Theory*, 16(4), pp. 411–426.

Hamden, Mohamed (1993), Introduction to the History of the Press in Tunisia (1838–1988. Institute of Journalism and Information Sciences. Tunis: STP.

Julien, Charles-André (1985), *Et la Tunisie devint indépendante (1951–1957)*. Tunis: Les éditions Jeune Afrique S.T.D.

Karam, S. (2005), *Continuous Clamping Down on Free Speech in Tunisia in spite of the International Protests*. *D.W.*, 17 November. Retrieved from https://bit.ly/2RWR2Fs. Accessed 19 January 2020.

Karimi, Ali (2011), *Press Law in the Arab Maghreb: Challenges and Prospects*. Rabat: ISESCO.

Kheshana, R. (2018), Tunisia after the 2011 Revolution: Hard Task Facing the Transformation of the Media from Government Media to Public Service Media. *Swissinfo*, 21 January. Retrieved from www.swissinfo.ch/ara/business/43816644/تونس_-مصاعب-الانتقال-من-الإعلام-الحكومي-إلى-الإعلام-العمومي; Accessed 27 March 2020.

Middle East Eye (2002), *Media in Tunisia is Making Swift Progress*, 18 June. Retrieved from https://bit.ly/2VZ6RNp. Accessed 30 January 2020.

Poulet, B. (2009), *La fin des journaux et l'avenir de l'information*. Paris: Gallimard.

Rossignol, Gilles (1970), Le statut de la presse et des journalistes en Tunisie de 1859 à 1969. *Revue Servir, M.T.E, Tunis,* (6), pp. 38–49.

Truth and Dignity Commission (2018), *Documentary Film: The Propaganda and Misinformation System*, 17 December. Retrieved from https://bit.ly/2Vpqtej. Accessed 22 November 2019.

Wannas, Y. (2019), Has the Tunisian Media overcome Problems of the Past? *Anadul Agency*, 14 January. Retrieved from www.aa.com.tr/ar/. Accessed 25 January 2020.

35

BROADCASTING IN TUNISIA FROM INDEPENDENCE TO POST-2011 REVOLUTION ERA

Noureddine Miladi

Introduction

TV and radio broadcasting have witnessed a total transformation in Tunisia after the revolution of 14 January 2011, from a media controlled by successive undemocratic regimes to outlets that experience unprecedented transformations in terms of ownership, editorial control, and regulatory mechanisms. This significant revolution in media freedom has unleashed free speech and the circulation of information and brought to existence the public service broadcasting as well as independent media as new players in the broadcasting market. This chapter provides an analysis of the transformations in the broadcasting sector in Tunisia since independence and analyzes the hallmark changes in this regard. It discusses the sophistication of the role of political leadership in controlling the media during the 55 years of Tunisia's post-independence era up until the eve of the revolution that ousted the regime of Zein Elabidine Ben Ali.

In this chapter, I approach the transformation in the media scene through three historical phases: (1) the rule of the first president of the republic, Habib Bourguiba; (2) the Ben Ali era; and (3) the post-revolution restructuring of the radio and TV broadcasting market and its potential role in the democratic transition and social change.

Broadcasting under the rule of Habib Bourguiba (1956–1987)

The rule of the first president of Tunisia, Habib Bourguiba, marked the birth of the first republic after independence from France (1881–1956). This era is deemed significant in the history of the emerging nation at the time because it potentially represented a historical turn that could have paved the way for Tunisia to join the locomotive of democratic countries. Particularly with the establishment of independent media institutions, Tunisia was ready to embrace a democratic system built on liberal values of free speech, diversity, and justice.

Before delving into the analysis of the media scene during Bourguiba's rule, it is imperative to address the emergence of journalism practice in Tunisia under French colonization and the diverse newspaper and magazine outlets that existed throughout that period. During the French colonial epoch, the Tunisian press had considerable presence, fueled by the resistance against the colonists. The narrow space available for freedom of expression at the time contributed to the emergence of a few newspapers and periodicals which had helped echo the views of the

Tunisian national movement to the European, African, as well as Arab elites (Chouikha, 1992). Also, newspapers and newsletters that existed at the time carried the same spirit and thus linked the leaders of the national movement and activists throughout the country with news and latest developments, albeit among the educated elites. Among the important initiatives in this context was the establishment of the newspaper *L'Action Tunisienne* (Tunisian Labor) by Habib Bourguiba, Tahir Safar, and Salih Farhat after the launch of the new party in 1934 at the city of Qasr Hilal. This media platform represented a tool to disseminate news about anti-colonialism activism and views about how to induce reform in the country.

However, the stringent control on media outlets started appearing soon after Bourguiba took power as the first president of the republic in 1956. The Office of State Media was established on 31 May 1956 as the body through which Bourguiba governed the media scene (Hajji, 2004). On 31 May 1966, the first TV broadcasting had started under the name of Tunisian Radio and Television. The establishment of the first TV channel in the country was followed on 30 December 1967 with the inauguration of the first college of journalism in the country and indeed in the region, called Institut de Presse et des Sciences de l'information (IPSI). The institute served as an incubator for future generations of qualified journalists that fed both press and broadcast journalism institutions over the years.

Tight legislation governing the press and broadcasting started appearing with Article 8 of the 1 June 1959 Constitution. The document stipulated that freedom of speech and freedom of the press were guaranteed. But the legislation governing the field of media and communication was considered by media critiques and human rights groups as repressive and arbitrary. The International Media Support (2002: 12) reported, "The Tunisian government has set into motion a sophisticated security apparatus which creates an environment of fear among journalists, leads to self-censorship and a sense of deep humiliation."

In the mid-1960s, Tunisia witnessed another setback regarding media freedom, which included restricting freedom of speech and closing many media outlets and often chasing or forcing their owners to leave the country. This period coincided with the incarceration of the leaders of the Yousfi movement (named after its leader Ahmed ben Yousuf) and banning the activity of the Tunisian Communist Party (Haddad, 2008).

Bourguiba's long authoritarian rule

The close connection between media and state power is unmistakable when attempting to analyze the media scene during Bourguiba's rule. Throughout his long march of power, Bourguiba was aware of the significance of the media from the outset. TV and radio broadcasting were fully employed as tools for public opinion influence and nation-building. The media in his philosophy were tools to galvanize the public towards implementing the state policies. The communication strategy included various campaigns to guide public opinion towards certain practices and instill behaviors that Bourguiba saw as crucial in building a "civilized society" (Bourguiba, 1962). Organized campaigns, for instance, on birth control to convince Tunisian families of its importance in preventing poverty and increasing women's productivity remained for a whole decade during the 1970s. On 27 December 1974, the country's constitution was revised and Bourguiba declared himself head of state for life. This enabled him to legitimize further tight control on all affairs of the state. Central to his political communication strategy was the direct overseeing of all forms of mass media platforms at the time (newspapers, radio, and TV) (Haddad, 2008).

As a result of this strategy, Bourguiba was able to gradually extend his influence on the state apparatus. This became evident in his dominance as head of state on the content of news bulletins on state television and on national radio, as well as on official and pro-government newspapers. On the main news program of each day, coverage of the president's activities accounted for one-third of the news programs on national radio and TV. The ever-repetitive narrative consisted of his daily activities like speeches, meetings, and visits to various places in addition to the inauguration of new projects. Descriptive news reports such as "The president has today met with," "The president has visited," "The president has inau-gurated the new project," or "The president has said" were the main digest of national TV and radio news programs. Hardly any current affairs analysis or any attempts that amounted to a form of investigative journalism existed in the local and international news reporting (Miladi, 2019).

As for media ownership, the reign of Habib Bourguiba had overarching control of the media outlets especially broadcasting. The Tunisian Radio and Television Corporation was not a sovereign facility but a government-run apparatus. Senior and middle managers were directly appointed from the presidential palace. Leadership positions were also allocated based on strict party allegiance to the ruling party (Rassemblement Constitutionel Democratique [RCD; Constitutional Democratic Assembly]) (Chouikha, 2015). For instance, during 30 years of his rule, Bourguiba appointed 11 ministers of culture and media, all of whom were from the same ruling political party. The regime saw in this position authority to guide society, as no place for dissenting opinion was allowed to stand out or even have the slightest influence. The result of the media policy of the Bourguiba regime was a total absence of the media's role as a govern-ment watchdog and of protecting the interests of the public.

While Bourguiba, as argued by Haddad (2008), had fully engaged the state bureaucracy and institutions to build Tunisia based on Western modernity, he resisted the most significant value in the Western modernity project, freedom of expression, which the intellectuals of the Euro-pean Enlightenment cherish as the core of liberal democracy.

Media as weapons to harass political opponents

Bourguiba used the media to demonize and humiliate political opponents and human rights defenders. Although this scene changed in the era of Prime Minister Mohammed Mzali (1980–1986), who was known for his relative openness, the margins of freedom did not change much. Given the regime's complete control over the media landscape, either by owning media outlets and controlling the content or by intimidating violators, its opponents did not have any plat-forms to express their views. This happened successively with national figure Saleh ben Youssef (1907–1961), the nationalists (in the 1970s), the leftists (in the 1980s), and finally members of the Ennahda party, during the 1990s until 2011 (Hajji, 2004). Among the victims of Bour-guiba's tight grip on the media was Bashir ben Ahmed, who served as the first minister of infor-mation after independence. Unable to sustain the regime's grip on the media, he founded *Jeune Afrique* magazine in 1961 and settled in Paris in 1962 to continue his journalism career. *Jeune Afrique* has continued since then as an important platform for news and current affairs analysis about Tunisia and the African region.

Media scene during the Ben Ali Era (1987–2011)

Zein Elabidine Ben Ali, who had started his career in the 1980s as a member of the Tunisian security services, ascended the diplomatic ladder to become the ambassador of Tunisia to Poland, minister of the interior, then prime minister in 1986, appointed by the then presi-dent Habib Bourguiba. Ben Ali managed finally to stage a bloodless coup against the ailing president Bourguiba and declared himself the second president of the Republic of Tunisia on 7 November 1987.

Media ownership and control during his mandate (1987–2011) did not differ from that of his predecessor. However, a key feature of this era was the close Ben Ali family members who became influential in every sphere of public life, including the media (Buckley et al., 2012). Also, his party, RCD, smoothed his hegemonic influence on public life and normalized his police image for a civil leader able to outreach to the general public across the country.

The Ministry of Information and the External Communication Agency (known as ATCE), two official bodies, became instrumental in the media control apparatus that Ben Ali established during his 23 years of rule. In *The Black Book: Propaganda Machine under the Rule of Ben Ali,* Marzouki (2013) unravels the extent to which the External Communication Agency under the Ben Ali regime took in charge propaganda campaigns overseas for the Ben Ali regime. Mainly through bribing journalists and media companies, this propaganda tool used to generously pay writers and PR organizations in Europe and the USA to spread reports about fake economic successes of the regime, stability, freedom, and respect for human rights at a time when Tunisia witnessed one of the darkest periods of its modern history (Ben Letaief, 2018: 3). It also waged wars against all critical voices both inside and outside Tunisia and tended to terrorize journalists and writers who dared disseminate a negative image about Ben Ali, especially about his ineligibility to lead the country (Marzouki, 2013: 12). In addition to censoring newspapers, the government used to control the movement of journalists, especially when attending international gatherings relating to press freedom (Rugh, 2004).

Internally, total censorship on critical issues was always monitored. Human rights abuses, freedom of speech, the president's personal life along with that of his family and entourage, and issues related to poverty and underdeveloped regions in Tunisia were among the taboos that all media and critics must refrain from covering (Marzouki, 2013: 12). The national TV and radio channels remained propaganda tools directly controlled from the presidential palace.

Over the five decades before the 2011 revolution, the Tunisian regimes had established a sophisticated security apparatus and spread a climate of fear everywhere in the country. Reports from international organizations testified that the "media have always been subjected to a conundrum of legal restrictions, government interference, physical threats, arrest and many other types of abuse" (International Media Support, 2002: 3). The law controlling free speech included various prohibitions. Numerous methods used by the Bourguiba and Ben Ali regimes to censor information and keep tight control on free speech included the 1975 Press Code. The *legal deposit* requirement obliged all publishers to submit a copy of their publication before distribution. This gatekeeping policy allowed regime regulators to censor every form of media at the time critical to the regime. Heavy fines and sometimes prison sentences were typically enforced on any journalist who dared be critical. Under such a regime, defamation was a legislative tool used to accuse and imprison political dissidents and independent journalists. Tailor-made court sentences for "attempting to jeopardize state security and public order or causing offense to the head of the state and other government figures" were always in place (Human Rights Watch, 2005; Reporters Without Borders, 2010).

Also, through the Ministry of Information, Ben Ali managed to have control over the media scene. Public service media (two TV channels, nine radio stations, and the Tunisian national news agency) used to be directly controlled from the president's office. As a consequence,

> Ben Ali has gone to great lengths to appear "democratic" through sophisticated public relations overseas and the creation of an array of official national human rights

bodies including a human rights minister and human rights departments in at least four ministries.

(International Media Support, 2002: 3)

As far as appointments to media leadership positions were considered, all nominations of directors and chief editors come through a presidential decree. The Tunisian News Agency (TAP), supposedly a professional and independent news service provider, was also part of the regime's media machine. The same goes for private media organizations which started to appear only a few years before the revolution. Licensing of newspapers, magazines, and later a limited number of private radio and TV channels used to be granted solely to close members of the president's family (Barata, 2013). For instance, Mosaique FM, which was the first private radio station, was launched in 2003 by Ben Ali's son-in-law Belhassen Trabelsi. In 2004 the first private TV channel, Hannibal TV, was launched by Larbi Nasra, a businessman with close ties to the Ben Ali regime and a relative of Ben Ali's wife (Leila Trabelsi). Then consecutively afterward, a few more TV and radio channels were licensed to people from the close family circle. Radio Zitouna FM was launched in 2007 by Sakhr El Matri (Ben Ali's son-in-law). Nabil Karwi, a wealthy businessman and supporter of Ben Ali, launched his private TV channel Nessma TV in June 2009. Ben Ali's daughter (Cyrine) launched Radio Shams FM in August 2010, while the son of Ben Ali's doctor received a license to launch his private radio in October 2010 called Radio Express FM.

Overall, the Ben Ali government had leverage over commercial TV and radio outlets through economic means. Due to financial difficulties, such channels remain always vulnerable to government pressures. It was always the case that government advertising was associated with being in line with an editorial policy that pleases the regime. Tight control by the Ben Ali regime on public spaces was not limited to media outlets but also placed on all public spaces. Cafés, mosques, clubs, and town squares used to be heavily policed environments. All potential spaces for public gatherings, even if small, became spheres for intelligence gathering by the security services.

Consequently, in this environment, notorious for its tight control on basic freedoms, satellite TV coming from abroad remained the refuge for large audiences in Tunisia during the 1990s and the new millennium. Al Jazeera Arabic channel, in particular, had received competitive following due to its uncensored news and discussion shows on critical issues related to public interests like free speech, human rights, democracy, and corruption in the Arab countries (Mabrouki, 2016). However, in an attempt to downplay the impact of Al Jazeera, the Tunisian Parliament passed a law in 1995 making the approval of local councils mandatory for the installation of satellite dishes. Other channels that have had a share in the Tunisian TV market before the revolution were mainly broadcasting from London, such as Middle East Broadcasting Center (MBC) which later moved to Dubai, Al-Mustakilla TV, Iqra TV, Al-Hiwar TV, and Al-Magharibia.

Against this backdrop, it is worth noting that both Bourguiba's and Ben Ali's human rights records were not challenged by Western allies. Under the Euro-Mediterranean Association Agreement, Tunisia had a significant trade partnership with the European Union. European Union countries, as well as the USA, had no issues supporting the regime in Tunisia as long as Ben Ali kept serving their economic and strategic interests in the region. France was the main benefactor par excellence and the main supporter of the brutal regimes of Ben Ali and Bourguiba. Ben Ali's position was even further bolstered after the September 11 attacks on New York and Washington, ostensibly for being a model in the region for "fighting extremism."

In conclusion, regarding the aforementioned two critical periods in the history of Tunisia, and like most other Arab regimes, under Bourguiba and Ben Ali the successive governments managed to establish their dominance over the media, preventing every form of diversity. The general aim was to promote national unity and consolidate Tunisian identity, but this came under party propaganda and information control (International Media Support, 2002).

Transformation of the broadcasting market post-2011 revolution

The ousting of the Ben Ali regime has brought with it an entire shift in media ownership, diversity, editorial freedom, and free speech. The media as platforms for public opinion expression and spheres of debate on social and political affairs have become the heart of the democratic project which the country has been witnessing.

Firstly, freedom of expression has become enshrined in communication laws as well as the new constitution of the country. The global freedom index, Freedom House, for instance, rated Tunisia very high in terms of freedom of expression by 2015. On a scale from 1 (being the best) to 7 (being the worst) in the world, Tunisia rated second (Freedom House, 2015). The report also states, "The transitional government (at the time) proclaimed freedom of information and expression as a foundational principle for the country, and vast new press freedoms emerged from the revolution" (Freedom House, 2015).

Since then, Tunisia has made significant improvements in consolidating its citizens' constitutional rights, at the core of which is freedom of speech, thought, and faith. The new constitution ratified in 2014 established freedom of expression and freedom of religion as basic rights for every citizen. Article 31 states, "Freedom of opinion, thought, expression, media, and publication shall be guaranteed. These freedoms shall not be subject to prior censorship" (Constitution of the Republic of Tunisia, 2015). Also, Article 32 states, "The state shall guarantee the right to information and the right to access information. The state seeks to guarantee the right to access to information networks" (Constitution of the Republic of Tunisia, 2015).

At an early stage after the revolution, a constitutional body was set up to follow up on achieving the goals of the revolution. The High Authority for the Achievement of the Objectives of the Revolution, Political Reform, and Democratic Transition had committed itself, among other tasks, to oversee media reform according to international standards. Its mission became significant especially after the dissolution of the Ministry of Information and the Higher Council for Communication. It brought in regulatory models regarding media reform from various international media organizations such as the Office of Communication (OFCOM) in the UK, the BBC public service model, and the Higher Audiovisual Council in France, among other examples from around the world.

Moreover, a milestone change regarding complaints or infringements related to freedom of speech formerly dealt with by the Ministry of Interior is now managed by the justice system. Related to these developments are journalists' independence and freedom from all attempts to coerce or intimidate them for various political or financial reasons. Media organizations are now compelled by law to reveal for the first time their sources of income and their audited annual financial reports to avoid any forms of influence, both local and international.

Secondly, the radio and television broadcasting market has witnessed a rapid transformation too. Tens of new radio and TV channels have come into existence, which has increased competition and as a result diversified audience choice. This sector, which now hosts 11 TV channels and over 21 radio stations, remained for decades (during the rule of Bourguiba and Ben Ali) very much dominated by state-controlled channels. Since 2013 there still exist two TV broadcast systems in Tunisia, analog and digital; "*Al Watania 1, Al Watania 2* cover respectively

99.80% and 99.60% of the Tunisian territory, while the cover rate of Hannibal TV is 44.80%" (OECD, 2013). The digital TV broadcasting market includes 11 television channels: two public channels, which are Al Watania 1 and Al Watania 2, and nine private channels, namely Hannibal TV, Nessma TV, Attounissia, El Hiwar Ettounsi, TWT, Al Janoubia TV, Tounesna TV, Ezzitouna TV, and El Kalima TV. Audience share in the three largest governorates, namely Tunis, Sousse, and Sfax, is monopolized by four main channels: "Al Watania 1, Hannibal TV, Attounissia and Nessma TV acquire for a total audience share of 55.30%, 52.6% and 62.80% in Tunis, Sousse, and Sfax respectively" (OECD, 2013).

As for the radio broadcasting market in Tunisia, it is composed of 21 channels (nine public and 12 private). In the capital Tunis, Mosaïque FM has the highest audience share with 51% of the market. In Sousse and Sfax, Jawhara FM and Sfax Radio remain the most dominant in the radio broadcasting market with 52% and 35% of the audience share. This is because all of the aforementioned channels are well-established media organizations, even before 2011. The Tunisian Radio Authority (public service radio authority) hosts nine radio channels, two are general: The National Radio and Radio Tunis International, and two are thematic radio services: Youth Radio and Tunisian Cultural Radio. In addition, five regional radio stations are situated in key cities from the north of the country to the southern part. However, despite the geographic expansion of radio broadcasting in Tunisia, the Court of Accountability (2019) reports that there is poor reception of radio signals of public service radio, especially in the middle and southern parts of the country. Part of the problem, it has been argued, is that most of those radio stations broadcast on AM frequencies instead of FM, which affects the sound quality of the broadcasts (ibid.: 658).

The report has also criticized the radio channels for a lack of program planning and proper scheduling. It reads,

> there existed duplication in terms of program content for the national radio channels. The lack of coordination has meant no distinction between them. As a consequence, none of the public service radio channels have managed to compete in the radio market. The three radio services have mostly remained copy-cat in terms of their media discourse and the general trend of their programs.
>
> *(2019: 659)*

The editorial policy of radio broadcasting remains also problematic namely when it comes to sticking to objectivity and impartiality in news reporting and discussion shows. The report also observed that there is an absence of audience studies which should help understand what listeners are interested in, in terms of program preferences. This has enormously affected its audience share, which did not exceed 2% according to the report by late 2014 (Court of Accountability, 2019: 660).

Thirdly, the post-2011 period has witnessed landmark changes in terms of regulatory frameworks, which have helped organize ownership and control of media outlets in a way that does not infringe on competition rules. The audiovisual market in Tunisia saw the establishment of the first independent audiovisual regulatory authority, known as High Authority for Audio-Visual Communication (HAICA). The HAICA was the outcome of lengthy debates in the Constituent Assembly (first parliament after the revolution). Decree-Law No. 2011–10 dated 2 March 2011 and Decree-Law No. 2011–116 dated 2 November 2011 provided for the creation of an independent regulatory authority to be in charge of governing the radio and TV broadcasting sector at a national level. It was also granted power as a consultative body to approve the appointment of executive positions for public service media organizations. The legislative framework of HAICA repealed all legislative frameworks governing the television and broad-casting sector such as Law No. 93–8 dated 1 February 1993, regarding the creation of National Broadcasting Corporation, and Law No. 2001–1 dated 15 January 2001 promulgating the tel-ecommunications code Law No. 2007–33 dated 4 June 2007, relating to the public audiovisual establishments.

This independent body was also entrusted with guaranteeing fair and competitive market rules in radio and television broadcasting in Tunisia. Its raison d'être is to guarantee free speech, diversity and objectivity, and balanced journalism. In terms of market distribution, it controls media ownership by preventing unfair competition in the audiovisual market. The HAICA is also in charge of frequency licensing and monitoring of the media market. Observing the output of radio and TV broadcasting across the board entails guaranteeing the implementa-tion of professional journalism ethics, freedom of speech, and diversity. Along with the Higher Independent Authority for Elections, the HAICA also has power, according to the new regula-tory laws, to monitor radio and TV political broadcasts during election campaigns. In cases of violations of any of the laws regulating the audiovisual sector, HAICA may sanction warnings or even withdraw broadcasting licenses.

New challenges in the post-revolution media scene

Tunisia is no exception when it comes to the challenges faced by media organizations world-wide with regard to funding and ideological influences. Most of the private TV and radio stations in the country have been going through financial crises during the last few years. For example, Al-Mutawassit TV, Zaytouna TV, Nessma TV, Hannibal TV, and Al-Hiwar al-Tunisi channels laid off scores of their journalists and came to the verge of bankruptcy.

As a result, funding from advertisers and business conglomerates have affected the editorial line and agenda of these channels. The regulatory body HAICA has already filed a few cases about political influence on the media through funding. Nessma TV (founded in 2007) is a case in point whereby its founder Nabil Karoui was warned by HAICA for political mobilization of the channel. Through its news programs and discussion shows, the channel was considered politically motivated in support of Nidaa Tounes.

Moreover, corruption and manipulation of the public service media institutions by members from the extreme left infiltrating those institutions heightened even more after 2013 when the Troika-led government lost power to Nidaa Tounes. As quoted by Labidi (2017: 132),

> On July 18, 2016, the National Commission to Fight Corruption (INLC), the Tunisia League for Human Rights (LTDH), SNJT and FTDJ denounced mafia-like media outlets that had turned into criminal gangs, warning against their dangerous impact on Tunisia's transition to democracy.

The Troika government was the first elected government after the revolution and was a coalition of three victorious parties after the 2011 election: Ennahda, The Congress for the Republic (CPR), and Democratic Forum for Labor and Liberties (FDTL). During 2012–2014 the Troika-led government faced significant challenges partly due to the smear campaigns from ideologically driven media outlets. In fact, opposite to what Yacoub (2017: 115) had claimed that the three parties sharing power at the time "were accused of controlling public media and leading defamatory campaigns against the media," those parties were instead victims of system-atic negative coverage. Biased media coverage focused attention on problems and undermined the government's attempts to fix economic problems, unemployment, and other social and political issues. Scores of journalists known for their affiliation to the extreme left ideology drifted away from the standard norms of professional journalism and instead waged media wars against government ministers and state institutions.

As a consequence, instead of being watchdogs for the public, scores of ideologically driven media outlets turned into sources of misinformation and potential tools for stirring social disturbances. As suggested by Labidi (2017: 125), "A victory to liberate the press from government control may be meaningless if the sector is not also protected from potential capture by self-serving business leaders." Broadcast media should be, as suggested by Zran and Ben Messaoud (2014: 9), "a mirror reflecting the national interests. Public broadcasters in Tunisia are regarded as social institutions entrusted with a significant role of reporting news, circulating information, and discussing issues which concern the public."

Conclusion

Since 14 January 2011, Tunisia has witnessed a radical change in the media system and a historic transformation that has led to a complex period of democratic transition. As the country recovers from a long dictatorship, which lasted over 50 years, the emerging democracy in Tunisia remains fragile but more promising than any other among the Arab Spring countries. During this transitional period, the media remain a sophisticated area of manipulation and power struggle between the power structures of the country. An analysis of the media scene during this period leads to the conclusion that ideological battles between different parties have taken on multiple dimensions. Although most of this power struggle occurs in public spaces, much of it has been taking place on television and radio waves in addition to social media networks platforms.

The media's role in the transition to democracy has been considered significant. Free and diverse media outlets can potentially help rebuild political and social values of power-sharing, peaceful political change, democratic governance, and freedom of opinion. This requires regular news coverage of political affairs neutrally and impartially, routine handling of the activities of the elected government, and reporting the business of parliament in a transparent manner.

In this new environment, public service media can potentially spearhead a healthy democratic transition in Tunisia. It is worth noting that a new critical space is developing for civil society organizations to express their views regarding the shaping of the new democracy in the country. TV and radio channels have been hosting a growing number of discussion shows that address every aspect of the Tunisian society. Talk shows about political reform, corruption, education, the role of the police, civil society, human rights, culture, and sports have become the digest of scores of channels. This new scope of media freedom is exceptional given the fact that representatives of civil society organizations had never before had the opportunity to freely express their views on public service media, for instance during the Ben Ali era, especially when it comes to issues relating to human rights, workers' rights, and political participation.

This growth in the media market has also meant growing challenges for the regulatory bodies and genuine concerns regarding the influence of the new web of media outlets. As such, this post-revolution period has also witnessed unremitting tensions between the influential media enterprises and the elected governments. On the one hand, this is partly due to the conflicting understanding of the media's role in a transitional democracy, the manipulation of the media by rich entrepreneurs, and ideological interests. The global phenomenon termed by some as "tabloidization," which is the result of the increasing media market competition, already affected the Tunisian media decades ago. What has been happening to the world media, especially the press during the last 20 years or so, has already taken its toll on the media in Tunisia.

On the other hand, part of the challenge for the proper development of the media is the existence of old school bureaucrats, entrenched in the state bureaucracy, who are still influencing the political agenda from making any palpable progress in this area. The challenge to Tunisia's media and democracy comes not only from big businesses and a few politicians but also from known figures and organizations who pose for media reform, but in fact, they blindly mix ideology with media reform.

In conclusion, it can be argued that Tunisia's transition to democracy is difficult without a free media, whose role can effectively affect politicians and elites. It should be recommended here that the public media in Tunisia need structural reform that includes immediate implementation of professional editorial policy and high standards of professionalism to serve this role. The liberalization of the media sector has been valued as one of the achievements of the revolution. However, this development in the media landscape was not accompanied by vigorous reforms in the laws governing the sector, intensive training programs to change the high professional standards that the media should pursue in democracy, as well as fundamental changes in its management.

References

Barata, J. (2013), Tunisian Media under the Authoritarian Structure of Ben Ali's Regime and After. In T. Guaaybess (ed.), *National Broadcasting and State Policy in Arab Countries*. London: Palgrave Macmillan.

Ben Letaief, M. (2018), Freedom of Speech in Tunisia: Texts and Contexts. *Mena Media Law*. Retrieved from www.menamedialaw.org/sites/default/files/library/material/tunisia_chp_2018.pdf. Accessed 24 February 2019.

Bourguiba, H. (1962a), *Best Behavior is a Guarantor for Safe Society (public speech)*, 12 March. Retrieved from www.youtube.com/watch?v=0cNNkEGsUlk. Accessed 16 November 2019.

Buckley, S., Benchelha, M., and Ouarda, B. (2012), *Assessment of Media Development in Tunisia*. Paris: UNESCO. Retrieved from www.unesco.org/new/fileadmin/MULTIMEDIA/HQ/CI/CI/pdf/IPDC/tunisia_mdi_report_english.pdf. Accessed 11 November 2019.

Chouikha, L. (1992), Situation de la Liberte d'Information en Tunisie (Situation of Freedom Information in Tunisia). In *l'Information au Maghreb*. Tunis: Ceres Productions.

Chouikha, L. (2015), *La difficile transformation des médias: des années de l'indépendance à la veille des élections de 2014* (The Difficult Transition of Media in Tunisia: From Independence to the 2014 Elections). Tunis: Editions Finzi.

Constitution of the Republic of Tunisia (2015), Tunis. *Journal Officiel de la République Tunisienne*, 20 April. Retrieved from www.legislation.tn/sites/default/files/news/consti-tution-b-a-t.pdf/. Accessed 25 February 2019.

Court of Accountability (2019), *The Institution of Tunisia Radio*. Retrieved from www.courdescomptes.nat.tn/upload/rapport29/II-11.pdf. Accessed 23 March 2019.

Freedom House (2015), *Freedom in the World 2015*. Retrieved from https://freedomhouse.org/report/freedom-world/2015/tunisia#.VTJ_nfAUuwE. Accessed 26 February 2019.

Haddad, K. (2008), *Bourguiba, and the Media: The Dialectic of Power and Propaganda* (in Arabic). Tunis: Tunis Carthage Publishers.

Hajji, L. (2004), *Bourguiba and Islam: Headship and Religious Leadership* (in Arabic). Tunis: Dar Al-Janoub for Publishing.

Human Rights Watch (2005), *False Freedom: Online Censorship in the Middle East and North Africa*, 17(10) (e) (November). Retrieved from www.hrw.org/report/2005/11/14/false-freedom/online-censorship-middle-east-and-north-africa. Accessed 7 May 2019.

International Media Support (2002), *Tunisia's Media Landscape*. IMS Report. Copenhagen: IMS. Retrieved from www.yumpu.com/en/document/view/21846848/tunisias-media-landscape-international-media-support. Accessed 31 March 2019.

Labidi, K. (2017), Tunisia's Media Barons Wage War on Independent Media Regulation. In Aniya Schiffrin (ed.), *In the Service of Power: Media Capture and the Threat to Democracy*. Washington, DC: The National Endowment for Democracy, pp. 125–137. Retrieved from www.cima.ned.org/wp-content/uploads/2017/08/CIMA_MediaCaptureBook_F1.pdf. Accessed 25 March 2019.

Mabrouk, M. (2016), Democratic Transition and Media Transition: Characteristics of the Tunisian Experience. In J. Zran and N. Miladi (eds.), *Media and the Democratic Transition in the Arab World* (in Arabic). Tunis: AMCN and Sotumedias, pp. 317–342.

Marzouki, M. (2013), *The Black Book: Propaganda Machine under the Rule of Ben Ali* (in Arabic). Tunis: Media and Communication Unit, Tunisian President's Office.

Miladi, N. (2019), Public Service Broadcasting and Democratic Transition in Tunisia. In Jamel Zran and Noureddine Miladi (eds.), *Media & Democratic Transition in the Arab World*. Tunis: AMCN and Sotumedias, pp. 343–368.

OECD (2013), *Competition Issues in Television and Broadcasting*, p. 293. Retrieved from www.oecd.org/daf/competition/TV-and-broadcasting2013.pdf. Accessed 22 February 2019.

Reporter Without Borders (2010), *World Freedom Index 2010*. Retrieved from https://rsf.org/en/world-press-freedom-index-2010. Accessed 7 May 2019.

Rugh, W. (2004), *Arab Mass Media: Newspaper, Radio, and Television in Arab Politics*. London: Praeger Publishers.

Yacoub, S. (2017), Press Freedom in Tunisia. The Post-Revolution Challenges. In Elsebeth Frey, Mofzur Rahman, and Hamida El Bour (eds.), *Negotiating Journalism. Core Values and Cultural* Diversities. Göteborg: Nordicom, pp. 109–120.

Zran, J., and Ben Messaoud, M. (2014), *Public Service Media, Characteristics, Potential, and Challenges. The Radio and Television Institutions as an Example*. Tunis: Arab Radio Broadcasting Union.

36

SOCIAL MEDIA NETWORKS AND THE DEMOCRATIC TRANSITION IN TUNISIA

From censorship to freedom

Moez Ben Messaoud

Introduction

Researchers and observers will always recall that social media networks had a pivotal role in disseminating pictures and broadcasting the first videos of the Tunisian revolution (between 17 December 2010 and 14 January 2011) to the whole world. After the then president Zein Elabidine Ben Ali (1987–2011) was overthrown, Facebook and Twitter platforms facilitated the most popular virtual spaces for social, cultural, and political interaction amongst activists. Such platforms became even more important by the time that Mohamed Ghanouchi, interim prime minister, abolished the Ministry of Communication and resumed Internet service on 17 January 2011.

That environment turned social media into precious tools that helped unleash individuals' freedoms and consolidate people's sense of being citizens. Tunisians became able to interact with the various texts, ideas, and experiences on the Internet by consuming, diffusing, and commenting on them. "This interaction has created changes at the psychological, intellectual and cultural levels and in the individual's perception of himself and others" (Grami, 2013). Coming from a number of Arab countries, which more recently include The Sudan, where public protests started on 19 December 2018 after an official statement announced an increase in bread prices, and Algeria, where there has been a popular movement since February 2019 and where young people have managed to lead through their use of communication means.

> The latter have been dominated by social networks, for instance, in Egypt, Libya, Syria and Yemen. Indeed, Facebook became famous in the Arab world and spread at an amazing speed, as its users were able to benefit from its services in order to realize their goals in mobilizing the masses to overthrow authoritarian regimes.
>
> *(Mansouri, 2012)*

Accordingly, the democratization of the communication means has undergone a noticeable change, which has been recognized by those interested in the field of new media. This is despite the divergent viewpoints between those who associate new social media with a prominent role in the Tunisian revolution, in particular, and Arab revolutions, in general, and those who see the new social media as one of the several factors that have contributed to broadening people's potential for participation in shaping a new world. The actual role of these means remains an issue that is open for debate and requires a lot of scrutiny to understand the importance of the active participants and their roles in the Tunisian popular mobilization.

The emergence of the Internet in Tunisia and its transformation into an alternative platform

Since 1999, the Internet has been widely used by a significant segment of youth and the opposition, who have found it to be a window on the world and an alternative space in which they can enjoy freedom of speech. In fact, from the end of the 1990s to the present day, it is possible to identify three major periods in Tunisian online criticism, particularly as a function of existing communication devices, and they are being utilized for contentious purposes (Lecomte, 2011: 391). Initially, from the late 1990s to the mid-2000s, those who are often referred to as Tunisian "cyber-dissidents" (Lecomte, 2011: 392) were largely isolated from the vast majority of Tunisian netizens. They were involved in a small number of collective websites, mailing lists, and discussion forums. Debates were thus strongly centralized within a few communication spaces. The critical tone in these spaces was radical, most of the Internet users remained anonymous, and many resided abroad. Few examples to mention here were *Takriz* (created in January 1998), *Tunezine* (created in 2001), *Réveil Tunisien* (created in 2002), and *Nawaat*, co-founded in 2004 by two Tunisians abroad, Sami Ben Gharbia and Riadh Guerfali, who were already active on the forum *Tunezine*.

In the second period, around the mid-2000s, blogs began to gain importance. They were often run by individuals who did not know each other but were nonetheless connected, notably through "aggregators" and hypertext links. At this juncture, it is worth emphasizing that blogs would encourage the diversification and enrichment of forms of criticism, for example, the development of satirical criticism in the Tunisian dialect and through caricature. On the other hand, they would encourage the first movement towards the decompartmentalization of the citizen and the militant uses of the Internet. In the past, there were, on the one hand, a few critical collective spaces, vis-à-vis the regime, in place and, on the other, a multitude of spaces (forums and websites) devoted to various themes. But they avoided any speech that might be considered, even if only slightly, "political" or "subversive." This configuration of criticism within Tunisian cyberspace corresponded, in a certain way, to a phenomenon that Cass Sunstein and others have called "cyber-balkanization" (Rohde, 2005: 119); that is to say, this tendency would have Internet users utilize those digital spaces that are frequented by individuals who share the same opinions and the same interests as themselves.

Finally, one can identify a third period in Tunisian online spaces, characterized by the emergence of social networking platforms, especially Facebook and – to a lesser extent – Twitter. It is around the beginning of 2008 that Tunisians appropriated Facebook more and more for protest purposes. The "citizen netizens" have not deserted the blogs that continue to grow, often complementing Facebook. While, according to the available statistics, in early 2008 there were 16,000 Tunisian Facebook users, the number of users has since grown exponentially to about 1,800,000 in January 2011 and 7,300,000 in 2019 (Key Figures of Social Networks, Tunisia, 2019). These statistics, while probably imperfect, give an indication of the popularity of this platform in Tunisia. In addition to being popular in the country, this platform from the "third generation" of contesting Internet uses has allowed a new decompartmentalization of online criticism, and it was thus able to play a catalytic role during the Tunisian revolution.

These online platforms became akin to an incubator, nurturing a Tunisian civil society that yearns for freedom and a space for activity and expression in parallel to that freedom. Indeed, these websites enabled free voices to express their convictions in a public sphere that used to be dominated by political power.

Internet censorship under the Ben Ali regime was enforced against activists through a wide array of deterrent laws and administrative measures that conferred unlimited discretionary powers on the public administration. Among these legislations was the decision of the minister of communications on 22 March 1997, relating to the approval of the terms and conditions booklet that determines the conditions for value-added services, in terms of their presentation and use in Internet-based communications. This decision compels the service provider to trace its clients' browser content and to report a list of their names to the public intermediary (Tunisian Internet Agency [TIA]). Article 9 stipulates that "the director appointed by the services supplier, in accordance with Article 14 of Decree law n° 501–1997, and whose name must be submitted to the designated public intermediary, has the responsibility for web pages' content and the distributors that are hosted in their system, in accordance with the Journalism Law":

> Such measures as argued by activists from the youth group *Nawaat* reduced the citizen's possibilities to object, thus citizens always ended up as the victim of an oppressive administration whose influence relies on its broad powers and awareness of its own immunity.
>
> *(Nawaat, 2010)*

During Ben Ali's reign and following the introduction of the Internet in Tunisia, local public providers transformed the Internet into a closed network that was spread across the entire country. Usually, when someone sends a request from their device, it is transported via connectors until it reaches its destination. However, in Tunisia, this circuit gets interrupted at the time by a strong firewall that closes it, then redirects the request along a different path. It goes through a filter that analyzes it and decides whether to allow it to reach its destination. If the onward transfer is allowed, it is sent to a connector abroad and the requested page is loaded.

> However, if the request is on the black list, an error message appears to the user informing him/her that the requested page does not exist. The famous message "404" (Page not found) replaced the error message, and it was derided by Tunisian Internet users, who used to nick name it "Ammar 404."
>
> *(Nawaat, 2010)*

In order to justify forfeiture, the former regime mobilized all of the means possible to track Internet users by launching a special unit that was dedicated to information surveillance and tracking technology. This made many unrestrained writers point out dangerous issues that are related to individual liberties and privacy protection, which should have been protected in accordance with the Tunisian Constitution. The latter was abolished in March 2011 and replaced by a provisional law relating to the temporary organization of public authorities, before the new Constitution was ratified on 27 January 2014 by the National Constituent Assembly. Article 9 of the old Constitution of the Tunisian Republic, which was in force during the rule of the ousted Ben Ali, stipulates that "the right to the sanctity of a person's home and the confidentiality of correspondence shall be protected." Article 1 states,

> everyone has the right to the protection of personal data concerning him or her, as it is one of the fundamental rights guaranteed by the Constitution. Processing personal data shall respect transparency, fairness and respect of human dignity in accordance with the clauses of this act.
>
> *(Nawaat, 2010)*

The Internet police trusteeship of Tunisian citizens during the reign of Ben Ali came to an end with the outbreak of the Tunisian revolution in December 2010. This date marks the momentum witnessed in alternative media as ordinary citizens, politicians, and human rights advocates flocked to these online platforms.

New media amid the Tunisian revolution

Many saw such platforms as social networks and blogs as having an important role in accelerating the course of the Tunisian revolution. The question remained whether blogs and social networks, like Twitter and Facebook, were at the time real and direct causes of the Tunisian revolution and the spread of protests. Alternatively, was there simply an amplification of the role of these tools in the popular movement in Tunisia, which culminated in the overthrowing of the regime on 14 January 2011?

An observation of the Tunisian media and communication landscape during the last decade will tell about the significant acceleration in the use "new media," with a striking spread of blogs, websites, forums, and satellite channels on the Internet and Facebook pages, especially in the years immediately before the outbreak of the Tunisian revolution. For instance, the latest statistics for 2019 (Key Figures for Social Networks, Tunisia, 2019) estimate that the number of Facebook users in Tunisia is around 7,300,000, compared to 4,100,000 Messenger users, 1,900,000 Instagram users, and 115,000 Twitter users.

Activists such as Lina Ben Mhenni, Fatma Riahi, and Emna Ben Jemâa consider that users' interest in "new media" through the circulation of YouTube videos and exchanging tweets, pictures, and information on social media played a central role in the Tunisian revolution. Indeed, the easy access to these means of communication and thus their ability to rally, mobilize, and pressure people, as well as to quickly transmit information and to cross spatial and temporal boundaries, contributed towards raising awareness among those who were yearning for freedom, dignity, and justice and those aspiring to stop being marginalized, alienated, or isolated. In particular, the youth managed to effectively use these means of communication.

> They succeeded in organizing demonstrations, protests and campaigns, in addition to creating networks for solidarity and advocacy. They published critical articles, commented on events, and united street movements through these communication means. Thus, they grew more self-confident and confirmed their ability to act and change reality.
>
> *(Grami, 2013)*

They were also the source of news on which several Arab and foreign news channels relied in order to broadcast pictures and videos of the events that took place in Tunisia between December 2010 and 14 January 2011, given the blackout that was put in place by the former regime.

In contrast, others question whether the "new media" means were alone in playing the main role in the success of the Tunisian revolution. Many activists believe it to be an overstatement

> that is prejudiced against the role of generations of militants who promoted awareness and encouraged determination. Besides, that analysis merely observed one factor and marginalized the others. In fact, after study, the causes of the revolution proved to be compound, interrelated and complex. So, it is not possible to focus only on the role of communication means in studying the beginning of the revolution and the creation of a public opinion of quality.
>
> *(Grami, 2013)*

When studying the progress of the militant movement in Tunisia before the revolution, we notice several battles that had been experienced by human rights activists and politicians who contributed in raising awareness among Tunisians. This can be illustrated by the people's revolt at the mining basin in Gafsa, in the south of Tunisia, within the cities of Raidif, Um El-Araes, M'thila, and Al Metlawi, which lasted for around six months in 2008. Today, this may prove that peaceful popular protests in Tunisia had started before the revolution, despite the attempts of the previous regime to obscure and suppress them by isolating this region from other Tunisian cities.

We thus cannot comprehend the roles of the key actors in the Tunisian revolutionary movement without considering this topic from a historical perspective. Indeed, the historical approach discounts the generalization that views the new means of communication as the only contributor to the progress of the Tunisian revolution. Poverty and marginalization in Tunisia also limited access to those means of communication by all social categories. It has been proven that only a few young men were able to take pictures of what was happening and to transmit them via Internet (Lecomte, 2011: 393). The will to confront the authoritarian regime pushed men and women to mobilize in the streets, without caring about the oppression of the security services. "It is a will built on what the State under Bourguiba's rule gave to Tunisians in terms of gender equality, a compulsory and free education, and especially the Tunisian women's movement for freedom" (Grami, 2013).

This means that the Tunisian popular movement is the result of a historical process, during which the expertise and experiences of Tunisian civil society activists, intellectuals, jurists, journalists, and politicians accumulated and finally managed to destroy the fear barrier. They succeeded in organizing themselves into small blocs, believing in the need to protect justice and human rights, as well as the freedom of opinion and expression, and so on, for instance, through organizations such as the Tunisian League for the Defense of Human Rights, the Association of Tunisian Judges, the Tunisian Association of Democratic Women, the Association of Tunisian Women for Research and Development, Amnesty International, and the National Syndicate of Tunisian Journalists. Accordingly, it certainly cannot be argued that the "new media" means were alone in contributing to the Tunisian revolutionary process. Rather, they should be analyzed as one of the factors and as "a tool that enabled actors to make their sufferings visible, thus exposing the autocratic regime to the world in a historical moment, which could not have happened without a pre-existing awareness of the need to struggle" (Grami, 2013).

Social media networks and the democratic transition in Tunisia

More than eight years have passed since the first post-revolution elections took place on 23 October 2011; these were followed by second free and democratic presidential elections on 15 September 2019 and parliamentary elections on 6 October 2019. Such a time period allows an evaluation of the democratic transition that has been experienced in Tunisia, which has been seen around the world as a real test of the success of democracy in the region.

In this context, the most important observation that can be made is that,

> Tunisia has limited itself to a competitive approach in order to succeed in this transition, by promoting the latter as the central theme of its programs, investments and dialogues both at home and abroad. The situation has become akin to a mysterious game in a country where people used to dream of a qualitative improvement in their lives through the revolution, especially in terms of economic and social issues. Yet concern about democracy has become the priority that negated all other concerns.
>
> *(Al-Dababi, 2018)*

A few, such as Kamel Laabidi, freelance journalist and ex-president of the National Authority for the Reform of Information and Communication (INRIC) in Tunisia, Mohamed Laarbi Chouikha, Abdelkrim Hizaoui, and Saloua Charfi (INRIC Report, 2012), argued that what is currently happening in Tunisia is a transformation of democracy from a project for development and comprehensive change to a democratic struggle for democracy. "It is a battle between the elite themselves and for the benefit of the elite who are trying to control the scene, using all available means to maintain this status-quo" (Al-Dababi, 2018). In fact, this is evident in social networks' spaces and the various online communication means.

These virtual spaces represent alternative spheres that replace the lack of intermediaries faced by Tunisian citizens when they attempt to express their opinion about public order issues. This explains why political parties are interested in these means, as they opted to have a strong presence in them and through them. In fact, these spaces have become the refuge for all those who have been excluded from traditional media outlets, to the extent that social networks – mainly Facebook pages – have become a source of embarrassment and confusion for the traditional media. Relying on alternative media has even become a kind of reform movement for the traditional public media.

Politicians have realized that social networks are important means with which to communicate with both their sympathizers and neutral individuals during the democratic transition in Tunisia. Sometimes, they are a communication tool with which to respond to non-objective traditional media. They were also used sometimes to spread fake news and rumors, which means an attempt to mobilize public opinion and manipulate it.

On the other hand; it should be emphasized that social networks have played an important role in underlining even further the roles and functions of civil society during the democratic transition process in Tunisia, with all their complexities, multiple paths, and divergent outcomes. Indeed, in the aftermath of the Tunisian revolutionary process, the political and social participation system expanded, while the demands to change the rules for the practice of power increased. Additionally, social networks led to the crystallization of various civil interpretations. This has changed the nature of the relation with power as well as the way of managing public order and dealing with new social ties, under the auspices of diverse emerging interest groups and support circles. In addition, citizens' protests increased outside the traditional political frameworks of democracy as the latter made streets, public squares, traditional media, and modern social networks its spaces. All these indicators call for a reconsideration of the map of civil society roles and functions, in general, by consolidating social categories or increasing tensions between them. "There should also be a reconsideration of the different types of negotiations to ensure the necessary terms and conditions to establish democratic practice, assert its value and renew it" (Rosanvallo, 2006: 187), especially during the democratic transition process.

The term democracy has been broadened to include new conceptual issues which have branched out into participatory democracy, local democracy, governance, issues of inequality, disparity and corruption, surveillance roles and conflict management, interests, defense strategies, the emergence of lobbies, and the new forms of civic action, amongst others.

For some active participants, this appears to be

an erosion or reduction of traditional functions at the expense of the state and for the benefit of civil society organizations. The latter have been trying to impose themselves as a legitimate political actor that influences public policy and lobbies it, by mobilizing it during the political transition in particular, directing it toward plurality.

(Camau, 1991: 129)

It also appears as "consolidating the demand for democracy, along with the resulting stakes at the level of political legitimacy" (Ferrie and Santucci, 2006: 89). Hence the following questions: doesn't the growing citizens' movement in the streets, public squares, and virtual spaces, beyond traditional institutional frameworks, threaten "societal cohesion" and state sovereignty? Would a democracy based on representation and elections weaken the roles of elites and political parties, and then replace them with civil actors?

Answering these questions may require a deep understanding of what is shared in social networks, in particular, and in the alternative media, in general, about the details of the democratic transition and civil behavior in Tunisia, which ought to be written in a separate chapter of another book that would tackle the diagnosis of civil society's types of contribution to social, cultural, economic, and political life. It would also require observation to discover whether civil society in Tunisia has indeed become an "anti-authority" entity. Meanwhile, it can be argued that the contextualization of social networks in relation to civil society in Tunisia has succeeded, to some extent, in giving meaning to governance, in terms of individuals' relationships with the administration. It may also be a starting point from which to establish a Tunisian experience in the fields of alternative media and social networks. This experience would rely on open governance practices to consolidate the principle of transparency, unlike the accumulated claims made by political analysts about social networks or alternative media in Tunisia in the aftermath of the 2011 revolution.

Will the current legal framework protect free speech on social media?

Various experts argue that the Tunisian cybersphere has contributed to improving media freedom in Tunisia, especially after social networks transformed from being mere meeting and chatting virtual spaces to becoming an interface for opinion exchange and the expression of political viewpoints. This is a freedom that is sometimes inaccessible through written, audio, and visual media. In fact, this may often become a source of information for some of the media, while not being its competitor. The information revolution succeeded in revealing the aspects of cyber power, by combining the different dimensions of the digital revolution. As argued by Castells (2009: 119) "social conflict has changed into a struggle between the self, on one hand, and social networks, which are the new basis of society, on the other."

Tunisia has become one of the leading Arab countries in terms of media freedom. It ranked first on the Freedom of the Press index for Arab Countries in 2019, and it had moved up from the 97th place to the 72nd at the international level, according to a recent annual report by Reporters Without Borders (2019). Tunisia, reads the report, is the only country in North

Africa that has continued its transitional process towards democracy since the Arab Spring uprisings. In the Index, the country advanced its ranking by 25 places compared to the previous year. Reporters Without Borders (RWB) attributed the reasons for this improvement to the tangible decrease in the number of violations against journalists and the media, as well as Tunisia's commitment to a democratic approach through its participation in the "Information and Democracy" initiative that was launched by RWB in November 2018.

In light of this, the digital sphere, or cyberspace, which provides a significant number of the communication means which empower the citizen, has been consolidated. It has been turned into "a natural power with four main characteristics. It is a decentralized, global, coordinated and authority productive power" (Negroponte, 1995: 281).

However, Labib's (2016) fear is that the sum of these powers may be transformed into "cyber violence and terrorism" or Internet organized crime, if they are randomly misused or overused by the Tunisian people in this context; namely, during a revolutionary and fragile democracy-building process. In fact, social networks were categorized in some countries, such as Tunisia, Egypt, Syria, Libya, Iraq, Morocco, and Algeria, as being fertile ground for the creation and appearance of some of the subversive groups that are strongly linked to violent events.

The increasing use of Internet and social networks among the youth, and their interest in their intellectual and ideological contents, which have been promoted by some extremist religious groups through these networks, may be one of the main reasons that underline the need to enact new legislation in order to protect society from their growing influence, cyber terrorism and Internet crime. "As a result, observers and researchers are afraid of the restrictions that may be imposed on the freedom of opinion and speech, in particular, and the Tunisian virtual public sphere, in general" (Jamoussi, 2018: 16). This fear may be justified if we take into consideration the new reality that has been constructed by the liberation of the public sphere in Tunisia following the revolution, and this would concur with what the philosopher Michel Faulcault (1994) suggested

> power is no longer understood as being limited to the State in terms of its institutions, organs, police and laws. Instead, it is depicted as a number of current and present power relations in the social sphere with all its areas, departments and institutions.

Taking into consideration this new vision of power, the revolutionary conceptual shift of the public sphere, and the struggle of the governing power to maintain its historically traditional authority,

> Internet censorship has become one of the most problematic issues nowadays in the international pursuit of digital human rights. Indeed, digital rights have become equal to the human rights shaped by the Universal Declaration of Human Rights in 1948. There are different levels of States' political and democratic development in terms of cyberspace decisions, its new opinion and speech tools, as well as the balance between security and politics dimensions.
>
> *(Jamoussi, 2018: 16)*

For instance, like other Arab countries, and despite its policy of blocking websites before the revolution of January 2011,

> Tunisia has tried to provide and secure the means of electronic interactions, to support the trust of Internet users, and to safeguard their rights by establishing a regulatory

framework that has organized the virtual relationships of all Internet users in terms of practice and exchange, and by setting mechanisms that guarantee the safety of the data exchanged, its appropriate use, and cybersecurity. More than 70 regulations linked to Internet communication have been issued in relation to this topic, despite the controversial content of some, which contained violations of both individual and civil liberties under the pretext of fighting terrorism, among others.

(Jamoussi, 2012: 13)

In Tunisia, the inherited legal framework relating to this field reflects the confusion of, and contradictions in, the authoritarian regime before the revolution, between the logic of anarchy, and texts with a seemingly modern content that negate the very essence of freedom and independence.

The legislations related to private data protection and information safety prove it. Indeed, the previous regime used to see communication technologies in general through the duality of apprehension and utility. It was useful in embellishing its own image and achievements. On the other hand, they relied on legislations that seemed to be liberating, but whose essence suppressed liberties and restrained them.

(The National Authority for the Reform of Information
and Communication Report, 2012)

According to the report of the National Authority for the Reform of Information and Communication in the Republic of Tunisia, which was published immediately after the revolution, in April 2012, and more specifically, in Section 3, Part 1, which related to the legal framework and was entitled "Electronic Media: Between Anarchy and Extremely Restrained Liberties":

electronic media under the previous regime used to suffer from apprehension, containment and suppression. It reached the point where Tunisia was considered, by many human rights and internationally specialized organizations, as the worst enemy of Internet in general and electronic media in particular.

The non-democratic and non-liberator dimension of the legal framework related to press freedom and liberties in general deepened. During its last years, the extremely repressive nature of the regime became more pronounced. Article 61 bis of the Penal Code, amended in accordance with law n° 35, 2010, which added a second paragraph to the before mentioned Article, highlighted the gravity of the oppressive and withdrawn approach chosen by the regime.

(The National Authority for the Reform of Information
and Communication Report, 2012)

Some media and electronic communication laws in Tunisia, especially the Media Law or the Press Code, were reviewed, amended, and improved by the end of 2011, in accordance with Decree-Law No. 115, 2011, dated 2 November 2011, which related to the freedom of press, print, and publication, and with Decree-Law No. 116, 2011, dated 2 November 2011, which related to the freedom of audiovisual communication and the creation of the High Independent Authority for the Audiovisual Commission. The general trend is towards greater civil and individual freedoms, along with further respect for human rights, support for the media, as well as more security and responsibility for media and communication sector employees, in line with good governance and activists' access to free speech via social networks.

Conclusion

There are divergent opinions about the role of "new media" and social networks in the popular movement of the 14 January 2011 revolution and about the relevance of their role in cultivating a sense of citizenship in Tunisia during the democratic transition. However, it is clear that social media networks accelerated and strengthened the protest movements, even if they did not trigger them. These platforms acted as the mouthpieces of the dissidents, human rights activists, and critics of the former regime, as the latter had complete control of traditional media outlets. The Internet was one of the few media outlets that transmitted the people's dissatisfaction with unemployment, corruption, and poverty and that united the various strata of Tunisian society, including the poorest people and the middle-class intellectuals who live both in Tunisia and abroad. It also proved that there was an accumulation of militant struggles by generations of activists. Social media have contributed to making people go onto the streets under the umbrella of the civil society organizations that have played a huge role in the Tunisian revolutionary process and the birth of a democratic movement, after long years of a dictatorship that had impeded previous attempts to democratize the state and consolidate a culture of modern politics; a dictatorship that was inherited by the intellectual elite.

The Tunisian "revolution" thus brings together a generational and cultural dimension, and the revolutionary process in Tunisia in the aftermath of 14 January 2011 represented a good opportunity to put the intellectual elite at the forefront of events again, an elite that was depressed by defeat. Similarly,

> social networks, such as Facebook, Twitter, Instagram and others, provided the intellectual users with great places to interact with the web contents, especially media content, and allowed them to participate. They expressed their opinions and impressions by posting their comments, questions, articles, videos and pictures, etc. Eventually, they became a source of information and sometimes even rumors that are reported by some well-known newspapers websites without checking the credibility of the information.
>
> *(Ben Messaoud, 2016: 12)*

This "interaction has created new knowledge producers and a new knowledge structure that differ from the traditional structure based on the hegemony of elites, opinion leaders and traditional media control" (Ben Messaoud, 2019: 8). As a result, we have recorded many attempts to restrict the content shared on social platforms, for there is a legislative vacuum in relation to electronic publications and social networks in Tunisia and the Arab world. Sometimes, there have been attacks against the freedom of opinion and expression through new legal measures which give priority to narrow regime interests before taking into account legal principles and international treaties. This is why some authoritarian Arab regimes protest the content of some of these laws that support freedoms and treaties when they consider that there are what they call "contradictions" with the characteristics and ethics of society.

In Tunisia, for example,

> before the revolution of 14 January 2011, cyber activists used to feel suffocated in the virtual sphere for several reasons. In addition to the constant surveillance online, some social networks for shared videos and pictures, like YouTube and Flicker, were blocked to prevent Internet users from publishing content against the existing political

system. Internet activists found help in concealment systems (proxies) or anti-blocking systems, to access and use these websites.

(Jamoussi, 2018: 18)

After the 14 January 2011 revolution, "the chaos of media practice, especially in the so-called amateur-journalism and "asylum" press, transformed electronic media work into a field of illegal plagiarism. Moreover, some electronic media used extortion and defamation to secure more gains and profits, at the cost of their credibility, independence, and integrity." The professional practices of public relations have developed and flourished by enriching "the world of content preparation with innovative ways to feed information to the media in the new digital environment, though these practices are not professional and have no sense of responsibility towards citizens and society" (Ben Messaoud, 2019: 3). This has helped to increase the power of the authorities through further pressure on social network actors, through legal and judicial procedures, in cases of law violation, and whenever it has been felt necessary.

To conclude, questioning the role of social networks and the new media in Tunisia's revolutionary process and democratic transition has revealed to us that virtual reality has changed and the public digital sphere has become free, thus producing a new meaning for the public sphere, in particular, and for participatory democracy and democratic practice, in general. It can be argued that no matter how far cyber surveillance mechanisms are developed, and no matter how many restrictive legislations are drafted, the emerging virtual societies in Tunisia are not ready to lose the gains that have been achieved since January 2011, in terms of freedom of opinion and expression, even if this choice requires reorganizing and legalizing those freedoms so as to guarantee the respect of the media scene transformations, of the human rights regulating society and democracy, as well as of the special characteristics of the free, digital, virtual sphere.

References

Al-Dababi, M. (2018), *The Democratic Transition in Tunisia: 7 Years of Lost*. Retrieved from https://bit.ly/3cCAUkw 28 October 2018. Accessed 14 January 2019.

Ben Messaoud, M. (2016), *Newspapers in Arabic: Struggle for Survival and Digital Challenges*. Al Jazeera Center for Studies, pp. 1–21. Retrieved from https://studies.aljazeera.net/ar/mediastudies/2016/12/161206082318636.html. Accessed 4 December 2018.

Ben Messaoud, M. (2019), *Ethics of Arab Electronic Press: A New Vision for Professional Practice*. Al Jazeera Center for Studies, pp. 1–23. Retrieved from https://studies.aljazeera.net/en/node/2049. Accessed 4 April 2019.

Camau, M. (SD) (1991), *Political Changes in the Maghreb*. Paris: CNRS, French Edition.

Castells, M. (2009), *The Rise of the Network Society*. Hoboken, NJ: Wiley-Blackwell.

Faulcault, M. (1994), *"The Subject and Power" in "Sayings and Writings" tome VI text n 306*, French Edition. Paris: Gallimard, pp. 208–226.

Ferrie, J-N., and Santucci, J-C. (2006), *Democratization Devices and Authoritarian Devices in North Africa*. Paris: CNRS, French Edition.

Grami, A. (2013), What is the Role of Social Media in Tunisian Movement? *Deutsche Welle*. Retrieved from https://p.dw.com/p/18elv. Accessed 5 April 2019.

Jamoussi, J. (2012), *Introduction to Internet and Multimedia Law*. Tunisian Society for the Publication of the Development of Graphic Arts. Tunis: Tunisian Publishing Company, pp. 9–18.

Jamoussi, J. (2018), *Restrictions on Social Networks: Policies and Objectives*. Al Jazeera Center for Studies. Retrieved from https://studies.aljazeera.net/ar/mediastudies/2019/01/190102094150980.html. Accessed 14 April 2019.

Key Figures for Social Networks Tunisia (2019), Retrieved from www.digital-discovery.tn/chiffres-reseaux-sociaux-tunisie-2019/. Accessed 20 July 2019.

Labib, T. (2016), From Fear to Intimidation: Contribution to the Definition of a Culture of Fear. *Kapitalis*, 21 March. Retrieved from https://bit.ly/2KpzMob. Accessed 20 January 2019.

Lecomte, R. (2011), *Tunisian Revolution and the Internet: The Role of Social Media*, pp. 389–418. doi:10.4000/anneemaghreb.1288. Accessed 14 March 2019.

Mansouri, N. (2012), The Role of the Social Media in Stimulating Arab Revolutions. *Al- Akhbar*, 28 March. Retrieved from https://al-akhbar.com/Opinion/67495. Accessed 5 March 2019.

National Authority for the Reform of Information and Communication (2012), *INRIC Report*. Republic of Tunisia, Tunis, Prime Minister, pp. 40–72.

Nawaat (2010), *Report of the Tunisia Monitoring Group for the Freedom of Press, Publication and Innovation on the Reality of Internet in Tunisia*. Retrieved from https://bit.ly/3eGkjy0. Accessed 3 May 2019.

Negroponte, N. (1995), *The Digital Man*. Paris: Robert Laffont, French Edition.

Reporters Without Borders (2019), *RWB Report*. Retrieved from https://rsf.org/fr/classement-mondial-de-la-liberte-de-la-presse-2019-la-mecanique-de-la-peur. Accessed 3 February 2020.

Rohde, S. F. (2005), *Freedom of Assembly, Facts on File*. New York: Inc, Infobase Publishing, pp. 103–123.

Rosanvallo. P (2006), *Counter-democracy. Politics at the Age of Distrust*. Paris: Seuil, French Edition.

United Arab Emirates

37

MEDIA IN THE UAE – CREATING A NATIONAL VOICE

Najat AlSaied

Introduction

The United Arab Emirates (UAE) was officially formed on 2 December 1971, when six of the emirates – Abu Dhabi, Dubai, Sharjah, Ajman, Umm Al-Quwain, and Fujairah declared themselves a federation. In February 1972 another emirate, Ras Al Khaimah, joined the UAE as the seventh member. For a new union, the main function of media in general and broadcasting in particular was to act as a catalyst for sustaining national identity and economic development. For a federation keen on establishing itself as a modern state, it was no surprise that radio and television were being harnessed to promote socio-economic change while simultaneously preserving cultural traditions (Hasan, 2013).

The UAE's population stands at 9.54 million, between 10% and 15% of which, depending on your source, are UAE nationals while the remainder is made up of expatriates. The total number of expatriates is 8.447 million, which is mainly composed of South Asians, and there is an increasing presence of Europeans and mainly British nationals, particularly in cities like Dubai (United Arab Emirates Population Statistics, 2019). Based on these numbers, the power of media in the UAE is perceived to have arisen not only from its role in promoting national identity and fostering economic progress but also from its role in building bridges with far-flung regional and international audiences.

The fact that the UAE is a federation greatly complicates government administration, including control of the media. The unique federal nature of the UAE has produced several distinct systems within radio and television broadcasting. The programming philosophy of both media is oriented towards the tastes and interests of the population of all seven emirates. For example, the contrast between radio and television services in Dubai and Abu Dhabi is striking, primarily because of the completely different orientations of the two services. While Abu Dhabi-based national service programs respond to the needs of the seven emirates, Dubai concentrates on commercially oriented broadcasting. Abu Dhabi's media are more focused on matters of political and national security while Dubai's media is run as a business. Since the highest percentage of expatriates is located in Dubai, its radio and television services rely almost exclusively on expatriates. On the other hand, Ajman's and Sharjah's television channels vie for UAE viewers (Boyd, 1999).

This chapter discusses how media, including the press and broadcasting, media-free zones, and media events have contributed to socio-economic development in the federation. Though the national media continues to maintain its traditional role as a government voice on national and international issues, its function as a guardian of national identity and as a catalyst for economic development remains its most obvious purpose. Right from its inception, UAE media, primarily broadcasting, has been the main organ of the state for maintaining its national culture, heritage, and traditions. It also supports the nation's soft power ventures. The chapter begins with an overview of the UAE press and news agencies, then it presents an overview of the UAE broadcasting sector, shedding light on the importance of this sector in amplifying the UAE national identity. The last part of the chapter discusses the various media regulations as well as the role of UAE media in cementing the indigenous Bedouin culture as an authentic heritage.

Emirati press

The first printing facility was set up in Dubai in 1958, and it was used to print official bulletins and individual publications. The first issue of *al-Ittihad* appeared on 20 October 1969, one day before the meeting held in Abu Dhabi to agree on a new union among the seven emirates that form the UAE (Nafadi, 1996: 95). The first issue of *al-Khaleej* appeared in 1966 at the hands of Emirati brothers Tareem and Abdullah Omran (Nafadi, 1996: 113). Until 1972, there were no adequate publishing facilities and the few periodicals used to be printed in either Kuwait or Lebanon, but this changed with the newly accumulated wealth following oil discovery in Abu Dhabi in 1962, Dubai in 1970, and Sharjah in 1974 (Nafadi, 1996: 45–46). In 1970, the first information authority was set up in Dubai, and it was responsible for managing *Akhbar Dubai*, a weekly current affair magazine, circulating 8,500 copies inside and outside the UAE and subsidized entirely by the emirate of Dubai; the magazine was suspended in 1980 and its license was used to issue the new daily *al-Bayan* (Nafadi, 1996: 53–54). By the 1980s, the UAE recorded 20 official magazines, five women's magazines, six dailies, and, notably, many newspaper titles promoting a sense of "unity" among the seven emirates, including titles such as *al-Ittihad* (Union), *al-Wahda* (unity), *al-Ahd al-Jadid* (the new truce) (Gleissner, 2012, 2012: 69).

The printing industry in the UAE was booming by the early 1990s, partially because of the increasing demand from neighboring Kuwait, whose printing facilities were suspended during the Iraqi invasion in the first half of 1990 (Nafadi, 1996: 47). The years 1990–1991 witnessed the second Gulf War following Iraq's invasion of Kuwait and the subsequent liberation of Kuwait, an event that demanded editorial changes in Emirati newspapers to keep up with the fast-paced changes in the Gulf region and to compete with international news providers such as the CNN, which managed to attract a significant share of Arab audiences during the war. The period also marked an increase in prices across the Gulf states, which led the Emirati editors-in-chief of the five main newspapers (namely *al-Ittihad*, *al-Khaleej*, *al-Bayan*, *al-Wahda*, and *al-Fajr*) to raise their prices to meet the increasing publishing costs (Nafadi, 1996: 38). The decision had a mixed result: while it led to an increase in revenues, it also resulted in an overall distribution drop by 30%. The newspapers continued to abide by the new pricing strategy save for *al-Wahda* newspaper, which resorted to the old pricing in 1992 (Nafadi, 1996: 39).

The printing industry then witnessed a boom with the number of publications reaching 185 by 1996, ranging from Arabic-language and English publications, including *Khaleej Times*, *Gulf News*, *Gulf Today*, and *Emirates News* (Nafadi, 1996: 55). Today, the UAE records seven Arabic newspapers and eight English-language newspapers published locally; the portfolio of Arabic newspapers include *al-Khaleej* (set up in 1970), *al-Ittihad* (1972), *al-Wahda* (1973), *al-Fajr* (1975), *al-Bayan* (1980), *Emarat al-Youm* (2005), and *Akhbar al-Arab* (2011) in addition to several locally licensed magazines, including *Moujah*, *Zahrat al-Khaleej* (for women), *Majid* (for children), and *National Geographic* in Arabic (The UAE government portal, n.d.). The English titles include *Emirates News* (1975), *Gulf News* (1978), *Khaleej Times* (1978), *The Gulf Today* (1996), *7Days* (2003), *Emirates Today* (2005), in addition to a few online sites in Urdu and Spanish. The English-language *The National* was published in Abu Dhabi in April 2008, staffed by top journalists from the UK, USA, and Canada, and the editor-in-chief was the former editor of the UK's *Daily Telegraph*, whose annual salary was then claimed to be in the range of US $500,000 (Kadragic, 2010: 247). The English-language press usually caters to the large expatriate communities which form around 80% of all residents in the UAE, coming primarily from South Asia, Iran, other Arab countries, as well as citizens of Western countries (Kadragic, 2010: 249). Newspapers are now arguably the dominant platform holding about 40% of the advertising spend (Arab Media Outlook, 2015: 165).

Moreover, the Emirates News Agency was set up in 1974, depending on support from Reuters, and during the 1980s, the agency signed cooperation agreements with several other international agencies. The labor force consisted of mainly Arab expatriates who were sent for training in international newsrooms (Gleissner, 2012: 71). The Emirates News Agency aimed to monopolize news related to the rulers in the UAE and the various ministries; one reason behind this control was the increasing number of Arab and foreign staff across all newsrooms, triggering the local authorities' fear that the foreign journalists might push their own political and ideological agendas and not the UAE's main policies (Nafadi, 1996: 69). It was perhaps therefore that several UAE universities launched journalism degrees such as the American University of Sharjah and Zayed University; the latter hosts a media school for women – the College of Communication and Media Sciences. This is in addition to Zayed University Media Centre, which provides training and research to media companies in alliance with the Dubai Press Club (IREX, 2005: 247). As for syndicates, the UAE hosts the Journalists Association funded by the government. In some Gulf states, journalist syndicates take the form of private clubs or societies rather than formal labor unions (Mellor, 2010).

Emirati broadcasting

Though modern broadcasting in the UAE dates back to when the federation first came into being, the 1960s bore witness to the rise of numerous broadcasting operations. In 1962, a local radio station was established in Sharjah with the name Sawt Al Asahel (Voice of the Beach) by the Development Bureau of the Trucial States Rulers' Council, which was established in 1952. It aimed to work towards common interests in the UAE. The radio station was up and running for several years before the union was formed, but in 1970 it stopped broadcasting and was replaced by Radio Dubai, on the same frequency. The programs that were broadcast on Voice of the Beach included religious, health, and cultural programs, as well as news. Some of the most important broadcasters contributing to the development of the radio were announcers Hessa al-Osaily, Salim Arafat, and Riyad Shuaibi (Hasan, 2013). In February 1969, Abu Dhabi Radio was launched as the first official broadcaster in the country, followed on 6 August 1969 by Abu Dhabi Television (Boyd, 1999).

The Arab radio experiment has influenced other radio stations in the region, especially in the Arabian Gulf. Kamel Qustandi, a Palestinian media specialist, refers to a story about some Arab broadcasters at the opening of Abu Dhabi Radio.

> In 1969, we received a special invitation from Abu Dhabi to open the radio there.
> We went and stayed for a month. Others stayed for two months. The most prominent

contributor was Mohammed Al-Ghussein, a Palestinian media specialist. We opened the radio and trained a good group on radio art.

(Al-Tabour, 2000: 70)

The real start of broadcasting in the UAE dates back to the establishment of the seven-emirate federation on 2 December 1971. All broadcasting outlets carried the title "UAE Broadcaster from Abu Dhabi, Dubai, Sharjah." But when the UAE was established as an independent state, the need for more coherent and reliable broadcast operations was, more than ever before, a top priority on the nation's agenda. The establishment of the Ministry of Information and Culture in 1971 provided an umbrella for launching such services across the country (Ayish, 2013).

The name of Abu Dhabi Radio was changed on 2 December 1971 to the Radio of the United Arab Emirates from Abu Dhabi, thus becoming the official state radio. The types of programs on the radio are news, news analysis, religious programs, various cultural programs and services, music, and a program called "live broadcast." One of the most important programs is this live broadcast program, which began in 1986. In the morning, the focus is on citizens' service issues and contributes to solving these issues through direct contact with officials in governmental and private institutions to find suitable solutions. In the evening, the focus is on cultural and social issues to discuss them with the public. Part of the program is concerned with the national heritage of the country (Al-Tabour, 2000).

All radio channels in the UAE have this "live broadcast" program. The federal governments wanted to understand the needs and complaints of their citizens. Radio Dubai was launched in October 1971. It focuses on news programs and live broadcasts aimed at communicating with the public, listening to their concerns, and seeking to solve their problems. Also, there are music, cultural, and poetry programs (Hasan, 2013). Radio Sharjah was launched in August 1972 and focused on Islamic, cultural, and educational programs. Through its programs, it seeks to introduce Arab listeners to UAE culture. On 15 November 2000, the radio was relaunched and the focus became religious programs and local issues. The "live broadcast" program is one of its most important programs because it is a platform for the community to express its concerns and discuss issues directly with government representatives.

The UAE was, just like other Arab countries, keen to establish successful television channels. Abu Dhabi TV was first shown in August 1969, followed by Kuwait TV from Dubai in September 1969, then Dubai TV, Sharjah TV, Ajman TV, Fujairah TV, Sama Dubai, Fujairah TV, Noor Dubai, and Ras Al Khaimah TV (Hasan, 2013).

UAE TV, broadcast from Abu Dhabi, was the first television station in the UAE and its first broadcast in black and white was on 6 August 1969, and on 4 December 1974 it began its broadcasts in color. The channel's focus was on news programs, international events, documentaries, and the production of local films. On 15 October 1992, satellite transmission ensured it reached all corners of the globe. In October 2008, a new version of the channel was launched, and it was named Abu Dhabi El Oula or Abu Dhabi One TV. It features a series of entertainment, cultural and social programs, reports, films, and Arab dramas. Abu Dhabi TV has launched several specialized channels: Abu Dhabi Sports, Abu Dhabi UAE, Abu Dhabi Drama, and National Geographic Channel (Hasan, 2013).

Kuwait was the first Arabian Gulf country to establish an official television station on 15 November 1961. On 9 September 1969, under the patronage of Sheikh Rashid bin Saeed Al Maktoum and Sheikh Sabah Al-Ahmad Al-Sabah, the current emir of Kuwait, who was at that time the foreign minister, Kuwait, launched a television station in Dubai under the name of Kuwait TV from Dubai, which was broadcast in black and white, broadcasting to Dubai, Sharjah, and Ajman only (Hasan, 2013). Most of the programs came from Kuwait except for the news and local programs that were provided and supervised by broadcasters in Dubai. Kuwait TV from Dubai included several talented Emiratis such as Jassem Shehab, Saleh Al Shayji, Hessa al-Osaily, Majid Al Shatti, Ali Balraheef, Sultan Al Suwaidi, and many others who worked in the field of presenting, photography, and directing alongside Kuwaiti journalists. Kuwait TV from Dubai sent a group of UAE nationals working at the television station to Kuwait for training, developing Emirati broadcasters' skills, and giving them new experiences. Kuwait TV from Dubai was located in Al Qusais, the same location as the headquarters of the National Media Council (NMC). In December 1972, the television stopped broadcasting after the launch of Dubai Television (Dubai TV) in color (Hasan, 2013). Dubai Television in color was launched in 1970 and its programs were broadcast on 21 February 1971, under the name of UAE TV from Dubai. Dubai TV played a prominent role in covering events and activities and presenting news, political, and economic programs. In 1995, Dubai TV began its satellite broadcasts to reach countries around the world. Dubai TV has since launched several channels – Dubai 33, Dubai Sports, Dubai Economy, Sama Dubai, Noor Dubai, and Dubai Racing. On 18 November 1985, Sharjah TV Station was established. On 11 February 1989, Sheikh Sultan bin Mohammed Al Qasimi inaugurated Sharjah TV, one year on from when the station's building was completed. Sharjah TV broadcasts religious and educational programs in several languages, including Persian and Urdu, to serve all nationalities in the country. Sharjah TV has a huge archive (Hasan, 2013).

The early 1990s was the development phase for broadcasting in the UAE, which then became international thanks to its satellite services. By the end of the 1990s, local broadcasting operations like Dubai Media Incorporated and Emirates Media Incorporated were launched. Both specialize in journalism, publishing, media, and TV broadcasting (Khan, 2014). The 1990s also witnessed a growth in the number of local radio stations due to an advanced mobile telephone network, giving rise to live talk shows and entertainment programs (Ayish, 2013). When the Ministry of Information and Culture was abolished in 2006 and succeeded by the current NMC, the localization of broadcast operations (as opposed to federal) was already complete, leaving the NMC with only regulatory functions within media. The Abu Dhabi Media Company was established in 2005 to replace Emirates Media Inc. as a private media company with no institutional ties to the federal government. By the end of 2010, all broadcasting services in the UAE were operating as part of local government structures (Ayish, 2013).

At the beginning of the millennium, the UAE established free media zones, among them Dubai Media City (DMC), Free Zone of Technology, Dubai Production City, Dubai Outsource City, Dubai Internet City, Dubai Studio City, Abu Dhabi Media Free Zone (twofour54), Ras Al Khaimah (RAK) Media City, and Creative City Fujairah. The Dubai Technology and Media Free Zone (DTMFZ) was developed by Technology, Electronic Commerce and Media (TECOM) hosting hundreds of media operations, including regional and international radio and television services. Media institutions and companies located in the free zones function according to the laws and regulations of these free zones, which are consistent with the state's laws (Hasan, 2013). One of the most important characteristics of these free media zones is that they are exempt from paying tax while necessary services are still provided. The free media zones have been able to attract major international and regional organizations, companies, agencies, and media channels to the UAE (ibid.). DMC and twofour54 were set up to attract key international players. Organizations including Reuters, CNN, Sony, and Fox have offices in these media zones. DMC has also attracted major pan-Arab broadcasters such as the Middle East Broadcasting Center (MBC) Group. Sky News Arabia was launched in Abu Dhabi in 2012 (Khan, 2014). There were more than 1,213 specialized companies in DMC at the end of 2007, six years after its launch, and there were more than 60 television institutions in the city operating 160 different television stations. Twofour54 has attracted over 214 of the world's biggest companies in the field of media content generation. It provides training opportunities for young people on innovation and production and also services and benefits to all institutions; it encourages start-up companies by offering tax exemptions, 100% foreign ownership, and government, residential, and other corporate services as well (Hasan, 2013).

In May 2010, the NMC, Abu Dhabi Media Company, Dubai Media Incorporated, Sharjah Media Corporation, Etisalat, Du, and Kantar Media agreed to the development and implementation of a Television Audience Measurement (TAM) project across the UAE. The objective of this project is to develop a deep and detailed understanding of UAE TV viewership to ensure that the commissioning and development of television programming and television advertising in the UAE are strategic in their design and execution. Also, the project aims to generate ratings that will be used as a kind of currency for the media industry to trade with (Khan, 2014).

On 4 June 2007, Abu Dhabi Media[1] was established, and its main function is to create content that matters to audiences, to deepen their engagement. In 2010, The Government of Dubai Media Office[2] was established to implement strategic communication plans for the government of Dubai as well as to disseminate government-related news in cooperation with local government agencies. In September 2018, the Abu Dhabi Government Media Office was established to strategically promote Abu Dhabi's national interests.[3] The role of the Media Office is managed by the Abu Dhabi Executive Council. Even though all these media companies and offices are supposed to improve the UAE media's output and impact, it is also evident that there is a huge overlap between their functions, which may well be stifling their mission rather than furthering it. In some cases, those who manage and run these offices sometimes compete rather cooperate with each other.

As there are numerous media offices and companies, there are also many media events such as the Arab Media Forum, the Dubai Film Festival, the Abu Dhabi Media Summit, Abu Dhabi Film Festival, the International Government Communication Forum, and the Media and National Identity Forum. All these events aim to open a dialogue, deepen debate, and exchange ideas on media issues related to the region and the world. These events occur once a year except for the Media and National Identity Forum that took place just the once on 24 October 2011, after the events around the region related to the so-called Arab Spring. It was a joint initiative of the NMC and the Emirates Centre for Strategic Studies and Research (ECSSR) in cooperation with the Journalists' Association to raise awareness of the key role of the media in promoting national identity. The forum focused on four themes: media and identity in the era of globalization, the portrayal of national identity in UAE media, institutional and individual experiences of promoting national identity in the media, and experiences in the media of national identity from Gulf Cooperation Council (GCC) countries (Hasan, 2013).

Media regulations in the UAE

The press legislation began in 1973 with a new decree which was revised in 1980 affirming the state subsidy to the main newspapers, according to the sales of each newspaper (Nafadi, 1996: 67). There are several local bodies in charge of coordinating media activities within their emirate, such as the Department of Culture & Information in Sharjah, Media Zone Authority in Abu Dhabi, and Fujairah Culture & Media Authority. In Abu Dhabi, the media policy changed from supporting privately owned media to the nationalization of the media and ultimately concentrating media ownership in the hands of individual members of the ruling family (Al Nahyan); thus, *al-Ittihad*, *al-Bayan*, and *al-Wahda* newspapers were incorporated into the state-owned Emirates News Inc. (EMI) in 1989, an entity which later took over all media companies (Gleissner, 2012: 72).

The official portal of the UAE government publishes the rules and regulations of the UAE media including broadcasting (Government.ae 2019), and according to its published information, the Federal Law No. 11 of 2016 affirms the National Media Council as the federal government body entrusted to oversee and undertake all matters related to the media in the UAE on the mainland and free zones.

In 2018, the UAE National Media Council launched the New Electronic Media System to regulate electronic and digital media in the UAE and free zones. The new system covers all forms of expression including paintings, and all media producers are required to get approval before trading media content or publishing and advertising online. Moreover, the Telecommunications Regulatory Authority introduced the Internet Access Management policy, agreed with the main licensed Internet providers, Etisalat and Du; the new authority monitors online content available in the UAE and records any breaches of the policy by online operators inside the UAE. The new authority has the power to request the main telecommunication companies (Etisalat and Du) to block online content, particularly content that includes pornography, defamation, invasion of privacy, offences against the UAE, contempt of religion, gambling, and terrorism. In October 2019, the ruler of Dubai, Sheikh Mohammed bin Rashid, tweeted to urge all Emiratis to think of themselves as representatives of their country online and to adhere to the image and ethics of the founding father, Sheikh Zayed.

Moreover, all media institutions in the UAE, including the free zones, must comply with the standards set out in Federal Law 15 (1980) Concerning Press and Publications and other laws and regulations in force under Federal Law 11 (2016) on the regulation and powers of the NMC, Law 30 (2017) on Media Activities Licensing, and Law 26 (2017) on Media Content. According to the NMC's chairman (Decision No. 20 [2010]), all media outlets in the UAE must adhere to standards set out in Federal Law 15 (1980) Concerning Press and Publications and other media regulations in force. The chairman's decision is concerned with national standards for the prohibited media content (as set out in the Press and Publications Law) and requires media institutions to hold archives of all content that has been broadcast in the last three months. Monthly reports demonstrating compliance with these standards must be submitted to the NMC.

The UAE's national standards require outlets:

- to respect the regime of the UAE, its symbols, and the political system;
- to not offend the divine and Islamic beliefs, and show respect towards other religions;
- to respect the culture and heritage of the UAE;
- to not offend national unity or social cohesion and/or incite sectarian, regional, and tribal conflict;
- to respect directions and policies of the UAE at domestic and international levels;
- to not harm the economic system of the country, or spread rumors or misleading and biased news;
- to respect government policies to promote national identity and the integration of citizens into the media labor market;
- to respect the principles and codes of ethics of media work;
- to not broadcast information harmful to children, women, and other social groups, or information that would incite others towards hatred and violence;
- to respect copyright rules and regulations;

- to not disclose official confidential contacts, military matters, or conventions or treaties concluded by the government without proper authorization;
- to not report distorted proceedings and deliberations of courts or other regulatory bodies;
- to not disclose information about a criminal investigation, which has not been concluded and/or is deemed confidential;
- to not defame public officials; and
- to publish investigations that deal with more than one party, without giving an account of the views of all parties directly concerned.

All broadcasters operate as part of either Abu Dhabi Media (three television channels and five radio stations); Dubai Media Incorporated (DMI) (five television channels and nine radio stations); or Sharjah Media Corporation (two television channels and one radio station). Other broadcasters in Ras Al Khaima, Ajman, and Fujairah also operate as part of local government-controlled structures (Ayish, 2013). In media-free zones, broadcasters must have the appropriate license from the NMC, although local regulations in media zones offer greater autonomy to media institutions than is enjoyed by their national media counterparts. For example, Dubai Media City is subject to the Broadcasting and Publication Standards Tribunal (BPST) Regulations (Ayish, 2013).

In Abu Dhabi Media Zone Authority (twofour54), the Dissemination Licensing Regulations (2008) require that a license is held by anyone engaged in broadcast activities in the zone. Article 17.3 of the Regulations explains the following areas which constitute potential violations:

a   indecent or pornographic content;
b   promotion of violence or incitement to hatred based on race, sex, religion, or nationality;
c   undermining of basic social, cultural, and religious values in the UAE;
d   incitement to criminal activities or public disorder; and
e   violating any codes of practice and/or programming standards set by the Authority (Ayish, 2013).

The role of national media in reinforcing national identity and economic growth

Ever since the UAE was founded as a federation on 2 December 1971, national identity has been a defining issue in national policy discussions. Concern over a national identity being threatened by global cultural and local demographic developments has been a critical issue in a country where nationals constitute approximately 15% of a population dominated by expatriates. In 2011, the Emirates Centre for Strategic Studies and Research in cooperation with the National Media Council and the Journalists' Association organized the Media and National Identity Forum. The forum emphasized that media has a key role to play in boosting the UAE's national identity through inculcating and infusing a spirit of loyalty and belonging to its culture, heritage, and citizenship among every member of the community (Salama, 2011). Fatima Al Sayegh, Associate Professor, Department of History and Archaeology at the UAE University, said in the forum, "the UAE's national identity is threatened by the various cultures and identities of 200 nationalities living in the country and programs broadcast on satellite television channels" (cited in Salama, 2011).

National broadcasting in the UAE is entrusted, among other things, with the mission of shoring up the country's national identity. According to a study commissioned by the NMC in early 2010, national broadcasters seem to have scored highly on a National Identity Index (NII) (Ayish, 2013). Even though the findings of the study show high NII scores for national broadcasters, the findings of the Arab Media Outlook 2016–2018 show that UAE satellite television channels are not widely watched among Emiratis compared with other satellite television channels. The most popular is the MBC Group, which has an audience share of 36% (Dubai Press Club, 2018).

The transition from a state-controlled broadcasting model to a market-driven model suggests that broadcasting is no longer committed to national cultural and social development. Several Emirati critics and academics think that UAE television channels have been unable to act as successful catalysts in the formation of "cultural identity." A study by Amal Badr (2013), Assistant Professor at Ajman University, set out to display the extent to which broadcasting had been effective in educating and sustaining a national identity among young Emiratis. The results showed that television is the most influential and effective among all mass media outlets in establishing a national identity. The results also showed that even though broadcasting shapes national identity, the family is a far more powerful factor in identity formation when compared with broadcasting. Mass media came in third place after family and the Internet. The study's recommendation suggested a need for broadcasters to air educational programs that reflect national identity-formation processes in educational communities. Another study (2012) by an Emirati researcher, Fawzia Al Ali (2012), showed that the UAE public preferred Abu Dhabi One and Sama Dubai channels because of their local news coverage and the social and religious programs that attract Emirati viewers in particular. Examples of these programs are *Ulom Al Dar* (News of the House) and the religious program *Raheeq Al Iman* (Faith Nectar) on Abu Dhabi One channel and *Akbar Al Emirate* (Emirates News), *Ma'an Nastaea* (Together We Can) and *Shabab Al Youm* (Today's Youth) on Sama Dubai. The study recommended further inculcating a sense of national identity on Emirati satellite television channels by doing the following: increase the number of programs that address unconstrained social issues in UAE society, increase the number of programs that address all age groups, increase the time allocated to local news, and increase the number of talk shows. Most of the participants in the study complained that the majority of the programs on Emirati satellite television channels are imported from abroad and do not represent Emirati concerns. Finally, a study by Mohammed Carats (2011) was conducted with students at the University of Sharjah. The study indicates that the most popular radio stations for young Emirati adults are local radio stations as Radio Sharjah, Noor Dubai, and Al Rabia FM from Ajman. The main reason young Emiratis listen to these radio stations is for the programs on relevant social issues and because of the range of programs on offer. As for satellite television channels, the UAE satellite channels were not the preferred channels for Sharjah students. The most popular channels are MBC1, MBC2, and MBC4. The most important reason students watch these satellite channels is the diversity of their programs and their inclusive coverage. The students also noted that these channels have more freedom in selecting what they broadcast than UAE satellite television channels have. The best UAE satellite channel is Sama Dubai channel because of its various local programs, which cover both social and political issues. Young adults at this university found the weaknesses of the UAE satellite television channels to be the frequency of advertisements, programs repeated across more than one channel, and the proliferation of pointless programs and drama serials. To develop Emirati satellite channels, university students suggested there should be an increase in the number of programs discussing relevant and unconstrained social issues, including topics not discussed elsewhere, as well as innovation and diversification.

Suad Al Araimi (2017), Professor of Humanities at the University of Emirates, explained that in the founding period of the federation, the objective of mass media was to establish the rules of the state. Although the media at the time was in its infancy, it performed the required role successfully. Today, the rapid changes that the country is undergoing in terms of its development have outpaced the media's capacity to keep abreast. There is no clear vision in the media and there are several areas that need to be examined. Media agencies and television broadcasting outlets cannot continue to depend on non-specialized managers and executives who have come to work in the media by accident. Also, even though there are more local broadcasters, most of the producers, television writers, and news editors are not local and have not had direct experience of all the societal changes that have taken place in the UAE. Most of the media agencies and broadcasting outlets are led by Arabs who see media as a technical profession rather than as a vehicle for promulgating social messages committed to national issues. So the UAE's media has become a mere mouthpiece for messages that are unrelated to the local community. Broadcasting has not been properly harnessed in the service of national issues. On the contrary, its message has been characterized by a promotional approach of imported Western and foreign concerns and agendas, which are mainly focused on commercial entertainment rather than the more meaningful development of knowledge (Al Araimi, 2017).

The current broadcasting crisis is rooted in the fact that most programs are borrowed from abroad and do not have content that is relevant to a local audience. There is also no effective partnership between officials and decision-makers in television and the national audience. Ordinary people are isolated from those making decisions around programming, so national issues such as identity appear superficial because they are not debated at the grassroots. For broadcasting to promote a national identity, Emirati expertise is needed to create structured and informed programming based on understanding and analysis. National cadres exist and have a continuous presence in broadcasting, but they need to be trained to be more self-confident and must be given more freedom to take on greater responsibility. However, even if all of this can be achieved, there will remain several obstacles that influence broadcasting discourse. The most important obstacle is a lack of transparency over the official objectives of broadcasts (Al Araimi, 2017).

The following are arguably the most important requirements for broadcasting to be able to successfully establish a national identity, according to Al Araimi (2017):

- Regulated media should represent the fourth (supervisory) authority over the three powers: legislative, executive, and judicial. If the UAE's national media, mainly broadcasting, can achieve this, it would become an important partner in the formation of national identity.
- Strengthening the educational curriculum at universities and specialized institutes, because they are not currently sufficiently equipping media students, instead of teaching them outdated theories that are not compatible with the job market. Accordingly, these graduates are incapable of being proactive in initiating and establishing a national identity in broadcasting.
- The consolidation of national identity should not be carried out by way of direct, monotonous messages. This direct, monotonous discourse sometimes carries the characteristics of a primitive naive discourse that cannot achieve its aims. Generations change, learn, and participate in public life yet media discourse remains static and unchanging. An evidence-based approach is required even if the facts do not reflect the official discourse because national identity cannot be built by way of a promotional campaign. It is not unmarketable goods that need to be sold. Due to this monotony, programs dealing with national identity

are weak and do not appeal to younger generations, providing a key opportunity for others to attract this audience with more engaging programs.

- The UAE's media needs a crisis management strategy to devise media materials to manage and confront local and regional crises. This shortcoming was revealed during the Arab Spring crisis and in combatting the secretive Muslim Brotherhood movement.

Broadcasting and economic development

All broadcasters carry financial and business news in their daily national broadcasts, dealing with stock markets, real estate, the construction sector, trade, and energy. On the limited number of Arabic business-oriented shows like *Economy* on Abu Dhabi television and *Money Map* and *Economic Trading* on Dubai channel, audiences are introduced to new developments in the market. In addition to these programs, business ventures and projects are regularly featured in news broadcasts (Ayish, 2013).

The transition of broadcast organizations towards market-oriented business practices has had important implications for the volume of advertising spending. Since the late 1990s, the UAE, with the second-largest economy in the Arab world, has been positioned alongside Saudi Arabia in terms of advertising spending levels. According to the 2014 Advertising Monitoring Reports in the Pan Arab Research Centre (PARC), the top spenders are Saudi Telecomm at USD 22.174 million and Dubai Shop Festival at USD 14.923 million. Overall, according to the same Media Split Analysis, television spending on advertising is the highest at USD 11.930 million (PARC, 2014). According to the Arab Media Outlook Report, the UAE TV ad market was pegged at USD 344 million – set to increase to USD 436 million by 2018, registering a 6% growth over this period. Pay TV is the key driver of TV growth as it continues to be the second most lucrative after direct-to-home (DTH) television, which dominates pay TV and had 64% of the market share. Figures from 2018 show that within the UAE's TV market, revenue from paid-for television had reached 87% of market share and was higher than the revenue from advertisements, which only held 13% of market share (Dubai Press Club, 2018).

Given this emphasis on profit and revenue and a trend towards ever greater globalization, the media's objective to build a national identity has been unreservedly scuppered. Most programs focus on commercial, purposeless entertainment. For example, the free media zone in Dubai has become the focus of profit-driven media investment. UAE's media cannot instill a national identity while its output is shaped by commercial interests, which could not be further removed from what is important to its viewers (Al Araimi, 2017).

Conclusion

The media sector in the UAE has come a long way in its development since the establishment of the UAE federation in late 1971. From one black-and-white channel and three radio stations, the country now hosts more than 15 national television channels, 25 radio stations, and hundreds of broadcast outlets across several media zones. Even though there are numerous media companies and offices, without coordination these companies risk duplicating and even undermining each other, preventing the media from developing and maturing. Although the UAE's media, particularly its broadcasting outlets, has functioned as the state's primary organ for maintaining its national identity, emphasis must now be on the challenges that the region currently faces, especially the consequences of the events of the so-called Arab Spring. In 2011, the Media and National Identity Forum placed an emphasis on promoting national identity in the media and especially in broadcasting. It transpires that Emiratis, especially young adults, are more drawn to local radio stations than local satellite television channels due to their relevance to Emirati society. Emiratis generally do not find local television satellite channels appealing because they are lacking in relevance to their concerns. Studies, however, have shown that television, not radio, is the most influential and effective in mass media in establishing a national identity, irrespective of the availability and popularity of the Internet and social media.

The UAE authorities arguably aim to employ their media (and free zone policy) to boost its soft power, while consolidating its national identity and setting the national agenda (Subeh, 2017). The UAE presents a unique case of nation-state building as its borders were not drawn according to lines of ethnicity or religion; the state territory was drawn by negotiations between local actors, the Ottoman Empire, and imperial Britain (Gleissner, 2012: 36). The seven emirates that form the UAE entered into agreements with Britain to be treated as "The Trucial States" or the label given by Britain to tribal confederations in parts of Arabia. As such, the borders drawn among small Gulf states are arguably porous as all of these states (in addition to Saudi Arabia) share family ties, ethnicity, and religion. The initial union was not only limited to the seven emirates of the UAE, but it also included negotiations to include Bahrain and Qatar (Gleissner, 2012: 37). The UAE national identity, as propagated by state media and campaigns, is allegedly rooted in the Bedouin culture as the main heritage, with billboards featuring rulers wearing the Emirati Bedouin attire as a symbol of indigenous culture (Gleissner, 2012: 78). The UAE media then are deployed to cover national events and festivals aiming at reinforcing the national and cultural identity, including the National Day, the Flag Day, the Mother of the Nation Festival, and the Sheikh Zayed Heritage Festival (Subeh, 2017: 45).

However, to enhance its influence on sustaining national identity among Emiratis, especially young adults, Emirati satellite television programs need to develop their content and depend less on imported Western and foreign material, which is mainly celebrity entertainment shows, rather than anything more meaningful like educational content. The UAE's media and especially satellite television channels need more local skilled and creative broadcasters and producers to create programs related to ordinary people, where social issues relevant to Emiratis are discussed openly. These media agencies also need local managers and executives who have specialized media knowledge. Young Emiratis want more diverse and innovative programs that appeal to them. Besides, broadcasters and media officials should function as the fourth branch of government, acting as a watchdog in society by monitoring the three other arms of powers – legislative, executive, and judicial – to inculcate a sense of national identity on television programs. There will always be a conflict between commercial broadcasting that focuses on profits and meaningful programs of educational value. A balance needs to be struck between commercial programs and maintaining the state's emphasis on programs with national identity building as their objective. Moreover, striking a balance between the UAE as a modern cosmopolitan state that continues to attract multinational media corporations and as one that can maintain a sense of national unity for a small indigenous Emirati population through broadcasting media alone is no easy task.

Notes

1 Abu Dhabi Media at www.admedia.ae/en/Vision_Mission
2 The Government of Dubai Media Office at www.mediaoffice.ae/en/the-media-office/mission-vision-values.aspx
3 The National Role of Abu Dhabi Government Media Office increased, posted 28 October 2018 at www.thenational.ae/uae/role-of-abu-dhabi-government-media-office-increased-1.785206

References

Al Ali, Fawzia (2012), Evaluation of the Media Performance of the UAE Satellite Channels: A Comparative Study between the Attitudes of the Public and the Media Specialists. *The University of Sharjah Journal for Humanities and Social Sciences*, 9(3), pp. 161–205.

Al Araimi, Suad (2017), *The United Arab Emirates between the Consolidation of Identity and the Promotion of Belonging: An Analytical Sociological Study*. Abu Dhabi, UAE: The Emirates Centre for Strategic Studies and Research.

Al-Tabour, Abdullah (2000), *Development of Media Organizations in the UAE and Its Effects on Cultural Development*. Abu Dhabi, UAE: Cultural Foundation.

Arab Media Outlook (2015), *Forecasts and Analysis of Traditional and Digital Media in the Arab World*. Dubai: Dubai Press Club.

Ayish, Mohammed (2013), Broadcasting Transitions in the United Arab Emirates. In T. Guaaybess (ed.), *National Broadcasting and State Policy in Arab Countries*. London: Palgrave Macmillan.

Badr, Amal (2013), The Educational Role of the Media in Building and Consolidating Societal Values: An Applied Study on a Sample of the UAE Society. *Jerash Communication Research*, 15(June), pp. 149–172. Jerash University, Jordan.

Boyd, Douglas (1999), *Broadcasting in the Arab World: A Survey of the Electronic Media in the Middle East*. 3rd edition. Ames: Iowa State University Press.

Dubai Press Club (2018), *Arab Media Outlook 2016–2018: Youth . . . Content . . . Digital Media*. 5th edition. Dubai: Dubai Press Club.

Gleissner, Xenia Tabitha (2012), *Local for Locals or Go Global: Negotiating how to Represent UAE Identity in Television and Film*. Unpublished PhD dissertation, University of Exeter, UK.

Government.ae (2019), *Media in the UAE*. Retrieved from www.government.ae/en/media/media. Accessed 26 March 2019.

Hasan, Alia (2013), *Our Media Identity: From Al-Fareej Newspaper to the International Press*. Dubai, UAE: The National Media Council.

IREX (2005), *Media Sustainability Index. The Middle East and North Africa*. Washington, DC: IREX.

Kadragic, Alma (2010), Commentary: Media in the UAE: The Abu Dhabi Powerhouse. *Asia Pacific Media Educator*, 20, pp. 247–252. Retrieved from http://ro.uow.edu.au/apme/vol1/iss20/25

Khan, Mehmood (2014), UAE Mass Media and National Identity and Security. *Defense Journal*, 17(11). Retrieved from http://defencejournal.com/2014-6/index.asp

Mellor, Noha (2010), A Collective Diasporic Power? *Journalism Practice*, 4(4), pp. 492–506.

Nafadi, Ahmad (1996), *Sahafat al-Emirat*. 1st edition. Abu Dhabi, UAE: Cultural Foundation Publications.

Pan Arab Research Center (PARC) (2014), *Advertising Monitoring Reports*. Retrieved from www.arabresearch.com/knowledgeBase.php?submitBtn=1. Accessed 29 March 2019.

Salama, Samir (2011), Media's Vital Role in Building National Identity Emphasized. *Gulf News*. Retrieved from https://gulfnews.com/uae/government/medias-vital-role-in-building-national-identity-emphasised-1.918066. Accessed 27 March 2019.

Subeh, Ibrahim (2017), Understanding the Communication Strategies of the UAE. *Canadian Social Science*, 13(7), pp. 42–48.

The UAE Government Portal (n.d.), *Media in the UAE*. Retrieved from www.government.ae/en/media/media

Yemen

38

MEDIA IN YEMEN – NARRATIVES OF POLARIZATION AND FRAGMENTATION

Noha Mellor

Introduction

Yemen was named "Arabia Felix" by the Romans to distinguish it from the Arabian Desert, but Yemen's history – far from being felix – epitomizes the fierce political and military rivalries in the region. Yemen used to be divided into North and South Yemen; North Yemen was ruled by the Zaidi Imam Yahya (d. 1948), who was recognized by the Ottoman Empire as the de facto ruler of the northern part, while the British Empire controlled South Yemen from 1839 to 1967. Imam Yahya wanted to expand his imamate and rule over Greater Yemen but was deterred by the presence of the Idrisi dynasty, which ruled the Idrisid Emirate of Asir, or the area along the seaboard and the British protectorate of Aden. However, Imam Yahya managed to capture Hodeidah from the Idrisi, and the latter then asked Ibn Saud, ruler of Nejd, for assistance; the Saudis seized the chance to expand their rule into Asir and Nejran by 1934 (Baldry, 1977: 156). In 1948, an unsuccessful coup ended with the death of Imam Yahya; he was succeeded by his son Ahmad. The latter marked his reign with friction, not only with the British Empire in the South but also with the rising Arab nationalist regimes such as Nasser's (d. 1970) in Egypt.

When Imam Ahmed bin Yahya of the North died in 1962, army officers attempted another coup, which sparked a civil war between the imam's supporters, funded by Saudi Arabia and Britain, on the one hand, and the military rebels, supported by Egypt, on the other. In 1963, the resistance against the British presence intensified, forcing Britain to pull out of Yemen in 1967 (Müller, 2015: 195). The military rebels eventually declared victory in 1968, forming the Yemen Arab Republic, while in 1967, the People's Democratic Republic of Yemen was formed in the South. The two states entered into sporadic wars against each other in 1972. Ali Abdullah Saleh was named president of the Yemen Arab Republic in 1978, and, in 1990, the two states declared their unity, appointing Saleh as the president. The merger was between North Yemen or the Yemen Arab Republic and the People's Democratic Republic in the South, with Sana'a as the capital and Aden as the commercial center.

The Yemeni media, meanwhile, were being used by successive regimes as tools for promoting their interests. As argued in the following section, the media development in Yemen epitomizes the contradiction in the historiographical accounts of a united versus fragmented Yemen. In those accounts, the media have been utilized by each region to produce its historical narrative and political loyalties. In times of peace, however, the media have been used to claim unity and political cohesion. The following sections take a closer look at the development of Yemeni media, both before and after the unification in 1990 and during the ongoing civil war. The chapter covers development in print, broadcasting, and new media in Yemen.

Fragmentation – Yemeni media before 1990

The early development of the media in Yemen was very much linked to the British and Otto-man occupations. Printing was introduced to Yemen in 1853 when the British occupation authorities set up the first printing facility in Aden. During that period, the first periodical *Yemen* was issued followed by *Sanaa*, launched in 1878 in Turkish and Arabic, disseminat-ing propaganda for the Ottoman Empire (Al-Mo'yeed, 2003: 39). The British occupation set up *Aden* weekly in 1900, but, once free from Ottoman rule, the Yemenis launched *al-Iman* periodical in 1926, promoting the policies of the ruler of Northern Yemen, Imam Yahya; it appeared sporadically until 1962. Moreover, *al-Hikma* literary magazine was launched in 1938 representing the opposition to Imam Yahya but it ceased in 1940; it was followed by *Saba'* in 1949, representing those who supported the imam (Al-Mo'yeed, 2003: 43–57). The group that set up *al-Hikma* called themselves al-Nidal (The Struggle), and their members were at the fore-front of the 1948 attempted coup against the imam. Among other periodicals opposing Imam Yahya was *Sawt al-Yaman* (Voice of Yemen), set up in October 1946; it was also affiliated with the al-Nidal group, which later changed its name to Ahrar Party (Al- Mo'yeed, 2003: 71). *Sawt al-Yaman* ceased publication in 1962. Other short-lived periodicals and bulletins were produced by young revolutionaries opposing Imam Yahya such as *Aneen al-Shabab* in Taiz, set up in 1947 (Al-Mo'yeed, 2003: 85). The *Saba'* weekly newspaper was published in January 1949 in Aden, as the voice of Youth Society, and ceased publication in 1950. It published articles attacking the British and supporting Imam Yahya. It reappeared in Taiz in 1952 but ended with the revolution of September 1962 (Al-Mo'yeed, 2003: 61).

The revolution of 26 September in 1962 was marked with the new newspaper *al-Thawra* (The Revolution) claiming to be the voice of the people; by 1999, it multiplied its base of cor-respondents across Yemen as well as Cairo, London, New York, and Paris (Yemen Ministry of Information, n.d.). The newspaper was part of al-Thawra Publishing house, set up in Sana'a in 1990, and its portfolio included 30 outlets, such as the weekly *al-Wahda*, established on 22 May 1990 – the day on which the new united Yemen was declared. The portfolio also included the weekly sports magazine *al-Riyada*, as well as the monthly magazine *Ma'een*; by 2001, *al-Thawra* was said to have a distribution of 35,000 copies daily, *al-Wahda* had 15,000 weekly, *al-Riyada* around 13,000 weekly, and *Ma'een* 10,000 monthly (Al-Mo'yeed, 2003: 212). There were also specialized outlets such as *al-Ommal* (The Workers) launched in 1984, *al-A'mel* in 1962, and several weeklies such as *al-Sahwa* in 1985, as a weekly Islamic magazine – all in Sana'a (Al-Mo'yeed, 2003: 303–304).

Other newspapers were issued post-1962, which included *al-Shaab* (run for only two months in 1962), *al-Akhbar* (1963–1974), *al-Yaman* (1964–1967), and *al-Yaman al-Jadid* (1965–1967), which was launched from Cairo (Al-Zayn, 1992: 187). The 14 October publishing house was established in Aden on 19 January 1968, and it issued the *14 October* daily (circulation 10,000 copies a day), *Yemen Today* in English (weekly), and *al-Iqtisadi* (weekly supplement). Al-Jomhouriyaa, another publishing house, set up in Taiz in 1990 and published the daily *al-Jomhouriyya* (used to circulate 20,000 copies daily) and *al-Thaqafiyya* (7,000 weekly); other publishers included Dar al-Hamdani Publishing, set up in Aden in 1983 to distribute mainly school textbooks, and Dar Baktheer in Hadhramaut, set up in 1972, which later launched the weekly *Shibam* in 1998. There was a remarkably slow movement in the publishing industry, which was, arguably, due to the high illiteracy rate in the country and the high cost of importing and distributing books, coupled with a massive increase in the pan-Arab satellite television market (since the mid-1990s), providing attractive media content that largely supplanted printed matter (Al-Omari, 2006: 49–50).

The first news agency was launched in 1946 in cooperation with the Middle East News Agency bureau in Sana'a, but the partnership did not last long. By 1967, a new national news agency was launched in Sana'a. The agency was relaunched in 1975 as Saba Agency, headed by the minister of information in North Yemen; Reuters had a bureau in South Yemen that served as an agency for local outlets; the Aden Agency was launched in 1980 (Nasr, 2012). The Saba news agency merged with the Aden Agency and was relaunched in 1990 under the same name. This agency ran nine branch offices across the country: Al-Ghaydah, Taiz, Sayun, Lahj, Zinjibar, Aden, Ataq, Al-Hodeida, and Al-Mukalla, and served as the main source of news for state-owned media. The agency owns the daily newspaper *Al-Siyasiyah* based in Sana'a (Battaglia, 2018: 10).

As for the broadcasting sector, it began in 1940 with a small British radio station in Aden; it was subsequently closed in 1945. Another station, Sana'a Radio, was set up in 1946, closed in 1948, only to resume its activities in 1955. The first national radio broadcast was introduced in 1946 when the Yemeni army set up a simple station, but it lacked competent technicians and was only able to broadcast for an hour and a quarter, once a week, on a short wave frequency; it later managed to increase its broadcasting to two days a week (Nasr, 2012).

In 1964, television broadcasting began in Yemen, and after independence in 1967, the state dedicated more resources to television as one of the then main information sources. North Yemen had its first television station in Sana'a on 24 September 1975 (Nasr, 2012). The Ministry of Information used to control all broadcasting activities through the General Corporation for Radio and Television formed in 1990, merging the regulatory bodies in the North with those in the South; among the state channels are Yemen TV, launched in 1975, and Channel 2 launched in 1964. The Yamaniyya channel was originally founded in 1980 in South Yemen as Aden Channel and was renamed after the unification in 1990. It is to be noted that the separation between north and south did not affect tribal loyalties, nor the status of these tribes, as the main source of identity; even during Saleh's presidency, the Yemeni media highlighted the country's national identity in terms of tribal significance. State officials wore the traditional tribal dress signifying their tribal affiliations. The same identity coding can still be traced in daily media outputs through television programs, for example (Müller, 2015: 196).

Mobilization – Yemeni media in diaspora

Yemeni traders built up communities overseas, particularly in Indonesia, Malaysia, and Singapore, more than nine decades ago (Al-Zayn, 2003). It is estimated that about four million people in Indonesia and 10,000 in Singapore are of Yemeni descent. The large Yemeni communities in Singapore and Java are "where these Arab traders built up a powerful position under, respectively, British and Dutch colonial rule" (Halliday, 1992: 9). The Yemenis excelled in their exiled state – mainly because they were away from Yemen with all its local problems. Their main concern in diaspora was to trade and accumulate fortunes (Al-Zayn, 2003). They also formed an economic power that could support both Arab emigrants and the local authorities. It was even claimed that some of the powerful Yemeni families in Singapore issued their currency. There were some Yemeni in Indonesia who joined the Indonesian National Party and fought with the Indonesians against the colonial powers; they also contributed to the army and charity projects (Al-Zayn, 2003).

The Yemeni migrants were keen to spread Arab and Islamic cultures in their host countries through establishing their societies and clubs. Starting in 1905, the competition between these clubs led to a substantial increase in Arab publications, which were used by each faction or group as a platform to appeal to the Yemeni communities – they mainly played the role of educators and aimed at linking the Yemenis in Southeast Asia with their homeland. The publications at that time were very much linked to the cultural activities of Yemeni communities and clubs; in fact, the first half of the 20th century saw the establishment of more than 40 publications aimed at calling the Yemenis to hold onto their Arab roots and to care about Yemeni issues. Islamism and Arabism were the most important ideological ingredients for this émigré press, at least during the first quarter of the 20th century (Al-Zayn, 2003).

The peak of these journalistic activities was between the 1920s and 1930s; they shrank between the 1930s and 1950s when the Yemeni leaders resorted to traditional communication, such as preaching in mosques, to reach their audiences (Al-Zayn, 2003). The main goal of the Yemeni communities in Southeast Asia was to preserve their native cultural heritage (language and religion) and to remain together as much as possible, by resisting the influence of host societies.

The Yemenis immigrated in significant numbers across the region and the world and set up several publications in diaspora communities. *Al-Salam* periodical was established in Cardiff in 1948, for instance, by a group of Yemeni immigrants, with Abdullah Ali al-Hakimi as its editor-in-chief; it reached a distribution of around 2,000 copies at the time, but ceased publication in May 1952, when al-Hakimi returned to Yemen and the periodical lacked adequate financial support (Al-Mo'yeed, 2003: 77). The other diaspora outlets included *al-Sadaqa* in 1940 in Cairo, *Sawt al-Yaman* in 1955, also in Cairo, and *al-Rouwad* in London in 1962 (Al-Mo'yeed, 2003: 86); additional periodicals were launched in Singapore and Indonesia between 1906 and 1946 (Al-Mo'yeed, 2003: 110).

Records show that, between 1970 and 1990, around 30% of Yemeni men migrated to work outside Yemen, particularly in neighboring, oil-rich states; there were about 1.25 million Yemeni expatriates by 1990, whose remittances to Yemen helped transform the country, but the Iraqi invasion of Kuwait ended this temporary prosperity (Stevenson, 1993: 15). The invasion forced 45,000 Yemeni out of Kuwait: Yemen's neutrality in the subsequent war resulted in Saudi Arabia revoking the special status given to Yemeni workers who used to enter the KSA without work permits; Sana'a then lost more than $1.7 billion in foreign assistance from the neighboring Gulf states in addition to losing oil supplies and workers' remittances (Stevenson, 1993: 15–16).

Imagined community – media after the 1990 unification

By 1990, there were 14 state-owned press outlets and 31 others representing civil society. The unification of North and South Yemen on 22 May 1990 led to a surge in media outlets representing the new Yemen Republic, of which many were privately owned. These outlets included all forms of publications – from newspapers to bulletins – many of which disappeared as quickly as they appeared (Nasr, 2012). There were more than 150 outlets which appeared in the decade 1990 to 2000, of which 62 emerged between 1990 and 1991, but soon vanished (Al-Mo'yeed, 2003: 310). One of the new ventures was *al-Umma* periodical, launched in 1991 as an independent outlet, but was later acquired by al-Haq Party to become its official mouthpiece; other partisan outlets included *al-Tajamou'* weekly (launched in 1990) representing al-Tajamou' Party (Al-Mo'yeed, 2003: 438).

On 29 August 2007, the Yemeni embassy in Cairo held a symposium to discuss the development of Yemeni journalism, focusing on milestones recorded since the unification in 1990. According to participants, the number of state-run newspapers (as of 2007) was about 37 in total. The 1990 revised law allowed individuals to issue their publications, which increased registered publications; however, within a short period, the majority were forced to shut down due to lack of funding and professional staff (Yemen Embassy, 2007).

As for the Yemeni television industry, the official TV station, Yemen TV, joined Intelsat in 1995, and later, Nilesat; al-Islah political party launched its TV channel, Suhail Television, in July 2009, preceded by al-Iman channel launched in 2008 as an outlet dedicated to fighting radicalization; additional channels now include al-Saeedah (launched in 2007), Aden Live (run by southern separatists), Sama Yemen, Belqees (launched in 2014), Yemen Shabab, Yosr TV, Maeen TV, al-Saahaat TV (launched in 2014), Azal TV, Sheba TV (state-run), Yemen Today, al-Shareyyah (launched in 2015), and al-Masirah TV, launched in 2012 and run by the Houthis.

Media regulations

The government looked into drafting a new media policy in 1981, which resulted in a new law to replace the 1968 decree (Al-Zayn, 1992: 12). This new law (No. 43 of 1982) comprised 110 articles regulating the press, compared to the 1968 law, which included only 37 articles (Al-Zayn, 1992: 75); although it granted Yemeni citizens freedom of speech, it also granted the Ministry of Information the right to cease publication of any topic deemed to harm the public interest (Al- Mo'yeed, 2003: 606). The same law prohibited journalists from attacking the president as the symbol of Yemen, or attributing any saying to the president, without prior permission from the Ministry of Information and Culture. It also banned the press from reporting on other heads of neighboring states, lest this harmed Yemen's relations with them, or publishing information that could incite sectarianism. The law was revisited in 1990, re-enforcing several restrictions such as publishing any information that might harm the Islamic faith (Al-Mo'yeed, 2003: 607). The press law urged journalists to uphold national unity as one of the aims of the 1962 Yemeni revolution and the subsequent unity of 1990; Saleh's government used to ignore calls to revisit the law and repeal the articles penalizing journalists for violating this restrictive law.

According to the new law, local journalists must be Yemeni citizens and hold press cards from the Ministry of Information, while foreign journalists should obtain accreditation and press cards issued by the government; conversely, these could be revoked by the authorities without any reasons given. A draft bill was proposed in 2005 to reform the media, but it was rejected by the Yemeni Journalists' Syndicate for being even more repressive than the 1990 law; Saleh's promise to reform the media laws and abolish penalties for media offenses did not lead to any serious action. The new bill overlooked the issue of electronic media freedom and did not seek to end state censorship or the monopoly of broadcast media (The OpenNet Initiative, 2007).

There are two courts regularly employed to prosecute journalists: the Specialised Criminal Court, established in 1999 to handle national security cases, and the Specialised Press and Publications Court, set up in 2009 to handle cases relating to the media; both courts deployed the penal code to punish journalists, including political dissidents (Freedom House, 2015). Editors and journalists rarely won a judicial victory over the state save for a handful of cases, such as *al-Shaab* newspaper versus the Ministry of Information in December 1984. The West Sana'a Court ruled that the ministry had unlawfully confiscated two issues of the newspaper, and the newspaper was therefore allowed to resume publication (Ghanem, 2002: 274). The culture magazine *Aqlam* was confiscated four times in the early 1990s – either due to tackling topics deemed sensitive by the ministry or because the articles were penned by overseas contributors without prior permission from the ministry. It is worth noting that this magazine used to distribute its publications in Saudi Arabia via Okaz publishing house (Al-Zayn, 1992: 282). This demonstrates the financial dependence on Saudi's indirect subsidies to some publications, even before the 2011 uprising.

Under the same 1990 law, criticism could be leveled against journalists who were deemed to have crossed a line, and journalists could even be accused of being traitors, conspiring with foreign states against Yemen. In 2006, for instance, Samia al-Aghbari, a journalist affiliated with the opposition weekly *al-Wahdawi*, dared to criticize former president Saleh, after he had decided to stand for reelection in 2006, having previously claimed he would not do so. Al-Aghbari's criticism led to a wave of bad publicity targeted at the journalist, including misinformation about her in the quasi-official newspaper *al-Doustor*, alleging that she had had "immoral relations" with Syrian and Egyptian men. The campaign prompted al-Aghbari to sue those who wrote the articles. She won a court order for *al-Doustor* to print an apology, but this was never enforced (Article 19, 2009: 10–11). This continuous harassment has prevailed; in 2007, for instance, the Yemeni state arrested 12 independent journalists, while harassing many others (Article 19, 2009: 10).

In 2012, the country published its Freedom of Information law. It was the second Arab country, after Jordan, to implement such a law; but the mechanisms to implement the law, including an information agency, are yet to be established (Battaglia, 2018: 11). Since the Saudi-led coalition waged its war against the Houthis in Yemen, the Yemeni government has established a media policy aiming to highlight the Yemenis' resistance and to promote the coverage of Yemeni suffering, as a result of the ongoing war (Shayaa, 2019).

Yemeni journalists

Yemeni journalists have, historically, found it difficult to form unions because of the way the media have been used as tools in the hands of political rivals as detrimental to good journalism (Al-Mo'yeed, 2003: 484). The journalists' syndication began its activities with 2,000 media professionals forming the first organized society of journalists in Sana'a in 1963 (Al-Mo'yeed, 2003: 483). There was a parallel society in Aden, but none of these two societies could call itself a union. Syndicates and trade unions have been slow to develop in Yemen, although the country used to mark Labour Day each year, ever since the 1962 revolution (Al-Mo'yeed, 2003: 486). Following the unification of Yemen in 1990, the Journalists' Syndicate was set up in Sana'a to unite those affiliated with the ones in North Yemen with those in the South. The new syndicate's work faced obstructions, however, following the 1994 war, and did not manage to form a new board until 1999 (National Information Centre, n.d., 47). A conference to gather journalists from the North and South agreed to form a union for all journalists in June 1990; however, the journalists did not agree on the tasks of the union and its limited support; consequently, many of them suggested alternative societies, such as that in 1998, when a group of journalists proposed forming a different syndicate, but the project did not materialize (Al-Mo'yeed, 2003: 551–573). There was another idea raised in a statement published in *al-Ayyam* newspaper on 20 March 1999, signed by 11 veteran journalists, pleading to form a society whose main task was to defend journalists (Al-Mo'yeed, 2003: 575). The Yemen Journalists Syndicate (YJS) has its headquarters in Sana'a and branches in other parts of the country; it survived the 2011 uprising and the ongoing civil war, but its key leaders went into hiding. It listed over 1,400 members in 2018 (Battaglia, 2018: 9), and, in 2019, the total number of members was allegedly 3,000, in addition to technical and administrative staff (Labal, 2019).

The development, albeit slow, in the broadcasting sector was not accompanied by adequate investment in journalism training, which further curtailed the overall development in the sector (Al-Zayn, 1992: 13). Between 1982 and 1990, the government registered around 98 Yemeni graduates of media, PR, and communications studies, many of whom received their education in Saudi Arabia (around 35 Yemenis) or the USSR (26 Yemenis) (Al-Zayn, 1992: 138–141). A media training center was set up, according to Decree 222 of 1999, coordinating its activities with the Faculty of Mass Communication in Sana'a University, and providing training for students in broadcasting, journalism, and production. Female journalists have generally had fewer training and promotion opportunities compared to their male counterparts (Helal, 2006). Women working in the broadcasting sector in 2000 complained about the harassment they endured in the workplace. They not only felt that there were few incentives for women to join the journalism field but also that their intellectual abilities were being undermined by the continuous supervision of their male managers (Al-Mesaabi and al-Shaabi, 2000).

The ongoing civil war in Yemen has made the country one of the most hostile environments for journalists. The 2011 uprisings that swept through the region affected Yemen, resulting in sizeable Yemeni protests, demanding President Saleh's deposition. He agreed to hand over power to his deputy, Abdrabbuh Mansour Hadi, who was declared president in February 2012. A federal constitution was drafted in 2014 to accommodate Houthi grievances, but the Houthis, in the northern region, rejected it and seized control of Sana'a in 2014, forcing President Hadi to flee to Aden in 2015. This paved the way for radical Islamist groups such as ISIS to launch attacks in Yemen, targeting Shi'a mosques. The civil war began in earnest as the Saudi-led coalition of Arab Gulf states launched airstrikes against the Houthis in 2015.

The ongoing civil war led to the killing of scores of journalists, many of whom were used as human shields and others imprisoned (Studies & Economic Media Center, 2017: 8). There were around 148 journalists kidnapped or arrested and 150 websites blocked, not to mention the harassment of scores of activists who were using social media for their activities in the year 2015–2016 alone (Studies & Economic Media Center, 2017: 9). There have been recent reports which argue that the Yemeni media use inciting language in their coverage, thereby agitating the ongoing sectarian conflict (Studies & Economic Media Center, 2017: 24).

Self-censorship is imposed on several surviving outlets in Yemen: the Houthis block certain websites, while the Saudi-led coalition and Hadi government harass and arrest reporters; in April 2018, for instance, photographer Abdullah al-Qadry of the private outlet Belqees TV was killed in a missile attack while covering events in the province of Bayda, and three other journalists were injured; the attack was blamed on the Houthi forces. Anwar al-Rakan, a journalist detained by the Houthis, who previously worked for the government newspaper *al-Jomhouriyya* died two days after his release in June 2018. A Saudi airstrike, on the other hand, hit the Al-Maraweah Radio Broadcasting Centre in Hodeida in September 2018, killing four people (Freedom House, 2019).

The most recent account on 3 May 2019 reported on the occasion of World Press Freedom Day that the Yemeni Media Union, affiliated with rebel groups, issued a statement in which it condemned the Saudi-led coalition airstrikes which had allegedly killed 239 journalists and injured 21 others since the strikes began in 2015. The coalition was also criticized for launching airstrikes on 30 radio and television outlets, in addition to 21 other facilities, jamming some Yemeni media channels and preventing over 143 international journalists from visiting Yemen. The Yemeni Media Union has also allegedly monitored several cases of cloning satellite channels and websites (Yemeni Media Union, 2019).

Re-fragmentation – media post-2011

Before 2011, there were 15 state and partisan newspapers, 33 weeklies, and 42 monthlies, not to mention scores of news websites. Regarding broadcasting, there were 12 state-run radio stations, 10 private ones, and 14 television channels (of which five are state-run), in addition to 70 Arab and international outlets which had offices in Yemen (Labal, 2019). The Yemeni state has control of national TV stations broadcast from Sana'a, including Aden TV (also known as Channel 2), Saba TV, Al-Iman TV, focusing on religious programs, as well as 10 local radio stations in Lahj, Saada, and Zinjibar, all of which went off air in early 2012 (Infoasaid, 2012: 31–44). The other TV channels beaming from outside Yemen include the London-based Suhail TV and the Cairo-based al-Saidah TV and Yemen Shabab; the latter addresses the youth who support the rebellion against the government, funded by Qatar (Infoasaid, 2012: 46).

By the end of 2017, however, there was a substantial number of 258 outlets in Yemen: 22 TV stations, 37 radio stations, 22 publications, and 177 websites. Of the 37 radio stations, nine were affiliated with the authorities, and 28 affiliated with private organizations (Studies & Economic Media Centre, 2018: 6). Five of the radio stations working inside Yemen stopped in 2014 but managed to resume their work a couple of years later. As for online news outlets, there were 177 active sites, of which 34% set up between 2014 and 2017, but 37% of them were blocked by the Houthis (Studies & Economic Media Centre, 2018: 6). Eight of the satellite channels were run from inside Yemen, while 14 were run from Turkey, Lebanon, Saudi Arabia, UAE, Egypt, and the UK (Studies & Economic Media Centre, 2018: 7). There were also 22 newspapers: six dailies, 14 weeklies, and two bi-monthlies; nine of them were active before 2014, while 13 were launched after that year. Fifteen of these were privately owned newspapers, one party-affiliated, and six state-owned. Aden alone recorded 12 of those newspapers, while Sana'a hosted seven of them (Studies & Economic Media Centre, 2018: 13).

State control of the broadcasting sector was relinquished, following the Houthis' intervention in 2015, with the emergence of new outlets organized and controlled by the Saudi-led coalition, particularly KSA and UAE, on the one hand, and the Houthis, on the other. The lack of security in the country eventually led to immeasurable problems of production and distribution, not to mention extensive damage caused to the infrastructure which affected all facilities in the country. Journalists have inevitably been vulnerable to wide-ranging pressure from their political patrons, which has further agitated the internal conflict in the country. According to the Freedom House's reports on Yemen, journalists under Houthi control were exposed to serious threats and brutal force by the Houthis; journalists allied to the Hadi government and the Saudi-led coalition faced different pressures: enticed by economic incentives, they restricted their reporting to favorable coverage of the government and its allies. The result was a polarized media scene beginning in 2015, in which most of the outlets became mouthpieces for various factions and interest parties, who granted statements and interviews only to outlets loyal to them. The Houthis have reportedly raided several media outlets such as ransacking the Sana'a office of Al Jazeera pan-Arab channel, *al-Masdar* newspaper, and two other television stations, namely Suhail, and Yemen Shabab affiliated with the Islah Islamist party (Freedom House, 2017). The use of force inevitably led journalists to practice self-censorship to avoid being exposed to violence.

The Houthis and the Saudi-led coalition accused each other of preventing international journalists from entering the country. Those who managed to enter risked detention or even kidnapping; the Norwegian journalist Raymond Lidal, and the American, Casey Coombs, were abducted in 2015 by the Houthis but were later released after weeks of diplomatic negotiations. Yemeni journalists such as Khaled al-Washli and Majed Karout faced death, abduction, or detention. Al-Washli worked for the Houthi-affiliated al-Masirah TV and was killed in January 2017 while covering efforts to defuse a bomb; Karout, affiliated with an online news website, was sentenced to a year in prison in March 2014, accused of circulating false news about a former government employee implicated in a corruption activity (Freedom House, 2017).

At the time of writing, the media scene in Yemen is still chaotic, which makes it difficult for an entity like the Public Corporation for Radio and Television to actively regulate the sector or enforce any new measures.

New media in Yemen

The Internet was introduced in Yemen in 1996, but was monopolized by two companies (General Telecommunication Authority and TeleYemen); in 2004, the number of Internet users was 150,000, up from only 920 in 1997. The Yemeni ministries of Culture and Telecommunications, however, obstructed access to several sites; this led to a significant reduction of Internet users by 2004. The number of Internet cafés recorded a reduction in their revenues by 300% (ANHRI, 2004). There were 88,000 subscribers to ADSL services, and about 500,000 subscribers to slower speed dial-up services in 2011 (Battaglia, 2018: 7).

According to Internet World Stats,[1] Internet penetration was only 0.1% in 2000 (or around 15,000 users), rising to 1.6% in 2009 (or around 370,000 users) and around 24% in 2018 (or over seven million users). Internet penetration was about 25% in 2014, with unreliable connections and regular electricity shortages, which reduced the citizens' access to the Internet (Recorded Future, 2018). Even today, the majority of Internet customers use Internet cafés, which are exposed to the surveillance of both the state and the Houthis.

Saleh's government closed down several new sites in 2009, including Al-Shura.net, Ishtiraki. net, Adenpress.com, and the websites of four independent newspapers: *Al-Ayyam*, *Al-Taghyir*, *Al-Masdar*, and *Al-Wasat*, and also blocked Yemenhurra.net, a website dedicated to covering the Sa'ada conflict (Battaglia, 2018: 6–7). It is reported that the top 10 most-viewed media pages in Yemen were al-Mashhad al-Yamani, Belqees satellite channel, Aden Live, al-Saeeda satellite channel, Yemenia News, al-Jazeera.net, Yemen satellite channel, Mareb Press, Yemen Press and Aden al-Ghad (SEMC, 2018: 13).

The main two ISPs in Yemen have been YemenNet, as part of the government's Public Telecommunication Corporation, and TeleYemen, managed by France Telecom. The ongoing conflict between the various factions is reflected in cyberspace, where each party wages a secondary war through cyber means and controls Yemenis' Internet access (Recorded Future, 2018). The Houthis have controlled the main ISP YemenNet and TeleYemen since 2014, to monitor Internet activity by changing the government sites and the ".ye" domain space, while the Hadi-government in Aden produced a new ISP, Aden Net, in June 2018. The Houthis also seized control of the dominant mobile provider, MTN Yemen, in June 2018, and are using the resources under their control to block access to WhatsApp, Facebook, and Twitter (Recorded Future, 2018).

The poor infrastructure and difficulties in accessing information online pose problems for many journalists. Mohammed Jaber, a TV reporter, for instance, complained about the access restrictions to many news websites, which forced him to send low-quality videos and photographs to external agencies; other journalists resort to proxy servers to access information but complain that there is no escape from the inadequate Internet service in Yemen (SEMC, 2018: 9).

A recent study (Norman et al., 2018) maps the conversations on Twitter around the conflict in Yemen, identifying the networks, users, and how they have framed the conflict. The researchers identified the open web content used by the various political groups to promote their political outlook, testing access to different websites from Yemen, Saudi Arabia, Iran, and the UAE, or the main players in the Yemeni conflict. The study ran from April 2016 until November 2017, mapping three homogenous, politically divided networks, namely, the Hadi-government supporters, Houthi supporters, and Saleh loyalists. The study documents the polarization in political narratives throughout the networks, with users in each group framing the conflict on their terms and influencing sentiments towards daily political activities. It documents the way each one has sought to obstruct rival political jurisdiction: thus, the Houthi-controlled ISP blocks portions of the websites feeding the favorable narrative about the Hadi-government, while Saudi Arabia blocks websites informing the discourse of the Houthi and Saleh supporters. The researchers conclude that the censored content and the homogeneity of networks facilitate the diffusion of desired information, but participants in these networks are still exposed to censored content, despite the filtering regimes (Norman et al., 2018).

Conclusion

The media development in Yemen may be summed up in one word: "fragmentation." The role of media has been reduced to an information tool, producing a sensitized narrative in a polarized country that was historically divided into different regions – each region having different religious-political factions and conflicting loyalties, and where the ultimate gain in that struggle was to control a "Greater Yemen." The media are used to amplifying differences in times of war and claiming unity in times of peace. It is notable that, in times of war, the number of outlets tends to rise remarkably, while in peacetime, that number declines proportionally; for instance, before 2011, there were around 126 outlets, from print to broadcasting; whereas, in 2017, that number reached 258 outlets.

The development of Yemeni media was thus very much linked to the political rivalries, both within the country and the region as a whole, from the occupations (British and Ottoman empires) until the ongoing civil war among different factions, each one supported by a host of external actors or countries, making Yemen, yet again, the scene of proxy war and political rivalries. It is difficult for journalism to flourish as an autonomous or even semi-autonomous field, separated from the polarized political sphere, amidst this tension. What is worse, Yemen was historically targeted by different external actors who saw in it a remote, and therefore safe, place for terrorist activities – from al-Qaeda to ISIS, especially as Osama bin Laden's family originated from and has held close ties to Yemen (Müller, 2015: 191). Pockets of al-Qaeda in the Arabian Peninsula (AQAP) have held parts of the territories in the center of Yemen, and the group rebranded itself as Ansar al-Shari'a in 2011 (Recorded Future, 2018).

The acute problem now is the humanitarian crisis; by the end of 2018, the UN reported that around 20 million Yemenis are suffering from hunger and malnutrition, resulting in the region's worst humanitarian disaster. The country has no functioning central government, as the Hadi government is still dependent on its foreign patrons, especially Saudi Arabia and UAE. Yemen is far from being "Arabia Felix" separated from the neighboring Arabian Desert; mired in the problems of neighboring countries, Yemeni journalism has paid, and is paying, a hefty price.

Note

1 www.Internetworldstats.com/me/ye.htm

References

Al-Mesaabi, Rajaa A. A., and al-Shaabi, Khaled (2000), Al-hodour al-nisa'i fi was'il al-ilam al-yamaniyya. In *Bahithat*. Vol. 6. Yearbook of Lebanese Women Researchers. Beirut: Twafiq Tabaraa Centre.

Al-Mo'yeed, Abdel Wahhab Bin Ali (2003), *Mawsou'at al-Sahafa al-Yamaniyya*. Sanaa: Yemeni Journalists Syndicate.

Al-Omari, Intissar (2006), *Harakat al-nashr fi al-Yaman*. Sanaa: Markaz Abbadi lil Nashr.

Al-Zayn, Abdallah Yahya (1992), *al-I'lam wa horiyyat al-taabeer fil Yaman 1974–1990*. Beirut: Dar al-Fikr.

Al-Zayn, Abdallah Yahya (2003), *al-Nashat al-thawafi wa sahafi lil yamaneen fil mahjar*. Damascus: Dar el-Fikr.

ANHRI (2004), *al-Internet fi al-alam al-Arabi: mesaha jadida min al-qam*. Retrieved from www.anhri.net/reports/net2004/yemen.shtml. Accessed 3 February 2012.

Article 19 (2009), *Yemen: An Analysis of Women in the Media*, March, London, UK.

Baldry, John (1976–77), Anglo-Italian Rivalry in Yemen and ʿAsīr 1900–1934. *Die Welt des Islams*, New Series, 17(1/4), pp. 155–193.

Battaglia, Laura Silvia (2018), Yemen – Media Landscape. *European Journalism Centre (EJC)*. Retrieved from www.mediaLandscapes.org

Freedom House (2015), *Freedom of the Press*. New York: Freedom House. Retrieved from https://freedomhouse.org/sites/default/files/FOTP%202015%20Full%20Report.pdf

Freedom House (2017), *Yemen Report 2017*. Retrieved from https://freedomhouse.org/report/freedom-world/2017/yemen

Freedom House (2019), *Freedom in the World, Yemen*. Retrieved from https://freedomhouse.org/country/yemen/freedom-world/2019

Ghanem, Isam (2002), Prosecutions of the Press in Yemen. *Arab Law Quarterly*, 17(3), pp. 274–275.

Halliday, Fred (1992), *Arabs in Exile: Yemeni Migrants in Urban Britain*. London: I.B. Tauris.

Helal, Abdel Hakim (2006), *A Survey of Women Yemeni Journalists*. Retrieved from www.amanjordan.org/a-news

Infoasaid (2012), *Yemen, Media, and Telecoms Landscape Guide*. London: Infoasaid, February. Retrieved from https://reliefweb.int/report/yemen/yemen-media-and-telecoms-landscape-guide-february-2012

Labal, Salima (2019), al-I'lam al-Yamani bayna fakkiy kammasha. *Al-Qabas*, 29 April. Retrieved from https://alqabas.com/662720/

Müller, Miriam M. (2015), *A Spectre is Haunting Arabia – How the Germans Brought Their Communism to Yemen*. Transcript Verlag.

Nasr, Sari (2012), al-I'lam al-Yamani, mina al-dhahera ila 'asr al-fadaaiyyat, 25 September. Retrieved from http://althawrah.ye/archives/23845

National Information Centre (n.d.), *Directory of Unions and Syndicates in Yemen*. Retrieved from www.yemen-nic.info/download/union.pdf

Noman, Helmi, Faris, Robert, and Kelly, John (2018), *The Yemen War Online: Propagation of Censored Content on Twitter*. Berkman Klein Center for Internet & Society Research Publication. Retrieved from http://nrs.harvard.edu/urn-3:HUL.InstRepos:34878067

Recorded Future (2018), *Underlying Dimensions of Yemen's Civil War: Control of the Internet*. Insikt Group, CTA-2018–1128. Retrieved from www.recordedfuture.com

SEMC (2018), *Cyber-Blocked Restrictive Limitations and Policies of Internet Access in Yemen*. Taiz: Studies & Economic Media Center.

Shayaa, Mansour (2019), *Monaqashat al-khoutat al-i'lamiyya, al-Thawra*, 5 March. Retrieved from http://althawrah.ye/archives/568191

Stevenson, Thomas B. (1993), Yemeni Workers Come Home: Reabsorbing One Million Migrants. *Middle East Report, No. 181, Radical Movements: Migrants, Workers and Refugees* (March–April), pp. 15–20.

Studies & Economic Media Center (2017), *Media Coverage of the War in Yemen*. Taiz, Yemen: Studies & Economic Media Center.

Studies & Economic Media Center (2018), *Wasael al-Ilam al-Yamaniyya*. Taiz, Yemen: Studies & Economic Media Center.

The OpenNet Initiative (2007), *Yemen*. Retrieved from https://opennet.net/sites/opennet.net/files/ONI_Yemen_2007.pdf

Yemen Embassy (2007), *nadwa an al-sahafi fi al-Yaman*. Retrieved from www.yemenembassy-cairo.com/ndetail.asp?fr=2&nid=310&nabout=4&whichpage=1

Yemen Ministry of Information (n.d.), *Information about Yemeni Media* (in Arabic). Retrieved from https://bit.ly/2W419II

Yemeni Media Union (2019), *Union's Statement on the World Press Freedom Day*, 3 May. Executive Office-Sana'a, The Yemeni Media Union Statement on The World Press Freedom Day Occasion, 3 May. Retrieved from www.yemenimu.net/archives/12657

INDEX

Note: Page numbers in *italic* indicate a figure and page numbers in **bold** indicate a table on the corresponding page.

Printed in the United States
By Bookmasters